THE 100 BEST STOCKS YOU CAN BUY 2000

John Slatter

Adams Media Corporation
Holbrook, Massachusetts

Published by
Adams Media Corporation
260 Center Street, Holbrook, MA 02343

ISBN: 1-58062-169-4
ISSN: 1520-7692

Printed in Canada.

J I H G F E D C B A

This book is not designed or intended to provide or replace professional
investment advice. Readers should invest with care, including seeking specific professional advice, since investments by nature involve significant risk
and can result in financial losses. The past performance of the investments
reported in this book does not guarantee or predict future performance.

Cover design by Mike Stromberg.

This book is available at quantity discounts for bulk purchases.
For information, call 1-800-872-5627

Visit our exciting small business website: www.businesstown.com

Table of Contents

Dedication

To my family:
My wife, Beverly G. Slatter, R.N.
My daughter, Carol Louise Slatter
My son, Stephen W. Slatter

Acknowledgments

Writing a book is far easier than finding a publisher. My first book, *Safe Investing*, didn't find a home until I latched on to my dutiful agent, Edythea Ginis Selman. Edy knows how to find a publisher, and she knows how to convince the editor that I am worth paying a living wage.

My publisher, Adams Media, has treated me like a king. That could be because the editor is Edward Walters, an easy guy to do business with.

Part I
Preface

When I wrote the third edition of *The 100 Best Stocks You Can Buy*, I was warned by the editor that I might be called upon to update the book if investors in droves bought it. Apparently, that's what happened, so I was ordered back to my computer.

The editor didn't think this would be much of a chore, but he turned out to be wrong. Using the 1998 annual reports—and other information such as *Value Line*, newspaper and magazine articles, and Standard & Poor's reports—I found that about 80 percent of my write-ups were old news. In some instances I abandoned the entire text and started over.

Equally important, I added a batch of new stocks and dropped an equal number that I decided no longer interested me. Among the twenty-four new stocks are such intriguing companies as Microsoft, Lucent Technologies, Harley-Davidson, Home Depot, and Bed Bath & Beyond.

Adding new stocks means dropping old ones. One investor suggested that I give reasons for each stock being eliminated. Although this may seem sensible, I have elected not to comply. On the other hand, I see no reason to sell your shares of the stocks that do not appear in this edition. In most instances, switching from one stock to another doesn't work out. For one thing, every time you replace a stock, you have two commissions to pay. And don't forget the cash you have to ship to the IRS when you sell a stock that has risen in price.

In this edition, I have become somewhat more growth-oriented and aggressive. The number of stocks labeled *aggressive* *growth* has been climbing. This will probably surprise many of the people who know me well. They tend to regard me as a "value investor." They will be shocked that I am recommending such stocks as FDX, Washington REIT, and Intel.

And, for heaven's sake, don't fret when you can't find your favorite stock in my list of one hundred. Some of my own stocks are also missing, such as Royal Dutch Petroleum, Costco, Indiana Energy, and Lakehead Pipeline. What it amounts to is this: There are more than a hundred great stocks. Nor is my list necessarily the best one.

On the other hand, my wife and I own thirty of the one hundred stocks, which I guess makes us believers. It also makes us believers in the magic of common-stock investing.

It has now been over thirty years since I first joined the investment community. My philosophy over that span has not changed drastically, but there are a few fundamental truths that I cling to:

- You can't forecast the market, so quit trying.
- Common stocks are the only place to put your money. Everything else is inferior, such as real estate, bonds, coins, stamps, antiques, baseball cards, certificates of deposit, and money-market funds.
- Trading is the quickest way to the poorhouse. The only sensible strategy is to buy and hold.
- Don't bet the farm on one or two stocks. There are 3,000 stocks listed on the New York Stock Exchange.

Surely you can find fifteen or twenty that will help you become rich.

- Don't buy mutual funds. Why? They charge too much; they create unwanted tax liabilities; they are often inept. What's more, there are over 8,000 to choose from; many are managed by kids who are still in their twenties. Also, there is no way to know which ones are the best. Past history is of little help since managers move from one fund to another.

- Don't ask anyone for advice; make up your own mind. That way you won't have anyone to blame if you goof. And you will goof once in a while. But you don't have to be right too often to make a bundle. If the average stock returns 10 percent a year, here is how rich you'll be at age 65. If you invest $5,000 a year beginning at age 45, you'll have $286,375 at age 65. If you start at age 35, you'll have $822,470. It pays to start early. Here's proof. If you start at age 25 and invest only $2,000 a year, you'll reach age 65 with $885,185.

- Don't put off investing because you are saving for a car, saving for education, saving for a house, saving for a vacation. Put aside at least 10 percent of every paycheck. Even better, make it 15 or 20 percent. But don't do this unless you are prepared to reach retirement with stocks worth hundreds of thousands of dollars.

- Don't make the mistake of avoiding high-priced stocks such as IBM, Exxon, Intel, or GE. Investors often tell me, "I am just a small investor; I can't afford a high-priced stock. Don't you have something under $30 a share?" Rubbish. Buy 10, 20, or 30 shares if you can't afford 100.

- Don't buy a stock simply because my write-up appeals to you. Call the company and get a copy of the annual report. Study it as if your life depended on it. It does. If managing your own portfolio makes you nervous and fretful, call me at (802) 872-0637 and I'll give you some good reasons why I can do the chore for you. My minimum account is $100,000. You might also want to check my Web site: http://homepages.together.net/~bluechip. You can also reach me by e-mail: bluechip@together.net

Why Invest in Stocks?

Investing is a complex business. But, then, so is medicine, engineering, chemistry, geology, law, gardening, philosophy, cooking, paleontology, dentistry, photography, history, accounting—you name it.

In fact, investing is so daunting and intimidating that many otherwise intelligent individuals avoid it. Instead, they stash their money in certificates of deposit (CDs), annuities, bonds, or mutual funds.

Apparently they can't face buying common stocks. This is too bad, because common stocks are precisely where the money is made. To be sure, you don't make money every day, every week, or even every year. But over the long term, you will make the most out of your investment dollars in stocks.

Look at the Facts

One persuasive study, for instance, contends that common stocks will make money for you in most years. This study, which was done by the brokerage firm Smith Barney, looked at the thirty-five one-year periods between 1960 and 1995.

The study computed total return, which adds together capital gains and dividends. Over that span, stocks (as represented by the Standard & Poor's 500 index) performed unsatisfactorily in only eight of those thirty-five years. In other words, you would have been better off in money-market funds during those eight years. That's not a bad track record. Common stocks would have been more

successful in twenty-seven of those thirty-five years.

Investing for the Long Term

Investing, however, is not a one-year endeavor. Most investors start their programs in their forties and fifties, which means they could be investing over a twenty-, thirty-, or forty-year period.

If we look at the relative returns of different investments over five-year periods—rather than one-year periods—the results are even more encouraging. During the years from 1960 through 1994, there were thirty-one such periods. In only two of those five-year periods did the total return of the Standard & Poor's-based portfolio become negative.

Let's move ahead to all ten-year holding periods. There were twenty-six in that span. Exactly 100 percent worked out profitably. Equally important, the returns to the investor were impressive in all of these one-, five-, and ten-year periods. The one-year periods, for instance, gave you an average annual total return of 11.1 percent; for five-year periods, it was 10.5 percent, and for ten-year periods, it was 10.2 percent.

Based on this brokerage house study, then, we can say with a great deal of confidence that over a lifetime of investing, an investor will reap a total annual return of 10 percent or more.

If you compare this with the amount you could earn by owning CDs, annuities, government bonds, or any other conservative investment, the difference is considerable.

Some Profitable Comparisons

Let's see how that difference adds up. Suppose you invested $25,000 in a list of common stocks at the age of forty, and your portfolio built up at a 10 percent compound annual rate. By the time you reached sixty-five, your common stock nest egg would be worth $270,868.

On the other hand, let's say you had invested your money in government bonds, yielding 6 percent. The same $25,000 would be worth only $107,297, which is a difference of $163,571. Neither of these calculations has taken into account income taxes or brokerage commissions.

Now, let's look at the timid soul who invested $25,000 in CDs at age forty and averaged a return of 4 percent. By age sixty-five, that investment would be worth a paltry $66,646.

Why Doesn't Everyone Buy Common Stocks?

That's a good question, and I'm not sure I can provide you with a satisfactory answer. Part of the reason may be ignorance. Not everyone is willing to investigate the field of common stocks. These noninvestors may be too preoccupied with their jobs, sports, reading, gardening, travel, soap operas, hobbies, or whatever. Then there are the people who are heavily influenced by family members who have sold them on the idea that stocks are too speculative and better left to millionaires. (Of course, that's how many of these millionaires became millionaires.)

Even if you are convinced that I may be right about the potential of stocks, you are probably wondering how anyone can possibly figure out which stocks to buy, since there are tens of thousands to choose from. That, in essence, is the purpose of this book—and the subject of the chapter that follows.

Picking the Right Stocks for You

If you are a typical reader, it is unlikely that you will read this book straight through. You are more likely to treat it as a reference work, or have it handy on the coffee table for browsing while you munch on an apple or suffer through a lopsided football game.

As you flip through these pages, you'll probably skip over certain stocks that have no appeal. Others, on the other hand, will catch your attention and be read more carefully.

After you have thumbed through the book a few times, you will probably have flagged a "short list" of fifteen or twenty stocks that sound especially interesting to you. Even though this process may sound entirely subjective, you will have taken an important first step in choosing prime candidates for consideration. Here's why.

You may have noticed that the stocks listed in this book are broken down into four categories: aggressive growth, conservative growth, growth and income, and income. Roughly defined, these are:

- *Aggressive growth*: Stocks of companies that are growing fast. These stocks often have a low yield. Their chief shortcoming is their high volatility. They are not for the faint of heart.
- *Conservative growth*: Stocks of companies that are growing, but perhaps not as fast as those on the aggressive growth list. These companies are often more mature, larger, better known. They are generally financially strong, with a good balance sheet and a consistent earnings record. They typically pay a dividend, and often raise it every year.

- *Growth and income*: These stocks have a moderate dividend and a solid record of growth.
- *Income*: Stocks in companies that are more mature. These may have a yield of 3 percent or more. Most of the income stocks I have selected are those of companies that are still growing, but you are not likely to double your money in six weeks.

Each of these four types of stock corresponds to—and is best suited for—a specific investment personality or "temperament." By making subjective choices out of the list of 100 stocks, you have revealed important aspects of *your* investment temperament.

The next step is to list the fifteen or twenty stocks you've chosen, along with the category (income, etc.) listed in the report for each stock. Chances are you will find that most of the stocks you've chosen fall under one or two headings. For instance, you may have picked one aggressive growth stock, seven conservative growth stocks, five growth-and-income stocks, and two income stocks.

Your Investment Temperament

This kind of pattern is a sure indicator of what kind of investment temperament you have. In this case, you are obviously a middle-of-the-road, conservative investor who is not too aggressive. At the same time, it's clear from your choices that you are not urgently in need of income.

Another person might have chosen an entirely different assortment of stocks. For example, he or she may have picked six aggressive growth stocks, seven conservative growth stocks, two growth-and-income stocks, and no income stocks. This person's temperament is obviously different from yours. But at least both of you know where you stand. In effect, you know what kind of investor you are—and what kinds of stock you should be looking at.

At this juncture, it would pay you to review the stocks in the categories for which you have already shown a strong preference. This might result in your selecting as many as five more stocks for evaluation. Now you have a total of twenty stocks that seem to fit your needs.

Once again, you want to whittle this down to the one, two, or three stocks that you should consider for immediate purchase. Unfortunately, it is not always easy to make up your mind on which ones to buy.

Some Easy-to-Use Formulas

In order to help you pick only the best of these stocks, I have developed some simple formulas that use information found in the Standard & Poor's *Stock Guide*, which is readily available in any brokerage office. These formulas use four basic values that can be determined for each stock you're considering. Here they are:

• The Standard & Poor's *quality rating*. The highest rating—assuming you are a conservative investor—is A+, followed by A, A−, B+, and so on. An average rating would be B+.

• The *dividend yield*, which can be found in the Money & Investing section of the *Wall Street Journal*. As discussed earlier, this is the annualized dividend as a percentage of the stock price—2.7 percent, 5.3 percent, and so on.

• The *price–earnings ratio* is calculated by dividing the price of the stock by the earnings per share for the most recent twelve months. The earnings figure is in the *Stock Guide* under the heading "Last

12 Mos." For instance, as of this writing, Minnesota Mining's last twelve months' earnings were $5.07. The price of the stock in today's paper was $94.375. Dividing this by 5.07, you get a P/E of 18.6.

• The *dividend payout ratio* is calculated by dividing the annualized dividend by the most recent twelve months' earnings. Let's use 3M again. The dividend in today's *Wall Street Journal* is $2.20. To arrive at the payout ratio, divide this figure by the earnings per share (EPS). You'll get a payout ratio of 0.434, or 43.4 percent. This is *not* especially attractive. A growth investor would prefer a company with a lower payout ratio, since it would indicate a company that believes in plowing back earnings into the business. Income investors, however, might be quite happy with 43.4 percent. But they wouldn't—or shouldn't—be happy with an 85 percent payout.

Now that you understand these four factors, we can look at how to apply them to the stock selection process. A good way to proceed is to list your chosen stocks down the left side of the page and list the relevant factors across the top. (Several of the formulas use only two or three of the factors; one uses all four.)

Stocks for Income
The S&P Rating

To start out, let's look at the formula you should use if you're most interested in income stocks. The first factor to look at for this category is the Standard & Poor's rating. Look for the stocks with the best S&P rating, probably an A+. Give one point to each A+ stock. (As in golf, a low score will be best in these formulas.) Next, find the second-best stocks, which will probably be A stocks. If there were six A+ stocks, each A stock will be given 7 points. (This reflects the fact that the six A+ stocks can be considered "tied," and so the first stock with an A rating is, at best, your seventh-best stock in terms of this factor. If there were only two A+ stocks, each A stock would be given 3 points.) Once you have taken care of the A stocks, rate the two or three A– stocks. The total number of A+ and A stocks will determine the grade for the A– stocks.

To make this rating system crystal clear, here is a list of stocks from the Dow Jones Industrial Average, along with their S&P ratings and the number of points that should be awarded:

Name of Stock	S&P Rating	Point Score
American Express	B	7
Alcoa	B-	12
AlliedSignal	B+	4
Bethlehem Steel	C	15
Chevron	B	7
DuPont	B+	4
Eastman Kodak	B	7
General Electric	A+	1
General Motors	B-	12
International Paper	B+	4
Minnesota Mining	A+	1
Procter & Gamble	A	3
Sears, Roebuck	B-	12
United Technologies	B	7
Westinghouse Electric	B	7

The Dividend Yield

Next, let's grade these same stocks on their dividend yield. The procedure changes somewhat, since there are rarely ties to deal with—particularly if you take the yield out to the second decimal place. Again, a high dividend yield is better for income stocks than for stocks in other categories, but the best stock gets the lowest score in our system. Here is how our stocks looked using the *Stock Guide.*

Name of Stock	Dividend Yield	Point Score
American Express	2.18%	10
Alcoa	1.70	12
AlliedSignal	1.64	13
Bethlehem Steel	Nil	15
Chevron	3.82	1
DuPont	2.98	2
Eastman Kodak	2.39	6
General Electric	2.56	5
General Motors	2.27	9
International Paper	2.64	4
Minnesota Mining	2.83	3
Procter & Gamble	1.93	11
Sears, Roebuck	2.36	7
United Technologies	2.32	8
Westinghouse Electric	1.22	14

The Price–Earnings Ratio

The final factor in selecting an income stock is the price–earnings ratio, which is calculated by dividing the price of the stock by the latest earnings per share for the past twelve months, which is readily available by consulting the S&P *Stock Guide.* As noted earlier, a lower P/E is better in this case. Here is a tabulation of the same fifteen stocks.

Name of Stock	Price/Earnings Ratio	Point Score
American Express	13.79x	7
Alcoa	9.36	4
AlliedSignal	15.89	8
Bethlehem Steel	11.19	5
Chevron	17.29	10
DuPont	12.89	6
Eastman Kodak	18.21	11
General Electric	22.22	14
General Motors	7.49	1
International Paper	9.24	3
Minnesota Mining	19.81	12
Procter & Gamble	21.50	13
Sears, Roebuck	8.44	2
United Technologies	17.13	9
Westinghouse Electric	NM*	15

*NM=not meaningful, since there were no earnings.

The Final Score

Our final step is to put these three scores together, as follows:

Name of Stock	S&P Score	Yield Score	PE Score	Final
American Express	7	10	7	24
Alcoa	12	12	4	28
AlliedSignal	4	13	8	25
Bethlehem Steel	15	15	5	35
Chevron	7	1	10	18
DuPont	4	2	6	12
Eastman Kodak	7	6	11	24
General Electric	1	5	14	20
General Motors	12	9	1	22
International Paper	4	4	3	11
Minnesota Mining	1	3	12	16
Procter & Gamble	3	11	13	27
Sears, Roebuck	12	7	2	21
United Technologies	7	8	9	24
Westinghouse Electric	7	14	15	36
	Mean (average)			22.87
	Standard deviation			7.14
	Best buys			15.73

If you add up these scores, the mean (or average) score is just under 23 points. The standard deviation is about 7.

(The standard deviation is a statistical concept that enables you to determine what is very far from the average in either direction. If you don't know how to calculate the standard deviation, you can estimate it by using 16 percent of the total. Thus, if there are twenty-five stocks, the 16 percent best ones amount to four.)

Subtract the standard deviation from the mean, and you get about 16. Any stock with a score less than or equal to this value can be considered top-notch. In this case, the three stocks that are the best choice for income investors are:

DuPont	12
International Paper	11
Minnesota Mining	16

Stocks for Growth and Income

Let's assume that you would prefer to invest in stocks that provide a combination of growth and income. If that's the case, you would go through a similar exercise, using a different set of factors.

The dividend yield would be calculated in the same way, and it would be combined with one other factor, the payout ratio. This is simple to calculate, using the *Stock Guide.* You divide the indicated dividend by the latest twelve months' earnings per share. Thus, if a stock had a dividend of $1.25 and earning of $3.67, the payout ratio would be 0.361, or 36.1 percent. The lower the payout ratio, the better. The theory is that growing companies plow back earnings into new facilities, equipment, research, and so forth. If we examine the same fifteen stocks, here is how they looked, along with the corresponding point scores.

Name of Stock	Payout Ratio	Point Score
American Express	0.300	6
Alcoa	0.159	1
AlliedSignal	0.261	5
Bethlehem Steel	NM	14
Chevron	0.660	13
DuPont	0.384	7
Eastman Kodak	0.437	10
General Electric	0.568	12
General Motors	0.170	2
International Paper	0.244	4
Minnesota Mining	0.561	11
Procter & Gamble	0.414	9
Sears, Roebuck	0.199	3
United Technologies	0.397	8
Westinghouse Electric	NM	14

If the two scores are combined, they look like this:

Name of Stock	Yield Score	Payout Score	Total
American Express	10	6	16
Alcoa	12	1	13
AlliedSignal	13	5	18
Bethlehem Steel	15	14	29
Chevron	1	13	14
DuPont	2	7	9
Eastman Kodak	6	10	16
General Electric	5	12	17
General Motors	9	2	11
International Paper	4	8	12
Minnesota Mining	3	11	14
Procter & Gamble	11	9	20
Sears, Roebuck	-7	3	10
United Technologies	8	8	16
Westinghouse Electric	14	14	28
	Mean (or average)		16.20
	Standard deviation		5.83
	Best buys		10.37

The Final Winners

If we add these up and calculate the mean, it comes to just over 16. We subtract the standard deviation, which is 5.83, and we determine that a stock can be bought for growth and income if the score is 10 or less. These stocks qualify:

DuPont	9
International Paper	8
Sears, Roebuck	10

Stocks for Conservative Growth

If you are looking for stocks that are best for conservative growth, you should go through a similar process, using all four factors discussed earlier: the Standard & Poor's quality rating, the yield, the P/E, and the payout ratio.

Stocks for Aggressive Growth

Now, it's time for a change of pace. Not everyone is conservative. Many are more growth-oriented and are willing to forgo yield if they can get better-than-average growth of capital. I have developed an exceptional method of picking stocks for aggressive growth. It is rather complicated, but let's look at the basics. In this exercise, four factors come into play.

• The P/E ratio using the most recent twelve months' earnings. This is subtracted from 100. Thus, a P/E of 18 would give you a score of 82, a P/E of 32 would result in a score of 68, and so forth.

• The median P/E ratio. In this instance, you use the median earnings per share for the past five years. For instance, let's say the company earned $2.57, 3.02, 1.78, 2.80, and 1.92. These figures come from the *Stock Guide*. To arrive at the median, simply discard the two lowest numbers and use the next lowest. The two lowest in this illustration are $1.78 and $1.92. The next lowest is $2.57, which is the one you divide into the current price of the stock. Once again, you subtract the result from 100 to arrive at the score for this factor.

• The payout ratio is now calculated using the most recent earnings per share and the indicated dividend. Let's say the company earned $3.46 and paid out $1.50 in dividends. By dividing $1.50 by $3.46, you find a payout ratio of 43.35 percent. Subtract this from 100, for a final score of 56.65.

• The last factor is the median payout ratio. The earnings figure you will use is calculated in the same way as for the median P/E ratio. Again, subtract this figure from 100 for the score for this factor.

The last step is easy. Add up the first four and divide by 4. Suppose the scores for your four factors were 78.21, 75.90, 65.43, and 43.33. The total is 262.87. After dividing by 4, you get your final score, 65.72. In this system, higher scores are best—not lower, as in my other methods. According to tests I have made with this system, it works about 90 percent of the time.

Nothing, of course, is simple. This system will not work on stocks that give you a meaningless score. For instance, if the company had earnings of 35 cents, 10 cents, 2 cents, $3.50, and $2.99, you are going to get a meaningless score with the three low EPS numbers.

One thing more: If the score for a payout ratio is more than 80, reduce it to 80. This will happen with a company that pays a very skimpy dividend, such as Compaq.

Final Summary

Here is a brief recap of my "mechanical" approach, listing the factors to use, depending on what you are trying to accomplish:

Factors for selecting income stocks:
- The S&P quality rating, such as A, B+, or B–.
- The dividend yield, such as 2.78, 3.41, or 5.49.
- The P/E ratio, using the most recent twelve months' earnings, such as 18.89, 21.42, or 29.02.

Factors for selecting growth-and-income stocks:
- The dividend yield, such as 1.43, 3.98, or 4.12.
- The dividend payout ratio, using the most recent twelve months' earnings per share and the indicated dividend.

Factors for selecting stocks for conservative growth:
- The S&P quality rating, such as A+, A, or C.
- The dividend yield, such as 2.89, 4.18, or 3.20.
- The P/E ratio, such as 14.19, 18.38, or 22.47.
- The dividend payout ratio, such as 82.90, 23.87, 34.89, or 78.14.

Factors for selecting stocks for aggressive growth:
- The P/E ratio using the most recent earnings per share. Subtract from 100.
- The P/E ratio using the median EPS. Subtract from 100.
- The dividend payout ratio using the most recent twelve months' EPS. Subtract from 100, but do not use a figure in excess of 80. For instance, if you get a score of 91.39, reduce it to 80.
- The dividend payout ratio using the median EPS. Again, reduce all high scores to 80.

Divide the four factors by 4 and buy the stocks with good scores, normally between 75 and 80.

If all of these calculations seem thoroughly confusing to you, keep in mind that it is possible to use this book without going through these exercises. As I pointed out earlier, these 100 stocks have already been subjected to rigorous analysis. Once you've identified your investment personality and done your homework on the current status and prospects of the stocks that interest you, you're ready to start investing.

One final note: When this book was written, I had 1998 annual reports to refer to. Before you invest, it would be wise to read the company's latest report, which is available at no charge.

Common Mistakes You Should Avoid

Dr. Quetzal was obviously listening intently to my investment observations when I spoke at the South Burlington Rotary Club. He was feverishly taking notes. I was not surprised when he pushed his way toward the speaker's table at the end of the meeting.

"You make a lot of sense," he said. "But I question your thesis on diversification. I have never owned more than one stock. I know it intimately, and I keep in touch with management, read the company reports, pay attention to developments in the Wall Street Journal, and . . ."

"In other words, you know more about that company than most analysts. Is that right?"

"Exactly," said Dr. Herbert Quetzal (not his real name). "I'm a busy urologist in Peoria, Illinois. I'm in Burlington visiting my daughter who is a student at the University of Vermont. My waiting room is nearly always full. What I'm trying to say is this: With only a limited amount of time, I can't spend an hour a day reading *Business Week, Forbes, Fortune,* and all the rest. I have to zero in on one stock."

"I assume that one stock is a pharmaceutical," I said.

"No, as a matter of fact, it isn't. I have avoided drug stocks because I don't want my ownership to influence my prescription writing. For the past several years, I have invested exclusively in Caterpillar. Since I live and work in the same town with Caterpillar, I know several of their key people—play golf with them, attend the same church, and so forth. Frankly, my system of concentrating on one stock suits me just fine. When the day comes that

their fortunes start heading south, I'll know before anyone on Wall Street."

Failure to Diversify

Although I didn't say so then, I was certain that Dr. Quetzal was not likely to pick up any inside information from his pals at a Peoria golf course. It is a federal offense for a corporate insider (such as an officer or board member) to reveal developments not already public knowledge.

Since common stocks are inherently risky—volatility is their chief shortcoming—it makes sense to diversify. If done properly, this can be accomplished with ten or fifteen stocks. However, a longer list might be a little better. My typical client owns twenty or thirty stocks, depending on the size of the portfolio.

By contrast, many investors concentrate heavily in three industries: public utilities, oils, and banks. Yet, there are ninety-six different industries to choose from, according to *Value Line Investment Survey,* a widely read advisory and statistical service.

When I chide investors for owning too many utilities, they often tell me that they are well diversified geographically, one in San Diego, one in Florida, one in Chicago, and so forth. Or, they may defend their strategy by pointing out that they own six electric utilities, four gas distributors, a water company, and three telephone stocks. Even so, all are public utilities, and all will retreat at the first sign of higher interest rates. This is because utilities have high yields and thus fall into the same category as bonds and preferred stocks, which react negatively to rising interest rates. Worse yet, public utilities are heavily regulated by government commissions that have voters in mind—not investors—when they make their decisions.

To be sure, Dr. Quetzal had not fallen into the trap of concentrating on public utilities. Even so, his fascination with Caterpillar, the world's foremost manufacturer of earthmoving equipment, is not prudent. For one thing, CAT is not a classic growth stock, with steadily increasing earnings. Rather, it is subject to the vagaries of economic cycles and may suffer from lack of earnings. During the past fifteen years, for instance, Caterpillar had red ink in 1982, 1983, 1984, 1991, and 1992. This is not to criticize Herbert Quetzal for owning Caterpillar. In a diversified portfolio, this big blue chip may well play a part.

Undue Concentration on Local Stocks

Like many investors, Dr. Quetzal was enamored of a local stock. This is understandable, since physicians are often prominent in their communities and get to know corporate officers. They say to their stockbrokers that "if Harry Grebe is on the board of directors of Plover Manufacturing Company, it makes sense for me to own stock in it."

Without question, there are some fine stocks in your city, but there are far more in other parts of the country. If you buy electricity from Western Idaho Power & Light Company, that may not be a sound reason to buy stock in the company. On the other hand, it could be if you live in Milwaukee or Charlotte. Wisconsin Energy and Duke Energy are among the best electric utilities. But if you live in Cleveland or Buffalo, you may regret owning shares in the public utilities that serve those regions.

A better way to buy stocks is to examine a host of companies in that industry. Then buy the best one—not the one that operates down the street, even if the treasurer of the company sits next to you in church.

Failure to Keep Track of Your Stocks

Sometimes it makes sense to journey south during the winter months, particularly if you live in Vermont, which is better known for its balmy summers. Recently, I had occasion to attend a wedding in Natchez, Mississippi.

That's where I bumped into Gila Vickers, a diplomat, American Board of Family Practice. At the reception, I was wandering around trying to find someone to talk to. Nearly everyone was busy talking about their salad days. One person who seemed to be equally at sea was a rather tall and distinguished, middle-aged woman who was sipping a drink when I accosted her.

"You must not be a native of this historic city," I said. "All the natives are talking with the other natives."

"You sound like a Yankee," she said, with a pronounced southern drawl. I can't believe you want to talk with someone from the deep South. My name is Gila Vickers. I patch up the lame and the halt in New Orleans. The only person I know is the bride."

Like most good conversationalists, she made no effort to talk about herself, but asked me how I came to write five books on the stock market. Once we got beyond that, she admitted she didn't spend much time studying her stock portfolio.

"It takes most of my spare time keeping up with diabetes, hypertension, migraine headaches, brittle fingernails, constipation, and a score of other assorted ailments. The only time I do my homework on a stock is when I buy it. After that, I leave it up to the gods to protect me from declining earnings, takeovers, and management ineptitude. So far, I have had more winners than losers."

As we talked, it turned out the she preferred to talk more about her winners, such as Procter & Gamble, Merck, and Intel than she did about the ones that had fallen by the wayside. True, Dr. Vickers had some handsome winners, but she had also held onto her losers too long. More careful attention to developments might have benefited her portfolio.

Every day, changes occur in the stocks you own. These developments are reported in the financial press. Equally important, all companies publish reports. Annual reports are particularly helpful in understanding your companies. To be sure, you may find it difficult to understand every word in those reports. If so, why not call the "investor contact." The names of investor contacts are sometimes available in your annual report. You can also find their names at the bottom of the Standard & Poor's tear sheet, readily available in libraries and brokerage house branch offices.

The best time to call is when the investor contact is out to lunch. Leave your number, and the cost of the call will be borne by the company. Make sure you are prepared with a list of at least ten questions. A good place to look for questions is the one-page report issued by *Value Line*. Read the commentary at the bottom of the page, and every time you are in doubt about a statement, ask the investor contact to "elaborate on what some analysts say is troubling your foreign operations."

When you have exhausted your list of specific questions, say this: "I suppose there are some Wall Street analysts who are recommending your stock. What are the reasons they give for their favorable comments?" Then take the other tack and say, "No doubt some analysts are critical of your prospects. What are they saying in this regard?"

Above all, when you ask a question, never interrupt until the investor contact has said everything on her mind. She is almost certain to give you far more information than you had bargained for.

Too Much Trading

When you sell a stock, there is a commission to pay. This may amount to $100, $200, or $300. If you reinvest in another stock, there is still another commission. And don't forget to keep Uncle Sam in mind when you sell a stock that has risen above the purchase price. Admittedly, some selling is healthy, perhaps two or three switches a year. But excessive trading could drain your portfolio of assets.

Incidentally, don't try to avoid commissions by dealing with a discount broker unless you are a veteran investor and don't need anyone to talk with. A good broker provides valuable information and service that may be lacking with a discount broker. By the same token, make sure you deal with a broker who is knowledgeable and is interested in your welfare. Avoid brokers who encourage you to trade or who sell you "packaged products." Common stocks should be the core of your portfolio—not bonds, CDs, preferred stocks, options, or mutual funds.

Too Little Trading

Some investors hang on to their stocks year after year, never making any changes. This strategy is better than excessive trading, but it may not be ideal. At least once a year, examine each stock and say to yourself, "Is this really the best stock in its industry? If I didn't own it, would I buy it now?" If the answer to these questions is "no," perhaps you should prune such stocks out of your portfolio.

Obsession with Market Timing

Aaron Kestrel is an engineer in Rome, New York. I can't tell you what he looks like, since he is merely a voice on the telephone. "I read your book, *Straight Talk*

About Stock Investing, and decided to call you, since you put your phone number on page 11."

"It's also on page 251," I told him. "Managing money is a rather lonely business, Mr. Kestrel. I enjoy hearing from my readers. Of course, I am always hoping the caller will see the light and become a client. But, alas, most of them don't. I must not have a very mellifluous voice."

He didn't comment. "The reason I called is to ask you if now is the time to bail out; the market is certainly due for a collapse, don't you think?"

"The nature of the stock market is that it goes up for a few years and then retreats for a year or so. Back in 1973 and 1974, it sagged over 40 percent. I expect that we will have some bad days ahead. My only problem is deciding *when*."

"I was hoping for something more definite," he said.

"If you buy common stocks, Mr. Kestrel, you have to be prepared for a bumpy ride once in a while. If you can't stand the occasional volatility, you might like CDs or bonds. But if you want to make money, stick with common stocks."

"So far, your advice has made me a lot of money, but I am not prepared to give it all back."

"I know what you mean. Let me tell you a little story. A firm in Boston—I think it was Dalbar—made a study of mutual funds from January 1984 to March of 1996. They found that a typical mutual fund during those years gained 491%. You'll have to agree that 491% is a lot better than you would have done in CDs or bonds. But the ironic fact is that most investors did not do nearly as well. They made a mere 97% during that 1984–1996 period."

Mr. Kestrel interrupted, "That doesn't make sense!"

"I agree," I said. "What happened is this. Those investors tried to be market timers. Every time they thought the market

was due for a correction, they bailed out and put their cash in a money market fund."

"That's rather sobering," he said. "In other words, you're telling me not to be a Nervous Nellie."

The Fallacy of Market Timing

In theory, market timing is a great idea. You pull your money out of stocks just before prices hit the skids, then reinvest right before shares resume an uptrend. Putting that theory into practice, however, isn't so easy. While you may succeed in getting out of stocks in the early stages of a market downturn, you're apt to be caught unawares by the recovery, since strong upward moves in stock prices often come in short, unexpected spurts. And being out of the market for even a brief period during an upswing can dramatically reduce your returns.

Even if you manage to time your investments perfectly and buy exactly when stock prices are lowest, the gain isn't as substantial as you might think, says Sheldon Jacobs, editor of *The No-Load Fund Investor*.

He cites a study showing that an investor who put $500 into stocks at the beginning of each quarter for a twenty-year period ending in 1989 would have earned an average annual return of 11.8 percent.

Meanwhile, an investor who, instead, put in the same $2,000 annually as a lump sum on the day the market hit its low for the year would have earned 13.4 percent. "That's better than 11.8 percent but not all that much better, considering that it would be nearly impossible to consistently hit the low points for buying," says Jacobs. "The advantage of being a buy-and-hold investor is that the market is up three years out of four. Thus, three times out of four you're going to be right to stay in. Over time, that will give you the best returns."

Investing in Mutual Funds Exclusively

If you are busy or don't have an interest in common stocks, you may seek the refuge of mutual funds. Unfortunately, there are 9,000 to select from, which means it is more difficult to pick a fund than a common stock. Using past performance as a way to pick a fund is seriously flawed. There is very little correlation of future performance with past performance. Then, too, successful managers don't always stay put. The new manager may not have the same talent as the previous one.

Equally important, funds are expensive—even no-load funds—since they have all sorts of hidden charges that can approximate 1.5 percent or more a year. You can hire a professional manager for less and get personal attention, geared specifically to your particular situation.

Investing Solely for Income

Sharon Raggi, a schoolteacher in northwestern Vermont, asked me to autograph a copy of my most recent book. I met her at the Barnes & Noble store on Dorset Street on a chilly day in January. "I hope there are income stocks in this book, Mr. Slatter. I'm too old for growth stocks."

I assured her that about twenty-five stocks described in the book had better-than average dividend yields. I was surprised that she thought she was too old for growth stocks, since she looked no more than sixty. Naturally, I didn't ask her age.

Although I can understand the need for income for those who are retired, I have found that it is a mistake to concentrate too heavily on stocks with a high yield. An extensive study of this question was carried out by portfolio manager John Fields of the Delaware Group. To prove his case, the author looked at the 500 stocks that make up the Standard & Poor's 500. He divided these stocks into five equal groups, based on yields at the beginning of each year, from 1926 to 1995.

Mr. Fields found that the worst results were turned in by the stocks with extremely low yields and the group with very high yields. For instance, the 20 percent with low yields had an annual total return (dividends coupled with price appreciation) of only 10 percent. Similarly, the high-yield segment did only modestly better, with a total return of 10.8 percent during the same span.

By contrast, the best performers were the ones in the middle. The stocks sporting the second-highest yields provided investors with an average annual return of 13.2 percent. This surpassed the other two groups, which provided their holders with 11.8 percent and 10.6 percent. What it amounts to is this: avoid the extremes and stick with stocks with above-average yields. Stocks with inordinately high yields tend to have problems and lack growth potential. Owning a few such stocks is okay, but concentrating on them will doom your portfolio to mediocrity.

Ignoring the Price/Earnings Ratio

It pays to examine the price/earnings ratio before you buy a stock. You can calculate the P/E ratio by dividing the price of the stock by the per-share earnings during the most recent twelve months. These earnings can be found in *Value Line* or in the Standard & Poor's *Stock Guide*.

As an example, in a recent copy of the *Stock Guide*, the price of Coca-Cola was $68.50. Its latest earnings were $1.38. Divide $1.38 into $68.50, and you get a P/E of 49.6, which is far above most stocks. By contrast, Emerson Electric, selling at $63.875, had twelve-month earnings per share of $2.87. Divide that number into Emerson's price, and you get a P/E of 22.3. This is somewhat below average. Based on the quality of the company and the consistency of its earnings stream, I would be inclined to invest in Emerson, rather than Coca-Cola.

A stock selling for forty or fifty times reported earnings may be a great company with a super record of growth—but it may be overpriced and vulnerable to a sharp decline at the first sign of bad news. Try to pick stocks that have a P/E ratio that is at or below the market.

Ignoring the Dividend Payout Ratio

Finally, make sure you examine the dividend payout ratio. A company that earns $4 a share and pays a dividend of $3 is not reinvesting enough in its future. It would be better to pay out $1, plowing back the rest in marketing, research, acquisitions, and new facilities. Companies that reinvest their profits tend to grow. Those that don't often stagnate.

Final Comments

Investing in the stock market can be an intimidating pursuit, fraught with a multitude of mistakes. But even if you eliminate all the mistakes, you may not outperform the market. But at least you will do better than most people. Here are ten tips that should help you to become a more successful investor:

- Buy at least fifteen stocks, representing a minimum of ten different industries.
- Don't be obsessed with local stocks.
- Once you buy a stock, make an effort to keep abreast of developments.
- Don't trade frequently. Every time you make a switch, it costs you money in commissions; it may also help the IRS.
- Review your holdings at least once or twice a year, with the idea of making a change or two. Don't make the mistake of buying and holding forever.
- Don't go overboard with dividend yield. An extremely high yield often indicates problems, and a dividend cut may be in the offing.
- Make sure you avoid stocks selling at a high price compared to earnings, the P/E ratio.
- Don't buy stocks that pay out a high percentage of earnings to shareholders. Utilities are famous (or infamous) for this practice.
- Don't think you are smart enough to forecast the next dip in the market. You aren't. Nor is anyone else.
- Don't think mutual funds are the royal road to wealth. They might make sense for beginners, but they are tough to pick, they charge too much, and the tax consequences are bad for your financial health.

Some Simple Formulas for Asset Allocation

Serious investors spend a lot of time deciding which stocks or mutual funds to buy. I can't quarrel with that. If you are going to invest $10,000 in Merck, Illinois Tool Works, Praxair, Leggett & Platt, or United Technologies, you shouldn't do it without some research and thought.

On the other hand, some financial gurus maintain that it is far more important to make an effort to achieve an effective approach to asset allocation. They believe that you should place your emphasis on how much of your portfolio is invested in such sectors as:

Government bonds
Corporate bonds
Municipal bonds
Convertible bonds
Preferred stocks
Large-capitalization domestic stocks
Small-capitalization domestic stocks
Foreign stocks
Foreign bonds
Certificates of deposit
Annuities
Money-market funds

There are probably a few other categories you could include in your portfolio, but I think that examining this list gives you an idea of what is meant by asset allocation.

To illustrate the importance of asset allocation, look at 1998. You may recall that the long bull market temporarily aborted in mid-July of that year. Prior to that time, the big blue chip stocks had been making heady progress. Beneath the surface, however, the small and medium-size stocks were already in their own bear market. Thus, if you had avoided these smaller companies in the first six months of 1998, you would have sidestepped the devastation that was taking place in this sector.

After mid-July, however, the big stocks—particularly the financial stocks such as J. P. Morgan, Travelers (now Citigroup), and American Express—took a real tumble. The best place to be during this period was in U.S. government bonds. Once again, we are talking about asset allocation and how it can help or hurt you.

My Approach to Asset Allocation

From the comments made so far, you can see that asset allocation, like everything else in the world of finance, can get rather complex and confusing. It is no wonder that many people don't delve into this arcane realm. That's where John Slatter comes to the rescue. My idea of investing is to make it simple. After all, there are just so many hours in the day. If you are still gainfully employed, you probably work eight hours a day making a living. In the evenings, you may spend a few hours a week reading journals and other material so that you don't get fired. Obviously, that doesn't leave much time for studying the stock market.

For my part, I don't invest in many small-cap stocks, foreign stocks, bonds, convertibles, preferred stocks, or most of the other stuff on my list. I prefer to invest mostly in big-cap stocks (such as Exxon, GE, Merck, IBM, Procter & Gamble, and Johnson & Johnson) and money-market funds (a safe alternative to cash).

This reduces my categories to two, not a dozen. All you have to do is decide what percentage of your portfolio is in stocks. The rest is in a money-market fund. Of course, the *percentage* is vitally important.

A Few Alternatives to Consider

Some people may be shocked that I am not concerned about foreign stocks. One firm I once worked for insisted that we strive to invest 20 percent of each investor's portfolio in foreign stocks, such as Schlumberger, Repsol, Royal Dutch Petroleum, British Telecommunications, or Elf Aquitaine.

I have no objection to such stocks, but I see no urgency to adhere to a rigid percentage. For one thing, foreign stocks are more difficult to research. Their annual reports are far less revealing than those put out by corporations here at home. They also have different and less informative accounting.

In any event, the United States has hundreds of great companies. We are the envy of the world when it comes to business. The Japanese—at least for a decade or two—tried to convince people otherwise. But they have spent that last several years wallowing in a serious recession.

As far as bonds are concerned, they don't have a particularly impressive record. Except for a year here or there, common stocks have always been a better place to be. What's more, the return on bonds today is not much better than the rate you can get on a money-market fund.

One more thing: bonds, even U.S. Treasuries, have an element of risk; they decline in value when interest rates go up. Long-term bonds, moreover, slide precipitously when rates shoot up.

I don't want to spend too much time discussing the shortcomings of the rest of the list. I would prefer to point out the virtues of major stocks, such as McDonald's, Wal-Mart, Hewlett-Packard, J. P. Morgan, AT&T, Chevron, Alcoa, Eli Lilly, Minnesota Mining, and Walt Disney.

Blue chip companies are not likely to go bankrupt. To be sure, they have their troubles, but they are big enough to hire a CEO who can bring them back to life. Among the thirty companies in the Dow Jones Industrial Average, for instance, such companies as IBM, Eastman Kodak, AT&T, Sears, Roebuck, United Technologies, and AlliedSignal were restructured in recent years by a few dynamic executives.

Major corporations are also found in most institutional portfolios such as mutual funds, pension plans, bank trust departments, and insurance companies. One reason they like these big-capitalization stocks is liquidity. Since institutions have huge amounts of cash to invest, they feel comfortable with these stocks. The reason: the number of shares outstanding is huge, which means they won't disturb the market when they buy or sell. By contrast, if they try to invest a million dollars in a tiny Nasdaq company, the stock will shoot up several points before they complete their investing. It could be just as disruptive when they try to get out. As a consequence, major companies are in demand and are not left to drift. On the other hand, there are thousands of small companies that no one ever heard of. The only investors who can push them up are individuals—not institutions.

Another reason I like big companies is because they can afford to hire top-notch executives and they have the resources to allocate to research and marketing. In addition, their new products, acquisitions, management changes, and strategies are discussed frequently in such publications as the *Wall Street Journal,* the *New York Times, Barron's, Fortune, Forbes,* and *Business Week,* all of which I subscribe to.

How Much Should You Invest in Stocks?

When it comes to deciding on the percentage you should devote to common stocks, there are several alternatives that should be considered. All have some merit, and none are perfect.

In fact, there is no such thing as a perfect formula for asset allocation. It depends on such factors as your age and your temperament. It might also depend on what you think the market is going to do. If it's about to soar, you would want to be fully invested. But if you think stocks are poised to fall off a cliff, you might prefer to seek the safety of a money-market fund.

Forget About Everything Else and Buy Only Stocks

Believe it or not, there are some investors who are convinced that common stocks—and common stocks alone—are the royal road to riches. A good friend of mine has never bought anything but stocks, and he's been doing it for many years. He even went through the severe bear market of 1973–1974, when stocks plunged over 40 percent. He wasn't exactly happy to see his stocks being ground to a pulp, but he hung on. Today, he is a millionaire many times over. He's now sixty years old, still a comparatively young investor. His name is David A. Seidenfeld, a businessman in Cleveland.

Dave got his start by listening to the late S. Allen Nathanson, a savvy investor who wrote a series of magazine articles on why common stocks are the best way to achieve great wealth. Dave Seidenfeld recently collected these essays and published them as a hardcover book, *Bullishly Speaking*, which is available in bookstores.

If you start investing early, such as in your forties, this method can work. If you systematically invest, setting aside ten or fifteen percent of your earnings each year and doing it through thick and thin, you won't need any bonds, money-market funds, or any of the other alternatives that financial magazines seem to think you must have. You will arrive at retirement with a large portfolio that will enable you to live off the dividends.

However, if you arrived late to the investment party—let's say in your late fifties or early sixties—you may not be able to sleep too well if you rely entirely on common stocks. After all, stocks have their shortcomings too. They tend to bounce around a lot, and they can cut their dividends when things turn bleak.

Some Options to Consider

If you are an ultraconservative investor, I suggest you invest only 55 percent of your portfolio in common stocks. To be sure, when the stock market is marching ahead, as it has in recent years, you won't be able to keep pace. But if it falters and heads south for a year or two, your cautious approach will keep you out of the clutches of insomnia. Frankly, I don't think such a timid approach is the best way to approach asset allocation. However, I worked for a firm a few years ago that used this formula on nearly everyone. As far as I know, there weren't too many people complaining.

A better way to handle the uncertainty is to invest 70 percent in stocks, with the rest in a money-market fund. Once you decide on a particular percentage, stick with it. Don't change it every time someone makes a market forecast. These market forecasts don't work often enough to pay any attention to them. To my knowledge, no professional investor has a consistent record in forecasting. Every once in a while, one of these pundits makes a correct call at a crucial turning point, and from that day on, every one listens intently to the pronouncements of this person—until the day the pronouncement is totally wrong. That day always comes.

My Favorite Formula for Asset Allocation

I think age is the key to asset allocation. The older you are, the less you should have in common stocks. If you are age 65, you should have 65 percent in common stocks, with the rest in a money-market fund. If you are younger than 65, add 1 percent per year to your common stock sector. As an example, if you are 60 years old, you will have 70 percent in stocks.

If you are older than 65, deduct 1 percent a year. Thus, if you are age 70, you will have only 60 percent in stock. When you reach 80, you will be 50–50. And if you are much younger than 65, let's say 45, you will have 85 percent in stocks.

If you are not sure what this all means, here is a table breaking down the two percentages by age:

Age	Stocks	Money-Market Funds
40	90%	10%
45	85	15
50	80	20
55	75	25
60	70	30
65	65	35
70	60	40
75	55	45
80	50	50
85	45	55

Basic Terminology

If you are new to the investment arena, you may have difficulty understanding parts of this book. To get you over the rough spots, I have listed some common expressions that appear frequently in books on investing. You will also encounter them in the *Wall Street Journal, Forbes, Financial World, Business Week, Barron's,* and other periodicals devoted to investing.

This is not a glossary but merely a brief list of terms that are essential for understanding this book. If you would like a more complete glossary, refer to either of my previous books: *Safe Investing* (Simon & Schuster, 1991) or *Straight Talk About Stock Investing* (McGraw-Hill, 1995).

Analyst

In nearly every one of the one hundred articles, you will note that I refer to "analysts" and what they think about the prospects for a particular stock. Analysts are individuals who have special training in analyzing stocks. Typically, they have such advanced degrees as M.B.A.s or C.F.A.s. Many of them work for brokerage houses, but they may also be employed by banks, insurance companies, mutual funds, pension plans, or other institutions. Most analysts specialize in one or two industries. A good analyst can tell you nearly everything there is to know about a particular stock or the industry it's part of.

However, analysts can be dead wrong about the future action of a stock. The reason is surprises. Companies are constantly changing, which means they are acquiring, divesting, developing new products, restructuring, buying back their shares, and so forth. When they make a change and announce this change to Wall Street, the surprise can change the course of the stock. In short, analysts can be helpful, but don't bet the store on what they tell you.

Annual Report

If you own a common stock, you can be certain that you will receive a fancy annual report a couple of months after the close of the year. If the year ends December 31, look for your annual report in March or April. If the fiscal year ends some other time of the year, such as September 30, the annual report will appear in your mailbox two or three months later.

Not all investors read annual reports, but they might be better off if they did. Although most companies will not list their problems, you can usually get a pretty good idea how things are going. In particular, read the report by the president or CEO. It's usually one, two, or three pages long and is written in language you can understand.

If you want detailed information on the company's various businesses, the annual report will often overwhelm you with details that may be difficult to fathom. If you are really curious about what they are trying to say, feel free to call the investor contact. I have provided the name of this person in all one hundred stocks listed. Have a list of questions ready, and call during the person's lunch hour, leaving your name and phone number. This sneaky little strategy means the cost of the call back will be paid by the company, not you. By the way, don't assume you will be intimidated by the investor contact. Investor contacts are usually quite personable and helpful.

Asset Allocation

This is not the same as diversification. Rather, it refers to the strategy of allocating your investment funds among different types of investments, such as stocks, bonds, or money-market funds. In the long run, you will be better off with all of your assets concentrated in common stocks. In the short run, this may not be true, since the market occasionally has a sinking spell. A severe one, such as that of 1973–74, can cause your holdings to decline in value 20 percent or more. To protect against this, most investors spread their money around. They may, for instance, allocate 50 percent to stocks, 40 percent to bonds, and 10 percent to a money-market fund. A more realistic breakdown might be 70 percent in stocks, 25 percent in bonds, and 5 percent in a money-market fund.

Balance Sheet

All corporations issue at least two financial statements: the balance sheet and the income statement. Both are important. The balance sheet is a financial picture of the company on a specific date, such as December 31 or at the end of a quarter.

On the left side of the balance sheet are the company's assets, such as cash, current assets, inventories, accounts receivable, and buildings. On the right side are its liabilities, including accounts payable and long-term debt. Also on the right side is shareholders' equity. The right side of the balance sheet adds up to the same value as the left side, which is why it is called a balance sheet.

In most instances, corporations give you figures for the current year and the prior year. By examining the changes, you can get an idea of whether the company's finances are improving or deteriorating.

Bonds

Entire books have been written on the various kinds of bonds. A bond, unlike a stock, is not a form of ownership. A bond is a contractual agreement that means you have loaned money to some entity, and that entity has agreed to pay you a certain sum of money (interest) every six months until that bond matures. At that time, you will also get back the money you originally invested—no more, no less. Most bonds are issued in $1,000 denominations. The safest bonds are those issued by the U.S. government. Not since the War of 1812 has there been a default on government bonds. The two advantages of bonds are safety and income. If you wait until the maturity date, you will be assured of getting the face value of the bond. In the meantime, however, the bond will fluctuate, because of changes in interest rates or the creditworthiness of the corporation. Long-term bonds, moreover, fluctuate far more than short-term bonds. But enough about bonds. This book is about stocks.

Capital Gains

When you buy common stocks, you expect to make money in two ways: capital gains and dividends. Over an extended period of time, about half of your total return will come from each sector. If the stock rises in value and you sell it above your cost, you are enjoying a capital gain. The tax on long-term capital gains is less than it is on dividends—a maximum of 20 percent if the stock is held for 12 months.

Common Stocks

We might as well define what a common stock is, since this whole book is devoted to them. All publicly owned companies—those that trade their shares outside of a small group of executives or the founding family—are based on common stocks. A common stock is evidence of partial ownership in a corporation. Most of the stocks described in this book have millions of shares of their stock outstanding, and the really large ones may have in excess of 100 million shares. When you own common stock, there are no guarantees. If the company is successful, it will probably pay a dividend four times a year. These dividends may be raised periodically, perhaps once a year. If, however, the company has problems, it may cut or eliminate its dividend. This can happen even to a major company, such as Commonwealth Edison, Woolworth, IBM, Goodyear, or General Motors. As I said, there are no guarantees.

Investors who own common stock can sell their shares at any time. All you do is call your broker, and the trade is executed a few minutes later at the prevailing price—which fluctuates nearly every day, sometimes by a sixteenth of a point (a point is a dollar) or sometimes two or three points.

Current Ratio

The current ratio is calculated by dividing current assets by current liabilities. Current assets include any assets that will become cash within one year, including cash itself. Current liabilities are those that will be paid off within a year. A current ratio of 2 is considered ideal. Most companies these days have a current ratio of less than 2.

Diversification

Since investments are inherently risky, it pays to spread the risk by diversifying. If you don't, you may be too heavily invested in a stock or bond that turns sour. Even well-known stocks such as Alcoa, International Paper, Eastman Kodak, and American Express can experience occasional sinking spells.

To be on the safe side, don't invest more than 5 percent of your portfolio in any one stock. In addition, don't invest too heavily in any one sector of the economy. A good strategy is to divide stocks among twelve sectors: basic industries, capital goods/technology, capital goods, consumer growth, consumer cyclical, credit cyclical, financial, energy, transportation, utilities, and conglomerates.

Here's a rule of thumb that will keep you out of trouble: Invest at least 4 percent in each sector but not more than 12 percent. That means that you should own at least twelve stocks so that you have representation in all twelve sectors.

Dividends

Unlike bonds, common stocks may pay a dividend. Bonds pay interest. Most dividends are paid quarterly, but there is no set date that all corporations use. Some, for instance, may pay January 1, March 1, July 1, and September 1. Another company may pay February 10, May 10, August 10, and November 10. If you want to receive checks every month, you will have to make sure you buy stocks that pay dividends at different times of the year. The Standard & Poor's *Stock Guide* is a source for this information, as is the Value Line Survey. Most companies like to pay the same dividend every quarter until they can afford to increase it. Above all, they don't like to cut their dividends, since investors who depend on this income will sell their shares, and the stock will decline in price. If you use good judgment in selecting your stocks, you can expect that your companies will increase their dividends nearly every year.

Dividend Payout Ratio

If a company earns $4 per share in a given year and pays out $3 to its shareholders, it has a payout ratio of 75 percent. If it pays out only $1, the payout ratio is 25 percent. A low payout ratio is preferred, since it means that the company is plowing back its profits into future growth.

The Dividend Reinvestment Plan

Unless you are retired, you might like to reinvest your dividends in more shares. Many companies have a plan (also known as a DRIP) that will allow you to do this, and the charge for this service is often minimal. Most of these companies also allow you to mail in additional cash, which will be used to purchase new shares, again at minimal cost.

In recent years, a few companies have created "direct" dividend reinvestment plans. Unlike most plans, direct plans enable you to buy your initial shares directly from the company. To alert you to which companies have direct plans, I have inserted the word *direct*. Companies having such plans include Exxon, McDonald's, Procter & Gamble, Merck, and Lilly. Incidentally, you can rarely buy just one share. Many companies have a minimum, such as $500.

This may sound like a good way to avoid paying brokerage commissions, but there are some drawbacks to bear in mind. For one thing, you can't time your purchases, since it may be a week or more before your purchase is made.

Even worse is calculating your cost basis for tax purposes. By the time you sell, you may have made scores of small investments in the same stock, each with a different cost basis. Make sure you keep a file for each company so that you can make these calculations when the time comes. Or, better still, don't sell.

Dollar Cost Averaging

Dollar cost averaging is a systematic way to invest money over a long period, such as ten, fifteen, or twenty years. It entails investing the same amount of money regularly, such as each month or each quarter. If you do this faithfully, you will be buying more stock when the price is lower, and less stock when the price is high. This tends to smooth out the gyra-tions of the market. Dollar cost averaging is often used with a mutual fund, but it can just as easily be done with a company that has a dividend reinvestment plan (DRIP).

Income Statement

Most investors are more interested in the income statement than they are the balance sheet. They are particularly interested in the progress (or lack of it) in earnings per share. The income statement lists such items as net sales, cost of sales, interest expense, and gross profit. As with the balance sheet, it makes sense to compare this year's numbers with those of the prior year.

Investment Advisor

Investors who do not have the time or inclination to manage their own portfolios may elect to employ an investment advisor. Most advisors charge 1 percent a year. Thus, if you own stocks worth $300,000, your annual fee would be $3,000. Advisors differ from brokers, since they do not profit from changes. Brokers, by contrast, charge a commission on each transaction, which means they profit from changes in your portfolio. Advisors profit only when the value of your holdings increases. For instance, if the value of your portfolio increases to $500,000, the annual fee will be $5,000. You, of course, will be $200,000 richer. In case you wondered, I am an investment advisor and my minimum fee is $1,000 a year.

Preferred Stock

The name sounds impressive. In actual practice, owning preferred stocks is about as exciting as watching your cat take a bath. A preferred stock is much like a bond. It pays the same dividend year in and year out. The yield is usually higher than a common stock. If the company issuing the preferred stock does well, you do not benefit. If it does poorly, however, you may suffer, since the dividend could be cut or eliminated. My advice is: Never, never buy a preferred stock.

Price–Earnings Ratio

This is a term that is extremely important. Don't make the mistake of overlooking it. Whole books have been written on the importance of the P/E ratio, which is sometimes referred to as "the P/E" or "the multiple."

The P/E ratio tells you whether a stock is cheap or expensive. It is calculated by dividing the price of the stock by the company's earnings per share over the most recent twelve months. For instance, if you refer to the *Stock Guide*, you will see that Leggett and Platt had earnings of $2.23. At the time, the stock was selling for $52. Divide that figure by $2.23 and you get a P/E of 23.32.

In most instances, a low P/E indicates a stock that Wall Street is not too excited about. If they like a stock, they will bid it up to the point where its P/E is quite high, let's say 25 or 30. Coca-Cola is such a stock. In this same *Stock Guide*, Coca-Cola had annual earnings per share of $1.59. Based on the price of the stock at that time (it was $75), that works out to a P/E ratio of 47.17. Of course, Coca-Cola is extremely well regarded by investors and is expected to do well in the future—but is it really worth 47 times earnings?

Stock Split

Corporations know that investors like to invest in lower-priced stocks. Thus, when the price of the stock gets to a certain level, which varies with the company, they will split the stock. For instance, if the stock is $75, they might split it three-for-one. Your original 100 shares now become 300 shares. Unfortunately, your 300 shares are worth exactly the same as your original 100 shares. What it amounts to is this: Splits please small investors, but they don't make them any richer. One company, Berkshire Hathaway, has never been split. It is now worth a huge amount per share: over $68,000. It also pays no dividend. The company is run by the legendary Warren Buffett. He has made a lot of people very wealthy without a stock split or dividend.

Yield

If your company pays a dividend, you can relate this dividend to the price of the stock in order to calculate the yield. A $50 stock that pays a $2 annual dividend (which amounts to 50 cents per quarter) will have a yield of 4 percent. You arrive at this figure by dividing $2 by $50. Actually, you don't have to make this calculation, since the yield is given to you in the stock tables of the *Wall Street Journal*. Here are some typical yields from mid-1999. Coca-Cola, 1.0 percent; Exxon, 2.1 percent; General Electric, 1.2 percent; Illinois Tool Works, 0.7 percent; Kimberly-Clark, 1.8 percent; and Minnesota Mining and Manufacturing, 2.6 percent. Although the yield is of some importance, you should not judge a stock by its yield without looking at many other factors.

Part II
100 Best Stocks You Can Buy

The following table lists the 100 stocks discussed in this book. A brief explanation of the table follows.

The ticker symbol is given so that you can use the quote machine in your broker's office. Or, if you call your broker on the phone, it makes it easier if you know the ticker symbol, since your broker may not.

In the table, "Industry" refers to one of the company's main businesses. This is not always easy to express in one or two words. For instance, United Technologies is involved in such industries as aircraft engines, elevators, and air conditioning equipment. To describe the company succinctly, I arbitrarily picked the designation "aircraft engines." Similarly, General Electric presents an even more daunting problem since it owns NBC, makes appliances, aircraft engines, medical devices, and a host of other things.

The designation "Sector" indicates the broad economic industry group that the company operates in, such as Transportation, Capital Goods, Energy, Consumer Cyclicals, and so forth. As described elsewhere, a properly diversified portfolio should include at least one stock in each of the twelve sectors. However, I see no problem in having stocks in nine or ten sectors.

"Category" refers to one of the following: (1) Income (Income), (2) Growth and Income (Gro Inc), (3) Conservative Growth (Con Grow), or (4) Aggressive Growth (Aggr Gro). It might make sense to have some representation in each category, even though you have a strong preference for only one.

I have not included the page numbers because of space limitations. In any event, it is easy enough to find a particular stock, since they appear alphabetically in the book.

Company	Symbol	Industry	Sector	Category
—A—				
Abbott Laboratories	ABT	Med Supplies	Cons Staples	Con Grow
Air Products	APD	Chemical	Basic Ind	Con Grow
Alberto-Culver	ACV	Cosmetics	Cons Staples	Con Grow
Albertson's	ABS	Grocery	Cons Staples	Con Grow
Alcoa	AA	Metals	Basic Ind	Aggr Gro
AlliedSignal	ALD	Diversified	Conglomerates	Aggr Gro
American Home Prod.	AHP	Drugs	Cons Staples	Con Gro
American Water Works	AWK	Water	Utilities	Gro Inc
AT&T Corp.	T	Telephone	Utilities	Con Grow
Automatic Data Proc.	AUD	Comp Soft	Cap Goods-Tech	Aggr Gro
—B—				
Baldor Electric	BEZ	Elect Equip	Capital Goods	Gro Inc
Bank of New York	BK	Bank	Financial	Con Gro
Becton Dickinson	BDX	Med Supplies	Cons Staples	Aggr Gro
Bed, Bath & Beyond	BBBY	Retail	Credit Cycl	Aggr Gro
BellSouth	BLS	Telephone	Utilities	Grow Inc
Bergen Brunswig	BBC	Drg Wholesaler	Cons Staples	Con Grow
Bristol-Myers Squibb	BMY	Drugs	Cons Staples	Con Grow
—C—				
Cedar Fair	FUN	Entertain	Cons Staples	Income
Chevron	CHV	Oil	Energy	Gro Inc
Clayton Homes	CMH	Housing	Credit Cycl	Aggr Gro

Clorox	CLX	Household Pd	Cons Staples	Aggr Gro
Coca-Cola	KO	Beverages	Cons Staples	Aggr Gro
Colgate-Palmolive	CL	Household Pd	Cons Staples	Con Grow
Compaq Computer	CPQ	Computers	Cap Goods-Tech	Aggr Gro
—D—				
Dexter Corp.	DEX	Chemicals	Basic Ind	Income
Disney, Walt	DIS	Entertain	Cons Staples	Aggr Gro
Dover Corp.	DOV	Machinery	Capital Goods	Aggr Gro
Duke Energy	DUK	Elect Util	Utilities	Income
—E—				
Edwards, A. G.	AGE	Stockbroker	Financial	Aggr Gro
Emerson Electric	EMR	Elect Equip	Capital Goods	Con Grow
Energen Corp.	EGN	Natural Gas	Utilities	Income
Ethan Allen	ETH	Furniture	Credit Cycl	Aggr Gro
Exxon Mobil	XON	Oil	Energy	Gro Inc
—F—				
FDX Corporation	FDX	Air Freight	Transportation	Aggr Gro
Federal Signal	FSS	Elect Equip	Capital Goods	Gro Inc
FelCor Lodging	FCH	REIT	Cons Services	Income
Fifth Third Bancorp	FITB	Bank	Financial	Aggr Gro
FPL Group	FPL	Elect Util	Utilities	Income
—G—				
Gannett Co.	GCI	Publishing	Cons Services	Con Grow
General Electric	GE	Elect Equip	Capital Goods	Con Grow
General Motors	GM	Automobile	Cons Cyclical	Gro Inc
Genuine Parts	GPC	Parts Distrib	Cons Cyclical	Gro Inc
Gillette	G	Toiletries	Cons Services	Aggr Gro
Grainger, W. W.	GWW	Elect Equip	Cap Goods-Tech	Con Grow
—H—				
Hannaford Brothers	HRD	Grocery	Cons Staples	Con Grow
Harley-Davidson	HDI	Recreation	Cons Staples	Aggr Gro
Hewlett-Packard	HWP	Computers	Cap Goods-Tech	Aggr Gro
Home Depot	HD	Retail	Credit Cycl	Aggr Gro
Houghton Mifflin	HTN	Publishing	Con Services	Con Grow
Hubbell	HUB.B	Elect Equip	Capital Goods	Gro Inc
—I—				
Illinois Tool Works	ITW	Machinery	Capital Goods	Con Grow
Ingersoll-Rand	IR	Machinery	Capital Goods	Con Grow
Intel	INTC	Computers	Cap Goods-Tech	Aggr Gro
Int'l Business Mach	IBM	Computer	Cap Goods-Tech	Aggr Gro
Interpublic	IPG	Advertising	Cons Cyclical	Con Grow
—J—				
Jefferson-Pilot	JP	Insurance	Financial	Gro Inc
Johnson & Johnson	JNJ	Med Supplies	Cons Staples	Con Grow
Johnson Controls	JCI	Elect Equip	Capital Goods	Con Grow
—K—				
Kimberly-Clark	KMB	Tissues	Basic Ind	Gro Inc
Kimco Realty	KIM	REIT	Cons Services	Income

—L—

Leggett & Platt	LEG	Furn Compon	Credit Cycl	Con Grow
Lilly, Eli	LLY	Drugs	Cons Staples	Aggr Gro
Lilly Industries	LI	Chemicals	Credit Cyclic	Con Grow
Lucent Technologies	LU	Tel Equip	Cap Goods Tech	Aggr Gro

—M—

McCormick & Co.	MCCRK	Spices	Cons Staples	Con Grow
McDonald's	MCD	Restaurant	Cons Services	Con Grow
McGraw-Hill	MHP	Publishing	Cons Services	Con Grow
MDU Resources	MDU	G&E Utility	Utilities	Income
Merck & Co.	MRK	Drugs	Cons Staples	Con Grow
Microsoft	MSFT	Comp Soft	Cap Goods-Tech	Aggr Gro
Minnesota Mining	MMM	Diversified	Cap Goods-Tech	Income

—N—

National City	NCC	Bank	Financial	Income
New Plan Excel	NXL	REIT	Cons Cyclical	Income
Newell Rubbermaid	NWL	Cons Durables	Cons Staples	Con Grow
Nicor Inc.	GAS	Natural Gas	Utilities	Income
Nordson	NDSN	Machinery	Capital Goods	Cons Gro
Norfolk-Southern	NSC	Railroad	Transportation	Income

—P—

Pfizer	PFE	Drugs	Cons Staples	Aggr Gro
Philip Morris	MO	Tobacco	Cons Staples	Gro Inc
Pitney Bowes	PBI	Postage Mtrs	Cap Goods-Tech	Gro Inc
PPG Industries	PPG	Glass	Basic Ind	Con Grow
Praxair	PX	Indust Gases	Basic Ind	Con Grow
Procter & Gamble	PG	Household Pd	Cons Staples	Con Grow

—S—

Sara Lee	SLE	Foods, App'l	Cons Staples	Con Grow
Sherwin-Williams	SHW	Paint	Credit Cyclic	Con Grow
SIGCORP	SIG	G&E Utility	Utilities	Income
Sysco Corporation	SYY	Food Distrib	Cons Staples	Con Grow

—T—

Textron	TXT	Diversified	Conglomerates	Con Grow

—U—

United Technologies	UTX	Aircraft Eng	Cap Goods-Tech	Aggr Gro
U. S. Foodservice	UFS	Food Distrib	Cons Staples	Con Grow

—V—

Valspar	VAL	Paint	Credit Cyclic	Con Grow
VF Corporation	VF	Apparel	Cons Cyclical	Con Grow
Vulcan Materials	VMC	Const Materi	Credit Cyclic	Gro Inc

—W—

Wachovia	WB	Bank	Financial	Gro Inc
Walgreen	WAG	Drug Stores	Cons Staples	Aggr Gro
Wal-Mart Stores	WMT	Retail	Cons Cyclical	Aggr Gro
Wash. Gas Light	WGL	Natural Gas	Utilities	Income
Washington Real Est.	WRE	REIT	Cons Cyclical	Income
Weingarten Realty	WRI	REIT	Cons Cyclical	Income
Weyerhaeuser	WY	Forest Prod	Basic Ind	Gro Inc

CONSERVATIVE GROWTH

Abbott Laboratories

100 Abbott Park Road, Abbott Park, IL 60064-3500 □ Investor contact: John Thomas (847) 938-2655 □
Dividend reinvestment plan available (888) 332-2268 □ Web site: www.abbott.com □ Ticker symbol: ABT □
S&P rating: A+ □ Value Line financial strength rating: A++

Abbott Laboratories is one of the largest diversified health care manufacturers in the world, with 1998 revenues of $12.5 billion. The company's products are sold in more than 130 countries, with about 40 percent of sales derived from those international operations.

Abbott's major business segments include Pharmaceuticals & Nutritionals (prescription drugs, medical nutritionals, and infant formulas) and Hospital & Laboratory Products (intravenous solutions, administrative sets, drug-delivery devices, and diagnostic equipment and reagents).

Although revenue growth in Abbott's infant formula and diagnostics businesses has slowed in recent years, new drugs (such as the antibiotic clarithromycin), new indications (including the BPH claim for Hytrin), the launch of disease-specific medical nutritionals and costcutting (diagnostics and hospital supplies) continue to boost the company's profits.

Brand names include Erythrocin, Similac, Isomil, and Selsun Blue. What's more, Ensure (an over-the-counter medical nutritional for adults) is an important cornerstone of the company's nutritional products franchise and one of the largest OTC health care and nutritional products sold in the United States.

Shortcomings to Bear in Mind

- Abbott's solid performance in 1998 did not come without problems. For example, health care markets in Southeast Asia and Japan suffered under considerable macroeconomic pressure. What's more, markets in many parts of the world continue to face significant pricing pressures. In all of Abbott's markets, moreover, the forces of increased competition, customer consolidation, and technology advances continue to challenge the company. "Even so," says management, "health care remains an outstanding business for companies with a commitment to scientific innovation, long-term growth, sound financial management, and operational excellence. Abbott is one of those companies."

- Around the world, governments and private payers seek to reduce the growth of health-care spending. This results in pressure on utilization and pricing in many parts of Abbott's business. In addition, negative effects of foreign exchange and difficult economic conditions in Asia will continue to be a challenge for the company.

Reasons to Buy

- In a major step to expand its pharmaceuticals segment, Abbott agreed to acquire Alza Corporation in June of 1999 for $7.3 billion in stock. The combined company will not only become a formidable maker of cancer and incontinence medicines, but it will be the nation's leading maker of sustained-release drugs. According to one analyst, "The two companies are a perfect fit. Alza has excellent drug-delivery programs and good technology." Miles D. White, Abbott's CEO, cited Alza's current pharmaceutical offerings and its pipeline of drugs under development. Alza focuses on drugs used in the urology and oncology sectors.

- In 1998, diluted earnings per share rose 12.7 percent. This marked Abbott's twenty-sixth consecutive year of double-digit growth in earnings per share. Cash flow from operations exceeded $2.7 billion. At year-end, the board of directors declared the company's 300th consecutive dividend, a record dating back to 1924.
- In 1998, Abbott's scientists made excellent progress on the development of the next-generation protease inhibitor for HIV and AIDS that recently moved into late-stage clinical trials. Data suggest that, for patients, this drug is well-tolerated, convenient, and more potent than Abbott's Norvir, the most potent protease inhibitor on the market today.
- In early 1999, Abbott acquired U.S. co-marketing rights to the drug Mobic, one of a new class of highly promising pain medications known generally as "Cox-2 inhibitors." Abbott sells the drug along with its maker, Germany's Boehringer Ingelheim GmbH. The Cox-2 drugs, so-called because they act on an enzyme called cyclooxygenas e-2, represent a potential breakthrough in the treatment of arthritis. Wall Street analysts say they will constitute a market of several billion dollars soon. That is because they treat pain as well as current drugs, but hold the potential of doing so without causing severe gastrointestinal difficulties, such as bleeding ulcers, as current arthritis drugs do in some patients.

For Abbott, the deal with Boehringer is a major departure and is an example of things to come. The venture reflects the more aggressive style of its new chief executive, Miles D. White. In interviews, Mr. White makes it clear that Abbott, which long has shunned pharmaceutical co-marketing deals and largely avoided mergers, now will be more assertive in pursuing both. Apart from acquiring rights to Mobic, Abbott also began co-marketing the Boehringer hypertension drug Micardis, also among a promising new class of drugs called angiotensin II receptor blockers.

- In 1998, Abbott launched TriCor, a lipid-lowering drug licensed from Groupe Fournier of France. The product has been well received by patients and physicians.
- In late 1998, Abbott and Idun Pharmaceuticals, Inc. signed a worldwide research agreement to focus on the discovery and development of new treatments for people with cancer. Abbott and Idun, moreover, will collaborate on the discovery of drugs that regulate the activity of select proteins involved in the cell pathway leading to programmed cell death, or apoptosis.
- The cornerstone of Abbott's neuroscience business is Depakote, a versatile agent for the treatment of epilepsy and bipolar disorder and the prevention of migraine headaches. In 1998, Depakote surpassed lithium, the longstanding market leader, to become the agent most prescribed by psychiatrists for treating patients who experience manic episodes associated with bipolar disorder (also known as manic depression).
- To supplement the company's strong market position in urology—which includes pharmaceuticals such as Hytrin, for benign prostatic hyperplasia, and diagnostic tests for prostate conditions—Abbott is developing a compound for urinary stress incontinence. This is one of a new wave of medications in clinical development aimed at improving the lifestyles of active adult patients.
- In diagnostics, Abbott launched many new products in 1998. Most notable is ARCHITECT, Abbott's next-generation family of laboratory systems that ultimately will enable customers to combine immunoassay testing with

clinical chemistry testing in one integrated, labor-efficient system.

- In the company's Ross products division, Abbott's collaboration with Med-Immune, Inc., led to the introduction of an important new product for the pediatric market: Synagis, for the prevention of respiratory syncytial virus (RSV), a serious and sometimes deadly disease that affects hundreds of thousands of children throughout the world.

- TAP Pharmaceuticals Inc., Abbott's partnership with Takeda Chemical Industries, Ltd. of Osaka, Japan, remains an important growth contributor for the company. Sales of PREVACID, for instance, nearly doubled in 1998, to $1.3 billion. Sales of Lupron and PREVACID together now exceed $2 billion.

- As powerful as Abbott's internal programs are, no drug company can succeed alone in today's markets. There is too much new information and too much new technology for any company to rely exclusively on internal development. This is the impetus for one of Abbott's growth strategies—external collaborations. Collaborations bring the company new technologies, such as combinatorial chemistry and genomics that hold great promise for speeding up the drug discovery process. In the case of genomics, Abbott is also using this technology to develop diagnostic capabilities that will allow earlier and more accurate diagnosis of medical conditions.

Collaborations also bring the company promising new clinical candidates. An alliance with MedImmune, Inc. of Gaithersburg, Maryland, provides the company access to a humanized monoclonal antibody that is being developed for prevention of respiratory syncytial virus, a serious lung disease in children. What's more, Abbott has entered the important medical category of lipid-lowering agents through an agreement with Groupe Fournier of France.

Abbott's strategic focus in the realm of diabetes disease management led to an alliance with Metabolex, Inc., of Hayward, California, to discover drugs to treat diabetes and to develop nutritional products for diabetics. Further, Abbott entered into an agreement with Biorex Research and Development Rt. of Hungary to develop and market a drug to treat diabetic complications.

- Clarithromycin is the treatment of choice for the eradication of *Helicobacter pylori* (*H. pylori*), a bacterium that is believed to be responsible for about 90 percent of active or recurrent duodenal (small intestine) ulcers. Clarithromycin is prescribed in 85 percent of all antibiotic regimens for ulcers.

- Abbott's adult nutritional business, led by the Ensure brand, has been growing in international markets. Sales are strengthened by Abbott's presence in emerging markets where economic growth is spurring demand for quality health care.

- Abbott is focusing on global opportunities for its pediatric nutritional products, particularly the new, reformulated Similac infant formula. This product has been launched in more than 20 countries, including the United States.

The reformulation has made Similac closer than ever to breast milk. The new formulation is marketed as Improved Similac in the United States and as Similac Advance and other Similac trademarks in the rest of the world. It is the only infant formula with added nucleotide levels patterned after the potentially available nucleotides from breast milk. Nucleotides, the building blocks of DNA and RNA, are compounds found naturally in all cells and in breast milk. The new formula is the product of a seven-year research effort—the largest such program ever conducted by Abbott's nutritional research scientists.

- Anesthesia is a cornerstone of Abbott's hospital pharmaceutical strategy. The company's worldwide leadership in anesthesia is providing the catalyst for growth in other hospital business segments, particularly outside the United States.

Abbott's newest inhalation anesthetic, sevoflurane (marketed as Ultane in the United States and Sevorane in other countries), has had the most successful new hospital product launch in Abbott history. Anesthesiologists in 56 countries now use this versatile agent. Sevoflurane has broad applicability for both induction and maintenance of anesthesia in pediatric and adult patients. And because it allows patients to emerge from anesthesia rapidly and smoothly, it has helped the company penetrate the growing market for outpatient surgery. Sevoflurane has experienced steady growth since its introduction in 1994. It is the induction agent of choice for anesthesiologists who have administered it.

- Abbott is a world leader in hematology technology. Hematology measures various components of whole blood, including red and white blood cells and platelets. These tests are a basic measure of health and are the most commonly ordered blood tests. Abbott's technological leadership is most clearly illustrated by the company's flagship hematology analyzer, the Cell-Dyn 4000. This new state-of-the-art instrument is the first to automate a number of hematological measurements. This improves laboratory efficiency and reduces the time it takes to report test results, making the Cell-Dyn 4000 perfectly suited to the needs of high- volume reference laboratories as well as labs that routinely handle abnormal samples.

- Abbott Laboratories, already a major player in drugs for the treatment of AIDS, moved to strengthen its position further in mid-1999 with a $335-million alliance with Triangle Pharmaceuticals Inc. to produce new antiviral compounds. Abbott said it will develop and co-promote products for the AIDS-causing HIV virus and for hepatitis B that are being developed by Triangle. Abbott already sells Norvir, generically called ritonavir, and is developing a highly promising new compound called ABT-378 that is in phase III, the final stage of human trials. Arthur Higgins, Abbott's senior vice president of pharmaceutical operations, said the alliance with Triangle could "potentially launch at least one new antiviral each year over the next four years."

Total assets: $13,216 million
Current ratio: 1.09
Common shares outstanding: 1,518 million
Return on 1998 shareholders' equity: 43.6%

	1998	1997	1996	1995	1994	1993	1992	1991
Revenues (millions)	12,477	11,883	11,014	10,012	9,156	8,408	7,852	6,877
Net income (millions)	2,333	2,094	1,882	1,689	1,517	1,399	1,198	1,089
Earnings per share	1.51	1.34	1.21	1.06	.94	.85	.71	.64
Dividends per share	.60	.54	.48	.42	.38	.34	.30	.25
Price: high	50.1	34.9	28.7	22.4	16.9	15.4	17.1	17.4
low	32.5	24.9	19.1	15.4	12.7	11.3	13.1	9.8

Air Products and Chemicals, Inc.

7201 Hamilton Boulevard, Allentown, PA 18195-1501 ◻ **Investor contact: Michael F. Hilton (610) 481-5775** ◻ **Direct dividend reinvestment plan available (888) 694-9458** ◻ **Web site: www.airproducts.com** ◻ **Listed: NYSE** ◻ **Fiscal year's end September 30** ◻ **Ticker symbol: APD** ◻ **S&P rating: A** ◻ **Value Line financial strength rating: B++**

Air Products and Chemicals, Inc., with operations in thirty countries and 1998 revenues in excess of $4.9 billion, is a leading supplier of industrial gases and related equipment, specialty and intermediate chemicals, as well as environmental and energy systems.

Air Products' industrial gas and chemical products are used by a diverse base of customers in manufacturing, process, and service industries.

In the environmental and energy businesses, Air Products and its affiliates own and operate facilities to reduce air and water pollution, dispose of solid waste, and generate electric power.

Industrial Gases
• APD is the fourth-largest supplier in the world.

• Its products are essential in many manufacturing processes.

• Gases are produced by cryogenic, adsorption, and membrane technologies

• They are supplied by tankers, on-site plants, pipelines, and cylinders

• International sales, including the company's share of joint ventures, represent more than half of Air Products' gas revenues.

The markets served by Industrial Gases include chemical processing, metals, oil and gas production, electronics, research, food, glass, health care, and pulp and paper. Principal products are industrial gases, such as nitrogen, oxygen, hydrogen, argon, and helium, and various specialty, cutting, and welding gases.

Chemicals
• APD has a leadership position in over 80 percent of the markets served.

• Markets include a wide range of attractive, diversified end uses that reduce overall exposure to economic cycles.

• World-scale, state-of-the-art production facilities and process technology skills ensure consistent, low-cost products while enhancing long-term customer relationships.

• International sales, including exports to over one hundred countries, represent a quarter of the business.

The markets served by the Chemicals operation include adhesives, agriculture, furniture, automotive products, paints and coatings, textiles, paper, and building products. Its principal products are emulsions, polyvinyl alcohol, polyurethane and epoxy additives, surfactants, amines, and polyurethane intermediaries.

Environmental and Energy Systems
• Facilities, owned and operated with partners, dispose of solid waste, reduce air pollution, and generate electrical power.

• Strong positions are built by extending core skills developed in the industrial gas business.

• Forces driving this market are environmental regulations, demand for efficient sources of electrical power, utility deregulation, and privatization. Principal products are waste-to-energy plants, electric power services, and air pollution-control systems.

The markets served by Environmental and Energy Systems include solid waste disposal, electrical power generation, and air pollution reduction.

Equipment and Services

• Cryogenic and noncryogenic equipment is designed and manufactured for various gas-processing applications.

• Equipment is sold worldwide or manufactured for Air Products industrial gas business and its international network of joint ventures.

The markets served by Equipment and Services include chemicals, steel, oil and gas recovery, and power generation.

Shortcomings to Bear in Mind

■ Air Products has a rather leveraged balance sheet. Its common stock represents only 53 percent of capitalization. As a consequence, its coverage of long-term debt interest is only 4.9 times.

Reasons to Buy

■ In 1998, Air Products commissioned new tonnage hydrogen plants to serve customers in Europe and Latin America, bringing to thirteen the hydrogen supply arrangements the company has undertaken for refiners worldwide within the past five years. APD also began work on a new hydrogen and synthesis gas facility in Louisiana to serve BASF and Shell and announced plans to build, own, and operate a world-class hydrogen plant for refineries in California. As part of a joint venture, Air Products signed a contract to supply the syngas and hydrogen requirements for Eastman Chemical's oxo-alcohol facility in Singapore.

■ In 1998, Air Products and Chemicals began tripling the capacity of its Liberal, Kansas facility, won new business from the Arianespace program in France and Germany, and extended its domestic magnetic resonance imaging (MRI) cryogenic fill contract with Siemens

Medical Systems, Inc. through the year 2004.

The company also celebrated the tenth anniversary of its "KeepCOLD" Cryogenic Fill Services Program that supplies cryogenic gases and services to more than half of the total MRI magnets worldwide.

■ Demand for industrial gas has been strong. This high demand is more than a cyclical phenomenon and is being fueled by new applications and new industrial gas production technology.

■ Beyond its leadership in tonnage hydrogen, Air Products also has a substantial liquid hydrogen business. The National Aeronautics and Space Administration (NASA) is the world's largest customer of liquid hydrogen. The company has been serving NASA since the 1960s, when APD first began supplying hydrogen for the Apollo space program. Over the last twenty years, Air Products has safely and reliably provided hydrogen for NASA's space shuttle engine-testing program and all eighty-five shuttle launches.

■ Today, some 60,000 customers in North America—once served by eighty different locations—are now managed from the company's Single-Point-Of-Contact Center, using state-of-the-art information technology systems. The number of errorfree deliveries is improving, customer runouts are significantly lower, and APD's customers are increasingly positive about the changes made.

■ Air Products is well positioned to benefit from increased demand from new plants being built in the chemical, paper, and other basic industries. In particular, the company is seeing an acceleration in bidding for new gas contracts in the electronics market and in gaseous hydrogen for oil refineries.

- Air Products's reputation for reliability and innovation has made the company a preferred supplier to the electronics industry. As the market leader in North America and Europe and a strong competitor in Asia through joint ventures, APD's global infrastructure assures its electronics customers that they can count on receiving the same high-quality products and services, regardless of where they are.
- Air Products continues to be among the lowest-cost, highest-quality manufacturers in the chemicals industry. To maintain that leadership, the company implemented a systematic process for setting productivity goals and monitoring progress throughout its operations.

- The chemical and process industries (CPI) market is the company's largest. At the forefront of the shift from "make" to "buy" hydrogen decisions, Air Products has over fifty hydrogen plants around the world, plus extensive pipeline systems in the United States, Europe, and Asia, to meet unprecedented demand from refiners for hydrogen needed to produce a cleaner slake of fuels and carbon monoxide and synthesis gas for petrochemical producers.
- Earnings and dividends have been advancing at a healthy clip. EPS climbed from $.98 in 1988 to $2.22 in 1998, a compound annual growth rate of 8.5 percent. In the same ten-year stretch, dividends expanded from $.28 to $.64, a growth rate of 8.6 percent.

Total assets: $7,490 million
Current ratio: 1.40
Common shares outstanding: 211 million
Return on 1998 shareholders' equity: 20.8%

	1998	1997	1996	1995	1994	1993	1992	1991
Revenues (millions)	4,919	4,638	4,008	3,865	3,485	3,328	3,217	2,931
Net income (millions)	489	429	416	368	264	268	235	216
Earnings per share	2.22	1.95	1.69	1.62	1.03	1.16	1.19	1.05
Dividends per share	.64	.58	.54	.51	.48	.44	.42	.37
Price: high	45.3	44.8	35.3	29.8	25.2	24.3	24.8	18.5
low	29.0	33.2	25.2	21.9	19.4	18.8	18.2	12.8

CONSERVATIVE GROWTH

Alberto-Culver Company

2525 Armitage Avenue, Melrose Park, IL 60160 ◻ Investor contact: Daniel B. Stone (708) 450-3005 ◻ Web site: www.alberto.com ◻ Dividend reinvestment plan not available ◻ Fiscal year's end September 30 ◻ Listed: NYSE ◻ Ticker symbols: ACV and ACV.A ◻ S&P rating: A ◻ Value Line financial strength rating: B++

Alberto-Culver is a leading developer and manufacturer of personal-care products, primarily for hair care, retail food products, household items, and health and hygiene products.

Alberto-Culver is comprised of three strong businesses built around potent brands and trademarks:

- Alberto-Culver USA develops innovative brand name products for the retail, professional beauty, and institutional markets. Personal-use products include: hair fixatives, shampoos, hair dressings, and conditioners sold under such trademarks as Alberto VO5, Bold Hold, Alberto, Alberto Balsam, Consort, TRE-

Semme, and FDS (feminine deodorant spray). Retail food product labels include: SugarTwin, Mrs. Dash, Molly McButter, Baker's Joy, and Village Saucerie. Household products include: Static Guard (antistatic spray) and Kleen Guard (furniture polish).

• Alberto-Culver International has carried the Alberto VO5 flag into more than one hundred countries and from that solid base has built products, new brands, and businesses focused on the needs of each market.

• Sally Beauty Company is the engine that drives Alberto-Culver. With over 2,000 outlets in the United States and the United Kingdom, Sally is the largest cash-and-carry supplier of professional beauty products in the world.

The typical Sally Beauty store averages 1,800 square feet and is situated in a strip shopping center. It carries more than 3,000 items. About three-quarters of Sally Beauty's sales are to small beauty salons and barber shops, with the rest to retail customers.

Sally is the only national player in the United States in cash-and-carry beauty supplies sold primarily to professionals. It is the market leader by a wide margin. Sally capitalizes on its dominance in that niche, which provides beauty professionals the opportunity to purchase products from a wide selection of vendors at wholesale prices without having to manage and carry inventory in their stores.

The company's products do not have a common origin. They have come to Alberto-Culver in diverse ways. For instance, the original Alberto VO5 Hairdressing was a small regional brand that the company acquired because it felt it had national sales potential.

In another instance, the FDS products and its mousse products had counterparts in the marketplace in Europe. Consequently, ACV brought the ideas to the United States and introduced its products to an American audience.

Mrs. Dash, Static Guard, and Consort were all developed internally by the company's research and development team because its customers identified a need that these products met.

SugarTwin and TRESemme were acquired by the company as tiny brands and grown to the strong positions they hold today.

Perhaps the company's most important acquisition, after the original purchase of Alberto VO5 Conditioning Hairdressing, was the purchase of the Sally Beauty Company, originally a chain of twelve stores, many of which were franchised. Today, the chain has over 2,000 company-owned stores, including more than one hundred in Great Britain, Germany, and Japan. Sally is the largest distributor of professional beauty supplies in the world.

The primary customer for Sally is the salon and barber professional who can find at Sally an unmatched selection of professional beauty supplies available at discount prices. In addition to the supplies they need, these professionals find in Sally a valuable source of information about trends and products that they can take back to their customers.

One of the keys to Sally's success is the ability to move product quickly from warehouse to shelf. This process starts with proprietary point-of-sale registers in each Sally store that record and report each sale. Sally is now investing millions of dollars to add a second POS register to each store to enhance its ability to serve customers.

Sally greatly improved its inventory-control ability with the opening of a new computer-controlled, state-of-the-art warehouse in northern Nevada. The company has a similar distribution center in Columbus, Ohio.

Shortcomings to Bear in Mind

- Fiscal 1998 was a challenge for Alberto-Culver. There were very large competitive hair-care product introductions that put pressure on the company's packaged-goods businesses. Then too, the weakness of key foreign currencies reduced ACV's dollar-reported sales by over $25 million. As a consequence, the company's growth rate slowed, compared with the previous three years, which were helped by acquisitions. Even so, Alberto-Culver was still able to achieve record sales and profits.

- For the longer term, the fundamental outlook for the personal-care industry differs geographically. Domestically, this industry is mature, consolidated, and competitive. According to the Commerce Department, wholesale shipments of beauty-care products are expected to inch ahead between 3 percent and 5 percent annually in the years ahead. In order to preserve or gain precious shelf space, these manufacturers have elected to consolidate, roll out new products, and spend more on marketing and advertising. Significant earnings growth for personal-care companies as a whole in the United States is rather unlikely. If there is much earnings growth at all, it is likely to come from acquisitions, cost reductions, and international expansion. For its part, Alberto-Culver has a strong balance sheet and seems likely to continue to make solid acquisitions in the future.

Reasons to Buy

- Alberto-Culver has taken steps to strengthen its new product capabilities. Management has established a New Business Development Group that will coordinate new product development for both the domestic and International sector. With creative R&D labs in several of its facilities, Alberto-Culver is in an excellent position to accelerate its new product efforts and is committed to making the investments necessary in development and marketing to bring these products to market successfully.

- Throughout 1998, the company continued to strengthen and enhance its product lines with consumer-tested new products:
  - Alberto VO5 added herbal formulas to its shampoo and conditioner line and fortified the original shampoo line with a five-vitamin formula.
  - St. Ives introduced a novel spray-on body lotion, St. Ives Swiss Formula Body Lotion Mist. Fast, convenient, and messfree, the soothing botanical mists have been a strong addition to the brand's lineup.
  - St. Ives also completely relaunched its shampoo and conditioner line with new packaging, new fragrances, and new formulas sold under the St. Ives Swiss Spa banner. The line features six shampoo and six conditioner botanical formulas.
  - FDS came to market with StayFresh, a product for consumers with light bladder control problems, that neutralizes odor on clothing and bedding.
  - TRESemme debuted a line of antifatigue shampoos called TRESemme Changes.

- Alberto VO5 Conditioning Hairdressing remains by far the number one brand in its category and the best-selling hairdressing in the world. VO5 is among the market leaders in the United States, Great Britain, Scandinavia, Canada, Mexico, Australia, and Japan.

- In over 120 countries, Alberto-Culver International markets or manufactures many of the consumer brands that it markets in the United States, including Alberto VO5 and St. Ives Swiss Formula brands.

In addition, some of the company's international units offer products unique to their markets. In the Scandinavian countries, for example, ACV is the market leader in a wide range of toiletries and household products. In the United Kingdom, the company is a market leader in hair-styling products. What's more, it has introduced several items in the hair-coloring segment. Finally, in Canada, Alberto-Culver produces the top-selling Alberto-European styling line, and its SugarTwin artificial sweetener is number one in its category.

Total assets: $1,068 million
Current ratio: 1.89
Common shares outstanding: 57 million
Return on 1998 shareholders' equity: 15.6%

	1998	1997	1996	1995	1994	1993	1992	1991
Revenues (millions)	1,835	1,775	1,590	1,358	1,216	1,148	1,091	874
Net income (millions)	83.1	75.6	62.7	52.7	44.1	41.3	38.6	30.1
Earnings per share	1.37	1.25	1.06	.94	.79	.72	.68	.53
Dividends per share	.24	.20	.18	.16	.14	.14	.12	.11
Price: high	32.4	32.6	25.0	18.3	13.7	14.1	16.0	17.1
low	19.8	23.6	16.3	12.9	9.7	10.1	10.6	10.3

CONSERVATIVE GROWTH

Albertson's, Inc.

P. O. Box 20, Boise, ID 83726 □ Investor contact: Renee Bergquist (208) 395-6622 □ Dividend reinvestment plan available (800) 982-7649 □ Fiscal year's end Thursday nearest January 31 □ Web site: www.albertsons.com □ Listed: NYSE □ Ticker symbol: ABS □ S&P rating: A+ □ Value Line financial strength rating: A+

In terms of sales volume, Albertson's is the fourth-largest retail food-drug chain in the United States. Although Albertson's operates in twenty-five states, with a total of 983 stores, its greatest concentration is in two states: California (177 stores) and Texas (197), with Florida (104) and Washington (77) also having a large number of outlets. By contrast, the number of stores in several states is low, such as South Dakota (1 store), Arkansas (2), and Kansas (6).

Combination food and drug stores range in size from 35,000 to 75,000 square feet. Conventional supermarkets range from 15,000 to 35,000 square feet and offer a full line of grocery items and, in many locations, feature in-store bakeries and delicatessens.

Retail operations are supported by eleven company-owned distribution centers. About 78 percent of all products purchased by the stores are supplied from facilities operated by Albertson's. Distribution facilities operate as profit centers. Profits earned by a distribution center are rebated to each store, based on merchandise purchased from the center.

American Stores Company Merger

The company's merger with American Stores Company, approved by stockholders of the two companies in November of 1998, will increase Albertson's operating area sharply. At its fiscal year-end on January 30, 1999, American Stores operated 1,580 stores, including 773 freestanding drugstores, and ten distribution operations in twenty-six Eastern, Midwestern, and Western states.

The merger created a company with revenues of more than $35 billion, based on 1998 reported results. An estimated 200,000 employees now operate some 2,500 stores throughout thirty-eight states.

The merger strengthens Albertson's position in existing markets such as California and the Southwest, as well as taking the company into important new urban markets, such as Chicago and Philadelphia. It also provides the company with a new format, the standalone drugstore.

Shortcomings to Bear in Mind

- Food retailing is a competitive business and is often subject to price wars.
- Not only do supermarkets have to compete with each other (usually with nearly identical products priced competitively), they also have to be concerned with the inroads being made by warehouse clubs, such as Sam's and Costco, and by supercenters that sell food and general merchandise, such as those being rolled out by Wal-Mart and Kmart.

Reasons to Buy

- Albertson's distribution system continues to keep pace with the rapid growth of its retail stores. The company's distribution centers encompass nearly 7.4 million square feet and are situated strategically throughout the twenty-five-state operating region.
- Albertson's has been able to increase sales through an everyday-low-pricing strategy, coupled with strong in-store merchandising programs and increased efficiencies from its expanded distribution system.
- As one of the most conservative food retailers in the business, Albertson's prefers to let others test market new

products and services. If they work for other retailers, Albertson's is content to jump on their train.

- In the past ten years, earnings per share climbed from $.61 to $2.31, a compound annual growth rate of 14.2%. In the same 1988–1998 period, dividends per share advanced from $.14 to $.68, a 17.1 percent growth rate.
- The company believes good retail site selection is the foundation of its success. Unlike grocery chains that cluster their stores, Albertson's is careful to place each store far enough away from another Albertson's store so they do not hurt their own business.
- Albertson's is one of the main beneficiaries within the food retailing group of the improved drug store industry fundamentals. The key factors are:
  - Renegotiated third-party prescription drug margins (in favor of the retailer)
  - Burgeoning generic drug sales (which have higher profit margins)
  - Reformatted/remerchandised stores with more focused general merchandise
  - Stabilized prescription drug inflation
- Albertson's is well organized when it comes to property development. Here are some highlights of its strategy:
  - Cross-functional teams were created to increase efficiency and continuity on new store construction projects. Each team is comprised of store planners, real estate specialists, economic analysts, lawyers, architects, engineers, and construction supervisors.
  - A new, single-entrance store format that is more employee- and customer-friendly was implemented in 1994.
  - A micromarket approach is used to select store sites that maximize sales and profits within individual trade areas.

- All prospective store sites are personally visited by top management before approval.
- Albertson's primarily constructs combination food-drug stores of 50,000 square feet, with only a limited number of 40,000 square-feet stores for smaller cities, and builds a limited number of Max warehouse stores, as needed.
- All stores are continually reviewed and marginal performers are eliminated. Surplus stores are sold, leased, or subleased.
- In-house design and construction departments enhance speed and efficiency on new store and remodel projects, using computer-aided design equipment.
- Stores are located in eighteen of the twenty fastest-growing domestic metropolitan areas, as identified by Market Metrics.
- Management continues to review all potential acquisitions that meet the company's tough criteria.
- Albertson's uses an efficient, phased remodeling process that minimizes shopper disruption.

- About 90 percent of Albertson's square footage is "combo stores" (essentially a complete drugstore under the same roof as a complete supermarket), with about 80 percent of these actually having a pharmacy.
- The company's distribution centers service Albertson's stores exclusively.
- Information systems and technology play a key role in the ability of the company to grow and prosper by providing information across all boundaries of the organization.
- The company's gross margin is expanding modestly, The improvement, moreover, is largely the result of distribution efficiencies, such as savings realized from buying in larger quantities and gains resulting from spreading out fixed costs over a larger sales base. A more profitable sales mix is another plus. Analysts believe that Albertson's can expand gross margins even further over the next four or five years.

- Computer Guided Training is going online at Albertson's. New computers that help entry-level employees learn their jobs better and faster are being installed in all Albertson's stores. They will make learning fun and easy through a simple touch-screen interface. Behind the simplicity are sophisticated software programs designed exclusively for Albertson's. Computer Guided Training will add structure and consistency to the hands-on training already provided by management. The combined methods of instruction will teach employees how to do their jobs better and more effectively while providing top-notch customer service.
- A private data communications network links all retail stores, distribution centers, the division office, and the corporate office. This network, along with the large-scale computers, in-store processors, and numerous personal computers, provides the infrastructure for companywide messaging and information access.
- A fully computerized, demographic and lifestyle-based site selection and neighborhood mapping system is used for real estate site evaluation, merchandising, and advertising.
- All stores with pharmacies have computers that provide information on drug interaction, initiate third-party billings, and enhance customer service.
- The company's customers are looking for quicker and easier ways to provide tasty and nutritious meals for their families. Albertson's storewide Quick Fixin' Ideas help them to do just that. Customers can collect meal ideas and

recipes to prepare quickly at home. Or they can pick up a variety of meals already prepared.

In new stores and remodels, meal centers help satisfy its customers' need for ready-to-eat meals. Meal centers are self-service food cases placed around a food preparation area. They allow customers to find a variety of prepared entrees, meats, cheeses, and side dishes all in one area.

- In 1998, Albertson's completed its twenty-ninth consecutive year of increased sales and earnings. The company has paid dividends on its common stock for the last thirty-nine years and has increased the dividend in each of the past twenty-eight years.
- *Fortune* magazine recognized Albertson's as one of "America's most admired companies" in 1999, for the fifth consecutive year.

Total assets: $6,234 million
Current ratio: 1.29
Common shares outstanding: 246 million
Return on 1998 shareholders' equity: 21.9%

	1998	1997	1996	1995	1994	1993	1992	1991
Revenues (millions)	16,005	14,690	13,777	12,585	11,894	11,284	10,174	8,680
Net income (millions)	567	517	494	465	417	352	276	258
Earnings per share	2.31	2.08	1.96	1.84	1.65	1.39	1.05	.97
Dividends per share	.68	.64	.60	.52	.42	.36	.32	.28
Price: high	67.1	48.6	43.8	34.6	30.9	29.6	26.7	25.7
low	44.0	30.5	31.5	27.3	25.1	23.4	18.4	16.3

AGGRESSIVE GROWTH

Alcoa Inc.

201 Isabella Street at 7th Street Bridge, Pittsburgh, PA 15212-5858 ◻ **Investor contact: Edgar M. Cheely, Jr.** **(412) 553-2451** ◻ **Dividend reinvestment plan available (800) 317-4445** ◻ **Web site: www.alcoa.com** ◻ **Listed: NYSE** ◻ **Ticker symbol: AA** ◻ **S&P rating: B** ◻ **Value Line financial strength rating: A**

Alcoa (formerly Aluminum Company of America), founded in 1888, is the world's leading integrated producer of aluminum products. These products are used worldwide by packaging, transportation, building, and industrial customers. In addition to components and finished products, Alcoa produces alumina, alumina-based chemicals, as well as primary aluminum for a multitude of applications.

Alcoa competes against such companies as Alcan Aluminium (note the Canadian version of aluminum) and Reynolds Metals. Alcoa, with 1998 revenues of $15.3 billion, is the largest factor in the aluminum industry. The company has 215

operating locations in thirty-one countries. Alcoa's operations are broken down into the following segments:

The alumina and chemicals segment includes the production and sale of bauxite, alumina, and alumina chemicals.

Aluminum processing comprises the manufacturing and marketing of molten metal, ingot, and aluminum products that are flat-rolled, engineered, or finished.

The nonaluminum products segment includes the production and sale of electrical, ceramic, plastic, and composite materials products, manufacturing equipment, gold, separations systems, magnesium products, as well as steel and titanium forgings.

Since aluminum is expensive and has difficulty competing against steel—even though it has some admirable qualities—it might appear to be a rare element. Not so. Aluminum is an abundant metal and, in fact, is the most abundant metal in the earth's crust. Of all the elements, only oxygen and silicon are more plentiful. Aluminum makes up 8 percent of the crust. It is found in the minerals of bauxite, mica, and cryolite, as well as in clay.

Until about one hundred years ago, aluminum was virtually a precious metal. Despite its abundance, it was very rare as a pure metal. The reason: it was so difficult to extract from its ore. This is because aluminum is a reactive metal, and it cannot be extracted by smelting with carbon. To solve the problem, displacement reactions were tried, but metals such as sodium or potassium had to be used, making the cost prohibitive. Electrolysis of the molten ore was tried, but the most plentiful ore, bauxite, contains aluminum oxide, which does not melt until it reaches 2050° Celsius.

The solution to the problem of extracting aluminum from its ore was discovered by Charles Hall in the United States and by Paul Heroult in France, both working independently. The method now used to extract aluminum from its ore is called the Hall-Heroult process.

I won't describe all the steps in this process. The important fact to remember is that it is far from cheap. Even so, it can be done economically enough to make aluminum the second most widely used metal. However, it is not likely to replace iron and steel any time soon. Iron makes up more than 90 percent of the metals used in the world.

The main cost in the Hall-Heroult process is electricity. So much energy is required that aluminum smelters have to be situated near a cheap source of power, normally hydro-electric. The price of entry into the business is so high that it discourages most upstarts from taking the plunge. On the other hand, this frustrating effort to produce commercial aluminum is worth the cost, since the white metal has a number of valuable attributes:

- It has a low density.
- It is highly resistant to corrosion.
- It is lightweight—one-third the weight of steel.
- It is an excellent reflector of heat and light.
- It is nonmagnetic.
- It is easy to assemble.
- It is nontoxic.
- It can be made strong with alloys.
- It can easily be rolled into thin sheets.
- It has good electrical conductivity.
- It has good thermal conductivity.
- Aluminum doesn't rust.

Highlights of 1998

- Net income of $853 million was 6 percent above 1997.
- Aluminum shipment of 3,951 metric tons, was up 34 percent. A metric ton, often abbreviated mt, is equal to 1,000 kilograms, or 2,204.6 pounds.
- Revenues were $15.3 billion, driven by the record volume of shipments.
- Improved financial results for 1998 relative to the prior year were the result of higher volumes, aided in part by the Alumax and Inespal acquisitions, as well as to continued operating improvements. Partially offsetting these positive factors were lower overall aluminum and alumina prices and the impact of the company's increased amount of debt.

Shortcomings to Bear in Mind

■ Gone are the days when almost every soda and beer product on store shelves came in identical aluminum cans. Underneath the paint to identify the product was the same sturdy, flip-top container. Today, beverage makers, looking to distinguish their product from the others on the shelf, are demanding new shapes and features. Just as technical advances allowed the aluminum industry to seize the can business from steel in the 1960s, innovations from plastic, glass, and even good old steel, are undermining aluminum's hegemony.

That's a problem for Alcoa and its competitors in the aluminum industry. Over the past twenty years, they have come to dominate the $11-billion beverage-container market. Cans account for one-fifth of the aluminum sold in North America, which makes it the industry's biggest business—bigger than airplane parts or siding for houses.

Reasons to Buy

■ While the aluminum industry in general suffers through a protracted slump in aluminum prices, Alcoa has seen its profits rise. Part of that is due to the effects of recent acquisitions. But much of the improvement can be traced to a new corporate philosophy, called the "Alcoa Business System." Essentially, it calls for plants to produce more, produce it faster, and not let it sit on the docks for too long. The new production processes are "deceptively simple and seemingly obvious," says one analyst. But, on top of other cost-cutting efforts already in the works, they are helping Alcoa weather what otherwise might be a dismal year. As aluminum prices recover—either because of growing demand or because excess capacity is shuttered—Alcoa stands to see earnings jump dramatically. Analysts say that each penny increase in the LME price of aluminum boosts Alcoa's per-share earnings by about $.12. LME refers to the spot price of aluminum ingots on the London Metals Exchange. Normally, the prevailing world price of aluminum is an important determinant of aluminum companies' profits. From 1982 through 1995, Alcoa's earnings and the LME price moved in lock step. Since then, however, the LME price has dropped while Alcoa's earnings have held steady or drifted up. According to the company's chief financial officer, Richard Kelson, "We are breaking away from the LME pricing."

■ Consumers will find 1998 Alcoa innovations in the automobiles they drive, the planes they fly, the tractor trailer delivering goods to their stores, the lighting fixtures that brighten their way, the lithographic sheet used to print their newspapers and magazines, and the CDs their teenagers play. During 1998, Alcoa received eighty-six U.S. patents, the highest number awarded since 1987.

■ Two years ago, Alcoa's business unit presidents agreed to a revenue target of $20 billion by the year 2000. Today, that ambitious goal is clearly within reach. In early 1998, Alcoa acquired Inespal, Spain's state-owned aluminum producer. In mid-1998, the company completed a $3.8-billion merger with Alumax. These two expansions followed acquisition of the Italian state aluminum company and the second half of Alcoa Kofem in Hungary, where Alcoa operations have since been further enlarged. In the fall of 1998, Alcoa agreed to acquire an extrusion plant and distribution facilities in Spain and a bright sheet products plant in France.

In the meantime, internal growth has continued in worldwide operations such as Alcoa World Alumina, Alcoa Closure Systems International, and the fiberoptics business of Alcoa Fujikura. Less profitable operations at several locations have been sold or closed.

■ Aluminum usage in automobiles and light trucks has been climbing steadily. It's a new and potentially powerful trend, and Alcoa has played a major role in getting it started. As recently as

1990, there were no aluminum-structured passenger cars in production anywhere in the world. Aluminum shipments to the automotive sector grew by $400 million in 1998, fueled by acquisitions as well as by internal growth.

In North America, from 1996 to 1999, aluminum use in brakes, drive lines, chassis, and suspensions rose 46 percent; in steering systems, 47 percent; and closure panels, 65 percent. Aluminum use by automakers in North America, western Europe and Japan over the next ten years is expected to climb by 52 percent. Areas of growth include body parts, engine blocks, and safety systems.

Total assets: $17,462 million
Current ratio: 1.40
Common shares outstanding: 367 million
Return on 1998 shareholders' equity: 16.3%

	1998	1997	1996	1995	1994	1993	1992	1991
Revenues (millions)	15,340	13,319	13,061	12,500	9,904	9,056	9,492	9,884
Net income (millions)	859	759	555	796	193	67	196	280
Earnings per share	2.44	2.18	1.59	2.22	.54	.20	.57	.82
Dividends per share	.75	.49	.67	.45	.40	.40	.40	.45
Price: high	40.6	44.8	33.1	30.1	22.6	19.6	20.2	18.3
low	29.0	32.1	24.6	18.4	16.1	14.8	15.3	13.4

AGGRESSIVE GROWTH

AlliedSignal Inc.

101 Columbia Road, P. O. Box 1219, Morristown, NJ 07962-1219 ◻ Investor contact: John Stauch (973) 455-2222 ◻ Dividend reinvestment program is available (800) 432-0140 ◻ Web site: www.alliedsignal.com ◻ Ticker symbol: ALD ◻ S&P rating: B+ ◻ Value Line financial strength rating: A++

AlliedSignal is an advanced technology and manufacturing company serving customers worldwide with aerospace and automotive products, chemicals, fibers, plastics, and advanced materials.

For years, the vast majority of AlliedSignal's revenues came from mature or cyclical businesses—as evidenced by the company's erratic earnings and stagnant stock price. Beginning in 1991, AlliedSignal began to revitalize its business portfolio, selling some businesses while improving and acquiring others. Today, more than half of the company's revenues are generated by growth businesses, making a solid platform on which to build further sales and earnings gains.

A Breakdown of AlliedSignal's Operations

Aerospace is the largest of ALD's groups. As the broadest supplier of commercial aircraft systems (except large engines), with strong market positions in auxiliary power units (APU's), wheels and brakes, and environmental controls, ALD should benefit from the early part of the commercial aircraft cycle, as high-margin aftermarket business recovers.

The Automotive segment, which accounts for 38 percent of sales, manufactures safety restraints, spark plugs, turbochargers, and filters for passenger cars and light trucks.

Finally, Engineered Materials, which accounts for 26 percent of revenues, manufactures nylon and polyester carpet fibers, fluorine products, plastics, refrigerants, solvents, films, and laminates.

The Purchase of Honeywell

In June of 1999, AlliedSignal agreed to acquire Honeywell Inc. in a stock transaction valued at $13.8 billion, creating an aerospace parts-and-electronics powerhouse that also would be one of the country's largest industrial conglomerates. The friendly deal resolves the question of who will succeed the company's high-profile CEO, Lawrence A. Bossidy. Under the agreement, Honeywell's CEO, Michael R. Bonsignore, 58 years old, will become CEO of the combined company, while Mr. Bossidy, 64, remains as chairman until he retires in April 2000. The deal is expected to add $.17 a share to AlliedSignal's earnings in 2000, rising to $.32 by 2002.

The deal also accomplishes several of Mr. Bossidy's long-running aims: broadening AlliedSignal's operations, damping the cyclical ups and downs of the business, and boosting the company's revenues to more than $20 billion a year. The combined company could have revenues of about $25 billion in 1999, putting it in the same league as top diversified manufacturers such as United Technologies.

The combined company will be renamed Honeywell, but will be based in Morristown, New Jersey. Honeywell is a leading maker of control systems and components for buildings, homes, industry, aerospace, and aviation. Its home- and building-control products include building-automation systems, energy-management equipment, and fire-protection and security-control devices. Honeywell's industrial products division makes automation and control products and field instrumentation. The space and aviation unit manufactures equipment for companies in the aviation industry.

Shortcomings to Bear in Mind

- The company's Truck Brake Systems (TBS) is one of the world's largest manufacturers of air brake systems and components for heavy trucks. However, critics point out that the auto parts industry has been labeled as "low margin and cyclical." To be sure, sales of new heavy trucks are cyclical. On the other hand, 40 percent of Truck Brake Systems sales are in the heavy truck aftermarket segment, which is far less sensitive to economic swings. Since 1993, TBS achieved 9 percent compound growth in sales revenue. In the same period, AlliedSignal's return on investment in this business has grown from 18 percent to 25 percent, proving the company can be consistently profitable in this industry.

  Over the years, TBS has positioned itself to be the leader in the majority of product segments it serves. The company, moreover, holds one of the most respected and well-known brand names in the industry—Bendix. What's more, the company's end-user customers, the truck fleet owners, rely on high-quality, trusted products made by a company they know, indicating the Bendix brand is a major asset.

Reasons to Buy

- What has transpired during these past eight years can be credited to Larry Bossidy, the CEO of AlliedSignal since mid-1991. It is Mr. Bossidy who is the architect of the changes that have transformed the company in this brief span.

  In the chemicals business, for example, Bossidy moved AlliedSignal out of commodity chemicals and into specialty chemicals, where profit margins are higher. In AlliedSignal's auto-parts operation, Bossidy chose to do business with auto parts retailers, who will pay a good price, rather than with car manufacturers, who are known for squeezing their suppliers. When it comes to the notoriously cyclical aerospace market, AlliedSignal has increased revenues and profits by constantly coming out with new services and products, including a safety device that American Airlines has been installing throughout its fleet—at a cost of nearly $100,000 per plane.

Clearly, AlliedSignal has undergone a transformation since 1991. Back then, 87 percent of its businesses were mature, cyclical, or closely related to commodities. Today, that percentage has shrunk to 35 percent, while the remaining 65 percent of the business is in higher growth areas. Bossidy's goal: to get the mix to 25 percent cyclical-mature and 75 percent growth by the year 2000.

- The aerospace unit is benefiting from improving demand for engine spare parts and strong sales of safety equipment, such as wind-shear-detection instruments, ground proximity warning systems, and collision-avoidance systems (which are now being required on smaller planes). Repair and overhaul services are proving to be a growth area for this division.
- With global demand rising for custom-produced specialty fine chemicals, AlliedSignal's Specialty Chemicals business is well positioned for future growth. Its Pharmaceutical Intermediaries business, which sells products used by the pharmaceutical industry to make medications, is particularly vibrant and an area targeted for expansion.

With annual revenues of $200 million in 1998, Pharmaceutical Intermediaries is expected to grow to $425 million in sales within the next three years. The business enables pharmaceutical companies to outsource the production of the intermediate compounds used in their products and to focus their resources on their core competencies—research and development and drug discovery. The outsourcing portion of the $20 billion pharmaceutical bulk actives and intermediates industry is about $3 billion and is expanding at an annual rate of 8 to 10 percent.

To keep up with market demand, the business has grown significantly in the past three years through key acquisitions. In the second quarter of 1998, the business acquired Pharmaceutical Fine Chemicals S.A. (PFC) of Lugano, Switzerland, a custom producer and distributor of bulk active ingredients. PFC strengthened the company's foothold in Europe, expanded FDA-approved production capacity, and broadened the company's product offerings.

- Three Latin American airlines—Lan Chile, TACA of El Salvador, and TAM of Brazil—have selected AlliedSignal's Enhanced Ground Proximity Warning System's 131-9 (A) Auxiliary Power Unit (APU) and Data and Cockpit Voice Recorders for their fleets. The combined contracts are valued at more than $100 million. It is the largest order to date for the APUs.

China Eastern Airlines and Alitalia have also placed orders for 34 of the 131-9 (A) APUs for their Airbus aircraft in contracts worth more than $35 million. More than 200 of these new units have already been delivered to other customers.

- In 1998, AlliedSignal Polymers acquired Web Technologies, a leading manufacturer of nylon film used in electronics packaging. The purchase builds on the purchase of Gomar National Industries in 1997 and makes AlliedSignal the leading supplier to this high-growth segment. Web adds new customers, advanced technologies, and valuable process equipment.
- In 1998, AlliedSignal added to its list of honors. For the first time, the company was ranked the number one aerospace company in the world in *Fortune* magazine's "Global Most Admired Companies."

The company was also lauded by *Industry Week* as one of the "World's 100 Best Managed Companies." And *Money* magazine listed AlliedSignal sixth in its ranking of the *Fortune* 100's employee health plans.

Larry Bossidy was chosen by a committee of his peers as 1998 Chief Executive of the Year" by *Chief Executive* magazine. In selecting Bossidy, the committee cited AlliedSignal's successful restructuring under his leadership, the consistent delivery of shareowner value, and the development of a deep, talented management team.

■ AlliedSignal earned its reputation with superior technology. What's more, Larry Bossidy says that "continued technological leadership will provide us with a steady stream of highly profitable products. The legacy of Garrett, Bendix, and Allied Chemical lives on. Consider the following list alone, which should generate $10 billion in new revenues over the next five years:

- TurboGenerator power system
- AS900 aircraft engine
- Enhanced Ground Proximity Warning System
- Predictive wind shear detection systems
- Garrett variable nozzle turbocharger and HydraCharger
- Aclar packaging film for food and pharmaceuticals
- AZ-20 non–ozone depleting refrigerant
- Low k electronic and packaging materials for semiconductor chips
- Pharmaceutical intermediates engineered to custom specifications

Total assets: $15,560 million
Current ratio: 1.33
Common shares outstanding: 560 million
Return on 1998 shareholders' equity: 27.8%

	1998	1997	1996	1995	1994	1993	1992	1991
Revenues (millions)	15,128	14,472	13,971	14,346	12,817	11,827	12,042	11,831
Net income (millions)	1,331	1,138	1,020	875	759	659	541	342
Earnings per share	2.32	2.02	1.81	1.55	1.34	1.16	.96	.63
Dividends per share	.60	.52	.45	.39	.32	.29	.25	.40
Price: high	47.6	47.1	37.2	24.9	20.3	20.0	15.5	11.3
low	32.6	31.6	23.6	16.7	15.2	14.4	10.2	6.5

CONSERVATIVE GROWTH

American Home Products Corporation

Five Giralda Farms, Madison, NJ 07940 ▫ Listed: NYSE ▫ Investor contact: Thomas G. Cavanagh (973) 660-5000 ▫ Dividend reinvestment plan available: (800) 565-2067 ▫ Web site: www.ahp.com ▫ Ticker symbol: AHP ▫ S&P rating: A+ ▫ Value Line financial strength rating: A+

American Home Products is a global leader in discovering and commercializing innovative, cost-effective health care and agricultural products.

AHP's broad, growing lines of prescription drugs, vaccines, nutritionals, over-the-counter medications, and medical devices benefit health care worldwide. Among the company's leading products are such names as Triphasal, Norplant, Premarin, Cordarone, Redux, Naprelan, Orudis, Advil, Anacin, Dimetap, Robitussin, Preparation H, Centrum vitamins, Primatene, SMA, Lodine, and Effexor.

Here is a breakdown of the company's segments:

Women's Health Care

Wyeth-Ayerst's research, products, and educational initiatives benefit millions of women. (Wyeth-Ayerst is a major pharmaceutical arm of American Home Products.) A leader in oral contraception and the world's largest provider of hormone replacement therapy, Wyeth-Ayerst's products include Lo/Ovral, Triphasil, and Premarin, the most-prescribed medication in the United States.

Cardiovascular Therapies

Wyeth-Ayerst is focused on improving cardiovascular health through research initiatives and product innovation aimed at advancing the treatment of cardiovascular diseases, including arrhythmia and hypertension. The company's antihypertensives include products such as Verelan and Ziac. The company's antiarrhythmic franchise, which includes Cordarone and Cordarone I.V., leads the U.S. market, reflecting recognition of Cordarone's important role in the management of life-threatening ventricular arrhythmias.

Mental Health Products

Wyeth-Ayerst offers various important anti-anxiety products as well as the fast-growing antidepressant, Effexor. Effexor XR, a new, once-daily formulation, was introduced in 1997. It has demonstrated the same unique efficacy profile of Effexor, with more convenient dosing.

Vaccines

Wyeth-Lederle Vaccines and Pediatrics is a major supplier of vaccines that prevent childhood and adult diseases, including: whooping cough, diphtheria, poliomyelitis, meningitis, pneumonia, and influenza. Important products include: HibTITER, a major contributor to the reduction of diseases in children caused by the Haemophilus influenza type b organism; Orimune, the only oral polio vaccine sold in the United States; and Acel-Imune for infants, a vaccine that provides advanced protection against whooping cough, diphtheria, and tetanus.

Oncology/Hematology

Anticancer agents from AHP are used by oncologists (cancer specialists) throughout the world. In the United States, Novantrone and Leukine, marketed by Immunex Corporation, are important products widely used in cancer treatment.

Pain and Inflammation

Wyeth-Ayerst's solid position in the pain and inflammation category was strengthened in 1997 with the introduction of Duract and Synvisc. Duract—a potent nonnarcotic analgesic for the short-term management of pain—achieved quick success in the United States. Synvisc, licensed from BioMatrix, is a new treatment designed to alleviate pain associated with osteoarthritis of the knee by restoring and supplementing the natural elastic properties of synovial joint fluid.

Anti-Infectives

Wyeth-Ayerst offer important antibiotic products that are used to treat infectious diseases globally. The company's anti-infective franchise includes Minocin, Pipracil, Suprax, and Zosyn. Zosyn has been gaining increased usage for the treatment of nosocomial (hospital-acquired) pneumonia throughout the world.

Nutritionals

The Wyeth-Ayerst nutritional franchise is among the world leaders. AHP's line-up of first-age, second-age, third-age, and other formulas designed for special needs includes S-26/SMA, Promil,

Progress, and Nursoy and is scientifically designed to meet the nutritional and therapeutic needs of infants and children.

Consumer Health Care

Leading brands such as Advil, Centrum, Dimetap, and Robitussin give Whitehall-Robins Healthcare one of the largest global over-the-counter product franchises. It is a world leader in the sale of analgesics, vitamin and mineral supplements, and respiratory products.

Agricultural Products

Cyanamid's growth as a leader in the global agricultural products market is a based upon innovative herbicide, insecticide, fungicide, and biotechnology products that meet increasingly stringent safety and environmental demands.

Animal Health Care

By completing the acquisition of the global animal health business of Solvay S. A. in 1997, Fort Dodge Animal Health has become the world's third-largest provider of animal health care products. Recognized as a leader in pharmaceuticals and biologicals for companion animals and livestock, the company continued to expand its line of moxidectin-based antiparasitic products in 1997 and 1998, introducing Quest Gel dewormer and boticide for horses and Cydectin Pour-On for cattle.

Shortcomings to Bear in Mind

- American Home Products had some problems in 1998, partly due to the voluntary market withdrawal of its anti-obesity products in the latter part of 1997, as well as Duract in mid-1998. There was also intense generic competition for Oruvail and Lodine, two of the company's anti-inflammatory drugs, and for Cordarone, an anti-arrhythmia medication.

What's more, the U.S. agricultural products industry experienced unfavorable weather conditions and increased competition from genetically engineered products. This affected AHP's domestic agricultural products business. Despite all these negatives, pro forma net sales for American Home Products increased 2 percent in 1998.

- In the spring of 1999, AHP announced that it is in early-stage talks to settle thousands of liability lawsuits on behalf of patients who took its diet drugs Pondimin and Redux. Since the drugs' withdrawal from the market, the company has been hit with more than 2,500 lawsuits seeking a variety of damages for alleged injuries, or medical monitoring expenses for patients who took the drugs but are not currently sick.

Reasons to Buy

- Over the past ten years, American Home Product has transformed itself from a diversified company with $6.7 billion in net sales to a world leader in health care and agricultural products, with $13.5 billion in net sales. AHP today has 82 percent of net sales coming from prescription pharmaceuticals, vaccines, nutritionals, and consumer health-care and animal health-care products.

  Net income, moreover, has risen sharply, increasing from $1.1 billion ten years ago to nearly $2.5 billion today. The company's dividend has risen steadily in the past decade and, in fact, has increased for forty-seven consecutive years.

- Through continual efforts to improve its business portfolio and its operating efficiency, AHP has been able to sustain income and dividend growth while dramatically increasing investment in research and development. The company's R&D spending has risen from

$345 million in 1989 to a record $1.65 billion in 1998. Of this, more than 80 percent was dedicated to pharmaceutical innovation, with an emphasis on biotechnology.

■ Several highly differentiated pharmaceutical products that will provide growth for AHP are awaiting global approval in 1999. These include Sonata, for the treatment of general insomnia; ReFacto, a recombinant blood-clotting factor for hemophilia A; Protonix, for erosive esophagitis (to be marketed in the United States only); and Rapamune, an immunosuppressive therapy for prophylaxis of renal transplant rejection.

Expedited regulatory review of pneumococcal conjugate vaccine, for the prevention of pneumococcal disease in infants and young children, began in 1999. In addition, the company expects Effexor XR to receive market clearance for the treatment of general anxiety disorder, as well as labeling for rapid onset of action.

■ In 1998, Wyeth-Ayerst launched new products, including:

• Neumega, a blood platelet growth factor that promotes production of the body's platelet supply in cancer patients undergoing chemotherapy.

• RotaShield, the first vaccine for use in the prevention of rotavirus gastroenteritis.

• Enbrel, a first-in-class, breakthrough product for the treatment of rheumatoid arthritis, discovered by Immunex Corporation, an AHP majority-owned company, and jointly marketed in the United States by Wyeth-Ayerst and Immunex. Wyeth-Ayerst has exclusive marketing rights for Enbrel outside the United States and expects European approval and launch during 1999.

■ Whitehall-Robins Healthcare remains a global leader in consumer health care products, with revenues of $2.2 billion in 1998. It maintained one of the largest over-the-counter (OTC) product franchises in the United States, marketing three of the five top-selling brands in the nation: Advil, Robitussin, and Centrum. In the international OTC market, Advil, Centrum, and Caltrate continued to increase sales through geographic expansion.

■ Although drug companies tend to rise and fall on the strength of their research departments, some of the older drugs are still important. For instance, American Home Products still does well with Premarin. To be sure, the drug has been on the market since 1942. But it was not until the 1980s that scientists showed that it could ward off bone loss as well as symptoms of menopause.

Total assets: $21,079 million
Current ratio: 1.75
Common shares outstanding: 1,318 million
Return on 1998 shareholders equity: 25.7%

	1998	1997	1996	1995	1994	1993	1992	1991
Revenues (millions)	13,463	14,196	14,088	13,376	8,966	8,305	7,874	7,079
Net income (millions)	2,474	2,160	1,883	1,338	1,528	1,469	1,371	1,375
Earnings per share	1.85	1.67	1.48	1.10	1.24	1.18	1.09	1.09
Dividends per share	.87	.86	.79	.76	.74	.72	.67	.60
Price: high	58.8	42.4	33.3	25.0	16.8	17.3	21.1	21.6
low	37.8	28.5	23.5	15.4	13.8	13.9	15.8	11.6

GROWTH AND INCOME

American Water Works Company, Inc.

1025 Laurel Oak Road, P. O. Box 1770, Voorhees, NJ 08043 ◻ Investor contact: Thomas G. McKitrick (609) 346-8207 ◻ Dividend reinvestment program available (800) 736-3001 ◻ Web site: www.amwater.com ◻ Ticker symbol: AWK ◻ S&P rating: A ◻ Value Line financial strength rating: A

In addition to being the most capital-intensive of all utilities, the water business in the United States is highly fragmented. Ninety percent of the country's estimated 60,000 separate water systems serve fewer than 3,000 people each and are finding it increasingly difficult to provide the capital required to remain profitable and to provide adequate service. Thus, regional approaches are emerging as the preferred solution to the nation's water service challenges.

For its part, American Water Works Company, Inc. is a holding company of water utilities. Together with its twenty-three wholly-owned water service companies, it represents the largest regulated water utility business in the United States.

Subsidiaries serve a population exceeding 7 million people in more than 879 communities in twenty-two states, from Pennsylvania and Tennessee in the East and Southeast to Indiana and California in the Midwest and West. AWK serves a total of 1.9 million customers.

The American Water Works Service Company, a subsidiary, provides professional services to affiliated companies. These services include accounting, administration, communication, corporate secretarial, engineering, financial, human resources, information systems, operations, rates and review, risk management, and water quality. This arrangement, which provides these services at cost, affords affiliated companies professional and technical talent otherwise unavailable economically or on a timely basis.

Highlights of 1998

- Customers served at year-end 1998 totaled 1,952,000, or 3 percent higher than a year earlier.

- Water sold totaled 257 billion gallons, slightly above 1997.

- Construction expenditures for essential water service facilities totaled $392 million, or 11 percent higher than at year-end 1997.

- Revenues increased 7 percent, to $1,018 million.

- Net income to common stock totaled $127 million, or 10 percent above the prior year.

- Earnings per share increased 9 percent, to $1.58.

- The common stock dividend increased 8 percent. It was the twenty-fourth consecutive annual dividend increase.

Shortcomings to Bear in Mind

- The weather plays an important part in the fortunes of a typical water company. They do best during hot, dry summers, since this stimulates the use of water for showers, lawns, and gardens. However, if the weather is excessively dry, the government may step in and ration the use of water for car washing, gardens, and lawns.

  On the other hand, if the region is deluged with rain, there is far less reason for customers to water their lawns and gardens. They may even take fewer showers if the temperature is cool.

  American Water Works, for its part, is not as seriously hurt by a dry summer in one or two of its territories, assuming the weather is not severe in its other jurisdictions. Smaller water companies, by contrast, usually serve parts of a single state or city and are more vulnerable to droughts or other vagaries of weather.

- A water utility, like all public utilities, is closely regulated by a state commission. Each state has its own commission, some of which are more politically motivated than others. They tend to settle rate cases by favoring the consumer, rather than the company. In recent years, most state commissions have reduced the amount they will permit the company to earn on common equity. Typical awards are in the 11 percent or 12 percent range. If the company disagrees with the decision of the commission, it may go to court, in hopes of overturning a harsh award. More often than not, the courts side with the politicians.

  American Water Works has to cope with twenty-two different commissions, since it operates in twenty-two states. This has one disadvantage: it means keeping track of twenty-two commissions, trying to keep from offending them or incurring their wrath. It has an important benefit, however. The company does not stake its whole livelihood on one commission, which may be unreasonable. What it amounts to is the protection of geographic diversification.

- Public utilities fret about interest rates. There are two reasons: they borrow a lot of money, and high interest rates boost their costs. Second, they offer investors a good source of income. However, when interest rates rise, some investors may sell their utility shares and go elsewhere to take advantage of the higher interest rates. When this happens, the shares of the utility decline.

Reasons to Buy

- During 1998, the company continued its efforts to acquire water and wastewater systems. That quest is strategic because broadening the scope and geographic diversity of the company's investments enables it to improve service. It also helps make American Water Works more cost-efficient, and it increases earnings per share. In 1998, AWK completed twenty-two transactions. In total, those transactions expanded the population served by more than 77,000 people. The company also expanded its service territory, establishing operations in the state of Hawaii for the first time.

- The water utility industry is extremely fragmented, but it is becoming less so, as takeovers reduce their ranks. Even so, there are still more than 60,000 independent water systems. Most are owned by financially constrained local municipalities or private investors. The attraction of many of these smaller utilities for the larger water companies is the risk reduction they could provide through geographic diversification.

  The smaller entities have another serious problem: Water utilities have had to spend large sums of money in recent years in order to bring their plant and equipment up to the standards mandated by the Safe Drinking Water Act, the Clean Air Act, and other regulations. In this realm, the larger investor-owned utilities are much better suited to tap the financial markets in order to raise the needed cash to solve regulatory mandates.

  To meet today's standards of quality, reliability, and affordability requires ever-increasing technical expertise, financial resources, and operational efficiencies. In this environment, size and financial strength become essential elements in satisfying the water service needs of customers. Yet 90 percent of the water systems in the nation serve fewer than 3,300 people each, and 97 percent serve fewer than 10,000.

- There should be ample opportunities for growth. The Environmental Protection Agency predicts it will take $138.5 billion of restructuring during the next twenty years to update and maintain the nation's 55,000 water systems, almost all of which will need fixing up within those two decades.

- American Water Works has been active on the acquisition front. As of early 1999, twenty-three more acquisitions were in the works. Most have been privately owned systems. The biggest acquisition in the works for American Water Works is a $700 million agreement to buy family-owned National Enterprises Inc. of St. Louis. The company is aggressively on the lookout for new candidates and employs scouts such as Chuck Johnson, one of ten scouts employed by the company. Mr. Johnson sometimes puts 1,200 miles a week on his car as he drives through Pennsylvania in search of water systems that might be looking for a buyer. With 2,800 water systems in the state, he is constantly meeting with town officials to convince them that they would be making a good move by selling out to AWK.

- The water utility business is less competitive than other utility businesses. For one thing, it is not threatened by the competitive pressures weighing down the electric and telephone utility businesses. Water is a relatively inexpensive commodity to obtain but a difficult one to transport, which makes competition in the industry less likely. Barriers to entry include the immense cost of infrastructure development and necessary proximity to a water supply.

- One of the key characteristics of the consolidation of the water utility business is the demand for high water quality. Unlike any other utility service, water companies must protect the safety of their product because people drink it. Pollution of water sources, better testing technology, and government regulation are requiring additional water filtration, chemical treatment, and extensive water monitoring.

For many water systems, that means skyrocketing costs and greater technical expertise in the operation and monitoring of water treatment facilities. Assuring water quality today requires an ongoing investment in research, construction, testing, and monitoring.

A leader in the water business, American Water Works and its subsidiaries have long committed the capital and employee resources needed to maintain a high level of water quality across the twenty-one-state system of water utilities.

Recently, new regulation and public concern have centered on naturally occurring parasite contaminants such as giardia and cryptosporidium. American Water Works has reacted in anticipation of these regulations with the incorporation of particle-count monitoring, improved disinfection, and upgraded filtration. In addition, with regulation targeting more stringent control of by-products from the use of chlorine and other chemicals, process modification and alternative disinfectants are being introduced into existing facilities.

Another potential future treatment requirement is the removal of radon from some well water sources. American Water Works has tested every source of well water in its operations and is prepared to introduce either aeration or granular activated carbon filtration when needed.

Total assets: 1,548 million
Current ratio: .85
Common shares outstanding: 81 million
Return on 1998 shareholders' equity: 11.1%

	1998	1997	1996	1995	1994	1993	1992	1991
Revenues (millions)	1,017	954	895	803	770	718	657	633
Net income (millions)	127	115	102	92	74	79	72	76
Earnings per share	1.58	1.45	1.31	1.26	1.17	1.15	1.04	1.14
Dividends per share	.82	.78	.70	.64	.54	.50	.47	.43
Price: high	33.8	29.7	22.0	19.6	16.1	16.1	14.2	13.4
low	25.3	19.9	17.8	13.4	12.6	12.3	10.3	7.8

CONSERVATIVE GROWTH

AT&T Corporation

32 Avenue of the Americas, New York, NY 10013-2412 ◻ Investor contact: Mary Ann Nibeojeski (212) 387-5400 ◻ Dividend reinvestment plan available (800) 348-8288 ◻ Web site: www.att.com/ir/ ◻ Listed: NYSE ◻ Ticker symbol: T ◻ S&P rating: B+ ◻ Value Line financial strength rating: A++

AT&T is among the world's communications leaders, providing voice, data, and video telecommunications services to large and small businesses, consumers, and government agencies. The company provides regional, domestic, international, local, and Internet communication transmission services, including cellular telephone and other wireless services.

Some History

A multitude of changes have transformed AT&T since the huge enterprise spun off its seven Baby Bells back in 1984. The regional companies have since reduced their number by mergers, including Bell Atlantic's takeover of NYNEX and Southwestern Bell's acquisition of Pacific Telesis. It's now called SBC Communications and is bent on adding Ameritech to its empire.

AT&T recently took a big stride toward entering the local services market by acquiring Teleport Communications Group for $11.3 billion in stock. The multinational alliance is expected to produce $10 billion in revenues by 2000 and to increase earnings in the first year.

In mid-1998, the company acquired Tele-Communications, Inc., (TCI) one of the nation's largest cable companies, in a stock transaction valued at a hefty $48 billion. C. Michael Armstrong, AT&T's chairman, made the risky move to buy TCI in an attempt to do an end-run around the local Bell phone companies, which have been slow to open their markets to rivals, including AT&T. TCI and its various partners potentially give AT&T access to one third of American homes, enabling it to provide local telephone and Internet access on a mass scale.

In 1998, AT&T's sources of revenues broke down as follows:

Business long distance	41%
Consumer long distance	40
Wireless services	11
Local and other	8

AT&T Wireless Services operates on a TDMA (Time Division Multiple Access) digital technology platform. It serves 7.2 million subscribers.

AT&T WorldNet Internet access service has gone from a startup in March 1996 to a leading provider of online services, with nearly 1.3 million subscribers at the end of 1998.

In 1998, the company sold its Universal Card Services unit to Citicorp, for $3.5 billion in cash. In March of 1998,

AT&T sold its Solutions Customer Care business to Cincinnati Bell for $625 million in cash. These moves were part of an effort to focus only on businesses that fit AT&T's communications strategy.

In 1996, the company completed a plan to split into three, separate publicly traded companies. The largest of the companies consists primarily of core long-distance operations and wireless services, as well as 25 percent of the Bell Laboratories unit, which designs and develops new products and carries out basic research. This company retains the widely recognized AT&T name. The company provides its long-distance services throughout the United States and internationally to virtually all nations and territories. Its wireless operations are the largest of any domestic carrier.

In the fall of 1996, AT&T spun off Lucent Technologies. Lucent's operations include telecommunications equipment manufacturing and the remaining 75 percent of Bell Laboratories. The spinoff of the third company, the NCR computer unit, completed the separation.

Shortcomings to Bear in Mind

- AT&T's acquisition of the cable-television giant, Tele-Communications Inc., means the phone company will inherit the public-relations problems of the cable industry, one of Washington's least-favorite interest groups.
- Though the cable industry is hardly known for its warm ties with consumers and local government, AT&T was surprised at the poor state of Tele-Communications's customer-care centers on which it will have to put its own blue-chip brand name. Although TCI was known to have skirmished with local regulators, AT&T apparently wasn't prepared for the extent of the acrimony between the cable company and some localities.
- While the Internet, telephone, and television are converging, the underlying technologies that make convergence possible—long-haul bandwidth, local access, and interactive content—are pulling apart. So AT&T will have to compete in three increasingly distinct markets. Each is highly competitive. Each plays by increasingly different rules.

Reasons to Buy

- In May of 1999, AT&T bought MediaOne Group, paying $58 billion. This move made the company the largest cable company in the nation. It gives AT&T access to 26 million American households and minority stakes in cable systems that have access to 34 million more. Starting in 2000, the company plans to use cable wires to deliver the entire menu of telecom products to consumers—not merely long distance, but also local telephone service, high-speed Internet access, and cable television. By delivering bundled services, AT&T believes it can offer lower prices and effectively compete with the local telephone companies that are gearing up to provide a similar array of services.
- In another stunning move in the spring of 1999, the company cut a deal with Microsoft to provide software for AT&T's cable boxes. Under the agreement, which included a $5-billion investment by Microsoft, AT&T will use Windows CE software in at least 2.5 million set-top boxes that will deliver digital television, telephone, and Internet service.
- In June of 1999, AT&T's wireless unit introduced an unlimited-use calling plan for businesses in a bid to draw customers away from Nextel Communications. While AT&T's new service won't offer Nextel's convenient "walkie-talkie" feature that enables users to reach many people at once, it does allow users to make unlimited calls to five different land-lines, or traditional phone num-

bers. The landline service should appeal to subscribers who use their cell phones to check voice mail or touch base with colleagues back in the office.

■ AT&T and British Telecommunications P.L.C. bought a stake in the Japan Telecom Company in the spring of 1999, adding a third partner to their $10-billion alliance and speeding their entry into the Japanese market. British Telecom bought 20 percent and AT&T 10 percent of Japan Telecom, the country's fourth-largest phone company, for about 150 billion yen ($1.3 billion). British Telecom and AT&T needed direct links to customers in the $111 billion Japanese market to compete with rivals like MCI WorldCom.

Before this deal, AT&T already had a joint venture with twenty-five Japanese corporations, including KDD Corporation, Fujitsu Ltd., and Hitachi Ltd., to offer Internet access and other service to business. The venture, formed in 1984 and called AT&T Jens, was the country's first commercial Internet service provider.

■ A key element in the transformation of AT&T is its new CEO, C. Michael Armstrong, who took the reins in late 1997. Since then, he has been making wholesale changes, beginning with the purchase of the cable giant, TCI, with plans to rebuild its creaking rural systems so that he can deliver telephone calls, video, and data all on the same wires. He formed a joint venture with British Telecom to combine international phone operations. He bought Teleport Communications Group, a phone company that serves big businesses in city centers, and sold AT&T's credit card business to Citibank. He also signed long-term contracts with Citibank and later Banc One, among others, to manage their communications networks. Armstrong brought in new managers to run AT&T's major

businesses, designating outsiders to take over the consumer, commercial, and international telecom operations. He began cutting the company's bloated costs, leaving AT&T more or less debt-free—all while completing an 18,000-person middle management staff cut a year ahead of schedule.

■ In the fall of 1998, AT&T launched a new brand, Lucky Dog Telephone Company. Its mission: to help AT&T compete against "dial-around" phone carriers, such as MCI WorldCom's Telecom USA. The upstart dial-arounds have grabbed business from AT&T by encouraging customers to dial a special code—in the case of MCI WorldCom, 10-10-321—as a way to bypass their home carrier. In its ad campaign, Lucky Dog doesn't reveal it is a subsidiary of AT&T. The decidedly downscale ads are a far cry from AT&T's "Reach out and touch someone."

Dial-arounds are an attractive option to some consumers because there is usually no monthly fee, and rates are comparable to some of MCI and AT&T's heavily advertised regular discounts. On the other hand, sometimes dial-around customers don't save much and might require more time. Lucky Dog has a $.10 hookup fee for every call, which can add up for customers who make many calls a month.

■ AT&T, seeking to expand its presence in Canada, signed an agreement that enables it to merge partially with, and eventually buy, MetroNet Communications Corporation, in a deal valued at about $2.4 billion (in American dollars). MetroNet, based in Calgary, is Canada's largest provider of local phone hookups to businesses. The pact, which was signed in the spring of 1999, merges AT&T Canada's national long-distance network with MetroNet's local connections in major Canadian cities and MetroNet's Internet interests.

The alliance enables AT&T to offer businesses that operate in Canada a sweeping range of telecommunications services. AT&T officials said the move helps bolster the company's dominance of the North American market.

- In 1999, AT&T won a coveted bid to sell its prepaid calling cards in thousands of stores operated by Wal-Mart Stores and its Sam's Club unit. The loser was MCI WorldCom, which previously had the contract. AT&T's Wal-Mart pact reflects the company's determination to invade the fast-growing, $2-billion prepaid calling-card business. Ironically, AT&T had previously viewed calling cards as a small, low-margin business. Today, the company sees the cards as an opportunity to sign up long-distance customers. As of early 1999, it had tripled the number of outlets that distribute its prepaid cards during the prior eighteen months.

One reason that phone-card sales are on the rise is their growing acceptance by small businesses. Companies buy them from outlets such as Sam's Clubs, where the cards hold as much as 300 minutes, and then account for them as one-time expenses. The cost per minute on a prepaid card is determined by the retailer. Users make calls by dialing an 800 number and punching in an access code on the back of the card.

- In 1999, AT&T and Time Warner decided to team up to offer a package of telecommunications services via cable TV wires, moving closer to the day when customers get one bill for their television service, phones, and Internet access.

Combined with earlier moves—notably AT&T's purchase of Tele-Communications—this latest development allows AT&T to offer these services to 40 percent of U.S. households, or 35 million homes, within five years. Finally, the pact marks another big step by AT&T to get back into local phone service, which it left after being dismantled by the government in 1984.

Total assets: $59,550 million
Current ratio: .91
Common shares outstanding: 2,630 million
Return on 1998 shareholders' equity: 25.3%

	1998	1997	1996	1995	1994	1993	1992	1991
Revenues (millions)	53,223	51,319	52,184	79,609	75,094	67,156	64,904	63,089
Net income (millions)	5,235	4,472	5,608	1,866	4,879	4,258	3,807	522
Earnings per share	1.94	1.83	2.31	.79	2.09	2.10	1.91	.27
Dividends per share	.88	.88	.88	.88	.88	.88	.88	.88
Price: high	52.7	42.7	45.9	45.7	38.1	43.3	35.4	26.9
low	32.3	20.5	22.2	31.8	31.5	33.5	24.4	19.3

Automatic Data Processing, Inc.

Corporate Accounting, One ADP Boulevard, Roseland, NJ 07068-1728 ❑ Investor contact: William M. Rice (201) 535-7512 ❑ Web site: www.adp.com ❑ Dividend reinvestment plan not available ❑ Fiscal year's end June 30 ❑ Listed: NYSE ❑ Ticker symbol: AUD ❑ S&P rating: A+ ❑ Value Line financial strength rating: A++

ADP, with over 425,000 clients, is one of the largest companies in the world dedicated to providing computerized transaction processing, data communications, and information services. The company's services include: payroll, payroll tax, and human resource management; brokerage industry data, securities transaction processing, and investor communication services; industry-specific computing and consulting services for auto and truck dealers; and computerized auto repair estimating, auto parts availability services, and fee and utilization audits of bodily injury claims.

Employer Services, Brokerage Services, Dealer Services, and Claims Services are the company's four largest businesses. Together, they represent over 95 percent of ADP's revenue and are the key strategic elements of the company's growth.

Employer Services

ADP's oldest and largest business is Employer Services (ES), which contributes more than half of the company's revenues. ES provides a comprehensive range of payroll, human resource, benefits administration, time and attendance, and tax-filing and reporting services to more than 400,000 employers in the United States, Canada, South America, and Europe.

Brokerage Services

ADP's second-largest business, Brokerage Services, contributes over 20 percent of the company's overall revenues. Brokerage Services is a leading provider of securities processing, real-time market information, and investor communications services.

Dealer Services

ADP Dealer Services is the world's largest provider of computing, data, and professional services to auto and truck dealers and manufacturers. Nearly 19,000 dealers in the United States, Canada, Europe, and Latin America use ADP's on-site systems and communications networks to manage virtually every area of operations.

Claims Services

ADP's Claims Services, the leading claims information provider to the property and casualty insurance industry, offers a broad line of products to help clients accurately estimate auto damage, bodily injury, and property claims. Clients include fourteen of the fifteen largest auto insurance carriers, more than 250 additional insurance carriers and independent adjusting companies, over 7,000 collision repair facilities, and more than 3,600 auto parts recycling facilities in the United States and Canada.

Significant Events in 1998

• ADP extended its unparalleled record of growth by reporting its 148th consecutive quarter of record highs in both revenue and earning per share.

• Revenue growth by major business unit was:

Employer Services 21 percent
Brokerage Services 23 percent
Dealer Services 7 percent
Claims Services 13 percent

• Employer Services paid a record 26 million workers worldwide and issued 37 million W-2s to U.S. workers and 800,000 T-1s to Canadian wage earners.

- Employer Services moved over $300 billion, electronically, on behalf of the company's clients and their employees. This included payroll taxes from clients to government agencies in the United States and Canada and direct deposit of earnings to employee bank accounts.

- Employer Services completed several international acquisitions in 1998, growing international revenue by 55 percent.

- Employer Services accelerated its penetration of the rapidly expanding, multibillion-dollar benefits administration market by acquiring the Mercer benefits administration business. This favorably positions Automatic Data to be a major service provider in this important market.

- Employer Services is one of the top ten processors of small business 401(k) plans, serving 6,500 clients whose plans total more than $1.3 billion in assets. As a result of the Mercer acquisition, AUD now also provides a number of larger companies with 401(k) record-keeping services.

- Employer Services's revenues from its time-and-attendance services grew over 40 percent in 1998, to $50 million. The company's third quarter acquisition of Time Resource Management, Inc., which serves the hospital and hospitality industries, provides AUD with an excellent vertical market opportunity to further accelerate the growth of the company's time-and-attendance business.

- Brokerage Services processed over 160 million trades—30 percent more than the prior year, including over 1 million trades on October 28, 1997.

- Brokerage Services now conducts the transaction processing for half the major firms that offer trading services on the Internet.

- Brokerage Services signed a letter of intent with Bridge Information Systems,

Inc., to create a long-term, strategic alliance that will provide integrated offerings of market data, desktop applications, and transaction processing services to the financial services industry.

Shortcomings to Bear in Mind

- Although a slowdown in the U.S. economy could cause some dislocations in the company's core customer base, the recurring nature of much of Automatic Data's business, coupled with investors's flight to large-cap quality in times of economic uncertainty, help add stability to the stock in market downturns. On the other hand, Automatic Data Processing comes at a hefty price. To be sure, AUD is a superb company, but it rarely sells at a rock-bottom price. Quite often, it trades at a price/earnings ratio of 30 or more.

Reasons to Buy

- As market trends increasingly favor both outsourcing and software as preferred payroll solutions, ES is uniquely positioned to be the logical vendor of choice for more and more companies. ADP's "Payroll Any Way" strategy presents to businesses of virtually every size and type an extensive menu of outsourced and on-site payroll solutions, from turnkey service to client-site software.

- Many of the world's largest corporations are ADP's National Accounts clients. In many instances, ES provides solutions for their entire human resource, payroll, and benefits needs. For those companies who choose to process these applications, ES delivers valuable standalone services such as tax-filing, check-printing and distribution, year-end statements (W-2s), and benefits administration.

- ADP is the largest provider of securities processing services in North America. In

1998, the company processed about 15 percent of the retail equity transactions in the United States and Canada, handling an average of over 620,000 trades per day.

- ADP Investor Communications Services (ICS) is the largest processor and provider of shareholder communications services and serves more than 14,000 publicly traded companies on behalf of more than 800 brokerage firms and banks and 450 mutual fund families. During 1998, Automatic Data's ICS operation signed contracts with Merrill Lynch, Prudential Securities, and Paine Webber, while adding 80 other new clients. ICS processed over 360 mailings—a 30 percent increase over 1997—and tabulated over 40 million shareholder ballots, representing over 250 billion shares.

- ADP Dealer Services is the leading service provider to the emerging retail auto "superstore" market. The company helps these very large dealers design and implement enterprisewide information and technology strategies, including state-of-the-art retailing systems that enable customers to easily select and even purchase a vehicle at touch-screen kiosks.

- Over 3,600 auto parts recycling facilities and salvage yards now manage their inventories using ADP Parts Services, which helps the flow of parts information between insurers, body shops, and parts recyclers. ADP is also the data collector for the ARA International Database. Updated daily, it contains over 10 million items and is the preferred resource for locating recycled auto parts.

Total assets: $5,175 million
Current ratio: 1.52
Common shares outstanding: 604 million
Return on 1998 shareholders' equity: 20.1%

	1998	1997	1996	1995	1994	1993	1992	1991
Revenues (millions)	4,798	4,112	3,567	2,894	2,469	2,223	1,941	1,772
Net income (millions)	605	534	455	395	334	294	256	228
Earnings per share	.99	.90	.79	.69	.59	.52	.46	.41
Dividends per share	.26	.22	.20	.12	.11	.10	.08	.07
Price: high	42.2	31.3	22.9	20.6	14.9	14.2	13.9	11.6
low	28.8	19.8	17.8	14.4	11.9	11.7	9.7	6.3

GROWTH AND INCOME

Baldor Electric Company

P. O. Box 2400, Fort Smith, AR 72902 ◻ Investor contact: John A. McFarland (501) 646-4711 ◻ Dividend reinvestment plan available (800) 633-4236 ◻ Web site: www.baldor.com ◻ Listed: NYSE ◻ Ticker symbol: BEZ ◻ S&P rating: A ◻ Value Line financial strength rating: B++

With annual sales of less than $600 million, Baldor Electric Company is a pygmy among giants. Baldor makes electric motors that power pumps, fans, conveyor belts, and all the other automated components that keep modern factories humming. It competes successfully against much larger

firms such as Reliance Electric, Emerson Electric, and General Electric. But what Baldor lacks in size, it more than makes up for in flexibility and profitability.

Baldor Electric designs and manufactures a broad product line to serve its customers' diverse needs. Industrial AC and

DC electric motors, ranging from 1/50 through 800 horsepower, are the mainstay of the company's products.

Baldor's new line of Standard-E motors are designed to meet the efficiency requirements of the Energy Policy Act. Baldor's premium efficient Super-E motors are widely recognized as offering some of the highest efficiencies. These higher efficiencies translate into lower operating costs to the end user.

Baldor also offers customers a wide range of "definite-purpose" motors. Examples include Baldor's Washdown Duty motors, which are ideal for food processing and other wet environments. Baldor's Chemical Processing line of cast-iron motors are built for the harsh environment of mills and processing plants. Baldor Farm Duty motors meet the rugged outdoor requirements in the agricultural market. Also included are broad lines of brakemotors, explosion-proof, C-Face, pump motors, and gearmotors.

The fastest-growing segment of Baldor's product line is adjustable-speed drives. The company offers DC SCR controls, AC inverters, and vector control, and a wide range of servo and positioning products. Baldor markets matched performance by offering customers matched motor and control packages with lab-tested performance.

Baldor recently introduced the Baldor SmartMotor, an integrated motor and adjustable-speed control. Now available from 1 to 10 horsepower, this breakthrough new product is easy to install and offers many performance advantages.

Shortcomings to Bear in Mind

- Of late, Baldor's operations have experienced some softness. The company's top-line growth has slowed to a low single-digit pace. The causes were several. For one thing, the economic uncertainties in such regions as Asia and Latin America have cut back on demand. Even in the United States, the slowdown is evident, since some of the company's customers have been hurt by problems abroad.

Reasons to Buy

- What sets Baldor apart, analysts believe, is its innovative approach to the business. For one thing, Baldor offers a broad selection of motors. What's more, it produces motors in small lot sizes that only fit the needs of a small group of customers. About one-third of what it sells are custom products.

    Second, the company is a domestic manufacturer. Even so, Baldor's margins are about the same as most of its competitors. Some of these rivals, moreover, also include higher-margined mechanical transmissions linkage products. What's more, Baldor has the highest margins of any domestic industrial motor manufacturer. Analysts think part of the explanation relates to Baldor's fragmented customer base—it has over 8,000 customers. Additionally, the company sells only a modest volume into the consumer market where the customers are large and can exercise significant pricing leverage.

    Third, Baldor doesn't have its own sales force. Instead, it relies on independent sales representatives who are paid on commission. Each of these agents has an exclusive territory and sells all of Baldor's products in that region. In addition, the mix of Baldor's business is more heavily weighted to distributor sales—50 percent of sales, compared with 33 percent for the industry. This is a plus factor because distributors tend to concentrate on the replacement market; it's more recession-resistant than the original-equipment realm.

- BEZ has a solid record of growth. In the 1988–1998 period, earnings per share climbed from $.31 to $1.17, a compound annual growth rate of 14.2 percent. In the same ten-year stretch, dividends per share expanded from $.10 to $.40, a growth rate of 14.9 percent.

- Baldor Electric spends thousands of hours every year talking with customers to see how the company is perceived. Baldor consistently receives high grades. In recent surveys, for instance, 82 percent of those interviewed named Baldor first when asked, "What motor line do you prefer?"

- In 1998, Baldor Electric was selected by *Fortune* magazine as among the "100 Best Companies to Work for in America." In making their selection, *Fortune* reviewed the practices of over 1,000 companies with at least 500 employees that had been in business for ten years or more.

- Management's philosophy toward inventories is not typical. Although many efficiency experts argue that manufacturers should strive for just-in-time operations, Baldor has a different approach. Baldor believes that, given the nature of its customers, the benefits of having inventories on hand outweigh the costs. Quick delivery times are very important to Baldor's customers, especially the distributors. Therefore, having available products and being able to deliver nearly any motor in less than twenty-four hours helps the company to obtain sales. What's more, the margins on short-lead-time sales are also higher.

- Baldor's products are available at more locations than any other brand. The company's thirty-nine district offices across North America offer immediate availability of Baldor products to thousands of distributors in the United States, Canada, and Mexico.

- Information is an important competitive advantage for Baldor. The company's CD-ROM electronic catalog, first introduced in 1994, is now in its fifth edition. It is used by over 30,000 customers. BEZ's Internet Web site, moreover, is visited daily by users around the world. In 1998, Baldor added 285 new motors and drives to its catalog. The company now offers more than 5,000 different products—far and away the industry's broadest line of stock motors and drives.

- In 1998, the new Baldor Standard-E line of motors earned the distinction of "Product of the Year" from the readers of *Plant Engineering* magazine. The entire Standard-E line meets and exceeds new government efficiency standards. These motors also run cooler and quieter and are balanced to half of industry vibration standards. What's more, they maintain high torques, have low starting currents, and carry a new two-year warranty.

- In a recent move, Baldor acquired Northern Magnetics (NORMAG), a highly respected designer, innovator, and manufacturer of linear motors for more than twenty-five years. Linear motors are a fast-growing part of the motor business. They are found on many applications requiring flexibility, speed, and repeatability, such as packaging materials handling, medical equipment, machine tools, and semiconductor manufacturing. Through NORMAG, Baldor offers the industry's widest range of linear motor technologies.

- The long-awaited move to factory automation is gaining momentum, which is good news for Baldor. Such core industries as pulp and paper, mining, and petrochemical, for instance, are devising new, more efficient methods of operation. These include applications perfect for Baldor's extensive line of high-performance drives, from logging and sawmilling to textiles and plastics.

- Electric motors and drives are used in virtually all industries. Take, for example, the high-precision, robotic positioning needs of medical equipment and semiconductor manufacturers. These represent new and fast-growing markets for Baldor servos, especially the company's new palm-size BSM 50 brushless servo motor.
- Baldor engineers have been working for several years on a line of commercial-duty motors. These motors are designed for use in commercial applications, such as ventilation blowers used in shopping malls and fast-food restaurants, where industrial motors are "too much" for the job. Baldor has also developed special flange-mount pump commercial motors. The company estimates the domestic market for these commercial motors to be as much as $400 million.
- Baldor has been promoting energy efficiency since the 1920s, long before it was the popular consideration it is today. In recent years, BEZ pioneered new motor technology development through such products as washdown motors, common keypad language drives, the Baldor SmartMotor, and motors wound with ISR magnet wire.

- Today, the industrial drives business is growing much faster than the motor business. In fact, within a couple of years, the company believes it will be as big as the entire industrial motor business. This nearly doubles BEZ's opportunities for growth domestically and abroad.

  Baldor high-performance drives are now being used in applications previously handled by fixed-speed motors. The result is far greater productivity, flexibility, and reduced operating costs.
- Baldor likes to give customers a choice. Today, the company offers two basic types of AC drives. The most common is an "inverter." The more advanced technology is the "vector." Both can control a motor's speed, but only the vector drive can control the motor's torque, independent of speed, in precise, small increments.

  Baldor vector drives also offer "auto-tuning." This exclusive Baldor feature automatically matches the vector to the motor it's controlling.

  In 1989, BEZ became one of the first companies to offer a general-purpose vector drive. Today, the company's present generation vectors are one of the fastest growing segments of its drives business.

Total assets: $412 million
Current ratio: 3.04
Common shares outstanding: 38 million
Return on 1998 shareholders' equity: 17.6%

	1998	1997	1996	1995	1994	1993	1992	1991
Revenues (millions)	589	558	503	473	418	357	319	286
Net income (millions)	45	40	35	32	26	19	15	12
Earnings per share	1.17	1.09	.97	.84	.70	.52	.42	.33
Dividends per share	.40	.35	.29	.26	.21	.16	.14	.13
Price: high	27.2	23.8	18.8	19.9	13.6	12.3	9.4	6.9
low	10.1	18.2	13.9	12.9	10.6	8.1	6.1	4.3

The Bank of New York Co., Inc.

Church Street Station, P. O. Box 11258, New York, NY 10286-1258 ◻ Investor contact: Gregory A. Burton (212) 495-1784 ◻ Direct dividend reinvestment plan available (800) 432-0140 ◻ Web site: www.bankofny.com ◻ Listed: NYSE ◻ Ticker symbol: BK ◻ S&P rating: A- ◻ Value Line financial strength rating: A

Bank of New York is far from huge, nor does it dominate the New York landscape. Even so, the bank is thriving after several years of shuffling its businesses and swallowing a string of small, niche-oriented acquisitions.

While largely sitting out the recent merger wave that is reshaping the banking group, Bank of New York has carved out a growing and highly profitable role as one of the nation's major processors of basic securities transactions. In fact, analysts say it resembles a processor more than a bank, especially considering its relatively modest consumer banking operation.

The Bank of New York is one of the largest bank holding companies in the United States, with total assets of more than $63 billion at the end of 1998. The company provides a complete range of banking and other financial services to corporations and individuals worldwide through its core businesses. These services include: securities and other processing, corporate banking, retail banking, trust, investment management, and private banking and financial market services.

The company's principal subsidiary, the Bank of New York, is one of the largest commercial banks in the United States. It was founded in 1784 by Alexander Hamilton and is the nation's oldest bank operating under its original name.

The bank is an important lender to major domestic and multinational corporations and to midsize companies nationally. It is the leading retail bank in suburban New York. The bank is also the largest provider of securities-processing services to the market and a respected trust and investment manager. It also provides cash-management services to corporations located primarily in the mid-Atlantic region.

BNY Financial Corporation is the second-largest factoring operation in the United States and the largest in Canada. (Factoring takes place when borrowers sell their accounts receivable to a lender at some discounted value.) For over fifty years, the company has served the factoring needs of leading designers and manufacturers of apparel, as well as the textile, carpet, service, furniture, electronics, and toy industries, among many others.

The Bank of New York Commercial Corporation specializes in secured lending to a broad spectrum of midsize companies throughout the United States, including retailers, distributors, manufacturers, and service companies. It ranks among the top ten companies engaged in asset-based lending.

The Bank of New York Mortgage Company originates and services single and multifamily mortgages in New York, New Jersey, and Connecticut. Through its nine loan production offices, it offers a broad range of mortgage products and is a leading lender in affordable housing programs.

BNY Associates, Inc. is an investment bank providing a broad range of financial advisory services, primarily to middle market companies, throughout the United States.

BNY Leasing Corporation is a leading provider of domestic and cross-border leveraged lease products, offering investment capital to major equipment-intensive industries throughout the world. Its Transportation Finance Division originates, invests in, and syndicates an array of asset-backed lending products to the global aviation and rail industries.

Highlights of 1998

The bank's capital ratios remain well in excess of published regulatory requirements for a "well capitalized" bank. These ratios, combined with the bank's favorable ratings from Moody's and Standard & Poor's, are an important advantage in competing for new business around the world, especially in the Securities Servicing sector.

Asset quality continued to improve throughout 1998, as nonperforming assets decreased 7 percent, to $193 million. Nonperforming assets represent only 0.5 percent of total loans and other real estate assets owned. The reserves as a percentage of nonperforming assets were 329 percent at year-end.

Return on average assets was a strong 1.89 percent, and return on average common equity reached an all-time high of 24.25 percent. Both ratios are among the highest in the industry.

Bank of New York maintains a fundamental commitment to cost containment in all that it does, a discipline that is reflected in the company's efficiency ratio. That ratio, which measures expenses as a percent of revenues, was 50.5 percent in 1998, again one of the best in the industry.

A significant factor in BK's consistent earnings growth is its business mix. In 1998, Securities Servicing fee revenues grew by 27 percent and reached the $1-billion level, despite volatility in global markets. Internal growth in these businesses was 16 percent, with the remainder provided by acquisitions. Trust & Investment fees rose by 15 percent, reaching $208 million. Driven by this growth in the bank's

fee-based businesses, noninterest income accounted for 58 percent of total revenues, up from 54 percent in 1997 and 43 percent five years earlier.

Shortcomings to Bear in Mind

- Bank of New York operates only 370 branches in the New York metropolitan area, mostly in affluent suburbs. Its size is dwarfed by such competitors as Chase-Manhattan and Citicorp. Though the bank has finally started opening supermarket branches and exploring other retail-bank innovations, the growth prospects are limited, especially in view of the heavy costs that would be involved in such a move. In its defense, management points out that its retail banks provide it with low-cost deposit funds, which in turn fund the corporate lending business. This, in turn, brings customers into the processing business. Some analysts—although they don't argue with the logic—are not convinced that the strategy is sound.

Reasons to Buy

- In June of 1999, General Motors finance unit agreed to buy a commercial-finance unit of Bank of New York for $1.8 billion. The sale marks the latest step in the company's effort to focus on fee-based businesses that have higher growth potential. The sale to GMAC will result in a drop of 2 percent to 3 percent from analysts' original projections for the bank's 1999 earnings. But "increased concentration on our fee-based businesses will enhance our overall earnings growth," said Thomas Renyi, the chairman of Bank of New York. One immediate use for the proceeds is a program to buy back 30 million company shares at the end of 1999.
- It has been the strategy of the Bank of New York to maintain and enhance the

mix of its business toward fiduciary and securities servicing businesses.

One important way to augment strong internal growth is though acquisitions. During 1998, the company made eleven acquisitions. In Securities Servicing, BK acquired five corporate and municipal trust businesses: Mark Twain Banc Shares, Bank of Montreal's UK-based fiscal agency business, Deposit Guaranty, AmSouth, and Trotter Kent.

With the acquisition of Coutts & Company's unit-trust trusteeship and institutional custody business in July of 1998, the company expanded its asset-servicing capabilities in the United Kingdom. The acquisition of EVEREN Clearing Corporation in November marked the company's entry into the correspondent clearing business, an important product for the bank's broker/dealer client base. Finally, the acquisition of Alpha Management late in 1998 added to capabilities of BNY ESI, Bank of New York's agency brokerage operation.

These transactions made new products available to the company's existing customer base and attracted new customers, further leveraging the bank's technology investments, expanding its ability to cross-sell, and enhancing its leadership positions in these areas.

- American depositary receipts enable U.S. investors to invest in dollar-denominated equity and debt securities of foreign companies and government agencies and provide the issuers of these securities access to the U.S. capital markets. Growth in this business has been very strong, driven by the increased globalization of the capital markets. Trading volume for listed depositary receipts has been growing at a compound annual rate of 22 percent since 1990.

- The Bank of New York is one of the largest custodians for mutual fund management companies, providing domestic and global custody, portfolio accounting, and pricing and fund administration services. In total, the bank acts as custodian for well over 1,000 mutual funds for eighty-three management companies.

- The Bank of New York has consistently invested in the technology necessary to improve its processing efficiency and accommodate incremental volume. As an example, BK designed a personal computer-based information delivery system called "Workstation" that allows the bank's processing customers to access a range of securities-related data captured by the bank from their own office. Software the bank has developed, moreover, has allowed the bank to adapt this technology for use in virtually all of its securities-processing businesses.

- At an analysts' meeting, the company demonstrated its new "Inform" Web browser technology software that provides a secure Internet connection with real-time information combined with the ability to customize reports. The software provides easy access to information and is expected to reduce Bank of New York's processing costs.

In addition, the company's enhanced security data warehouse provides complete information on securities. The data warehouse is targeted to provide a single source of information for clients, increases coverage from 1 to 5 million securities, and provides Bank of New York clients with the foundation for modeling strategic projects.

Total assets: $63,141 million
Return on average assets: 1.89%
Common shares outstanding: 773 million
Return on 1998 shareholders' equity: 22.25%

	1998	1997	1996	1995	1994	1993	1992	1991
Loans (millions)	37,790	34,486	36,229	36,031	32,291	29,600	26,388	26,988
Net income (millions)	1,192	1,104	1,020	914	749	559	369	122
Earnings per share	1.53	1.36	1.21	1.08	.93	.68	.53	.16
Dividends per share	.54	.49	.42	.34	.28	.21	.19	.21
Price: high	40.6	29.3	18.1	12.3	8.3	7.8	6.8	4.5
low	24.0	16.4	10.9	7.1	6.2	6.3	3.8	2.1

AGGRESSIVE GROWTH

Becton Dickinson and Company

1 Becton Drive, Franklin Lakes, NJ 07417-1880 ❑ Investor contact: Ronald Jasper (800) 284-6845 ❑ Direct dividend reinvestment plan available (800) 955-4743 ❑ Web site: www.bd.com ❑ Fiscal year's end September 30 ❑ Ticker symbol: BDX ❑ S&P rating: A ❑ Value Line financial strength rating: A

Becton Dickinson is the world's largest manufacturer of syringes, needles, insulin-delivery devices, and blood-collecting devices and a major producer of infectious disease diagnosis systems and high-end cellular analysis instruments.

While Becton is considered a broad-based hospital-supply company, four businesses account for a good 65 percent of total corporate revenues and at least 80 percent of operating profits. These four core operations are:

- Diabetes-care products
- Hypodermic needles and syringes
- Blood-collecting devices
- Microbiology products

These products are ubiquitous in almost all health-care settings. Becton's core business consists of some of the most basic tools used to deliver medical care in the United States (and internationally, to a large extent), so that the company carries a high name recognition in the health care community.

Becton Dickinson is a global company. Today, about half the company's revenues come from outside the United States, and it has facilities and organiza-

tions in virtually every country in the world. The company has well-established infrastructures throughout Western Europe, as well as in Australia, Brazil, Canada, Japan, Mexico, Singapore, and South Korea. Increasingly, BDX has a growing presence in countries such as China and India, where health-care delivery, like the economy, is still developing.

In 1998, the company's revenues climbed 11 percent to a record $3.1 billion. Excluding the estimated impact of foreign currency translation, worldwide revenues grew 14 percent. Net income was $236.6 million, a 21.2 percent decrease compared with $300.1 million the prior year. However, net income would have been $360 million, excluding restructuring and other charges and the impact of the acquisition of the medical device business of the BOC Group (MDD).

Gross profit margin, a key measure of productivity, rose to 50.6 percent in 1998, compared with 49.7 percent in the preceding fiscal year. Research and development expense increased to $218 million in 1998, compared with $181 million in 1997.

Shortcomings to Bear in Mind

- It took one hundred years for Becton Dickinson to reach $2.7 billion in annual revenue. Clateo Castellini, chairman of BDX, thinks it will take just five years to double those yearly sales. Mr. Castellini seeks to increase the company's size through acquisitions, along with internally generated new products, geographic expansion, and a corporate-culture change. Reaching the CEO's goal would require revenue growth of about 15 percent a year—an ambitious target for a company whose sales have risen between 2 percent and 6 percent in recent years.
- During 1998, there was considerable evidence of insider selling. In early 1999, the stock was much weaker than the general market.
- Becton Dickinson, like many health-care companies, often sells at a lofty P/E multiple.

Reasons to Buy

- Analysts believe that Becton Dickinson can record double-digit earnings gains for at least the next five years. They attribute their optimism to accelerating sales growth overseas, an improving sales mix in the United States, and sharply rising free cash flow, which is being used to make selected acquisitions and in an aggressive share-repurchase program.
- Becton Dickinson has been growing at a solid pace. In the 1988–1998 period, earnings per share climbed from $.46 to $1.37, a compound annual rate of 11.5 percent, nor did earnings dip in any of those years. In the same ten-year span, dividends per share expanded from $.11 to $.30, a growth rate of 10.6 percent.
- An important element in analysts' more positive view of Becton Dickinson is its accelerating sales overseas, where Becton's major markets tend to be highly fragmented. In addition, the rate of conversion to disposable medical products abroad has been less than half that in the United States.
- Becton Dickinson expects to benefit from increasing demand for its products around the world. Markets such as Latin America—where trade barriers are continuing to fall—and China—which is experiencing strong economic growth—are but two examples of potential growth opportunities for Becton Dickinson.
- Domestic sales of insulin needles and syringes are expected to increase in the high-single digits during the next few years, fueled by the estimated 5 percent annual growth in the number of Americans suffering from diabetes, plus the trend toward multiple insulin injections. Recent scientific studies have shown that the use of multiple daily injections of insulin reduces the severity of the disease's longer-term deleterious effects. Becton Dickinson, which accounts for about 90 percent of the domestic insulin syringe market, has entered into an arrangement with Eli Lilly, the largest domestic producer of insulin products, and Boehringer Mannheim, a major manufacturer of glucose monitoring devices, to provide information to diabetics regarding the best manner in which to control their disease. Over time, this program should accelerate the trend toward multiple, daily insulin injections. The company is also reviewing a number of noninvasive techniques to monitor glucose levels in diabetics. This device could reach the market before the end of the decade and further enhance the company's overall position in the diabetic sector.
- There are 25 million people with diabetes in India—the most in any country in the world. For India, the challenge of diabetes isn't simply large numbers. It's that today less than half the cases are

being treated, and among those being cared for, less than 3 percent use insulin, well below world norms. Ominously, the number of diabetics is expected to double by 2005.

The opening of Becton Dickinson's first plant in India in 1997 is helping make treatment more accessible for people with diabetes in India. Located in Haryana, about an hour from Delhi, the plant is dedicated to producing insulin syringes.

Making quality insulin syringes available in mass quantities is the opening salvo in a larger war. Far more complex challenges lie in logistics and education. India is a vast country with an intricate and fragmented distribution system consisting of hundreds of thousands of points of consumption. In response, Becton Dickinson has built a distribution network anchored by ten warehouses in different parts of the country. The company initially appointed 270 distributors focused on specific customer segments. Another 80 distributors were added in 1998. What's more, the company launched an education campaign by hiring nurses to work with its own sales force as well as with hospital staff and physicians.

- Becton is the leader in flow cytometry, an innovative technology in the area of cellular analysis, enabling health care professionals to obtain new information on a wide range of immune system diseases, such as AIDS and cancer.

- Becton Dickinson's products and instruments for infectious disease diagnosis are used to screen for microbial presence, to grow and identify organisms, and to test for antibiotic susceptibility. Accurate and timely diagnostic information helps target the use of drugs and other therapies, thereby increasing a patient's chances for rapid recovery and reducing total health care costs.

- With a strong base of proprietary technology, Becton Dickinson holds a leading worldwide market position in peripheral vascular access devices for infusion therapy and is an important supplier of components and procedural kits for regional anesthesia.

- Becton holds a strong market position in hypodermic needles and syringes and pre-fallible systems and offers a wide array of safety products for medication delivery in many areas of the world.

- As a world leader in evacuated blood collection systems, Becton Dickinson makes products that ensure the safe and accurate collection of blood and other samples to meet the needs of the rapidly changing laboratory environment.

- Becton's tissue culture business serves research scientists in the academic and biopharmaceutical industries. The company's innovative plasticware and reagents are used to advance the fundamental understanding of diseases and potential therapies.

- The company's use of computer-aided design and manufacturing technology enables Becton to bring quality products to market faster and at a lower cost. One such technology is stereo lithography, which uses a laser system to quickly create a three-dimensional physical object from a computer-aided design model. Engineers can use this extremely accurate model as a prototype, improving both the quality of the product design and the speed of the product development process.

- The company continued its acquisition strategy with the purchase of the medical device division of the BOC Group (MDD). In addition to being an excellent strategic fit, this move substantially increases BDX's European infusion-therapy revenues. The company also purchased the Boston-based consulting firm, Concepts in Healthcare, Inc., giving the company's Consulting and Services Group a strong entry into the health care service business.

To augment Becton's Asian presence, the company purchased Boin Medica, the leading South Korean med-

ical device manufacturer. Also in its medical segment, BDX acquired Visitec ophthalmic surgical products, as well as the TRU-FIT lines of sports medicine support products.

Total assets: $3,846 million
Current ratio: 1.41
Common shares outstanding: 247 million
Return on 1998 shareholders' equity: 15.8%

	1998	1997	1996	1995	1994	1993	1992	1991
Revenues (millions)	3,117	2,810	2,770	2,712	2,560	2,465	2,365	2,172
Net income (millions)	362	313	283	252	227	213	201	190
Earnings per share	1.37	1.21	1.06	.90	.75	.68	.64	.61
Dividends per share	.30	.26	.23	.21	.19	.17	.15	.15
Price: high	49.6	27.8	22.8	19.0	12.5	10.2	10.5	10.2
low	24.4	20.9	17.7	12.0	8.5	8.2	8.0	7.3

AGGRESSIVE GROWTH

Bed Bath & Beyond Inc.

650 Liberty Avenue, Union, NJ 07083 ◻ Investor contact: Catherine Ferraro (908) 688-0888 Ext. 4552 ◻ Web site: www.bedbath.com ◻ Dividend reinvestment plan not available ◻ Fiscal year's end on the Saturday nearest February 28 ◻ Listed: Nasdaq ◻ Ticker symbol: BBBY ◻ S&P rating: Not rated ◻ Value Line financial strength rating: A

Bed Bath & Beyond sells home furnishings and decor items for every room in the house. The company was incorporated in 1971, following the opening of its first two stores. BBBY is included in the Standard & Poor's MidCap 400 Index.

In early 1999, the company had 189 stores in thirty-five states. The states with highest concentrations include California (22 stores), Florida (20), Texas (16), New Jersey (10), Virginia (10), New York (13), and Illinois (11). The company's stores usually range in size from 30,000 to 50,000 square feet, with some stores exceeding 80,000 square feet.

The stores are proliferating at a feverish pace, from thirty-eight as recently as 1993. In fiscal 1998 (ended February 27, 1999), Bed Bath & Beyond opened forty-

five new superstores, the largest number of new units added in company history. Another fifty units are slated for 1999.

The company's stores offer more than 30,000 better-quality domestic items and home furnishings at low prices. Domestic products include such items as bed linens, sheets, comforters, bedspreads, draperies, pillows, and blankets. Bath accessories include towels, shower curtains, wastebaskets, hampers, and rugs. Kitchen textiles include tablecloths, place mats, napkins, and dishtowels. Bed Bath & Beyond also sells home furnishings and kitchen and tabletop items, such as cookware, cutlery, flatwear, and glasswear. Finally, a typical store may also feature storage items, closet items, small electric appliances such as blenders, coffee makers, vacuum cleaners, toaster ovens, and hair dryers, along with gift items, picture frames, luggage, small toys, and seasonal merchandise.

The company's superstores may be found in strip malls and freestanding buildings, as well as in off-price and conventional malls. For marketing, Bed Bath and Beyond relies exclusively on circulars, mailings, and word-of-mouth.

Highlights of 1998

Net sales for the year ended February 27, 1999 were just shy of $1.4 billion, an increase of 31 percent from the prior year. Comparable store sales advanced by 7.6 percent. Net earnings of $97.3 million ($.68 per share) improved by 33.1 percent, from $73.1 million ($.51 a share), representing the seventh consecutive year of earning increases that exceeded 30 percent.

BBBY's debtfree balance sheet became even stronger in 1998, with working capital increasing by 42.1 percent. Average returns on shareholders' equity and total assets were 27.6 percent and 17.8 percent, respectively—among the highest in the retailing sector.

Shortcomings to Bear in Mind

- You may find it difficult to invest in this stock if you are a value investor. Unless the bottom falls out of the market, you will find yourself buying Bed Bath & Beyond when it has a multiple of 40 or more.
- Retailing is always subject to new and innovative competition. Bed Bath & Beyond is known as a "category killer."

  The company has taken a sector of the products normally sold in department stores, thus "killing" that category for department stores such as Sears and J. C. Penney.

Reasons to Buy

- Bed Bath & Beyond has an impressive growth record. In the 1991–1999 period, earnings per share shot up from $.09 (adjusted for three 2-for-1 stock splits) to $.68, a compound annual growth rate of 28.8 percent. The company's initial public offering took place in mid-1992, which explains why Value Line does not provide figures for prior years.
- Standard & Poor's recently assigned an investment grade credit rating to Bed Bath & Beyond, based on the company's "leadership position in the highly competitive home furnishings industry, successful merchandising strategy, strong financial profile, and stable outlook."
- According to management "Our stores are fun places to shop. The racetrack layout, high impact displays, and constantly changing merchandise mix all contribute to item sales greater than anyone else in the industry selling the same item. By focusing on consumer satisfaction and by offering customers new and exciting products, the company continues to achieve outstanding sales results."

  For my part, my wife and I have been shopping in Bed Bath & Beyond since we first discovered the chain when we were living in Chagrin Falls, Ohio. Now we have a brand new outlet in Taft Corners, Vermont (the only one in the state) that is even more fun. There is no way you can push a shopping cart through the aisles of a Bed Bath & Beyond and not make several purchases that you hadn't planned on.
- Prices charged by company stores can be 20 to 40 percent below those prevailing in department stores. Despite this pricing strategy, Bed Bath & Beyond posts healthy margins by shipping prod-

ucts directly from the manufacturer to the stores; there is no need for warehouses.

- The company maintains an entrepreneurial culture and decentralized management. A major portion of everyday decision-making is vested in the personnel who run the stores. They reorder most of the merchandise and understand the profitability and productivity of each item, as well as the relationship between volumes and margins. According to Steven H. Temares, executive vice president and chief operating officer, "Our store merchants consistently identify high-markup items and drive the volume on these products. They decide what items to feature and reorder the merchandise that will produce optimal results in their particular store."

- Bed Bath & Beyond has an enviable record in retaining its people. Since 1992, turnover at the supervisory level (store managers and above) has been below 5 percent. Similarly, turnover in the company's merchandising organization has been exceptionally low.

- The company has been expanding aggressively. In 1998, 45 new superstores were opened, compared with 33 the prior year. In addition, BBBY expanded into several new states: Delaware, Nebraska, South Carolina, Utah, and Vermont. Total store space, moreover, increased to 7.7 million square feet, an increase of 33.3 percent over 1997. In 1999, it also plans to expand several stores and enter several new states. In the next few years, Bed Bath & Beyond's goal is to have 600 domestic outlets.

- Bed Bath & Beyond operates in a highly fragmented sector of the retail industry. Whereas other sectors are dominated by 2 or 3 operators with market shares from 20 percent to 35 percent, the largest home goods superstore operators have relatively minor market shares. BBBY's share, for instance, is only 2 percent, another indication that the company has substantial room to grow.

- Favorable demographic and societal trends also support the company's belief that it can continue to expand. The home has increasingly become a focal point in people's lives. Whereas total consumer expenditures grew by about 28 percent during a recent six-year period, increases in expenditures for home goods exceeded 35 percent during that same span.

  Despite this generally favorable background, few operators in this retail sector have been successful. In fact, most have done poorly or failed. What's more, the few that have been profitable have achieved operating margins considerably lower than those of Bed Bath & Beyond.

- Officers and directors of the company own 18.1 percent of the common stock. This high ownership by management is a solid indication that they are motivated to keep the company growing.

- Since BBBY funds its new stores with operating cash flow, the company has no long-term debt. Each new outlet has managed to show an operating profit within the first twelve months of operation.

- In addition to benefiting from favorable socioeconomic trends, the company is blessed with a robust housing market and strong consumer spending that indicate that consumers are moving into new homes and have the money to furnish them with items from stores like BBBY. In today's fast-paced society, Bed Bath & Beyond is a welcome one-stop shop, offering convenience and reasonable prices to busy people who are concerned with enjoying a relaxing and fulfilling time at home.

Total assets: $633 million
Current ratio: 1.87
Common shares outstanding: 139 million
Return on 1998 shareholders' equity: 23.7%

	1998	1997	1996	1995	1994	1993	1992	1991
Revenues (millions)	1,397	1,067	823	601	440	306	217	168
Net income (millions)	97	73	55	40	30	22	16	12
Earnings per share	0.68	0.52	0.39	0.29	0.22	.16	.12	.09
Dividends per share	nil							
Price: high	35.2	19.6	15.8	9.9	8.6	8.9	4.8	
low	17.1	11.4	8.2	4.5	5.7	3.3	1.8	

GROWTH AND INCOME

BellSouth Corporation

1155 Peachtree Street, N. E., Room 14B06, Atlanta, GA 30309-3610 ◻ Investor contact: Nancy Humphries (404) 249-3428 ◻ Listed: NYSE ◻ Direct dividend reinvestment plan available: (888) 266-6778 ◻ Web site: www.bellsouth.com/investor ◻ Ticker symbol: BLS ◻ S&P rating: B+ ◻ Value Line Financial Strength A+

BellSouth is a $23-billion communications company serving nearly 34 million customers in nineteen countries. Bell-South provides local telecommunications, long distance access, wireless communications (including long distance), digital and data services, cable and digital TV, advertising and publishing, and Web hosting, Internet access, and other electronic commerce services to consumers, businesses of all sizes, and to competitive communications carriers.

Business services include connection, networking, and Managed Network Solutions. Residential products include MemoryCall voice messaging services, CallerID, Busy Connect, and other calling features.

BellSouth is one of the world's largest wireless communications companies, serving more than 8.2 million mobile phone customers in major markets throughout the United States and in key areas around the world. The BellSouth Intelligent Wireless Network delivers interactive paging and other two-way data communications in seconds to more than 93 percent of the urban business population in 266 U.S. metropolitan areas.

BellSouth is also one of the world's leading advertising and publishing companies, including *The Real Yellow Pages ONLINE* (www.yp.bellsouth.com) and the *At Hand Network Yellow Pages* on the Internet (www.athand.com).

With one of the largest shareholder bases in America, BellSouth has assets of more than $39 billion.

Shortcomings to Bear in Mind

■ Although BellSouth has staked out a growth program abroad, CEO Duane Ackerman admits that "There are challenges to economic growth in Latin America. These challenges do not shake our commitment to the region. We have more than ten years' operating experience in Latin America. BellSouth has always been a long-term investor, and we have weathered previous periods of economic fluctuations on the continent. I am convinced Bell-South's investments there will continue to be a growth engine for your company. Latin America is one place international business simply has to be over the next decade."

- Mr. Ackerman is also concerned about regulation. Here are his views of the matter. "Even while BellSouth is setting the pace in opening our markets to competitors, we still are prohibited from entering the long distance market in our region. More than three years after the Telecommunications Act of 1996, there are also big decisions still to be made in the regulatory arena on universal service and on access charges for interconnection to the BellSouth network. As I shared with you a year ago, we are continuing to work on every front to make sure that these decisions are made with a sense of balance and fairness."

Reasons to Buy

- In 1998, the company's stock appreciation, coupled with a dividend increase, provided BellSouth's investors a total return of over 80 percent. This compares to a 42 percent total return for the company's peer group and a 28.5 percent total return for the Standard & Poor's 500.
- In 1998, BellSouth's Communications Group's net income climbed 17.2 percent on a gain of 7.8 percent in revenues.
- I am impressed that most of the Board of Directors are major shareholders in BellSouth, even though only one of them is an employee of the company. In the 1998 annual report, here is how many shares were owned by each board member: Ronald A. Terry, retired chairman of the board, First Tennessee National Corporation (54,955 shares); Phyllis Burke Davis, retired senior vice president Avon Products (42,548); Reuben V. Anderson, partner Phelps Dunbar; Jackson, MS (21,899); Leo P. Mullin, president and CEO of Delta Air Lines (11,681); James H. Blanchard, CEO of Synovus Financial Corporation

(49,068); William S. Stavropoulos, CEO of The Dow Chemical Company (6,997); C. Dixon Spangler, Jr., chairman of the board C. D. Spangler Construction Company (49,453); Kathleen F. Feldstein, president Economics Studies, Inc. (1,165); J. Tylee Wilson, retired chairman of the board and CEO of RJR Nabisco, Inc. (59,253); F. Duane Ackerman, CEO of BellSouth (574,261); Armando M. Codina, CEO of Codina Group Inc. (47,607); J. Hyatt Brown, CEO of Poe & Brown Inc. (81,753); Robin B. Smith, CEO of Publishers Clearing House (17,974); John G. Medlin, Jr., chairman emeritus of Wachovia Corporation (52,019).

- BellSouth is at the heart of the communications revolution. The company has more than 2.6 million miles of fiberoptic technology in its network. What's more, in 1999, it deployed fiberoptics all the way to more than 200,000 homes. The company's digital and data services revenues surged in 1998, reaching more than $1.9 billion, a 42 percent increase over the prior year.
- BellSouth's SONET capabilities lead the industry, with over 10,000 SONET rings in service at the end of 1998. Capacity in this area is growing over 20 percent per year.
- BellSouth also has nearly 250 ATM and Frame Relay-based Fast Packet switching systems. These technologies combined with extensive Native Mode LAN (Local Area Network) interface technology, related digital multiplexing, and bridging technologies have given the company's customers the services they require today—and BellSouth the experience it will require for tomorrow.
- BellSouth has developed the first integrated fiber-in-the-loop system. It is delivering voice, video, and data over one single fiber for the company's resi-

dential customers in multiple neighbor-hoods today. It will be further deployed to 200,000 homes in Atlanta and Miami in 1999.

- BellSouth has deployed its own Internet access platform that serves forty-seven markets. The company's deployment of its own Internet access platform gives its customers the best quality in the industry (rated A+ by Inverse).
- BellSouth's wireless data leadership is evident nationwide. The company's two-way, wireless packet network covers 93 percent of U.S. urban popu-lation centers, with more than 1,600 base stations with related data switching and support systems. Bell-South expects to serve 2 million wire-less data and interactive paging cus-tomers by 2002.
- In 1998, BellSouth captured the highest ranking in the J. D. Power and Associ-ates Local Residential Telephone Service Satisfaction Study. The company has won this award for three straight years.
- BellSouth has been moving aggressively abroad. Latin America is the focus of the company's international strategy. The reason is simple: that's where the growth is. Fueled in part by Brazil—one of the most successful telecommu-nications start-ups anywhere, ever—Latin American revenues nearly doubled in 1998, to $1.5 billion. Bell-South's share of wireless customers grew more than 117 percent, to 2.3 mil-lion. In less than eight months, Bell-South's two companies in Brazil added a total of 1 million customers—and the growth, according to management, "remains huge." Fewer than one person in thirty in the company's Latin American markets purchases service from BellSouth, compared to about one in eight in its U.S. markets.

- To make it easy for customers to buy its wireless products, BellSouth has always been a leader in distribution. The company is adding to its channels while lowering costs. BLS now has 275 company-owned retail stores. It will provide its customers with bundled wireless and wireline services as regula-tions permit.
- In the 1950s, the average American household spent only about $7 per month for basic telecommunications services. In that era, the vast majority of residences in the United States still used party lines, with millions even sharing the same line with four or more other customers. Rotary-dial local and long distance service were about all that customers used because that's about all the telecommunica-tions services that were then widely available.

Today people need much more from their telecommunications company. Many customers spend $200 or more per month for local, long distance, wireless, video, Internet, and other ser-vices. That figure is expected to keep going up.

- Half the people in the world have never placed a telephone call, and in the high-growth wireless markets that BellSouth serves around the globe, the company has an even bigger opportu-nity to bring new services to customers. There are nearly 70 million potential customers in the thirteen countries where BellSouth operates cellular sys-tems, and only one out of every thirty-seven people currently use the com-pany's service. Compare that with the United States, where about one person in five uses wireless phone service. With those numbers in mind, you can see the potential of the emerging inter-national markets BellSouth serves.

Total assets: $39,140 million
Current ratio: 0.95
Return on 1998 equity: 20.6%
Common shares outstanding: 1,950 million

	1998	1997	1996	1995	1994	1993	1992	1991
Revenues (millions)	23,123	20,561	19,040	17,886	16,845	15,880	15,202	14,446
Net income (millions)	3,259	2,790	2,519	2,227	2,092	1,773	1,658	1,507
Earnings per share	1.65	1.41	1.27	1.12	1.05	.90	.85	.78
Dividends per share	.73	.72	.72	.71	.69	.69	.69	.69
Price: high	50.0	29.1	22.9	21.9	15.9	15.9	13.8	13.8
low	27.1	19.1	17.6	13.4	12.6	12.6	10.8	11.3

CONSERVATIVE GROWTH

Bergen Brunswig Corporation

4000 Metropolitan Drive, Orange, CA 92868 ❑ Investor contact: Lisa Riordan (714) 385-4079 ❑ Web site: www.bergenbrunswig.com ❑ Dividend reinvestment plan not available ❑ Fiscal year's end September 30 ❑ Listed: NYSE ❑ Ticker symbol: BBC ❑ S&P rating: A– ❑ Value Line financial strength rating: B++

Bergen Brunswig Corporation is one of the nation's largest distributors of pharmaceuticals and medical-surgical supplies to the managed-care market and is the second-largest wholesaler to the retail pharmacy market.

The company distributes a full line of products, including pharmaceuticals, proprietary medicines, cosmetics, toiletries, personal-health products, sundries, and home-health-care supplies and equipment. The company operates sixty-seven distribution centers across the country.

BBC's products are sold to a large number of hospital pharmacies, managed-care facilities, health-maintenance organizations, independent retail pharmacies, pharmacy chains, supermarkets, food-drug combination stores, and other retailers in all fifty states, as well as the District of Columbia, Guam, and Mexico.

In another sector, Bergen Brunswig offers logistics-management solutions, information technology, and commercializations services to more than 60,000 customers nationwide.

The company's segments include:
- Bergen Brunswig Drug Company
- Regional Drug Distribution Centers
- Bergen Brunswig Medical Corporation
- ASD Specialty Healthcare
- Bergen Brunswig Corporate Office
- Integrated Commercialization Solutions

Shortcomings to Bear in Mind

- BBC has exhibited steady growth, as earnings per share climbed from $.40 in 1988 to $1.02 in 1998, which represents a compound annual growth rate of 9.8 percent. In the same ten-year stretch, dividends advanced from $.07 to $.24, a growth rate of 13.1 percent. Neither of these growth rates is extraordinary, which might make you think the stock's P/E ratio is too high.

Reasons to Buy

- In 1998, Bergen Brunswig Drug Company (BBDC) generated more than 700 new accounts and showed strong gains in all regions and across all customer segments. Good Neighbor Pharmacy (GNP), Bergen's brand identity program for independent pharmacies, continued to show increased utilization of the full spectrum of initiatives offered under the

GNP umbrella—most notably in the growth of advertising support, which today puts the GNP name in markets representing 75 percent of U.S. households. The company's independent network of stores under the GNP banner places BBDC among the leading chains in both store count and total retail sales.

In addition, Bergen recently acquired J. M. Blanco, Inc., Puerto Rico's largest pharmaceutical distributor, which creates opportunities to move GNP, as well as other Bergen retail health system initiatives, into new markets in Puerto Rico and the Virgin Islands.

- Bergen Brunswig Specialty Company (BBSC), launched only five years ago as a distributor of oncology products, has exceeded expectations by achieving operating earnings growth of more than 150 percent for the second year in a row and continues to exhibit rapid expansion in both its ASD Specialty Healthcare and integrated Commercialization Solutions (ICS) divisions.

ASD's introduction of new products and services in the oncology, plasma, nephrology, vaccine, and other specialty markets has built a solid infrastructure that is well respected in the industry and has already increased revenues from $30 million in 1995 to an annualized rate of over $800 million today.

- Diversification broadens the scope of programs and services a company offers its customers. For Bergen, diversifying into complementary businesses has also been a key strategy for enhancing margins and well as shareowner return.

In 1994, the company launched ASD, a specialty distribution group which has diversified quickly from its oncology focus to include a wide variety of specialty products. In 1997, under the auspices of Bergen Specialty Company, Bergen moved into the burgeoning field of commercialization outsourcing by forming integrated Commercialization Services (ICS) as a sister company to ASD.

ICS develops and implements customized distribution, marketing, and clinical programs to support the launch of new products for pharmaceutical and biotechnology companies. Already respected in the industry, ICS broadened its scope in fiscal 1998 with the acquisition of The Lash Group, a leading reimbursement consulting firm that works with providers, manufacturers, and patients to ensure that healthcare products are made available to all eligible patients. This addition to the ICS portfolio of services is a prime example of Bergen's aggressive expansion into new and growing markets, which, in turn, drives revenues and profitability.

- Early in 1999, the company acquired Stadtlander Drug Company, a leading distributor of AIDS, transplantation, and mental-health drugs. Stadtlander is a complement to BBSC's ASD Specialty Healthcare Group, which serves the oncology, plasma, vaccine, and nephrology markets. BBSC has been Bergen's fastest growing subsidiary.

- Bergen Brunswig has been an innovator in the development and utilization of computer-based retailer order-entry systems and electronic data-interchange systems, including computer-to-computer ordering systems. Substantially all orders received from customers are received via electronic order-entry systems. BBC is expanding its electronic interface with its suppliers and now electronically processes most of its purchase orders, invoices, and payments.

Since 1986, BBC has opened eight regional distribution centers, replacing twenty older, smaller, less-efficient facilities. The company believes that the new centers help improve customer service levels because of wider product selection.

- Bergen Brunswig has grown rapidly in recent years, reflecting:
  - The explosion of drug therapy programs in the United States
  - The rapid increase in the number of newly introduced, expensive and one-of-a-kind pharmaceutical products on the market
  - Greater reliance by the large pharmaceutical manufacturers on third-party distributors
  - Surging demand from managed care companies and hospitals seeking to lower their drug-related expenses
- The medical product distribution field has consolidated significantly as industry participants seek to gain additional cost advantages in an increasingly competitive field. However, BBC still ranks among the largest distributors, with annual revenues exceeding $17 billion.
- Bergen's increasing productivity stems from many sources: efficiency, automation, and telemarketing, to name a few. One interesting example is the productivity generated by ASD Specialty Healthcare, the specialty products distribution arm of Bergen Brunswig Specialty Company, which led productivity figures in 1998 with operating earnings per employee of $75,000.

One of the reasons for ASD's productivity is its ability to demonstrate remarkable growth with few additions to staff. Much of the credit for this may be attributed to its internal account management team, which is able to create and maintain close relationships with customers over the phone.

- In 1998, Bergen Brunswig celebrated the tenth anniversary of the first A-frame technology installed in a company distribution center. Bergen was first in the industry to utilize this technology, which automates the order-filling process. The company has also installed it with much success in its larger regional distribution facilities.

Automation technology has improved order-filling productivity by fifteen times. It has not only maximized distribution center capacity but has also enabled the company to handle significant growth in business while maintaining the most efficient processing cycles and improving levels overall.

The A-frame is stocked with fast-moving inventory items, which account for over 50 percent of the total items shipped each day, and its lines-per-hour speed has resulted in overall warehouse productivity gains of 45 percent. These improvements have not only maximized the return on investment in the company's automated regional distributions centers—which process as many as 14 million invoice lines annually—but have greatly assisted the company in meeting its commitment to quality service.

Total assets: $2,490 million
Current ratio: 1.31
Common shares outstanding: 101 million
Return on 1998 shareholders' equity: 15.1%

	1998	1997	1996	1995	1994	1993	1992	1991
Revenues (millions)	13,720	11,659	9,943	8,448	7,480	6,824	5,048	4,838
Net income (millions)	104	82	74	64	54	48	56	64
Earnings per share	1.02	.81	.73	.64	.56	.53	.54	.55
Dividends per share	.24	.22	.19	.19	.18	.15	.15	.13
Price: high	35.0	23.0	13.2	11.6	8.0	9.3	8.5	10.0
low	16.8	11.0	9.6	7.7	5.2	5.4	6.3	6.1

Bristol-Myers Squibb Company

345 Park Avenue, New York, NY 10154-0037 ❑ Listed: NYSE ❑ Investor contact: Tim Cost (212) 546-4103 ❑ Dividend reinvestment plan available: (800) 356-2026 ❑ Web site: www.bms.com ❑ Ticker symbol: BMY ❑ S&P rating: A ❑ Value Line financial strength rating: A++

Bristol-Myers Squibb is a leading, diversified health care and personal-care company. Its list of products includes ethical (prescription) drugs, over-the-counter preparations, diagnostics, infant formulas, orthopedic implants, as well as health and beauty aids.

Bristol-Myers is a global leader in chemotherapy drugs and ranks near the top in cardiovascular drugs and antibiotics. Heart drugs (17 percent of 1998 sales) include Pravachol, a cholesterol-reducing agent, Capoten/Capozide and Monopril, which are antihypertensive preparations. Through a joint venture with Sanofi, SA, BMY produces Plavix, a platelet aggregation inhibitor for the prevention of stroke, heart attack, and vascular diseases; and Avapro, an angiotensin II receptor blocker that treats hypertension. Principal anticancer drugs (16 percent of sales) consist of Taxol, Paraplatin, VePesid, and Platinol.

The company features a wide variety of anti-infective drugs (13 percent of 1998 sales), including Duricef/Ultracef, Cefzil, and Maxipime antibiotics; and Videx and Zerit AIDS therapeutics.

The company's nutritionals (10 percent of sales) encompass infant formulas such as Enfamil and ProSobee, vitamins, and nutritional supplements.

Beauty-care items (13 percent of 1998 sales) include Clairol, Ultress, Matrix Essentials, and Herbal Essence lines of hair-care products, Nice 'n Easy and Clairesse hair colorings, Final Net hair spray, Vitalis hair preparation, and other products.

Highlights of 1998

In 1998, Bristol-Myers Squibb achieved record sales, with all four of its business segments reporting increases, excluding the effects of foreign exchange and divestitures. Worldwide sales grew to $18.3 billion, a 9 percent increase over the prior year. Domestic sales, which represent 61 percent of worldwide sales, increased 15 percent, to $11.1 billion.

In 1998, the company's most important products, most of which experienced double-digit sales increases on a worldwide basis, made significant contributions to the company's sales growth. Two products, Pravachol and Taxol, exceeded $1 billion in sales for 1998. An additional seven products exceeded over a half billion dollars in annual sales. By the end of 1998, BMY had sixty-four product lines with more than $50 million in annual sales, thirty-six of which had more than $100 million in annual sales.

Shortcomings to Bear in Mind

■ Bristol-Myers is well known for aggressively developing and marketing drugs that it licenses from other companies or academic institutions, but its internal research efforts have lagged other top drug companies. Its two biggest products, Pravachol for lowering cholesterol and Taxol for cancer, are drugs that it licensed.

Under new research chief Peter Ringrose, a former star research manager at Pfizer, the company plans to increase its scientific staff 50 percent, to 6,000 workers by 2002. With this greater emphasis on research, BMY is hoping to reach its goal of tripling the number of new drugs approved to three a year by 2003, compared with the current rate of about one a year.

Reasons to Buy

- Bristol-Myers ended 1998 with an exceptionally strong balance sheet, one of only eight industrial companies in the United states with a triple-A credit rating from both Moody's and Standard & Poor's. The company had $2.2 billion in cash on hand at year-end. What's more, cash flow from operations reached an all-time high of $4.1 billion. Finally, BMY returned over $3.1 billion to shareholders, about half of which was use to repurchase company stock, with the rest for dividends.
- Bristol-Myers Squibb has an enviable pipeline of drugs under development. This pipeline, moreover, has expanded from twenty-nine compounds in active development five years ago to forty-two today. At the same time, the number of research licenses and alliances has nearly tripled.
- In 1998, *Fortune* magazine ranked Bristol Myers the second-most-admired pharmaceutical company in the world; it moved up from seventh place just a year earlier. This was a bigger leap than was made by any of the other 277 companies surveyed in twenty-one industry categories. Further, *Working Woman* and *Working Mother* magazines included Bristol-Myers in their lists of top employers in the United States. Most important, Bristol-Myers Squibb was awarded the 1998 National Medal of Technology, the nation's highest honor for technological innovation. The award was given to BMY for extending and enhancing human life through innovative pharmaceutical research and development and for redefining the science of clinical study.

- In 1998, the company initiated filings with the Food and Drug Administration (FDA) for two important compounds: Orzel, the first oral agent for colorectal cancer in the United States, and Tequin, a broad-spectrum oral quinolone antibiotic. Over the next year, BMY expects to file for additional medicines, including omapatrilat, the company's new hypertensive drug.
- The company has four strong businesses—pharmaceutical, nutritionals, consumer products and medical devices—each of which fields a broad line of high-quality products. These products are first or second in sales in ten of its fifteen largest product lines.
- During the past two decades, the business environment in which Bristol-Myers Squibb operates has become increasingly complex. The company has responded in a number of ways. It has entered new therapeutic areas, made major commitments to R&D, expanded marketing, and added or divested businesses as needed, culminating in one of the largest events in the history of corporate America, the merger of Bristol-Myers and Squibb in 1989.
- Bristol's nonpharmaceutical businesses, which include medical devices and non-prescription health and consumer products, should outpace the substantially larger pharmaceutical business, in terms of sales and earnings growth, over the next few years.
- Bristol-Myers Squibb has paid a dividend to its shareholders for an unbroken sixty-six years since becoming a public company in 1933. What's more, the company has increased the dividend each year since 1972.
- Glucophage is a novel antidiabetic agent indicated for first-line or combination treatment of type II diabetes. Type II diabetes is the most prevalent form. It affects over 13 million of the 14

million who suffer from diabetes. Glucophage is believed to work by increasing peripheral utilization of glucose (sugar), increasing the production of insulin, decreasing hepatic glucose production and altering intestinal absorption of glucose. The advantage of Glucophage over standard diabetic therapy is its action outside the liver. Conventional antidiabetic agents work solely by increasing insulin production. They sometimes lead to excessive insulin levels and associated low blood glucose levels (hypoglycemia), a complication that Glucophage avoids.

- Sustagen, a nutritious, flavored milk-substitute for pre-school and school-age children and pregnant or lactating mothers, is particularly popular in Latin America and Asia. As Mead Johnson seeks to standardize the product's formulation, Sustagen has become a cornerstone of the division's efforts to globalize its business.

- In 1998, the Food and Drug Administration (FDA) approved extra-strength Excedrin as the first over-the-counter medicine for migraines. The extra-strength version of the twenty-year-old painkiller is potent enough to treat mild-to-moderate migraines, FDA officials said. The approval gives Bristol-Myers a competitive advantage in the nation's $4-billion pain-reliever market, analysts said. As many as 18 million suffer from migraine headaches that can last for twenty-four hours or more. Many of these people cannot afford prescription drugs or a visit to the doctor to obtain a prescription.

- In the cancer research sector, Bristol-Myers said it is in the late-stage tests of a new colon and rectal cancer drug that is likely to have comparatively few side effects and could become the drug of choice for these diseases. In the longer term, the company is testing several ambitious new approaches, including what could be one of the first vaccines to prevent the reoccurrence of severe skin cancer. It also is nearing clinical testing of new genetic approaches to attacking cancer that would turn off signals from mutant genes that tell cancer cells to divide.

- Avapro and Plavix are both important additions to BMY's strong cardiovascular franchise that the company plans to develop aggressively. Resulting from the research staff of Sanofi, a leading French pharmaceutical company, these important drugs are being co-developed and co-marketed by Sanofi and Bristol-Myers. Avapro, the company's advanced antihypertensive medication, received initial approvals in the fall of 1997. But Bristol-Myers has already seen strong interest in this compound, which it believes is the best in its class. The reason is simple: With Avapro, physicians need not compromise efficacy by reducing dosage levels to reduce side effects in the treatment of hypertension. Avapro has tolerability similar to a placebo at all doses. Plavix, an antiplatelet agent, received approval from the U.S. Food and Drug Administration in November of 1997. It is used for the reduction of atherosclerotic events (myocardial infarction, stroke, and vascular deaths).

- The company's tussle with breast implant liability is about over. Bristol Myers took an $800 million pretax charge in the fourth quarter of 1998 to make final settlement of the 17,000 pending lawsuits. Although a few minor charges related to the insurance recoveries are possible in 1999, these should mark the end of the liability costs. With this albatross out of the way, it frees cash flow for share buybacks, acquisitions, and dividends.

Total assets: $16,272 million
Current ratio: 1.66
Return on 1998 equity: 49.2%
Common shares outstanding: 2,010 million

	1998	1997	1996	1995	1994	1993	1992	1991
Revenues (millions)	18,284	16,701	15,065	13,767	11,984	11,413	11,156	11,159
Net income (millions)	3,630	3,205	2,850	2,600	2,331	2,269	2,108	2,056
Earnings per share	1.80	1.61	1.42	1.28	1.15	1.10	1.02	.99
Dividends per share	.78	.76	.75	.74	.73	.72	.69	.60
Price:　high	67.6	49.1	29.1	21.8	15.3	16.8	22.5	22.3
low	44.2	26.6	19.5	14.4	12.5	12.7	15.0	15.3

INCOME

Cedar Fair, L. P.

P. O. Box 5006, Sandusky, OH 44871-5006 ❏ Investor contact: Brain C. Witherow (419) 627-2233 ❏ Dividend reinvestment plan available (800) 756-3353 ❏ Web site: www.cedarfair.com ❏ Listed: NYSE ❏ Ticker symbol: FUN ❏ S&P rating: Not rated ❏ Value Line financial strength rating: B+

Cedar Fair, L. P. owns and operates five amusement parks, two major water parks, three resort hotels, several year-round restaurants, a marina, and an RV campground. The company's parks attract more than 10 million visitors a year.

Cedar Fair prides itself on the growth of its roller coasters. Cedar Point alone boasts twelve—more than any other park in the world. All told, Cedar Fair parks have thirty-six roller coasters, including some of the tallest, steepest, and highest-rated coasters ever built.

Cedar Fair's Five Parks

Cedar Point, which is located on Lake Erie between Cleveland and Toledo, is one of the largest amusement parks in the United States; it serves a total market area of 22 million people. Valleyfair, located near Minneapolis/St. Paul, draws from a total population of 8 million people in a multistate market area. Dorney Park & Wildwater Kingdom is located near Allentown, Pennsylvania; it serves a total market area of 35 million people in the Northeast. Worlds of Fun/Oceans of Fun, in Kansas City, Missouri, draws from a total market area of 7 million people.

Knott's Berry Farm, near Los Angeles, is one of several, major, year-round theme parks in southern California. It serves a total market area of 20 million people and a large national and international tourist population.

How They Operate

The parks are family-oriented, providing clean and attractive environments with exciting rides and entertainment. Except for Knott's Berry Farm (which is open all year), the operating season is generally from May through September.

The parks charge a basic daily admission price that provides unlimited use of virtually all rides and attractions. Admissions account for about 52 percent of revenues, with food, merchandise, and games contributing 42 percent and accommodations the other 6 percent.

Tax Considerations

Cedar Fair is a publicly traded master limited partnership (MLP). The MLP structure is an attractive business form because it allows the partnership to pay out the majority of its earnings to its owners without first paying significant federal and state income taxes at the entity level, avoiding what is known as the corporate form as double taxation of earnings.

Ownership of Cedar Fair, L. P. units is different from an investment in corporate stock. Cash distributions made by the partnership are treated as a reduction of basis and are generally not taxable. Instead, unitholders must pay tax only on their pro rata share of the partnership's taxable income, which is generally lower. The partnership provides the tax information necessary for filing each unit holder's federal, state, and local tax returns on I.R.S. Schedule K-1 in late February each year.

The tax consequences to a particular unit holder will depend on the circumstances of that unit holder; however, income from the partnership may not be offset by passive tax losses from other investments. Prospective unit holders should consult their tax or financial advisors to determine the federal, state, and local tax consequences of ownership of units in this limited partnership.

Ownership of limited partnership units may not be advisable for IRAs, pension and profit-sharing plans and other tax-exempt organizations, nonresident aliens, foreign corporations and other foreign persons, and regulated investment companies.

Shortcomings to Bear in Mind

- About two-thirds of the company's revenue is derived from the Midwest and Mid-Atlantic regions. Adverse economic conditions in these regions could hurt attendance at Cedar Fair parks. On the other hand, the acquisition of Knott's Berry Farm lessens this risk somewhat.
- When you file your income tax, you may find that Cedar Fair has failed to send you the usual paperwork. In 1998, I didn't get mine till March 18th. I had already given my CPA the rest, and he

had completed my return before I realized my blunder. Unfortunately, it was back to square one at my expense. One other thing, since Cedar Fair operates in several states, you may find you have to pay a few of them some tax money. Otherwise, it is a great stock.

- Each of the company's parks faces some direct competition from other parks. For instance, Dorney Park competes with Hershey Park in central Pennsylvania and Six Flags Great Adventure in the New York and New Jersey metropolitan area. Out West, the newly acquired Knott's Berry Farm has to compete with six parks, all within fifty miles. They include Adventure City, Castle Amusement Park, Disneyland, Six Flags Magic Mountain, Scandia Family Fun Center, and Pacific Park. Cedar Point, the company's biggest park, competes with three nearby parks: Paramount Kings Island in southern Ohio, and Sea World and Geauga Lake, both near Cleveland. Valleyfair faces the least competition: Adventureland, 250 miles away in Des Moines, and Camp Snoopy, an indoor park at the Mall of America fifteen miles away, now owned by Cedar Fair. Worlds of Fun's competition consists of Silver Dollar City in Branson, Missouri, and Six Flags Over Mid America, outside St. Louis.

Reasons to Buy

- At the end of 1997, the company acquired Knott's Berry Farm, which got off to a shaky start in 1998, due to the impact of El Niño on West Coast weather patterns in the winter and spring. However, attendance increased sharply with the debut of Supreme Scream in early July of 1998. This new ride was the first major new thrill ride at Knott's in several years. According to management, it "really made a difference and communicated to the very competitive Southern California market that Knott's is committed to being a park with great rides as well as great attractions." In the same year, Knott's unveiled its second major ride, GhostRider, which had been under construction when Cedar Fair made its purchase. In the 1998 annual report, the company says, GhostRider "opened to great reviews from both roller coaster buffs and park-goers."

- The company's status as a limited partnership was in doubt until recently, since it was feared Congress would end this favorable business form. To remain a limited partnership, Cedar Fair began paying a tax on its gross profits in 1998. Publicly traded limited partnerships were scheduled to expire at the end of 1997 but were indefinitely extended if the company agreed to a 3.5 percent tax on gross profits.

- Although the Cedar Fair Partnership is relatively young (it was created in April of 1987), it owns four amusement parks with considerable longevity. In 1998, Cedar Point, the flagship park, celebrated it 129th anniversary. That same year, Valleyfair celebrated its twenty-fourth season. Dorney Park opened its 116th season in 1999. Finally, Worlds of Fun first opened in 1973 and celebrated its twenty-seventh summer in 1999.

- According to one analyst, Cedar Fair's management team "exhibits both strength and depth." The general managers at the five parks have an average tenure of nearly twenty-three years with the company.

- Cedar Fair operates in an industry with high barriers to entry, with scant likelihood of new competition. The absence of direct competition gives the parks pricing power in their regions, bolstering profit margins.

- The acquisition of Knott's Berry Farm gives Cedar Fair exposure to the faster growing western states. In 1999, the company purchased the Buena Park Hotel, located adjacent to this theme park. The addition of this 320-room hotel should further reduce the cyclicality inherent in the company's business. Management hopes to duplicate the success it has enjoyed at its Cedar Point resort, which offers numerous amenities typical of a full vacation destination.

- One way of promoting success in the amusement park business is to offer the public new and exciting attractions. Toward this end, Cedar Fair has upgraded its capital expansion program; $48 million worth of improvements are on tap for 1999. Cedar Point, the company's park in Sandusky Ohio, introduced Camp Snoopy (a family playground based on the comic-strip characters from Peanuts). It also added a new, 230-room hotel at that location, Breakers Tower. With this new structure, the Hotel Breakers is now the second-largest hotel in Ohio. At Dorney Park, the company has a new 200-foot-tall thrill ride, tabbed Dominator. Meanwhile, Worlds of Fun now boasts a new family attraction at its water park, as well as a major new food complex and go-cart track.

- The Magnum roller coaster propelled Cedar Point to a record attendance year in 1989. When it was opened in May of that year, Magnum was the tallest, steepest, and fastest roller coaster on earth. A decade later, Magnum is still a major draw to the park and remains the park's most popular roller coaster. In a recent Amusement Today poll, it was named the best steel roller coaster on the planet. The same poll ranked Cedar Point as the nation's best amusement park by a wide margin.

Total assets: $631 million
Current ratio: 0.39
Common shares outstanding: 52 million
Return on 1998 partners' capital: 24.4%

	1998	1997	1996	1995	1994	1993	1992	1991
Revenues (millions)	420	264	250	218	198	179	153	128
Net income (millions)	84	68	74	66	61	50	43	36
Earnings per share	1.58	1.47	1.59	1.45	1.37	1.13	.98	.84
Dividends per share	1.29	1.26	1.20	1.14	1.06	.95	.87	.77
Price: high	30.1	28.3	19.5	18.6	18.3	18.3	14.9	9.5
low	21.8	17.7	16.1	14.1	13.4	13.5	8.9	6.3

GROWTH AND INCOME

Chevron Corporation

575 Market Street, Room 3444, San Francisco, CA 94105-2856 ◻ Investor contact: Peter M. Trueblood (415) 894-5690 ◻ Direct dividend reinvestment plan available (800) 842-7629 ◻ Web site: www.chevron.com ◻ Listed: NYSE ◻ Ticker symbol: CHV ◻ S&P rating: B+ ◻ Value Line financial strength rating: A++

Chevron is a worldwide petroleum company with important interests in chemicals and minerals. It is a leading domestic producer of crude oil and natural gas and a marketer of refined products. Chevron is active in foreign exploration and production and overseas refining and marketing.

Supply and Demand

The price of oil stocks tends to be a reflection of crude oil prices, which are a function of worldwide supply and demand. Demand is determined primarily by weather and economic conditions. Supply, on the other hand, is influenced by inventories and production levels.

In recent years, OPEC (the Organization of Petroleum Exporting Countries) has been able to control, at least to some extent, production by setting quotas that keep crude prices high enough to benefit them, but low enough to keep non-OPEC producers from getting too competitive with their exploration and drilling or consumers from finding something else to burn.

A Breakdown of Chevron's Operations

Exploration and Production

Chevron explores for and produces crude oil and natural gas in the United States and twenty-five other countries. The company is the third-largest domestic natural gas producer.

Major producing regions include the Gulf of Mexico, California, the Rocky Mountains, Texas, China, Canada, the North Sea, Australia, Indonesia, Angola, Nigeria, Kazakhstan, Alaska, Republic of Congo, Papua New Guinea, Colombia, Peru, and Ireland. Exploration areas include the above, as well as Alaska, Azerbaijan, Bahrain, and Qatar.

Refining

CHV converts crude oil into a variety of refined products, including motor gasoline, diesel and aviation fuels, lubricants, asphalt, chemicals, and other products. Chevron is one of the largest refiners in the United States.

The company's principal U.S. locations are El Segundo and Richmond, CA;

Pascagoula, MS; Salt Lake City, Utah; El Paso, TX; and Honolulu, Hawaii. The company also refines in Canada (through its Caltex affiliate), Asia, Africa, Australia, and New Zealand.

Marketing

Chevron is one of the leading domestic marketers of refined products, including motor gasoline, diesel and aviation fuels, lubricants, and other products. Retail outlets number 7,900 in the United States, and 200 in Canada; Caltex supplies about 9,000 retail outlets worldwide.

Supply and Distribution

The company purchases, sells, trades, and transports, by pipeline, tanker, and barge, crude oil, liquefied natural gas liquids (such as propane and butane), chemicals, and refined products.

Chevron has trading offices in Houston, Walnut Creek, CA, London, Singapore, Mexico City, and Moscow. Moreover, the company has interests in pipelines throughout the United States and in Africa, Australia, Indonesia, Papua New Guinea, Europe, and the Middle East. Chevron has tanker operations worldwide.

Chemicals

The company's main products are benzene, styrene, polystyrene, paraxylene, ethylene, polyethylene, and normal alpha olefins. Chevron also produces a variety of additives used for fuels and lubricants.

Chevron operates plants in nine states and in France, Brazil, Mexico, Singapore, and Japan. Through affiliates and subsidiaries, the company operates or markets in more than eighty countries.

Shortcomings to Bear in Mind

- According to management, "1998 was a tough year for Chevron and for the petroleum industry. The depressed economic conditions in Asia reduced the demand for petroleum product, and the resulting worldwide oversupply of crude oil hammered prices. The price of U.S. benchmark crude dropped to its lowest annual average in twenty years, down some 30 percent from 1997. Chevron's net income fell 59 percent, to $1.339 billion, from the record $3.256 billion earned in 1997."

- The company's operations on the Caspian Sea are speculative. The crux of the problem lies in simple geography; they don't call Kazakhstan Central Asia for nothing. The vast, mostly empty country, one-third the size of the continental United States with only 16 million people, is equally remote from the world's two main oil importing regions: Western Europe and East Asia. Such distance is not a serious problem in the oil business if it can be covered by ship—an easy enough proposition for producers in West Africa, East Asia, or the Persian Gulf. But the Caspian, though called a sea, is surrounded by land—five different nations, in fact—and none of them easy places to do business. The northern shore is dominated by Russia, the southern edge, by Iran. Azerbaijan is on the west side of the Caspian, Kazakhstan and tiny Turkmenistan on the east side. All of them present tricky problems, not easily solved.

Reasons to Buy

- In June of 1999, Chevron said it had formed a joint venture with Sasol Ltd. of South Africa to take a technology for converting natural gas to liquids worldwide, a move that could make Chevron one of the oil industry's most aggressive players in this emerging business. Sasol is the world's largest synthetic-fuel producer.

  Several companies, including Royal Dutch, Exxon, and BP Amoco, are scrambling to develop natural-gas-to-liquid technology, which could make the world's vast, but isolated, natural gas reserves profitable to produce. When natural gas is turned into a form of petroleum, it can be more easily and less expensively transported and sold in world markets. A Chevron spokesman said the two companies anticipate spending billions of dollars on the technology over the next five to ten years.

- Several major large projects will drive the company's projected growth in international oil and gas production over the next several years. Offshore Angola, the deepwater Kuito and Benguela oil fields will be developed, with first production scheduled for 1999 and 2002, respectively. Chevron's share is 31 percent.

Chevron has a goal of producing 600,000 barrels a day from its properties offshore Angola by 2001. In late 1998, the company set a single-day production record of more than 510,000 barrels a day. Several new water-injection projects, designed to increase production from older oil fields, are under way.

North Sea and the Boscan and LL-652 fields in Venezuela are expected to contribute significantly over the next several years to the increase in Chevron's international oil and gas production. Additional projects in Angola, Nigeria, and Congo will also make significant contributions.

- Chevron's ability to reduce operating costs since 1991 has been critical to its success. It is, in fact, the key to funding vital growth projects. The company's current business plan calls for cost reductions of $500 million in 1999.

Improvements in energy efficiency, project management, and procurement are contributing significantly to savings. When compared to 1993, savings in energy efficiency alone amount to $200 million a year. By managing capital projects better, the company cut costs 15 percent since 1991 and in 1999 is making additional improvements that are expected to reduce costs another 10 percent.

- Not many oil companies are boosting their investment in new oil wells. But Chevron is. Kenneth Derr, CEO of Chevron, is increasing the company's exploration and production budget by 12 percent, to $3.7 billion, making it the only major oil company to bolster its drilling budget in 1999. Exxon, for instance, is whittling down its spending by 12 percent; BP Amoco by 22 percent; and Conoco by 40 percent. As a group, the fifteen largest petroleum companies are slashing an average of 17 percent, according one leading analyst.

Chevron's CEO says, "If you are going to go for something, make sure it's big enough to matter." What this means is this: Most oil companies are choosing profits over production growth. Derr wants both. Chevron got in early in several rich drilling regions abroad, such as Angola and Kazakhstan. Those fields are profitable even at the depressed prices in 1999. This means that Derr can afford to pump more money into production. And if prices go back up, as they should before the fields run dry, the projects become even more lucrative.

After Derr took the reins in 1989, he channeled an increasingly larger percentage of Chevron's budget into big oil and gas projects overseas. The result is that over the past five years, as Chevron has pumped 2.6 billion barrels, it has added 4.3 billion others, for a 165 percent replacement rate. By contrast, the average big oil company replaced just 116 percent of what it sold. It now costs Chevron $3.91 per barrel to find oil, considerably less than what it cost the company a decade ago.

- Worldwide exploration and production earnings fell by half in 1998, from $2.169 billion in 1997 to $1.098 billion in 1998. However, Chevron's production gains were one of the highlights of the year. The company's worldwide net liquids production climbed 3 percent, to 1.1 million barrels a day. International net liquids production—the company's main area of focus—increased for the ninth straight year, up 7 percent over 1997. What's more, Chevron more than replaced this production with new reserves.
- In 1950, world crude oil reserves were estimated at 76 billion barrels, which was about a twenty-year supply at the rate of consumption at that time. In the forty-five years since, the world has used 600 billion barrels, and there's an estimated 1 trillion barrels in proved reserves. The world's oil supply now is greater than it has ever been, if we didn't find another drop of oil, we would still have a fifty-year supply left.
- In February of 1999, Chevron and a unit of Atlantic Richfield, ARCO Permian,

announced an agreement to exclusively pursue a combination of the two companies' oil and gas producing assets in the Permian Basin of West Texas and southeast New Mexico. ARCO and Chevron each own 50 percent of the new company. The new entity develops and produces oil and natural gas and market-crude oil, natural gas, natural gas liquids, and related products in the Permian Basin. Operations consist of more than 7,000 wells and 150 fields, representing 600 million barrels of proved reserves and producing over 170,000 barrels per day of oil equivalents.

- Chevron Chemical Company began commercial production in January 1999 at its new $215 million Singapore plant, the largest fuel and lubricating additives manufacturing plant in Asia. The plant manufactures twenty-six additive components from over forty different raw materials and makes more than 150 additive package blends tailored to customer needs.

Total assets: $36,540 million
Current ratio: 0.91
Common shares outstanding: 652 million
Return on 1998 shareholders' equity: 7.8%

	1998	1997	1996	1995	1994	1993	1992	1991
Revenues (millions)	26,187	40,583	42,782	37,082	30,340	32,123	37,464	36,461
Net income (millions)	1,976	3,256	2,607	1,962	1,693	1,819	1,593	1,293
Earnings per share	3.01	4.95	3.98	3.01	2.60	2.80	2.35	1.85
Dividends per share	2.44	2.28	2.08	1.93	1.85	1.75	1.65	1.63
Price: high	90.2	89.2	68.4	53.6	47.3	49.4	37.7	40.1
low	67.8	61.8	51.0	43.4	39.9	33.8	30.1	31.8

Clayton Homes, Inc.

P. O. Box 15169, Knoxville, TN 37901 ❑ Investor contact: Carl Koella (423)380-3206 ❑ Web site: www.clayton.net ❑ Dividend reinvestment plan available (800)937-5449 ❑ Fiscal year's end June 30 ❑ Listed: NYSE ❑ Ticker symbol: CMH ❑ S&P rating: A- ❑ Value Line financial strength B+

Clayton Homes, Inc. is a vertically integrated manufactured housing company headquartered in Knoxville, Tennessee. Employing more than 6,700 people and operating in twenty-eight states, the company builds, sells, finances, and insures manufactured homes. It also owns and operates residential manufactured housing communities.

The company makes a wide variety of single- and multisection manufactured homes. They are factory-built, completely finished, constructed to be transported by trucks, and designed as permanent, primary residences when sited. In fiscal 1998, CMH's homes had retail prices ranging from $10,000 to $75,000. Their sizes ranged from 500 to 2,330 square feet.

The Manufacturing Group is a leading producer of manufactured homes, with eighteen plants supplying homes to 1,046 independent and company-owned retail centers.

The Retail Group sells, installs, and services factory-built homes. At the end of fiscal 1998, there were 273 company-owned retail centers in twenty-one states.

Financial Services provides financing and insurance for homebuyers at company-owned and selected independent retail sales centers through Vanderbilt Mortgage and Finance, a wholly-owned subsidiary.

The Communities Group owns and operates seventy-one manufactured housing communities, with 18,964 home sites in twelve states.

In 1998, Clayton Homes completed its eighteenth consecutive record year. Net income has increased at a rate of 29 per-cent per year since the initial public offering in 1983. Earnings per share, moreover, have grown at 23 percent annually. Shareholders who purchased 1,000 shares in June of 1983 for $16,000 now have 14,551 shares worth $276,469. That amounts to an annual return of 21 percent.

The fourth quarter of 1998 marked the company's forty-eighth consecutive record quarter, while achieving positive comparisons in 60 out of 61 quarters since the initial public offering.

Since June 1983, the expansion includes:

- Company retailers, expanded from 39 to 273
- Independent retailers, from 109 to 702
- Manufacturing plants, from 3 to 18
- Communities, from 0 to 71
- Annual mortgage originations, from $14 million to $802 million
- Service portfolio, from $27 million to $2.9 billion
- Capital investments, from $405,000 to $62 million
- Shareholders' equity, from $28 million to $881 million
- Market capitalization, from $86 million to $2.3 billion
- Employees, from 800 to 6,700

Shortcomings to Bear in Mind

■ Clayton Homes was disappointed that its target for retail stores in 1998 was missed; management felt that it was not in the long-term interest of its shareholders to pay unreasonably high premiums for new retail stores or other acquisitions. To facilitate growth for

1999, the Retail Group was restructured into four zones, each supervised by a group vice president with fifteen or more years of industry experience.

- During fiscal 1998, the company leveraged its balance sheet to make strategic portfolio acquisitions and to improve the return on equity. Long-term debt increased from $23 million to $248 million. Although higher debt is a short-coming—particularly for conservative investors—the company's debt is still not onerous. At the end of 1998, common stock represented a solid 78 percent of total capitalization.

Reasons to Buy

- Growth among the company's four groups has varied from quarter to quarter and year to year, but the synergies involved in this very difficult to execute concept have enabled the company to consistently achieve records. While one group is undergoing a period of slower growth, another group is enjoying high growth. The challenge of balancing and maintaining the model should not be underestimated—especially since other industry leaders have taken multiple charges to restate their securitization models. On the other hand, Clayton Homes has taken a conservative approach to growth and risk management.

- In 1998, Clayton Homes's Manufacturing Group achieved record performance in sales revenue, productivity, quality, and income. Revenue grew to $600 million, up 15 percent over the prior year. The number of floors produced increased 14 percent, to 39,892, and home production increased 7 percent, to 27,640.

   The company's distribution now reaches twenty-eight states via 1,046 long-term partners, including 702 independents, 273 company-owned sales

centers, and 71 communities. Multisection homes represented 44 percent of Clayton's shipments for the fiscal year, up from 35 percent, as the company kept pace with the industry's shift to multisection homes. New plants will be designed and located to support the growing multisection segment. However, single-section home production remains strong and will continue to be an important component of the company's strategic focus.

- During Clayton Homes's fifteen years as a public company, the Retail Group has navigated many market trends. In 1983, the group sold 3,354 homes, generating more than $42 million, while multisection homes comprised only 19 percent of the product mix. In 1998, revenues climbed to $535 million from the sale of more than 16,500 homes. The heightened demand for multisection homes is credited to several factors: affordability, lower interest rates, the increasing price of site-built homes, and the efforts of the company's sales force, which strives to match the needs and expectations of its buyers.

   The Retail Group opened 33 distribution outlets in 1998 and closed five underperforming outlets. Since 1983, the group increased the number of sales centers from 39 to 273. To ensure future expansion, the group has devoted additional resources to the development of new sales centers in attractive markets and to the acquisition of independent retailers, when available at reasonable prices.

- In 1998, the company's Communities Group increased by 1,167 its number of home sites, or 7 percent. Contributing to this growth was the acquisition of four communities in Virginia, South Carolina, and Florida that added 945 sites. Expansion in existing communities contributed 222 sites. Clayton Homes now owns and operates 71 communities, with 18,964 home sites in twelve states. Three states, Texas, Florida, and Tennessee, account for 73 percent of these home sites.

Operating rental revenues rose 21 percent to a record level in 1998. This was accomplished by the increase in occupied sites, along with a 7-percent increase in the company's average site rent. For properties owned at least one year, occupancy increased to 72 percent, from 70 percent in 1997. Overall occupancy was also at 72 percent—three of the four communities purchased during the year had high occupancy levels.

- In 1998, the company's Financial Services group set new records for loan origination, servicing, securitization, and written insurance premiums. Vanderbilt Mortgage and Financial's loan origination for 1998 totaled $802 million, of which the Million Dollar Business Units (MBUs) generated $269 million, and net written insurance premiums totaled $51 million.

In 1983, the year of the company's initial public offering, Vanderbilt's servicing portfolio totaled $27 million. Fifteen years later, the portfolio had grown to $2.9 billion. In 1998, Vanderbilt and the MBUs continued to enjoy a relatively low cost of funds. This was attributable to their experience, reputation as a premier servicer, and to the low interest rate environment. What's more, the company's diligent collection efforts resulted in a delinquency rate of only 1.98 percent for the year.

The MBUs produced one-third of the total loan originations in 1998, as their originations increased more than 70 percent. Financial Services now has six MBUs up and running: Direct Lending, Private Mortgages, Independent Lending, Commercial Unites, Home Security, and Insurance Marketing. MBUs seek to leverage the core competencies of Financial Services and to produce profit potential of at least $1 million per year by the end of their third year.

Total assets: $1,458 million
Current ratio: 7.90
Common shares outstanding: 116 million
Return on 1998 shareholders' equity: 16.8%

	1998	1997	1996	1995	1994	1993	1992	1991
Revenues (millions)	1,128	1,022	929	758	628	476	371	321
Net income (millions)	138	120	107	87	69	54	39	29
Earnings per share	.92	.80	.72	.59	.47	.37	.29	.24
Dividends per share	.06	.06	.05	.03				
Price: high	18.1	15.6	14.5	15.0	11.5	10.6	8.9	5.1
low	10.7	10.1	9.9	6.8	6.6	7.1	3.8	2.7

The Clorox Company

P. O. Box 24305, Oakland, CA 94623-1305 ▢ Investor contact: Steve Austenfeld (510) 271-7270 ▢ Web site: www.clorox.com ▢ Dividend reinvestment plan available (888) 259-6973 ▢ Fiscal year's end June 30 ▢ Listed: NYSE ▢ Ticker symbol: CLX ▢ S&P rating: A ▢ Value Line financial strength rating: A+

Over the years, the name Clorox has become synonymous with household bleach. No wonder. Since the company introduced its first pint of Clorox bleach in the 1920s, The Clorox Company has come to dominate the domestic bleach market, with nearly a 70 percent share.

Today, Clorox has evolved into a diversified consumer-products company whose domestic retail products include many of the best-known brands of laundry additives, home cleaning and automotive-appearance products, cat litters, insecticides, charcoal briquets, salad dressings, sauces, and water-filtration systems.

Background

In 1913, a group of Oakland businessmen founded the Electro-Alkaline Company, a forerunner of The Clorox Company. The company originally produced an industrial-strength liquid bleach. It was sold in 5-gallon crockery jugs to industrial customers in the San Francisco Bay area.

A household version of Clorox liquid bleach was developed in 1916 and subsequently was distributed in sample pint bottles. Demand for the product grew, and its distribution was gradually expanded nationally until it became the country's best-selling liquid bleach.

Clorox was a one-product company for its first fifty-six years, including the eleven years from 1957 through 1968 when it was operated as a division of The Procter & Gamble Company. Following its divestiture by Procter & Gamble in 1969, the company has broadened and diversified its product line and expanded geographically. Today,

Clorox manufactures a wide range of products that are marketed to consumers in the United States and internationally. It is also a supplier of products to food service and institutional customers and the janitorial trades.

Although the company's growth in the first few years after divestiture came largely through the acquisition of other companies and products, strong emphasis is now being given to the internal development of new products.

The company's line of domestic retail products includes many of the country's best-known brands of laundry additives, home cleaning products, cat litters, insecticides, charcoal briquets, salad dressings, sauces, and water-filtration systems. The great majority of the company's brands are either number one or number two in their categories.

Included in Clorox products are such well-known names as Formula 409, Liquid-Plumr, Pine-Sol, Soft Scrub, S.O.S., Tilex, Armor All, Kingsford charcoal, Match Light, Black Flag insecticides, Fresh Step cat litter, Hidden Valley salad dressing, and Kitchen Bouquet.

Clorox's Professional Products unit is focused on extending many of the company's successful retail equities in cleaning and food products to new channels of distribution, such as institutional and professional markets and the food-service industry.

Internationally, Clorox markets laundry additives, home cleaning products, and insecticides, primarily in developing countries. What's more, Clorox is investing heavily to expand this part of its business. Overall, Clorox products are sold in more than seventy countries and are manufactured in thirty-five plants at locations in the United States, Puerto Rico, and abroad.

Highlights of 1998
- Case volume grew by a strong 9 percent.
- Net sales increased a healthy 8 percent.
- Net earnings and diluted earnings per share climbed 19 percent.
- Operations generated cash flow of $313 million.
- The company's return on equity increased from 25.4 percent to 28.4 percent.

Shortcomings to Bear in Mind

- Because of its consistent success, Clorox often sells at a high multiple.
- Shipments of Hidden Valley mixes for salads and dips were off during 1998. According to management, "We plan to get the mixes up and running like the rest of the division by improving presence on store shelves and increasing marketing activity."

Reasons to Buy

- In 1998, several of the company's Combat and Maxforce products entered the market with a significant competitive advantage. They now contain Fipronil, a powerful new active ingredient for which Rhone-Poulenc granted Clorox license rights. According to Clorox, "Fipronil is a major advance in insecticide technology and holds great promise for the company's business."
- You might wonder why anyone would want to be the nation's number one maker of cat litter. Apparently, Clorox likes the idea. The CEO of the company says he wants Clorox to be number two or better in every category in which it competes. In fiscal 1999, Clorox acquired the First Brands Corporation, a firm that makes Glad trash bags, STP car care products, as well as three kinds of cat litter. The $1.52-billion stock gives Clorox a leading share of the market in all three categories. Not least, the cat litter business has very high margins.

The deal added STP to the company's Armor-All, the car protectant maker it bought a year earlier. Not only is Clorox now number one in car care products, but it now has a 30 percent stake in plastic bags and plastic wrap, with the addition of the Glad lines.

- In 1998, Clorox continued to build portfolio; that is, the company carefully chose businesses and focused its efforts where it can add value. For instance, six years ago, international business was only 4 percent of sales. Today, foreign revenues have climbed to 18 percent. In 1998, moreover, the company improved its position in Brazil and Chile with acquisitions of solid bleach franchises, and Clorox is now in seventy-nine countries worldwide.
- In 1998, Clorox continued to introduce new products at a fast pace. The company introduced a record forty-one new products. For instance, it made a strong entry into a dynamic new category of "daily cleaners" with Tilex Fresh Shower. Management believes this is going to be a significant contributor to its Tilex business. The Pine-Sol franchise was strengthened with the successful launch of the company's new Lemon Fresh Pine-Sol antibacterial product.

Integration of Armor All, purchased in 1996, is complete and now adding to earnings.

- In a market that Clorox created and which has attracted a host of competitors, the company's Brita water filtration systems business completed another year of record shipments and profits, as well as clear category leadership.

Growth in this business was propelled by continued household penetration by Brita systems, coupled with strong growth in the sales of replacement filters. What's more, distribution gains have seen a 40 percent increase in the number of stores offering Brita products.

■ Clorox continues to expand where the company sees an opportunity to enter a market with a competitive advantage. Once Clorox acquires a business, it expands it by modernizing plants. What's more, the company builds mass through line extensions and strategic acquisitions.

Clorox also upgrades packaging and leverage marketing expertise gained in the United States by putting it to use in a new country with the company's just-acquired brands. In sum, that's how Clorox built leadership positions in the majority of its worldwide markets.

For example, in Argentina, the company's liquid bleach brand, Ayudin, holds a 70 percent share in the market. Arco Iris and Ayudin Ropa Color, Clorox's brands of color-safe bleach, dominate the competition. The company's two brands in the stain-remover category, Arco Iris and Trenet, have a combined share of over 90 percent, and the company's sponge business, Mortimer, holds nearly one-half of the market.

There are similar success stories in Brazil, Chile, the Republic of Korea, and Malaysia. And, in close step with the company's domestic business, the bulk of its international sales volume is represented by Clorox Company brands that are either number one or number two in their respective categories. Today, the company's international business (including exports) accounts for 16 percent of sales, up from 4 percent a few years ago.

■ The company's charcoal business continues to thrive. In 1998, the Match Light brand saw the highest gains in the group. Consumers appreciate the convenience that instant-lighting briquets provide. The company's scientists knocked another five minutes off the time that it takes Match Light briquets to be ready for cooking. They're now ready to go in about ten minutes.

Kingsford added a NASCAR sponsorship to its marketing program in 1998. NASCAR is the world's fastest-growing spectator sport and a new and exciting way to build the charcoal business. Clorox's share of charcoal consumption in the southeast portion of the United States has climbed as a result of this program.

■ Effective advertising, coupled with expanded distribution into warehouse club stores such as Sam's Club and Costco, catapulted shipment of the full-calorie bottled Hidden Valley dressings and the K. C. Masterpiece barbecue sauces to record levels, despite intense competition. Four new flavors of bottled dressings introduced in 1998 also helped volume and sales.

Total assets: $3,030 million
Current ratio: .71
Common shares outstanding: 104 million
Return on 1998 shareholders' equity: 28.4%

	1998	1997	1996	1995	1994	1993	1992	1991
Revenues (millions)	2,741	2,533	2,218	1,984	1,837	1,634	1,717	1,646
Net income (millions)	298	249	222	201	180	168	144	131
Earnings per share	2.82	2.41	2.14	1.89	1.68	1.54	1.33	1.22
Dividends per share	1.28	1.16	1.06	.96	.93	.86	.80	.74
Price: high	117.5	80.4	55.1	39.6	29.8	27.7	26.0	21.2
low	74.4	48.6	35.0	27.6	23.5	22.0	19.8	17.5

The Coca-Cola Company

One Coca-Cola Plaza, P. O. Drawer 1734, Atlanta, GA 30301 ◻ Investor contact: Larry M. Mark (404) 676-8054 ◻ Dividend reinvestment plan available (404) 676-2777 ◻ Web site: www.thecoca-colacompany.com ◻ Listed: NYSE ◻ Ticker symbol: KO ◻ S&P rating: A+ ◻ Value Line financial strength rating: A++

The Coca-Cola Company is the world's largest producer and distributor of soft-drink syrups and concentrates. Company products are sold through bottlers, fountain wholesalers, and distributors in nearly 200 countries. The company's products represent about 48 percent of total soft-drink unit-case volume consumer worldwide. (A unit-case is equal to 24 eight-ounce servings.)

Trademark Coca-Cola accounts for about 68 percent of the company's worldwide gallon shipments of beverage products (excluding those distributed by The Minute Maid Company).

The company's allied brands account for the remaining 32 percent of gallon sales. These brands are: Sprite, diet Sprite, TAB, Fanta, Fresca, Mr Pibb, Hi-C, Mello Yello, Barq's, POWERaDE, Fruitopia, and specialty overseas brands.

The company's operations are managed in five operating groups and The Minute Maid Company. Excluding those products distributed by The Minute Maid Company, the company's unit-case volume by region is as follows: North America Group, 31 percent; Latin America Group, 25 percent; Greater Europe Group, 21 percent; Middle and Far East Group, 19 percent; and Africa Group, 4 percent.

The Minute Maid Company, headquartered in Houston, Texas, is the world's largest marketer of juice and juice-drink products. Major products of The Minute Maid Company include the following:

• Minute Maid chilled ready-to-serve and frozen concentrated citrus and variety juices, lemonades, and fruit punches

• Hi-C brand ready-to-serve fruit drinks

• Bright & Early breakfast beverages

• Bacardi tropical fruit mixes

Shortcomings to Bear in Mind

■ The company had a disappointing year in 1998. Operating income was $4.97 billion, off 1 percent from the prior year. Net income was $3.53 billion, a decline of 14 percent. Similarly, earnings per share fell 13 percent, to $1.42. The company blamed its setback on "The weakened currencies we continued to see around the world." Without the currency factors and transactions pertaining to bottling system changes, the company's 1998 operating income would have increased nearly 10 percent over 1997.

■ Coca-Cola's plans to buy Orangina faded in April of 1999, when France's highest administrative court refused to overturn a government ruling that had blocked the sale. While Coca-Cola officials sought to put a positive spin on the decision, it was clearly a setback for the company. The transaction dated back to December of 1997, when Coca-Cola announced that it would buy Orangina, a highly popular orange-flavored drink owned by Pernod Richard SA, for $844 million. The French disappointment was the second ruling against Coke's strategy of buying popular international brands. In the same month, Australian regulators rejected the company's plan to buy brands now owned by Cadbury Schweppes PLC.

■ Coca-Cola has been a stellar performer in recent years. The stock has been one of the best components of the Dow

Jones Industrial Average. As a consequence, its price/earnings ratio is extremely high. Those who prefer low P/E stocks may choose to select from among those with lower multiples.

Reasons to Buy

- Although management is difficult to evaluate, Coca-Cola's new CEO, M. Douglas Ivester, has a lot going for him. Mr. Ivester succeeded Roberto C. Goizueta, who died of lung cancer in October of 1997. Mr. Ivester, the son of a factory foreman from Gainesville, Georgia, joined Coke in 1979 as assistant controller after a stint as outside auditor for the company. He stood out quickly, long before being tapped in 1994 for president and chief operating officer. Donald Keough, the company's president from 1981 to 1993, says that at the end of every year, he used to turn in a report about who should succeed him as president if he was incapacitated. He began penciling in Mr. Ivester's name as early as 1987. "He has this passion to succeed," Mr. Keough says. "Every job he took, he thought he could master."

- This is a classic growth stock. In the 1988–1998 period, earnings per share climbed from $.36 to $1.42, for an impressive compound annual growth rate of 14.7 percent. Dividends also performed well, advancing from $.15 to $.60, a growth rate of 14.9 percent. What's more, the stock was split three times during this period.

- In the United States, the company reached an agreement to make Coca-Cola classic the official drink of NASCAR racing, connecting with millions of the sporting world's most loyal fans.

- Meanwhile, POWERaDE became the official sports drink of the fast-growing National Hockey League. And Surge continued its very strong performance

as the company's biggest new product launch in more than a decade. This "fully loaded citrus soda" is a hit with young people and will soon reach 90 percent of the United States.

- As Coca-Cola continues sharpening its bottling and customer networks, it is applying the same intensity and focus to the logistical and technical support it provides that system.

  For instance, to boost the system's procurement capabilities, it reorganized its Global and Trading Group and brought in new talent to extend the company's expertise in that function. What's more, to strengthen Coca-Cola's distribution and customer service systems, it formed two aligned groups within its Marketing and Technical Operations Divisions: one focused on the execution of sales and merchandising programs, the other on logistics, warehousing, and delivery.

- In 1998, Coca-Cola widened its domestic market lead over PepsiCo. What's more, Coke's Sprite volume rose three times the rate of sales growth in the overall soft drink industry. Coca-Cola's share of the estimated $56.3 billion U.S. soft drink market increased by six-tenths of a percentage point. At the same time, PepsiCo's share rose five-tenths of a percentage point. Overall, Coca-Cola had a 44.5 percent share of case sales in 1998, compared with PepsiCo's 31.4 percent. The last time Pepsi gained market share on Coca-Cola was in 1989.

- In the summer of 1999, Coke began selling a bottled water called Dasani in the United States and Canada, tapping into the fastest-growing segment of the beverage industry. Dasani, a purified, noncarbonated water with minerals added, is sold in light blue bottles in 20-ounce, 1-liter, and 1.5-liter sizes. Bottled water sales increased 9.8 percent in 1998, to $4.3 billion.

101

- Coca-Cola has invested and grown during world wars, hyperinflation, and depression. In the company's 113 year history, volume has declined only twelve times; the last setback was 44 years ago.

- The worldwide strength and resources of Coca-Cola enables the company to stay and invest where other companies do not. The company has invested heavily in marketing and infrastructure. For example, more than $500 million has been invested in India over the past five years. And more than $400 million in the past three years has been poured into the beverage industry in the Philippines. What's more, the company plans to invest nearly $1 billion in Brazil in the next three years.

- For the ninth consecutive year, Coca-Cola has increased its share of the soft-drink sales in the United States. Notably, the company made major strides in its lower per capita markets such as Southern California and New York, where sales significantly outperformed the industry average.

- The company's brands continue to grow in the United States, with Coca-Cola classic still refreshing more people every day. Additionally, diet Coke has been dramatically increasing its growth rate. And Sprite again significantly outperformed the industry average as it gained market share in 1998.

- In the United States, sales of Minute Maid Premium juices outpaced the industry in 1998. Minute Maid created the calcium-fortified orange juice segment. In 1998, the company built on its market leadership by introducing Minute Maid Premium orange tangerine juice, targeted to children. Sales of Minute Maid Premium ready-to-drink orange juice grew 12 percent in 1998, with the company's calcium-fortified orange juices accounting for 50 percent of that growth.

- The company accelerated its international momentum in Europe, Latin America, Africa, and Asia in 1998. Consumers in eight European countries, including the United Kingdom, Austria, and Poland, now enjoy Minute Maid Premium refrigerated ready-to-drink juices. Coca-Cola, moreover, successfully launched Minute Maid Premium juices in South Africa. And the company worked with a key bottler in Chile to create a new structure for the juice business in that region.

- Although the shares of Coca-Cola have lagged of late, they have performed better than analysts might have expected. One reason that Coke has such stamina may be its ownership base. Much of the stock is in the hands of people who either view it as sacrilege to sell or who can't sell. For instance, long-term institutional owners like Berkshire Hathaway, SunTrust, and Fayez Sarofim together own 16 percent of the stock. Then there are S&P 500 index funds, which must own Coke as part of the index and which own 10 percent of the stock. Add to that loyal individuals (who own about 40 percent of the stock), many of whom made a fortune from the company over the years. Add these up, and you aren't left with many investors who are eager to unload the shares.

Total assets: $19,145 million
Current ratio: .76
Common shares outstanding: 2,463 million
Return on 1998 shareholders' equity: 45.1%

	1998	1997	1996	1995	1994	1993	1992	1991
Revenues (millions)	18,813	18,868	18,546	18,018	16,172	13,967	13,074	11,572
Net income (millions)	3,533	4,130	3,492	2,986	2,554	2,188	1,884	1,618
Earnings per share	1.42	1.64	1.40	1.19	.99	.84	.72	.61
Dividends per share	.60	.56	.50	.44	.39	.34	.28	.24
Price: high	88.9	72.6	54.3	40.2	26.7	22.5	22.7	20.4
low	53.6	50.0	36.1	24.4	19.4	18.8	17.8	10.7

CONSERVATIVE GROWTH

Colgate-Palmolive Company

300 Park Avenue, New York, NY 10022-7499 ❑ Investor contact: Kathya R. Guerra (212) 310-3312 ❑ Dividend reinvestment plan available (800) 756-8700 ❑ Web site: www.colgate.com ❑ Listed: NYSE ❑ Ticker symbol: CL ❑ S&P rating: A- ❑ Value Line financial strength rating: A+

Colgate-Palmolive is a leading global consumer products company, marketing its products in 213 countries and territories under such internationally recognized brand names as Colgate toothpaste and brushes, Palmolive, Mennen Speed Stick deodorants, Ajax, Murphy Oil Soap, Fab, and Soupline/Suavitel, as well as Hill's Science Diet and Hill's Prescription Diet.

With two-thirds of its sales and earnings coming from abroad, Colgate is making its greatest gains in overseas markets. Travelers, for instance, can find Colgate brands in a host of countries:

• They'll find Total toothpaste, with its proprietary antibacterial formula that fights plaque, tartar, and cavities, in more than seventy countries.

• The Care brand of baby products is popular in Asia.

• Colgate Plax makes Colgate number one in mouth rinse outside the United States.

• The Colgate Zig Zag toothbrush, popular in all major world regions outside the United States, helps make Colgate the number one toothbrush company in the world.

• Axion is an economical dishwashing paste popular in Asia, Africa, and Latin America.

Oral Care

Colgate is the global leader in oral care, and number one worldwide in toothpaste and toothbrushes. Colgate's oral care products include toothbrushes, toothpaste, mouth rinses, and dental floss, as well as pharmaceutical products for dentists and other oral health professionals.

Success in the realm of oral care is due in large measure to Colgate's 200 oral care scientists and dentists. Recognized worldwide for leadership in their field, these professionals enable Colgate to provide consumers with advanced oral care technologies and products, from patented plaque-fighting toothpaste and mouth-rinse formulas to toothbrushes that provide precise cleaning action.

Personal Care

Colgate leads many segments of the Personal Care market, including some of the fastest growing. For instance, Colgate is the number one market leader in liquid soaps in the United States and globally. It is number two in baby care products and underarm protection worldwide.

Strong brands include:

- Irish Spring
- Softsoap
- Palmolive—one of the world's most popular personal-care names, available as a soap and, in many countries, as shampoo and conditioner
- Mennen deodorants, baby care products, and men's toiletries

Strong research and development capabilities enable Colgate to support these and other brands with technologically sophisticated products for consumers' personal-care needs.

Household and Fabric Care

Ajax, Palmolive, and Murphy Oil Soap are three of the household names through which Colgate markets its wide variety of household cleaning and laundry products. These products include powder and liquid soaps for use in the sink and dishwasher; powder and liquid laundry detergents, including convenient super-concentrates and refills; and the highly regarded Murphy Oil Soap, North America's leading wood cleaner.

Pet Nutrition

Colgate, through its Hill's Pet Nutrition subsidiary, is the world's leader in specialty pet food. Hill's markets its pet foods primarily under two well-established brands:

- Science Diet, which is sold by authorized pet supply retailers, breeders, and veterinary hospitals, enables pet owners to provide their dog or cat a nutritionally balanced diet every day.
- Prescription Diet, available only through veterinarians, is specially formulated for dogs and cats with disease conditions.

Shortcomings to Bear in Mind

- Like other multinationals, Colgate has been facing negative currency translations and reduced purchasing power in some regions. Still, unit volume grew 3.5 percent in 1998, driven by strong performance in North America, Latin America, and Hill's Pet Nutrition. On the other hand, sales were $9 billion, a decrease of close to 1 percent. On a more positive note, exclusive of foreign currency translations, and divestitures, Colgate's sales expanded by 6 percent in 1998.

Reasons to Buy

- In addition to capturing toothpaste leadership in the United States, Colgate has strengthened its number one rankings in such countries as Canada, the United Kingdom, and Mexico. What's more, the company holds leadership positions in toothpaste in 175 countries. Colgate whitening toothpaste, for example, has captured almost 50 percent of the world's whitening segment, and distribution has been expanded to seventy-five countries. Colgate's global market share for toothpaste, moreover, is at a record high.
- The company's leadership positions extend throughout all core categories. Colgate leads the market in liquid soaps, men's stick deodorant, liquid cleaners, and fabric softeners in scores of countries. In 1998, new variants of Palmolive shower gel introduced in Europe helped increase market shares in nine countries. Halfway around the world, in Argentina, a new variant of the same shower gel quickly achieved an 11 percent share of this segment after launch.
- Around the world, a record $3 billion of sales, or 33 percent of the total in 1998, came from new products introduced in the last five years. What's more, Col-

gate says, "our pipeline is full of new products that will offer consumers real value and benefits."

■ Colgate entered 1999 just having announced a promising new toothpaste for the large domestic market. Total Fresh Stripe, a striped gel, is the second variant of the Colgate Total line to receive U.S. Food and Drug Administration approval—the only toothpaste cleared to make claims for gingivitis and plaque reduction. Colgate Total was one of *Business Week's* "Best New Products of 1998."

Abdul Gaffar, a Ph.D. chemist who holds more than one hundred patents, was part of a Colgate team of 200 scientists that spent ten years and some $35 million developing Total. Their main challenge: how to embed Triclosan, a highly soluble, broad-spectrum antibiotic used in soaps and deodorants to fight bacteria, into a mint-flavored paste and then make sure it didn't get immediately washed away. Working with dental schools in the United States and Europe, this research team developed polymers capable of binding Triclosan to teeth and gums for fourteen hours, thus providing round-the-clock treatment with two daily brushings. Total also contains fluoride to prevent cavities. The FDA took four years of scrutiny before it finally approved Total for sale in the United States.

Diseases like gingivitis, which cause gums to bleed from a buildup of plaque and tartar, cost some $40 billion per year around the world to treat, estimates Dr. Abdul Gaffar, vice president for advanced technology. Colgate says its treat-as-you-brush strategy is cheaper.

■ Colgate's growing leadership in oral care extends beyond toothpaste. New toothbrushes are selling briskly. The premium Colgate Total Professional toothbrush cleans down and around teeth. It has added incremental U.S. toothbrush market share since it was introduced in mid-1998.

■ In the United States, introductions of Palmolive antibacterial, Ajax antibacterial, and Palmolive for pots and pans have boosted dishwashing liquid market share to record levels.

■ Adding to region-specific initiatives is the company's vast consumer intelligence. Colgate interviews over 500,000 consumers in more than thirty countries annually to learn more about their habits and usage of the company's product.

■ To support new products and existing brands, Colgate increased the ratio of total advertising to sales to its highest level in more than a decade and boosted absolute total spending to 12 percent. Enhanced productivity/cost-savings programs provide the funds to do this.

■ Colgate continues to invest in its future by focusing 60 percent of its capital spending on savings-oriented projects that improve margins and increase operating profit quickly.

■ Colgate's global reach lets the company conduct consumer research in countries with diverse economies and cultures to create product ideas with global appeal. The new product development process begins with the company's Global Technology and Business Development Groups analyzing consumer insights from various countries to create products that can be sold in the greatest possible number of countries. Creating universal products saves time and money by maximizing the return on R&D, manufacturing, and purchasing. To assure the widest possible global appeal, potential new products are test-marketed in lead countries that represent both developing and mature economies.

- A global leader in pet nutrition, Hill's continues to strengthen its ties to veterinarians. Record levels of advertising supported a U.S. campaign for Science Diet, themed, "What Vets Feed Their Pets." New Science Diet products include dry varieties for cats, new canned varieties in chunk and gravy form for cats, and dry varieties for dogs.

In 1998, Hill's business contributed 11 percent of sales, or $1 billion. Unit volume expanded 4 percent, and sales rose 3 percent. Selling its products in sixty-eight countries, Hill's has almost all of its sales in the developed world.

Total assets: $7,685 million
Current ratio: 1.06
Common shares outstanding: 586 million
Return on 1998 shareholders' equity: 39.8%

	1998	1997	1996	1995	1994	1993	1992	1991
Revenues (millions)	8,972	9,057	8,749	8,358	7,588	7,141	7,007	6,060
Net income (millions)	849	740	635	541	580	548	477	368
Earnings per share	1.41	1.22	1.05	.90	.96	.85	.73	.65
Dividends per share	.55	.53	.47	.44	.39	.34	.29	.26
Price: high	49.5	39.4	24.2	19.4	16.4	16.8	15.2	12.3
low	32.6	22.5	17.2	14.5	12.4	11.7	11.3	8.4

AGGRESSIVE GROWTH

Compaq Computer Corporation

P. O. Box 692000, Houston, TX 77269-2000 ◻ Investor contact: No name available (800) 433-2391 ◻ Direct dividend reinvestment plan available (888) 218-4373 ◻ Web site: www.compaq.com ◻ Listed: NYSE ◻ Ticker symbol: CPQ ◻ S&P rating: B- ◻ Value Line financial strength rating: A++

Compaq Computer Corporation is the second-largest computer company in the world and the largest global supplier of computer systems. Compaq develops and markets hardware, software, solutions, and services, including industry-leading enterprise computing solutions, fault-tolerant business-critical solutions, enterprise and network storage solutions, commercial desktop and portable products, and consumer PCs. Compaq products are sold and supported in more than one hundred countries through a network of authorized Compaq marketing partners.

During 1998, Compaq introduced and implemented a model based on customer choice. In other words, the company does business with its customers the way they choose to do business, whether it is through one of the company's resellers, a customer account team, or directly via the Web or telephone.

This strategy is superior to the direct-only model because it reflects the way customers actually buy. For example, many customers prefer to purchase PCs and other volume products directly from the manufacturer. For more complex solutions, however, they often want the expertise and support of a value-added reseller or a systems integrator.

Historically, Compaq has sold its products almost exclusively through resellers and other channel partners. But in 1998, after extensive consultation and with its partners to implement its customer choice model, the company began to expand its ability to sell direct.

In Compaq's consumer business, for example, the company now sells over the

Web, through customer call centers, and through its retail configuration program. What's more, the company introduced a new family of products for small and medium businesses that are sold directly over the Web and the phone, as well as through its reseller agents. Finally, Compaq began rolling out Web-based "extranets" that enable major customers to configure and order the products they want.

Shortcomings to Bear in Mind

- Compaq doesn't make itself easy for shareholders to embrace. It took investors over a cliff in the first quarter of 1998, cutting its earnings targets after shipping far more computers than were actually sold over the 1997 holiday season. And in the wake of the early-1999 ouster of the firm's CEO, Eckhard Pfeiffer, Compaq officials have been vague about exactly what led to the 1999 first-quarter disaster.

  On the other hand, several fund managers and analysts are making a case that a $35-billion company attempting a complicated restructuring is entitled to more than a couple quarters to turn itself around. One of them commented, "The changes Compaq is trying to make are sticky, and they are always harder and always take more time than investors expect."

- In one sense, the fundamentals in the computer industry remain strong, mainly due to a growing global appetite for technology products that increase productivity. On the other hand, the industry is still dominated by intense competition that can quickly turn today's leaders into tomorrow's losers. That's because buyers are rarely content to use outdated models. They demand that vendors constantly introduce new, more powerful, and cheaper versions of successful products while keeping a tight rein on operating expenses.

Reasons to Buy

- In May of 1999, Compaq announced that it would slash the number of distributors who sell many of its business-class products to four from about forty. In the company's first major move since it ousted Eckhard Pfeiffer in April, Compaq said it was streamlining its distribution system by solidifying relationships with fewer distributors. By cutting the number of destinations to which units are shipped, Compaq hopes to better manage inventory levels to make the entire distribution process more efficient.

- Unfortunately, it's a world that includes hackers. But bad news for them, Compaq has installed more high-security e-commerce firewalls than anyone. According to the company, no hacker has ever broken through.

- Compaq is moving into new areas of Internet growth. When the company acquired Digital, it also acquired the world's fastest Internet search and navigation guide, AltaVista. Early in 1999, Compaq made it a separate company, The AltaVista Company, with the goal of establishing it as the leading destination site for information and e-commerce on the Internet. Compaq is the first major computer company to deploy such broad Internet service capabilities.

  The company sees a significant opportunity to increase Compaq's share of the rapidly growing market for Internet content and services. Moreover, Compaq plans to take the new company public, which will enable it to unlock AltaVista's value for Compaq shareholders.

- A profitable trend in the computer industry is the continued movement toward client-server computing. This model promotes the use of networks of cheap, yet powerful, PCs and servers, in contrast to the larger, more expensive, and proprietary mainframe computers.

- Another key trend is the growing implementation of corporate "intranets," which are internal corporate networks based on existing Internet technologies. These intranets require high-powered servers that are fueling a new product class for many hardware companies. Fundamentals in the PC industry will remain challenging to all participants, according to analysts, as new competitors and price pressures challenge profitability. Even so, analysts expect that strong international growth and a strong upgrade cycle will boost prospects. They view Compaq as an attractive investment, as these developments unfold.

- Some analysts believe that "the crown jewel" of Compaq is its Systems Business. The company is the world's leading supplier of servers and super-servers in a market that's undergoing dramatic growth. According to market research from IDC, Compaq supplies 36 percent of the worldwide market for servers, or two-and-a-half times that of its nearest competitor, IBM.

  In fact, Compaq's servers are the reference platform for Microsoft, Oracle, Novell, SAP, and many other leading software developers. More and more global customers are standardizing on the company's servers to run their businesses.

- In 1998, Compaq bought struggling Digital Equipment Corporation for $8.55 billion in cash. The purchase of Digital puts Compaq in a position to compete directly with IBM and Hewlett-Packard. In a ruthlessly competitive market, the move gives Compaq the ability to move beyond PCs into a whole new realm: high-end computing—for which Digital makes powerful workstations and Internet servers—and servicing computer operations for big companies, which alone is estimated to bring in about $6 billion a year for Digital.

- The Digital acquisition furthers Compaq's goal of increasing its presence in the enterprise market for computers. It also complements its 1997 acquisition of Tandem Computer, a leader in complex enterprise-class networks. Before these acquisitions, Compaq had broadened its product offering to this market and introduced new clustering and Internet-working solutions. In 1996, the company entered the workstation market with its Professional Workstation line, featuring Intel's Pentium Pro (and now also Pentium II) processor and Windows NT operating system.

  Under its Presario line, Compaq offers consumers and home office users PCs rich with multimedia capabilities. Compaq also has offerings in the fast-growing networking product arena. The company's Internet-working Product Group includes NetWorth Inc. (acquired in 1995), a provider of Fast Ethernet networking products, and Thomas-Conrad Corp., a maker of network interface cards and hubs.

- Compaq's marketing alliance with Canon Sales Company is now bearing fruit. In 1998, Compaq unveiled a new, low-priced desktop personal computer tailored to the Japanese consumer. The new machine represents a fresh attempt by Compaq to expand its share of Japan's PC market. Compaq and Canon Sales said that Canon Sales would become the sole distributor for Compaq's Presario-brand consumer-oriented PCs in Japan. Both companies gain from the alliance. Compaq wins an established distribution network with a powerful local ally, and Canon Sales get a big-name computer brand with a pricing edge.

Total assets: $23,051 million
Current ratio: 1.43
Common shares outstanding: 1,683 million
Return on 1998 shareholders' equity: NM

	1998	1997	1996	1995	1994	1993	1992	1991
Revenues (millions)	31,169	24,584	18,109	14,755	10,866	7,191	4,100	3,271
Net income (millions)	(2,743)	2,107	1,313	1,030	867	470	248	230
Earnings per share	(1.71)	1.35	.93	.75	.64	.36	.20	.17
Dividends per share	.06	nil	nil	nil	nil	nil	nil	nil
Price: high	44.8	39.8	17.4	11.4	8.4	5.1	3.3	4.9
low	22.9	14.2	7.2	6.2	4.8	2.8	1.5	1.5

INCOME

Dexter Corporation

One Elm Street, Windsor Locks, CT 06096-2334 ◻ Investor contact: John D. Thompson (860) 292-7640 ◻ Dividend reinvestment program available (800) 288-9541 ◻ Web site: www.dexter.com ◻ Ticker symbol: DEX ◻ S&P rating: B+ ◻ Value Line financial strength rating: A

Founded in 1767, Dexter Corporation is the oldest company listed on the New York Stock Exchange. All but two of Dexter's businesses are based on polymer chemistry. The company uses its polymer technology to formulate and process specialty coatings, encapsulants, and adhesives, mainly for the electronics, food-packaging, and aerospace markets.

Dexter's proprietary nonwovens technology is used to formulate and produce long-fiber, wet-formed, and hydroentangled materials, principally for the food-packaging and medical markets.

The company's Life Technologies (LTI) segment develops and manufactures precise, reproducible biological and biochemical products for life sciences research and commercial applications.

In 1998, the research-market segment of LTI's business was stronger in the United States and Europe than it was in Asia. However, on a currency-adjusted basis, LTI achieved growth in Asia.

Among strong performers in 1998 were research products developed to meet unique customer needs. These products include custom primers, the Platinum Taq

family of products, transfection materials, and the Concert product line.

LTI's technology leadership in generic research has resulted in several break-through discoveries in molecular cell biology disease processes, aging, as well as many critical-to-life sectors.

Shortcomings to Bear in Mind

- Although the company operated well within its debt-to-capital goal of 30 to 35 percent through 1998, in late December of that year, Dexter increased its leverage to nearly 50 percent because of the acquisition of an additional 22 percent of Life Technologies, Inc. It is expected that upon application of the proceeds from the sale of the Packaging Coatings business, the debt-to-capital ratio would return to the low 30 percent range, but would increase again to the 50 percent level if the company acquires the remaining minority interest in Life Technologies.

- I have classified this company as an income stock because of its lackluster record of growth. In the 1988–1998 period, earnings per share advanced from $1.61 to $2.50, an annual compound growth rate of 4.5 percent. In the same ten-year stretch, dividends did not do any better, inching ahead from $.80 to $1.00, a growth rate of only 2.3 percent. On the other hand, the stock provides a liberal dividend that is well covered by earnings.

Reasons to Buy

- Medium- and long-term prospects for earnings growth were enhanced by the strategic decision to sell the Packaging Coatings business, along with its associated operation, Dexter SAS in France, and to acquire the minority interest in Life Technologies, Inc. (LTI). These steps were designed to further simplify the company and concentrate resources on those global opportunities where Dexter has powerful market and technology positions.

- The company's Life Technologies had another strong year in 1998, with revenues and earnings from operations setting new records. LTI is the world's largest manufacturer of consumable products needed to grow and study cells. The company sells its products to the life sciences research, biomedical, and pharmaceutical industries. In 1998, LTI achieved strong double-digit increases for research products sold to industrial customers and for production materials. Success has been fueled by strong funding by key customers of commercial research, the new product approval process, and the transfer into production of approved new drugs.

  Life Technologies is also seeing the benefit of a dramatically expanded base of companies that utilize its materials for the new product approval process. As these products enter production, LTI benefits again. In Europe, the business has additionally focused efforts on several biotechnology start-up companies that are beginning to live up to expectations.

  Given a consolidating and competitive base, Dexter either needed to double the size of the Packaging Coatings business to ensure continued future success or to exit. The company concluded that shareholders's money would be better invested in LTI. The stronger growth characteristics of life science markets, and consequently the longer-term prospects for Life Technologies, are attractive. The acquisition of LTI will be dilutive in 1999 because of noncash amortization charges. However, the improved growth and profitability resulting from the acquisition of an additional 22 percent of LTI stock and divestiture of the coatings businesses should position the company to expand earnings at strong double-digit rates in year two and beyond.

- Dexter is the world's leading manufacturer of tea bag paper. The introduction in 1998 of several new products for the next generation of packaging machinery creates competitive advantages for the future. New fusion products also meet a compelling need for customers to differentiate their products in the marketplace. Technology investments made during 1998 are expected to support new-generation products that have clear advantages that translate into lower costs or better performance for Dexter's customers.

- In the medical arena, new gamma fabrics that can be sterilized have enhanced sales for wet-formed materials in the historically flat American market. International sales for medical products have been improving with the wider distribution of Dexter spunlace materials. These products are manufactured with aesthetic appeal and better performance for demanding applications in the surgical realm.

- Hydroentangled nonwoven fabrics are also creating new opportunities in other markets. There has been strong demand for these new fabrics in automotive interior applications and in selected large niches within the industrial wiping market. Dexter's hydroentangled technology is expected to create strong growth opportunities in Europe, North America, and the Far East.

- Dexter's nonwoven materials were employed to meet unique customer needs in a wide variety of ways in 1998. A whole new generation of Dexter Hydraspun patterned and embossed baby wipes material was introduced for North American distribution. A flushable wipe material for Asian distribution represented a significant new technology. Products utilizing hydroentangled composites dramatically simplified automotive customers's production processes by reducing the number of individual materials.

- Dexter sells the majority of its specialty polymers to the aerospace and electronics markets. In the aerospace market, Dexter SynSpand is the fastest-growing patented technology. It is formulated to provide design engineers with new-generation composite assemblies and a product that enhances in-service durability and simplifies manufacturing operations.

    Dexter Eclipse aerospace topcoat is becoming the industry standard for ease of application, coupled with attractive appearance and better in-service performance. This new topcoat technology, coupled with Dexter's low-VOC primer, becomes the first environmentally compliant system in the industry approved for exterior decorative airframe applications—exceeding all global emission standards.

- In the electronics market, Dexter joined an industry consortium to develop an underfill for flip chip applications. The new material reduces flow and cure time dramatically, with no loss of functional performance, thereby delivering considerable savings in customers's cost-of-use. Dexter has developed a unique Quantum conductive adhesive material that cures in seconds. It has very low moisture absorption, establishing a new standard of performance in the die attach process.

- In response to sluggishness in the electronics market, Dexter Magnetic Technologies is leveraging its strengths in designing very precise magnetic fields to meet specialized customer requirements in other markets. Magnetic coating techniques that were developed for the semiconductor industry have found new applications in the production of architectural glass. Highly specialized magnetic fields developed by Dexter are also being employed in research labs to separate cells in medical applications. Dexter teamed up with a customer to develop a revolutionary Frekote release agent that cuts the production process from twenty-four hours to fifty-six minutes.

Total assets: $1,208 million
Current ratio: 2.02
Common shares outstanding: 23 million
Return on 1998 shareholders' equity: 8.3%

	1998	1997	1996	1995	1994	1993	1992	1991
Revenues (millions)	1,168	1,147	1,100	1,089	975	887	951	938
Net income (millions)	58*	56	48	41	38	34	38	def
Earnings per share	2.50	2.41	2.02	1.67	1.56	1.40	1.58	def
Dividends per share	1.00	.96	.88	.88	.88	.88	.88	.88
Price: high	43.4	43.9	33.6	26.9	26.0	28.9	28.1	26.1
low	23.5	28.8	23.1	20.4	19.9	20.4	20.9	18.5

* Excluding one-time charges

The Walt Disney Company

500 South Buena Vista Street, Burbank, CA 91521-0949 ❑ Investor contact: Winifred Markus Webb (818)560-5758 ❑ Fiscal year's end September 30 ❑ Direct dividend reinvestment plan is available (818) 553-7200 ❑ Web site: www.disney.com ❑ Listed: NYSE ❑ Ticker symbol: DIS ❑ S&P rating: A- ❑ Value Line financial strength rating: A

The Walt Disney Company is a family entertainment company engaged in animated and live-action film and television production; character merchandise licensing; consumer products retailing; book, magazine, and music publishing; television and radio broadcasting; cable television programming; and the operation of theme parks and resorts.

Creative Content

The Creative Content segment produces live-action and animated motion pictures, television programs, and musical recordings, and licenses the company's characters and other intellectual property for use in connection with merchandise and publications. The Creative Content segment also publishes books and magazines.

Theatrical Films

Walt Disney Pictures and Television, a subsidiary of the company, produces and acquires live-action motion pictures that are distributed under the banners Walt Disney Pictures, Touchstone Pictures, and Hollywood Pictures. Another subsidiary, Miramax Film Corporation, acquires and produces motion pictures that are primarily distributed under the Miramax and Dimension banners.

In fiscal 1999, the company expects to distribute some twenty-one feature films under the Walt Disney Pictures, Touchstone Pictures, and Hollywood Pictures banners. It also expects to distribute about thirty-six films under the Miramax and Dimension banners. In addition, the company periodically reissues previously released animated films. As of September 30, 1998, the company had released 547 full length, live-action features (primarily color), 36 full-length color features, and 478 cartoon shorts.

Books and Magazines

The company has book imprints in the United States offering books for children and adults as part of the Buena Vista Publishing Group. Disney also produces several magazines, including *Family Fun, Disney Adventures,* as well as *Discover,* a general science magazine. Finally, the company produces *ESPN The Magazine* as part of a joint venture with ESPN, Inc. and The Hurst Company.

Broadcasting

The company operates the ABC Television Network, with 224 primary affiliated stations operating under long-term agreements reaching 99.9 percent of all U.S. television households. Disney also operates the ABC Radio Networks, which reaches more than 144 million domestic listeners weekly and consists of over 8,900 program affiliations on more than 4,400 radio stations. The company owns nine very high frequency (VHF) television stations, five of which are located in the top ten markets in the United States; one ultra high frequency (UHF) television station; fifteen standard AM radio stations; and fifteen FM radio stations. All of the television stations are affiliated with the ABC Television Network, and most of the thirty radio stations are affiliated with the ABC Radio Networks.

Shortcomings to Bear in Mind

- For Disney, 1998 was a rough year. Its blockbuster, *Armageddon*, barely turned a profit. ABC, its beleaguered network, saw ratings plunge 10 percent. Three top executives quit. And worst of all, for the first time in nearly a decade, earnings came in flat. Nor is 1999 shaping up any better, as earnings seemed headed for another lackluster performance. On the other hand, Disney continues to boast one of the great brands on the planet, according to money managers and analysts. However, some professionals warn that Disney's spell of bad quarterly earnings could drag on into 2000.

- ABC is mired in a ratings slump. In the crucial November 1998 sweeps, it again placed number three, trailing NBC and CBS. ABC's $9.2 billion gamble on National Football League rights got off to a shaky start. And the network's woes, alongside concerns about slowing growth at cable sports network ESPN, helped prompt analysts in late 1998 downgrade Disney stock.

  On the other hand, some parts of ABC are doing well, including ESPN and ABC's ten TV stations and thirty radio outlets. Even so, in the fourth quarter of 1998, operating income for ABC dropped 18 percent, compared with the prior year.

- Walt Disney's chief executive Michael Eisner isn't exactly whistling while he works on improving results in his movie division. Despite a string of hits such as *Enemy of the State, A Bug's Life, A Civil Action,* and *The Waterboy,* Disney has a few flops, including *Mighty Joe Young.*

  These disappointments have prompted Disney to revamp its studio operation. Animated-film chief Peter Schneider was put in charge of Disney's family film unit. In addition, the company is also seeking deals with other studios to share in the cost of big-budget films, and Disney will make more lower-priced family films.

Reasons to Buy

- Part of the Disney legacy is innovation. Walt Disney pioneered the first cartoon with sound, the first color cartoon, the first feature-length animated film, the first use of the multiplane camera, the first use of stereophonic sound, first 3D cartoon, the first theme park, and the first use of audio-animatronic entertainment.

- Disney is trying to wean itself from one of Hollywood's most unusual and entrenched practices: granting long-term employment contracts to mid- and even low-level executives. Entertainment companies have long been notorious for making big exit payouts to high-profile executives, such as former Disney president Michael Ovitz and former Universal Studios Inc. chairman Frank Biondi, Jr., both of whom were fired in the early stages of a long-term contract. But it is less well-known that the same companies routinely grant three- or five-year contracts to junior publicists, fledgling development executives, and a host of others below the top ranks. The practice is so rampant that some industry executives crack, only half in jest, that nearly everyone's dream in Hollywood is to sign a five-year contract so they can be fired in the first year and then force the studio to pay off the remaining four years.

  Now Disney is looking to rob the joke of its punch line. It has implemented a company-wide initiative to eliminate as many employment contracts as possible in coming years. In the process, it will convert all but a handful of top executives in each division to "at-will" employees, who can be let go without the obligation to pay future salaries.

- In the first quarter of fiscal 1999, Disney's theme park unit was a bright spot in an otherwise disappointing period. Its operating income was up 17 percent, to $335 million. The gains were partly driven by the new Animal Kingdom theme park in Orlando, Florida. To be sure, that park siphoned off some visitors from Disney's three other Orlando parks, but nonetheless carried the division to a strong overall increase.

- To propel Disney anew, after a disappointing 1998, Mr. Eisner is investing aggressively in what he describes as an "inside-outside" strategy. He wants to keep luring people out of their homes to see Disney's movies and visit its theme parks, while giving them an increasing number of products to entertain and inform themselves when they do stay home.

  The "outside" part of the equation includes a new chain of regional entertainment centers that feature ESPN restaurants and high-tech Disney Quest arcades. Disney has ambitious plans to expand its recently introduced cruise-ship and live-theater operations and will continue growing in traditional ways, a prime example being the California Adventure theme park now under construction near Disneyland in Anaheim, California.

  Most notable on the "inside" track is Disney's emergence as a player on the Internet through its decision to acquire 43 percent of Infoseek Corporation. Disney also has a team of people trying to develop a model for interactive television. In more tradi-

tional forms of home entertainment, the company is aggressively rolling out local ESPNs and Disney Channels around the world. And after a decade of embarrassing failure in the music industry, Disney in mid-1998 had its first-ever hit records.

- On the movie front, the company seems to be heeding the critics who have complained in recent years that Disney's animated films have begun to look and sound alike. The studio's next few releases all offer something different. In 1998, *A Bug's Life*, a co-production with Pixar Animation Studios, is computer-animated. And big hopes are pinned to the summer of 1999, with the new *Tarzan*, a more action-oriented animated film that has a Phil Collins soundtrack, but isn't a musical like most other Disney cartoons.

- When Disneyland Paris opened a few years ago, it was anything but magical. Rather, it had exorbitant prices, bad American-style food, rides still under construction, and groups of bewildered Europeans sheltering their children from the likes of Goofy, Donald Duck, and Pluto.

  Since then, all has changed. Instead of going bankrupt, the park is now booming. In fact, Disneyland Paris (as the company now insists on calling the park commonly referred to as EuroDisney) has now overtaken the Eiffel Tower as the number one tourist spot in France, largely because of some key changes. Among them, lower prices, better food, and the addition of some adult amenities, such as wine with dinner.

Total assets: $41,378 million
Current ratio: 1.01
Common shares outstanding: 2,049 million
Return on 1998 shareholders' equity: 10.0%

	1998	1997	1996	1995	1994	1993	1992	1991
Revenues (millions)	22,976	22,473	21,238	12,112	10,055	8,529	7,504	6,182
Net income (millions)	1,871	1,886	1,533	1,344	1,110	889	817	637
Earnings per share	.90	.92	.74	.84	.68	.54	.51	.40
Dividends per share	.20	.17	.14	.12	.10	.08	.07	.06
Price: high	42.8	33.4	25.8	21.4	16.2	16.0	15.1	10.8
low	22.5	22.1	17.8	15.0	12.6	12.0	9.5	7.8

AGGRESSIVE GROWTH

Dover Corporation

280 Park Avenue, New York, NY 10017-1292 □ Investor contact: John F. McNiff (212) 922-1640 □ Dividend reinvestment plan not available □ Web site: www.dovercorporation.com □ Listed: NYSE □ Ticker symbol: DOV □ S&P rating: A □ Value Line financial strength rating: A+

Dover Corporation is a diversified manufacturer of a wide range of proprietary products and components for industrial and commercial use. The company is comprised of more than fifty independent operating units, most of which are number one in their niche markets. Dover is an enterprise supplying value-added products and services to thousands of customers in more than one hundred countries. Dover's businesses are divided into four segments.

Dover Technologies (the company's largest business, with 1998 revenues of $1,211 million) concentrates on the manufacture of sophisticated automated assembly equipment for the electronics industry, industrial printers for coding and marking, and, to a lesser degree, specialized electronic components. This segment is made up of nine companies, such as Universal Instruments Corporation, Everett Charles Technologies, Inc., and DEK Printing Machines Ltd. (United Kingdom).

These companies have a stake in such products as: automated assembly equipment for printed circuit boards, spring probes, high-frequency capacitors, Dow-Key coaxial switches, ferrite transformers, and continuous inkjet printers.

Dover Industries (1998 revenues of $1,012 million) makes products for use in waste handling, bulk transport, automotive service, commercial food service, and machine tool industries. Dover Industries is comprised of twelve companies, including Heil Trailer International, Tipper Tie/Technopack, and Texas Hydraulics.

Dover Industries produces such items as: liquid and dry bulk tank trailers, refuse-collection vehicles, packaging systems, automotive lifts, welding torches, car wash equipment, commercial refrigeration, benchtop machine tools, and commercial food service cooking equipment.

Dover Diversified (1998 revenues were $958 million) builds sophisticated assembly and production machines, heat-transfer equipment, and specialized compressors, as well as sophisticated products and control systems for use in the defense, aerospace, and commercial building industries. Dover Diversified is made up of twelve companies, such as Hill Phoenix, Waukesha Bearings, and A-C Compressor.

Among the products produced are: heat exchangers, transformer radiators, rotary compressors, refrigerated display cases, aircraft fasteners, fluid film bearings, high-performance specialty pistons, autoclaves, and machinery for corrugated boxes.

Dover Resources (revenues in 1998 were $801 million, making this segment the company's smallest) manufactures products primarily for the automotive, fluid handling, petroleum, and chemical industries. This part of the company includes nineteen operations, such as OPW Fueling Components, Midland Manufacturing, Tulsa Winch, Petroleum Equipment Group, and Duncan Parking Systems.

Some typical products include: key card systems, tank monitors, air-operated double-diaphragm pumps, tank car and barge valves, tank monitoring and control systems, loading arms, toggle clamps, EOA robotic and automation components, industrial gas compressors, peristaltic pumps, filtration systems, quartz-based pressure transducers, worm and planetary gear winches, packings for gas compressors, and progressing cavity pumps.

Highlights of 1998

• During 1998, the company raised $350 million in new long-term debt, repurchased 3.3 million Dover shares, raised the dividend for the thirty-eighth consecutive year, and invested $126 million in new capital equipment. The combined investment in capital equipment, acquisitions, and stock repurchases set a record by a wide margin, at $788 million. The comparable number in 1997 was $470 million.

• The $556 million Dover invested in the purchase of new businesses in 1998 enabled the company to acquire four standalone companies—Wilden, PDQ, Wiseco, and Quartzdyne—and ten add-ons that are now part of ten different operating companies.

Wilden Pump and Engineering, of Grand Terrace, California, was the largest acquisition in Dover's history in terms of purchase price. Wilden is a leader by a substantial margin in its niche of the worldwide pump market. Nearly half of Wilden's sales are international, and its distribution strength is substantial.

Wilden became part of Dover Resources, which is also home of the Blackmer group of pump companies, which specialize in positive displacement pumps. This gives Dover Resources leadership in two of the many technology niches within the fragmented, multibillion-dollar specialty pump market.

Quartzdyne, based in Salt Lake City, Utah, is the world leader in the design and production of quartz-based pressure transducers, used primarily in gas and oil drilling and the management of existing reserves. These transducers allow highly accurate, real-time feedback without the need to interrupt operations to insert a measuring device.

Wiseco, located in Mentor, Ohio, is the country's leading producer of high-performance pistons, used in racing engines for autos, motorcycles, boats, and snowmobiles. Racing enthusiasts typically buy Wiseco products to replace standard OEM components to improve engine power output.

PDQ is the leading manufacturer of touchless car washing equipment, which is the fastest-growing segment of the car wash equipment business. The equipment uses environmentally safe chemicals, high-pressure spray, solvent-recovery systems, and electronic sensing and programming to provide a fast, reasonably-priced car wash, with minimal manpower requirements.

Shortcomings to Bear in Mind

■ In the face of a market collapse, the company combined Norris, Norriseal, and AOT companies into a new Petroleum Equipment Group. In 1998, profits declined more than 50 percent, and this company was only marginally profitable in the second half of that year. These businesses contributed more than 40 percent of Dover's income during an oil boom in the early 1980s but less than 2 percent of the company's operating profits in 1998.

- Dover Technologies's profits declined 25 percent in 1998 as a result of the contraction of capital spending for electronic assembly and test equipment that began late in 1997. Even so, profits that year exceeded every year prior to 1997. After six consecutive years of growth, the market for assembly and test equipment plunged in 1998, primarily because of the fall-off in Asian economies, coupled with the caution it generated within the electronics industry worldwide, as well as excess capacity resulting from heavy spending in 1995–1997.

  This pattern is typical of the industry. The most recent expansion followed a downturn in 1989–1991, which itself followed a growth period after a downturn in 1985.

Reasons to Buy

- Dover has a strong record of earnings increases. In the 1988–1998 period, earnings per share climbed from $.56 to $1.69, a compound annual growth rate of 11.7 percent. In the same span, dividends expanded from $.16 to $.40, a growth rate of 9.6 percent.
- In 1999, Universal Instruments (part of Dover Technologies) purchased Alphasem, an established Swiss manufacturer of semiconductor packaging equipment. As chip technology continues to put more processing power into less space, the distinction between Universal's advanced assembly and Alphasem's "back-end" semiconductor packaging technologies is expected to blur. The acquisition of privately owned Alphasem reflects both companies' belief that they will make each other stronger in their pursuit of the markets that these technology changes will produce.

- In 1998, Dover Industries, Dover Resources, and Dover Diversified achieved higher profits, setting new earnings records with gains ranging from 10 percent to 25 percent. What's more, twenty-one of the forty-five companies that were owned by Dover throughout all of 1998 achieved record profits.

- Five years after Dover's acquisition of Heil, its two businesses—Heil Trailer and Heil Environmental—have more than doubled earnings, to over $50 million in 1998, on sales of about $350 million. Stronger markets, sharp focus on a few product areas, coupled with $36 million of capital investment, along with eight, small, add-on acquisitions, contributed to this success.

Total assets: $3,382 million
Current ratio: 1.40
Common shares outstanding: 223 million
Return on 1998 shareholders' equity: 20.5%

	1998	1997	1996	1995	1994	1993	1992	1991
Revenues (millions)	4,634	4,548	4,076	3,746	3,085	2,484	2,272	2,196
Net income (millions)	379	393	340	278	202	158	129	125
Earnings per share	1.69	1.74	1.51	1.23	.89	.69	.56	.53
Dividends per share	.40	.36	.32	.28	.25	.23	.22	.21
Price: high	39.9	36.7	27.6	20.8	16.7	15.5	11.9	10.9
low	25.5	24.1	18.3	12.9	12.4	11.3	9.6	8.6

INCOME

Duke Energy Corporation

526 South Church Street, Charlotte, NC 28202-1904 □ Investor contact: Sue A. Becht (704) 382-3853 □
Direct dividend reinvestment plan available: (800) 488-3853 □ Web site: www.duke-energy.com □ Listed:
NYSE □ Ticker symbol: DUK □ S&P rating: A- □ Value Line financial strength rating: A+

Duke Energy Corporation is an integrated energy and energy-services provider with the ability to offer physical delivery and management of both electricity and natural gas throughout the United States and abroad. Duke Energy provides these and other services through seven business segments.

Energy Operations generates, transmits, distributes, and sells electric energy in central and western North Carolina and the western portion of South Carolina (doing business as Duke Power or Nantahala Power and Light).

Natural Gas Transmission, through its Northeast Pipelines, provides interstate transportation and storage of natural gas for customers primarily in the Mid-Atlantic and New England states.

Field Services gathers, processes, transports, and markets natural gas and produces and markets natural gas liquids (NGL). Field Services operates gathering systems in ten states that serve major gas-producing regions in the Rocky Mountains, Permian Basin, Mid-continent, and Gulf Coast regions.

Trading and Marketing markets natural gas, electricity, and other energy-related products across North America. Duke Energy owns a 60 percent interest in Trading and Marketing's operations, with Mobil Corporation owning a 40 percent minority interest.

Global Asset Development develops, owns, and operates energy-related facilities worldwide. Global Asset Development conducts its operations primarily through Duke Energy Power Services and Duke Energy International.

Other Energy Services provides engineering, consulting, construction, and integrated energy solutions worldwide, primarily through Duke Engineering & Service, Inc., Duke/Fluor Daniel, and Duke Solutions.

Real Estate Operations conducts its business through Crescent Resources, Inc., which develops high-quality commercial and residential real estate projects and manages forest holdings in the southeastern United States.

Shortcomings to Bear in Mind

- Public utilities are always sensitive to changes in interest rates. This is partly because they often borrow money to finance new plants. Higher interest rates shove up the cost of these funds. High interest rates can also cause investors to sell their shares in order to invest their money where the return is greater.
- In recent years, the industry has been undergoing profound changes, with the specter of competition lurking.

Reasons to Buy

- Duke Power is uniquely positioned to capitalize on its expertise in designing, building, and operating generating facilities. Duke is one of only a few domestic utilities that has historically designed, built, and operated its own power plants. The expertise Duke gained in those areas over the years has been retained through Duke Engineering & Services, Inc. and Duke/Fluor Daniel (DE&S).
- Duke Power meets its customers' needs for electricity primarily through

a combination of nuclear-fueled, fossil-fueled, and hydroelectric generating stations.

Over the past twenty years, Duke's fossil-fueled generating system has consistently been cited by *Electric Light & Power* magazine as the country's most efficient fossil system as measured by heat rate. Heat rate is a measure of efficiency in converting the energy contained in a fossil fuel such as oil, natural gas, or coal into electricity. A low heat rate means Duke burns less coal to generate a given quantity of electricity, lowering operating costs and helping keep rates competitive.

■ In 1998, Duke Energy established a major Canadian presence. The company signed a fifteen-year agreement to deliver up to 50 billion Btus per day of natural gas to BC Gas Utility Ltd. It also signed a five-year agreement to provide comprehensive natural gas supply management to Alliance Gas Management—the largest Canadian retail load aggregator.

■ Duke Energy International investment in Aguaytia Energy, Peru's first integrated energy project, began commercial operation in 1998. It features:

● 125 miles of natural gas pipeline
● Natural gas processing facilities to extract NGLs from 55 MMcf per day
● 65 miles of NGL pipelines
● Natural gas fractionation, storage, and distribution facilities
● 155 megawatt natural gas-fired power plant
● 250-mile high-voltage transmission line to move energy from central Peru across the Andes to the coast

■ Duke Energy's presence in some regions is anchored by its subsidiaries that provide engineering, construction, and related services. Duke Engineering & Service, through its offices in South Africa, announced two major projects in 1998:

● A major engineering contract for a rural electrification project serving 300,000 people in South Africa.
● In Mauritius, construction began on DE&E's largest renewable energy project to date, a 70-megawatt cogeneration plant to generate steam and power from sugar cane byproducts.

■ Duke Power offers attractive incentive rates for businesses to relocate and expand within its service territory. Duke's Economic Development Rate awards an initial 20 percent discount during the first year for industrial customers who expand their electricity consumption by one megawatt and either hire a minimum of seventy-five new employees or invest at least $400,000 in capital upgrades. Several dozen companies have qualified for the program.

■ Duke Energy International moved swiftly to establish significant interests in Australia in 1998:

● Purchased the 389-mile Queensland Pipeline and energy trading and marketing operations from PG&E Corporation
● Purchased from Broken Hill Proprietary Company Ltd. (BHP) and Westcoast Energy the right to build the Eastern Gas Pipeline, a 500-mile interstate pipeline to be completed in 2000
● Agreed to purchase from BHP its power business, including 392 megawatts of power-generation facilities, electric transmission facilities, and an 11.8 percent interest in Goldfields Gas Transmission pipeline

■ For the second straight year, Duke Power led the electric utility industry in customer satisfaction in the American Customer Satisfaction Index. The data was collected by the National Quality Research Center and compiled by the University of Michigan. The rankings were published in *Fortune* magazine.

- Two of the company's coal-fired plants in the Carolinas were ranked the most efficient in the United States in 1998, according to *Electric Light & Power* magazine. For more than a quarter of a century, no company has been able to generate more electricity from a ton of coal than Duke Power.

- DukeNet Communications tripled fiberoptic capacity and revenues in 1998. The explosive growth in Internet and wireless communications, along with steady growth in long-distance telephone communications, continued to drive strong growth in revenues and system expansion of DukeNet's fiberoptic system in 1998. System capacity was expanded by installing additional electronic equipment on existing fiberoptic routes. DukeNet will expand service to several midsize cities in the Carolinas in 1999, such as Burlington and Hickory, North Carolina.

- DukeSolutions was created in 1997 to provide integrated energy services for large energy users across North America. Their mission is to be the premier business-to-business retail energy services provider. Consistent with that goal, DukeSolutions established a strong presence in Canada and the United States. They delivered on that promise to be profitable in the fourth quarter of 1998 and built an excellent foundation for future profitability by signing more than twenty-four contracts with a future revenue stream of $1.2 billion.

- Duke/Fluor Daniel was awarded eleven major contracts in 1998. In addition to the Ingleside Project and Maine Independence Project, an affiliate of the partnership began construction of a 220 megawatt natural gas-fired simple cycle plant on the Island of Trinidad in the Republic of Trinidad and Tobago. It was awarded a turnkey contract by Dearborn Industrial Generation, L.L.C. to build a 550-megawatt cogeneration plant serving Rouge Steel and Ford Motor Company facilities in Dearborn, Michigan. Overall, Duke/Fluor Daniel was awarded five major engineering, procurement, and construction contracts in 1998.

- In 1998, Crescent Resources expanded, with projects across the Southeast:
  - Two new buildings totaling more than 300,000 square feet at Primera office park north of Orlando.
  - Three office buildings at its Hidden River development on Tampa's east side.
  - The 260-acre mixed-use CrossTown Center south of Tampa.
  - In Nashville, Crescent Resources is developing CentrePoint, a 220-acre warehouse/distribution park. It is also continuing the development of its Corporate Centre office park with two new buildings totaling 266,000 square feet.
  - In Charlotte, Crescent Resources is moving toward a build-out of Coliseum Centre with the opening of Five Coliseum Centre and construction of six-story Four Coliseum Centre.

Total assets: $26,806 million
Current ratio: 0.98
Return on 1998 equity: 15.3%
Common shares outstanding: 362 million

	1998	1997	1996	1995	1994	1993	1992	1991
Revenues (millions)	17,610	16,309	4,758	4,677	4,279	4,282	3,962	3,817
Net income (millions)	1,260	974	730	715	639	626	508	584
Earnings per share	3.43	2.51	3.37	3.25	2.88	2.80	2.21	2.60
Dividends per share	2.20	2.16	2.08	2.00	1.92	1.84	1.76	1.68
Price: high	71.0	56.6	53.0	47.9	43.0	44.9	37.5	35.0
low	53.1	41.9	43.4	37.4	32.9	35.4	31.4	26.8

AGGRESSIVE GROWTH

A. G. Edwards, Inc.

One North Jefferson Avenue, St. Louis, MO 63103 ❑ Investor contact: Robert Proost (314) 955-4321 ❑ Dividend reinvestment plan not available ❑ Web site: www.agedwards.com ❑ Fiscal year's end February 28 or 29 ❑ Listed: NYSE ❑ Ticker symbol: AGE ❑ S&P rating: A ❑ Value Line financial strength rating: B+

A. G. Edwards, Inc. is a holding company whose subsidiaries provide securities and commodities brokerage, investment banking, trust, asset management, and insurance services.

Its principal subsidiary, A. G. Edwards & Sons, Inc., is a financial services company with 639 locations in forty-nine states and the District of Columbia. A. G. Edwards & Sons provides a full range of financial products to individual and institutional investors and offers investment banking services to corporate, governmental, and municipal clients.

A. G. Edwards continued to expand both the number of its registered investment professionals and its nationwide branch office network in fiscal 1999 (ended February 28, 1999), further strengthening its securities distribution capability.

In the past year, the number of A. G. Edwards registered representatives continued to expand, closing the year at 6,300, an increase of 3.6 percent. A. G. Edwards is the fourth-largest domestic brokerage firm focused on individual investors, or relatively affluent men and women who manage their personal portfolios with the help of a registered represen-

tative. Many of these people are professionals or business owners.

Shortcomings to Bear in Mind

- Rising interest rates or a falling stock market would have an adverse impact on investors. Since A. G. Edwards is heavily dependent on commission business, its revenues would be hurt by such developments.

- Without a doubt, the brokerage business is more competitive today than ever before. Full-service firms are expanding. Banks are offering brokerage services. Discount brokers are thriving. Mutual funds are marketing directly to investors. And "do-it-yourselfers" are benefiting from the longest bull market in recent history. Despite all these negatives, A. G. Edwards has continued to grow.

Reasons to Buy

- A. G. Edwards received several national accolades during fiscal 1999, reflecting the value of the firm's full-service, relationship-centered approach to it clients.

    In the publication's annual survey, *Smart Money* magazine ranked A. G. Edwards as the number one full-service retail brokerage firm. In addition to taking first place overall, A. G. Edwards finished first in four of the eight categories evaluated, including stock research, fees and commissions, breadth of products (tied for first), and mutual fund selection and performance.

- The quality of the firm's stock recommendations also received attention in the "All-Star Analysts Survey," developed by Zacks Investment Research and published annually in the *Wall Street Journal.* For the second consecutive year, eleven Securities Research analysts earned "All-Star" status for either stock-picking skill or earnings-estimate accuracy. Nine of the department's eleven "All-Stars" have been selected at least twice in the annual survey's six-year history.

- A. G. Edwards' asset allocation recommendations ranked first for 1999 in studies conducted by Zacks Investment Research, Wilshire Associates, and Carpenter Analytical Services, all of which were published in the *Wall Street Journal.*

- The A. G. Edwards Focus List of recommended stocks also received prominent attention in the national media during 1999. *Money* magazine ranked the Focus List number one for its three-year performance. The Focus List also earned the number two ranking for its five-year results in a stock-selection study conducted by Zacks Investment Research and published in the *Wall Street Journal.*

- The firm also was selected as one of "The Best Companies to Work For in America" in an annual survey published by *Fortune.*

    This marks the fourth consecutive time the firm has been included on this elite list—one of only fourteen firms to achieve this distinction.

- A. G. Edwards's Investment Banking Division reported record results in 1999,

with revenues increasing 15 percent. Corporate Finance management fee revenue increased 39 percent in fiscal 1999—a record high. The firm completed the largest lead-managed equity transaction in its 112-year history, with an equity offering by Reinsurance Group of America, Inc., and acted as financial advisor to Milwaukee-based Reiman Publications, a privately held publisher of lifestyle magazines, in its sale to a private equity investment firm in Chicago.

- The combined value of assets managed increased by 24 percent during 1999. These assets includes such programs as: A. G. Edwards Managed Accounts; A. G. Edwards Trust companies; Investment Management Consulting Services (formerly known as Asset Performance Monitor); and the Pathways, Spectrum, Fund Navigator, Fund Advisor, and Strategic Asset Account investment advisory programs.

- Over the past ten years (1989–1999), the dividend expanded from $.19 per share to $.55, a compound annual growth rate of 11.2 percent. In the same ten-year span, earnings per share climbed from $.73 to $3.07, a compound annual growth rate of 15.4 percent.

- A. G. Edwards is well prepared to ride out a market correction. The company has one of the strongest balance sheets in the industry and no long-term debt. What's more, with the majority of its costs variable in nature (mostly commissions paid to brokers), the brokerage house can easily ride out the vagaries of a cyclical industry with only moderate impact on margins.

- At A. G. Edwards, the practice is to manage its bond inventory for the primary purpose of meeting client demand for products, rather than to generate profits for the firm's account. Management believes that committing capital to pursue trading profits as an important source of revenue would expose the firm to excessive risk and compromise its commitment to putting its clients' needs ahead of those of the firm.

- The company is known for its practice of keeping its customers's success as its primary focus. One aspect of this philosophy is the company's agency approach. That is, A. G. Edwards does not offer in-house mutual funds or other products; rather, brokers are free to select the best outside products for clients. In addition, registered representatives do not have production quotas.

- Alex Bigelow, A. G. Edwards Vice President and Branch Manager, West Palm Beach, Florida, states his belief in the philosophy espoused by the firm:

"What I enjoy most about working for A. G. Edwards is that the culture here allows me to concentrate on being the best branch manager I can be. There are no 'products of the month' or monthly sales goals for my branch to contend with. There's much more of an emphasis on people, with the belief that if you hire the right people, the business will naturally follow. A. G. Edwards doesn't offer up-front money to attract new brokers.

"When I recruit new investment brokers, I look for people with character who have a drive to succeed but aren't looking for the shortest route to success. For investment brokers to succeed at A. G. Edwards, they have to care about what they do and care about what's best for the client."

- A. G. Edwards is one of the lowest-risk firms in the volatile brokerage industry because of its extremely strong capital position, solid earnings record, and above-average dividend yield. AGE has avoided the troubles currently afflicting other brokers because investment

banking and trading comprise a much smaller part of its total business.

- The Edwards Information Network (EIN) presents live broadcasts of world, market, and A. G. Edwards news throughout the day to each investment broker. The network programming was expanded in 1993 and improved to include more timely and useful information, including hourly updates with late-breaking news. EIN operates with a full-time staff of broadcasting professionals that gathers and reports news from the major services, including Dow Jones, Reuters, Bloomberg, and CNN. The network broadcasts 12 hours of news and informational programming every business day to the firm's investment brokers throughout the country.

- In the unlikely event that you are not convinced that this is a superior firm, here are some remarks by Louis Harvey, President of DALBAR, Inc., Boston, Massachusetts:

"For the last twenty years, my company has conducted nationwide market research on the financial services industry through customer and employee satisfaction surveys and other means. Today, it appears financial services firms are genuinely trying to change to be more customer-driven, rather than product- or profit-driven. The customer orientation is nothing new to A. G. Edwards, which has historically had a client focus and often receives high marks from both clients and its own brokers in DALBAR surveys. In my opinion, one of the things that distinguishes A. G. Edwards is that it doesn't build its own products. If you have your own products, there are pressures to sell your products. Not having them allows A. G. Edwards brokers to focus on clients without the burden of responsibility for products."

Total assets: $3,803 million
Common shares outstanding: 95 million
Return on 1999 shareholders' equity: 18.9%

	1999	1998	1997	1996	1995	1994	1993	1992
Revenues (millions)	2,241	2,004	1,696	1,454	1,178	1,279	1,074	939
Net income (millions)	292	269	219	171	124	155	119	106
Earnings per share	3.07	2.81	2.29	1.80	1.35	1.75	1.40	1.28
Dividends per share	.55	.51	.44	.40	.37	.35	.29	.25
Price: high	48.8	39.9	35.0	27.0	24.4	25.4	25.7	24.6
low	30.9	20.5	22.5	17.5	16.5	18.0	13.8	8.3

CONSERVATIVE GROWTH

Emerson Electric Company

P. O. Box 4100, St. Louis, MO 63136-8506 ◻ Listed: NYSE ◻ Investor contact: Nancy L. Wulf (314) 553-2197 ◻ Dividend reinvestment plan available (888) 213-0970 ◻ Web site: www.emersonelectric.com ◻ Ticker symbol: EMR ◻ Fiscal year's end September 30 ◻ S&P rating: A+ ◻ Value Line financial strength rating: A++

Emerson Electric is a leading manufacturer of a broad list of intermediate products such as electrical motors and drives, appliance components, and process-control devices. The company also produces hand and power tools, as well as accessories.

Founded some 107 years ago, Emerson is not a typical high-tech capital goods producer. Rather, the company makes such prosaic things as refrigerator compressors, pressure gauges, and In-Sink Erator garbage disposals—basic products that are essential to industry.

Without question, Emerson Electric is one of the nation's finest companies and should be a core holding in any portfolio devoted to growth of capital. Let's glance at the company's eight segments:

Process Control

Emerson is the worldwide leader in measurement and analytical instrumentation, valves, regulators, distributed control systems, and automation software for process and industrial markets. This business is leading the nation's change from centralized control to field-centered solutions that incorporate digital technologies, standard communication protocols and software advances in diagnostic and predictive maintenance capabilities.

Fractional Horsepower Motors

Emerson is the world's largest manufacturer of motors for appliances; heating, ventilating, and air conditioning (HVAC); refrigeration equipment; and specialty applications. This business continues to build strong global relationships with appliance and HVAC customers and is a recognized technology leader as evidenced by the state-of-the-art Motor Technology Center and the 1994 acquisition of Switched Reluctance Drives Ltd.

Heating, Ventilating, and Air Conditioning Components

Emerson is the global leader in compressors; hermetic terminals; and thermostats and valves for heating, ventilating, air conditioning (HVAC), and refrigeration markets. As the technological leader, this business is leading the industry's transition from reciprocating to scroll compressors. Copeland Compliant Scroll technology is being expanded into a full product offering for air conditioning and refrigeration applications worldwide.

Tools

Emerson is a major producer of power tools and accessories, plumbing tools, hand tools, ladders, fans, and disposers for consumer and professional markets. This business is well positioned to serve fast-growing home-improvement centers in North America and Europe. The company's joint ventures with Robert Bosch GmbH continue to provide a significant source of value creation.

Industrial Components and Equipment

Emerson is the leading supplier of ultrasonic and vibration welding, ultrasonic cleaning, materials testing, industrial electric heating, fluid control, emergency power control, index drives, fine particle separation, electrical enclosures, and lighting equipment for industrial markets. This business serves the capital goods equipment needs of the world's emerging economies and continues to strengthen its North American, European, and Asia Pacific positions with innovative new products.

Appliance Components

Emerson is the leading producer of controls, thermal-protection devices, sensors, and electric heating elements for major appliance manufacturers worldwide. This business benefits from the continuing globalization of appliance manufacturers and their incorporation of electronic appliance controls.

Industrial Motors and Drives

Emerson is the global leader in industrial motors, variable-speed drives, mechanical power transmission equipment, bearings, and diesel generator sets for industrial applications.

The acquisition of Leroy-Somer, F. G. Wilson, and Control Techniques expanded the Industrial Motors and Drives' global market and technology leadership positions. They also provided Emerson with the capability to engineer application-specific industrial motor and variable-speed drive solutions.

Electronics

Emerson is a leading producer of Uninterruptible Power Supplies (UPS), power conditioning equipment, environmental control systems, site monitoring systems, power conversion equipment, and electronic components for the world's computer, telecommunications, and industrial markets. This business continues to penetrate the Micro-UPS market, expand its European and Asia Pacific presence, and strengthen its telecommunications and industrial market positions.

Shortcomings to Bear in Mind

- Five years ago, Emerson's global expansion efforts focused on Asia-Pacific markets. The 1993 annual report stated, "Our total scope of operations, including joint ventures, reached $1.3 billion in sales in fiscal 1993." The report went on to say, "and plans are in place to utilize this base to double our sales in the region over the next five years."

So much for crystal balls. In fiscal 1998, Emerson's sales in Asia were substantially below the five-year target. This was primarily the result of the recession in Japan; sales in Asia outside Japan more than doubled. However, additional programs that evolved over the period to expand sales in other developing markets, such as Latin America and Eastern Europe, exceeded $1 billion and grew at an annual rate of 20 percent over the last five years. This performance more than compensated for the recent decline in Asia Pacific. On a combined basis, sales in all developing markets have grown at an annual rate of 18 percent since 1993. Total international sales, including the company's substantial operations in Europe, reached $5.4 billion in 1998, representing 40 percent of Emerson's total revenues.

Reasons to Buy

- The increase in sales of new products and services over the past five years has been impressive, with an average growth rate of 18 percent. In 1998, these new products and services represented 33 percent of the company's total sales. This level compares with 24 percent in 1993. The company's goal is to reach the 40 percent level by 2003.

- In May of 1999, Emerson Electric bolstered its presence in the oil-and-gas equipment business with the purchase of Daniel Industries Inc. The purchase price was $460 million. Houston-based Daniel, with 1998 revenues of $283.2 million, is the leading North American maker of measurement equipment for the natural gas industry. The purchase of Daniel "will strengthen our ability to provide services and solutions in this important market segment, especially natural gas," said Charles F. Knight, Emerson's chairman. About 8 percent of the $26 billion global process-control market is directed at oil-and-gas companies.

- Earnings have advanced with monotonous regularity for forty-one consecutive years. What's more, dividends have been boosted for forty-two straight years. To my knowledge, this is the longest period of sustained growth in both earnings and dividends of any publicly traded, U.S.–based manufacturer of industrial products. This earnings and dividend consistency can be attributed to a management process that emphasizes tight cost controls, growth in niche markets, and intelligent acquisitions. In the past ten years (1988–1998), for instance, EPS climbed from $1.16 to $2.77, a compound annual growth rate of 9.1 percent. In the same span, dividends advanced from $.50 to $1.18, a growth rate of 9 percent.

- Analysts regard Emerson as being extremely well positioned over the next several years. Its industrial end-market orientation, focus on manufacturing, global presence in its core activities, and superior financial attributes should serve it in good stead. What's more, analysts are particularly impressed with the concentration on products that allow end users to lower their production costs while at the same time paying heed to environmental concerns.

Total assets: $12,660 million
Current ratio: 1.24
Common shares outstanding: 438 million
Return on 1998 shareholders' equity: 21.9%

	1998	1997	1996	1995	1994	1993	1992	1991
Revenues (millions)	13,447	12,299	11,150	10,013	8,607	8,174	7,706	7,427
Net income (millions)	1,229	1,122	1,018	908	789	708	667	632
Earnings per share	2.77	2.52	2.28	2.03	1.76	1.58	1.49	1.42
Dividends per share	1.18	1.08	.98	.89	.78	.72	.69	.66
Price: high	67.4	60.4	51.8	40.8	33.0	31.2	29.0	27.5
low	54.5	45.0	38.8	30.8	28.2	52.8	23.4	18.4

INCOME

Energen Corporation

605 21ˢᵗ Street North, Birmingham, AL 35203-2707 ◻ **Investor contact: Julie S. Ryland (800) 654-3206** ◻
Direct dividend reinvestment plan available (800) 654-3206 or on the Web at www.netstockdirect.com ◻
Web site: www.energen.com ◻ **Listed: NYSE** ◻ **Ticker symbol: EGN** ◻ **Fiscal year's end September 30** ◻
S&P rating: A ◻ **Value Line financial strength rating: B++**

Based in Birmingham, Alabama, Energen Corporation is a diversified energy holding company, with a stake in two main lines of business: the distribution of natural gas and the exploration and production of oil and natural gas.

The holding company dates back to 1978 with the reorganization of its natural gas utility and largest subsidiary, Alagasco. This natural gas utility was launched in 1948, with the merger of Alabama Gas Company and Birmingham Gas Company. Energen's principal subsidiaries are Alagasco and Taurus Exploration.

Alagasco

Alagasco is the largest natural gas distributor in Alabama. The utility serves 468,000 homes and businesses in central and northern Alabama. The service territory covers 22,000 square miles and 175 communities in thirty counties, including Birmingham and Montgomery, with an estimated combined population of 2.4 million. The distribution system includes 8,800 miles of mains and more than 9,600 miles of service lines. In addition, two liquefied natural gas facilities are used to meet peak demand.

Alagasco serves about 70 percent of the potential customers along its gas mains. In addition, about 88 percent of the 5,400 new homes constructed in its service area during 1998 incorporated natural gas for space and water heating. Penetration in the new multifamily housing market was up, with 53 percent of the new multifamily starts using natural gas.

In an effort to supplement normal growth, Alagasco continues to pursue the acquisition of municipal gas systems in Alabama. The company has added more than 42,000 customers through the acquisition of twenty-two municipal gas systems in Alabama over the last thirteen years, but did not acquire any new systems in 1998. Alagasco believes the remaining seventy-eight municipal systems in Alabama offer the company future growth opportunities.

Energen Resources Corporation

Energen Resources Corporation (formerly Taurus Exploration) has a stake in the exploration and production of oil and natural gas. During fiscal 1998, Energen Resources invested about $85 million to acquire an estimated 120 billion cubic feet equivalent (Bcfe) of oil and gas reserves. Over the last three years, Energen Resources has invested about $365 million in acquisitions, adding some 740 Bcfe of reserves.

In 1998, the company established a solid operating presence in the Permian Basin in west Texas through a property acquisition. It later improved that position by trading most of Energen's shallow Gulf of Mexico interests for additional properties there. For a number of years, the offshore Gulf was the focus of the company's limited exploration program. The property swap was important strategically because it signaled the company's decision to concentrate future exploration activities in those areas onshore where it has, or may gain, a substantial operating presence.

Shortcomings to Bear in Mind

- Natural gas utilities are hostage to the weather. If the winter is mild, utilities sell less gas. The summer weather, on the other hand, is not very important, since only a small amount of gas is used in air conditioning, even though that sector holds considerable promise for the future. An electric utility, in contrast, can be hurt by a mild summer, since air conditioning can generate huge revenues during a torrid June, July, and August.

- Public utilities are subject to the vagaries of interest rates. There are two reasons: investors are often on the lookout for a better return. If interest rates rise, income-oriented investors may be tempted to sell their utility shares and invest elsewhere, which depresses the price of utility shares. The second reason is that utilities tend to be major borrowers, since they have to invest in new distribution facilities. By the same token, when interest rates fall, it augurs well for public utilities.

Reasons to Buy

- Alagasco's net income increased $2 million in fiscal 1998, to $20.6 million, marking the eighth consecutive year of record earnings for the Birmingham-based utility. Alagasco earned a return of 13.5 percent on an increased level of equity that represents investment in utility plant.

  With the help of temperatures that were 15.4 percent colder in 1998 than in 1997, coupled with a healthy industrial marketplace, Alagasco's gas delivery volumes climbed 8.3 percent, to a record throughput of 115.3 billion cubic feet (Bcf). Residential, small commercial and small industrial, and transportation volumes all increased 7 percent to 10 percent.

- Alagasco's financial stability, in part, is due to Alabama's progressive regulatory environment. The company's ratepayers and shareholders both benefit from the utility's unique rate-setting mechanism, Rate Stabilization and Equalization (RSE), the prime example of this environment.

- Natural gas utilities have some advantages over electric utilities. For one thing, they are not as concerned about competition. Natural gas is a preferred fuel, compared with coal, oil and electricity. It is plentiful and clean-burning. Thus, it is not a target of antipollution activists. It can be burned in vehicles instead of gasoline and has some advantages. It is less expensive than gasoline and does less harm to the engine. Of course, it is unlikely to dislodge gasoline anytime soon, except as a fuel for interurban vehicles such as buses, delivery vans, and taxis.

- Many natural gas utilities are entirely dependent on their revenues from their utility function. This has some disadvantages. For one thing, utilities are regulated and are unlikely to experience high growth. If the state regulators are tough to deal with—most state regulators are consumer-oriented—the utility may languish.

  On the other hand, when the company is active in exploration, there is the opportunity to increase earnings without the fear of regulation. For its part, Energen derives a hefty portion of its earnings from its oil and gas exploration. What's more, exploration is not tied to weather or season. On the other hand, if natural gas prices are weak, this segment of the company will be hurt.

- Alagasco was voted one of the 100 Best Companies to Work For in America. According to the survey's authors,

Energen was included because of its management's willingness to listen to employee suggestions and its infatuation with stamping out "dinosaur thinking."

- Energen Resources' production has increased dramatically, from 10.1 Bcfe in 1995 to 57.4 Bcfe in 1998 and is expected to reach 87 Bcfe in 1999. In addition, over the three-year period, the company's reserves increased 700 percent, from 95.2 Bcfe to 764.9 Bcfe.

Net income, moreover, has risen substantially, increasing more than 335 percent from a base of $3.5 million in 1995 to over $15 million in 1998.

- Over the next four years, the company plans to drill some 60 development wells in the San Juan Basin and perform 150 well recompletions at a net cost of about $58 million. In the Permian Basin, Energen plans to drill some 28 wells and perform 15 recompletions at a net cost of about $11.5 million.
- Energen Resources's acquisition of TOTAL Minatome Corporation got 1999 off to a good start with the addition of about 200 Bcfe of proved oil and gas reserves. Energen Resources's net investment was $132.6 million. What's more, the company plans to invest about $70 million over the next several years to exploit fully the 45 percent of behind-pipe and proved and undeveloped reserves.
- In February of 1999, Energen Resources announced that it had reduced its exposure to oil prices for the remainder of fiscal 1999 through the use of futures hedging instruments. With the addition during that month of crude oil futures contracts and third-party derivatives, Energen Resources now has more 55 percent of its estimated oil production for the year hedged at an average price of $14.83 per barrel.

Oil comprises about 25 percent of Energen Resources's estimated production in 1999. Natural gas is the largest component of Energen Resources's production mix and comprises about 70 percent of the company's 1999 production of 80 billion cubic feet equivalent. The company hedged more than 85 percent of its gas production at an average price of $2.31 per Mcf.

Total assets: $993 million
Current ratio: 0.80
Common shares outstanding: 29.2 million
Return on 1998 shareholders' equity: 11.1%

	1998	1997	1996	1995	1994	1993	1992	1991
Revenues (millions)	503	448	399	321	377	357	332	325
Net income (millions)	36	29	21	19	22	18	16	14
Earnings per share	1.23	1.16	.98	.89	1.01	.89	.77	.71
Dividends per share	.63	.61	.59	.57	.55	.53	.51	.48
Price: high	22.5	20.6	15.6	12.6	11.9	13.4	9.6	9.4
low	15.1	29.0	21.8	20.1	19.3	18.1	15.0	16.0

Ethan Allen Interiors, Inc.

P. O. Box 1966, Danbury, CT 06813-1966 ❑ Investor contact: Ms. Margaret (Peg) W. Lupton (203)743-8234 ❑ Web site: www.ethanallen.com ❑ Dividend reinvestment plan not available ❑ Fiscal year's end June 30 ❑ Listed: NYSE ❑ Ticker symbol: ETH ❑ S&P rating: Not rated ❑ Value Line financial strength rating: B+

Ethan Allen, one of the ten largest manufacturers of household furniture in the United States, sells a full range of furniture products and decorative accessories through a network of 315 retail stores, of which 72 are company-owned. Retail stores are located in the United States, Canada and Mexico, with 20 located abroad.

The company's stores are scattered across the country, with outlets in nearly every state. However, there are more than a dozen outlets in such states as California (27), Texas (19), and Florida (23). There is a also a concentrated cluster of Ethan Allen stores along the Eastern Seaboard in such states as New Jersey, Connecticut, and Massachusetts.

The company's twenty-one manufacturing facilities and three sawmills are located in the United States.

Within this fragmented industry, the company has the largest domestic furniture retail network utilizing the gallery concept. Comparable-store sales have benefited from a repositioning of the product mix to appeal to a broader consumer base, a program to renovate or relocate existing stores, coupled with more frequent advertising and promotional campaigns.

Ethan Allen is pursuing an aggressive growth strategy, including investments in technology, employee training, and new stores. Margins have been enhanced by manufacturing efficiencies, lower interest expense, and a strengthening of the upholstery and accessory lines.

With an efficient and flexible vertically integrated structure, a strong, dedicated retail network, an impressive 95 percent brand name recognition, and a sixty-six-year reputation for exceptional quality and service, Ethan Allen is uniquely positioned as a dominant force in the home furnishings industry.

As Ethan Allen approaches the new millennium, the company's philosophy of design remains the same as it was when it was founded sixty-six years ago. Styles may have changed from colonial to eclectic, but the company's commitment to exceptional quality, classical design elements, innovative style, and functionality will continue to position Ethan Allen as a preferred brand for years to come.

In keeping with the way consumers live today, the company has organized its product programs into two broad style categories. "Classic" encompasses more historically inspired styles, from early European and French influences to designs from the eighteenth- and nineteenth-century masters. "Casual," on the other hand, captures a clean, contemporary line and an updated country aesthetic.

Shortcomings to Bear in Mind

- This stock is labeled "aggressive growth," because it has a high beta coefficient of 1.70. A beta of 1 indicates a stock that fluctuates with the market. High betas are indicative of stocks that can be volatile.
- The stock of Ethan Allen can be sensitive to the cyclical whims of furniture demand. For instance, when interest rates rise, housing starts are hurt, as is the furniture industry.

Reasons to Buy

- The company has been reducing its debt in recent years. In 1995, debt as a percentage of capitalization was 40 percent. In the years since, this figure has declined to 28 percent, 20 percent, and 4 percent (at the end of 1998).
- During the last seven years, Ethan Allen increased its sales by 106.7 percent. In the same period, its plants increased production by 64.6 percent. Interestingly, nearly all of this growth emanated from the same number of stores. What's more, the number of plants declined by seven. During this same span, the company changed more than 90 percent of its products, in terms of style and affordability. In addition, the company developed a $60 million annual advertising campaign to project its new identity. Finally, Ethan Allen renovated 89 percent of its storefronts.
- In 1998, the company increased production by nearly 20 percent from existing facilities. To do this, Ethan Allen invested in technology, improved work processes, and dramatically revamped its product line.

  At the company's Andover, Maine, facility, management started the process of doubling its sawmill capacity. At Beecher Falls, Vermont, the company's new rough mill is helping it to increase capacity, and the construction of ten new kilns will enable the company to process twice as much lumber. Finally, in the New York and Pennsylvania regions, Ethan Allen has plans for a major expansion.
- To enhance marketing, Ethan Allen is developing proprietary products that combine attractive design, quality, and an affordable price. The company is also strengthening its position as a total home furnishings enterprise in both classic and casual styles, with strong programs in wood furniture, upholstery, and decorative accents.
- These efforts are paying off. In fiscal 1998, the company's sales increased by 18.8 percent, to $679.3 million. Net income, before an extraordinary charge (arising from the early redemption of debt) increased by 47.6 percent, to $71.9 million. By the end of 1998, the company was virtually debtfree, and its net worth increased by $48.9 million, to $314.3 million. During the year, ETH implemented a 2-for-1 stock split and boosted its cash dividend by 33 percent. Finally, the company invested $29.7 in capital expenditures and repurchased $23.3 million of its stock in the open market.
- Operating a store in today's environment is a complicated business if management doesn't have the right structure in place. Ethan Allen is convinced that "You need to be able to keep the store beautiful and inspiring, help customers select the right products, train and motivate the sales staff, grow a complicated custom business, make accessory house calls and anticipate customer service requests—all at the same time."

  To respond to these demands, Ethan Allen began testing new ways to staff its stores in 1998. For example, at its corporate headquarters in Danbury, Connecticut, management looked at its needs, especially on high-traffic weekends, and created an environment to better support the designers who were working on the front lines.

  First, the company established the right sales management structure so that designers were able to obtain the training and direction they needed to build their businesses. Then Ethan Allen added specialists in the soft goods and accessories areas to help designers sell more of these complicated product programs. In addition, the company also added a merchandise manager to keep the store beautiful and a customer service specialist to address delivery and service issues.

Since this structure has been in place, traffic in the Danbury store increased about 19 percent. During that same period, the store's written business jumped up 35 percent.

- In 1998, Ethan Allen increased case goods production by nearly 14 percent, without increasing physical space. According to management, "that was a tall order for our thirteen case goods plants, and investments in technology and work processes have helped us to meet the increased demand."

  In order to improve the company's ability to process the wood it uses in its products, it invested $1 million in new equipment in its three sawmills, $4 million in new kilns, and $2.5 million in rough mill technology. In the company's machining rooms, moreover, it spent over $2.1 million in new technology to improve its ability to quickly carve and sand parts. In addition to increasing output, these investments are helping to augment quality and consistency throughout the entire manufacturing process.

- To further increase capacity and improve the company's ability to serve its customers, Ethan Allen is editing its line by about 10 percent and retiring underperforming items. Management is convinced that this strategy will free up capacity immediately while the company begins construction on expansion projects in all four of its manufacturing regions.

- Running a custom business that offers hundred of frames, thousands of fabrics, and endless combination in a challenge in itself. Running it profitably is even harder. At Ethan Allen, the company does it by marrying state-of-the-art technology with smart work processes and trained processionals.

  For instance, new technology like the fabric-cutting machine in operation at the company's Maiden, North Carolina, facility is changing the way Ethan Allen does business. Using a computerized mapping system and automated cutting mechanism, the machine can cut perfectly matched pieces on a very complicated fabric pattern with precision and accuracy. In addition to eliminating the cost of human error, the machine allows the company to triple its output using fewer people. Plans are underway to install this technology in Ethan Allen's other upholstery plants.

Total assets: $433 million
Current ratio: 2.35
Common shares outstanding: 41.4 million
Return on 1998 shareholders' equity: 22.9%

	1998	1997	1996	1995	1994	1993	1992	1991
Revenues (millions)	693	572	510	476	437	384	351	n/a
Net income (millions)	72	49	28	23	23	def.	def.	
Earnings per share	1.63	1.11	.65	.52	.51	def.		
Dividends per share	.09	.06	.01	nil	nil			
Price: high	44.4	28.6	13.0	8.33	10.7	10.5		
low	15.7	12.3	6.5	5.7	6.5	5.4		

* Ethan Allen went public on March 23, 1993, and thus this table is incomplete.

Exxon Mobil Corporation

P. O. Box 140369, Irving, TX 75014-0369 ◻ Investor contact: Mr. Peter Townsend, V.P. (214) 444-1900 ◻ Direct dividend reinvestment program available (800) 252-1800 ◻ Web site: www.exxon.com ◻ Listed: NYSE ◻ Ticker symbol: XON ◻ S&P rating: A ◻ Value Line financial strength rating: A++

Exxon, one of the two largest oil companies in the world (the other is Royal Dutch Petroleum) has a stake in every facet of the industry, including exploration for and production of crude oil, refining, natural gas, petrochemicals, and metals.

Exxon's merger with Mobil has been completed. Shareholders of the two companies overwhelmingly voted to approve the merger in May of 1999. In 1998, Exxon agreed to acquire Mobil in a deal valued at $75.9 billion, paying 1.32 Exxon shares for each of Mobil's 796.5 million shares outstanding. At the time, Lee Raymond, Exxon's CEO, estimated that 9,000 of the two companies' 123,000 jobs worldwide would be axed. More recently, Mobil insiders believe the number could be closer to 15,000. Over a three-year period, the combined company is expected to save $2.8 billion. To be sure, the merged company is huge; it's the world's biggest. Even so, the combined company will control less than 4 percent of oil production worldwide and less than 11 percent of sales.

Exploration and Production

With exploration in about thirty countries, the company has built a diverse portfolio through high-quality additions to its oil and gas resource base. (The resource base includes proved reserves and other resources that will likely be developed in the future.) Exxon's 1998 exploration program boosted the company's resource base by 1.2 billion oil-equivalent barrels of newly discovered resources in eleven countries at a cost of just over $1 a barrel. More than 900 million of these barrels came from new-venture areas, which are expected to yield significant production in the future.

Refining and Marketing

Exxon, which has ownership in thirty-one refineries in eleven countries, serves both mature and emerging markets. Exxon markets a wide range of petroleum products around the world and sells some 65 million gallons of motor fuel to 8 million customers each day. This success results from the company's focus on being the most efficient retailer in the business.

Chemicals

Despite economic problems in Asia Pacific, primary petroleum demand worldwide grew by 2 percent in 1998. Capitalizing on the addition of new capacity and building on strong customer relationships, Exxon Chemical achieved earnings of $1.2 billion, the fourth-highest ever. However, overall margins were weaker than in 1997 because increased industry supplies exceeded demand growth for several key products.

Exxon's unique mix of chemicals business lines and strong competitive positions delivers superior performance throughout the business cycle. The company's portfolio includes cyclical commodity chemicals such as olefins, polyolefins, and aromatics, as well as less cyclical specialty businesses such as elastomers, plasticizers, solvents, oxo alcohols, and adhesion products.

Coal, Minerals and Power

In 1998, average realized coal and copper prices fell 13 percent and 28 percent, respectively, leading to a $177-million decline in product realizations from the prior year. These declines, however, were offset by lower operating costs and record production. As a result, earnings for

Exxon's coal, minerals and power businesses were flat compared with those of 1997.

Shortcomings to Bear in Mind

- Oil companies of all stripes are getting squeezed by low petroleum prices, coupled with the high capital costs of exploration. Given the exotic locales of the most promising untapped fields, it is unlikely that exploration will get any cheaper. And with oil selling below $20 a barrel, it seems a safe bet that oil won't be selling for $100 a barrel in the next year or two—something analysts were predicting during the oil price runup of the early 1980s.

Reasons to Buy

- Exxon has the resources and expertise to take advantage of the best oil and gas opportunities around the globe—both in areas where the company has a history of operating experience and, increasingly, in parts of the world where only minimal hydrocarbon exploration has taken place.
- Exxon benefits from wide light/heavy crude oil price differentials because of the complexity of the company's refineries, which are geared to the processing of heavy crude oils.
- Exxon is the world's largest producer of the base stocks used to make lubricants, including oil for cars, manufacturing equipment, and other machinery.
- Technology for finding and producing oil and gas is evolving rapidly. For example, recent advances in deep-water production capabilities, horizontal drilling, and 3D seismic processing have helped to add reserves and decrease finding and producing costs. Exxon holds a leadership position in exploration and production technology and is committed to maintaining that position.

Key to Exxon's strategy for technical leadership is an active research program.

Exxon Production Research Company is a premier technical organization that invests more than $100 million annually to develop new technology for a wide spectrum of operational challenges. The following are some examples of recent research accomplishments:

- Advanced Exxon technology for geochemical analysis can differentiate the molecular components of very small hydrocarbon samples. The new techniques, using only a drop of oil, provide a better understanding of the origins of oil and gas, which leads to improved predictions of where new fields may be found.
- 3D seismic analysis and geological mapping have been integrated with computer-driven visualization to fundamentally improve the speed and accuracy of subsurface geological interpretations. These improved interpretations reduce the risk associated with wildcat and appraisal wells.
- Hydrates—icelike, crystalline mixtures of light hydrocarbons and water—can plug an oil or natural gas flowline. The problem is particularly severe where discoveries are in deeper, colder water and at greater distances from processing facilities. Exxon has established an advanced test facility to develop improved techniques for controlling hydrates. This research will reduce the cost of field developments, especially gas fields in frontier regions.
- Exxon's refining and marketing business builds upon a longstanding presence in the large, mature markets of North America and Western Europe, where extensive efficiency and rationalization programs have greatly improved the company's position as a leading competitor.

Exxon's well-placed network of refining and distribution facilities in western European markets has provided a competitive advantage for the company's expansion into eastern European countries.

- Univation Technologies, a worldwide joint venture with Union Carbide Corporation, began operation in 1997. The new company researches, develops, markets, and licenses advanced technologies for making polyethylene, the world's most widely used plastic, combining Exxon's metallocene catalysts and Union Carbide's processes.

- Exxon is one of the world's largest oil and gas producers, but it's also a major consumer of energy. Because energy is a cost of doing business, it makes sense to use it efficiently.

  Over the past twenty-five years, the refineries and chemical plants of Exxon and its affiliates have cut energy consumption by 35 percent—for a total savings of 1.2 billion equivalent barrels of oil. That's more than the annual oil use of any single country except the United States, Russia, Japan, and China. What's more, Exxon is continuing to save the equivalent of 80 million barrels of oil a year. Some of these savings at refinery and chemical plants come from making steam and electricity at the same time, a process called cogeneration. It uses 30 percent less energy than conventional processes that produce steam and electricity separately.

  Worldwide Exxon and its affiliates operate or have an interest in twenty-six cogeneration plants, with 1,100 megawatts of capacity. Plant capacity, moreover, could more than double by the year 2003.

- Although oil and gas companies have begun to explore only half the deepwater basins, they have already found them to contain the equivalent of more than 40 billion barrels of oil. Geoscientists predict that well over 100 billion barrels remain to be discovered in ocean basins where the water is deeper than

400 meters (1,300 feet). More than two-thirds of the earth is covered by oceans, which average two miles deep. With over fifty years of offshore experience, Exxon is one of just a handful of international oil companies with the operating and technical expertise to operate in this deepwater frontier.

Despite intense competition, Exxon has been successful in gaining access to the best deepwater opportunities. Since 1990, Exxon's deepwater acreage holdings have increased dramatically to more than 30 million acres (47,000 square miles).

- Three-dimensional imaging is an important tool for locating oil and natural gas in sedimentary basins. Vessels towing long streamers of listening devices record low-frequency sound waves bounced off layers of rock far below the ocean floor. Exxon pioneered many of the technologies for gathering seismic data and developed the industry's most sophisticated computer software to process and interpret the information.

  The ability to produce sharp three-dimensional images of rock formations in deepwater basins is an important competitive advantage. It's one way Exxon has raised the success rate in wildcat exploration wells to more than 50 percent. It has also helped Exxon to reduce average finding costs to about $1.00 per barrel, while adding billions of barrels of oil and natural gas to the company's resource base.

- Since 1991, when initial studies of the deepwater region where completed, Exxon has established a major position in the attractive deepwater basins offshore West Africa. Once final negotiations were completed in 1998, Exxon had interests in eighteen high-potential deepwater blocks in Angola, Republic of Congo (Brazzaville), and Nigeria, totaling about 14 million gross acres.

Total assets: $92,630 million
Current ratio: 0.96
Common shares outstanding: 2,431 million
Return on 1998 shareholders' equity: 14.5%

	1998	1997	1996	1995	1994	1993	1992	1991
Revenues (billions)	118	137	134	123	114	111	117	116
Net income(millions)	6,365	8,460	7,510	6,470	5,100	5,280	4,770	5,600
Earnings per share	2.61	3.37	2.99	2.59	2.04	2.10	1.91	2.23
Dividends per share	1.64	1.62	1.56	1.50	1.46	1.44	1.42	1.34
Price: high	77.3	67.3	50.6	43.0	33.6	34.5	32.8	30.9
low	56.6	48.3	38.8	30.1	28.1	28.9	26.9	24.8

AGGRESSIVE GROWTH

FDX Corporation

6075 Poplar Avenue, P. O. Box 727 Department 1854, Memphis, TN 38194-1854 ❑ Investor contact: J. H. Clippard, Jr. (901) 395-3478 ❑ Web site: www.fedex.com ❑ Dividend reinvestment plan not available ❑ Fiscal year's end May 31 ❑ Listed: NYSE ❑ Ticker symbol: FDX ❑ S&P rating: B- ❑ Value Line financial strength rating: B++

FDX Corporation was founded on January 27, 1998 as a holding company comprising Federal Express Corporation and Caliber System, Inc. FDX, a $16-billion global transportation and logistics powerhouse, offers a broad portfolio of services through its network of independent operating companies.

FedEx invented express distribution twenty-five years ago and remains the industry's global leader, providing rapid, reliable, time-definite delivery to more than 210 countries, connecting markets that comprise more than 90 percent of the world's gross domestic product. Unmatched air route authorities and transportation infrastructure make FedEx the world's largest express transportation company, providing fast and reliable service for more than 3 million shipments each business day.

RPS, Inc. is North America's second-largest provider of business-to-business ground small-package delivery service. RPS also provides service to Puerto Rico and twenty-eight European countries. Like FedEx, RPS is a pioneer in applying advanced information technology to meet customer information needs.

Viking Freight, Inc. is the leading regional freight carrier in the western United States, offering premium next- and second-day less-than-truckload freight service to eleven states, along with direct ocean service to Alaska and Hawaii.

Roberts Express, Inc. is the world's largest surface-expedited carrier, offering nonstop, time-specific, door-to-door delivery (with a guarantee) of time-critical and special handling shipments with the United States, Canada, and Europe. In keeping with the core competencies of FDX, Roberts's point-to-point surface and air-charter delivery solutions are driven by sophisticated and proprietary shipment-control technology.

FDX Global Logistics, Inc. designs, develops, and applies integrated logistics and technology solutions that provide a competitive edge for customers worldwide. Services include transportation management, dedicated contract carriage, intermodal transportation, dedicated and shared warehousing, order fulfillment, and value-added services such as kitting, subassembly, and returnable containers management.

Shortcomings to Bear in Mind

- The company's biggest business, the Priority Overnight service, is fairly mature. This segment accounted for about 40 percent of the company's revenues in the most recent fiscal year, down from 43 percent a year earlier. This shrinkage was caused partly by the shift to billing customers according to the distance of the delivery and partly by increased competition from the U.S. Postal Service.

- According to management, "We are a very capital-intensive business. To do what we do takes big, wide-bodied planes—and lots of them. It takes trucks and vans and large, costly operating hubs, both across America and abroad. It takes a lot of information and telecommunications devices, whether it be scanners and radios in the trucks or what-have-you." On the other hand, FedEx's global network is now more or less complete, and that will make a big difference, not least because investors can expect the pace of capital spending to decline sharply.

Reasons to Buy

- Increasingly, businesses are seeking strategic, cost-effective ways to manage their supply chains—the series of transportation and information exchanges required to convert parts and raw materials into finished, delivered products. According to the management: "Experience tells us that customers prefer one supplier to meet all of their distribution and logistics needs. And FDX has what it takes: Our unique global network, operational expertise, and air route authorities cannot be replicated by the competition. With FDX, our customers have a strategic competitive weapon to squeeze time, mass, and cost from the supply chain."

- In the spring of 1999, FDX and Netscape announced an agreement to make the shipping giant's package-delivery services easily accessible to users of Netscape's fast-growing Netcenter portal on the Internet. The agreement enables Netscape users to ship and track packages without leaving the Netscape site.

- In 1998, *Wired* magazine selected FDX as one of forty "New Blue Chips," companies that are "building the new economy using technology, networks, and information to reshape the world." Of the forty companies cited for possessing fundamental qualities necessary to succeed in a fast-changing economy—globalism, communication, innovation, technology, and strategic vision—FDX was the only company deemed to possess all five fundamentals as core business elements.

- Dell Computer Corporation revolutionized the computer industry with a custom-focused direct business model that's lean on inventory and cycle time, but long on logistics efficiencies, customization, and customer delight. The company turns inventory in fewer than eight days, compared with sixty to ninety days through more traditional indirect competitors. To keep its supply chain tight, Dell has FedEx deliver computers and parts from its factory in Malaysia to its largest Asian market, Japan. In North America, Caliber Logistics provides distribution and fleet management services for Dell facilities in Austin, Texas. FedEx, meanwhile, handles the express deliveries of several Dell products, displaying a commitment to velocity, quality, and customer service that mirrors Dell's own uniquely successful approach to business.

- When a large corporation decentralizes shipping, it's like a computer's circuitry firing at random: interesting pyrotechnics, but not very productive. That's why Unisys chose to harness the buying power of hundreds of sales offices, service locations, and manufacturing sites by utilizing the transportation management services of FDX. Unisys employees simply call a tollfree number staffed by Caliber Logistics. Caliber distribution expert rely on FedEx, RPS, Roberts Express, and Viking Freight to ship everything from critical replacement parts to Unisys enterprise servers directly to the customer site. Each shipping decision reflects the most appropriate and cost-effective delivery solution.

- With 2,000 employees and owner-operators, Roberts Express is the world's largest surface-expedited carrier. For shippers and their customers, Roberts's service guarantee and exceptional on-time performance deliver peace of mind, even in the most time-critical situations.

  To promote ever higher levels of productivity and service, Roberts recently installed a dynamic vehicle-allocation system. As customer orders are received, the system lets dispatchers evaluate at least twenty load and traffic variables to help ensure that delivery vehicles are where they need to be, when they need to be, for optimum customer service and fleet utilization.

- Nearly 1,000 times each business day, Roberts Express's engineers and executes time-specific, door-to-door surface and air-charter delivery solutions that solve special-handling challenges for FDX customers within North America and Europe.

  How special? Consider the 60-ton stamping press Roberts recently delivered from Brescia, Italy to Kokomo, Indiana. The largest shipment ever handled by Roberts, the press was delivered quickly and on time, keeping an automaker's assembly plant up and running at peak efficiency and quality levels.

- What the stock market seems to be overlooking right now is that for all the books, computers, and corduroy britches consumers buy from today's Internet retailers, someone has to deliver the goods. In millions of instances, that someone is FedEx. This helps explain how FedEx has been able to keep growing.

- FedEx has invested heavily in recent years to develop an international infrastructure. It presently can reach locations accounting for 90 percent of world GDP, with 24- or 48-hour service. International delivery services for documents and freight have been growing faster than domestic business in recent years. In fiscal 1998, international shipments accounted for 8.6 percent of volume, up from 6.6 percent in 1991. FedEx is the only foreign air carrier allowed to operate directly in China.

- The company's fastest-growing domestic services are deferred delivery services: FedEx 2Day and Express Saver. Express Saver, launched in July of 1997, provides guaranteed delivery of shipments in most of the United States within three business days.

Total assets: $9,686 million
Current ratio: 1.02
Common shares outstanding: 149 million
Return on 1998 shareholders' equity: 13.3%

	1998	1997	1996	1995	1994	1993	1992	1991
Revenues (millions)	15,703	11,520	10,274	9,392	8,480	7,808	7,550	7,688
Net income (millions)	526	348	308	282	204	110	64	106
Earnings per share	1.75	1.51	1.35	1.25	.92	.51	.30	.50
Dividends per share	nil							
Price: high	46.6	42.3	22.5	21.5	20.2	18.2	14.1	11.2
low	21.8	21.0	16.7	14.7	13.4	11.1	8.7	7.9

GROWTH AND INCOME

Federal Signal Corporation

1415 West 22nd Street, Oak Brook, IL 60523-2004 ▫ Investor contact: Henry L. Dykema (630) 954-2020 ▫
Dividend reinvestment plan available (312) 461-3309 ▫ Web site: www.federalsignal.com ▫ Listed: NYSE ▫
Ticker symbol: FSS ▫ S&P rating: A+ ▫ Value Line financial strength rating: A

Federal Signal, founded in 1901, is an acquisition-oriented manufacturer and worldwide supplier of safety, signaling, and communications equipment. The company has a stake in the manufacture of fire trucks, ambulances, street sweeping and vacuum loader vehicles, parking-control equipment, custom on-premise signage, carbide cutting tools, precision punches, as well as related die components.

Federal Signal is managed on a decentralized basis and is comprised of four major operating groups.

The Safety Products Group (with 1998 sales of $254 million) includes the Signal Products Division, Aplicaciones Tecnologicas VAMA S. L., Justrite Manufacturing, and Federal APD. These divisions primarily serve public and industrial safety, parking-control, and security markets. The Signal Products Division consists of Emergency Products, Electrical Products, Federal Warning Systems, and Commercial Products.

The Tool Group ($146 million) consists of Dayton Progress, Bassett Rotary Tool, Manchester Tool, and Dico. A broad range of consumable tools for metal stamping and metal cutting applications is manufactured for more than 14,000 industrial customers around the world.

The Sign Group ($66 million) manufactures on-premise identification signs and visual communications displays throughout the continental United States from twenty-three manufacturing and sales facilities.

The Vehicle Group ($537.8 million) includes Emergency One, Superior Emergency Vehicles, Elgin Sweeper, Guzzler Manufacturing, Vactor Manufacturing, and Ravo International. These companies are world leaders in the fire/emergency apparatus, street sweeping, industrial vacuum, and municipal combination catch basin/sewer cleaning equipment markets as a result of strong distribution channels and continuing product innovations.

Highlights of 1998

At just over $1 billion, Federal Signal's 1998 sales increased 8 percent over the prior year. The company crossed the $1 billion mark for the first time; it represented the thirty-third straight year of sales increases. Although 1998 earnings per share of $1.30 only slightly exceeded the prior year's $1.29, the company is encouraged by the accelerating earnings growth it experienced during the course of the year, capped by Federal Signal's best fourth quarter ever in new orders and sales. Three of Federal Signal's four operating groups reported earnings increases in 1998, but problems within the Vehicle Group weighed down total performance.

Cash flow from operations increased 18 percent, to $75 million, in 1998, clearly outperforming the company's increase in income. Federal Signal's focus on working capital programs is mainly responsible for this performance. Return on equity was 19.1 percent, below the company's 20 percent target for the first time since 1989.

Shortcomings to Bear in Mind

- In 1998, the performance of the Vehicle Group was hurt badly by vendor component shortages. The United States municipal fire business, the company's biggest segment, was hit the hardest. These shortages were greatest during the first two quarters, leading to reduced sales, higher backlog, and reduced productivity. As components became available, Federal Signal acted to raise production, including hiring manufacturing employees and changing certain manufacturing methods. While these actions adversely affected productivity in the short run, they were effective in raising production levels in the fourth quarter and set the stage for higher plant productivity in 1999.

Reasons to Buy

- The Safety Products Group posted record sales and profits in 1998, as all major businesses increased operating performance. Sales grew 14 percent, to $253 million, and profits increased 36 percent, to over $40 million.
- The Safety Products Group develops new products as an essential part of its growth strategy. About 20 percent of the group's 1998 sales came from prod-

ucts introduced over the last five years. The group launched several new products during 1998. A new speaker for emergency vehicles produced and sold in the United States met with, according to management, "unprecedented market acceptance." A motorcycle lighting package manufactured at the Spain plant was successfully introduced into the domestic market.

The United Kingdom hazardous area lighting unit designed and manufactured a new product that helped secure a large new order in the Middle East. The group introduced a new line of hazardous liquid containment cabinets to further penetrate key international markets.

- In 1998, overall sales for the Tool Group increased 5 percent, and income improved 2 percent. The group achieved record sales levels in both the die components and cutting tool segments, maintaining their number one market share positions in the United States in their principal segments.
- Analysts believe that Federal Signal will continue to benefit from strong municipal demand for its increasingly diverse line of emergency/maintenance vehicles and safety products (municipal revenue streams typically lag the cycle), a strengthening presence in international markets, operating improvements and synergies generated at recently acquired companies, an ongoing, focused acquisition strategy, and a probable escalation in investor interest in companies with proven resistance to economic downturns.
- Federal Signal has a consistent record of growth. In the 1988–1998 period, earnings per share climbed from $.41 to $1.30, a compound annual growth rate of 12.2 percent. In the same ten-year stretch, dividends per share advanced from $.16 to $.71, a growth rate of 16.1 percent.

■ The cornerstone of Federal's growth over the last two decades has been acquisitions. These acquisitions have either taken the form of standalone companies that maintain their own unique identities or add-on acquisitions of businesses or product lines that are usually fully integrated into an existing Federal Signal business. The common thread between standalone and add-on acquisitions is that they are all related in important ways to the company's existing businesses.

Federal Signal's acquisition strategy is focused on expansion of the company's current lines of business. In addition, they must exhibit these characteristics:

• Operate in attractive industries
• Offer leadership positions in niche markets
• Have good prospects for growth
• Would either benefit significantly from synergies with the company's existing strengths in marketing and manufacturing or would expand its markets geographically, especially internationally.

A critical part of the acquisition process is the valuation of each acquisition candidate. Federal's valuation methodology is based on its expectation of the future cash flows of the candidate and an estimate of its future business value.

■ Each of Federal Signal's operating units has defined its own specific critical success factors that are the most important variables for growth and profitability. These factors are targeted for improvement each year and are monitored appropriately. Other success factors cover areas such as customer satisfaction, speed of new product development, and supplier relationships. To be sure, the largest improvements most often occur in the company's newly acquired businesses. Even so, Federal Signal is making steady progress in long-held businesses as well.

■ All of the company's domestic sales are from businesses that have the leading position in their main markets. Certain of Federal Signal's businesses have a leading position in individual foreign countries, but it has many foreign markets where the company can expect to substantially improve share.

For example, substantial share improvements can be expected in markets such as Europe's emergency signaling markets; here Signal Products has the innovative products to break down competitive barriers.

■ Diversity of markets is a key reason that Federal Signal has consistently improved performance over the years.

Total assets: $836 million
Current ratio: 0.90
Common shares outstanding: 45 million
Return on 1998 shareholders' equity: 19.1%

	1998	1997	1996	1995	1994	1993	1992	1991
Revenues (millions)	1,003	925	896	816	677	565	518	467
Net income (millions)	59	59	62	52	47	40	34	31
Earnings per share	1.30	1.29	1.35	1.13	1.02	.86	.75	.68
Dividends per share	.71	.67	.58	.50	.42	.36	.31	.27
Price: high	27.5	27.5	28.3	25.9	21.4	21.0	17.6	15.2
low	20.0	19.9	20.9	19.6	17.0	15.7	12.4	9.3

FelCor Lodging Trust Inc.

545 E. John Carpenter Freeway, Suite 1300, Irving, TX 75062-3933 □ Investor contact: Molly E. Morrow (972) 444-4974 □ Dividend reinvestment plan not available □ Web site: www.felcor.com □ Listed: NYSE □ Ticker symbol: FCH □ S&P rating: Not rated □ Value Line financial strength rating: Not covered

FelCor Lodging Trust is one of the nation's largest real estate investment trusts (REITs). At the end of 1998, FelCor had 193 hotels, with nearly 50,000 rooms and suites. The company operates in thirty-four states and Canada.

FelCor is the owner of the largest number of Embassy Suites, Crowne Plaza, Holiday Inn, and independently owned Doubletree-branded hotels. Other leading hotel brands under the FelCor umbrella include Sheraton Suites, Sheraton, Promus, and Westin.

Shortcomings to Bear in Mind

- Management expects hotel rates and occupancies in 1999 to be similar to 1998, reflecting continued softness because of the competition from hotels currently under construction. The supply additions are primarily in the limited-service sector, but they will add new rooms to the market and will have some competitive impact. Since new hotel construction starts are decreasing, however, the company anticipates that if demand growth continues or accelerates, the company should begin to see a firming in rates, occupancy, and revenues.
- 1998 was a year of both progress and disappointment. Much like the farmer who harvests a phenomenal crop, only to sell it at depressed market prices, FelCor's growth and profit were not rewarded with an increased stock price in 1998 or 1999. In fact, the stock price decreased 35 percent from its high, primarily due to concerns about the REIT and lodging industries from the investment community. According to man-

agement, "Sadly, hard work and productivity are not always rewarded by the market, at least not in the short term."

Reasons to Buy

- The hotel industry is changing rapidly because of several factors:
  - Increasing demand for full-service products from business and leisure travelers.
  - Significant changes in the ownership structure through increased REIT participation in the industry.
  - A flattening in the supply of upscale, luxury, and full-service hotel rooms.
  - A proliferation of brands and products, primarily in the limited-service sector.

  FelCor's response to these changes has been to focus on matching a product brand with effective management. The company has continued to expand its brand/manager relationships beyond the Promus brands of Embassy Suites hotels, Doubletree Guest Suites hotels, and Doubletree hotels.
- In identifying acquisition candidates, some hotels have stable operating histories, and others have poor management or weak franchise affiliations. FelCor's acquisition team uses its extensive hotel industry experience to determine the most effective means of enhancing each hotel's ability to generate revenue. Underperforming properties frequently require extensive renovation, and FelCor has demonstrated its ability to invest the capital wisely to improve RevPAR (revenue per available room).

- Few of FelCor's hotel improvement programs are more dramatic than the renovation to the Embassy Suites hotel in New Orleans. Situated downtown near the city's convention center and famed French Quarter, the hotel's former owners failed to capitalize on the area's unique character. The trademark Embassy Suites atrium was a combination of drab brick and ventilation grates from the wall of the neighboring parking garage. FelCor's solution was to transform the atrium into a vibrant recreation of a Bourbon Street scene. This innovative approach maintained the structural requirements of the space while providing a festive atmosphere that appeals to the leisure traveler. With downtown access for business travelers, this hotel now offers a mix of convenience, fun, and Embassy Suites value that makes it one of FelCor's top performers.

- FelCor has taken a very conservative approach to financing, with common equity and preferred stock representing 80 percent of its total capitalization. This conservative approach has been rewarded with unsecured debt and lines of credit, which allows FelCor's management to respond quickly to acquisition opportunities without the extensive documentation requirements that usually accompany secured loans. In fact, FelCor was the first REIT to obtain an unsecured line of credit and is the only REIT to have registered unsecured debt securities outstanding—a testament to the company's lenders' confidence in management's ability to invest wisely.

- FelCor's dividends provide an attractive yield to shareholders. As a REIT, FelCor is required to pay dividends equal to at least 95 percent of its annual taxable income. FelCor's historical growth in net income has enabled FelCor's common stock dividends to grow from an annualized rate of $1.54 per share in 1994 (inception) to a total of $2.545 per share in 1998. Included in the 1998 dividend is a special one-time distribution of $0.345 per common share, representing accumulated earnings and profits from its July 1998 merger with Bristol Hotel Company.

- Analysts are encouraged by FelCor's prospects in 1999 and beyond. They believe the company's merger with Bristol Hotels marks FelCor's alliance with another "best of class" hotel operator in Bristol Hotels. They also think the merger will fuel the company's growth in 1999 and 2000, once the newly acquired Bristol properties complete their renovation and repositioning programs.

- FelCor is noted for the quality of its assets, achieved through strategic investment in the renovation, redeployment, and rebranding of its hotels and aggressive asset management. During 1998, FelCor and Bristol Hotel Company, prior to its merger with FelCor, spent an aggregate of about $180 million on the renovation, redeployment, and rebranding of forty hotels. In addition, continuing capital replacements and improvements of about $40 million enabled FelCor to maintain the high standards of its previously renovated hotels.

- Diversification of brands and locations is a hallmark of FelCor's portfolio. The company's hotels are located in thirty-four states and Canada, with concentrations in Florida, Texas, and California. The hotels are situated primarily in major markets near airports, suburban, or downtown areas.

- FelCor is committed to maintaining a sound financial structure. The company's conservative approach was evidenced by the following at the end of 1998:

- Consolidated debt equal to 38 percent of total assets
- Interest coverage of 3.8 times
- Borrowing capacity of $114 million under its existing credit facilities
- Fixed interest rate debt equal to 56 percent of total debt
- Debt of only $16 million maturing prior to December 31, 1999

■ FelCor's focus is on upscale and full-service hotels, which the company believes provides its shareholders with the best opportunity for revenue growth and accounted for 95 percent of total revenues in 1998. For the year, FelCor's comparable hotel portfolio achieved a 6.2 percent increase in revenue per available room (RevPAR), nearly double that of the industry average. This exceptional RevPAR performance reflects the quality of FelCor's assets.

■ Analysts believe that continued earnings growth in the lodging industry, combined with fears of an overbuilt hotel market, have created an opportunity for value- and income-oriented investors to buy shares of FelCor Lodging Trust at very attractive valuations. Further, they are convinced that the recent slowdown in new hotel construction, combined with improving prospects for the U.S. economy, should enhance the future of the lodging industry.

Total assets: $4,175 million
Common shares outstanding: 58 million

	1998	1997	1996	1995	1994	1993	1992
Revenues (millions)	340	177	101	26	6	*	
Net income (millions)	93	52	33	12	2		
Earnings per share	1.86	1.64	1.43	1.71	.64		
Dividends per share	2.20	2.05	1.92	1.84	.66		
Price: high	39.5	42.8	36.7	31.7	23.7		
low	17.4	33.5	27.1	18.5	17.0		

* FelCor did not go public until mid-1994.

AGGRESSIVE GROWTH

Fifth Third Bancorp

Fifth Third Center, Cincinnati, OH 45263 ❏ Investor contact: Neal E. Arnold (513) 579-4356 ❏ Dividend reinvestment program is available (800) 837-2755 ❏ Web site: www.53.com/investor ❏ Traded: Nasdaq ❏ Ticker symbol: FITB ❏ S&P rating: A+ ❏ Value Line financial strength rating: A

Fifth Third Bancorp—a $28.9-billion, regional bank holding company—provides commercial banking, retail banking, trust and investment, and third-party data-processing services to customers primarily located in the tri-state region of Ohio, Indiana, and Kentucky, through some 468 full-service branch offices. Fifth Third is among the top thirty largest bank holding companies in the country and among the fifteen largest in market capitalization.

Fifth Third Bank traces its origins to the Bank of the Ohio Valley, which opened its doors in Cincinnati in 1858. In 1871, the bank was purchased by the Third National Bank. With the turn of the century came the union of the Third National Bank and the Fifth National Bank, eventually to become known as Fifth Third Bank.

Fifth Third focuses on the consumer and small and medium-sized businesses within its marketplace and electronic processing businesses on a national basis. Since 1979, the company's return on assets has been at least 1.60 percent (on an originally reported basis), and equity usually is 10 percent of average assets. The business focus tends to be on developing the deposit and fee side of a relationship first. The company's financial condition is excellent, and the operation is the most efficient of the top fifty bank holding companies in the nation. Fifth Third Bancorp is an anomaly in the banking industry. Its financial strength is unquestioned, with a common equity ratio of 9.8 percent. Yet despite its significant equity position, the company has no problem sustaining its 17-plus percent return on common equity. This revolves around a number of factors:

• First and foremost, a superior use of technology has enabled the company to operate more efficiently, as exemplified by its exceptional overhead ratio. Its overhead ratio is the best of the top fifty banking companies in the country.

• Second, the company has an aggressive marketing (an incentive) culture that penetrates all employee levels.

• Third, the company is small enough to go into other geographical markets and initially underprice business until a critical mass has been developed. This tactic is currently being deployed successfully in Cleveland, Toledo, and Indianapolis.

• Fourth, the company has one of the best credit cultures in the business, with consistent low net charge-off ratios and a reserve-to-loan ratio that never varies outside of a range of 1.50–1.80 percent.

• Finally, a well-balanced approach to its four main business lines virtually ensures consistently superior financial results.

Investment Qualities

In 1998, Fifth Third completed twenty-five consecutive years of record increased earnings and growth. What's more, during the last twenty years, the bank's growth has been at a double-digit rate. To illustrate this growth, $1,000 invested in Fifth Third stock twenty years ago was worth $202,093 on December 31, 1998.

Over the past twenty-five years:

• FITB's earnings compounded at 18.7 percent per year.

• Fifth Third has beaten the S&P 500 13-fold.

• One share of stock has grown to fifty-one shares because of nine stock splits since 1983.

• The bank is number eight among all public companies for consistency of earnings and dividend growth.

• Revenue growth exceeded twice the industry average.

• Fifth Third has the lowest overhead ratio of the top fifty bank holding companies.

Shortcomings to Bear in Mind

■ There is no question that Fifth Third is a superior bank. However, it is not cheap; in fact, it is rarely cheap. Its P/E multiple is typically two or three points higher than most other regional banks. Although this bank is not too large to be a possible target of an acquisition, its high P/E ratio might be somewhat of a deterrent.

■ Shareholders have been so well-served by the price runup that it would be hard for a potential buyer to persuade them to trade their stock for that of another bank. Employees and directors own 7 percent to 8 percent of shares outstanding.

Reasons to Buy

■ In mid-1998, Fifth Third closed the two largest acquisitions in its history. CitFed Bancorp, Inc., a thrift with $3.1 billion in assets based in Dayton, Ohio and

State Savings Company, a $2.8 billion thrift headquartered in Columbus, Ohio. As a consequence, the bank's presence in Dayton and Columbus has doubled, and it has the number one market share along the I-75 corridor from Northern Kentucky to Cincinnati, through Dayton and up to Toledo.

- Through focused selling and follow through, the bank's Retail Banking operation delivered more loans, leases, and checking and savings accounts in 1998 than any time in its 140-year history. Fifth Third provided convenient access for 3 million customers at 468 Banking Centers and Bank Mart locations inside grocery stores, as well as 14 Quick Source locations, also in grocery stores and 1,264 Jeanie Automated Teller Machines throughout Ohio, Kentucky, Indiana, Florida, and Arizona.

    Jeanie, Fifth Third's proprietary ATM network, was welcomed at 41 new institutions and merchants in 1998. In 1999, over 500 Winn-Dixie stores throughout the Southeast will add Jeanie convenience. The network is now available in nineteen states and serves 5.2 million cardholders.

    The MPS (Midwest Payment Systems) Merchant Processing Group added 3,351 new credit, debit, and EBT retailers in 1998, including Amoco's 2,000 convenience marts; 2,700 Eckerd drugstores in the Southeast; and Carlton Cards, American Greetings's retail division, with over 450 stores in forty-one states. Sterling Jewelers, which operates a 780-store chain of twelve jewelry companies, including J. B. Robinson's and Kay Jewelers, also joined MPS in 1998, as did 125 Damon's Restaurants nationwide and the Boat/U.S. 45-store chain on the eastern seaboard.

- Mortgage lending was explosive during 1998. Through hard work, a favorable interest rate environment, and record

referrals from the its Banking Centers, the mortgage loan team originated $5.4 billion in residential mortgage loans in 1998. Mortgage banking fee income exceeded $72 million, a 57 percent increase over 1997. Fifth Third is now the number one home loan lender in Cincinnati, Butler County, Northern Kentucky, Dayton, and Toledo.

- During 1998, Fifth Third's Commercial Bankers continued to build and maintain solid business relationships, while new acquisitions broadened product offering and capabilities and added new markets. Revenue increased 29 percent with an overall commercial deposit growth of 17 percent, highlighted by a 13 percent rise in demand deposits. Finally, strong loan and lease originations all contributed to a 16 percent increase in net income for Commercial Banking in 1998.

- Fifth Third's Investment Advisors Group continued to build wealth for its growing base of personal, institutional, and not-for-profit clients by staying close to them, working to understand their needs, and offering the best investment and planning solutions available. These efforts resulted in a net income gain of 35 percent in 1998 and total revenue growth of 40 percent. Fifth Third now has $148.4 billion in assets under care, of which the Group manages $18.1 billion, making FITB one of the largest money managers in the Midwest.

- Fifth Third's data-processing subsidiary, Midwest Payment Systems, delivered a 34 percent increase in net income during 1998. Strong sales to new Electronic Funds Transfer (EFT) and Merchant Processing customers, along with successful expansion of service to existing EFT customers, fueled 27 percent revenue growth for Midwest Payment Systems. By combining technological expertise, innovation, and hard work, the Group developed EFT and Merchant Credit, Debit, and Electronic Benefits Transfer (EBT) data processing solutions for 51,000 retail locations and financial institutions throughout the world.

- The Fifth Third culture promotes a hard-work ethic, aggressive selling skills, and quality earnings growth. Fifth Third bankers take a disciplined approach to lending, and frugality is an ingrained part of the employees' mode of operation. Emphasis is on profitability and profitable growth. The consistency of the bank's operating philosophy and a well-integrated incentive program reinforce the Fifth Third culture. In addition to incentive programs, all employees participate in the bank's profit-sharing plan, which has contributed, on average, 13 percent to 14 percent of their total compensation.

Total assets: $28,518 million
Common shares outstanding: 267 million
Return on 1998 assets: 2.09%
Return on 1998 shareholders' equity: 19.5%

	1998	1997	1996	1995	1994	1993	1992	1991
Loans & Leases	17,779	13,438	12,514	11,513	10,286	8,811	7,475	5,807
Net income (millions)	476	401	335	288	244	196	164	138
Earnings per share	2.04	1.69	1.40	1.29	1.13	.97	.81	.69
Dividends per share	.71	.57	.49	.43	.36	.30	.27	.23
Price: high	74.1	55.7	33.0	22.7	16.3	17.5	16.0	13.5
low	47.5	27.0	19.3	13.9	13.3	14.7	11.8	5.8

INCOME

FPL Group, Inc.

700 Universe Boulevard, P. O. Box 14000, Juno Beach, FL 33408-0420 ◻ Investor contact: Scott W. Dudley, Jr. (561) 694-4697 ◻ Dividend reinvestment plan available (888) 218-4392 ◻ Web site: www.fplgroup.com ◻ Listed: NYSE ◻ Ticker symbol: FPL ◻ S&P rating: B+ ◻ Value Line financial strength rating: A

FPL Group, Inc. is the parent of Florida Power & Light Company, one of the largest investor-owned electric utilities in the nation. Other operations include FPL Energy, a leader in producing electricity from clean and renewable fuels. FPL Energy has projects in twelve states, South America, and the United Kingdom.

In December of 1998, FPL had 9,845 employees, serving 7 million people, nearly half of the state's 15 million population. Power is delivered from thirty-four major generating units, plus nonutility sources, over some 66,000 miles of electric lines.

FPL serves an area covering almost the entire eastern seaboard of Florida and the southern third of the state. Cities served by Florida Power & Light include St. Augustine, Daytona Beach, Melbourne, Stuart, West Palm Beach, Fort Lauderdale, Miami, Bradenton, Sarasota, Fort Myers, and Naples. The region continues to experience vibrant growth, driven by Florida's attractive climate, natural beauty, and exceptional quality of life.

Throughout the 1990s, FPL Group narrowed the focus of its other businesses to concentrate on the independent power industry outside Florida. It divested several businesses, including insurance, consulting, and real estate and strengthened its independent power operations. In 1998, the company completed the sale of its citrus subsidiary, Turner Foods. In 1999, the company reached an agreement to sell its cable TV interests. These transactions essentially complete FPL's program of divesting unrelated businesses that were acquired in the 1980s.

In 1998, FPL Group earned a record net income of $664 million. Earnings per share increased 7.8 percent. Investors in FPL Group realized a five-year total return of 96 percent, as the company's stock outperformed the Dow Jones Electric Utilities Index.

During the 1990s, FPL Group focused on reducing costs, improving quality and customer satisfaction, and investing outside of Florida in environmentally favored generation technologies. As a consequence, the company is one of the largest, cleanest, most efficient, and financially sound providers of electricity in the country.

FPL Group took an important step in early 1998 that supports its strategy, forming a new company called FPL Energy. This new organization brings together the domestic independent power business formerly operated under FPL Group's ESI Energy subsidiary and the overseas power projects previously part of FPL Group International. FPL Energy also includes gas-fired cogeneration facilities purchased at the beginning of 1998 in Massachusetts and New Jersey and generating plants being acquired in Maine.

In addition to combining all FPL Group's independent power resources, this new structure builds on the company's world-class skills in gas-fired combined-cycle generation and its leadership position in other clean-fuel technologies such as geothermal, solar, and wind.

Shortcomings to Bear in Mind

- Electric utilities are not recommended for growth-oriented investors. According to one analyst, "Earnings growth from the regulated utility will be limited to 2 percent. Thus, if FPL is to realize (after 2000) annual EPS growth of 6 or 7 percent, it will have to come from the growth of the non-regulated operations, primarily through FPL Energy's development and operation of low-cost generation facilities."

- Until recent years, electric utilities were not unduly concerned with competition. In particular, there was little concern over competition from other electric utilities. By their very nature, they were natural monopolies, with each utility serving exclusively its own area, such as a city or part of a state. In fact, since there was no competition, it was necessary to regulate electric companies. Without regulation, it was feared that power companies would charge whatever the traffic would bear. That era may be passing. There seems to be a groundswell in favor of letting large users buy their power from the company with the lowest rates, regardless of whether it is 10 miles away or 1,000 miles away.

  Of great importance is the nature of the company's customers. Most of them are residential or commercial. Only a tiny percentage of revenues come from industrial customers: 4 percent. By contrast, a typical utility might obtain one-fourth of its revenues from the industrial sector. It is these large customers who are the most likely to seek lower rates.

Reasons to Buy

- FPL added nearly 65,000 new accounts in 1998, a 1.8 percent increase over the prior year. Annualized customer growth from year-end 1993 through 1998 was

1.9 percent in FPL's service territory, compared to 1.3 percent nationally.

- FPL's continued aggressive cost-control efforts have resulted in a reduction of operating and maintenance costs per kilowatt-hour (kwh) for the eighth consecutive year—and 33 percent since 1990. Operation and maintenance costs in 1998 were 1.22 cents per kwh, compared to 1.82 cents in 1990.

- In March 1999, FPL announced a price reduction for its customers—on average a 6 percent per kilowatt-hour price decrease. For example, under FPL's new rates, a customer whose electric bill totals $100 will save about $5.60 a month.

  FPL residential electric rates are lower than any major investor-owned electric utility in Florida and 19 percent lower than the national industry average. While the price of electricity declined, the Consumer Price Index increased; it's up 56 percent since 1985. In that same span, FPL's rates edged down 15 percent.

- FPL uses a diverse energy mix to produce power. This diversity provides operating flexibility and helps lower fuel costs by taking advantage of energy price changes. This means lower bills for FPL customers.

- In 1998, FPL's fossil plant (those that burn coal or oil) availability (the percentage of the time they are in operation) reached an all-time high of 94 percent, well above the industry average. Similarly, nuclear plant availability was 93 percent, also above the industry norm.

- The Turkey Point plant south of Miami became the first nuclear facility in the country to receive three consecutive "superior" ratings from the Nuclear Regulatory Commission.

- FPL plans to add 3,600 megawatts of new generation by upgrading four, older oil-fired power plants with high-efficiency, gas-fired, combined-cycle generators. The upgrades will increase FPL's generating capacity by 20 percent within ten years. Meanwhile, the company will "repower" the Fort Myers plant first, nearly tripling its output by early 2002.

- FPL has a long history of offering cost-effective programs that meet the energy conservation-related needs of its customers. In the past two decades, the company successfully reduced demand for energy by more than 2,600 megawatts, meaning that FPL customers aren't paying for six additional power plants.

- FPL Energy's generation portfolio reflects a focus on clean energy: almost 80 percent is either gas-fired or derived from renewables such as wind, hydro, geothermal, and solar energy. FPL Energy is the nation's largest generator of wind energy.

  FPL Energy owns more than 3,000 net megawatts (mw) of generating capacity currently operating. About 97 percent of this capacity is located in the United States. When other projects currently planned or under construction are completed, the company will have close to 4,400 megawatts of capacity.

- FPL Energy has already added significantly to its generation fleet in 1999. In January and February, plans were announced for the development of 1,250 megawatts of natural gas-fired power plants: a 1,000-megawatt plant in Texas to begin operation in mid-2000 and a 248-megawatt plant in Washington to be producing power by mid-2001.

- FPL Group continues to be favorably perceived by the business and investment communities. In *Fortune* magazine's recent 1998 survey of America's most admired companies, FPL Group was the highest-rated utility in the nation.

- The population of Florida has grown dramatically, doubling since 1970, to 15

million residents today. FPL has been part of Florida's growth for more than seventy years, expanding its generation system to keep pace with the substantial increases in customers and average power usage.

Total assets: $12,029 million
Current ratio: 0.77
Common shares outstanding: 173 million
Return on 1998 shareholders' equity: 13.5%

	1998	1997	1996	1995	1994	1993	1992	1991
Revenues (millions)	6,661	6,369	6,037	5,593	5,423	5,316	5,193	5,249
Net income (millions)	664	636	603	553	557	556	511	473
Earnings per share	3.85	3.57	3.33	3.16	2.91	2.75	2.65	2.65
Dividends per share	2.00	1.92	1.84	1.76	1.88	2.47	2.43	2.39
Price: high	72.6	60.0	48.1	46.5	39.1	41.0	38.4	37.3
low	56.1	42.6	41.5	34.1	27.4	35.5	32.0	28.1

CONSERVATIVE GROWTH

Gannett Company, Inc.

1100 Wilson Blvd., Arlington, VA 22234 ▫ Investor contact: Gracia Martore (703)284-6000 ▫ Web site: www.gannett.com ▫ Dividend reinvestment plan available (703) 284-6960 ▫ Listed: NYSE ▫ Ticker symbol: GCI ▫ S&P rating: A ▫ Value Line financial strength rating: A++

Gannett is a diversified news and information company that publishes newspapers and operates broadcasting stations. The company also has a stake in marketing, commercial printing, a newswire service, data services, and news programming. Gannett has operations in forty-five states, the District of Columbia, and Guam.

In terms of circulation, Gannett is the largest domestic newspaper group, with seventy-five daily newspapers, including *USA Today*, a variety of nondaily publications, and *USA Weekend*, a weekly newspaper magazine. Total average paid daily circulation of Gannett's daily newspapers is about 6.7 million.

Gannett owns and operates twenty-one television stations in major markets.

Highlights of 1998

For the seventh year in a row, Gannett achieved record revenues and profits in 1998. Buoyed by strong advertising demand across the board, operating revenues increased 8 percent, to $5.1 billion. Each of the company's three major businesses reported higher earnings for the year. As a result, Gannett's earnings advanced 15 percent, to $816 million. The company's operating cash flow in 1998 totaled $1.75 billion, a new company record. In addition, Gannett was able to reduce its debt by $444 million and make capital investments of $244 million.

The company's newspaper division expanded its presence in New Jersey, acquiring two dailies, for a total of seven in the Garden State. The *Daily Record* in Morristown and the *Ocean County*

Observer in Toms River joined the Gannett chain in July.

USA Today had another solid year in 1998, as advertising revenues gained 12 percent, on top of strong gains for the past few years. Circulation of the nation's newspaper expanded to a daily average of 2,271,767. Among new contents in 1998: a Friday travel section in Life; a weekly health/behavior feature to complement a weekly science page; and more coverage of entrepreneurs and the global economy in the Money section. In 1999, *USA Today* completed a press expansion project, which helps meet increased demand for color from the paper's advertisers.

USATODAY.com is the most-visited newspaper Web site. It turned profitable in the fall of 1998. Gannett aims to look for ways to increase e-commerce opportunities and expand content of USATODAY.com in the years ahead.

Shortcomings to Bear in Mind

- During 1998, there was a steady stream of selling by insiders, such as officers and board members. Apparently, they were aware of negative developments that might depress the shares. During the year, GCI retreated from the yearly high of $75.

- Retail advertising revenues increased only 4 percent in 1998, hurt by soft results from the company's major advertisers. The chief causes of the lackluster results were store closings, bank mergers, and the decision by some customers to move their advertising from inside-newspaper pages to preprinted inserts. As expected, however, preprint revenues and volume rose. More important, business from medium and smaller retail advertisers expanded for the fifth consecutive year, with revenues up nearly 7 percent. This group continues

to be a top priority in the company's strategy of diversifying its account base to reduce reliance on the major advertisers. Gannett newspapers are focusing on increasing ad frequency for advertisers by packaging several insertions of the same ad, at an attractive price, over a given period of time. As a result, ad count was up dramatically in 1998.

- Circulation gains from the newspaper segment have been modest. In 1998, daily net circulation grew about 1 percent, a turnaround after a slight decline the prior year. The better results of 1998 were attributed to an increase in daily home-delivery volume. On a more positive note, circulation revenue finished up 2 percent for the year.

Reasons to Buy

- Consistent growth of all advertising categories in 1998 led to another year of record revenues and operating profits for Gannett's newspaper division. Overall, pro forma ad revenue increased 6 percent in 1998, for a two-year gain of more than 13 percent. Classified, moreover, remained especially strong for the eighth consecutive year.

- In June of 1999, Gannett bought the British regional newspaper group, Newsquest PLC, for about $1.5 billion in cash.

    Newsquest's publications include such major regional newspapers as the *Northern Echo*, based in Darlington, north England, the *Oxford Mail*, the *Evening Argus* in Brighton, south England, and *Westmoreland Gazette*, in the Lake District in north England. Newsquest had a pretax profit of $204.3 million in 1998 on sales of $483.5 million.

- In late July of 1999, Gannett elected to get out of cable television, selling all of its properties to Cox Communications of Atlanta for 42.7 billion in cash. Gannett President Douglas H. McCorkindale said the company didn't make a strategic decision to get out of the cable business but decided to sell because "someone just offered us a lot of money." The price of cable franchises has been rising rapidly recently, and Gannett was able to get one of the highest per-household prices ever paid—$4,500 to $5,100, depending on how the value is calculated—for its 525,000 subscribers. McCorkindale said the sale would have a "positive" effect on Gannett's earnings. Gannett had owned the cable TV operations for only three and one-half years.

- *USA Weekend* remains the country's fastest-growing newspaper magazine. A total of forty-three newspapers added the magazine in 1998. *USA Weekend* began 1999 with a circulation of 21.2 million in 541 newspapers. In addition to *USA Weekend*, Gannett has a stake in about 200 other nondaily publications. Many are aimed at specific niche markets, such as *Nursing Spectrum* and Army Times Publishing Company's military and defense publications. The Army Times military newspapers recently were redesigned, offering readers several new features and a more attractive look.

- As the Internet continues to be a growing part of people's lives, more Gannett newspapers are jumping into the World Wide Web. What's more, the online pioneers continue to enhance content and add new products, including those stemming from Gannett's participation in Classified Ventures and CareerPath.com. As leading information providers for their communities, the company's newspapers are aware that fresh information is essential to success online. *Florida Today's* Space Online (www.spaceonline.com), for instance, covers space shuttle launches, literally as they blast off. Reporters with laptop computers file stories from the beach at Cape Canaveral, supplying live news online within moments of a launch.

Some fifty-eight of the newspaper division's publications and operations have Web sites, offering more than 200 products; more are on the way. This expansion has fueled revenue growth. Total online revenues, including advertising and Internet service provider (ISP) fees collected by the company's newspapers, shot up 84 percent in 1998.

- Gannett's television division posted a 6 percent revenue increase in 1998, despite some slackness in the advertising environment. The company's sales staffs successfully navigated a winding road that began with early boosts from the Winter Olympics, the Super Bowl and increased tobacco spending, but later had to cope with softness from the auto sector, tied to the General Motors strike. The movement of NFL programming from the company's twelve NBC stations to its six CBS affiliates hurt results in the third and fourth quarters of 1998. On the other hand, political spending exceeded expectations. In 1999, Gannett's priority is to continue building new business in a year that brings no special events such as the Olympics or elections.

- Gannett has more than doubled its roster of television stations in the last five years. They now reach 16.7 percent of domestic viewers. WLTX-TV at Columbia, South Carolina, became the company's twenty-first station in mid-1998.

Local news is the foundation of Gannett's TV stations. Many are leaders in their markets. Three—KSDK-TV in St. Louis, KUSA-TV in Denver, and KARE-TV in Minneapolis-St. Paul—consistently rank among the nation's five, highest-rated Nielsen stations for late evening news among adults age 25–54. This is the key demographic segment for advertisers. In most of the company's markets, the Gannett station ranks number one or number two in morning and late news with this same group of adults.

Total assets: $6,979 million
Current ratio: 1.15
Common shares outstanding: 282 million
Return on 1998 shareholders' equity: 21.9%

	1998	1997	1996	1995	1994	1993	1992	1991
Revenues (millions)	5,121	4,730	4,421	4,007	3,824	3,642	3,469	3,382
Net income (millions)	816	713	531	477	465	398	346	302
Earnings per share	2.86	2.50	1.89	1.71	1.62	1.36	1.20	1.00
Dividends per share	.78	.74	.71	.68	.67	.64	.63	.62
Price: high	75.1	61.8	39.4	32.4	29.5	29.1	27.0	23.5
low	47.6	35.7	29.5	24.8	23.1	23.4	20.6	17.6

CONSERVATIVE GROWTH

General Electric Company

3135 Easton Turnpike, Fairfield, CT 06431 ▫ Investor contact: Mark L. Vachon (203) 373-2816 ▫ Direct dividend reinvestment plan available (800) 786-2543 ▫ Web site: www.ge.com ▫ Ticker symbol: GE ▫ S&P rating: A+ ▫ Value Line financial strength rating: A++

General Electric is one of the world's largest corporations, with 1998 revenues of $100.5 billion. Although GE can trace its origins back to Thomas Edison, who invented the light bulb in 1879, the company was actually founded in 1892.

The company's broad diversification is clearly evident if you examine its components. Operations are divided into two groups: product, service, and media businesses and GE Capital Services (GECS).

Product, service, and media includes eleven businesses: aircraft engines, appliances, lighting, medical systems, NBC, plastics, power systems, electrical distribution and control, information services, motors and industrial systems, and transportation systems.

GECS operates twenty-seven financial businesses clustered in equipment management, specialty insurance, consumer services, specialized financing, and mid-market financing.

Highlights of 1998
• Revenues rose to $100.5 billion, up 11 percent.
• Earnings increased 13 percent to $9.3 billion.
• Earnings per share grew 14 percent to $2.80.
• Operating margin rose to a record 16.7 percent, up a full point from the record 15.7 percent of 1997.
• Working capital turns rose sharply, to 9.2, up from the 1997 record of 7.4.

- This performance generated $10 billion in free cash flow, which, in combination with an AAA debt rating, allowed GE to invest $21 billion in 108 acquisitions in support of two of the three companywide initiatives: globalization and services.

- Record cash flow allowed General Electric to raise dividends by 17 percent and to further increase shareowner value by repurchasing an additional $3.6 billion in GE stock.

- In 1998, GE was named *Fortune* magazine's "Most Admired Company in America" and "World's Most Respected Company" by a worldwide business audience in the *Financial Times*.

- The total return on a share of GE stock was 41 percent in 1998. GE has averaged a 24 percent per-year total return to shareowners for the past eighteen years.

Shortcomings to Bear in Mind

■ With CEO John R. Welch set to retire in two years, there are few more tantalizing questions in corporate America than who will replace the legendary executive. Neither Welch nor the company will discuss succession, and no obvious heir-apparent has surfaced.

That doesn't mean the race to succeed Jack Welch is not well underway. He has a stable of seasoned lieutenants vying for the job. And over the past two years Welch has given new tasks to a younger crop of possible heirs and fast-trackers in their forties. His two-pronged strategy: test the front-runners while also developing GE's farm team.

It's a delicate balancing act. If Welch anoints an heir, he could face a brain drain of GE's most seasoned players. With the race still open, however, headhunters say it has been remarkably difficult to lure would-be CEOs away from the giant conglomerate.

■ The loss of *Seinfeld* in 1998 was a blow to NBC. But it was merely another indication that all is not well for network TV. With more on the line than ever before, as costs of programming mount and advertisers are increasingly courted by the expanding number of cable stations, the networks, by their own reckoning, failed to add even a single new show in 1998 that falls into a category known as "appointment viewing." These are shows that viewers make a point of watching every week.

What's more, the networks' share of the television audience has fallen steadily for years, but 1998's performance was particularly stark, with network viewer totals down about 9 percent from the prior season. Not coincidentally, the ratings for cable channels were up about 10 percent. Unfortunately, a disturbing amount of the network falloff took place at NBC, the network that has been providing most of the big hits.

Reasons to Buy

■ Hoping to get a foot in the door of Internet retailing, NBC bought a stake in ValueVision International Inc., the number three cable home-shopping network. In the spring of 1999, NBC, along with the private equity arm of GE Capital, bought 19.9 percent of ValueVision for about $56 million. The company has an option to increase its ownership to 39.9 percent. GE's hope is that by using the marketing muscle of it broadcast network, along with cable holdings like CNBC and MSNBC, it can boost ValueVision's presence on cable and on the Web, generating a new source of revenue. However, ValueVision's subscriber base is less than one-third of QVC, the home-shopping market leader.

- Jack Welch has developed a defect-reduction program called Six Sigma. Six Sigma contributes mightily to GE's earning growth. Think of sigma as a mark on a bell curve that measures standard deviation. Most companies have between 35,000 and 50,000 defects per million operations, or about 3 sigma. For GE, a defect could be anything from the misbilling of an NBC advertiser to faulty wiring in locomotives. Four years ago, engineers determined that the company was averaging 35,000 defects per million operations—or about 3.5 sigma. (The higher the sigma, the fewer the errors.) That was a better-than-average showing but not good enough for Welch's restless mind. He's now maniacal about hitting his goal of reducing defects to the point where errors would be almost nonexistent; 3.4 defects per million, or 6 sigma.

- Six Sigma project work consists of five basic activities: Defining, Measuring, Analyzing, Improving, and then Controlling processes. In the words of management, "These projects usually focus on improving our customers' productivity and reducing their capital outlays, while increasing the quality, speed and efficiency of our operations."

- GE is strong financially, with 98 percent of its capitalization made up of shareholders' equity. Coverage of bond interest, moreover, is a hefty twenty-six times.

- Despite its huge size, the company continues to demonstrate growth. In the 1988–1998 period, earnings per share climbed from $.94 to $2.80, a compound annual growth rate of 11.5 percent. (The company, moreover, has had twenty-two consecutive annual earnings increases.) In the same ten-year span, dividends per share advanced from $.37 a share to $1.25, a growth rate of 13.0 percent.

- Scientists from GE Plastics and Corporate R&D have developed a new process to improve quality and reduce cycle times in manufacturing Lexan polycarbonate for compact disks.

- NBC has moved aggressively to expand into cable television. The network has stakes in seventeen cable networks, including CNBC, Court TV, and the History Channel. NBC has also moved swiftly in recent years to introduce new entertainment and new channels in Europe, Asia, and Latin America.

- GE Aircraft Engines delivered a stellar financial performance in 1998, achieving strong double-digit gains in revenues and earnings, while expanding market share. Consistent with General Electric's industry leadership during the 1990s, GE Aircraft Engines and CFM International (the company's 50/50 joint venture with Snecma of France), again won the majority of the world's large commercial engine orders. Important 1998 airline orders included American Airlines, Continental Airlines, Delta Air Lines, Iberia Airlines, Korean Airlines, Lufthansa German Airlines, Sabena Belgian Airlines, Southwest Airlines, and VARIG.

- GE Medical Systems posted a record year of double-digit revenue and earnings growth despite the effects of continued global price erosion and consolidation among health care providers. With the introduction of the Light-Speed scanner system, GE Medical System created a new paradigm in medical imaging capability. Developed at a cost of more than $60 million to serve the $1.7 billion global CT market, LightSpeed is the world's first scanner that enables doctors to capture multiple images of a patient's anatomy simultaneously and at a speed that is six times faster than traditional single-slice scanners. Customers are ordering Light-Speed systems at a rate faster than any of GE Medical Systems's previous product introductions.

- The NBC television network finished the 1997–1998 TV season as America's most-watched network for the third year in a row, placing first in the prized adult 18–49 demographic category by a 34 percent margin. For the third consecutive season, NBC had five or more of the nation's top-rated prime-time shows. CNBC cemented its position as the world leader in business television when it signed an alliance with Dow Jones in early 1998. By providing access to the editorial resources of the *Wall Street Journal* and other Dow Jones properties, the alliance strengthens CNBC in Europe, Asia, and the United States. Finally, advertising revenue increased 36 percent, and U.S. distribution rose 7 percent, to 68 million subscribers.

- In 1998, GE acquired the business infrastructure and sales force of Toho Mutual Life, and—because of the high respect the Japanese have for Thomas Edison—the company renamed it GE Edison Life and quickly became a force in the Japanese insurance industry.

General Electric also acquired the consumer loan business of Japan's Lake Corporation, with $6.2 billion in assets, and added it to the company's already rapidly growing consumer finance business there. These acquisitions, along with several other ventures, partnerships, and buyouts by GE's industrial businesses, together with the growth of the company's existing businesses in Japan, should enable GE to more than double its over $300 million in 1998 Japanese earnings within three years.

- The company's Japanese initiatives are part of an intense multiyear focus on globalization that produced $43 billion in revenues in 1998 and a growth rate for GE outside the United States that has been double that of the company's domestic growth rate for ten years.

Total assets: $355,935 million
Current ratio: 0.68
Common shares outstanding: 3,268 million
Return on 1998 shareholders' equity: 25.5%

	1998	1997	1996	1995	1994	1993	1992	1991
Revenues (millions)	100,469	54,515	46,119	43,013	60,109	55,701	53,051	51,293
Net income (millions)	9,296	82,033	7,280	6,573	5,915	4,184	4,137	3,943
Earnings per share	2.80	2.50	2.20	1.95	1.73	1.52	1.26	1.28
Dividends per share	1.25	1.04	.95	.85	.75	.65	.58	.52
Price: high	103.9	76.6	53.1	36.6	27.4	26.8	21.9	19.5
low	69.0	47.9	34.8	24.9	22.5	20.2	18.2	13.3

General Motors Corporation

3044 West Grand Boulevard, Detroit, MI 48202-3091 □ **Investor contact: None given (313) 556-2044** □ **Dividend reinvestment plan available (800) 331-9922** □ **Web site: www.gm.com** □ **Listed: NYSE** □ **Ticker symbol: GM** □ **S&P rating: B** □ **Value Line financial strength rating: B++**

General Motors Corporation, founded in 1908, is the world's largest vehicle manufacturer. GM designs, manufactures, and markets cars, trucks, automotive systems, heavy-duty transmissions, and locomotives worldwide. Other substantial business interests include Hughes Electronics Corporation and General Motors Acceptance Corporation. GM cars and trucks are sold in close to 190 countries, and the company has manufacturing, assembly, or component operations in more than 50 countries.

General Motors' Operations

General Motors North American Operation manufactures vehicles for the following nameplates: Chevrolet, Pontiac, Oldsmobile, Buick, Cadillac, GMC, and Saturn.

General Motors International Operations meets the demands of customers outside North America, with vehicles designed and manufactured for the following nameplates: Opel, Vauxhall, Holden, Isuzu, and Saab.

General Motors Acceptance Corporation provides a broad range of financial services, including consumer vehicle financing, full-service leasing and fleet leasing, dealer financing, car and truck extended-service contracts, residential and commercial mortgage services, and vehicle and homeowner's insurance. GMAC's business spans thirty-three markets around the world.

Hughes Electronics Corporation manufactures advanced technology electronic systems, products and services for the telecommunications and space, automotive electronics, and aerospace and defense industries on a global scale.

General Motors Locomotive Group manufactures diesel-electric locomotives, medium-speed diesel engines, locomotive components, locomotive services, and light-armored vehicles to a global customer base.

Allison Transmission Division is the world's largest producer of heavy-duty automatic transmissions for commercial-duty trucks and buses, off-highway equipment, and military vehicles.

Shortcomings to Bear in Mind

- In 1999, Ford Motor made its latest incursion into the big sport utility vehicle market by introducing the biggest SUV yet, the Excursion. General Motors, which has dominated the market for decades with its hulking Chevrolet and GMC Suburban, was not willing to back down without a fight. In March of 1999, the company displayed a prototype of its redesigned 2000 Suburban at the New York International Auto Show. At the same time, GM also displayed its redesigned 2000 GMC Yukon, a slightly smaller SUV whose Chevy twin is called the Tahoe.

  The 2.5-ton, nine-seat Suburban is a critical product for General Motors—one of its most profitable and enduring. It was introduced in 1935, predating even the Volkswagen Beetle and making it the longest-running automobile nameplate ever.

  According to one analyst, "The Suburban market is one of the few segments where GM can really claim leadership at the moment. But that leadership position is being threatened by a very aggressive Ford innovation."

- In 1999, United Auto Workers President Stephen Yokich said he strongly opposes GM's plan to slash vehicle production costs by shifting work from assembly plant to suppliers's factories, under a strategy known as modular assembly. The union leader also denounced GM's handling of the spinoff of its Delphi Automotive Systems Corp. unit. Mr. Yokich's sharp criticism of General Motors indicates that the nation's leading auto maker still has a long way to go to heal the rift with the UAW that sparked 1998's seven-and-a-half-week strike and a series of walkouts prior to that. Mr. Yokich agrees, "People say Ford has a better relationship with the UAW than GM, and Chrysler has a better relationship than GM, and they're right." The UAW represents about 220,000 workers at General Motors, 101,000 at Ford and 75,000 at Daimler-Chrysler AG.

Reasons to Buy

- One auto columnist recently wrote: "Whoever says GM is not radically different than it was just five years ago simply isn't paying attention."
- In May of 1999, General Motors pushed Delphi, its auto parts maker, out of the nest and into its shareholders' portfolios. For GM, the spinoff ends a ninety-year tradition of vertical integration—a strategy of making most of the parts as well as the final product.

  The divestiture is a milestone in the auto maker's continuing struggle to transform itself from a complacent and noncompetitive company into a streamlined, more agile organization. Instead of relying on its in-house auto-parts maker, GM wants to farm out the business to leaner, cheaper parts makers worldwide, as other auto makers have done for years.

- Shanghai GM, General Motors' joint venture with a Chinese automaker, announced in the spring of 1999 that it would begin regular production of Buick sedans. The $1.5-billion venture with Shanghai Automotive Industry Corporation is the biggest foreign joint venture in China. The company said it will produce about 20,000 Buicks in 1999 and gradually increase annual production to 100,000.

- A quick look at three other financial measurements demonstrates the company is changing the way it does business. Five years ago, GM's pension funds were underfunded by $12 billion; the company had no net liquidity; in that year alone, General Motors posted a loss of $2.6 billion. Today, the company's pension funds are essentially fully funded.

- Competing on a global basis is a priority that is driving the largest international production capacity expansion in the company's history. General Motors has five new manufacturing facilities either under development or up and running in Argentina, China, Brazil, Poland, and Thailand. These plants are the cornerstone of GM's expansion into new markets.

- Michael J. Burns, the president of GM Europe, says that his operations will profit from a number of favorable developments: full availability in 1999 of the high-volume Astra compact, which was rolling out slowly during most of 1998; from the introduction of the Zafira, a small minivan that GM says opens a new vehicle category in Europe; from higher sales of Saab luxury cars; and from a modest increase in imports of Chevrolets and Cadillacs from the United States.

- As shock waves from collapsing Asian economies started to subside in 1998, General Motors saw a rare opportunity. Vast unused manufacturing capacity in Asia meant it could save big bucks on heavy metal, stamping dies, machinery, and rolls of steel. So, in March of that year, GM dispatched eleven executives and senior engineers, armed with clipboards and detailed questionnaires. They converged on such countries as Thailand, Taiwan, South Korea, and Japan. Their mission: to evaluate twelve toolmakers in twelve days, as potential sources of stamping dies, the superhard steel molds used to shape sheet metal into fenders, hoods, and other parts of a vehicle's body. In the end, the team awarded contracts to companies in Korea and Japan. GM people say the deals were valued at a combined $50 million and represented a 25 percent savings from the company's previous die purchase. In similar fashion, GM has been taking advantage of the new age of deflation in order to lock in the bargains available on virtually everything that goes into making its cars and trucks.

- In 1999, General Motors spun off Delphi Automotive Systems Corporation. The CEO of Delphi, J. T. Battenberg III, has his work cut out for him, in his effort to slim down this $28-billion auto parts giant. GM dumped this albatross because it is saddled with low productivity, high labor costs, as well as strife with the United Auto Workers.

- In 1999, General Motors agreed to buy more than $1 billion of recycled aluminum from IMCO Recycling Inc. over the next thirteen years. The pact is the latest in a series of long-term supply deals that GM has put together in an effort to reduce costs and eliminate wide price fluctuations for the metals it uses to make cars and trucks.

John Stiles, a company executive, said the agreement allows GM designers and engineers to plan for increased aluminum use in future vehicles without fear that a sudden change in market prices would make the cost prohibitive. GM's current models use an average of 271 pounds of aluminum for each vehicle, up 29 percent from 1988. Because aluminum is lighter than steel, it offers a variety of fuel-economy and emissions benefits.

- GM Locomotive Group (GMLG) designs, manufactures, and markets diesel-electric locomotives, medium-speed diesel engines, locomotive components, light armored vehicles, and turret systems to a global customer base. During 1998, GMLG increased locomotive assembly capacity by integrating associate manufacturing partners in four countries. This enabled the company to increase unit production by 50 percent and to expand revenue per employee by 15 percent. In 1998, GMLG completed the restructure of its LaGrange, Illinois, operations, which cut costs substantially by reducing floor space by 65 percent and machine tools by 75 percent.

- Allison Transmission Division leads the world in the design, manufacture, and sales of medium- and heavy-duty automatic transmissions for commercial-duty trucks, buses, off-highway equipment, and military vehicles.

Headquartered in Indianapolis, the division has three international regional offices, situated in The Netherlands, Japan, and Brazil. Through its more than 1,500 distributors and dealers, Allison has a presence in more than eighty countries. It provides service and technical support to some 250 original equipment manufacturers, and 47,000 fleet owners and operators, as well as more than 14,000 end users. In 1999,

Allison launched the new 1000/2000 Series transmission, which could significantly increase the division's annual production volume.

■ General Motors finance unit, GMAC, in its largest acquisition so far, agreed to buy a commercial finance unit of Bank of New York for $1.8 billion in June of 1999. The cash agreement for BNY Financial, which is involved in asset-based lending and factoring operations, continues General Motors Acceptance Corporation's search for growth areas outside its profitable but mature core business in automotive lending. GMAC already is the largest commercial lender in the United States. While the bulk of its business remains auto finance, the company has been expanding in recent years into mortgage lending, insurance, and commercial finance, in search of faster growth rates. BNY Financial will also give GMAC a bigger presence in the United Kingdom, which the company will use as a platform for expanding into Europe, according to William Muir, chief financial officer of GMAC.

Total assets: $257,389 million
Current ratio: 1.45
Common shares outstanding: 654 million
Return on 1998 shareholders' equity: 18%

	1998	1997	1996	1995	1994	1993	1992	1991
Revenues (millions)	161,315	153,782	164,069	168,829	154,951	138,220	132,429	123,056
Net income (millions)	2,956	6,698	4,668	6,932	5,659	2,466	def	def
Earnings per share	5.21	8.70	5.72	7.28	6.20	2.13	def	def
Dividends per share	2.00	2.00	1.60	1.10	.80	.80	1.40	1.60
Price: high	76.7	72.4	59.4	53.1	65.4	57.1	44.4	44.4
low	47.1	52.3	45.8	37.4	36.1	32.1	28.8	26.8

GROWTH AND INCOME

Genuine Parts Company

2999 Circle 75 Parkway, Atlanta, GA 30339 ◻ Investor contact: Jerry W. Nix (404) 953-1700 ◻ Dividend reinvestment plan available (800) 568-3476 ◻ Web site: www.genpt.com ◻ Ticker symbol: GPC ◻ S&P rating: A+ ◻ Value Line financial strength rating: A++

Genuine Parts Company, founded in 1928, is a service organization engaged in the distribution of a wide range of products. Here are the segments that make up the company:

The Automotive Parts Group

The Automotive Parts Group, the largest division of Genuine Parts Company, distributes automotive replacement parts, accessory items, and service items. This Group operates 62 NAPA distribution centers, 3 Balkamp distribution centers, 6 Rayloc facilities, and 5 Johnson Industries facilities and serves about 5,600 NAPA Auto Parts stores throughout the United States. This Group also includes UAP Inc., with 16 distribution centers in Canada that serve 652 corporate and associate wholesalers. In addition, this Group has a joint venture with Auto Todo, with 18 distribution centers and 18 company-owned stores in Mexico.

The Automotive Parts Group operates six remanufacturing plants that distribute products under the name Rayloc.

Also in this Group is Balkamp, Inc., a majority-owned subsidiary that purchases packages and distributes service and supply items under the trade name Balkamp to NAPA distribution centers.

The NAPA program strives to improve market penetration, reduce costs, and focus on specific customer needs. The great success of the NAPA program has enabled Genuine Parts to become the leading independent distributor of automotive replacement parts and expand in sales and earnings at a faster rate than the industry.

The Industrial Parts Group

The Industrial Parts Group distributes replacement parts and related supplies. This Group stocks over 1.6 million items, including industrial bearings, belts, hoses, mechanical and fluid power transmission equipment, and material-handling components. The Industrial Group distributes from 446 operations located across the United States and Canada. This Group serves more than 165,000 customers in all types of industries throughout North America.

The Office Products Group

The Office Products Group distributes a broad line of office products, ranging from furniture and desk accessories to business electronics and computer supplies. This Group, operating under the name of S. P. Richards Company, distributes over 20,000 items, from forty-eight distribution centers. These distribution centers serve over 6,000 office supply dealers. The items it distributes include office furniture, filing supplies, computer supplies and accessories, office machines, desk accessories, paper products, and janitorial and sanitation supplies. Since its beginnings as a modest retailer in 1848, S. P. Richards has evolved into one of the largest office products wholesalers in the nation.

The Lesker division distributes an extensive office furniture selection to ten states throughout the Mid-Atlantic and Midwest regions from four distribution centers.

Electrical/Electronic Materials Group

EIS Supplies and manufactures a full range of critical products for electronic and electrical apparatus. Distribution of more than 100,000 items is made from forty-six distribution centers nationwide. From insulation and conductive materials, to assembly tools, test equipment, and customized parts, EIS serves as an important single source to original equipment manufacturers, repair shops, printed circuit board manufacturers, and the electronic assembly market.

Highlights of 1998

• The company achieved record sales for the forty-ninth consecutive year, and profits improved for the thirty-eighth consecutive year.

• Cash dividends paid to shareholders in 1998 were increased for the forty-second consecutive year. The company has paid a dividend every year since going public in 1948 and has increased the payout every year since 1955.

• A new business segment was added in mid-1998, with the acquisition of EIS Inc., an electrical and electronic materials provider to the original equipment market (OEM) and aftermarket customers throughout the United States. Annual revenues are about $500 million.

• The Motion Industries Industrial Group moved ahead with its strategy of growth through both acquisitions and the opening of new branches. Another three were added with the acquisition of Hub Supply, Inc. located in Wichita, Kansas; Blytheville Bearing and Supply in Blytheville, Arkansas; and Cascade Bearing and Hydraulics in Yakima and

Pasco, Washington. More recently, in early 1999, this Group completed the acquisition of Lou's Bearing in eastern Canada and a joint venture with RIMSA, a partner in Mexico.

• At the end of 1998, Genuine Parts completed the acquisition of UAP Inc., Canada's leading automotive parts distributor, with locations covering markets throughout the country.

• In early 1999, the company completed the acquisition of Johnson Industries, an independent distributor of ACDelco Motorcraft and other automotive supplies.

• In 1998, S. P. Richards Company, GPC's distributor of office products, continued its expansion by acquiring Norwestra Sales, Inc., a privately held company located in Vancouver, British Columbia, Canada. This is S. P. Richards's first operation in Canada and is expected to be the foundation for future growth and a national presence in the Canadian market.

Shortcomings to Bear in Mind

■ Do-it-yourselfers and professional customers alike have more options than ever when they choose where to buy parts. All of the company's wholesale customers, repair shops, service stations, body shops, and national accounts are also facing more challenges in pleasing their customers. Nor it is merely the do-it-yourself customers who are increasing their demands for quality products and service at a competitive price. The automotive aftermarket is becoming increasingly crowded with retailers who know how to please the retail trade and are now seeking to acquire wholesale customers as well. NAPA, for its part, has designed programs to improve its penetration of each of these markets with the intent to continue to gain market share each year.

■ Although Genuine Parts has an impressive record of earnings growth, the pace of this grow is lackluster. In the 1988–1998 period, earnings per share advanced from $1.04 to $1.98, a compound annual growth rate of only 6.7 percent. That's why I have designated the stock for "growth and income." On the other hand, I believe this growth rate could accelerate and be most rewarding to patient investors.

Reasons to Buy

■ Genuine Parts is exceptionally strong and is rated A++ for financial strength by Value Line, as well as A+ by the Standard & Poor's Stock Guide. It's easy to see why. The company has very little debt, and its ratio of current assets to current liabilities is a solid 3.0 times. Most companies, by contrast, have current ratios below 2.0. Management contends that future expansion will be financed with internally generated funds.

■ The automotive aftermarket has experienced an upturn beginning in 1993 that is expected to continue. There are several factors contributing to this growth:

• The average age of cars and trucks is increasing. Currently, the average age of the vehicle fleet is over eight years; it is expected to surpass nine years by the year 2000.

• Vehicle usage is up. Miles driven by personal and commercial drivers are increasing at a 3 percent annual pace.

• The vehicle population is climbing steadily at an average annual rate of 2.6 percent since 1970.

• There appears to be significant pent-up demand in discretionary repairs to add potential sales growth. It is estimated that unperformed maintenance approaches $50 million at retail levels.

• Government regulations will be one of the key drivers in the future growth of the automotive after-market. The most widely known initiative has been the IM240 testing programs mandated by the Clean Air Act of 1990. More stringent emissions programs have always benefited the repair business and created additional parts sales. It is believed that government agencies will continue to tighten emissions regulations in the future and will provide solid support for aftermarket growth.

■ The Industrial Parts Group supplies plant surveys, inventory management programs, national supply agreements, and technical instruction.

The implementation of programs such as Extra Value Service Process (XVS), Electronic Data Interchange (EDI), and Continuous Service Improvement (CSI) helps to secure the extended quality service that customers expect.

With the advent of an electronic catalog system (ECAT), Motion Industries leads the industry in electronic data retrieval. The electronic catalog provides branches and customers with immediate access to manufacturers' technical and parts information. The Group's state-of-the-art computer system, representing the first VSAT satellite system in the industry, gives the Industrial Parts Group the edge on technological advancement.

■ While consolidation continues throughout all aspects of the office products industry, dealers have increased their efforts to reduce investment and expense by stocking fewer products. S. P. Richards is well positioned to be the source for those products. Moreover, the company has concentrated its merchandising efforts on bringing new products to market quickly and capitalizing on new growth-market opportunities. Its product offering has been broadened with expansion into the fast growing computer and imaging supply area, janitorial and breakroom supplies, and furniture. Further, the company's private label offerings include additional products distributed under the following brand names: Sparco, Nature Saver, and CompuCessory.

Total assets: $3,600 million
Current ratio: 3.04
Common shares outstanding: 179 million
Return on 1998 shareholders' equity: 19.1%

	1998	1997	1996	1995	1994	1993	1992	1991
Revenues (millions)	6,614	6,005	5,720	5,262	4,858	4,384	4,017	3,764
Net income (millions)	356	342	330	309	289	258	237	224
Earnings per share	1.98	1.91	1.82	1.68	1.55	1.39	1.28	1.21
Dividends per share	1.00	.96	.88	.84	.77	.70	.67	.64
Price: high	38.3	35.8	31.7	28.0	26.3	26.0	23.2	21.9
low	28.3	28.7	26.7	23.7	22.4	21.9	19.3	15.5

The Gillette Company

Prudential Tower Building, Boston, MA 02199-8004 ❑ Investor contact: Danielle M. Frizzi (617)421-7175 ❑ Listed: NYSE ❑ Direct dividend reinvestment plan available: (800) 643-6989 ❑ Web site: www.Gillette.com ❑ Ticker symbol: G ❑ S&P rating: A ❑ Value Line Financial Strength A+

Founded in 1901, The Gillette Company is the world leader in male grooming, a category that includes blades, razors, and shaving preparations. Gillette also holds the number one position worldwide in selected female grooming products, such as wet shaving products and hair epilation devices.

The company is the world's top seller of writing instruments and correction products, toothbrushes, and oral-care appliances. In addition, Gillette is the world leader in alkaline batteries.

Gillette manufacturing operations are conducted at sixty-two facilities in 25 countries. Products are distributed through wholesalers, retailers, and agents in over 200 countries and territories.

Shortcomings to Bear in Mind

- In 1998, the company's results were dampened by sales growth that was held well below the company's usual performance, due to a number of significant factors:
  - The strength of the U.S. dollar relative to foreign currencies reduced the sales growth rate by three percentage points. The growth rate was lowered an additional two points by the divestiture of Jafra Cosmetics in April of 1998.
  - In the first half of 1998, in North America and Western Europe, Gillette intentionally shipped twin blade systems at a rate below consumer take-away to reduce trade inventory levels before the launch of the Mach3 system. Following its introduction, the company's trade

partners in the United States continued to purchase the older systems, including Sensor and SensorExcel, at a level well below retail consumer take-away.
  - Economic developments in Asia and Russia negatively affected the company's business. For example, the recession in Japan significantly affected sales and profit for Braun. In Russia, the banking crisis halted the flow of Gillette products to the trade for several months, disrupting Gillette's previously fast-growing business.

Reasons to Buy

- For the ninety-third consecutive year, Gillette paid cash dividends on its common stock. Dividends declared rose 19 percent, to $.51, up from $.43 in 1997. This marks the twenty-first successive annual increase in dividends per share, reflecting strong business fundamentals. Since 1993, the dividend rate has more than doubled, climbing at a 19 percent annual rate.
- In 1998, 47 percent of Gillette sales came from products launched in the past five years. The company's goal is to maintain this new product ratio at well above 40 percent of sales annually, a goal Gillette has achieved in each of the last five years. During 1998, Gillette launched more than twenty new products, maintaining the accelerated pace of recent years.
- Following a $750-million investment in research, development, and capital, the long-anticipated Mach3 shaving system

was launched at mid-1998 in North America, followed by a rollout into Western Europe that began in September. According to management, "The Mach3 system has achieved unprecedented sales and market share results in every market where it is available. In the first six months, sales of Mach3 blades and razors in the United States were more than triple those of the Sensor system in the first six months of its launch."

In every major European market, Mach3 razors gained the leading position, and blade shares matched or exceeded the outstanding domestic results. In only six months, worldwide sales of the Mach3 razor surpassed the cumulative sales of the Sensor razor in its first two years.

- In 1998, Duracell introduced a new line of alkaline batteries in AA and AAA sizes, formulated for use in high-technology devices such as digital cameras, palm-sized computers, remote-control toys, and cellular phones.

Called the Duracell Ultra, the new battery has been in development for four years and will last up to 50 percent longer than ordinary alkaline batteries. The new line is priced about 20 percent higher than Duracell's traditional line. It represents the first significant new product from the battery maker since it was acquired by Gillette at the end of 1996.

The development of the Duracell Ultra is the latest salvo in a traditionally vitriolic marketing battle between Duracell and Eveready Battery Co., a unit of Ralston Purina Co., which sells its products under the Energizer brand. In 1997, Energizer introduced its own reformulated AA and AAA batteries.

Duracell is breaking with tradition by selling the new line alongside its regular alkaline batteries, representing a rare attempt to segment the alkaline-battery market into distinct categories. Energizer, by contrast, simply replaced its old AA and AAA battery with the reformulated version.

According to Brian Barnett, director of battery-industry studies at Arthur D. Little Inc., "Anytime you introduce another brand, there's a real risk of diluting the message to the customer. If you have a high-powered brand that's premium-priced, you're telling the customer your other brand isn't as good."

For its part, Duracell executives decided that its new Ultra deserved a novel strategy since high-tech customers are in a fast-growing sector. The company says that about 17 percent of AA and AAA alkaline batteries are sold for high-tech devices, and it expects the high-tech segment to mushroom to 28 percent within five years. AA and AAA sizes represent about 75 percent of all battery sales.

The Ultra represents classic Gillette strategy. Gillette is known for its ability to squeeze greater profits out of ordinary items, such as razor blades, by upgrading consumers to better-performing, premium-priced brands.

- As expected, Duracell has improved on the company's sales and profit performance, reconfirming that Duracell was an exceptional addition to Gillette. Since the merger, the Duracell operating profit margin has increased more than three points, reflecting merger synergies, an upgraded product line, and more efficient manufacturing.

- After a long obsession with men's faces, Gillette is paying more attention to women's legs. Following years of stubbly advertising support for female shaving products, Gillette raised ad spending in 1998 by 58 percent, almost all of it concentrated in the peak summer season.

Part of its drive is an ambitious new campaign with the slogan "Gillette for Women: Are You Ready?" As a counterpart to its "Gillette: The Best a Man Can Get" slogan, the new theme aims to unify the company's growing array of women's shaving offerings and inject some glamour into what most American women consider a routine grooming chore.

Women's products, it turns out, have generated much of the growth in Gillette's core shaving business in recent years. From almost a standing start, six years ago, Gillette's shaving line for women has expanded into a $400-million global business, growing nearly 20 percent a year.

The big shift came in 1992, when Gillette introduced Sensor for Women, a version of its hit Sensor razor, but with a flat, wafer-shaped handle crafted by a female industrial designer to give women better control while shaving. Shunning stereotypical pink, its colors were white and green, and the product was an instant success. Gillette followed with SensorExcel for Women, as well as a high-end disposable razor called Agility and a line of shaving creams and aftershave products sold under the Satin Care brand.

■ Building on the record results of 1997, Oral-B again in 1998 strengthened its position as the clear leader of the global toothbrush market. Sales moved slightly higher in 1998, while profits climbed sharply from the prior year. Oral-B has long been recognized for its broad range of superior oral care products. Chief among these are Oral-B toothbrushes, the brand used by more dentists and consumers than any other in the United States and many major international markets.

The most recent addition to Oral-B's arrays of powerful brands, the new CrossAction premium toothbrush, was introduced in the United States at year-end 1998, following three years of development. Featuring uniquely engineered CrissCross bristles angled in opposing directions for a more effective brush stroke, this innovative toothbrush is clinically proven to offer a new standard in plaque removal. Trade and consumer response has been excellent.

Superior new products developed in partnership with dental professionals, a broader geographic presence, and momentum from its 1998 performance offer Oral-B excellent prospects for the future.

Total assets: $11,902 million
Current ratio: 1.56
Return on 1998 equity: 31.4%
Common shares outstanding: 1,105 million

	1998	1997	1996	1995	1994	1993	1992	1991
Revenues (millions)	10,056	10,062	9,698	6,795	6,070	5,411	5,163	4,684
Net income (millions)	1,428	1,427	1,232	824	698	591	513	427
Earnings per share	1.27	1.28	1.11	.93	.79	.67	.58	.49
Dividends per share	.51	.43	.36	.30	.25	.21	.18	.16
Price: high	62.7	53.2	38.9	27.7	19.1	15.9	15.3	14.0
low	35.3	36.0	24.1	17.7	14.4	11.8	11.0	7.0

W. W. Grainger, Inc.

100 Grainger Parkway, Lake Forest, IL 60045-5201 ◻ **Investor contact: Robert D. Pappano (847) 535-1000** ◻ **Dividend reinvestment plan not available** ◻ **Web site: www.grainger.com** ◻ **Listed: NYSE** ◻ **Ticker symbol: GWW** ◻ **S&P rating: A** ◻ **Value Line financial strength rating: A++**

With 1998 sales of $4.3 billion, W. W. Grainger is the North American leader in the distribution of maintenance, repair, and operating (MRO) supplies and related information. The company does business in the commercial, industrial, contractor, and institutional markets. W. W. Grainger regards itself as a service business.

The company does not engage in basic or substantive product research and development activities. New items are added regularly to its product line on the basis of market information as well as on recommendations of its employees, customers, and suppliers, coupled with other factors.

The company distributes motors, HVAC (heating, ventilation, and air conditioning) equipment, lighting, hand and power tools, pumps, and electrical equipment, along with many other items.

In another sphere, W. W. Grainger provides support functions and coordination and Benefits, Data Systems and Data Processing, Employee Development, Finance, Government Regulations, Human Resources, Industrial Relations, Insurance and Risk Management, Internal Audit, Legal, Planning, Real Estate and Construction services, Security and Safety, Taxes, and Treasury Services.

Grainger sells primarily to contractors, service shops, industrial and commercial maintenance departments, manufacturers and hotels, and health care and educational facilities.

The company purchases from more than 1,000 suppliers for its General Catalog, most of whom are manufacturers, in support of Grainger Integrated Supply Operations (GISCO).

Grainger offers its line of products at competitive prices through a network of stores in the United States and Mexico (349 at December 31, 1998).

Shortcomings to Bear in Mind

■ Acklands-Grainger, Canada's largest broad-line MRO distributor, is important to the company's future. However, the unfavorable Canadian exchange rate was a drag on 1998 earnings. A weakness in the Canadian lumber, mining, and oil markets also hurt Acklands-Grainger in 1998.

■ Overall company profitability has been hurt by the transition to multiple business units. (In 1998, the company broke itself into several separate business units based on diverse market needs. Each is focused on providing customized, lowest-cost MRO solutions to a unique market segment.) Businesses in transition include Grainger Integrated Supply (the company's outsourcing business) and Grainger Custom Solutions (its large-customer commodity management unit). On the other hand, these segments should make strong contributions, once their transitions are complete.

Reasons to Buy

■ The Internet is an important growth engine for Grainger Industrial Supply. Access to Grainger 24 hours a day, 7 days a week through Grainger.com is a major convenience for many customers and a competitive advantage for this business. Enhancements in 1999 to Grainger's Internet offering included more products, better search capabilities, and the ability to accept credit cards.

- In the spring of 1999, the company announced that it was extending its commitment to digital commerce; it formed an alliance with SAP AG, the world's leading provider of enterprise business solutions. Grainger is integrating its online catalog into the SAP Business-to-Business Procurement solution (SAP B2B), providing direct access to Grainger products and product information through one standardized Internet procurement solution. This access allows users seamless electronic commerce transactions between both supplier and buyer Internet sites for reduced overall purchasing costs and improved efficiency. The alliance with SAP represents greatly expanded customer access to Grainger.com, which has been recognized as one of the top ten business-to-business Web site two years in a row by *Advertising Age*.

- During 1998, Grainger reinvested $167 million in its business through capital expenditures. These included new information systems, expansion of its branch network, and continued construction of the company's new Lake Forest, Illinois headquarters facility. By centralizing Chicago area employees, the move to this new facility in 1999 will enhance productivity, communication, and efficiency.

- At the end of 1998, the company's branch network totaled 532 branches, including 352 in the United States, Puerto Rico, and Mexico; and an additional 180 in Canada through Acklands-Grainger Inc.

- Grainger Industrial Supply is the domestic leader in branch-based MRO distribution. Its network of 349 branches and Grainger.com Web site offer an unmatched combination of product assortment, rapid availability, and ease of service. In 1998, the business experienced strong financial performance despite the launch of several future growth initiatives and infrastructure projects.

- Grainger's industry expertise enables it to build market share by enhancing product availability in unique markets. For example, at Boston's "Big Dig" construction project, the business introduced a mobile branch, complete with wireless computer links to Grainger's order entry systems. In Manhattan, the company replaced large branches with a number of small branches in convenient locations. Frequent replenishment of these small units maintains Grainger's commitment to availability while leveraging its investment in inventory.

- In 1998 and 1999, *Fortune* magazine selected Grainger as one of the 100 "Best Companies to Work for in America."

- Grainger offers to customers services that reduce the hidden costs of MRO (maintenance, repair, and operating) supplies. In many cases, these costs can exceed the cost of the product itself. They include the customer's procurement process, the costs associated with possessing and maintaining inventory, the interface with multiple suppliers, and the use of MRO supplies.

- Small businesses represent over 1.1 million of Grainger's customers. Strong relationships with these customers are best achieved using direct marketing methods. Many customers cite a preference for this form of contact. With relatively simple operations and little MRO inventory, small businesses can reduce their total cost of MRO supplies with easy-to-use product information and selection assistance, one-stop service, and inventory nearby. The company's industry-leading General Catalog, broad product line, and network of local stores are a good solution for these customers.

- Large businesses represent about 210,000 of Grainger's customers but constitute over two-thirds of the revenues. The Grainger direct sales force is the key relationship builder with this customer group. Customers served by the direct sales force range from medium-sized manufacturing plants to Fortune 500 companies. The common thread for these customers is their desire to reduce the total cost of MRO supplies.

Larger businesses generally have more sophisticated purchasing processes, more MRO suppliers, and more inventory. While product price is always important, the keys to reducing total MRO costs are improving the purchasing process, reducing the interface with multiple suppliers, and applying better inventory management methods. The company's network of leading manufacturers, product availability, order processing systems, and customer inventory management tools form a powerful solution.

- The company increased its 1999 dividend for the twenty-seventh consecutive year. Over the past ten years, the dividend climbed from $.22 to $.59, a compound annual growth rate of 10.4 percent. In the same 1988–1998 span, earnings per share advanced from $.98 to $2.44, a growth rate of 9.6 percent. What's more, there were no dips along the way.

- Sales in Mexico (through Grainger, S.A. de C.V.) increased significantly in 1998. Grainger's broad assortment of products, rapid availability, and simple ordering process is filling a need that has been largely unmet in Mexico. The efforts of sixty-six sales representatives, along with direct marketing, public relations, and advertising, placed Grainger number one among MRO suppliers in customer awareness. In Monterrey, companies rated Grainger as their first choice for miscellaneous MRO purchases. In order to spur and accommodate growth, Grainger doubled its branch capacity in Monterrey to 80,000 square feet. At year-end 1998, over 60,000 products were available to customers, an increase of 54 percent over the prior year.

- Lab Safety Supply is the leading direct marketer of safety products and other industrial supplies to American business. Located in Janesville, Wisconsin, Lab Safety Supply reaches its customers through its award-winning General Catalog, targeted catalogs, and other marketing material throughout the year.

Customers select Lab Safety Supply for its extensive product depth (over 400,000 products in the 1998 General Catalog), its superior technical knowledge, and its industry-leading service. It is a primary supplier for many small- and medium-sized companies and a critical back-up supplier for many larger companies.

Total assets: $2,104 million
Current ratio: 1.76
Common shares outstanding: 93 million
Return on 1998 shareholders' equity: 18.5%

	1998	1997	1996	1995	1994	1993	1992	1991
Revenues (millions)	4,341	4,137	3,537	3,277	3,023	2,628	2,364	2,077
Net income (millions)	238	232	209	187	178	149	137	128
Earnings per share	2.44	2.27	2.02	1.82	1.74	1.44	1.29	1.19
Dividends per share	.59	.53	.49	.45	.39	.35	.33	.31
Price: high	54.7	49.9	40.8	33.8	34.6	33.4	30.5	27.8
low	36.4	35.3	31.3	27.8	25.8	25.8	19.5	15.1

CONSERVATIVE GROWTH

Hannaford Brothers Company

P. O. Box 1000, Portland, ME 04104 ◻ Investor contact: Charles H. Crockett (207) 885-2349 ◻ Dividend reinvestment plan available (212) 509-4000 ◻ Web site: www.hannaford.com ◻ Listed: NYSE ◻ Ticker symbol: HRD ◻ S&P rating: A ◻ Value Line financial strength rating: B+

Hannaford Brothers is a multiregional food retailer. At the end of 1998, Hannaford operated 150 supermarkets. Of these, 46 were located in Maine, 21 in New Hampshire, 8 in Vermont, 6 in Massachusetts, 23 in New York, 27 in North Carolina, 1 in South Carolina, and 18 in Virginia. There were pharmacies in 108 of these stores, and 90 had branch banking facilities.

The stores in the Northeast operate under the names Shop'n Save and Hannaford. The supermarkets in the Southeast use the name Hannaford. Having the company's name on its stores and private brand products helps forge a strong identity in the marketplace and leads to clearer communication with customers. During 1997, Hannaford moved closer to this goal by converting the remainder of the Shop'n Save stores in the Albany, New York, area to the Hannaford name. In addition, the company put the Hannaford name on the Shop'n Save stores operating under the Wilson's name in the Southeast.

The company operates four distribution centers to supply its stores. Two are in Maine, one in New York, and the fourth in North Carolina. These distribution centers also provide merchandise to nineteen independent supermarkets.

Hannaford operates Hannaford Trucking Company, a wholly-owned subsidiary; it is licensed as an irregular route common carrier with forty-eight-state authority. Hannaford Trucking often contracts with third parties to haul various commodities; this reduces to a minimum the number of miles that these vehicles return empty after making their deliveries to company supermarkets.

Hannaford is a relatively small grocery chain, with 1998 revenues of $3.3 billion. By contrast, Albertson's had 1998 revenues of $16 billion; Great Atlantic & Pacific had about $10 billion; Winn-Dixie had over $13 billion; and Kroger (the largest) had over $28 billion.

Shortcomings to Bear in Mind

- Some analysts believe that the outlook for retail supermarket chains remains neutral. They point out that consumer spending for food is expected to continue to show only modest gains. They concede, however, that "operators are developing new merchandising techniques and controlling expenses to improve overall profitability."

- There is always the specter of competition. On the other hand, the consolidation in the warehouse club industry has slowed the building of clubs. Although supermarkets have not yet been declared the victors in their struggle to maintain market share against warehouse clubs and discounters, they are increasingly holding their own. But competition will remain vigorous.

What's more, there is a new threat on the horizon—supercenters that sell food and general merchandise are being rolled out by Wal-Mart and Kmart. Over time, these powerhouse retailers could pose the next threat to traditional grocery stores.

Reasons to Buy

- In today's busy world, many people want quick, easy meals that require little or no home preparation. Hannaford is satisfying this need by offering more prepared foods in its meal centers. In the company's newest stores, moreover, the meal centers offer and assemble complete meals, in addition to providing a selection of foods that are separately prepared and packaged.

  This selection also includes fresh vegetables that are cut and packaged in serving-size containers. Hannaford's meal centers also provide a range of special services, including menu planning, nutrition consulting, party planning, special order assistance, and demonstrations of food preparation techniques.

- Hannaford operates high-quality stores that are brightly lit and clean and have high ceilings. The company's stores typically range in size from 40,000 to 55,000 square feet, each featuring wider aisles and broader selection than non-chain, local competitors. Hannaford stores are generally younger than competitor stores, particularly in the Southeast, where its average supermarket is less than three years old.

- The company has strong market share in New England, where it has been operating for a half century. Nearly two-thirds of Hannaford's Northeast sales come from major markets where it is ranked in the top three in market share.

- Hannaford is one of the few supermarket chains that combine high-quality stores and product offerings with a strategy of emphasizing everyday low prices. As a result, analysts believe that Hannaford has created a loyal customer base, as compared with competitors who do not use this strategy but prefer to lower prices temporarily on particular items, rather than across the board.

- Hannaford's stores are often situated in smaller markets, such as Bangor, Maine, and Manchester, Vermont. There are barriers to entry in these markets, based on their low population densities and slower growing economies.

- The company's new, full-line Southeast distribution center is situated in Butner, North Carolina, about fifteen miles north of Raleigh, near major transportation routes that can get product to Hannaford's stores with a minimum of traffic.

  The main distribution building contains 431,000 square feet, and there are 112 truck doors to handle both incoming and outgoing product. In addition to the main distribution building, the center also includes a truck-maintenance facility and a product-recovery center.

  The center was built in less than one year at a cost of $43 million and commenced shipping product to the company's stores in November of 1996.

  The Butner distribution center supplies Hannaford stores in the Southeast with dry groceries, frozen foods, and perishables. The building was specifically designed for newer, more efficient forms of materials handling. The freezer, for instance, is situated near the grocery area to more easily combine loads for shipping. A mezzanine level turns overhead storage space into ergonomically enhanced selecting slots.

- Richmond, Virginia is a good example of how Hannaford builds market presence. From a single site in 1994, the company presence in Richmond has grown to eight stores, with a ninth under construction. This expansion resulted from new construction, as well as from store acquisitions that the company remodeled or relocated to facilities meeting Hannaford's standards for layout and customer service. This process will be repeated in the company's other Southeast markets, mainly through new construction.

■ Hannaford has demonstrated consistent growth in earnings per share. In the 1988–1998 period, earnings per share climbed from $.77 to $2.21, a compound annual growth rate of 11.1 percent. In the same span, dividends expanded from $.16 to $.60, a growth rate of 14.1 percent. Equally important, the company pays out a low percentage of its earnings, giving it more capital to invest in its future. In 1998, its $.60 dividend represented only 27 percent of earnings.

■ The company is making use of information technology to improve operating results. One way is with Hannaford's Strategic Information Process (SIP), a leading-edge, computer-based, decision support system that the company developed in-house. The system is based on sales to customers, rather than on inventory coming into the store ("front door" versus "back door" sales). It focuses on front-door contribution rather than back-door mix. The information gathered by SIP will be integrated through Hannaford's operations, so that it can easily see how an action in one part of the business affects all

others. In this way, management can evaluate its impact on profits. One of the key features of SIP is a common inventory measurement tool called ACIS, or Average Cost Inventory System. The SIP program, including ACIS, has been implemented in the company's 101 stores in the Northeast. During 1998, it was rolled out company-wide. As part of the SIP program, Hannaford is able to analyze its check-out scanning data to learn more about its customers' shopping preferences. This knowledge helps management make marketing decisions.

■ The company has been experimenting with home delivery, which it calls Hannaford's Home Runs. However, the start-up has taken longer and been more costly than anticipated. Since it is a new venture, there are no models to follow or computer systems available to operate the business. Through Hannaford's own research and experience, the company is learning about customer needs and the logistical system required to deliver groceries through this channel. Management's goal is to capitalize on the potential of this new venture and to evaluate whether it can provide a healthy return for Hannaford shareholders.

Total assets: $1,285 million
Current ratio: 1.11
Common shares outstanding: 42 million
Return on 1998 shareholders' equity: 14.7%

	1998	1997	1996	1995	1994	1993	1992	1991
Revenues (millions)	3,324	3,226	2,958	2,568	2,292	2,055	2,066	2,008
Net income (millions)	95	84	75	70	62	55	49	43
Earnings per share	2.21	1.99	1.78	1.67	1.50	1.33	1.21	1.08
Dividends per share	.60	.54	.48	.42	.38	.34	.30	.26
Price: high	53.0	44.1	34.3	29.0	26.6	25.0	28.5	22.8
low	38.8	30.5	23.0	23.9	19.8	20.0	16.0	16.4

Harley-Davidson, Inc.

3700 West Juneau Avenue, P. O. Box 653, Milwaukee, WI 53201 □ Listed: NYSE □ Investor contact: Rod Copes (414) 343-8002 □ Dividend reinvestment plan available: (877) HDS-TOCK □ Web site: www.harley-davidson.com □ Ticker symbol: HDI □ S&P rating: B+ □ Value Line financial strength rating: B++

Harley-Davidson, the only major American-based motorcycle manufacturer, is a leading supplier of premium quality, heavyweight motorcycles to the global market. The company benefits from having one of the world's most recognized and respected brand names. The company primarily manufactures and sells twenty-four models of heavyweight (engine displacement 651 cc or more) touring and custom motorcycles, along with a broad range of related products. These include motorcycle parts, accessories, riding apparel, and collectibles.

The company's legendary, high-powered motorcycles include the Electra Glide, the Sportster, and the Fat Boy. Many of Harley-Davidson's biking brethren are members of the Harley Owners Group, cruising along with 430,000 devotees. The company sells twenty-four models of touring and custom heavyweight motorcycles, with suggested domestic retail prices ranging from about $5,200 to $19,300. Distribution is handled by more than 1,000 dealerships, including some 600 in the United States. The touring segment of the heavyweight market includes motorcycles equipped for long-distance riding. They include fairings, windshields, and saddlebags. Custom motorcycles are differentiated through the use of trim and accessories.

Harley-Davidson competes with such companies as Honda, Suzuki, Kawasaki, and Yamaha. Despite continuous production increases, domestic consumers often have to wait to purchase a new Harley-Davidson bike at list price.

Studies conducted by Harley-Davidson indicate that a typical U.S. customer is a male in his mid-forties. He has a household income of about $68,000. He uses the bike for recreational purposes and is an experienced motorcycle rider.

In February of 1998, the company acquired Buell Motorcycle Company, a business in which HDI held a 49 percent interest since 1993. Buell makes sport and sport-touring motorcycles.

Eaglemark Financial Services, Inc. provides wholesale and retail financing, insurance, and credit card programs to Harley-Davidson dealers and customers and similar programs for other leisure products manufacturers.

Shortcomings to Bear in Mind

- In the 1988–1998 period, earnings per share climbed from $.21 to $1.38, a compound annual growth rate of 20.72 percent. To be sure, this is an exceptional growth rate. As you might expect, the price of the stock reflects this exemplary record and is rarely cheap.

- New competition is entering Harley-Davidson's core market. A host of new motorcycles are ready to hit the streets, seeking some of Harley's dominant market share. For instance, Excelsior-Henderson, Polaris, BMW, and others will be targeting the heavyweight motorcycle market. Analysts are concerned that some HDI customers may not have the patience to wait for a Harley and may be tempted to buy a bike made by one of these competitors.

Reasons to Buy

- In 1998, Harley-Davidson achieved two major milestones in its capacity expansion plan. The company became fully operational in the manufacture of engines and transmissions at its new 479,200-square-foot facility near Milwaukee. It also began Sportster motorcycle production in the new 330,000-square-foot assembly plant in Kansas City, Missouri.
- In 1998, HDI's revenues grew by more than 17 percent, to over $2 billion. What's more, earnings climbed even faster, at a rate exceeding 22 percent, to $213.5 million. It was the company's thirteenth consecutive year of record revenues and earnings. Moreover, all of the Harley-Davidson product lines grew at double-digit rates. Buell Motorcycle Company's revenues spurted ahead by better than 32 percent. Eaglemark Financial Service, which has achieved record growth in each of the its six years of existence, posted more than a 60 percent jump in earnings.
- In 1998, Harley-Davidson produced and sold record numbers of motorcycles: 150,818 Harley-Davidson models and 6,334 Buell motorcycles, which were increases of 14 percent and 44 percent, respectively.
- Harley-Davidson has delivered twelve consecutive years of record revenue and earnings.
- The company has a strong balance sheet that is virtually debt-free outside of its financial services company.
- Between 1995 and 1998, HDI invested over $650 million in capital expenditures, all of which was internally generated. It was invested in production capacity, infrastructure, and new product development.
- The worldwide heavyweight motorcycle market is experiencing growth. It's up 60 percent since 1991.

- Demand continues to be greater than supply for Harley-Davidson motorcycles in the United States, even as production has quadrupled since 1986.
- Harley-Davidson is in the midst of the most aggressive new product development plan in its history. The introduction of an all new engine, the Twin Cam 88 for the 1999 model year, was just the beginning. The creation of the 1450 cc Twin Cam 88 set new standards for research, development, and testing. It was designed with the best computer-aided technology in the world, then run more than 2.5 million test miles before its introduction. The result is one of the most durable, reliable, and powerful engines in Harley history.
- Overseas, Harley-Davidson motorcycles are popular in a host of countries:
  - In 1998, Harley-Davidson motorcycle registrations in the Netherlands were up 5.4 percent, while the overall heavyweight market was down 10.1 percent. Introducing new dealers, relocating established dealerships, and delivering more customer-focused marketing has set the ground work for sustainable growth in the Dutch market.
  - Harley-Davidson is expanding its business in Brazil by capitalizing on a surge of enthusiastic support for the company's motorcycles. For years, owning a Harley-Davidson motorcycle has been attainable only by the wealthy in Brazil because of steep import tariffs. In 1999, Harley-Davidson established a limited assembly operation in the Brazilian city of Manaus. This has reduced tariffs and makes the company's vehicles affordable to more Brazilian consumers.
  - Harley-Davidson motorcycle registrations were up 23.2 percent in Spain in 1998. To keep the momentum

going, the company's local distributor, Onex S. A., is adding new dealers to its network and relocating some existing dealerships to meet the rapid changes taking place in the lifestyle and prosperity of Spanish customers.

- In 1998, Harley-Davidson's share of the heavyweight segment in the United Kingdom expanded by 49 percent. This is the company's highest share of the heavyweight custom segment in any European market. The XL883 Sportster is the number one selling heavyweight custom bike in the United Kingdom. Buell also experienced tremendous growth in that country in 1998, with registrations up 88 percent.

- Today, there is a vibrant heavyweight motorcycles market in Japan, due in part to a relaxation of motorcycle license requirements. Both Harley-Davidson and Buell have found a place in this very competitive environment. The Harley-Davidson brand is well established and supported by more than 14,000 members in the Harley Owners Group.

- Harley-Davidson has always found innovative ways to reach its customers. Adapting to Sweden's challenging geography, the company's independent distributor, Harley-Davidson Sweden, has launched creative marketing initiatives. These include a floating store and theme restaurant that bring the Harley-Davidson experience to the customer. This traveling dealership features an extensive offering of motorcycles, parts, and accessories, as well as general merchandise.

- After more than eighty years of bringing Harley-Davidson to motorcycle enthusiasts to Australia, the company's share is nearly 40 percent of the heavyweight motorcycle market, and the brand is recognized by 95 percent of the population. This gives HDI a tremendous advantage over its competitors when it introduces new products.

Total assets: $1,920 million
Current ratio: 1.80
Return on 1998 equity: 21.1%
Common shares outstanding: 153 million

	1998	1997	1996	1995	1994	1993	1992	1991
Revenues (millions)	1,763	1,531	1,350	1,542	1,217	1,105	940	865
Net income (millions)	214	174	143	111	104	78	54	37
Earnings per share	1.38	1.13	.95	.74	.69	.49	.38	.26
Dividends per share	.16	.14	.11	.09	.07	.03	nil	nil
Price: high	47.5	31.3	24.8	15.1	14.9	9.7	7.6	4.3
low	24.9	16.7	13.2	11.0	10.8	7.9	5.4	2.2

Hewlett-Packard Company

3000 Hanover Street, Palo Alto, CA 94304 ◻ Investor contact: Steve Pavlovich (415) 857-2387 ◻ Dividend reinvestment plan available (800) 286-5977 ◻ Web site: www.hp.com/go/financials ◻ Fiscal year's end October 31 ◻ Ticker symbol: HWP ◻ S&P rating: A ◻ Value Line financial strength rating: A++

Hewlett-Packard designs, manufactures, and services electronic products and systems for measurement, computing, and communication.

Hewlett-Packard's products are used by people in industry, business, engineering, science, medicine, and education.

The company's more than 23,000 products include computers and peripheral products, electronic test and measurement instruments and systems, networking products, medical electronic equipment, instruments and systems for chemical analysis, handheld calculators, and electronic components.

HWP is one of the nineteen largest industrial companies in the United States and one of the world's largest computer companies. The company had revenues of $47.1 billion in its fiscal 1998 year (ended October 31, 1998).

Nearly 60 percent of Hewlett-Packard's business is generated abroad; two-thirds of that is in Europe. Other principal markets include Japan, Canada, Australia, the Far East, and Latin America. HP is one of the top eight U.S. exporters.

Hewlett-Packard's domestic manufacturing plants are situated in twenty-eight cities, mostly in California, Colorado, the Northeast, and the Pacific Northwest. The company also has research and manufacturing plants in Europe, Asia Pacific, Latin America, and Canada.

HWP sells its products and services through some 600 sales and support offices and distributorships in more than thirty countries.

Most of the company's revenue comes from a broad range of computer products and services, including workstations, personal computers, and peripherals, such as tape, disk and optical storage devices, plotters, and printers.

HP is the world's number two supplier of powerful desktop workstations for engineering, business, and multimedia applications. HP also is one of the fastest-growing personal-computer companies in the world.

Hewlett-Packard's PC products include the checkbook-size 200LX palmtop PC with built-in Pocket Quicken, and the HP OmniBook family of notebook PCs for mobile professionals.

A Spinoff in the Works

In the spring of 1999, the company announced that it plans to spin off its measurement business ($7.6 billion in sales). By mid-2000, it will be a separate, publicly traded entity. While HWP has said its broad product portfolio has served it well, with revenue growth averaging more than 20 percent during 1995 and 1996, revenue growth had slowed sharply since the second half of fiscal 1998 because of weak Asian demand and weakness in semiconductor test equipment. After the spinoff, the computing and imaging segment will carry the HWP name, including servers, PCs, and laser/inkjet printers, plus related services and software. Initially, no CEO was named for this segment. However, the smaller segment, which sells medical products and test and measurement devices, is headed by Ned Barnholt, an executive whose previous post was head of HP's test and measurement.

Hewlett-Packard's CEO, Lew Platt, explains the reasons for the move: "A couple years ago, we realized that HP was beginning to have some of the characteristics of a large company—complexity, breadth, a lost of accountability." He also explained why he did not put himself in the head position at the new HP: "I'm going to be 59-plus. Senior people here retire at 60. We just thought it didn't make sense to put everybody through one major transition, only to put them through another less than a year later."

Shortcomings to Bear in Mind

- In 1998, Hewlett-Packard's earnings dipped for the first time in several years. The company attributes this disappointing showing to "unacceptably high expense growth and competitive pricing pressures in PCs in the first half, and a weak macroeconomic environment in the second half."

- According to Hewlett-Packard, 1998 "was a challenging year overall in our measurement businesses, particularly in test and measurement, where the situation in Asia and the downturn in the semiconductor industry were key factors in a 4-percent revenue decline. Our component business was also affected by weakness in Asia." On a more positive note, there were better tidings in other sectors. Strength in fiber-optic and optical electronics enabled the components business to achieve 8 percent revenue growth in 1998. What's more, strength in the United States and Europe helped the medical business achieve an 11-percent revenue increase. Finally, the company's chemical-analysis business's focus on pharmaceutical and biopharmaceutical markets was key to its 6 percent revenue growth.

- Analysts believe that Hewlett-Packard's competition has increased in the past two or three years. More companies are selling low-cost printers, while Sun Microsystems competes fiercely in the market for Unix-based computers.

HWP is a leader in computers that use the Unix operating systems.

Reasons to Buy

- In mid-1999, Hewlett-Packard unveiled several partnerships and a software technology dubbed e-speak that helps manage service requests among different Web sites, part of an ambitious effort to position itself as a leader in Internet-based services. E-speak is a software architecture designed to allow electronic services to communicate in a dynamic, automated way with each other over the Internet. That is difficult to do today because there is no standard way for services to recognize each other. For instance, an Internet travel service using e-speak could put out requests for airline tickets, hotel reservations, and automobile rentals over the Internet on behalf of a client and let individual Web sites offering such services "bid" for the business automatically.

  The announcement is the latest sign of the company's intention to challenge dynamic rivals such as Sun Microsystems and IBM. Both have made major pushes to sell the equipment and software needed to run Web sites and offer Internet-based services.

- In June of 1999, Hewlett-Packard said that it planned to unveil a strategy to sell personal computers and other products directly to corporate customers, stepping into an arena that has plunged some competitors into chaos. The company said that it will extend to corporate customers the ability to buy most of its product line through its Web site. H-P sells its entire customer line of PCs, printers, scanners, and supplies over the Internet but has been slower to take the same route for corporate sales, where the company has traditionally been more dependent on its network of third-party dealers.

Instead of cutting its dealers out of its sales process, H-P plans to give them an opportunity to compete for the company's online business. For instance, a corporate customer that wants to buy ten laser printers could either order them directly from a Hewlett-Packard Web page or follow a link from that page to a list of recommended local dealers that could sell the printers and assist with installation. The company's strategy is explained by a company official, "We just want to serve those who would otherwise go to Dell Gigabuys for a solution."

- In 1998, the company's computer activities accounted for 84 percent of its revenues, and many businesses achieved good results. Printers, software and services, high-end UNIX systems, and PCs had solid growth and profitability.

Both the company's laser and inkjet businesses posted solid growth, achieved good profits, and held or strengthened their market share leadership in 1998. Late in the year, Hewlett-Packard introduced twenty new printing and imaging products across its LaserJet, DeskJet, and ScanJet families—the largest hardcopy rollout in the company's history and an introduction that positions HWP very well for 1999.

What's more, these products deliver on the company's digital workplace strategy, enabling the seamless exchange between paper and digital information. Hewlett-Packard also unveiled two inkjet printers in 1998 that incorporate breakthrough technology that it calls the Modular Ink Delivery System.

- In the spring of 1999, Hewlett-Packard announced a new line of midrange servers, plugging a gap in its product line and putting it back into competition with Sun Microsystems Inc. and IBM. Analysts said that the company's N-Class servers, priced starting at $48,000,

should help Hewlett-Packard catch up to its competitors in the market for servers, which are powerful computers that increasingly run everything from corporate networks to Internet-based electronic commerce. The new machines are designed to pick up the slack from the company's aging K-Class line, whose sales started to wane in 1998.

- Hewlett-Packard' medical-products division makes defibrillators and is a leading provider of the machines to hospitals, clinics, and physicians' offices. It has also been expanding into portable defibrillators. In 1998, Hewlett-Packard acquired Heartstream Inc., a pioneer in portable heart defibrillators.

- Taking aim at rivals' low-priced computers, Hewlett-Packard unveiled its first line of personal computers to use Intel's most powerful technology. Introduced in January of 1998, the new line of computers retail for less than $800. In the past, PCs costing less than $1,000 were typically available from a major vendor if they used older technology or were cloned versions of less-powerful Intel chips.

Hewlett-Packard says that its HP Pavilion 3260 is the first to hit the market at the $800 level that is based on Intel's powerful 200-megahertz Pentium chip. The chip uses Intel's MMX technology for advanced display of graphics and other multimedia features.

- The company's new HP LaserJet 4000 printers produce 1,200 dots per inch print equivalent at full engine speed— an important innovation over competitors who must cut engine speed by half to achieve the highest quality output possible on their printers. The HP LaserJet 4000 is the first product to incorporate HP's new JetSend technology, which allows printers, scanners, and other devices to exchange information directly without a PC.

Total assets: $33,673 million
Current ratio: 1.60
Common shares outstanding: 1,037 million
Return on 1998 shareholders' equity: 17.4%

	1998	1997	1996	1995	1994	1993	1992	1991
Revenues (millions)	47,061	42,895	38,420	31,519	24,991	20,317	16,410	14,494
Net income (millions)	3,065	3,119	2,675	2,433	1,599	1,177	881	755
Earnings per share	2.88	2.95	2.54	2.32	1.54	1.16	.87	.76
Dividends per share	.60	.56	.42	.35	.26	.23	.18	.12
Price: high	82.4	72.9	57.7	48.3	25.6	22.3	21.3	14.3
low	47.1	48.1	36.8	24.5	18.0	16.1	12.6	7.5

AGGRESSIVE GROWTH

The Home Depot, Inc.

2455 Paces Ferry Road, NW, Atlanta, GA 30339-4024 □ Investor contact: Kim Schreckengost (770) 384-4388 □ Direct dividend reinvestment plan available (800) 557-0177 □ Web site: www.homedepot.com □ Fiscal year's end Sunday closest to January 31 of following year □ Listed: NYSE □ Ticker symbol: HD □ S&P rating: A+ □ Value Line financial strength rating: A++

Founded in 1978, The Home Depot is the world's largest home improvement retailer and ranks among the ten largest retailers in the United States, with fiscal 1998 (ended January 31, 1999) sales of $30.2 billion. At year-end, the company was operating 761 stores, including 707 Home Depot stores and 8 EXPO Design Center stores in the United States, 43 Home Depot stores in Canada, 2 Home Depot stores in Chile, and 1 Home Depot store in Puerto Rico, as well as the wholly-owned subsidiary Maintenance Warehouse and National Blinds and Wallpaper, Inc.

Home Depot has been publicly held since 1981 and is included in the S&P 500. The company has been named America's most admired specialty retailer by *Fortune* magazine for six consecutive years.

Home Depot targets the do-it-yourself market and stresses customer service, low prices, and a broad product assortment. The company also serves professional builders. Stores average about 130,000 square feet and stock over 40,000 items, including lumber, floor and wall coverings, plumbing and gardening supplies, hardware, tools, and paint.

Highlights of 1998

Net sales for fiscal 1998 increased 25.1 percent, to $30.2 billion, from $24.2 billion the prior year. This increase was attributable to:

• Full-year sales from the 112 new stores opened during fiscal 1997

• A 7 percent comparable store-for-store sales increase

• One hundred thirty-eight new store openings and 4 store relocations during 1998

In 1998, gross profit as a percent of sales was 28.5 percent, compared with 28.1 percent the prior year. The rate increase was primarily attributable to a lower cost of merchandising resulting from product line reviews and other merchandising initiatives. In addition, sales mix changes, better inventory shrinkage results, and benefits from import strategies contributed to the overall gross profit margin.

Operating expenses as a percent of sales were 19.7 in 1998, compared with 20.2 percent for 1997. Operating expenses for 1997 included a $104 million nonrecurring charge related to the settlement of a class action gender discrimination lawsuit and three other gender discrimination law-suits. Excluding the nonrecurring charge, operating expenses as a percent of sales were 19.8 percent for 1997.

Shortcomings to Bear in Mind

- During 1998, insiders, such as officers and board members, were heavy sellers of the stock.
- For the past thirteen consecutive years, earnings have increased to record levels. In the 1988–1998 period, earnings per share climbed from $.07 to $1.06, a compound annual growth rate of 31.2 percent. Is it any wonder that the stock sells for an extremely high multiple? "Value players" had better pass this one up.

Reasons to Buy

- During 1998, the company opened a net of 137 stores in a variety of new and existing markets. Home Depot ended the year with 761 stores. In the years ahead, the company plans to open new stores at the rate of 21 to 22 percent a year. The goal is to have 1,600 stores by the end of 2002.
- The U.S. home improvement industry continues to grow, as new and existing home sales reach record levels, home ownership rates increase, and existing houses and their owners age. In addition, the quality of home life has become more important to many home-owners, prompting them to make improvements or enhancements to kitchens, bathrooms, and other fre-quently used rooms. All of these factors spell opportunity for The Home Depot.

The company intends to capture these opportunities in new and existing Home Depot stores, which will con-tinue to drive consistent sales and earning growth for the foreseeable future. Longer term, increasing the company's sales in other segments of the industry will become progressively more important to supporting a consis-tent growth pattern.

- Home Depot's EXPO Design Center division is beginning an aggressive store growth program. According to manage-ment, "There's no other retailing con-cept that comes close to matching its product and service offerings or cap-turing its look, feel, and excitement. EXPO will allow us to gain a larger share of the home decor market and provide an alternative to Home Depot shoppers whose remodeling preferences sometimes go beyond a Home Depot store."
- The company is taking steps to increase its share of the professional business customer market. In some respects, this has been a balancing act for Home Depot, since do-it-yourself customers are still the company's most important customers, and the company is com-mitted to continuing to serve their needs. However, Home Depot is also focusing on gaining more sales from the pros already shopping in its stores. According to management, "As we refine the tests we are conducting today to expand our professional programs to more stores, we expect this customer segment will drive incremental sales."
- To be sure, the bulk of Home Depot sales are in the United States, but a move abroad is in the works. During 1998, the company opened two stores in Santiago, Chile, and one in San Juan, Puerto Rico. Home Depot's experiences so far in both markets are offering encouragement for future success in global retailing. According to manage-ment, "Every day we learn more about serving the diverse needs of customers in other areas of the world. We are also learning that the Home Depot culture is, indeed, transferable, and customer service is valued around the world."

- The company's long-term plans are also addressing alternative methods of distribution to attract more customers, enhance their shopping experiences, and obtain a larger share of the total market. Through the company's acquisition of Maintenance Warehouse in 1997, Home Depot has learned how to serve the property maintenance and repair market through direct mail distribution. The company is now beginning to leverage Maintenance Warehouse's business expertise with The Home Depot brand and capabilities. This is resulting in more aggressive sales growth at Maintenance Warehouse, the pursuit of new target markets, and steps toward a more seamless integration of the two companies.

- The company has been strengthening its telephone sales and special-order capabilities through The Home Depot Special Order Center. Currently in the testing phase, the center was created during 1998 by National Blinds and Wallpaper, Inc., also a Home Depot subsidiary. It has been dramatically simplifying the special order process for window coverings and wallpaper in the Home Depot stores participating in the test. The process is faster and more accurate, adding value to the customer shopping experience and allowing employees to serve more customers.

- Of late, the company has been venturing further into cyberspace. Its Internet home page is undergoing a major content transformation that will affect Home Depot's industry leadership position. It will also, according to management, "provide the platform for e-commerce plans later in 1999." As the company implements its Internet strategy, it is focusing on three key sectors:

  - The first is to use the interactive capabilities of the Internet to learn more about the company's customers. This will allow Home Depot to respond more quickly to their needs and enhance their shopping experience in the company's stores.

  - The second focus is to use the company's Web page as an educational tool for its customers. Home Depot expects these two focus areas to drive additional sales in its stores.

  - The third focus area, selling products on the Internet, has the mind-boggling potential to put The Home Depot "store" within reach of customers around the world. Most retailers, including Home Depot, are just scratching the surface with the Internet. With more and more homes becoming Internet-enabled each year, this medium is destined to develop into a much more important brand-building and sales vehicle in the future.

- The company is making a move to create its own brands—products developed by and sold only at The Home Depot. These will supplement the nationally branded products in many categories. During 1998, the company introduced three successful new product lines that are growing rapidly. A new line of RIDGID bench top and stationary power tools, in addition to RIDGID wet/dry vacuums and air filtration systems, appeals to pros and do-it-yourself woodworking enthusiasts.

  In addition, the company joined forces with John Deere for the manufacture and servicing of Scotts' lawn tractors. Late in 1998, The Home Depot began offering GE SmartWater water heaters and softeners, with added features and extended warranties.

- The company also has a stake in the rental sphere. Do-it-yourself and professional customers now have the option to rent up to 200 tools to complete one-time projects, or simply to try a tool out before purchasing it. Tool rental centers were in forty-six Home Depot stores at the end of 1998, and the company plans to add more new and existing stores during 1999. This service establishes The Home Depot into a nearly $20-billion, highly fragmented market.

- In another new venture, The Home Depot is testing a concept called Vil-

lager's Hardware, with test stores being opened in 1999. The Villager's Hardware format will test the best products and methods for gaining market share in the $50-billion hardware convenience market, a home improvement segment whose customers tend to be doing smaller fix-it projects and prefer convenient store locations with quick in-and-out service.

Total assets: $13,465 million
Current ratio: 1.73
Common shares outstanding: 1,475 million
Return on 1998 shareholders' equity: 18.5%

	1998	1997	1996	1995	1994	1993	1992	1991
Revenues (millions)	30,219	24,156	19,536	15,470	12,477	9,239	7,148	5,137
Net income (millions)	1,614	1,160	938	732	604	457	363	249
Earnings per share	1.06	.78	.65	.51	.44	.34	.27	.20
Dividends per share	.12	.10	.08	.06	.05	.04	.03	.02
Price: high	62.0	30.3	19.8	16.6	16.1	17.0	17.2	11.7
low	27.7	15.9	13.8	12.2	12.2	11.7	9.9	3.8

CONSERVATIVE GROWTH

Houghton Mifflin Company

222 Berkeley Street, Boston, MA 02116 ◘ Investor contact: Susan E. Hardy (617) 351-5114 ◘ Dividend reinvestment plan available: (800) 730-4001 ◘ Web site: www.hmco.com ◘ Listed: NYSE ◘ Ticker symbol: HTN ◘ S&P rating: B+ ◘ Value Line financial strength rating: B++

Houghton Mifflin is a leading publisher of books for schools and colleges. Textbooks and related educational products provided 90 percent of 1998 revenues. Houghton Mifflin also publishes trade books, such as scholarly biographies and novels. In the mid-1990s, HTN embarked on a strategy to reach revenues of $1 billion by the year 2000; it is well on its way to reaching that goal. It began with the 1994 acquisition of McDougal Littell, followed by D. C. Heath (then part of Raytheon) a year later.

Added products and staff from D. C. Heath significantly strengthened three divisions, while yielding $30 million in cost savings. The College division is now a leader in mathematics, history, modern languages, chemistry, English, and political science.

The Secondary School division, bolstered by McDougal Littell, has strong positions in modern languages, social studies, literature, and mathematics.

The School division (kindergarten through eighth grade) has broadened its offerings in mathematics and reading. The acquisitions also contributed to HTN's successful entry into the supplemental-materials market.

Houghton Mifflin is actively developing integrated multimedia programs in all subject areas. It offers computer-assisted and computer-managed instructional programs for all education levels, computer tools and operating systems for the college market, and a computer-based career and college guidance information system in versions for junior and senior high school students.

The company's Riverside Publishing Company unit provides educational and psychological test and measurement materials to schools and colleges, in addition to providing guidance information and products.

In mid-1998, the company acquired Computer Adaptive Technologies, a developer of computer-based testing solutions. It also widened Riverside's product offerings and Houghton's role in the testing market.

In the non-school sector, which operates under General Publishing, the company's products include fiction, nonfiction, children's books, dictionaries, and reference materials in a variety of formats and media.

Houghton Mifflin Interactive, a unit of the Trade and Reference division, develops CD-ROM titles for sale in the multimedia consumer product markets. Trade and reference works are largely sold to retail stores.

Highlights of 1998

Houghton Mifflin's results in 1998 exceeded management's original expectations, in a year when school adoption opportunities were quite limited. The outstanding performance of the company's K–12 Publishing group boosted net sales to a record $862 million. Excluding extraordinary and infrequent items, income after tax was $40.8 million, or $1.40 per share.

The School Division's reading and spelling programs did exceptionally well in 1998. The reading intervention products that the company's creative team developed to help students reading below grade level improve their skills not only led the market, they created new opportunities in teacher training for the division.

Late in 1998, HTN acquired DiscoveryWorks, a best-selling K–6 science program, from Silver Burdett Ginn Inc. Science was the only major discipline in which the School Division had no product offerings, and it has been one of the company's strategic goals to enter this market. DiscoveryWorks will allow the company to participate in many state adoption opportunities in 2000 and beyond, including those in California, Florida, and Texas. Although the investment required to revise the series will cause earnings dilution of between $.17 and $.22 per share in 1999, management expects *Discovery Works* will generate incremental earnings of $.35 to $.40 per share in 2000.

Shortcomings to Bear in Mind

- Creating textbooks is complicated by the adoption process. Some twenty-one states are referred to as "adoption states," which means that the company's proposed textbook must be approved by state officials before it can be sold to specific schools within the state. Among the major states that have this approach are California, Texas, and Florida.

The problem is further complicated because one state may approve the publisher's book, but that same book may not appeal to another major state. Obviously, it doesn't pay to print separate books for both states. However, there are times when changes can be made if the state is a major one such as Texas or California.

As noted, not all states are "adoption states" that require books be approved by a central authority. A total of twenty-nine states leave purchasing and decision-making up to local school districts. These states are referred to as "open territories." In an adoption state, an approved list is published after the book and other parts of the program have been examined. However, once a publisher gets on an approved list, the sales process from that point forward is the same as it is in an open territory. In other words, in order to make sales, the marketing team still has to convince each school board that their program is the best. In 1998, adoption opportunities were "quite limited," according to management. Even so, earnings held up well. On a more positive note, the future looks much better, since this is a cyclical business. Most states adopt every five to seven years. In the meantime, they continue to use the old books. The years 2000 through 2002 are expected to bring a solid batch of adoption opportunities. This is a major factor in favor of investing in a textbook company such as Houghton Mifflin.

Reasons to Buy

- The company is ably led by CEO Nader Darehshori, who has been chairman since 1990, when the company was much less profitable. At that time, HTN relied primarily on producing reading materials for primary schools. If it was a good year for reading, it was a good year for Houghton Mifflin, otherwise earnings suffered. Mr. Darehshori has spent his entire tenure divesting unprofitable operations and building the performing assets, as well as making key acquisitions. Now the company has a much broader base, with participation in grade school, high school, and college. This has led to greater stability.
- Houghton Mifflin has only a few major competitors, notably McGraw-Hill, Pearson (owned by Pearson PLC, a British concern), Harcourt General, and Scholastic. Assuming you like educational publishing, Houghton Mifflin is the clear choice, since about 90 percent of the company's revenues come from textbooks and related material. The other companies are all involved in

other ventures. In other words, HTN is essentially a "pure play."
- There are a number of macro industry factors that favor educational publishing. For one thing, the current period is, according to management, "the best funding environment we have seen in many years." The purchase of educational books are primarily funded by state and local governments; very little comes from the federal government (only 6 or 7 percent). Compared with the early 1990s, the economic picture has improved dramatically, including many states having budget surpluses. What's more, education is currently a priority throughout the country. Businesses, parents, and other groups have made education a key issue for government spending. Of course, employing more and better teachers is a part of this picture, but better books are also important. Still another factor is demographic: the number of students is growing at a steady 1 or 2 percent pace.
- McDougal Littell, Houghton's secondary division, was the clear leader in its market in 1998, according to *Educational Marketer.* Its literature and language arts programs gained market share in California, Maryland, New York, as well as in other states. Its mathematics product line took commanding share in Alabama, Oklahoma, Texas, and many open territory districts. The division's new programs in American and world history also outsold the competition. In 1999, McDougal Littell published a new Spanish program, which is eliciting strong support from educators.
- A new edition of the division's outstanding literature series, *The Language of Literature*, has been completed and is being marketed throughout the country. The series introduces students in grades 6–12 to the finest literature, connecting

the selections to their own lives. It includes print and technology components and resources on the World Wide Web. According to management, *The Language of Literature* is "expected to be an extremely strong competitor in the many literature adoption opportunities in 2000–2002."

■ *Calculus* by Larson/Hostetler/Edwards has helped well over 1.5 million students grasp the intricacies of calculus in college and high school classrooms over the past twenty years. Still a bestseller in its sixth edition, *Calculus* has expanded its reach and is now available as a printed textbook, in CD-ROM format, and as Houghton Mifflin's first subscription-based Web site that provides the entire contents of a textbook online. *Internet Calculus* is the first such Web site offered to the marketplace by any college textbook publisher.

■ DiscoveryWorks, a best-selling K–6 science program, engages students in active investigations of scientific concepts. With this welcome edition to the School Division's product line, Houghton Mifflin now has offerings in all major elementary school disciplines. DiscoveryWorks will enable the company to participate in many state adoption opportunities in 2000 and beyond,

including those in California, Florida, and Texas.

■ With the increasing diversity in America's classrooms, accurately measuring students' abilities has become a critical issue. Riverside's *Universal Nonverbal Intelligence Test* (the UNIT) provides a comprehensive standardized assessment of general intelligence designed to ensure fairness for all students, regardless of race, ethnicity, sex, language, country of origin, or hearing status. Unlike the typical nonverbal intelligence test that measures only one narrow aspect of intelligence, the UNIT is a multidimensional measure, yielding several broad-based indexes.

■ Since he first appeared in print more than fifty years ago, Curious George has captivated readers of all ages. The Curious George line at Houghton Mifflin now includes books, CD-ROMs, and a wide variety of licensed products from toys to clothing and games, and the irrepressible monkey is helping educate children as well as entertain them. The line is a good example of the company's strategy of publishing in different forms for different audiences and leveraging the value of HTN's publishing assets across the broadest possible market.

Total assets: $975 million
Current ratio: 1.43
Common shares outstanding: 30 million
Return on 1998 shareholders equity: 10.2%

	1998	1997	1996	1995	1994	1993	1992	1991
Revenues (millions)	862	797	718	529	483	463	455	467
Net income (millions)	41	43	31	19	34	38	27	25
Earnings per share	1.40	1.48	1.11	.70	1.22	1.37	.96	.88
Dividends per share	.50	.49	.48	.47	.44	.42	.40	.38
Price: high	47.3	40.3	28.4	27.4	26.5	25.2	19.9	15.2
low	26.8	26.3	20.2	19.8	18.1	18.2	13.3	11.1

Hubbell Incorporated

P. O. Box 549, Orange, CT 06477-4024 □ Investor contact: Thomas R. Conlin (203) 799-4293 □ Dividend reinvestment plan available (800) 851-9677 □ Web site: www.hubbell.com □ Listed: NYSE □ Ticker symbol: HUB.B □ S&P rating: A- □ Value Line financial strength rating: A+

For over a century, Hubbell has manufactured high-quality electrical and electronic products for a broad range of commercial, industrial, telecommunications, and utility applications. Since 1961, Hubbell has expanded its operations into other areas of the electrical industry and related fields.

Hubbell products are manufactured or assembled by twenty-two divisions and subsidiaries in the United States, Canada, Puerto Rico, Mexico, the United Kingdom, and Singapore. The company also participates in joint ventures with partners in South America, Germany, and Taiwan. In addition, Hubbell maintains sales offices in Malaysia, Mexico, Hong Kong, South Korea, and the Middle East.

The company is primarily engaged in the engineering, manufacture, and sale of electrical and electronic products. They can be divided into three general segments:

1. Products primarily used in low-voltage applications
2. Products primarily used in high-voltage applications
3. Other products that are either not directly related to the electrical business, or if related, cannot be clearly classified on a voltage-application basis

Hubbell's Three Segments

Low-voltage products are in the range of 600 volts or less. They are sold principally to distributors and represent stock items of standard and special-application wiring-device products, lighting fixtures, low-voltage industrial controls, and cable-management product.

High-voltage products are in the more-than-600-volt range. They are sold through distributors, independent sales representatives, and directly to customers by sales engineers. Segment products are comprised of test and measurement equipment; wire and cable; and electrical transmission and distribution products, such as insulators, surge arresters, switches, cutouts, sectionalizers, fuses, connectors, and related hardware.

The Other segment consists of products not classified on a voltage basis. This segment includes standard and special-application cabinets and enclosures, fittings, switch and outlet boxes, wire management component and systems, construction materials and tools for building and maintenance of overhead and underground power and telephone lines, data transmission and telecommunications equipment, and components for voice and data signals. Segment products are sold to customers in a wide range of markets, including industrial, commercial, and residential construction; hardware and home-center outlets; original equipment manufacturers; and electric and telephone utilities.

Shortcomings to Bear in Mind

■ The past year (1998) was one of striking contrasts that affected the performance of Hubbell. On a global scale, the domestic economy by all macroeconomic indicators stayed remarkably strong, even as Asian economies continued to struggle. Europe began slowing down in the second half of 1998. What's more, questions about Latin America's near-term future grew with the devaluation of the Brazilian currency.

To be sure, Hubbell's exposure to these overseas economies is relatively minor. However, Hubbell's slack sales to international customers clearly hurt year-over-year comparisons. Further, the decline in export trade for the wide range of North American industrial manufacturers that the company does supply had a negative impact on Hubbell's order volume.

- Some analysts look upon Hubbell as being too conservative. For instance, they point out that the company has too little debt: only 11 percent of its capitalization is in the form of long-term debt. In its defense, management insists that it prefers to maintain a low level of debt so that it has the ability to make acquisitions.
- Analysts don't expect the company will change its stripes, since the Hubbell family and other insiders own 40 percent of the voting stock—the Class A shares. Although the families' shares are held in trust, the trustees who vote these shares are board members, including G. Jackson Ratcliffe, the CEO.

Reasons to Buy

- One of the keys to Hubbell's high level of profitability and consistency in its distribution franchise for its traditional electrical products. Hubbell receives a premium price for these products because of its quality and reliability as a supplier. In addition, Hubbell does not compete with its suppliers, whereas some of its competitors do. These factors enable Hubbell to maintain solid relationships with its network of independent suppliers. What's more, the company's strong distribution network also facilitates acquisitions, since Hubbell can generally reduce administrative costs of acquired companies by incorporating the new products into its existing structure.

- Even though Hubbell has made a number of key acquisitions in recent years, there are still more opportunities to explore. For example, the 250 largest electrical distributors in the United States have aggregate sales of $25 billion. To be sure, Hubbell does not serve the entire market. Even so, Hubbell has total distribution of sales on the order of $700 million. Analysts believe that the industry is destined for further consolidation.
- Hubbell has been known for it excellence in manufacturing and continuous cost-reduction efforts. As a result, it has one of the highest productivity levels and after-tax margins in the electrical component/connector industry.
- Hubbell's growth has been consistent, although not spectacular. Its solid record of consistency is all the more impressive when you take into account that it operates in a cyclical industry. Over the 1988–1998 period, earnings advanced from $1.07 to $2.50, a compound annual growth rate of 8.9 percent. In the same ten-year span, dividends per share climbed from $.43 to $1.22, an 11 percent growth rate. The company has raised its dividend thirty-eight times in the past thirty-eight years.
- In most years, Hubbell has an above-average return on equity, typically 17 percent or 18 percent.
- Hubbell's businesses have a late-cycle orientation and are primarily related to maintenance and repair activities. This high maintenance-and-repair component lends stability to demand. In addition, Hubbell has very low exposure to the automotive, appliance, and residential sectors.
- The proliferation of microprocessors—in production machinery, desktop computers, and hospital equipment—has increased the consequences of transient voltage surges. Contrary to popular

belief, only one-third of power transients are caused by lightning or utility grid switching. Rather, the majority originate within a building, from HVAC equipment, elevators, photocopiers. Unfortunately, each surge has the potential to destroy electronic circuits in a millisecond. Hubbell has a full range of protection solutions sold under the *SpikeShield* name: service entrance, branch panel, modular panel, wired-in blocks, and point-of-use devices.

- Wirecon is the market share leader of self-contained devices for the manufactured home and recreational vehicle markets. Self-contained wiring devices are similar in appearance to standard residential and wall outlets and switches, but they do not require a mounting box. They incorporate specialized insulation displacement terminations. Growth in these markets is strong; manufactured housing, for example, is the fastest-growing segment of the single-family home market, with annual production more than doubling in the past five years.

- Hubbell manufactures devices that attach to or are associated with wires, whether they transmit data, voice, or electricity. These include plugs, receptacles, wall plates, electrical fittings, cable assemblies, wire management systems, lighting equipment, insulators, channel banks, and so on. These devices control, connect, direct, and protect, and thus are essential to delivering electricity or data in a usable fashion.

- Hubbell's products are evolutionary, not revolutionary. Complete obsolescence is rare. The pull-chain switch light bulb socket that launched Hubbell is still sold and in use to this day. Such long product lifecycles mean that more of Hubbell's new products are incremental to the revenue base and are not cannibalizing its own product line.

- Hubbell tends to target niche applications where the customer desires a high-quality product and does not worry about breakage, maintenance, and replacement. Safety is a concern as well. Many of Hubbell's products are designed for heavy duty or hazardous environments. Ease of installation also differentiates the company's products. In other words, Hubbell products are positioned to be sold based on performance; this enables the company to charge a premium price. Its success can be measured by the numerous competitor advertisements over the years that point out, "we are as good as Hubbell."

- While product lifecycles are very long, Hubbell is constantly redesigning products to reduce parts count, lower materials content, and facilitate automated assembly. Its success can be seen from its rising revenue per employee. Hubbell is also reducing costs by moving manufacturing to low-labor-cost regions. Some 2,300 of its 8,200 employees are currently located in Mexico and Puerto Rico, with more than 1,000 jobs slated to move there over the next three or four years.

Total assets: $1,390 million
Current ratio: 1.64
Common shares outstanding: 66 million
Return on 1998 shareholders' equity: 20.2%

	1998	1997	1996	1995	1994	1993	1992	1991
Revenues (millions)	1,425	1,379	1,297	1,143	1,014	832	786	756
Net income (millions)	169	130	142	122	106	66	94	91
Earnings per share	2.50	1.89	2.10	1.83	1.60	1.00	1.41	1.37
Dividends per share	1.22	1.13	1.02	.92	.81	.78	.76	.69
Price: high	52.8	51.1	43.9	33.1	29.9	28.0	28.6	25.7
low	33.9	40.8	31.8	24.8	25.0	24.2	21.5	19.1

CONSERVATIVE GROWTH

Illinois Tool Works Inc.

3600 West Lake Avenue, Glenview, IL 60025-5811 □ Investor contact: Linda Williams (847) 657-4104 □
Dividend reinvestment plan available (888) 829-7424 □ Web site: www.itwinc.com □ Listed: NYSE □ Ticker
symbol: ITW □ S&P rating: A+ □ Value Line financial strength rating: A

Illinois Tool Works is a multinational manufacturer of highly engineered fasteners, components, assemblies, and systems. ITW's businesses are small and focused, so they can work more effectively in a decentralized structure to add value to customers' products.

The company has subsidiaries and affiliates in thirty-four countries on six continents. Foreign sales, moreover, account for 38 percent of sales and 29 percent of profits.   Some 400 ITW operating units are divided into five business segments:

Engineered Products—North America

Businesses in this segment are located in North America and manufacture short-lead-time components and fasteners and specialty products such as adhesives, resealable packaging, and electronic component packaging. In 1998, these units primarily served automotive (38 percent), construction (27 percent), and general industrial (14 percent) markets.

Engineered Products—International

Businesses in this segment are located outside North America and manufacture short-lead-time components and fasteners and specialty products such as electronic component packaging and adhesives. In 1998, these operations primarily served the automotive (37 percent), construction (33 percent), electronics (10 percent), and general industrial (10 percent) markets.

Specialty Systems—North America

Businesses in this segment operate in North America and produce longer-lead-time machinery and related consumables and specialty equipment for applications such as industrial spray coating, quality measurement, and static control. In 1998, these companies concentrated their efforts in such sectors as general industrial (30 percent), construction (15 percent), food and beverage (15 percent), and automotive (12 percent).

Specialty Systems—International

Operations in this segment do business outside North America. They have stakes in longer-lead-time machinery and related consumables and specialty equipment for industrial spray coating and other applications. In 1998, these units served such markets as general industrial (37 percent), food and beverage (15 percent), industrial capital goods (10 percent), and paper products (10 percent).

Leasing and Investments

This segment makes investments in mortgage-related assets, leveraged and direct-financing leases of equipment, properties and property developments, and affordable housing.

A Classic Growth Stock

To be sure, Illinois Tool Works is not a household name, since it does not produce products that are familiar to the average investor, such as Coca-Cola, Rubbermaid, Goodyear Tires, or Hewlett-Packard calculators. ITW is, nonetheless, a classic growth stock with a long history of increasing earnings and dividends. What's more, it is still small enough (only $5 billion in sales) so that it should continue to expand for many years to come, often enhanced by acquisitions. By contrast, all of the "household names" named above are vastly larger.

How Illinois Tool Works Got Started

Founded in 1912, Illinois Tool Works' earliest products included milling cutters and hobs used to cut gears. Today ITW is a multinational manufacturer of highly engineered components and systems.

In 1923, the company developed the Shakeproof fastener, a patented twisted tooth lock washer. This product's success enabled ITW to become the leader in a new industry segment, engineered metal fasteners. Illinois Tool soon expanded the Shakeproof line to include thread-cutting screws, preassembled screws, and other metal fasteners. By the late 1940s, the line grew to include plastic and metal/plastic combination fasteners. Today, ITW units produce fasteners for appliance, automotive, construction, general industrial, and other applications.

After World War II, the company also expanded into electrical controls and instruments, culminating in the formation of the Licon division in the late 1950s. Today, ITW units provide a wide range of switch components and panel assemblies used in appliance, electronic, and industrial markets.

In the early 1960s, the newly formed Hi-Cone operating unit developed the plastic multipack carrier that revolutionized the packaging industry. Hi-Cone multipacks today are used to package beverage and food products as well as a variety of other products.

Also in the 1960s, the company formed Buildex to market existing Shakeproof fasteners as well as a line of masonry fasteners to the construction industry. Buildex today manufactures fasteners for drywall, general construction, and roofing applications.

In the mid-1980s, ITW acquired Ramset, Phillips Drill (Red Head), and SPIT, manufacturers of concrete anchoring, epoxy anchoring, and powder actuated systems; and Paslode, maker of pneumatic and cordless nailers, staplers, and systems for wood construction applications. Today, the construction industry is the largest market served by Illinois Tool Works.

In the 1970s, ITW purchased Devcon Corporation, a producer of adhesives, sealants, and related specialty chemicals. Today the company's engineered polymers businesses offer a variety of products with home, construction, and industrial applications.

In 1986, Illinois Tool acquired Signode Packaging Systems, a multinational manufacturer of metal and plastic strapping stretch film, industrial tape, application equipment, and related products. Today, ITW offers a wide range of industrial packaging systems, including Dynatec hot-melt adhesive application equipment.

In 1989, Illinois Tool Works acquired Ransburg Corporation, a leading producer of finishing equipment.

ITW expanded its capabilities in industrial finishing with the purchase of DeVilbiss Industrial/Commercial division in 1990. Today, DeVilbiss and Ransburg manufacture conventional and liquid electrostatic equipment, while Gema Volstatic (acquired with the Ransburg and DeVilbiss purchases) produces electrostatic powder coating systems.

The company acquired the Miller Group in 1993. Miller is a leading manufacturer of arc welding equipment and related systems. Miller's emphasis on new product development and innovative design fits well with ITW's engineering and manufacturing strategies.

Shortcomings to Bear in Mind

- The stock has historically traded at a premium to the market, but based on its exceptional performance over the years, it would appear to be warranted. With some 400 businesses, Illinois Tool offers investors wide diversification by product line, geographic region, and industry. This helps insulate the company from weakness in any one sector. Over the years, this has resulted in consistent performance, despite the cyclicality of the automotive and construction sectors.
- At present, about 20 percent of the company's business is automotive. According to CEO W. James Farrell, "that has been a growth market for us forever, but if you look at automotive production—the number of cars and trucks and vehicles that they produce—you have a tough time thinking of that as a growth market. It's flat as a pancake.

  "Well, in a flat-as-a-pancake scenario, we want to grow. In order to do that, you have to get more products on that automobile, more dollars per car. We organize our business to do that, to get more dollars on every car. We do that partly with new products." The other strategy is acquisitions.

Reasons to Buy

- When Volkswagen decided to reintroduce its famous Beetle, VW engineers approached ITW's Shakeproof business to design a fastening system for the car's front and rear fenders. Shakeproof, a leading manufacturer of threaded fastening systems for the automotive industry, faced the challenge head-on. Fastening of a Beetle fender is complex, because of its size. Each fender consists of one solid piece of plastic that extends all the way around the front or rear wheels. Not only did the screw assembly have to securely fasten each of these large one-piece fenders to the frame of the car, but it also had to allow the fender to move with thermal expansion from changes in temperature. Shakeproof's Stems screw assembly met both of these needs. The company has fully automated its manufacturing process to meet the high-volume demand for this part.
- Illinois Tool Works has an exceptional record of growth. In the 1988–1998 period, earnings per share climbed from $.67 to $2.67, an annual compound growth rate of 14.8 percent. In the same ten-year stretch, dividends advanced from $.12 to $.54, for a growth rate of 16.2 percent.
- ITW's Fastex business manufactures injection-molded, non-threaded fastening systems for a variety of industries, including the electronics industry. Working closely with Intel, it developed the NLX Motherboard Rail System, a proprietary system that allows easy installation and removal of circuit boards in computers. The system features rail guides that snap into the bottom of chassis and help guide the rail and board assembly into place, and an eject lever to release the board, for easy maintenance or upgrades without tools. With the trend toward standardization of components in the computer industry and the influence of Intel as an industry leader, other computer manufacturers also are considering adopting this design. Fastex is developing automated work cells to support what is anticipated to be a strong demand for this product.

Total assets: $6,118 million
Current ratio: 1.51
Common shares outstanding: 250 million
Return on 1998 shareholders' equity: 21.9%

	1998	1997	1996	1995	1994	1993	1992	1991
Revenues (millions)	5,648	5,220	4,997	4,152	3,461	3,159	2,812	2,640
Net income (millions)	673	587	486	388	278	207	192	181
Earnings per share	2.67	2.33	1.97	1.65	1.23	.92	.36	.82
Dividends per share	.54	.46	.36	.31	.28	.25	.23	.21
Price: high	73.2	60.1	48.7	32.8	22.8	20.3	18.2	17.4
low	45.2	37.4	26.0	19.9	18.5	16.3	14.3	11.4

CONSERVATIVE GROWTH

Ingersoll-Rand Company

200 Chestnut Ridge Road, P. O. Box 8738, Woodcliff Lake, NJ 07675-8738 ◻ Investor contact: Joseph P. Fimbianti (201) 573-3113 ◻ Dividend reinvestment plan available (800) 524-4458 ◻ Web site: www.ingersoll-rand.com ◻ Listed: NYSE ◻ Ticker symbol: IR ◻ S&P rating: A- ◻ Value Line financial strength rating: A

Ingersoll-Rand, a leading diversified industrial manufacturer, produces and sells primarily nonelectric machinery and equipment under the company name as well as numerous other brands. About 55 percent of its products are capital goods; the remaining 45 percent are expendables.

Ingersoll-Rand is strategically positioned as a leading manufacturer of a broad line of products for the automotive, construction, energy, and general industry markets.

The company's product lines include: air compressors, construction and mining equipment, bearings and precision components, tools, golf carts, locks, architectural hardware, temperature-control equipment, and industrial machinery. Through joint ventures, Ingersoll-Rand is also a leading supplier of pumps and hydrocarbon processing equipment and services.

Ingersoll-Rand's strategic objective is to be number one or number two in every market it serves, a position it already commands in most of its markets. For instance, Bobcat skid-steer loaders, produced by the company's Melrose unit, hold the top position in the worldwide market. Blaw-Knox is North America's largest producer of asphalt road-paving equipment. Club Car is a strong contender for world leadership in the golf car industry. Torrington is North America's leading broadline bearing manufacturer. Finally, Ingersoll-Rand's Architectural Hardware Group has the broadest line of door-related products in the United States, including such well-known brands as Schlage locks, Von Duprin exit devices, LCN closers, and Steelcraft steel doors.

Highlights of 1998

• The company achieved its fifth consecutive year of record sales, earnings, and earnings per share.

• Sales have more than doubled since the end of 1993.

• For the first time, the company recorded more than $1 billion in operating income for a full year. Operating income has nearly quadrupled since the end of 1993.

• The company's 1998 earnings of $509 million are more than triple the level of 1993 net earnings. During this period, earnings outpaced the company's sales growth rate, which demonstrates the success of its cost-reduction and productivity efforts.

• The company's 1998 diluted earnings per share increased 33 percent over the prior year's EPS of $2.31.

• Over the last five years, adjusted diluted earnings per share have grown at an average compound annual rate of 24 percent.

• In the last two years, IR has generated more than $1 billion in free cash flow.

• The cash-generating capability helped reduce the company's debt-to-capital ratio to 43 percent by the end of 1998. This compares to a debt ratio that reached 60 percent in late 1997, immediately after the company acquired Thermo King.

• The company's operating income margin has risen steadily, from 7.3 percent of sales at the end of 1993 to 12.6 percent of sales at the end of 1998.

Shortcomings to Bear in Mind

■ The outlook for world markets is mixed. Management anticipates that growth in Europe will be somewhat below the pace expected for the United States. Further, the company expects that activity in Asian markets will be flat compared to 1998, suggesting that the worst economic storms may have passed. Still, management does not expect a rapid turnaround in the region's outlook. Finally, a slowdown in the Latin American region appears likely.

For perspective, it is important to note that Asia comprises less than 8 percent of Ingersoll-Rand's overall sales. China and India represent almost half of this total and, to date, these economies have been resistant to the adverse conditions elsewhere in the region. Latin America accounts for about 4 percent of the company's total sales.

Reasons to Buy

■ Ingersoll-Rand pursues acquisitions and joint ventures that meet exacting criteria and extend the company's participation in markets around the world. The company's last major acquisition was that of Thermo King Corporation from Westinghouse Electric in 1997. With a premier brand name and an excellent management team, Thermo King is the world leader in the transport temperature-control market, and its business complements Ingersoll-Rand's compressor product technology. Thermo King exceeded management's expectations by adding $.15 to Ingersoll-Rand's earnings per share in 1998.

Going forward, Ingersoll-Rand will continue to seek "bolt-on" acquisitions of smaller companies in niche markets that add complementary products, broaden technology, or expand geographic scope.

Dresser-Rand and Ingersoll-Dresser Pumps, Ingersoll-Rand's two largest joint ventures, are increasingly contributing to earnings as a result of significant gains in productivity and internal operating efficiencies.

■ About 40 percent of Ingersoll-Rand's sales are derived outside the United States. In addition, roughly half of the company's manufacturing facilities are outside the United States, providing a variety of bases from which to source key product lines and to participate in markets that would otherwise prove difficult to enter.

The relatively healthy economies in China and India, which account for a significant portion of Ingersoll-Rand's international sales, helped to support overall overseas performance in 1998, despite the broader economic slowdown in Asia Pacific and Latin America.

■ Ingersoll-Rand is in its sixth year of a dramatic shift in how the company conducts its business. Work processes are constantly being improved, and management estimates that it has tapped into only half of its identified potential targets for boosting efficiency in operations and manufacturing.

One compelling example is a strategic sourcing initiative started in 1995, which leverages and consolidates corporatewide purchasing power in such areas as motors, steel, castings, and indirect materials and services. The effort saved more than $50 million in 1997, $80 million in 1998, and is expected to save $80 million again in 1999.

■ In January of 1999, Ingersoll-Rand reported its fifth consecutive year of record sales and earnings. Sales of $8.3 billion were 17 percent higher that in 1997, and operating income improved 37 percent, to $1,044 million. The company reduced its operating working capital-to-sales ratio to about 10 percent of sales at the end of 1998, compared with 23 percent at year-end 1993. In addition, after capital expenditures and dividends, the company generated $580 million in free cash flow during the year. This is more than the combined amount generated between 1994 and 1996.

Over the past five years, Ingersoll-Rand has exceeded its goal of increasing its compound annual growth rate (CAGR) in earnings. What's more, management has set its target to achieve 12 to 15 percent CAGR for the foresee-

able future. The company has paid dividends on its common shares every year since 1910.

■ A strong patent performance is a good measure of the company's innovative capabilities. Over the past five years, Ingersoll-Rand has been issued 566 U.S. patents, including 112 in 1998. This brings the number of the company's total domestic patents to 1,255 and worldwide patents to nearly 2,500.

■ Through a patented condensate-elimination system, the company's new IQ System portable air compressors not only can provide construction-standard compressed air but also clean instrument-quality air with zero waste condensate. For example, the IQ System has been used to help make snow for a New England ski resort.

■ Advanced metallurgical processing technology helped the company's Torrington subsidiary launch a unique series of stainless steel airframe bearings that provide longer life in the harsh operating conditions encountered by landing gear and wing flaps on airplanes.

■ A new utility vehicle from the company's Club Car unit is configured to conquer extremely rough terrain, such as found on new golf-course construction and other site-development work. Besides featuring rugged construction, the vehicle's cargo box can hold 300 pounds more than the closest competitive vehicle.

Total assets: $8,310 million
Current ratio: 1.31
Common shares outstanding: 169 million
Return on 1998 shareholders' equity: 18.8%

	1998	1997	1996	1995	1994	1993	1992	1991
Revenues (millions)	8,292	7,103	6,703	5,729	4,508	4,021	3,784	3,586
Net income (millions)	509	380	347	270	211	164	148	145
Earnings per share	3.08	2.31	2.14	1.70	1.33	1.04	.95	.94
Dividends per share	.60	.57	.52	.49	.48	.47	.47	.44
Price: high	54.0	46.3	31.8	28.3	27.8	26.6	22.8	18.3
low	34.0	27.8	23.4	18.9	19.7	19.2	16.7	11.7

Intel Corporation

RN5-24, 2200 Mission College Boulevard, Santa Clara, CA 95052-8119 ◻ Investor contact: Alex Lenke (408) 765-1773 ◻ Dividend reinvestment plan available: (800) 298-0146 ◻ Web sites: www.intc.com and www.intel.com ◻ Listed: Nasdaq ◻ Ticker symbol: INTC ◻ S&P rating: A- ◻ Value Line financial strength rating: A++

It has been more than twenty-five years since Intel introduced the world's first microprocessor, making technology history. The computer revolution that this technology spawned has changed the world. Today, Intel supplies the computing industry with the chips, boards, systems, and software that are the "ingredients" of computer architecture. These products are used by industry members to create advanced computing systems.

Principal Products

Processor Products

• Microprocessors (also called central processing units, CPUs, or chips) are frequently described as the "brains" of a computer, because they control the central processing of data in personal computers, servers, workstations, and other computers.

• Motherboards combine Intel microprocessors and chipsets to form the basic subsystem of a PC or server.

Computer Enhancement Products

• Chipsets perform essential logic functions surrounding the CPU in computers, based on Intel architecture processors.

• Flash memory provides easily reprogrammable memory for computers, mobile phones, and many other products. Flash memory has the advantage of retaining data when the unit's power is turned off.

• Embedded control chips are designed to perform specific functions in products such as automobile engines and braking systems, hard disk drives, laser printers, input/output control modules, cellular phones, and home appliances.

Networking and Communications Products

These products enhance the capabilities of PC systems and networks and make them easier to use and manage. They are sold through reseller, retail, and original equipment manufacturer (OEM) channels.

Major Customers

• Original equipment manufacturers of computer systems and peripherals

• PC users, who buy Intel's PC enhancements, business communications products, and networking products through reseller, retail, and OEM channels

• Other manufacturers, including makers of a wide range of industrial and telecommunications equipment

Shortcomings to Bear in Mind

■ In the past, when Intel brought out new chips, they went into desktop systems priced well above what had been the top of the line. However, when it introduced the Pentium III in early 1999, it was a different story. This time, the company was faced with a softening consumer market and competition from the likes of Advanced Micro Devices, with its new K6–III. In trying to persuade customers to upgrade to the Pentium III, Intel and the computer manufacturers faced a tough dual challenge. First, they had to sell people on the need for more speed. Then they had to convince them that the Pentium III delivers.

- Though Intel's profits have held up well so far, many analysts believe that the rise of the Internet will inevitably erode its margins. Consumers are increasingly expected to use simpler, lower-cost devices, from handheld machines to television set-top boxes, to access the Internet. The proliferation of these so-called Internet appliances, they note, will not replace personal computers by any means. But the Internet will fuel more diverse computing technologies and other access devices.

Reasons to Buy

- In June of 1999, the company agreed to acquire Dialogic Corporation for $780 million. The acquisition, Intel's second-largest ever, illustrates the chip maker's intention to exploit the convergence of voice and data networks, at a time when phone companies offer Internet service, cable companies offer phone and Internet service, and Internet service providers offer phone service.

    Dialogic makes software and add-on cards for computer servers that allow telecommunications companies to offer "unified" messaging services to businesses and consumers. That is, the software and hardware consolidate voice mail, electronic mail, facsimile, and paging services into a single network so that a user can retrieve all messages.

    With Dialogic's technology, PCs with an Internet connection can be used instead of the telephone to speak with other people or listen to voice mail. That can be especially important for electronic-commerce transactions, where a user can visit a shopping Web site and simultaneously talk with a salesperson via computer telephony software.

- Late in 1998, Intel disclosed that it is doing a huge business on the Internet. Since instituting a system to take orders on the Internet in mid-1998, the monthly bookings rate has ballooned to $1 billion, or nearly half the company's total revenue. Intel's management noted that the bookings are coming from its own customers, not new accounts. However, the volume has exceeded expectations. Analysts say that Intel leads most other companies in the amount of business it conducts over the Internet's World Wide Web.

- In the spring of 1999, Intel announced that it will pour more than $1 billion over the next few years into a new Internet Data Services unit. The unit will manage computer centers on behalf of Internet service providers, a hodge-podge of 14,000 companies that connect users to the Internet. Forrester Research Inc. estimated the business of managing computer centers could grow from $876 million in 1998 to $14.6 billion in 2003, as the service providers choose to rent computing resources rather than buy and manage machines themselves.

- In June of 1999, Intel said it will accelerate plans to adopt the next major generation of semiconductor-manufacturing technology, a move likely to spur a multi-billion-dollar retooling of the industry. Intel announced plans to begin manufacturing chips using silicon wafers that are 12 inches in diameter and incorporate other technology advances for making cheaper, faster chips. What's more, Intel will start by spending $1.2 billion to upgrade a research factory in Hillsboro, Oregon, with equipment that can handle 12-inch wafers. Today's silicon wafers, which are processed with chemicals and then sliced into individual semiconductor chips, typically are eight inches across. The change in size roughly doubles the surface area of each wafer and allow 2.4 times the number of chips that can be produced at one time.

- Intel has developed a technology that it says can speed up surfing for millions of Internet users, but speed demons have to pay extra for the service. In 1998, Intel unveiled what it calls Quick Web Technology, which allows Internet service providers to speed up their customers' access to Web pages containing graphics. The technology compresses some of the information from graphics so that there is less data to transmit. The result is lower-quality graphics, but served at a higher speed.

  Intel's technology also offers Internet services a way to "cache" or store copies of Web pages downloaded by their users, another way to achieve a speedier response. When users request such pages again, they can be delivered directly from the Internet service provider, rather than the Web site that produced it.

- Not satisfied with selling the brain for nearly every personal computer, Intel wants a bigger role in hooking them together. In 1998, the company unveiled a series of computer-networking devices that move Intel into one of the most lucrative segments of high technology. Intel won't immediately threaten the market leaders such a Cisco Systems. But it will increasingly compete with chip customers that have networking sidelines, such as Compaq and Hewlett-Packard. Intel officials said their moves are measured, with particular emphasis on consumer and small-business markets that the big companies have ignored. To be sure, established networking companies dismiss Intel as a bottom feeder. Not deterred, Intel believes that its role will inexorably expand because of its central role in the evolution of PC technology, which gives the company an inside position in improving the way those machines communicate. Craig Barrett, the president and CEO of Intel, said, "The big guys in networking can still laugh at us. But we're going to grow faster."

- In the spring of 1999, Intel unveiled a new, low-powered microprocessor design intended for use in so-called information appliances, in what analysts call an aggressive attempt to stake out a new market. The new Intel chip architecture is the second generation of StrongArm, a product family originally acquired from Digital Equipment Corp. Analysts say the new StrongArm architecture is likely to be a powerful contender as those devices require increasing computer power. The most powerful StrongArm chips to date consume roughly a watt of power and operate at a maximum speed of 233 megahertz; the new design requires less than half the power, only 450 milliwatts, while running at a speed of 600 megahertz.

- Late in 1998, Intel said it would expand its network products for small businesses and remote offices by buying Shiva Corporation. Shiva makes remote access servers and "virtual private network" equipment in a $4 billion segment of remote access technologies, which enable people to dial into their company's computer network from afar. The deal was Intel's biggest purchase yet of a networking company. In the past couple of years, Intel spent about $150 million in acquisitions of Case Technology Ltd., and Dayna Communications Inc., and a minority stake in Xircom Inc. These deals have helped Intel gain a position in providing networking equipment for consumers and small businesses.

- In 1998, Intel revamped its microprocessor lineup with new products created specifically for each computing segment:

- The company's Celeron microprocessor, introduced in April and followed in August with an advanced version, offers entry-level PC buyers a good value and reliable Intel technology. By the end of 1998, it was the second-highest volume PC microprocessor in the world, second only to the Pentium II microprocessor.

- The company's Pentium II microprocessor remains the heart of Intel's business. Ideal for the performance desktop and entry-level servers and workstations, this powerful processor makes up the majority of units the company sold worldwide in 1998.

- The powerful Pentium II Xeon microprocessor, introduced in August of 1998, is specifically designed for mid- and high-range servers and workstations. Manufacturers can benefit by designing systems to harness the power of multiple high-performance processors. Demand for servers and workstations is increasing, and within both of these segments, sales of systems based on Intel architecture are growing much faster than the overall segment.

■ Intel is looking for big savings in production costs. For instance, it has accelerated by six months, to mid-1999, its move to next-generation chip manufacturing technology: Shrinking the width of circuits on chips from 0.25 microns (about one-four-hundredths of the thickness of a human hair) to just 0.18 microns. That lets Intel make 75 percent more chips per silicon wafer, dramatically slashing unit costs. What's more, instead of buying all-new production gear, the company is reusing 70 percent of its current equipment as it shifts to 0.18-micron widths. These and other moves should raise gross profits by more than $1 billion in 1999.

Total assets: $31,471 million
Current ratio: 2.32
Common shares outstanding: 3,315 million
Return on 1998 shareholders equity: 26.4%

	1998	1997	1996	1995	1994	1993	1992	1991
Revenues (millions)	26,273	25,070	20,847	16,202	11,521	8,782	5,844	4,779
Net income (millions)	6,178	6,945	5,157	3,491	2,562	2,277	1,077	795
Earnings per share	1.77	1.94	1.45	.99	.73	.65	.31	.24
Dividends per share	.05	.06	.05	.04	.03	.03	.01	nil
Price: high	63.1	51.0	35.4	19.6	9.2	9.3	5.7	3.7
low	32.8	31.4	12.5	7.9	7.0	5.3	2.9	2.4

International Business Machines Corporation

New Orchard Road, Armonk, NY 10504 ▫ Investor contact: Hervey C. Parke (914) 499-5008 ▫ Direct dividend reinvestment plan available (202) 324-0405 ▫ Web site: www.ibm.com/investor ▫ Listed: NYSE ▫ Ticker symbol: IBM ▫ S&P rating: B ▫ Value Line financial strength rating: A++

IBM is the largest manufacturer of data processing equipment and systems. Its products run the gamut from personal computers to mainframes.

There's good reason to believe that IBM has more upside potential. For one thing, IBM owns some big, fast-growing businesses that don't always make the headlines. Its disk-drive unit, barely visible a few years ago, now generates an estimated $3 billion in revenue, putting it at the top ranks of the industry. What's more, sales of IBM software actually exceed those of Microsoft. And IBM's tech-services unit has been growing 23 percent a year; it passed EDS in 1997 as the leader in the field. The company also generates over $5 billion in free cash each year, a big chunk of which is earmarked for a huge stock buy-back plan.

Recent History

IBM acquired chip-maker CommQuest Technologies, Inc. for $180 million, a move IBM hope will speed development of more efficient, more compact wireless products and beef up its chip business. Analysts believe that the closely held CommQuest is a natural mesh for IBM's new "silicon germanium" semiconductor technology, which it plans to use to make low-cost chips for wireless devices. CommQuest makes chips for cell phones, satellite communications, and other radio-based applications, a realm in which IBM has little experience. IBM said the development of this technology will allow wireless capability to be built more compactly; think of a Dick Tracy–type cellular phone built into a wrist watch. Silicon germanium

chips can operate at higher speeds and emit less heat than those made of the more traditional plain silicon.

Shortcomings to Bear in Mind

- Not all was clear sailing in 1998. There were difficulties. Some were external: the economic distress in Asia and Latin America, soft memory chip prices, and a PC price war. And some were of IBM's own making, wrestling with important product transitions in its server line, for example.

- In mainframes, the company is losing market share to Hitachi, which has more than 20 percent of the market, up from less than 5 percent several years ago. Because a lot of the software IBM sells is tailored to its mainframes, weakness there is hurting software sales. IBM's minicomputers and workstations are losing share to servers built by Compaq.

- Some analysts are concerned about possible repercussions from a big cut in research and development spending imposed several years ago by IBM's CEO, Louis V. Gerstner, Jr., who joined the company in 1993. He cut R&D spending by $1 billion, to about $5 billion as he sought ways to turn around the then-ailing computer giant. Some observers wonder if IBM's cuts and its narrower focus on product-oriented research will prompt its scientists to avoid long-shot projects that nevertheless might yield a home run. Moreover, a decline in patents could hurt what has become a big IBM revenue stream: its patent portfolio generates about $1 billion in annual royalties, from about $350 million in 1993.

Reasons to Buy

- Hoping to lead the way to smoother on-line commerce, IBM introduced a new mainframe computer in May of 1999. It is capable of processing 1.6 billion instructions per second, more than 50 percent more powerful than any machine on the market. The high-speed business machines were introduced less than nine months after the company released the first mainframe to break the 1 billion mark for instructions per second. The S/390 G6, or sixth generation, is the first IBM mainframe to use the copper-semiconductor technology that the company introduced nearly two years earlier. In addition to increasing speed and capacity, copper chips cost less and use less electricity than those made with aluminum. The metals are used to carry signals between millions of transistors packed into each thumbnail-sized piece of silicon.

- IBM's market value, probably the most important measure of progress to investors, grew $69 billion in 1998. What's more, it has expanded by $146 billion since the company's major restructuring in 1993. In 1998, IBM's share price climbed an impressive 76 percent. Early in 1999, the company's board of directors approved the second IBM stock split in two years.

- In April of 1999, IBM agreed to sell Dell Computer Corporation $16 billion in parts over seven years, burnishing IBM's reputation in the technology market and further blurring the lines between competitor and ally in the computer industry. The two companies—fierce rivals for years in selling personal computers—called the deal the largest original-equipment manufacturing agreement ever reached in their industry. The deal positions IBM as a premier parts provider to one of the world's fastest-growing computer firms. Even before the deal, IBM was selling Dell about $350 million a year in computer components, mainly data-storing disk drives. But if the companies's seven-year estimate is attained, that figure would climb to an average of $2.3 billion annually, as IBM adds incremental sales in disk drives, chips, computer screens, and other electronics.

- In 1998, for the fourth straight year, the company reported record revenue, nearly $82 billion. Earnings rose to $6.3 billion, and the company set a new record in earnings per share.

- In 1998, IBM unveiled a much-anticipated new generation of powerful mainframe computers that have twice the processing speed of its prior models. Even so, IBM's new computers are still slower than those sold by Hitachi Data Systems. According to analysts, IBM's new mainframe could give the company a fighting chance to stop the erosion of revenue and market share in the important product line. One analyst said, "If IBM can get within spitting distance, there is some preference among large customers to go with IBM."

- In 1998, IBM unveiled a companywide initiative to move aggressively into business intelligence, a rapidly growing industry that helps companies stimulate revenue by extracting business trends from computer data banks. Business intelligence includes the gathering, management, and analysis of data for the purpose of using the acquired information to improve decision-making or to decrease operating profits.

Targeting a cross section of industries and large, medium, and small companies, IBM is introducing software, hardware, and consulting packages that start at $40,000 and reach multimillion-dollar figures.

The business intelligence industry, still largely an esoteric concept for many companies, is in its infancy and worth less than $10 billion. Projections from Palo Alto Management Group and Giga Information Corporation have it soaring to $50 billion or $70 billion by the turn of the century.

- IBM's services business is growing rapidly. The company's global reach helps it to win outsourcing contracts from companies with worldwide operations.

- IBM's expertise in networking is a plus in gaining contracts from the many businesses that are trying to tie together their vast computer resources.

- IBM is cashing in on the rapidly growing interest in electronic commerce, to help businesses speed up the exchange of information with suppliers and customers.

- The fundamentals in the computer industry remain strong, mainly because of the growing global appetite for technology products that increase productivity. Worldwide competition is forcing companies to become more productive, a task being accomplished largely through the employment of technology.

- Analysts see strong demand for the relatively new CMOS-based (complementary metal oxide semiconductor) mainframes, given their good price/performance characteristics. Although the machines are cheaper than older models, they are also less expensive to manufacture, which means margins are wider.

- The explosive growth of the Internet is helping IBM. The company expects the overall information technology industry to grow at an annual rate of 10 percent, to $1.6 trillion by 2002. Of that, the e-business segment will grow to $600 million, and it will grow twice as fast as

the industry overall. IBM management says, "We intend to capture a good chunk of that new business."

- Late in 1998, IBM teamed up with Santa Cruz Operation, Inc. and others, including Sequent Computer Systems, Inc., to present a more consolidated Unix software alternative to Microsoft in the corporate-computing market. The alliance is aimed at building a Unix operating system that can be used on computers ranging from laptop to supercomputers, whether they are based on IBM's own chips or the more common Intel microprocessors.

The joint effort brought together IBM, which has a robust Unix operating system called AIX that is used mostly in midrange computers, and SCO's UnixWare, the leading software at the low end of the Unix market. Sequent adds a technology, dubbed NUMA, that is used for high-end computers based on Intel chips.

The initiative could give a boost to Unix, a popular operating system for heavy-duty computing. Unix has been facing mounting competition from Microsoft's Windows NT software, in part because the Unix market has been split into multiple "flavors" offered by competing vendors. Application programs, such as databases, written for one version of Unix generally cannot run on computers that use another Unix variant.

- In 1999, IBM unveiled a more powerful model of its supercomputer in a move to help revive slumping computer hardware sales. The Power3 processor, the heart of the newest RS/6000 SP, performs up to 2 billion operations per second. That's twice as fast as the computer chip that ran Deep Blue, the machine that beat chess grandmaster Garry Kasparov in 1997. According to one analyst, "The RS/6000 was not getting enough attention. This product should give IBM a boost." IBM is also counting on the RS/6000's traditional strength with scientific and technical customers. The University of Utah in Salt Lake City, for instance, is using an early version of the computer to simulate drug effects.

■ Competing against everyone from Electronic Data Systems to Big Four accounting firms to boutique shops

offering only Web services, IBM has emerged as the world's largest purveyor of technology services, according to *Business Week*. It counsels customers on technology strategy, helps them prepare for mishaps, runs all their computer operations, develops their applications, procures their supplies, trains their employees, and even gets them into the dot.com realm.

Total assets: $86,100 million
Current ratio: 1.23
Common shares outstanding: 1,852 million
Return on 1998 shareholders' equity: 32.6%

	1998	1997	1996	1995	1994	1993	1992	1991
Revenues (millions)	81,667	78,508	75,947	71,940	64,052	62,716	64,523	64,792
Net income (millions)	6,328	6,093	5,429	6,334	2,965	13	1,435	2,112
Earnings per share	3.29	3.01	2.76	2.76	1.23	def.	.62	.92
Dividends per share	.44	.39	.33	.25	.25	.40	1.21	1.21
Price: high	95.0	56.8	41.5	28.7	19.1	15.0	25.1	34.9
low	47.8	31.8	20.8	17.6	12.8	10.2	12.2	20.9

CONSERVATIVE GROWTH

The Interpublic Group of Companies, Inc.

1271 Avenue of the Americas, New York, NY 10020 ❑ Investor contact: Eugene P. Beard (212) 399-8053 ❑ Dividend reinvestment plan available (201) 324-0498 ❑ Web site: www.interpublic.com ❑ Ticker symbol: IPG ❑ S&P rating: A+ ❑ Value Line financial strength rating: A+

The Interpublic Group of Companies is the world's second-largest advertising agency system. The advertising agency functions of the company are conducted in more than 120 countries through McCann-Erickson Worldwide, Ammirati Puris Lintas, The Lowe Group, Campbell Mithun Esty (50 percent-owned), Western International Media, and other affiliated companies.

The principal functions of the company's advertising agencies are to plan and create advertising programs for clients and to place the advertising in various media. The usual advertising commission is 13 percent of the gross charge (billings) for

advertising space or time, but discounting is common.

In addition to advertising agency activities, Interpublic is involved in publishing, market research, direct marketing, sales promotion, public relations, and product development.

With many globally oriented clients such as Unilever and Coca-Cola, Interpublic has long been considered Madison Avenue's most international advertising company. But lately, as the rest of the ad world scrambled to follow Interpublic's lead by scooping up ad agencies around the globe, Interpublic was looking harder for acquisitions here at home. This is where it found Hill, Holliday, which handles about $600 million a year in billings for clients that include Fidelity Investments, Advanced Micro Devices, FMR Corporation, the Gillette Company, Bay Networks, Harvard Pilgrim Health Care, John Hancock Mutual Life Insurance, and BankBoston.

The acquisition of one of Boston's leading midsize ad agencies by giant Interpublic underscores how important emerging advertiser categories such as financial services and technology are becoming to Madison Avenue's future growth.

Highlights of 1998

Interpublic had an exceptional year in 1998, as gross income climbed to nearly $4 billion, an increase of about 27 percent over the prior year. Net income advanced to $309.9 million, up nearly 30 percent over 1997. Based on these results, Interpublic continues to be one of the largest and most profitable organizations of advertising agencies and marketing communications services companies in the world.

What's more, 1998 was a year of dramatic growth for the company. Interpublic entered 1998 comprised of three global advertising networks, one global direct marketing network, plus a number of standalone regional and local businesses. The company closed the year with seven strong networks: the above-mentioned four, plus newly acquired International Public Relations, newly combined Western Initiative Media Worldwide, and dramatically expanded Octagon sports and event marketing.

Shortcomings to Bear in Mind

- It's no secret that Interpublic is doing well. In the last ten years, earnings per share advanced from $.60 a share to $2.21, a compound annual growth rate of 13.9 percent. Dividends in this same

1988–1998 period, also climbed at a good clip, expanding from $.17 to $.58, a growth rate of 13.1 percent. That's why the price/earnings ratio may be on the high side when you decide to examine this company.

Reasons to Buy

- The long-term outlook for the advertising industry is positive because of new markets, new advertisers, and new product introductions. A growing number of media outlets, increasing market segmentation, and other factors should guarantee expanding business opportunities.

- McCann-Erickson Worldwide offered more evidence in 1998 as to why it is considered the advertising industry's global standard. The first-ever ranking of global media buying units, published by *Advertising Age International*, showed that McCann led all media-buying competitors as the top-ranked in worldwide billings. The agency meanwhile continued its industry leadership in the core areas of overall billings, country coverage, number of agencies top-ranked in their own markets, and global brands handled.

  In its third successive year of winning more than $1 billion in new business, McCann-Erickson added major partners such as Sprint, Gateway, DuPont, and General Mills to its global client roster. It also added important new assignments from MasterCard, Motorola, Goodyear, and London International, among others.

- Under the guidance of CEO Martin Puris, Ammirati Puris Lintas delivered another year of solid growth in 1998. Revenue increased by 14 percent in constant dollars, with all regions showing gains. Of particular note was the global launch of Iridium, the global satellite-based telecommunications company. In partnership with Iridium management, seventeen Ammirati Puris Lintas offices created an innovative launch strategy, with advertising that will run simultaneously in forty-five countries, accompanied by a Web site that goes up in twelve languages. The success of Iridium is only one example of the agency's global and regional efforts for core clients such as Unilever, Johnson & Johnson, Nestlé, R.J. Reynolds International, and Burger King.

- The Lowe Group had its strongest year to date in 1998. Lowe & Partners Worldwide, the main advertising arm of The Lowe Group, continued to strengthen its network with new partnerships in Australia, Chile, Norway, South Africa, Spain, and Switzerland. Eight of the agencies won a Lion at the prestigious International Advertising Festival in Cannes in 1998. The offices in Belgium, Chile, Italy, Greece, and Switzerland were the best-performing agencies in their respective markets at Cannes. What's more, Lowe Partners/SMS was named second-best performing U.S. agency. For the third year running and the fourth time in its eight-year history, Roche Macaulay & Partners in Canada was voted Agency of the Year.

- In 1998, The Interpublic Group forged a new and powerful partnership to better serve its clients's media needs throughout the world. It created a new company, Western Initiative Media Worldwide, which extends the resources and the reach of Interpublic in every field of media planning and buying.

Western Initiative was formed through the merger of two of the world's leading independent media services companies: Western International Media, the largest media independent in the United States, and Initiative Media Worldwide, whose global network includes offices throughout Europe, Latin America, and Asia Pacific.

With more than $10 billion in billings, Western Initiative Media Worldwide is the largest independent media services company in the world. Its global network is unparalleled in its ability to offer client partners a coordinated media product in all major advertising markets.

- DraftWorldwide's reputation as a direct marketing powerhouse is built on its ability to bring clients the insight required to effectively translate business objectives to measurable results. That heritage has resulted in a *Fortune* 500 client list including advertising partnerships with long-standing clients: General Motors, American Express, Home Box Office, and Sprint.

The agency's strength in strategic research, media power, and database development and modeling led to much of its growth with existing and new clients. Today it provides the foundation for DraftWorldwide's position as one of the world's largest fully integrated marketing agencies.

In 1998, DraftWorldwide's billings expanded to nearly $2 billion. This growth came from existing clients, new business, and an aggressive acquisition strategy that was developed to increase market presence as well as add new specialty disciplines. DraftWorldwide now operates out of forty-four offices around the world, plus thirty-three field offices in the United States and Mexico.

In 1998, DraftWorldwide completed twelve acquisitions, including Chicago-based KBA Marketing, which established DraftWorldwide's entree into the lifestyle marketing category. Also in North America, the acquisition of Gingko Group Ltd., a Toronto-based integrated marketing communications agency, represented DraftWorldwide's entry in the Canadian market.

- In 1998, Interpublic acquired International Public Relations and its Shandwick International and Golin/Harris International business to complement existing and highly successful Weber Public Relations Worldwide operation. The acquisition establishes Interpublic as a global leader, in terms of geographic reach and scope of offerings. Interpublic ranks among the top three global public relations firms, with 1998 fee income of $300 million.

- Octagon, the Interpublic sports marketing unit, completed its first full year of operation in 1998. A key development was the completion of the merger of Advantage International and API at the end of 1998. Advantage International, based in Washington, D. C., with fourteen offices, specializes in sponsorship consultancy, as well as events, properties, and athletic management. API, based in London and with offices in twelve cities around the world, specializes in sponsorship sales, consultancy, and sports television programming and production.

Total assets: $6,943 million
Current ratio: 1.06
Common shares outstanding: 278 million
Return on 1998 shareholders' equity: 27.1%

	1998	1997	1996	1995	1994	1993	1992	1991
Revenues (millions)	3,969	3,126	2,538	2,180	1,984	1,794	1,856	1,678
Net income (millions)	310	239	205	168	152	125	112	95
Earnings per share	1.11	.95	.86	.72	.67	.56	.50	.44
Dividends per share	.29	.25	.23	.21	.19	.17	.15	.14
Price: high	40.3	26.5	16.8	14.5	12.0	11.9	11.9	9.6
low	22.6	15.7	13.2	10.6	9.5	8.0	8.6	5.7

GROWTH & INCOME

Jefferson-Pilot Corporation

P. O. Box 21008, Greensboro, NC 27420 ▢ Investor contact: John T. Still, III (336) 691-3382 ▢ Dividend reinvestment plan available (800) 829-8432 ▢ Web site: www.jpfinancial.com ▢ Listed: NYSE ▢ Ticker symbol: JP ▢ S&P rating: A+ ▢ Value Line financial strength rating: A+

Jefferson-Pilot has two business segments: insurance and communications. Within the insurance segment, JP offers individual life insurance products, annuity and investment products, and group insurance products through three principal subsidiaries: Jefferson-Pilot Life Insurance Company (JP Life), Alexander Hamilton Life Insurance Company of America (AH Life), and First Alexander Hamilton Life (FAHL).

Within the communications segment, JP operates television broadcasting stations

(three) and radio broadcasting stations (seventeen) and provides sports and entertainment programming. These operations are conducted through Jefferson-Pilot Communications Company (JPCC).

Highlights of 1998

Jefferson-Pilot's 1998 operating results were excellent. The company's operating earnings per share grew 21 percent to a record $3.37, and it again realized substantial capital gains that added $.54 to earnings per share, bringing the total to $3.91. Return on equity expanded to 16.4 percent. Cash dividends paid per share increased 11 percent, and total return to shareholders (dividends plus stock appreciation) reached nearly 48 percent in 1998.

The company implemented a plan to exit the volatile group medical insurance business, since JP was a relatively small competitor in a market increasingly dominated by large managed-care companies. What's more, it was a line of business that exposed the company's earnings to significant potential volatility. Thus, group medical insurance simply no longer fit JP's definition of an attractive core business, and getting out frees substantial capital for investment elsewhere.

The company also completed the assimilation of Jefferson-Pilot Financial Insurance Company (formerly Chubb Life, which was acquired the prior year).Variable universal life, not a part of the company's product portfolio two years earlier, now represents one-third of Jefferson-Pilot's current life insurance production. The company's average sale in the JP Financial franchise in 1998 was $417,000 in face amount of life insurance and $4,300 of annualized premiums. From these impressive figures, it's evident that Jefferson-Pilot caters to the "carriage trade." The company's sales of broker/dealer products approached $2 billion. What's more, it is extremely efficient, one of the lowest-cost producers in the industry.

Shortcomings to Bear in Mind

- According to management, the life insurance business faces several substantial challenges:
  - Traditional life insurance products and distribution channels are experiencing very modest growth.
  - The boundaries between products and sales channels that defined the industry in the past are becoming much less clear. Variable products and bank distribution are two excellent examples of this trend.
- New competitors are challenging the traditional players.
- The industry continues to have excess capacity, with some companies operating under unrealistically low capital return requirements.

However, there is good news at the same time:

- The nation's demographic characteristics are extremely favorable for life insurance and annuity products. The U.S. Census shows that the population in the age range of 40 to 59 years is growing much faster than any other segment of the population. In those years, people clearly reduce consumer spending and sharply increase savings for education and retirement.
- In response to inefficiencies, captive distribution systems are declining and being replaced by independent distribution. This trend benefits companies with flexible approaches to distribution.
- The industry's challenges, particularly overcapacity and inadequate capital returns, are bringing rationalization that will have the effect of removing excess capacity, reducing inefficiency, and improving returns.

Reasons to Buy

- Jefferson-Pilot has a history of steady, reliable growth without adverse surprises. Over the last five years, return on equity expanded from 13.3 percent to 16.4 percent. Operating earnings per share grew at a 16 percent compound rate. The company has produced consistent realized investment gains that have added, on average, 19 percent to

Jefferson-Pilot's earnings per share and in no year less than 12 percent.

- The company has a proven ability as a business operator, including demonstrated skill in building diversified distribution. Annualized premium sales have grown at a compound annual rate of 48 percent for the last five years. Individual life insurance in force ($18 billion in 1993) reached $139 billion in 1998, including $15 billion of variable universal life.

- Jefferson-Pilot has a leading role as an industry consolidator, with a track of sourcing, closing, and integrating strategic acquisitions. In the last five years, the company has closed nearly $1.6 billion of significantly accretive acquisitions.

- Jefferson-Pilot has one of the strongest capital positions in the life insurance industry. The company generated enough capital to support its growth plans while maintaining strong claims-paying ratings. Its financial leverage is moderate and its risk-based capital is strong. That means that Jefferson-Pilot has the financial capability to continue leading as an industry consolidator. What's more, the company has the flexibility to continue to make timely purchases of its own stock.

- JP owns a superior, value-creating Communications Company that holds a leadership position in some of the most attractive markets in the nation. The Communications Company's broadcast cash flow has grown at a compound annual rate of 20 percent during the last five years, to almost $76 million in 1998.

- The company has a clear priority of shareholder interests. Each of its acquisitions, for instance, has been accretive (additive to earnings). From 1993 through 1998, share repurchases amounted to $225 million (6.1 million shares) at an average cost of less than $37 per share. The company's cash dividend increased at a compound annual rate of better than 11 percent over that span. Finally, to align management and shareholder interests better, management compensation has been significantly more heavily weighted toward stock options. Moreover, the company has increased the importance of stock-based and variable compensation at all levels of the organization.

- JP is utilizing its channels to boost sales in synergistic ways. For example, in Chubb Life, the company acquired state-of-the-art capabilities in underwriting variable universal life insurance (VUL). Additionally, the VUL product has been extended into JP's pre-Chubb sales channels of career and independent life agents. At the same time, Chubb's agents have greatly expanded their sales platform to include Jefferson-Pilot's nonvariable life line.

- Jefferson-Pilot has transformed itself into a low-cost manufacturer. It has eliminated gaps between pricing assumptions built into its products and the actual expenses incurred, and its per-policy issuance and maintenance costs have been driven down to a level among the lowest in the industry. In the company's acquisitions, the company has targeted expense reductions of 40 percent or better.

- Jefferson-Pilot views the Internet as a very substantial opportunity. With 20 percent of U.S. households now possessing Internet connections, and with on-line banking established as a viable consumer product, there is no question as to its potential as a medium. According to management, "Certain of our product may achieve direct distribution via the Internet, but the real opportunity, we believe, is to upgrade our service levels and strengthen our relationship with our clients."

■ Jefferson-Pilot appears strategically positioned for a changing world. The financial services industry, and in particular the life insurance industry, is changing at a pace that will quicken further.

Jefferson-Pilot sees four key issues that will impact the life insurance business in the next several years. All involve the issue of industry consolidation, which JP management expects to continue and accelerate:

• Business and product lines focus are increasingly important to well-managed companies. That will drive rationalization and consolidation.

• Market demands for better return on equity will force efficiencies. For many companies, the most direct way to achieve efficiency will be consolidation.

• Demutualization is here. Of the twelve major mutual life insurance companies, two-thirds have either begun the process or publicly committed to it. Mutuals as a group have an excellent opportunity for efficiency improvement. Some of that will come from internal cost-cutting, and some will come via consolidation.

• Financial deregulation will happen. HR10 or some variant almost surely will be passed in Congress, perhaps in 1999. The melding of the insurance, banking, and securities industries will, no doubt, take unexpected turns and may follow an unpredictable schedule, but it will happen.

Total assets: $24,338 million
Common shares outstanding: 106 million
Return on 1998 shareholders' equity: 16.4%

	1998	1997	1996	1995	1994	1993	1992	1991
Premium income (millions)	1,049	1,135	994	810	655	670	658	658
Total income (millions)	2,610	2,578	2,125	1,569	1,334	1,247	1,202	1,174
Earnings per share	3.91	3.47	2.73	2.37	2.10	1.94	1.77	1.52
Dividends per share	1.16	1.04	.93	.83	.75	.69	.58	.48
Price: high	78.4	57.8	39.8	32.2	24.5	25.7	22.0	17.4
low	48.7	34.3	22.4	19.3	20.2	14.8	10.2	9.6

CONSERVATIVE GROWTH

Johnson & Johnson

One Johnson & Johnson Plaza, New Brunswick, NJ 08933 ❑ Investor contact: Helen E. Short (800) 950-5089 ❑ Dividend reinvestment plan available (800) 328-9033 ❑ Web site: www.jnj.com ❑ Listed: NYSE ❑ Ticker symbol: JNJ ❑ S&P rating: A+ ❑ Value Line financial strength rating: A++

Johnson & Johnson is the largest and most comprehensive health care company in the world, with 1998 sales of $23.7 billion. JNJ offers a broad line of consumer products, ethical and over-the-counter drugs, as well as various other medical devices and diagnostic equipment.

The company has a stake in a wide variety of areas: anti-infectives, biotechnology, cardiology and circulatory diseases, the central nervous system, diagnostics, gastrointestinals, minimally invasive therapies, nutraceuticals, orthopaedics, pain management, skin care, vision care, women's health, and wound care.

Johnson & Johnson has 180 operating companies in 51 countries, selling some 50,000 products in more than 175 countries. Its international presence includes not only marketing, but also production and distribution capability in a vast array of regions outside the United States. One advantage of JNJ's worldwide organization is that markets such as China, Latin America, and Africa offer growth potential for mature product lines.

One of Johnson & Johnson's premier assets is its well-entrenched brand names, which are widely known in the United States as well as abroad. The company's well-known trade names include Band-Aid adhesive bandages; Tylenol; Stayfree, Carefree, and Sure & Natural feminine hygiene products; Mylanta; Pepcid AC; Neutrogena; Johnson's baby powder, shampoo, and oil, and Reach toothbrushes. As a marketer, moreover, JNJ's reputation for quality has enabled it to build strong ties to health care providers.

More recently, through an acquisition, Johnson & Johnson now owns the Neutrogena line of skincare and beauty products. As a consequence, the company's stature in the skin and hair care market benefits from the acquisition of the Neutrogena Corporation. Renowned among consumers for its outstanding products for skin and hair care, Neutrogena enables JNJ to benefit from a broader access to this market.

The company's professional items include ligatures and sutures, mechanical wound closure products, diagnostic products, medical equipment and devices, surgical dressings, surgical apparel and accessories, and disposable contact lenses.

Shortcomings to Bear in Mind

- Birth-control pills (a sector in which JNJ's Ortho-McNeil participates) have lost market share to condoms and other forms of contraception in recent years. In addition to concern about sexually transmitted diseases, health worries about the pill are also driving some women away. A study by the National Center for Health Statistics found that 27 percent of U.S. women used the pill in 1995, down from 31 percent seven years earlier. The decline was even more pronounced for teens. Forty-four percent were using the pill, down from 59 percent. In the same period, condom use among women overall increased to 20 percent, from 15 percent.

On a more positive note, Ortho Tri-Cyclen is the only birth-control brand with FDA permission to advertise skin-clearing benefits. The company won approval for the product in 1997, after submitting clinical-test results in a six-month study involving 250 women. Ads in women's magazines such as Glamour, show a close-up of a young woman's face and pose a question riveting to teenagers: "Can a birth-control pill help clear up your skin?" Since Ortho-McNeil launched the campaign a couple years ago, the acne-clearing pill has surged past rivals, including other Ortho pills, to rank number one among domestic oral contraceptives, a $1.6-billion-a-year business.

- Five years ago, Johnson & Johnson sparked a revolution in the treatment of coronary-artery disease with a medical innovation called a stent. Few devices have yielded such an immediate eye-popping bonanza for their manufacturer. Doctors rushed to use the tiny metal scaffold to prop open obstructed heart vessels. In just thirty-seven months, Johnson & Johnson tallied more than $1 billion in stent sales and garnered more than 90 percent of this lucrative market.

All was well until Guidant Corporation entered the scene, introducing a competitive stent. According to a Guidant spokesman, "Within forty-five days, we had gained a 70 percent market position." Meanwhile, other rivals have joined the fray, including Arterial Vascular Engineering Inc. and Boston Scientific Corporation. By the end of 1998,

JNJ's share of the stent business had withered to less than 10 percent.

Reasons to Buy

■ Johnson & Johnson's broad range of products is one of the keys to its past success and its bright future. The company has dominant positions in a number of health care markets. It has been able to establish and enlarge leading market positions even in products areas in which it was not the innovator.

■ A new contact lens made by Johnson & Johnson promises to clear the fuzzy vision of aging Americans who would rather squint that be caught wearing bifocals. The Acuvue Bifocal disposable contact lenses are being heavily marketed by the company to the 80 million people who have presbyopia, a vision problem that usually begins shortly after forty. Caused by a loss of flexibility in the eye, presbyopia makes it hard to thread a needle, read a newspaper, or focus on a computer screen. The lenses are paper-thin and can be worn continuously for seven days or during waking hours for two weeks. Designed with five invisible concentric rings that bring distant and near objects into focus, they allow wearers to shift back and forth easily. They cost about $13 to $14 a pair.

■ Risperdal, the breakthrough drug discovered by the Janssen Research Foundation for the treatment of schizophrenia and other psychotic disorders, achieved another year of solid growth in 1998. The company's start in the central nervous system (CNS) realm goes back to Janssen's introduction in 1959 of haloperidol, which is still the most widely used antipsychotic in the world.

Current Janssen activities include the co-development, with the Britain's Shire Pharmaceuticals Group, of Reminyl for the treatment of Alzheimer's disease.

Johnson & Johnson recently completed Phase III clinical trials on Reminyl.

■ In 1998, Johnson & Johnson received approval from the federal government of its new artificial sweetener, called Sucralose. Some analysts believe that Sucralose could become a major factor in the giant market of sugarfree foods and beverages, now consumed by 144 million Americans. Many food and beverage companies have been eagerly awaiting a new generation of sweeteners, with the hope of giving a spark to sales of low-calorie products. Sucralose can now be used in fifteen types of foods and beverages, including soft drinks, baked goods, chewing gum, and sugar substitutes. The only artificial sweetener made from sugar, Sucralose is 600 times sweeter than sugar and could avoid many of the taste problems consumers have had with saccharine. Sucralose, made by McNeil Specialty Products, is one of only four artificial sweeteners available for use in the United States and one of only two without any substantive health warnings or usage restrictions. Aspartame, commonly known as Nutrasweet, is often used in diet sodas and carries only a minor health warning for people suffering from phenylketonuria, a rare genetic disease that mainly affects infants.

■ The company has a consistent record of growth. Earnings per share advanced from $.72 per share in 1988 to $2.67 in 1998, a compound annual growth rate of 14 percent. In the same ten-year span, dividends climbed from $.24 to $.97, a growth rate of 15 percent.

■ Cardiology and, more broadly, the management of circulatory diseases, is an important growth platform for JNJ. Through its Cordis affiliate, the company is well positioned for a profitable future in cardiology and the treatment of circulatory diseases. To be sure, this business is intensely competitive. However, Cordis is moving forward with a substantial pipeline of new stent, balloon, and endovascular products. Management is particularly pleased with the merger of Biosense, Inc. into Cordis, for its patented medical sensor technologies to facilitate a wide range of diagnostic and therapeutic procedures, particularly in the realm of correcting heart rhythm problems.

■ Skin care is the largest consumer market in which Johnson & Johnson participates—some $47 billion at retail. What's more, JNJ believes that it has the fastest-growing skin portfolio in the world. Its presence extends from its well-known heritage in baby products to consumer toiletries and prescription pharmaceuticals. Four of the company's five key skin care brands—Neutrogena, RoC, Clean & Clear, and Johnson's pH5.5—have been growing at double-digit rates.

■ LifeScan, a world leader in blood glucose monitoring, recently introduced meterless Smartstrip Test Strips in key markets outside the United States to allow people with diabetes to obtain accurate blood glucose values without a meter. LifeScan also launched the Surestep Pro System for hospitals.

■ In recent years, Johnson & Johnson has been making business-building acquisitions. They range from large ones such as DePuy in orthopaedics to smaller ones such as FemRx, a leader in the development of proprietary surgical systems that enable surgeons to perform less invasive alternatives to hysterectomy. Over the past ten years, moreover, Johnson & Johnson has made forty-five such acquisitions of companies and product lines. During the same span, the company divested eighteen businesses that no longer fit JNJ's long-term growth strategies and which management felt would be better off in someone else's hands.

■ Urology is among the newest growth platforms for Johnson & Johnson. The company entered this field through the 1996 acquisition of Indigo Medical and a subsequent alliance with Theragenics Corporation. Products marketed by Indigo include Theraseed, a Palladium-103 radioactive isotope, for treating localized cancer of the prostate—the second most common form of cancer in men. Theraseed implants are placed in the prostate gland in a one-time, minimally invasive procedure that typically has a lower incidence of side effects than traditional surgery. The objective is to deliver enough radiation to kill the targeted cancer while avoiding excessive damage to surrounding normal tissue. Johnson & Johnson has worldwide marketing rights to Theraseed Palladium-103 under an agreement with Theragenics Corporation.

Total assets: $26,211 million
Current ratio: 2.25
Common shares outstanding: 1,345 million
Return on 1998 shareholders' equity: 23.6%

	1998	1997	1996	1995	1994	1993	1992	1991
Revenues (millions)	23,657	22,629	21,620	18,842	15,734	14,138	13,753	12,447
Net income (millions)	3,669	3,303	2,887	2,403	2,006	1,787	1,525	1,461
Earnings per share	2.67	2.41	2.17	1.86	1.56	1.37	1.23	1.10
Dividends per share	.97	.85	.74	.64	.57	.51	.45	.39
Price: high	89.8	67.3	54.0	46.2	28.3	25.2	29.3	29.1
low	63.4	48.6	41.6	26.8	18.0	17.8	21.5	16.3

Johnson Controls, Inc.

P. O. Box 591, Milwaukee, WI 53201 ❑ **Investor contact: Denise M. Zutz (414) 228-1200** ❑ **Direct dividend reinvestment plan available (414) 276-3737** ❑ **Fiscal year's end September 30** ❑ **Web site: www.johncontrols.com** ❑ **Ticker symbol: JCI** ❑ **S&P rating: A** ❑ **Value Line financial strength rating: A**

Johnson Controls has expanded remarkably since Professor Warren Johnson founded the company to manufacture his invention, the electric room thermostat. Since its start in 1885, Johnson Controls has grown into a multibillion-dollar corporation, with worldwide leadership in two businesses: automotive systems and building controls.

Fundamental to this success, according to management, "is the Johnson Controls mission to continually exceed customers's increasing expectations."

Automakers, for instance, outsource their seating requirements to Johnson Controls to improve quality and reduce costs. They look to the company not merely to manufacture a complete seat or seat component. They also look to Johnson Controls to design it, engineer it, integrate it with surrounding parts, and deliver it globally.

Integration of electronics into vehicle interiors is one of the company's specialties, ranging from global positioning systems to digital compasses and Homelink. The company, moreover, is continuously developing new products and holds more patents than any other automotive interior supplier.

A fundamental component of the Johnson Controls mission is continuous improvement in quality, service, productivity, and time compression. Johnson Controls provides batteries for both original equipment and replacement automotive battery markets.

According to a spokesman for the company, "With more than 110 years of experience in the controls industry,

Johnson Controls understands buildings better than anyone else. That's why tens of thousands of commercial, institutional, and government building owners and managers around the world turn to Johnson Controls to improve the quality of buildings's indoor environments by maximizing comfort, productivity, safety, and energy efficiency."

The company engineers, manufactures, and installs control systems that automate a building's heating, ventilating, and air conditioning, as well as its lighting and fire-safety equipment. Its Metasys Facility Management System automates a building's mechanical systems for optimal comfort levels while using the least amount of energy. In addition, it monitors fire sensors and building access, controls lights, tracks equipment maintenance, and helps building managers make better decisions.

Building systems at some companies are critical to achieving their corporate missions. In the pharmaceutical industry, for example, the failure of a building's equipment or staff to maintain the proper laboratory conditions could mean the loss of years of new drug research and development. In a bank's data center, moreover, the failure of cooling equipment could shut down computer systems, delaying millions of dollars in transactions every minute.

Shortcomings to Bear in Mind

■ Although Johnson Controls has good prospects, its history of growth is good, but not spectacular. In the 1988–1998 period, earnings per share advanced from $1.36 to $3.25, an annual compound growth rate of 9.1 percent. During those years, moreover, earnings dipped from the prior year on two occasions. In the same ten-year span, dividends advanced from $.55 to $.92, a growth rate of only 5.3 percent.

Reasons to Buy

- In 1998, Johnson Controls completed its fifty-second consecutive year of increased sales, its eighth consecutive year of increased income, and its twenty-third consecutive year of increased dividends.

- *IndustryWeek* magazine included Johnson Controls in its roster of the "World's 100 Best-Managed Companies" for the third year in a row. It was also included in *Forbes* magazine's list of "America's Best Technology Users."

- The company's Automotive Systems Group achieved double-digit growth in sales in 1998 as JCI launched new seating and interiors programs. It also benefited from higher production of vehicles that it supplies in North America and Europe. What's more, Johnson Controls was able to achieve record results that year despite the impact of the strike at General Motors North American operations and lower-than-expected demand in South America, caused by an economic slowdown in the region.

- The company's automotive business is expected to expand in the years ahead as automakers continue outsourcing seating and interior systems in North America and Europe, as well as in emerging global markets.

  What's more, the company's development of innovative features and application of new technologies for the automotive interior will strengthen the company's leadership position as Johnson Controls makes its customers's vehicles more comfortable, convenient, and safe.

  The 1998 acquisition of Becker Group gives JCI a new platform for growth in interior systems, especially in Europe. Becker is a leading supplier of automotive door systems and instrument panels. The Becker acquisition should add about $1 billion to JCI's annual sales. In 1998, the company also acquired Commerfin SpA., an Italian manufacturer of door systems and a major supplier to Fiat. These acquisitions provide Johnson Controls with a new platform for further growth in Europe by integrating their products, processes, and manufacturing capabilities with those of JCI.

- Johnson Controls is the most innovative seating and interiors supplier in the industry, and automakers look to the company for new technologies that will differentiate their vehicles in the minds of the consumers. In 1998, the company introduced innovations such as seats with active temperature controls for heating, cooling, and ventilation; seats with built-in workspaces and child activity centers; and even seats with massage functions.

- Johnson Controls opened a state-of-the-art comfort technology lab in Plymouth, Michigan in 1998. The virtual-reality driving simulator replicates the exact sights, sounds, and motions that drivers experience. Researchers can better define seating comfort, as well as test interior ergonomics and performance on any human shape and size.

- In 1998, the company introduced TravelNote, a digital voice recorder that can be integrated into the sun visor or overhead console. It provides a safe and convenient way to store addresses, directions, or phone numbers.

- Johnson Controls is the largest automotive battery manufacturer in North

America. What's more, the company gained market share in 1998, as a result of a concerted effort to improve battery quality and life, coupled with its partnership with a select group of strong retailers and distributors.

The company's aftermarket battery customers include AutoZone, Interstate Battery, Sears, and Wal-Mart. In addition, JCI makes original equipment batteries for Daimler-Chrysler, Ford, Honda, Nissan, and Toyota.

- Investments in new products and process technology that bring value to the company's battery customers help Johnson Controls maintain its market leadership. One example, the Inspira thin metal film starting battery, is significantly smaller and lighter than traditional lead-acid batteries. This unique battery will help reduce the weight of vehicles by as much as 20 pounds, enhancing fuel efficiency. The Inspira is expected to be used in new vehicles beginning in the 2001 model year.

- In late 1998, the company announced new joint ventures in Mexico and South America that will allow it to bring advanced battery technology and improved product quality to these markets.

- The company's Metasys facility management system monitors and controls heating, ventilating, and air conditioning systems in buildings to ensure maximum occupant comfort with a minimum of energy costs. Hundreds of Metasys systems were installed in 1998, including new projects at the Pentagon, the Kremlin, and the new Beijing International Airport.

Metasys technology has been improved and expanded since its introduction to create new benefits for customers. Metasys leads the industry in its ability to integrate with other building systems such as lighting, access, and fire/safety systems. Today, Metasys can also integrate controllers made by other companies for power monitoring equipment, refrigeration systems, laboratory fume hoods, manufacturing process controls, and more.

Total assets: $7,942 million
Current ratio: 0.79
Common shares outstanding: 85 million
Return on 1998 shareholders' equity: 17%

	1998	1997	1996	1995	1994	1993	1992	1991
Revenues (millions)	12,587	11,145	10,009	8,330	6,870	6,182	5,156	4,559
Net income (millions)	303	265	235	196	165	138	123	95
Earnings per share	3.25	2.85	2.14	1.80	1.49	1.37	1.06	1.03
Dividends per share	.92	.86	.82	.78	.72	.68	.62	.60
Price: high	61.9	51.0	42.7	34.9	30.9	29.6	23.1	18.3
low	40.5	35.4	31.3	22.9	22.4	21.5	17.3	10.9

GROWTH & INCOME

Kimberly-Clark Corporation

P. O. Box 619100, Dallas, TX 75261-9100 ❏ Investor contact: Michael D. Masseth (972) 281-1478 ❏ Dividend reinvestment plan available (800) 730-4001 ❏ Web site: www.Kimberly-Clark.com ❏ Ticker symbol: KMB ❏ S&P rating: A- ❏ Value Line financial strength rating: A++

Kimberly-Clark is a worldwide manufacturer of a wide range of products for personal, business, and industrial uses. Most of the products are made from natural and synthetic fibers, using advanced technologies in absorbency, fibers, and nonwovens.

The company has manufacturing facilities in 38 countries and sales in more than 150. Kimberly-Clark has been one of *Fortune* magazine's "Most Admired" corporations since 1983.

The company's well-known brands include Kleenex facial and bathroom tissue, Huggies diapers and baby-wipes, Pull-Ups training pants, GoodNites underpants, Kotex and New Freedom feminine-care products, Depend and Poise incontinence care products, Hi-Dri household towels, Kimguard sterile wrap, Kimwipes industrial wipers, and Classic premium business and correspondence papers.

Shortcomings to Bear in Mind

■ The past year (1998) was a difficult one for Kimberly-Clark, with setbacks in Europe and Asia. European results suffered early in 1998 because of intense competition in tissue and the costs of expanding diaper manufacturing capacity, coupled with launching improved diapers and feminine-care products.

To turn around the company's business in Europe, Kimberly-Clark brought in a new management team that has done a solid job of moving quickly to improve results in the region. In Asia, KMB's management is also faring well. It has improved market share in many of its product categories despite the region's turmoil.

■ If Kimberly-Clark is to succeed, it must continually battle against relentless, determined Procter & Gamble, one of the most innovative and skillful companies in the world.

■ Growth in earnings per share has been rather pedestrian of late. In the 1988–1998 period, earnings per share advanced from $1.18 to $2.46, a compound annual growth rate of 7.6 percent. In the same ten-year stretch, dividends expanded from $.40 a share to $.99, a growth rate of 9.5 percent. This growth rate prompted me to keep the stock in the growth and income category.

Reasons to Buy

■ The cornerstone of Kimberly-Clark, according to management, is "brands and technology. Let's take our successful re-launch of Kleenex Cottonelle bathroom tissue. It's a great example of how we're now applying to tissue the same formula that's worked so well for us in personal care and health care—that is, employing technology to deliver superior-performing products that win in the marketplace."

Using a patented process first commercialized at the company's mill in Villey-Saint-Etienne, France, KMB has produced a tissue with superior bulk, strength, softness, and absorbency—while reducing manufacturing costs. As a result, Kleenex Cottonelle has achieved record profits for the company's premium bathroom tissue business in North America. In 1999, Kimberly-Clark expanded distribution of this product across the United States.

What's more, the company has begun applying this and other patented tissue technologies to improve the quality and reduce the manufacturing cost of many other Kimberly-Clark products. These include a significantly improved Kleenex Scottfold towel for commercial users, introduced in late 1998; a new Scott household towel that became available in domestic stores in 1999. Still another introduction in 1999 was an even better Andrex bathroom tissue, which is already one of the best-selling nonfood grocery brands in the United Kingdom.

- Technology's impact can be seen across all KMB brands. For instance, Huggies Little Swimmers disposable swimpants, introduced nationally in 1998, continue to garner awards for innovation. In addition, Depend protective underwear for adults, introduced late in 1998, reinforces the company's leadership in the North American incontinence market. Similarly, Kimberly-Clark's expertise in fibers, nonwovens, and absorbency technologies has led to improvements in Poise incontinence pads, Kotex feminine pads, Huggies diapers and baby wipes, Pull-Ups training pants, and GoodNites disposable underpants in many countries.

- As the world's foremost producer of nonwoven fabrics, Kimberly-Clark also brings sophisticated technology and cost advantages to bear on its health care products, which include sterile wrap, surgical drapes and gowns, and other protective apparel. In fact, the company holds an impressive 25 percent of the hundreds of patents granted in the non-woven field since 1995. In the opinion of KMB management, "health care is a business that continues to exceed expec-

tations and offers enormous potential for further growth."

- In 1997, the company acquired Tecnol Medical Products, which immediately gave Kimberly-Clark 50 percent of the domestic market for disposable face masks. Late in 1998, the company acquired Ballard Medical Products. This moves KMB into other health care categories and markets, as well. Ballard is a leading manufacturer of disposable medical devices for respiratory care, gastroenterology, and cardiology. What's more, Ballard sells more than 80 percent of all closed-suction catheters used in U.S. hospitals.

- The company's acquisitions are not limited to the United States. In 1998, Kimberly-Clark purchased a 50 percent equity interest in Klabin Tissue, the leading tissue manufacturer in Brazil and the second-largest in Latin America. Klabin supports the company's Latin American expansion and has given it such well-known consumer brands as Neve, Nice, Chiffon, and Gourmet.

- In 1998, the company also funded acquisitions or increased its investments in businesses in Bolivia, China, Colombia, Ecuador, Korea, and Peru. On the other hand, KMB decided to shut down its pulp mill in Mobile, Alabama in late 1999 and sell the related woodlands operation to Southstar Timber Resources. This is a continuation of its move out of the cyclical pulp business.

- In 1999, the company announced plans for additional facility consolidations, the charge for which was taken in 1998. With these moves, Kimberly-Clark has completed a three-year process of redesigning and rationalizing its asset base by eliminating excess, high-cost capacity and consolidating its operations into fewer, larger, and more efficient facilities. The company has realized significant savings from this process, with more savings to come.

- In the realm of professional health care products, the company has been achieving impressive results, much of it emanating from innovative surgical gowns, drapes, and wraps. The same is true of the performance of KMB's nonwoven materials segment, which supplies versatile fabrics to its consumer-products operations and other businesses at a cost advantage, compared with its competition.

- One of Kimberly-Clark's strengths stems from the leadership position it holds in three core technologies: fibers, absorbency, and nonwovens. It also comes from the company's capacity in high-speed manufacturing and from its constant emphasis on innovation, productivity, and cost reduction.

- Kimberly-Clark as it is now constituted is a much more balanced company. Before the Scott Paper merger and other acquisitions, the company derived almost half of its revenues from diapers and other personal-care products. That portion is now one-third. Consumer tissue also accounts for about one-third of revenues, with the balance coming from a combination of away-from-home and other products.

- The company's Huggies Utratrim diapers now feature hook-and-loop fasteners from suppliers such as Velcro USA Inc. KMB also added a breathable outer cover to its Huggies Supreme brand.

- In Central and Eastern Europe, Kimberly-Clark extended its line of consumer products in Russia, with the introduction of economy-priced diapers and feminine care products. The company also acquired Zisoft-Bobi, a Czech diaper and incontinence care

products manufacturer, making Kimberly-Clark the largest personal-care products company in that country. This presence provides a platform for offering products throughout Central and Eastern Europe. KMB has already introduced Kleenex and Scottex tissue products throughout the region and markets Huggies diapers in Russia, Romania, Croatia, Slovenia, and the Baltic states.

- In KMB's diaper business, Huggies remains the leading brand in North America. As part of the company's strategy to continuously improve the product, it has added hook-and-loop fasteners to Huggies Ultratrim and a leakage barrier at the waist to Huggies Supreme diapers.

- Kimberly-Clark has dominance in many of its brands throughout the world. In country after country, the company's position in its product is either number one or number two. In Australia, for instance, its Snugglers diapers and Thick & Thirsty paper towels fall into this group. The same holds true in such countries as Bolivia with Bebito diapers, Intima feminine pads, Sanex paper towels, and a host of other products. Similarly, in Brazil, this distinction includes Monica diapers, Chiffon paper towels, and Neve bathroom tissue; in China, it's Comfort & Beauty feminine pads; in the Netherlands, Page bathroom tissue and paper towels; in Mexico, Kleen Bebe diapers and Petalo bathroom tissue; in Spain, Monbebe diapers; in Germany, Camelia feminine pads and Tampona tampons; in Israel, Titulim diapers, Lily feminine pads, Molett bathroom tissue and paper towels, and Iris paper napkins. The list goes on and on.

Total assets: $11,510 million
Current ratio: 0.88
Common shares outstanding: 542 million
Return on 1998 shareholders' equity: 32.0%

	1998	1997	1996	1995	1994	1993	1992	1991
Revenues (millions)	12,298	12,547	13,149	13,789	7,364	6,973	7,091	6,777
Net income (millions)	1,676	1,403	1,404	1,104	535	511	517	508
Earnings per share	2.46	2.44	2.49	1.98	1.67	1.59	1.61	1.59
Dividends per share	.99	.95	.92	.90	.88	.85	.82	.76
Price: high	59.4	56.9	49.8	41.5	30.0	31.0	31.6	26.1
low	35.9	43.3	34.3	23.6	23.5	22.3	23.1	19.0

INCOME

Kimco Realty Corporation

3333 New Hyde Park Road, Suite 100, P. O. Box 5020, New Hyde Park, NY 11042-0020 ◻ Investor contact: Scott G. Onufrey (516) 869-7190 ◻ Dividend reinvestment plan available: (781) 575-3400 ◻ Web site: www.kimcorealty.com ◻ Listed: NYSE ◻ Ticker symbol: KIM ◻ S&P rating: Not rated ◻ Value Line financial strength rating: B++

Kimco Realty Corporation, a publicly traded real estate investment trust (REIT), owns and operates the nation's largest portfolio of neighborhood and community shopping centers (measured by gross leasable area), with interests in 440 properties comprising about 57.2 million square feet of leasable area in forty states. The company also manages an additional 27 properties comprising about 3.3 million square feet of leasable area.

Since incorporating in 1966, Kimco has specialized in the acquisition, development, and management of well-located centers with strong growth potential. Self-administered and self-managed, the company's focus is to increase the cash flow and enhance the value of its shopping center properties through strategic re-tenanting, redevelopment, renovation, and expansion, and to make selective acquisitions of neighborhood and community shopping centers that have below-market-rate leases or other cash flow growth potential.

A substantial portion of KIM's income consists of rent received under long-term leases, most of which provide for the payment of fixed-base rents and a pro rata share of various expenses. About 41 percent of the leases also provide for the payment of additional rent as a percentage of gross sales.

KIM's neighborhood and community shopping center properties are designed to attract local area customers and typically are anchored by a supermarket, discount department store or drugstore, offering day-to-day necessities rather than high-priced luxury items. Among the company's major tenants are Venture, Kmart, Wal-Mart, Kohl's, and TJX Companies.

Kimco's core strategy is to acquire older shopping centers carrying below-market rents. This space is then re-leased at much higher rates. A simple way to understand upside re-leasing is to compare the company's average base rent of $6.31 per square foot to what it believes current market rents are—about $9. Taking this spread, $2.69, and applying it to Kimco's 34-million-square-foot portfolio (excluding the Price REIT portfolio) infers that Kimco will receive $91.5 million, or $1.63 per share, as rents are bumped up to market. To be sure, such gains will not be realized at once, but they demonstrate the amount of built-in growth potential within the company's holdings.

Shortcomings to Bear in Mind

- As of March 31, 1999, Kmart was Kimco's largest tenant, representing 13.4 percent of annualized base rent. Management has indicated that it intends to either sell some of the properties leased to Kmart or finance out of the properties by putting non-recourse mortgage debt on the assets, thereby limiting the company's exposure to Kmart.

- Real estate, like many industries, is cyclical. KIM's performance will be, to some degree, dependent on the health of the economy in its markets. Kimco's prospects will also be dependent upon the balance between supply and demand for shopping center space in each of its markets.

- Kimco's CEO, Milton Cooper, believes that e-commerce will hurt commercial real estate. Mr. Cooper has always been aware of the supply/demand equation and retailer's financial status as it relates to retail centers. Even so, cyberspace was one factor he hadn't considered at the time of Kimco's initial public offering. He believes e-commerce could reduce the value for real estate and is watching how demand for space changes. The company is evaluating all tenants in its portfolio and would like to have most dominant tenants that are utilizing the Internet to enhance sales in its centers. Kimco has thrived on problems, he states, and believes the evolution of e-commerce will pose challenges to tackle. However, with Kimco's strong balance sheet and access to capital, Mr. Cooper believes the company can respond to changing demands.

Reasons to Buy

- In 1999, the company executed a joint venture agreement with the New York State Comptroller H. Carl McCall, as sole trustee of the New York State Common Retirement Fund (NYSCRF) to launch the Kimco Income REIT (KIR), an investment vehicle designed to acquire high-quality retail properties, financed primarily through the use of individual non-recourse mortgages. Under the agreement, Kimco contributed nineteen properties to the venture, with an aggregate equity value of about $105 million and has agreed to contribute an additional $12 million. NYSCRF has also subscribed for up to $117 million of equity in the venture, of which $70 million has been used to fund the venture's recent acquisition of four additional properties.

    As a result of the contributions, the KIR portfolio is comprised of twenty-three shopping centers with a value of about $430 million, comprising nearly 4 million square feet of gross leasable area located in 13 states. The portfolio is 98 percent leased and includes anchor tenants such as Home Depot, Target, Kmart, and others.

    Milton Cooper, Kimco's CEO, said, "This is only the first phase in the development of Kimco Income REIT. In fact, discussions are currently underway with other investors for an additional 20 percent equity interest, or about $58 million. In addition to proceeds from non-recourse mortgage financing, this new equity, as well as the remaining commitments from NYSCRF and Kimco, will provide the necessary capital to expand the asset base." Comptroller McCall said, "This investment complements the Common Retirement Fund's diversified portfolio. Given Kimco's expertise in retail properties, we look forward to excellent returns over the long term."

- A major area of activity in 1998 was the acquisition of the Price REIT, an owner/developer of large community shopping centers with a portfolio of properties concentrated in the western part of the United States. Kimco's investment of over $900 million in the Price REIT added forty-three new properties to the portfolio, comprising a total of about 8 million square feet. The Price REIT acquisition gives Kimco national distribution. In the past, the company operated mostly east of the Mississippi.

Additionally, Kimco acquired sixty-seven shopping center properties for a total investment of about $633 million, representing 8.6 million square feet of leasable area. Included in the total investment was the purchase of ninety-four leasehold interests from the bankrupt estate of Venture Stores, Inc., fifty-eight of which related to properties Kimco already owned. All told, Kimco added upwards of 16 million square feet to its portfolio in 1998. In sum, the company extended its operations across the country into a total of forty states, to become America's first truly national neighborhood and community shopping center REIT.

- Kimco has been delivering stable income plus growth since it became a public company in 1991. Kimco's funds from operations (FFO) on a per-share basis has grown at an average annual rate in excess of 10 percent, in line with the company's commitment to steadily increase shareholder value. In October of 1998, Kimco increased its quarterly dividend by 19 percent, from $.48 to $.57. The dividend was subsequently boosted to $.60. The company now pays out to shareholders double the amount paid in 1992.

- The company's merger with Price REIT has given Kimco unparalleled geographic diversity, providing access to major metropolitan markets in every region of the country. Kimco's tenant base is made up of an all-star list of national and regional retailers with strong credit and nationwide name recognition.

- Kimco's success comes not by accident but as the careful product of business principles that have remained firmly in place since the company was founded in the 1950s. The company invests in properties that are undervalued assets where management knows it will be able to capitalize on the margin between the price at which it can buy the property and the price at which it can lease it. The average rent on properties in Kimco's portfolio remains below the market, providing the company with significant upside potential.

- Known for its history of pursuing creative transactions and delivering value-added growth, Kimco's management depth, according to one analyst, is "unparalleled among its peers. The Price REIT transaction has increased this depth even further, particularly with respect to the development and leasing of 'big box' retailers."

- Management is clearly aligned with shareholders as indicated by their collective 19 percent ownership stake in the company, amounting to a $400 million investment.

- According to management, "it is vital to have constant and uninterrupted access to capital. You must have the financial reserves to keep you in the batter's box, ready at any moment to step up to the plate and throw all your talent and creativity into swing when opportunities arise. For us, this means a portfolio of over 300 unencumbered properties that can be easily financed or sold and a strong balance sheet characterized by low debt."

Total assets: $3,051 million
Current ratio: NA
Return on 1998 equity: 10.5%
Common shares outstanding: 60 million

	1998	1997	1996	1995	1994	1993	1992	1991
Revenues (millions)	339	199	168	143	125	99	79	NA
Net income (millions)	122	86	74	52	41	32	19	NA
Earnings per share	2.02	1.78	1.61	1.33	1.17	1.05	.83	NA
Funds from Operations	3.03	2.63	2.37	2.16	1.98	1.77	1.61	NA
Dividends per share	1.97	1.72	1.56	1.44	1.33	1.25	.99	NA
Price: high	41.6	36.2	34.9	28.1	25.9	26.2	20.8	14.3
low	33.4	30.3	25.3	23.6	22.1	20.3	14.1	12.8

CONSERVATIVE GROWTH

Leggett & Platt, Inc.

No. 1 Leggett Road, Carthage, MO 64836 ❏ Investor contact: J. Richard Calhoon (417) 358-8131 ❏ Dividend reinvestment plan not available ❏ Web site: www.leggett.com ❏ Listed: NYSE ❏ Ticker symbol: LEG ❏ S&P rating: A ❏ Value Line financial strength rating: A

Founded in 1883, Leggett & Platt is a leading manufacturer of engineered products serving several major markets. The company's products, many of which are proprietary, are offered through expanding business platforms:

• Furnishings—components for bedding, furniture, and other furnishings, plus select lines of finished products for homes, offices, and institutions

• Fixtures and Displays—store shelving and fixtures, point-of-purchase displays, storage, material handling, and other products for commercial use

• Aluminum Die Castings—components, custom tooling, machining, and other processes for manufacturers of consumer products, telecommunications and electrical equipment, and other products

• Materials and Technologies—specialized materials, manufacturing equipment, systems, and technologies for Leggett operations and other manufacturers

According to analysts, there are few companies that can match Leggett's impressive and steady returns. Since the company came public in March 1967, earnings per share have compounded in

excess of 15 percent per year, and the stock has averaged an annual return of more than 17 percent.

In addition, Leggett has consistently increased its dividend. What's more, the company's strategy has remained consistent during this span. Leggett & Platt looks to increase sales of existing products while pursuing an acquisition strategy that focuses on dominant companies in niche markets that can offer synergies and accretion once acquired.

Customers who buy the company's broad lines of components for bedding and furniture include several thousand manufacturers of home, office, institutional, and commercial furnishings. Manufacturers of today's bedding sets can buy almost all of their mattress and boxspring components from Leggett & Platt. They also purchase some of the company's highly specialized machinery and materials-handling equipment that LEG designs and builds for their needs. Some of the company's machinery and equipment is sold in international markets, primarily to manufacturers of bedding and other furnishings. For customers that manufacture upholstered furniture and other types of furniture, Leggett offers a leading line of specialized components designed for their needs.

Leggett & Platt's finished furnishings include select lines of sleep-related furniture, carpet underlay and nonskid pads, metal and wire displays, and shelving and fixtures for various residential and commercial applications. The diversified non-furnishings products the company manufactures are produced with technologies and processes very similar to those Leggett uses in making certain furnishings products or in producing some select raw materials.

Leggett & Platt maintains a strong emphasis on decentralized management responsibilities, coupled with centralized policies and controls, as well as central services and corporate support. Operations are organized in groups: Bedding and Furniture, Commercial Products, and Wire and Foam Components. There are several Leggett divisions within each group; and many operations produce products for sale in several niche markets.

Shortcomings to Bear in Mind

■ The market is concerned about a future slowdown in the economy and the potential impact on the furniture business. To an extent, Leggett's business is tied to home-buying and new housing starts. The two years after a home is purchased are normally years of heavy furniture purchases.

Reasons to Buy

■ According to a U.S. Department of Labor Study, the age group that spends the most amount on furniture is the 45-to-54-year-old bracket. The second-highest amount is spent by those 35 to 44. The Census Bureau says the number of consumers in the 45-to-54 age group expanded 14.1 percent from 1994 to 1999. The 35 to 44 age group advanced 7.3 percent. At the same time, the general population increased only 4.7 percent.

There are a number of reasons why middle-aged people spend more money on furniture:

● Their income is high during this span of their lives.

● They are more likely to be home-owners than are younger people.

● These more mature couples have sold their starter homes. Their new homes, moreover, are larger and may need a whole new set of more expensive furniture. In 1993, the average home had 2,100 square feet of living space, up 5 percent from 1988. According to surveys, the average home has now increased to 2,200 square feet. Larger homes require much more furniture than smaller ones. For instance, a home with 3,000 square feet needs 2.5 times as much as one with 2,000 square feet.

■ In 1999, *Fortune* magazine ranked Leggett & Platt in the top 5 percent of "America's Most Admired Companies." More than 10,000 executives, directors and securities analysts judged companies on innovativeness, quality of management, employee talent, quality of products/services, long-term investment value, financial soundness, social responsibility, and use of corporate assets. Only 22 of 469 companies had higher composite scores than Leggett & Platt.

■ Leggett & Platt boasts a remarkable record of growth. In the 1988–1998 period, earnings per share climbed from $.28 to $1.24, a compound annual rate of 16 percent. In the same ten-year stretch, dividends per share expanded from $.08 to $.315, a growth rate of 14.7 percent. What's more, Leggett & Platt has increased its dividend for twenty-eight consecutive years. In that span, the compound annual dividend growth rate was 15.3 percent.

- Leggett's commitment to research and development has kept pace with company growth. LEG has R&D facilities at both centralized and divisional locations. At those locations, engineers and technicians design and build new and improved products in all major lines and machinery. They also perform extensive tests for durability and function. Leggett's experience and accumulation of data in this highly specialized area of R & D is unmatched.
- Since 1967, acquisitions have been a key part of Leggett's growth strategy. Traditionally, the company pursues friendly acquisitions that fit with existing operations, either in marketing, technology, or both. Normally, Leggett's acquisitions broaden the company's product lines, providing entry into additional markets or secure sources of select raw materials.

  The company uses cash, stock, or combinations of the two in making acquisitions. In 1998 and the first two months of 1999, the company made twenty acquisitions, adding annualized sales of $370 million.
- There are no comparable companies to Leggett & Platt in the public sector. However, since the company is, in part, a supplier to the furnishings industry, the market tends to view LEG as a furniture company. This is not a correct perception. Here is why I believe this to be so:

  Residential furniture (whether a finished product or a component) represents less than 30 percent of Leggett's revenue base. What's more, bedding components, a much more stable product line, accounts for nearly 30 percent of revenue; this is a replacement business with just a minor decline in shipments during the last recession. The balance is composed of office, institutional, and commercial furnishings and fixtures (components and finished products) and the company's diversified nonfurnishings products.

The risk/reward parameters of Leggett's business are quite different from that of a furniture manufacturer. Keep in mind that LEG's components go into making the "insides" of furniture (springs, frames, motion mechanisms, and construction fabric), thus making Leggett immune to the fashion risk inherent in the furniture business. Since most manufacturers buy components from Leggett, there is little, if any, fashion risk related to Leggett's products. This risk is borne by the manufacturer and the way the finished product is differentiated with style or fabric.

Leggett has opportunities to grow even if overall demand does not grow. This is accomplished through internal growth, driven by market share gains and aggressive new product development, plus an aggressive acquisition program, responsible for two-thirds of the company's growth over the past fifteen years.

- Leggett & Platt has a proven strategy in place to expand its position in existing markets and selectively approach a larger portion of the total market for furniture and bedding components. A strong financial position also provides substantial capital resources and flexibility to pursue future growth opportunities, both internally and through selective acquisitions.
- Through its leadership role in new product development, new manufacturing techniques and technological improvements, analysts believe Leggett can gain market share vis-à-vis its smaller, less-well-financed competitors.
- Participation in such diverse furnishings categories as bedding and residential, office, and contract furniture gives Leggett & Platt the opportunity to

spread new product developments into several sectors at all price points while limiting its exposure to any one sector.

- Leggett & Platt has created a reputation for both innovation and confidentiality, often working with several larger manufacturers to develop exclusive components, giving each a competitive edge while utilizing Leggett & Platt's massive manufacturing capabilities. Consequently, LEG can manufacture a broad range of distinctive, cost-effective components for any customer, whether large or small.

Total assets: $2,535 million
Current ratio: 2.83
Common shares outstanding: 198 million
Return on 1998 shareholders' equity: 19.0%

	1998	1997	1996	1995	1994	1993	1992	1991
Revenues (millions)	3,370	2,909	2,466	2,110	1,858	1,527	1,170	1,082
Net income (millions)	248	208	153	135	115	86	62	39
Earnings per share	1.24	1.08	.93	.80	.70	.52	.41	.28
Dividends per share	.315	.27	.23	.19	.155	.135	.115	.11
Price: high	28.8	23.9	17.4	13.4	12.4	12.5	8.8	4.8
low	16.9	15.8	10.3	8.5	8.3	8.2	4.7	3.3

AGGRESSIVE GROWTH

Eli Lilly and Company

Lilly Corporate Center, Indianapolis, IN 46285 ☐ Investor contact: Patricia A. Martin (317) 276-2395 ☐ Direct dividend reinvestment plan available (800)451-2134 ☐ Web site: www.lilly.com ☐ Listed: NYSE ☐ Ticker symbol: LLY ☐ S&P rating: A- ☐ Value Line financial strength rating: A+

Eli Lilly is one of the world's foremost health care companies. With a solid dedication to R & D, Lilly is a leader in the development of ethical drugs (those available on prescription).

It is well-known for such drugs as Prozac (to treat depression), Ceclor (an antibiotic), insulin and other diabetic-care items. Some of its other important drugs include Keflex, Kefzol, Lorabid, Mandol, Nebcin, Vancocin Hcl, Tazidime, Darvon, Nalfon, and Axid. Lilly also has a stake in animal health and agricultural products.

Like most drug companies, Lilly is active abroad and does business in 120 countries.

Shortcomings to Bear in Mind

- Eli Lilly is concerned that economic turbulence will slow the availability of modern medical care, including the company's medicines, to people in many developing nations. Meanwhile, affluent countries are experiencing higher health care costs that are prompting concerns about the affordability of new medicines.

- The cost of developing new drugs, which was already high, is getting even higher. More emphasis is being placed on generic drugs by cost-conscious health care providers.

- The patent on one of Lilly's major antibiotic drugs, Ceclor, has expired. This means that generic versions are forcing the company to reduce prices.

- When depression hits, many suburban Chinese do what Americans do, they take Prozac, although they may have a different name for it. Chinese laws permit copying a patented drug. Although most drug companies have the same problem, they tend to do nothing, fearing reprisals from China's drug regulators. For its part, Lilly is fighting back, even though annual sales of the antidepressant drug are only $9 million, a tiny fraction of the worldwide sales of $2.8 billion. The reason: Drug sales are growing at a 20 percent rate in China, double the rate of other major markets.

Reasons to Buy

- Eli Lilly is emerging as an industry leader in forging productive alliances. The company is engaged in more than 100 R&D agreements, involving everything from new gene discoveries to new delivery technologies to late-stage drug candidates.

- Depression is a more serious and widespread illness than many realize. In the United States alone, one in five people will experience clinical depression at some time in their lives. Left untreated, depression can be dangerous. Discovered and developed by Lilly scientists, Prozac represented an important new treatment option, the first widely available product in a class of drugs called SSRIs (for selected serotonin reuptake inhibitors). In simple terms, SSRIs help the brain to maintain higher levels of an important natural substance called serotonin by selectively reducing its absorption or "reuptake."

- Lilly's own research into the brain and central nervous system (CNS) has led to the discovery and launch of additional important drugs, including Permax for the treatment of Parkinson's disease, and Zyprexa, the company's new product for the treatment of schizophrenia. Furthermore, Lilly is testing investigational compounds that may aid patients with Alzheimer's disease, migraine headaches, sleep disorders, epilepsy, and urinary incontinence.

- Lilly is leveraging its research and development resources by focusing them more sharply within five broad disease categories that match Lilly's strengths: central-nervous-system diseases, endocrine diseases, infectious diseases, and cancer and cardiovascular diseases. What's more, the company is seeking to be the world leader in each of those five categories.

- Diabetes, within the endocrine category, is a good example. As the developer of the first insulin product and one of the world's major suppliers of insulin, Lilly has long been a global leader in the field. But diabetes, which affects more than 100 million people worldwide, continues to cause severe long-term complications, suffering, lost productivity, and death.

  For many patients with this disease, diabetes is also inconvenient. Diabetics have to check their blood glucose several times a day. They may have to give themselves one or more shots of insulin. And they must take insulin at least 30 minutes before a meal or risk severe complications.

  Lilly believes that it has an answer that will give patients with diabetes a better quality of life and a good deal more convenience. More than 3,000 people in nineteen countries have taken Lilly's new insulin analog, Humalog, in clinical trials. The evidence from those trials show that Humalog acts faster than traditional insulin to control blood-glucose levels. Patients take it right before a meal, compared with 30 to 45 minutes before with current products. Humalog provides them with more freedom, better health, and fewer complications.

- The systematic antifungal market is the fastest-growing segment of the infectious diseases market, fueled by everything

ELI LILLY AND COMPANY 225

from toenail infections to the serious fungal infections that result from weakened immune systems, such as those in patients who have cancer or AIDS or those who have had organ transplants.

Lilly's investigational antifungal compound ECB is a derivative of a new class of compounds that work by disrupting synthesis of the fungal cell wall.

- Six products led Lilly's growth in 1998. The sales of the company's pioneering neuroscience medicine Prozac rose 10 percent to $2.8 billion. It was only the fourth pharmaceutical ever to generate sales of more than $2.5 billion in a single year. Meanwhile, the sales of the company's other neuroscience blockbuster, Zyprexa, increased 98 percent to $1.4 billion during only its second full year on the market.

Three other innovative products experienced excellent growth in 1998. Working with its partner, Centocor, Lilly achieved a 44 percent sales increase with the cardiovascular product ReoPro. Lilly's sale of the anticancer agent, Gemzar, rose 76 percent, and those of the insulin analog, Humalog, were up 91 percent.

- In January of 1998, Lilly introduced the new osteoporosis-prevention product, Evista. Although the early acceptance of this molecule was slower than expected, its first-year sales were $144 million. Meanwhile, Lilly has continued gathering clinical evidence supporting regulatory submissions for Evista as a treatment for osteoporosis. The company also initiated a large-scale clinical study of this medicine for the prevention of heart disease and prepared for a study of some 22,000 patients, under the auspices of the U.S. National Cancer Institute, that will focus on the prevention of breast cancer.
- In 1998, Eli Lilly's worldwide pharmaceutical sales grew 17 percent, while its

animal health sales rose 4 percent, resulting in a 16 percent increase in the company's total sales from continuing operations to $9.2 billion. What's more, Lilly's gross margin expanded at an even more robust rate, 20 percent, reflecting a more favorable product mix, influenced by the company's newer medicines as well as by improved manufacturing efficiencies.

- In 1998, Lilly increased its R&D investments by 27 percent, to $1.7 billion. With these resources, the company recruited outstanding scientists and invested in new research facilities. Lilly also invested in collaborations with twelve top-flight scientific organizations, bringing such collaborations to more than 100 worldwide.
- High among Lilly's new-product priorities is pioglitazone, a novel insulin-sensitivity enhancer discovered and developed by Takeda. On January 19, 1999, this alliance partner filed its regulatory submission for pioglitazone with the U.S. Food and Drug Administration.
- As Lilly builds its product line and confronts growing competition, the company is expanding its market presence in certain parts of the world. For instance, the company will go from 1,700 sales representatives in the United States two years ago to more than 2,600 by mid-1999, including a contracted sales team, as Lilly prepares for the promotion of pioglitazone and augments its support for Prozac and Zyprexa.

The company, on the other hand, is not simply depending on traditional sales and marketing tools. It is developing expertise in newer arenas for pharmaceutical companies, such as direct-to-consumer advertising.

- Lilly remains confident that its patents on Prozac are valid and enforceable. The company therefore does not expect to experience generic competition for

Prozac until 2004. Meanwhile, the company is planning for the Prozac patent expiration by building on its expertise and image in the field of depression. For instance, the company is developing a proprietary once-a-week formulation of Prozac for depressed patients who would benefit from alternatives to daily dosing. Lilly is also exploring the potential benefits of combining Prozac with another molecule. The company's lead approach pairs Prozac with Zyprexa. Lilly has encouraging, if preliminary, data regarding the potential of this combination for depressed patients who do not respond to current antidepressants.

Total assets: $12,596 million
Current ratio: 1.17
Common shares outstanding: 1,100 million
Return on 1998 shareholders' equity: 46.2%

	1998	1997	1996	1995	1994	1993	1992	1991
Revenues (millions)	9,237	8,518	7,346	6,764	5,712	6,452	6,167	5,726
Net income (millions)	2,098	1,774	1,524	1,307	1,269	1,347	1,393	1,315
Earnings per share	1.91	1.57	1.33	1.15	1.09	1.15	1.22	1.13
Dividends per share	.80	.74	.69	.66	.63	.61	.55	.50
Price: high	91.3	70.4	40.2	28.5	16.6	15.5	21.9	21.3
low	57.7	35.6	24.7	15.6	11.8	10.9	14.4	16.9

CONSERVATIVE GROWTH

Lilly Industries, Inc.

733 S. West Street, Indianapolis, IN 46225 ◻ Investor contact: John C. Elbin (317) 687-6703 ◻ Web site: www.lillyindustries.com ◻ Dividend reinvestment plan available (800) 942-5909 ◻ Fiscal year's end November 30 ◻ Listed: NYSE ◻ Ticker symbol: LI ◻ S&P rating: B+ ◻ Value Line financial strength rating: B+

Lilly Industries is among the five largest manufacturers of industrial paints and coatings in North America. Lilly formulates, produces, and sells coatings to other manufacturing companies. These coatings enhance the appearance and durability of such products as home and office furniture, cabinets, appliances, building materials, vehicles, construction equipment, and mirrors, as well as a variety of metal and fiberglass-reinforced surfaces.

The company sells its products into a number of industrial markets, using a technical sales force of nearly 600 people. In the past year, Lilly has sold its output to some 6,000 different customers, such as Caterpillar, Chrysler, Deere, Ethan Allan, Ford Motor, General Motors, Newell, Stanley Works, and Steelcase.

Industrial coatings generally make up close to 90 percent of the company's revenues. Lilly makes wood coatings for furniture, cabinet and building products; metal coil coatings for appliances and building products; powder coatings for various metal products, including shelving, pipe and rebars; metal liquids coatings for bicycles, lawn mowers, farm and construction equipment; gelcoats for fiberglass-reinforced products such as recreational boats; plastic coatings for automobile dashboards, hubcaps and computer casings; and glass solutions and coatings for mirrors. The rest of the company's sales emanate from

Guardsman Products, which Lilly acquired in 1996.

Shortcomings to Bear in Mind

- Although Lilly has not been seriously hurt by the slumping economies of Asia, it has, nonetheless, been affected by the strong U.S. dollar and adverse currency rate changes.
- At the end of 1998, the company's balance sheet was somewhat leveraged; it had more debt than equity. Coverage of bond interest, moreover, was only four times. I would prefer a coverage of six times. On a more positive note, Lilly's financial position continues to improve. In 1998, the company reduced total debt by nearly $21 million, to $204 million. Lower debt, combined with the 1997 debt restructuring, decreased Lilly's annual interest expense by more than $2 million. Finally, this debt reduction was accomplished while the company continued such growth initiatives as its German acquisition in fiscal 1998.
- Lilly's fortunes tend to track the ups and downs of the business cycle, as the pace of overall economic activity directly affects the demand for the durable good, such as cars, furniture, and farm and construction equipment, that use industrial coatings made by Lilly. Hence, while the loyalty of customers to Lilly as their coatings supplier is likely to be above that of most of their other input providers, it is reasonable to expect a recession to bring about a reduction in the volume of coatings orders.

On a more positive note, during a slack period the company would benefit from lower raw materials costs, coupled with less need for Lilly to maintain inventories at flat-out production levels. What's more, the general absence of product pricing volatility will help profits during a recession. Lilly's close customer relationships forged on the basis of quality coatings tend to keep product pricing from becoming a contentious issue.

Reasons to Buy

- In early 1999, Lilly announced that it had established a manufacturing presence in Mexico by acquiring an industrial coatings company, Pinturas Dygo, S.A. de C.V. Lilly stated that it will expand the Pinturas manufacturing operation to support its Mexican customers and to facilitate international growth.
- In early 1999, Lilly announced that it has entered into a strategic alliance with Dennis Chemical Company of St. Louis, Missouri. The alliance provides for cooperation between the two companies to supply plastisols to the coil coating industry.

Commenting on the purchase, Lilly's CEO, Douglas W. Huemme, said, "Dennis Chemical Company is a well-known supplier of plastisols with outstanding technology. Combining Dennis's technology with Lilly's sales and marketing expertise will enhance our ability to supply a full range of products to our coil customers."

- Lilly believes that the most important transaction in its 131-year history took place in 1996 when it acquired Guardsman Products, Inc. for $235 million. The acquisition brought complementary technology and related products to Lilly, with minimal customer overlap.

Guardsman's strengths are in specialty coatings for appliances and furniture, and two-component coatings for construction and agricultural equipment. The combined operations and technologies are resulting in significant cost reductions and access to an expanded customer base.

- Lilly Industries continues to sustain solid earnings growth in spite of the poor economic conditions in the Far East, an important market for the company. That's because the bulk of the business that Lilly conducts there relies on the sale of furniture typically slated for export. Since the Asia-Pacific economies are not primarily end markets for its products, the company has been largely protected from the effects of the financial crisis in that part of the world.

- Lilly Industries has developed a number of strategies designed to accelerate growth and improve operating margins. For instance, the company intends to continue on its path of global expansion by following its domestic customers into international markets and by acquiring complementary businesses. The company's international business now represents 24 percent of its business. Globalization helps Lilly in several ways. For instance, the company can accelerate sales growth because its international markets are growing more rapidly than the domestic economy. Then, too, Lilly's strategy of global penetration is a lower-risk strategy because the company is following major domestic customers overseas. What's more, these customers want the same quality coatings and leading-edge technology that it provides to them in the United States. Finally, once established abroad, Lilly then has the opportunity to serve local customers and other multinationals that are not currently U.S. customers. Increasingly, international manufacturers are recognizing the need for world-class finishes, as they seek to export their products to the United States and other highly developed countries.

- Technological leadership is another area of focus for Lilly Industries. The company has been working diligently on differentiating its products, developing new products, reducing costs, and creating pricing opportunities. Lilly's research and development and marketing initiatives are also focused on identifying new niche markets and securing new customers.

- Engineering cost reductions is another major strategy. The company's supply-chain management initiative will help Lilly reduce raw material costs and working capital. Enhanced process engineering is another major cost reduction tool that will also further improve quality.

- To enhance productivity domestically, support Lilly's growing powder coatings business, and expand the company's business globally, the company invested over $30 million in capital improvements in 1999. This move followed a $17 million capital improvements program the previous year. These two-year outlays were the largest such programs in the company's history. Finally, Lilly is making a multimillion-dollar investment in powder coatings technology, since worldwide demand for this product in increasing rapidly. In sum, the company's capital expenditures have been concentrated on modernizing plants in the United States, coupled with building or acquiring new facilities abroad, chiefly in attractive growth markets in Asia.

- Lilly has a solid record of growth. In the 1988–1998 period, earnings per share expanded from $.45 to $1.35, a ten-year compound growth rate of 11.6 percent. On the other hand, there were three years in which EPS declined during this span. Dividends during this same period climbed from $.16 to $.32, a growth rate of 7.3 percent. Although this is not particularly impressive, the dividend payout ratio of 24 percent indicates a company with solid growth prospects.

Total assets: $516 million
Current ratio: 1.73
Common shares outstanding: 23 million
Return on 1998 shareholders' equity: 20.5%

	1998	1997	1996	1995	1994	1993	1992	1991
Revenues (millions)	619	601	509	328	331	284	236	213
Net income (millions)	32	28	24	20	23	16	13	6
Earnings per share	1.35	1.20	1.04	.88	1.00	.70	.55	.27
Dividends per share	.32	.32	.31	.27	.24	.22	.22	.20
Price: high	24.6	24.6	19.8	15.0	18.0	16.2	10.8	6.0
low	14.4	16.5	12.1	11.0	11.8	9.6	5.7	3.8

AGGRESSIVE GROWTH

Lucent Technologies

600 Mountain Avenue, Room 3C-446 ☐ Murray Hill, NJ 07974-0636 ☐ Investor contact: Jeffrey A. Baum (908) 582-7635 ☐ Direct dividend reinvestment plan available (888) 582-3686 ☐ Web site: www.lucent.com ☐ Listed: NYSE ☐ Fiscal year's end September 30 ☐ Ticker symbol: LU ☐ S&P rating: Not rated ☐ Value Line financial strength rating: A

Lucent, the world's leading provider of telecommunications equipment, sells the hardware, software, and service that long-distance carriers, Baby Bells, and smaller companies need to ensure their customers' phone calls get through.

Embedded within Lucent is the brain power few companies can rival: It is home to Bell Labs, which has produced inventions such as the transistor and the laser. Lucent was formed from the systems and technology units that were formerly part of AT&T Corporation, including the research and development capabilities of Bell Laboratories. Prior to February 1, 1996, AT&T conducted Lucent's original business through various divisions and subsidiaries.

On February 1, 1996, AT&T began executing its decision to separate Lucent into a standalone company by transferring to Lucent the assets and liabilities related to its business. In April 1996, Lucent completed the initial public offering of its common stock, and on September 30, 1996, Lucent became independent of AT&T.

Lucent at a Glance

Systems for Network Operators—1998
Revenues: $18.8 billion

This segment produces switching and transmission systems for voice and data, data networking routing switches and servers, wireless network infrastructure, optical networking systems, optical fiber products, communications software, and Internet telephony servers. Lucent has a number one market share in optical networking, U.S. switching systems, and wireless infrastructure equipment.

Business Communications Systems—1998
Revenues: $8.1 billion

This group offers private branch exchange and key telephone systems; wireless systems; support services for voice, data, and video networks; network cabling within and between buildings; messaging systems and servers (offered through Lucent's Octel Messaging Division); call center offerings; conferencing systems; Internet-based products; and network management software.

Lucent has a number one market share in messaging, in-building wiring systems, call centers in the United States, and in-building wireless systems.

Microelectronics Products—1998
Revenues: $3.0 billion

Lucent provides integrated circuits for wireless and wired communications, computer modems, and networks; optoelectronic components for communications systems; as well as power systems. Lucent has a number one market share in communications integrated circuits (ICs), transmission, and modem ICs in personal computers; optoelectronic components for optical transmission systems; and power equipment. The company has a number two market share in local area network ICs and digital signal processors.

Richard A. McGinn, CEO

When Richard A. McGinn took over the CEO post at Lucent Technologies in October of 1997, he was following the footsteps of Henry B. Schacht, one of the nation's most respected corporate executives. Schacht, the former Cummins Engine Company CEO, brought in to head Lucent when the company was spun off from AT&T in 1996, had just guided Lucent to a spectacular first year.

But McGinn, age 52, didn't miss a beat after Schacht stepped down at age 63. His success may be related to his competitive spirit. He has a keen interest in golf and deep-sea fishing and will do anything to win. In the world of business, this competitive drive makes it imperative that he take market share from competitors like Motorola Inc. and Northern Telecom Ltd. In 1998, Lucent won a host of marquee deals, including contracts from wireless-service provider PrimeCo Personal Communications and Baby Bell SBC Communications Inc.

Despite a sunny disposition and an easy laugh, McGinn is not one to be taken lightly. He starts his day at 5 a.m. by working out on his treadmill and catching up on news from Asia and arrives at his office at 7. On the way to work, a 30-minute commute, McGinn is on his cell phone with other top executives.

Always a man in a rush, McGinn spent 1998 pushing Lucent into a host of new markets, including acquisitions in the fast-growing market for data gear. He's also aggressively expanding abroad. In 1998, Lucent won contracts in such countries as China, the Philippines, and Brazil.

Shortcomings to Bear in Mind

- Lucent continues to face significant competition and expects the level of competition on pricing and product offerings will intensify. The company expects that new competitors will enter its markets as a result of the trend toward global expansion by foreign and domestic competitors, as well as continued changes in technology and public policy.

  These competitors may include entrants from the telecommunications, software, data networking, and semiconductor industries. Such competitors may include Cisco Systems, Inc., Nortel Networks, Ericsson, Alcatel Alsthom, and Siemens AG.

- Lucent is less adept at packet switching than some competitors, and it must play catchup. Thus, notes one analyst, "it will be extremely difficult for earnings to grow faster than those of the overall market. As the market moves from circuit to packet switching, Lucent's sales will grow, at best, at the expense of circuit switchers, and, at worst, won't grow at all."

Reasons to Buy

■ Lucent, considered an ugly-duckling hardware business when it was spun off by AT&T in 1996, has emerged as a high-technology powerhouse and one of the decade's hottest stocks, defying predictions that the Internet would overwhelm the traditional telephone gear it makes.

In fact, the Net, by fueling demand for phone lines, has propelled sales of Lucent's bread-and-butter product, the circuit switches that route billions of phone calls a day over local and long-distance networks around the globe.

Lucent is convinced, however, that the future belongs not to the circuit switch but to the fancy packet networks sold by companies like Ascend Communications, maker of Internet switching equipment. In early 1999, conceding it had fallen behind in its efforts to devise similar products, Lucent agreed to acquire Ascend for $20 billion.

The new generation of networking equipment made by Ascend and such rivals as Cisco Systems and 3Com Corporation sends information across phone lines more efficiently by breaking the data into bits, called packets. The technology allows a single phone line to carry many messages simultaneously, promising savings for phone companies that now must allocate a separate line to each caller.

■ The communications industry is going through a revolution, centered on rapidly growing demand by commercial and residential users for voice, data, Internet, and wireless services. As a result, the industry has undergone a global consolidation of key players, including traditional telecommunications network manufacturers and data-networking companies, that compete in the same markets as Lucent. This consolidation, driven by the need for key technologies, new distribution channels in untapped markets, economies of scale, and global expansion, is expected to continue into the near future.

Lucent continues to evaluate its presence and product offerings in the marketplace and may use acquisitions to enhance those offerings where that makes good business sense. As part of Lucent's efforts to focus on the fastest-growing markets in the communications industry, the company acquired a number of businesses in 1998, complementing its existing product lines and its internal product development efforts:

● In September 1998, Lucent acquired JNA, an Australian telecom equipment manufacturer, reseller, and system integrator.

● In August 1998, Lucent acquired LANNET, an Israeli-based supplier of Ethernet and asynchronous transfer mode (ATM) switching solutions.

● In July 1998, Lucent acquired both SDX, a United Kingdom-based provider of business communications systems, and MassMedia, a developer of next-generation network interoperability software.

● In May 1998, the company acquired Yurie, a provider of ATM access technology and equipment for data, voice, and video networking.

● In April 1998, Lucent acquired Optimay, a developer of software products and services for chip sets to be used for Global Systems for Mobile Communications cellular phones.

● In January 1998, Lucent acquired Prominet, a participant in the emerging Gigabit Ethernet networking industry.

■ The global Bell Laboratories R&D community supports every Lucent business group from its centers in twenty different countries. The company earns more than three patents every business day, creating a remarkable stream of ideas for innovation and next-generation technology that sets Lucent's businesses apart from all others.

Bell Labs is focused on the leading-edge technologies that are transforming communications as thoroughly as earlier milestones like the laser, transistor, and cell phone. Today, researchers are engaged in both the practical application and long-term development of breakthroughs such as the all-plastic transistor and high-capacity optical fiber. Bell Labs' innovation in areas like photonics, digital signal processing, software, data networking, wireless, and semiconductors is constant and productive.

■ Lucent Technologies announced in May of 1999 that it had developed a computer chip for phones that will help small and midsize businesses use their companies' computer networks to deliver voice calls. The chip will help lower the cost of Internet phones from about $250 to $150 by decreasing the number of chips in a phone from five to one. The market for these Internet telephone sets is expected to average annual growth of more than 250 percent for the next three years.

■ The 30,000 people employed by the Business Communications Systems Group, the company's second-largest segment, provide more than 1.5 million business locations around the world and U.S. government customers with voice-related and computer telephony integrated products. Leaders in many business communication areas, they design, manufacture, and sell solutions for sales and service operations, conferencing and collaboration, mobility and distributed workforce, messaging, and intelligent networking. Offerings include the Definity family of private branch exchanges (PBXs), key telephone systems, call centers, structured cabling systems, voice processing and Octel Messaging Division solutions, wireless systems, and multimedia and Internet capabilities.

■ There is a revolution going on in the communications industry, and Lucent Technologies is at the center of it. It is a revolution driven by customer demand, bolstered by changing market dynamics, and fueled by technology.

First and foremost, it is a revolution in the way we all communicate. We want to do more with communications that we ever have before. We want mobility, we want immediate access to data, and we want all of our networking to be as easy as making a telephone call. Consider:

● 900 million voice-mail messages are exchanged each business day.

● 2.7 trillion e-mails were sent in 1998; that's 5 million every minute.

● Internet traffic is doubling every 100 days. More than 100 million additional Internet users are expected to come online by 2001.

● 75 million new customers signed up for cellular phone service in 1998, bringing the worldwide untethered population to roughly 285 million.

Those numbers add up to an insatiable appetite for "bandwidth," the amount of information that can be transmitted each second over a communications channel, such as a telephone line, as well as unprecedented opportunities for Lucent Technologies.

Total assets: $26,720 million
Current ratio: 1.35
Common shares outstanding: 2,643 million
Return on 1998 shareholders' equity: 41.3%

	1998	1997	1996	1995	1994	1993	1992	1991
Revenues (millions)	30,147	26,360	23,286	21,413	19,765	*		
Net income (millions)	2,287	1,507	1,054	806	482			
Earnings per share	.87	.59	.41	.39	.19			
Dividends per share	.08	.08	.04					
Price: high	56.9	22.7	13.3					
low	18.4	11.2	7.4					

* This table is incomplete, since Lucent was not a public company until recently.

CONSERVATIVE GROWTH

McCormick & Company, Inc.

18 Loveton Circle, Sparks, MD 21152-6000 ◻ Investor contact: Joyce L. Brooks (410) 771-7244 ◻ Web site: www.mccormick.com ◻ Direct dividend reinvestment plan available (800)424-5855 ◻ Fiscal year's end November 30 ◻ Listed: Nasdaq ◻ Ticker symbol: MCCRK ◻ S&P rating: A- ◻ Value Line financial strength rating: B++

When investors hear the name McCormick, they think of the spices they use every day. Indeed, McCormick is the world's largest spice company. Yet the company is also the leader in the manufacture, marketing, and distribution of such products as seasonings and flavorings to the entire food industry. These customers include foodservice and food-processing businesses, as well as retail outlets.

McCormick also has a stake in packaging. This group manufactures specialty plastic bottles and tubes for food, personal care, and other industries. Founded in 1889, McCormick distributes its products in about one hundred countries.

In 1998, the company's food products operation was by far the larger of the two segments, with revenues of $1.7 billion, compared with $188.8 million for packaging.

McCormick's U.S. Consumer business, its oldest and largest, is dedicated to the manufacture and sale of consumer spices, herbs, extracts, proprietary seasoning blends, sauces, and marinades. They are sold under such brand names as McCormick, Schilling, Produce Partners, Golden Dipt, Old Bay, and Mojave.

McCormick directly imports many of the spices and herbs purchased by the company from the countries of origin, including black pepper, vanilla beans, cinnamon, herbs, and seeds. However, significant quantities of some materials, such as paprika, dehydrated vegetables, onion and garlic, and food ingredients other than spices and herbs originate in the United States. The raw materials most important to the company are onion, garlic, and capsicums (paprika and chili peppers), which are produced in the United States; black pepper, most of which originates in India, Indonesia, Malaysia, and Brazil; and vanilla beans, a large portion of which the company obtains from the Malagasy Republic and Indonesia.

Shortcomings to Bear in Mind

■ The company's Industrial business was hurt by higher raw material prices in 1998, particularly pepper. Margins were reduced as competitive pricing pressure limited the company's ability to recover cost increases.

- Like most multinational firms, McCormick was affected by the sharp downturn in the economies of Asia and Latin America. The problems in Asia contributed to a difficult year for the company's Packaging business, which manufactures tubes and bottles for food, personal care, and other industries. What's more, lower demand by customers who sell cosmetics and other products caused a decline in revenues.

- The company's Venezuelan operation suffered from a severe economic recession in 1998. Expecting these conditions in that country to continue into 1999 and beyond, McCormick ceased production operations there and initiated a licensing agreement with a Venezuelan-based food company to market under the McCormick name.

- Japanese joint ventures also suffered from the economic woes of the Asian region. Sales shortfalls in both consumer and industrial ventures were due to lower discretionary income in Japan.

Reasons to Buy

- In 1998, the board of directors approved a 6 percent increase in McCormick's dividend. The company has paid dividends every year since 1925 and has increased this payout 380 percent over the past ten years.

- The company's past successes and future potential are rooted in the strength of the McCormick name. As a consequence, the company is now experiencing a 95 percent brand-awareness rating in the United States. This leadership role in the food industry ensures that consumers will enjoy a McCormick products at nearly every eating occasion. Grocery store aisles present more than 700 well-known products from major processors that rely on McCormick for seasoning or flavor.

- The company's quality products, high service level, and strong brand recognition, together with new marketing initiatives, were instrumental in McCormick gaining new distribution in 1998, such as Ahold USA, a major food retailer. The company's leadership, moreover, is also reflected in its success in obtaining widespread distribution. It is the primary spice supplier to sixteen of the top twenty retail and wholesale customers.

- In the United Kingdom, McCormick continued to be the market leader in 1998, with sales of its Schwartz brand reaching an all-time high. Consumers reacted favorably to "Make It Fresh," a new line of eleven different seasonings and flavorings for vegetables and fruit dishes. The line has exceeded sales expectations and is the most successful product launch in recent McCormick history. What's more, Potato Wedges, 1997's highly successful new product, maintained its position as the unit brand leader in the growing potato seasoning market.

- In Canada, new distribution gains in 1998 now make the company's Club House spice line available in most retail food locations. A successful product launch of Bag 'n Season in western Canada helped fuel growth, and this popular product line was introduced into Ontario in late 1998. A comprehensive advertising campaign begun in late 1998 and continuing through mid-1999 is building brand awareness in Ontario, one of McCormick Canada's most significant markets.

- In Australia, sales were accelerated with increased distribution, new product launches, and marketing support. What's more, the U.S. Produce Partner line met with success in Australia, and the well-known Aeroplane brand gained additional market share.

- Net sales for McCormick's Industrial and Food Service businesses grew 8.8 percent in 1998. The company's Industrial flavor and seasoning business supplies ingredients to a significant majority of the top one hundred food processors and restaurant chains worldwide. While the McCormick name may not appear on the food package, the company's flavors are in a wide range of snack foods, desserts, beverages, confectionery items, cereals, baked goods, and more.

The company's Food Service business supplies spices, seasonings, and other food ingredients, both direct and through distributor networks, to restaurants, warehouse clubs, and institutions worldwide. During 1998, a number of McCormick's major customers designated the company as a select supplier and/or awarded McCormick with supplier excellence recognition.

- In 1998, the company benefited from gains in membership warehouse companies. For instance, Costco, a leading U.S.-based membership warehouse club, awarded McCormick its total spice and seasoning volume for the United States and Canada.

- McCormick's record of growth is impressive. Earnings per share expanded from $.35 per share in 1988 to $1.43 in 1998, a compound annual growth rate of 15.1 percent. In the same ten-year span, dividends per share climbed from $.13 to $.64, a growth rate of 17.3 percent.

- In 1997, the company launched the Quest program, a pricing-and-promotional initiative between McCormick and the customer. The program's goal is to expand sales. Quest involves pricing most of the company's best-selling spice items and all of its dry seasoning mixes (DSM) to the customer net of discounts and allowances, with the objective of increasing consumer sales.

At the end of 1998, nearly 50 percent of the company's sales to its domestic customers were invoiced under Quest, with another 25 percent targeted for conversion in 1999. This effort was complemented by promotions and advertising targeted at potential high-growth items, such as Grill Mates, through a combination of couponing, sampling, and media advertising during key selling period. Resulting sales for the last three quarters of 1998 show unit growth in McCormick and Schilling branded products significantly outperforming the category growth as measured by store scanner data. Encouraged by these initial results, the company has continued to actively roll out the Quest program in 1999.

- Growth was likewise achieved in the United States with the DSM relaunch. Rolled out in 1998, this program's key element included package redesign, new product flavors, formula improvements, in-store merchandising, and promotion and advertising support. The merchandising of these products includes a section header, "Meal Idea Center," color-coded sections for pasta, beef, chicken, and other products, along with point-of-sale materials.

Total assets: $1,259 million
Current ratio: 0.88
Common shares outstanding: 10 million voting, 63 million nonvoting
Return on 1998 shareholders' equity: 27.7%

	1998	1997	1996	1995	1994	1993	1992	1991
Revenues (millions)	1,881	1,801	1,732	1,859	1,695	1,557	1,471	1,428
Net income (millions)	106	998	83	98	108	100	93	81
Earnings per share	1.43	1.30	1.03	1.20	1.32	1.22	1.14	.98
Dividends per share	.64	.60	.56	.52	.48	.44	.38	.28
Price: high	36.4	28.4	25.4	26.6	24.8	29.8	30.3	26.5
low	27.1	22.6	18.9	18.1	17.8	20.0	20.5	12.3

CONSERVATIVE GROWTH

McDonald's Corporation

McDonald's Plaza, Oak Brook, IL 60523 ◻ Investor contact: Lynn Irwin Camp (630) 623-8432 ◻ Direct dividend reinvestment plan available (800) 621-7825 ◻ Web site: www.mcdonalds.com ◻ Ticker symbol: MCD ◻ S&P rating: A+ ◻ Value Line financial strength rating: A+

McDonald's, which boasts one of the world's most valuable brand names, is the world's number one fast-food chain. The company operates more than 24,000 restaurants worldwide, and its more than 12,450 domestic outlets command a 42-percent share of the nation's fast-food hamburger business.

Most McDonald's outlets are the familiar freestanding variety, with a heavy emphasis on playgrounds to attract its devoted audience: kids. McDonald's is building mini-units with simplified menus at such alternative locations as Wal-Marts. Nearly 80 percent of the company's restaurants are franchised. Restaurants abroad account for about 60 percent of the company's sales and profits. Every day, McDonald's serves more than 40 million people in more than 24,000 restaurants in 114 countries around the world. Annually, that's nearly 15 million people served. Yet, on any given day, that amounts to less than 1 percent of the world's population. Obviously, the proliferation of McDonald's outlets is far from saturation.

Company Background

The company develops, operates, franchises, and services a worldwide system of restaurants that prepare, assemble, package, and sell a limited menu of value-priced foods. These restaurants are operated by McDonald's or, under the terms of franchise arrangements, by franchisees who are independent third parties, or by affiliates operating under joint-venture agreements between the company and local businesspeople.

The company's franchising program is designed to assure consistency and quality. What's more, McDonald's is selective in granting franchises and is not in the practice of franchising to investor groups or passive investors.

McDonald's restaurants offer a substantially uniform menu consisting of hamburgers and cheeseburgers, including the Big Mac and Quarter Pounder with Cheese, the Filet-O-Fish, several chicken sandwiches, French fries, Chicken McNuggets, salads, milkshakes, McFlurries, sundaes and cones, pies, cookies, and soft drinks and other beverages.

McDonald's restaurants operating in the United States and certain international markets are open during breakfast hours and offer a full or limited breakfast menu, including the Egg McMuffin and the Sausage McMuffin with Egg sandwiches, hotcakes and sausages, three varieties of biscuit sandwiches, and Apple-Bran muffins. The company believes in testing new products and introducing those that pass muster.

The company, its franchisees, and affiliates purchase food products and packaging from numerous independent suppliers. Quality specifications for both raw and cooked food products are established and strictly enforced.

The Beginning

The McDonald brothers' first restaurant, founded in 1937 in a parking lot just east of Pasadena, California, didn't serve hamburgers, nor did it have a playground. The most popular item on the menu was the hot dog, and most people ate it sitting on an outdoor stool or in their cars while being served by teenaged carhops.

For about a decade, that embryonic version of McDonald's was a big success. Then, America's tastes began to change, and the Golden Arches changed as well. As automobiles lost some of their romance, indoor restaurants took over. In the 1960s, however, some customers became bored with the menu and drifted away. Alert to what was happening, McDonald's responded by creating the Big Mac, and customers came flocking back. Later, beef was not always enough to keep draw in enough customers. Once again, the company was ready for the challenge; it introduced bite-size chunks of chicken in the early 1980s. Within four years, the company was the nation's second-largest poultry vendor.

Shortcomings to Bear in Mind

■ In the first quarter of 1999, McDonald's reported that Russia's and Brazil's economic problems dragged its international pretax earnings growth down to 9 percent, from what would have been 14 percent without those countries, based on constant currencies during the quarter. According the company's CEO, Jack M. Greenberg, Russia presents "more serious" problems. In that country, sales were down about 50 percent on a comparable-store basis. As a result, the company is proceeding cautiously, opening "just a handful of restaurants." On the plus side, even with Russia's problems, Europe during the quarter posted double-digit pretax earnings gains, as did the Asia-Pacific region.

Reasons to Buy

■ A behind-the-scenes transformation is underway at McDonald's. The company's relatively new chief executive, Jack M. Greenberg, is leading an overhaul of the long-insular restaurant company that has made both franchisees and investors more optimistic than they have been in years. In a break with tradition, Mr. Greenberg has turned to outsiders to fill key posts. As of early 1999, he had cut 23 percent of headquarters staff, the first layoff in company history. What's more, franchisees and corporate managers stationed in the field now make more of the decisions about when to discount and what food to test.

The result: McDonald's has found modest success with new products, including a bagel breakfast sandwich and the McFlurry sundae, coupled with regional discounts. Those were big reasons why average store sales climbed in 1998, and overall company revenues advanced 9 percent. In the words of one analyst, "Greenberg has done a fantastic job bringing a new sense of urgency and getting rid of their corporate arrogance."

- During 1999, McDonald's began upgrading its kitchens in a program dubbed "Made for You." In this $500 million transformation, instead of keeping food in taste-killing warming bins, the new system uses computers to project customer traffic and an assembly line to keep lettuce cold and burgers hot. Meanwhile, custom orders are available, as they are at such rivals as Burger King.

- In 1998, McDonald's extended its brand presence and reached millions of customers through sponsorship of the World Cup Soccer championship in France and the Winter Olympic Games in Nagano, Japan. McDonald's also sponsored the Dinoland exhibit at Disney's new Animal Kingdom in Florida and has two showcase restaurants on Disney's Orlando property.

- In 1998, the company bought a minority stake in World Foods, operator of Chipotle Mexican Grill, which has fourteen units in the Denver area. McDonald's indicated it was attracted to Chipotle not only as a way to "learn about new menu and restaurant format ideas" but also as a potential way to expand its franchise business. "Our longer-term vision for the Chipotle organization is to add it to our franchising mix, which would leverage the strengths of our existing franchising system," the company said. It added, however, that "it will take a couple years to evaluate the organization and determine its growth potential." The stake in closely held Denver-based World Foods is believed to be the first time McDonald's has made such an investment in another dining concept.

- McDonald's has long been popular with children because of its elaborate play-ground facilities and the frequent promotional tie-ins with major motion picture characters.

- McDonald's, selected by *Fortune* magazine as the most admired food service company in the world, has clung fast to its long-term strategy. While its domestic operations have struggled with sluggish growth and management blunders, the company's international business has prospered. Jim Cantalupo, president and chief executive officer of McDonald's International, credits the fast-food chain's infrastructure as the key to the company's continued global success. "We are second to none in sourcing our products," Cantalupo brags. He may just be right. McDonald's in Singapore typically imports its chicken from the United States. But within days of Thailand's currency devaluation, McDonald's Singapore restaurants were buying fowl from Thailand.

  McDonald's has found other ways to take advantage of wild swings in exchange rates. For example, to build its eighty restaurants in Indonesia it took out millions in construction loans in the local currency. After the rupiah crashed in 1998, McDonald's was able to pay off those loans at $.20 to the dollar. "Our assets were devalued, but so was our debt," Cantalupo said. He also moved to shore up troubled franchises in exchange for a greater equity stake in their restaurants.

- According to one analyst, "McDonald's has plenty going for it. The company plans to roll out a number of new key product offerings in 1999, including the Big Extra, which is aimed at the crowd that prefers Burger King's successful flame-broiled Whopper. Other new products include the Big McBacon cheeseburger and the McBagel breakfast sandwich."

- The company believes its greatest expansion opportunities are outside the

United States. While here at home there are 22,000 people per McDonald's, in the rest of the world there is only one McDonald's for every 605,000 people. At the end of 1998, 85 percent of systemwide restaurants were located in eleven markets: Australia, Brazil, Canada, England, France, Germany, Hong Kong, Japan, the Netherlands, Taiwan, and the United States. Some 65 percent of restaurant additions in 1998 were in these markets, and a similar percentage is expected in 1999. On the other hand, new and emerging markets, such as Central Europe, the Philippines, China, and Africa-Middle East, should account for a growing percentage of restaurants. Finally, rapid expansion is expected in Latin America.

Total assets: $19,784 million
Current ratio: 0.58
Common shares outstanding: 1,353 million
Return on 1998 shareholders' equity: 19.5%

	1998	1997	1996	1995	1994	1993	1992	1991
Revenues (millions)	12,421	11,409	10,687	9,794	8,321	7,408	7,133	6,695
Net income (millions)	1,769	1,642	1,573	1,427	1,224	1,082	959	860
Earnings per share	1.26	1.15	1.11	.99	.84	.73	.65	.59
Dividends per share	.18	.16	.15	.13	.12	.11	.10	.09
Price: high	39.8	27.4	27.1	24.0	15.8	14.8	12.6	10.0
low	22.3	21.1	20.5	14.3	12.8	11.4	9.6	6.5

CONSERVATIVE GROWTH

The McGraw-Hill Companies

1221 Avenue of the Americas, New York, NY 10020-1095 ◻ Investor contact: Donald S. Rubin (212) 512-4321 ◻ Direct dividend reinvestment program available (888) 201-5538 ◻ Web site: www.mcgraw-hill.com ◻ Listed: NYSE ◻ Ticker symbol: MHP ◻ S&P rating: not rated ◻ Value Line financial strength rating: A+

The McGraw-Hill Companies is a multimedia information provider. The company publishes textbooks, technical and popular books, and periodicals (*Business Week, Aviation Week, ENR*, and others). McGraw-Hill holds leadership positions in each of the markets it serves.

Financial Services
• Standard & Poor's Ratings Services is the number one rating service in the world and is applying its leadership to rating and evaluating a growing array of nontraditional financial instruments.
• Standard & Poor's Indexes, led by the S&P 500, are the world's benchmark measures of equity market performance.

• Standard & Poor's *Compustat* is the leading source of financial databases and advanced PC-based software for financial analysis.
• Standard & Poor's *MMS* supplies the world with real-time fundamental and technical analysis in the global money, bond, foreign exchange, and equity markets.
• Standard & Poor's *Platt's* is the key provider of price assessments with the petroleum, petrochemical, and power markets.
• Standard & Poor's *J. J. Kenny* produces the most comprehensive evaluating pricing information for the fixed-income investment community.
• Standard & Poor's *DRI* is the leading supplier of economics-driven

information to corporate and government clients.

Educational and Professional Publishing
- The McGraw-Hill School Division stands number one in providing educational materials to elementary schools.
- Glencoe/McGraw-Hill tops the grade 6–12 segment.
- CTB/McGraw-Hill is the preeminent publisher of nationally standardized tests for the U.S. K–12 market.
- Irwin/McGraw-Hill is the premier publisher of higher educational materials in business, economics, and information technology.
- The Professional Book Group is the leading publisher of business, computing, and reference books serving the needs of professionals and consumer worldwide.

Information and Media Services
- *Business Week* is the world's most widely read business publication, with a global audience of 6.3 million.
- F. W. Dodge is the leading provider of information to construction professionals.
- Sweet's Group is the premier supplier of building products information, in print and electronically.
- *Architectural Record* stands atop its industry as the official publication of the American Institute of Architects.
- *Aviation Week & Space Technology* is the world's most authoritative aerospace magazine.
- Tower Group International is the leading provider of customs brokerage and freight forwarding services.

Highlights of 1998
The company's financial results in 1998 represented the sixth consecutive year of record performance:
- Revenue grew to an all-time high of $3.7 billion.

- Net income rose 14.6 percent, to $333.1 million.
- Operating margins improved to 18.5 percent.
- Operating cash flow reached $755 million.
- Total return to shareholders increased 40.4 percent.
- The board of directors increased the dividend 10.3 percent, the 26th consecutive annual increase.

Shortcomings to Bear in Mind
- McGraw-Hill is an exceptional company and typically sells for a premium price.

Reasons to Buy
- McGraw-Hill's educational products are known for exemplary scholarship in technology. The company's Versatile Learning System, to cite one example, provides students and teachers with balanced, easy-to-use multimedia learning materials integrating textbooks, software, laser disks, audio, and video components.

  Reading products, which account for 40 percent of the company's School Division's revenue, led the nation in new sales in 1998. According to management, "Elementary math moves to the forefront in 1999." A new edition of *Math in My World* has been created to compete in six state adoptions, including Texas, the second-largest education market. (Textbook purchases in the twenty "adoption" states are guided by state-approved lists.)

  Glencoe/McGraw-Hill, the nation's number one secondary educational publisher, posted superb sales in grades 6–12 math adoptions in seven states during 1998, as well as in biology, science, social studies, and foreign languages.
- Every business day, Standard & Poor's Indexes are cited as key benchmarks of stock-market performance. The world-

wide reputation of the S&P 500 has nurtured a growing international family of indexes. Its newest offspring mirror the company's global objectives. In 1998, McGraw-Hill launched indexes for Europe, the S&P Euro and S&P Euro Plus, and a new equity index in Canada with the Toronto Stock Exchange. In 1999, the company introduced new indexes for Asia, Latin America, and the United Kingdom. What's more, McGraw-Hill is exploring opportunities with the Tokyo Stock Exchange. By year-end 1999, the company expects to launch the S&P Global 1200.

- S&P Indexes are the foundation for a growing array of investment funds and exchange-traded products that continue to generate new revenue. The company receives fees based on assets and trading activity. In addition, the recent volatility of the stock market has increased the revenue stream. Currently, more than $700 billion is invested in mutual funds tied to the S&P indexes.

- SPDRs (S&P depository receipts), linked to and directly tracking S&P indexes, consistently top the American Stock Exchange's most active list. Similarly, trading volume on the Chicago Mercantile Exchange of futures and options linked to S&P indexes is also high. Both exchanges introduced new trading instruments in 1998 tied to S&P indexes.

- Europe contributes almost half of McGraw-Hill's international revenue, growing at a double-digit rate. With a push from the new Monetary Union, the European market will be a springboard for growth in many of the company's key businesses. Here are some expectations:

  - European companies that once financed their growth mainly by borrowing from banks are shifting to the issuance of corporate bonds instead, while nontraditional financial instruments also boom. Those are both large opportunities for Standard & Poor's Rating Services, which has built the world's largest network of ratings professionals.

  - Increases in investments by Europeans building retirement funds—the result of a transition to privately funded pension plans—will accelerate demand for global financial information. These are pluses for Standard & Poor's Financial Information Services.

  - The continued growth of English in business communications and as a second language in everyday use widens. These will benefit the company's educational products and the European edition of *Business Week*.

  - The promise of the global economy depends on educational training. This is a plus for McGraw-Hill's global publishing activities—most notably the company's business, finance, engineering, information technology, and English instruction products.

- In Asia, economic problems have slowed growth but have not seriously affected the company's operations or diminished the region's long-term opportunities. McGraw-Hill's brands are strong in Asia. In a survey of 6,000 executives representing eleven Asian countries, MHP was chosen as one of Asia's 200 leading companies.

- The company is not only a beneficiary of global growth. McGraw-Hill helps spur global growth because its products provide information and analysis crucial to capital markets, business, and education—the cornerstones of progress. Revenue growth from international sources in the company's financial services business rose at a 17 percent compound annual growth rate during the

1993–1998 period. New information products helped spur that growth. Those introduced over the past three years accounted for 12 percent of the total revenue with the Financial Information Services group in 1998.

- In the past, many of McGraw-Hill's online financial services were distributed over networks controlled by third-party "quote vendors." With the Internet, the company now reaches many of its customers directly. As an example, Standard & Poor's MMS introduced its first Internet product in the spring of 1998. Now a subscription service, Global Markets Live offers real-time information and analysis on global bond, equity, currency, and commodity markets 24 hours a day.

- In the construction industry, the McGraw-Hill Construction Information Group (MH-CIG) is the foremost source of information crucial to new construction projects and planning. MH-CIG has increasingly turned to the Internet and other electronic tools to gather and distribute information. By the end of 2000, nearly half of its revenue will derive from electronic products.

Dodge Plans is the latest of several MH-CIG electronic products stemming from print media. It provides access— online or by CD-ROM twice weekly—to the plans, specifications, and bidding requirements for more than 60,000 new construction and renovation projects.

Total assets: $3,788 million
Current ratio: 1.23
Common shares outstanding: 197 million
Return on 1998 shareholders' equity: 22.9%

	1998	1997	1996	1995	1994	1993	1992	1991
Revenues (millions)	3,729	3,534	3,075	2,935	2,761	2,196	2,050	1,943
Net income (millions)	342	291	250	227	203	172	153	148
Earnings per share	1.71	1.46	1.25	1.14	1.03	.88	.78	.76
Dividends per share	.78	.72	.66	.60	.58	.57	.56	.55
Price: high	51.7	37.7	24.6	21.9	19.3	18.8	16.6	16.2
low	34.3	22.4	18.6	15.9	15.6	13.8	13.3	12.4

INCOME

MDU Resources Group, Inc.

P. O. Box 5650, Bismarck, ND 58506-5650 ◻ Investor contact: Warren L. Robinson (800) 437-8000 ◻ Dividend reinvestment plan available (800) 437-8000 ◻ Web site: www.mduresources.com ◻ Listed: NYSE ◻ Ticker symbol: MDU ◻ S&P rating: B+ ◻ Value Line financial strength rating: A

MDU Resources Group, Inc. is a natural resource company. The company's diversified operations, such as oil and gas and construction materials should help MDU Resources grow at a better rate than electric utilities that depend entirely on their electric business. However, investors should not ignore the increasingly competitive nature of the utility business. In this regard, MDU should fare better than utilities situated in more populated regions.

Montana-Dakota Utilities Company, the public utility division of the company, distributes natural gas and propane. It also operates power generation, transmission, and distribution facilities in North Dakota, eastern Montana, northern and western South Dakota, and northern Wyoming. Business development activities throughout the four states served by Montana-Dakota have produced a healthy economic climate. At the same time, increasing competitiveness and improved operating efficiencies have been providing financial rewards to the utility division.

Utility Services, Inc. installs and repairs electric transmission and distribution power lines and provides related supplies and equipment.

WBI Holdings, Inc. operates an interstate pipeline system that provides underground storage, transportation, and gathering services. In addition, it operates about 500 producing natural gas wells.

WBI Holdings owns and operates over 3,600 miles of transmission, gathering, and storage lines in the states of North Dakota, South Dakota, Montana, and Wyoming. Its system has links with five natural-gas-producing basins and interconnects with seven gas pipelines. Through three underground storage facilities located in Montana and Wyoming, storage services are provided to local distribution companies, suppliers, and other customers.

Knife River Corporation, through its wholly-owned subsidiary, KRC Holdings, Inc., and its subsidiaries, surface mines and markets aggregates and related construction materials in Oregon, California, Alaska, and Hawaii. In addition, Knife River surface mines and markets low-sulfur lignite coal at mines located in Montana and North Dakota.

KRC Holdings, including its interest in Hawaiian Cement, has aggregate reserves of about 153 million tons. Economically recoverable coal reserves approximate 229 million tons, of which some 67 million tons are subject to existing long-term contracts or commitments.

The Fidelity Oil Group is involved in the acquisition, exploration, development, and production of oil and natural gas properties. Fidelity Oil's operations vary from the acquisition of producing properties with potential development opportunities to exploration and are located throughout the United States, the Gulf of Mexico, and Canada.

The Economy of the Region

The company's traditional four-state service area is expected to experience moderate growth. The notable development of information processing and telecommunication operations, along with the population migration from small communities to metropolitan centers are anticipated to result in continued growth in Montana-Dakota's customer base. The company's construction materials operation can expect continuation of the healthy regional growth experienced in Oregon and Alaska and improving economies in northern California and Hawaii.

Highlights of 1998

• Consolidated revenues increased by 48 percent, approaching $900 million.

• The company celebrated fifty years on the New York Stock Exchange.

• Annual total return of 29 percent exceeded peer group and kept pace with the S&P 500 Index.

• Market capitalization exceeded $1 billion for the first time.

• First public stock offering in eighteen years completed in April of 1998, with proceeds going to support aggressive growth.

• Record high stock price reached in September of 1998.

• Second stock split this decade effected July 1998.

• Eighth consecutive annual dividend increase announced in August of 1998.

• The company invested over $230 million in business and property acquisitions, making 1998 the most active development year in the company's seventy-five-year history.

Shortcomings to Bear in Mind

■ In 1998, realized oil and natural gas prices were down 27 percent and 14 percent, respectively. These low prices prompted noncash writedowns that, when combined with slightly decreased production, reduced earnings from the oil and natural gas production unit. However, these factors were somewhat offset by lower production-related expenses. Excluding the noncash charges, earnings at this unit were $7.2 million, compared to $14.5 million for the same period in 1997.

Reasons to Buy

- Analysts consider MDU Resources to be an attractive investment for investors seeking to capitalize on the cyclical energy and construction-materials markets, coupled with the stability of a low-risk utility.

- In keeping with its strategy to expand its nonregulated business, two years ago MDU Resources began acquiring utility service companies. These operations provide full service utility engineering, construction, and maintenance to electric, natural gas, and telecommunications providers throughout the western United States. Through several strategic acquisitions in the last two years—three of which were completed since mid-April of 1998—these operations contributed $64 million in revenues and $3.3 million in earnings in 1998.

  Despite weather that was 6 percent warmer than normal, the natural gas distribution segment posted earnings of $3.5 million in 1998. The company continues to expand the nonregulated preferred service program, which offers customers insurance against unexpected appliance repairs. This program has been extremely successful since its introduction a few years ago. In 1998 alone, the number of customers subscribing to this service increased over 20 percent.

- MDU's diversified operations are becoming increasingly important. Although the electric and gas operations are still significant, most of the company's growth will come from the construction materials and oil and gas segments.

- The company's dividend reinvestment plan has been improved. The plan now enables investors residing in North Dakota, South Dakota, Montana, and Wyoming to purchase initial shares of the company's common stock through the program without payment of brokerage fees. Investors living in other states may buy MDU at low cost through NAIC (the National Association of Investors Corporation's Investment Plan).

- In the construction and mining business, earnings increased to $24.5 million in 1998, more than double that of the prior year. Increased aggregate and asphalt sales from existing operations, along with sales from construction materials operations acquired since mid-1997, were major factors in the earnings increase. Earnings from the coal operations almost doubled when compared to those of 1997. This was primarily due to the 1997 extended maintenance outage at a major electric utility generating station. Increased interest expense due to acquisition-related loans partially offset these gains.

- In 1997, the Montana State legislature passed an electric-industry-restructuring bill that provides for full customer choice by 2002, as well as full stranded-cost recovery and securitization. Based on other provisions of the legislation, however, MDU should be exempt from competition at least until 2002.

  In North Dakota and South Dakota, all of MDU's electric customers with loads of 10 megawatts or more are under special contracts of five years or more. In Montana, all new customers with these loads should be under similar special contracts. Currently, no significant deregulatory efforts are occurring in the other states in which the company operates. One significant plus factor: The company's rates are well below the national average, making inroads from competitors less likely. In addition, only

11.5 percent of MDU's electric utility retail revenue comes from industrial customers; industrial customers are considered to be the most likely to demand lower rates. Because of these factors, analysts consider MDU to be a utility with some of the lowest competitive risks in the United States.

- Knife River, through its wholly-owned subsidiary, KRC Holdings, Inc., made a number of acquisitions in 1998, making the year the most active for development since it began this program in 1992. In March, the company completed its acquisition of Morse Brothers, Inc.,

Oregon's largest construction-materials supplier. A premier full-service company, Morse supplies sand, gravel and crushed rock, ready-mix concrete, asphalt concrete, and prestress concrete products to customers throughout the Willamette Valley, one of the nation's fastest-growing regions. Morse Brothers specializes in materials for technically difficult construction jobs. One of the company's specialties is prestressed concrete beams for bridge construction. Prestressed concrete bridges are preferable to steel bridges in the Pacific Northwest's climate.

Total assets: $1,453 million
Current ratio: 1.42
Common shares outstanding: 53 million
Return on 1998 shareholders' equity: 6.5%

	1998	1997	1996	1995	1994	1993	1992	1991
Revenues (millions)	897	608	515	464	450	440	352	363
Net income (millions)	33.3	54.6	45.5	41.6	39.8	38.8	35.4	38.0
Earnings per share	.66	1.24	1.05	.95	.91	.89	.81	.87
Dividends per share	.78	.75	.73	.72	.70	.67	.65	.64
Price: high	28.9	22.3	15.7	15.4	14.3	14.7	11.9	11.1
low	18.8	14.0	13.3	11.5	11.3	11.5	9.7	8.8

CONSERVATIVE GROWTH

Merck & Co., Inc.

One Merck Drive, P. O. Box 100, Whitehouse Station, NJ 08889-0100 ◻ Investor contact: Laura Jordan (908)423-5185 ◻ Direct dividend reinvestment plan available: (800) 613-2104 ◻ Web site: www.merck.com ◻ Listed: NYSE ◻ Ticker symbol: MRK ◻ S&P rating: A+ ◻ Value Line Financial Rating: A++

Merck is a leading, research-driven pharmaceutical products and services company. Directly and through its joint ventures, the company discovers, develops, manufactures, and markets a broad range of innovative products to improve human and animal health. Merck also provides pharmaceutical and benefit services through Merck-Medco Managed Care.

Human Health Products

Human health products include therapeutic and preventative drugs, generally sold by prescription, for the treatment of human disorders. Among these are elevated-cholesterol products, which include Zocor and Mevacor; hypertensive/heart failure products include Vasotec, the largest-selling product among this group, Cozaar, Hyzaar, Prinivil and Vaseretic; anti-ulcerants, of which Pepcid is the largest-selling; antibiotics, of which Primaxin and Noroxin are the largest-selling; ophthalmologicals, of which Timoptic, Timoptic-XE, and Trusopt are the largest-selling; vaccines/biologicals, of which Recombivax HB (hepatitis B vaccine recombinant), M-M-R II, a pediatric vaccine for measles, mumps, and rubella, and Varivax, a live virus vaccine for the prevention of chickenpox, are the largest-selling; an HIV drug Crixivan, a protease inhibitor for the treatment of human immunodeficiency viral infection in adults, which was launched in the United States in 1996; and osteoporosis products, which includes Fosamax, for the treatment and prevention in postmenopausal women.

Animal Health Products

Animal health products include medicinals used to control and alleviate disease in livestock, small animals, and poultry. Crop protection includes products for the control of crop pests and fungal disease. In July 1997, the company sold its crop-protection business to Novartis. In August 1997, Merck and Rhone-Poulenc combined their animal health and poultry genetics businesses to form Merial Limited.

Merck-Medco

Merck-Medco primarily includes Merck-Medco sales of non-Merck products and Merck-Medco pharmaceutical benefit services, primarily managed prescription drug programs and programs to manage health and drug utilization.

Marketing

Merck sells its human health products to drug wholesalers, retailers, hospitals, clinics, government agencies, and managed-health care providers, such as health-maintenance organizations and other institutions. The company's professional representatives communicate the effectiveness, safety, and value of the company's products to health care professionals in private practice, group practices, and managed-care organizations.

Highlights of 1998

• In 1998, Merck launched five important new medicines: Singulair for asthma, Maxalt for migraine headache,

Aggrastat for acute coronary syndrome, Propecia for male pattern hair loss, and Cosopt for glaucoma.

• Merck achieved steady progress for its major products. Sales were up 14 percent over 1997. Net income also advanced 14 percent. And earnings per share climbed 15 percent.

• The company retained its number one position in the global market. Even in the complex, highly regulated European market, Merck enjoyed robust growth. The company rose to number two in the industry, growing at about twice the market growth rate and doubling its revenues in the past five years.

Shortcomings to Bear in Mind

■ Product patents for Vasotec, Vaseretic, Mevacor, Prinivil, Prinzide, Pepcid, and Prilosec (which Merck manufactures and supplies to Astra for the U.S. market) will go off-patent in 2000 and 2001. On the other hand, Merck contends that its newer products "will keep us competitive." Increasingly greater percentages of the company's overall sales derive from the 14 new drugs and vaccines it has introduced since 1995. These important medicines accounted for 22 percent of worldwide human health sales in 1998, up from 2 percent just three years ago. What's more, the five newest products are at the early stages of their lifecycles. As the company expands its marketing in Europe and the rest of the world in 1999, they will contribute even further to Merck's growth.

■ In 1998, Merck spent about $91 million to promote Propecia directly to domestic consumers. For the effort, the company posted only $68 million in U.S. sales and $83 million in worldwide sales. Even so, Merck's management is still optimistic about the prospects of Propecia, a drug Merck introduced in January of 1998 to treat mild to moderate hair loss. Propecia works by suppressing a hormone that shrinks hair follicles. The main side effect seen with Propecia is decreased libido and impotence, but only in a mere two percent of men. The problem clears up when the drug is discontinued. According to one analyst, "None of this helps to sell the product to men who are in their twenties and thirties and are sexual athletes."

- Competitive pressures will inhibit the growth of some of Merck's key products. For instance, Warner-Lambert's Lipitor has been gaining market share in the rapidly expanding market for cholesterol-lowering drugs, at the expense of Merck's Zocor and Mevacor. What's more, the company's Fosamax faces a formidable challenge from Eli Lilly's Evista. In addition, the protease inhibitor market is becoming ever more crowded; Agouron's Viracept has been showing solid growth. Finally, Bristol-Myers' Avapro will probably take some market share away from Merck's Cozaar.

- The markets in which the company's business is conducted are highly competitive and, in many ways, highly regulated. Global efforts toward health care cost containment continue to exert pressure on product pricing.

In the United States, government efforts to slow the increase of health care costs and the demand for price discounts from managed-care groups have limited the company's ability to mitigate the effect of inflation on costs and expenses through pricing.

Outside of the United States, government mandated cost-containment programs have required the company to similarly limit selling prices. Additionally, government actions have significantly reduced the sales growth of certain products by decreasing the patient reimbursement cost of the drug, restricting the volume of drugs that physicians can prescribe, and increasing the use of generic products. It is anticipated that the worldwide trend for cost containment and competitive pricing will continue and result in continued pricing pressures.

Reasons to Buy

- Crixivan, to treat HIV and AIDS, entered a new but crowded field, as the third product in its class. Based on its medical value, however, Crixivan established new standards for treatment and quickly rose to the number one market position globally in 1998.

- In 1998, Merck's once-a-day tablet, Singulair, had the most successful launch of any anti-asthma medicine in history. The Maxalt-MLT rapidly disintegrating tablet formulation for the treatment of migraine headaches was rapidly adopted for use, and it now accounts for half the medicine's new domestic prescriptions. In the United States, the 1,000 key hospitals that treat about 80 percent of the patients who suffer from acute coronary syndrome, purchased Merck's platelet blocker, Aggrastat, to help improve the survival chances of cardiac patients.

- Key Merck franchises, including Zocor, Fosamax, Cozaar, Hyzaar, and Crixivan, grew steadily in 1998, despite tough competition. With a new 80-milligram dose and a new indication to reduce the risk of first stroke in people with high cholesterol and coronary heart disease, Zocor enjoyed solid volume growth and is the most widely used cholesterol-lowering medicine in the world. Fosamax remains the leading nonhormonal medicine for the prevention and treatment of osteoporosis in postmenopausal women around the globe. Cozaar, the company's angiotensin II antagonist, enjoyed market leadership in 1998, extending its market presence with approvals to treat heart failure in fifteen countries. Cozaar is the only A-II antagonist approved for this use anywhere.

Crixivan, available in more than eighty countries, remains the most widely prescribed and cost-effective protease inhibitor for the treatment of HIV/AIDS throughout the world.

- In May of 1999, Merck received FDA approval for Vioxx, a new drug for arthritis and acute pain. Its principal claim is that is doesn't cause stomach ulcers, whereas most anti-inflammatory drugs may. Drugs now being used include aspirin, Relafen, Lodine XL, and Advil. An estimated 16,000 people a year die from deadly ulcers caused by conventional painkillers. Forty million people suffer from arthritis in the United States alone. Vioxx competes with Monsanto's Celebrex (which is also marketed by Pfizer, which paid Monsanto $240 million for this pact) arthritis medication, the first drug in the new cox-2 class to get FDA approval. Celebrex, which was introduced in January of 1999, has enjoyed one of the fastest new-drug launches in industry history. Now Merck will try to steal market share away from Celebrex as well as older drugs that still make up the majority of the market. Vioxx has one major advantage going for it: the FDA approval was for such afflictions as osteoarthritis, and acute short-term pain (such as menstrual cramps and pain following dental and orthopedic surgery). These uses are much broader than the FDA approval for Celebrex. Merck's drug has another advantage: it needs to be taken only once a day, regardless of the affliction being treated. Celebrex must be taken once or twice a day for osteoarthritis and twice a day for rheumatoid arthritis.

- Growth in earnings per share has been impressive. For instance, in the 1988–1998 period, earnings per share climbed from $.51 to $2.15, a compound annual growth rate of 15.5 percent. In the same ten-year span, dividends advanced from $.21 to $.95, a growth rate of 16.3 percent.

- There are about 4 million babies born in the United States each year who would be candidates for Varivax. About 8 percent to 9 percent of unimmunized children get chicken pox each year. It is currently estimated that there are 3.5 million cases of chicken pox each year in the United States, primarily in children between the ages of 5 and 9 years of age. Varivax has shown 93 percent efficacy in preventing the disease. Of the Varivax-vaccinated children, about 4 percent have gotten chicken pox, but with far fewer lesions than those experienced by unvaccinated children who get the disease.

The cost of Varivax to private physicians is $39 per dose. After discounts to various government funded programs and larger institutional buyers, Merck realizes about $28 per dose.

Total assets: $31,853 million
Current ratio: 1.78
Common shares outstanding: 2,382 million
Return on 1998 equity: 41.0%

	1998	1997	1996	1995	1994	1993	1992	1991
Revenues (millions)	26,898	23,637	19,829	16,681	14,970	10,498	9,662	8603
Net income (millions)	5,248	4,614	3,881	3,335	2,997	2,687	2,447	2,122
Earnings per share	2.15	1.92	1.60	1.35	1.19	1.17	1.06	.92
Dividends per share	.95	.85	.71	.62	.57	.52	.46	.39
Price: high	80.9	54.1	42.1	33.6	19.8	22.1	28.3	27.8
low	50.7	39.0	28.3	18.2	14.1	14.3	20.3	13.7

Microsoft Corporation

One Microsoft Way, Redmond, WA 98052-6399 ❑ Investor contact: Carla Lewis (425) 936-3703 ❑ Dividend reinvestment plan not available ❑ Web site: www.microsoft.com/msft/ ❑ Fiscal year's end June 30 ❑ Ticker symbol: MSFT ❑ S&P rating: A- ❑ Value Line financial strength rating: A++

Microsoft is the dominant player in the PC software market. It climbed to prominence on the popularity of its operating systems software and now rules the business-applications software market. Microsoft, moreover, has set its sights on becoming the leading provider of software services for the Internet.

By virtue of it size, market positioning, and financial strength, Microsoft is a formidable competitor in any market it seeks to enter. Earnings have shown explosive growth in recent years, enhanced by a strong PC market in general, along with new product introductions and market-share gains.

Microsoft is best known for its operating-systems software programs, which run on close to 90 percent of the PCs currently in use. Its original DOS operating system, of course, gave way to Windows, a graphical user interface program run in conjunction with DOS, which made using a PC easier.

Windows 98, the company's latest version of its flagship PC operating system, with sales closely tied to PC shipments, was introduced in mid-1998 and has already sold over 25 million copies. Its predecessor, Windows 95, has an installed base of more than 100 million users.

The company entered the business-applications market in the early 1990s via a line-up of strong offerings, combined with aggressive and innovative marketing and sales strategies. The company's Office 97 suite, which includes the popular Word (word processing), Excel (spreadsheet), and PowerPoint (graphics) software programs, is now by far the best-selling applications software package.

Shortcomings to Bear in Mind

- At times, Microsoft resembles a stumbling giant. In the federal antitrust case, for instance, the company's courtroom strategy was often described as inept.
- In the spring of 1999, the company's two most vigorous rivals, America Online and Netscape, merged to become a unified, potentially savage, competitor.
- Most of Microsoft's new wares merely match those introduced months, or even years ago, by competitors. Comparative shopping, for instance, which enables Netizens to check prices and products from a variety of vendors in one place, was introduced by Yahoo! Inc. in 1997. Microsoft's version of the service didn't come out until late in 1999.
- Microsoft has a long way before it can claim the lead in e-commerce software, programs used to manage on-line shopping and other transactions. Of course, Microsoft has been in this come-from-behind situation before, most notably when it saw Netscape Communications Corp. and others taking the lead in Internet technology. Microsoft leveraged its assets—mainly control over the Windows operating system—to make up for lost time. Virtually overnight, the company watched its share of the browser market go from the single digits to more than 50 percent today. Netscape, which had controlled close to 80 percent of the market, was nearly squashed in the process.

- In the spring of 1999, Steve Ballmer, the company's president, told a gathering of hardware executives in Los Angeles that it will release a consumer operating system in 2000 that will be based on its existing Windows 98 software. Previously, the company had said that it would phase out the software line in favor of a unified product line based on the code found in Windows NT and the coming Windows 2000.

   The strategy shift comes at a price because of the additional engineering required to maintain multiple software technologies. The move also is another sign of the wide-ranging impacts of the company's struggle to complete Windows 2000.

Reasons to Buy

- Microsoft Windows 98 is proving a great success. Customers appreciate its ability to work better and play better, while its robustness means that Windows 98 is generating less than half the customer calls of its predecessor. Integrated with the latest Internet Explorer technology, Windows 98 helps the company's customers leverage the interactivity of the Internet with the intelligence of the PC.

   Microsoft Windows NT Workstation is making deeper inroads into the desktop, based on its productivity, reliability, and lower total cost of ownership. What's more, Microsoft Windows CE, a compact version of the Windows operating system, designed for a wide range of intelligent devices, is finding its way into everything from interactive televisions to handheld computers.

- In May of 1999, Microsoft continued its spending spree with a $600 million investment in Nextel Communications Inc. The pact, which gave Microsoft a 4.25 percent stake in Nextel, is the latest in a string of deals by which Microsoft has used its huge cash hoard—cash reserves were nearly $22 billion in the spring of 1999—to cement relations with a major customer. A week earlier, Microsoft agreed to invest $5 billion in AT&T, in return for AT&T's commitment to use Microsoft's Windows CE software in many cable-television set-top boxes.

- Licensed sales of Microsoft Office 97 are strong, as the company's productivity applications continue to set the standard for features, functionality, and integration. Microsoft Office 2000, which came out in the first half of 1999, takes each of these factors into a significantly higher level, offering a simpler, personalized interface that learns each user's working style and adapts to it, plus many other productivity-enhancing features. Likewise, MSFT's development tools continue to lead the market with the release of Visual Studio 6.0.

- Microsoft Windows NT Server and Microsoft BackOffice applications continue to make solid progress in the marketplace and are now the clear enterprise solution of choice over the various UNIX-based platforms.

- The company's interactive media and services strategy continues to advance, focusing on on-line services, packaged software, and hardware. In Expedia travel service, CarPoint automotive service, Hotmail, Microsoft Investor, Gaming Zone, and Microsoft HomeAdvisor real estate service, the company is building some of the most powerful brands on the Internet. Its strategy going forward is to unify these sites around the MSN brand, so customers can easily reach all of them via a single portal, msn.com.

- In the spring of 1999, Microsoft released a new version of its Internet Explorer Web browser, a subtly improved edition that puts it once again ahead of Netscape in the continuing browser wars. To be sure, Internet Explorer 5.0 features no dramatic breakthroughs. However, it is filled with thoughtful little advances that make using the Web simpler for average, nontechnical folks.

In addition, Microsoft has upgraded Internet Explorer's free companion e-mail program, Outlook Express, adding features and sophistication while preserving its speed and ease of use. According to one analyst, "The changes strengthen my view that Outlook Express is the best Internet e-mail program, better even than Microsoft's much-touted but ponderous Outlook 98."

- One of the company's game plans is to beef up the Microsoft Network (MSN) into a more potent Web portal by adding an unparalleled menu of software products and services. Among other things, Microsoft will update its low-cost e-commerce software to enable on-line merchants to create more personalized Web stores. The key part of its initiative is BizTalk, a business-to-business tool that lets companies that operate on different systems do business with one another over the Net, even if they have never done business together before.

Microsoft believes that by offering the soup-to-nuts e-commerce system it will leapfrog the likes of Netscape/America Online. By controlling the operating system, software, services, and portal, the company can create seamless links between the different technologies and offer the whole package at a low price.

- In 1999, Microsoft Exchange Server set a new record, shipping 4.5 million client-access licenses in a single quarter. Through calendar 1998, Exchange outsold all competitors, with 14.4 million seats, demonstrating its leadership in the messaging and collaboration category.

- In early 1999, the company announced that Microsoft SQL Server 7.0 had been launched to over 45,000 customers in fifty-three countries. According to the company, "it made a clean sweep of COMDEX awards, bringing home the 'Best of Productivity Software' and 'Best of Show.'" As of the end of 1998, Microsoft is now, with SQL Server, the second-largest database vendor, moving up from fifth-largest in the prior two years. SQL Server is also growing at nearly twice the rate of the next-fastest competitor and nearly three times Oracle's CY98 growth rate.

- In 1999, the company announced availability of Microsoft Office 2000 beta 2 and the largest-ever early evaluation for Office. Responding to customer demand, the Office 2000 evaluation program has been expanded to an expected 700,000 customers participating in forty-three countries, making it ten times larger than all previous Office evaluation programs put together.

- Microsoft has recently expanded into the market for new consumer platforms. MSFT provides software for consumer devices, including handheld PCs, palm-sized PCs, wireless-communication devices, and Internet access devices. The company develops Windows CE, an operating system for communications, entertainment, and mobile computing devices.

Total assets: $5,363 million
Current ratio: 2.92
Common shares outstanding: 5,047 million
Return on 1998 shareholders' equity: 28.8%

	1998	1997	1996	1995	1994	1993	1992	1991
Revenues (millions)	14,484	11,358	8,671	5,937	4,649	3,753	2,759	1,843
Net income (millions)	4,786	3,454	2,176	1,453	1,210	953	708	463
Earnings per share	.89	.66	.43	.29	.25	.20	.15	.10
Dividends per share	nil							
Price: high	72.0	37.7	21.5	13.7	8.1	6.1	5.9	4.7
low	31.1	20.2	10.0	7.3	4.9	4.4	4.1	2.0

INCOME

Minnesota Mining & Manufacturing Company

3M Center, 225-1S-15, St. Paul, MN 55144-1000 □ Investor contact: Jon Greer (651) 736-1915 □ Web site: www.3M.com □ Listed: NYSE □ Dividend reinvestment plan available (800) 401-1952 □ Ticker symbol: MMM □ S&P rating: A □ Value Line financial strength rating: A++

Minnesota Mining & Manufacturing Company is an international manufacturer with a vast array of products (more than 50,000). The company has a stake in such items as tapes, adhesives, electronic components, sealants, coatings, fasteners, floor coverings, cleaning agents, roofing granules, fire-fighting agents, graphic arts, dental products, medical products, specialty chemicals, and reflective sheeting.

The company's Industrial and Consumer Sector is the world's largest supplier of tapes, producing more than 900 varieties. It is also a leader in coated abrasives, specialty chemicals, repositionable notes, home cleaning sponges and pads, electronic circuits, and other important products.

The Life Sciences Sector is a global leader in reflective materials for transportation safety, respirators for worker safety, closures for disposable diapers, and high-quality graphics used indoors and out. This sector also holds leading positions in medical and surgical supplies, drug delivery systems, and dental products.

MMM has a decentralized organization with a large number of relatively small profit centers, aimed at creating an entrepreneurial atmosphere. MMM is a highly diversified manufacturer of industrial,

commercial, consumer, and health care products that share similar technological, manufacturing, and marketing resources. Its business initially developed from its research and technology in coating and bonding.

MMM has many strengths:

• **Leading market positions.** Minnesota Mining is a leader in most of its businesses, often number one or number two in market share. In fact, MMM has created many markets, frequently by developing products that people didn't even realize they needed.

• **Strong technology base.** The company draws on more than thirty core technologies, from adhesives and nonwovens to specialty chemicals and microreplication.

• **Healthy mix of businesses.** MMM serves an extremely broad array of markets, from automotive and health care to office supply and telecommunications. This diversity gives the company many avenues for growth while cushioning the company from disruption in any single market.

• **Flexible, self-reliant business units.** MMM's success in developing a steady stream of new products and entering new markets stems from its deep-rooted corporate structure. It's an environment in which MMM people listen to customers, act on their own initiative, and share technologies and other expertise widely and freely.

• **Worldwide presence.** Minnesota Mining has companies in more than sixty countries around the world. It sells its products in nearly 200 countries.

• **Efficient manufacturing and distribution.** MMM is a low-cost supplier in many of its product lines. This is increasingly important in today's value-conscious and competitive world.

• **Strong financial position.** MMM is one of a small number of U.S. companies whose debt carries the highest rating for credit quality.

Shortcomings to Bear in Mind

■ Analysts and investors are disturbed that management has missed annual earnings projections for two years running. Sales, at $15 billion, are essentially flat. As of the spring of 1999, the stock had lost a third of its value since 1997. What's more, problems in overseas markets continue, both in Europe and Latin America. One analyst remarked, "We have been debating for a few months now whether MMM should even be considered a blue-chip stock anymore. It might be overstating it, but patience is waning."

■ MMM has been glacially slow to respond to the economic meltdown in Asia where it get 23 percent of its business. In the United States, a flood of cheaper products made by competitors like Korean polyester film outfits SKC and Kolon have cut into MMM's sales.

■ Over the past ten years, the company's growth, although steady, has not been dynamic. In the 1988–1998 period, earnings per share increased from $2.55 to $3.74, an annual compound growth rate of 3.9 percent. In the same ten-year stretch, dividends expanded from $1.06 to $2.20, a growth rate of 7.6 percent. With these lackluster numbers in mind,

I have changed this to a growth and income stock.

Reasons to Buy

■ While worldwide profits declined in 1998, the quality of MMM earnings continued to be high, excluding one-time charges:
  • Operating income was 16.9 percent of sales.
  • Net income was 10.2 percent of sales.
  • Return on stockholders' equity was 25.6 percent.
  • Return on invested capital was 15.9 percent, about six percentage points above the company's cost of capital.

■ During 1998, Minnesota Mining generated 31 percent of its sales from products new to the market during the prior four years. The company looks for an even higher proportion of sales to come from new products in 1999.

■ To sustain a strong flow of new product, MMM continues to make substantial investments, about $1 billion a year, in research and development. During 1998, the company was awarded 611 patents, placing MMM eleventh among domestic companies.

■ To resume healthy productivity gains, reduce costs, and further strength Minnesota Mining's competitiveness, it is implementing several actions. The company is streamlining its corporate structure, consolidating manufacturing operations, and withdrawing from product lines that have low returns or where MMM no longer sees a strategic fit.

■ Minnesota Mining is a global leader in industrial, consumer, office, health care, safety, and other markets. The company draws on many strengths, including a rich pool of technology, innovative products, strong customer service, and efficient manufacturing.

■ MMM invented and created a market for lightweight, maintenance-free respirators that help protect against certain airborne contaminants. Today, it is the global leader in the respiratory protection market. Workers and employers depend on Minnesota Mining not only for top-quality products but also for respiratory safety training worldwide.

To meet new, more stringent regulations, the company invented a new line of particulate respirators. Employing entirely new filtration technology, the company's respirators meet or exceed regulatory requirements while remaining comfortable to wear and easy to breathe through. What's more, Minnesota Mining has filed for two dozen patents and is launching this latest generation of respirators worldwide, further strengthening its market position.

- Pedestrians, bicyclists, and motorists have a new safety edge with MMM Scotchlite Diamond Grade Reflective Sheeting. The company's eye-catching fluorescent yellow-green sheeting was approved in 1998 for signs near schools, playgrounds, bike paths, and other areas where driver awareness is critical.

Another product in the line, Diamond Grade fluorescent orange sheeting, is rapidly becoming the standard in many states for signs in construction work zones. Durable fluorescent sheetings by 3M are the first to include a warranty for fluorescent-color retention. The company's Diamond Grade sheeting, which also makes large vehicles highly visible at night, draws on many MMM technologies and extends the company's leadership in reflective materials for transportation safety.

- The unrelenting drive toward smaller, lighter, more powerful, and more economical electronic products creates strong demand for leading-edge MMM Microflex Circuits. Minnesota Mining is the world's number one supplier of adhesive-less flexible circuitry. MMM microflex circuits connect components in many of the world's ink-jet printers.

They also link integrated circuits to printed circuit boards efficiently and reliably, making it possible to develop even smaller cellular phones, portable computer, pagers, and other electronic devices.

- Minnesota Mining supplies a wide variety of products to the automotive market, including high-performance tape attachment systems; structural adhesives; catalytic converter mounts; decorative, functional, and protective films; and trim and identification products.

- Under its Pacing Plus initiative, MMM has been accelerating the development of high-impact new products and bringing them to market faster. The company's Pacing Plus programs serve high-growth industries and largely produce new sales, rather than replace sales of existing products. These high-impact programs generated sales of $1 billion in 1998, up about 50 percent from 1997. The company expects sales of Pacing Plus programs to exceed $1.5 billion in 1999.

- The Life Sciences Sector produces innovative products that improve health and safety for people around the world. In consumer and professional health care, MMM has captured a significant share of the first-aid market with a superior line of bandages. The 3M Active Strips Flexible Foam Bandages adhere better to skin, even when wet, and 3M Comfort Strips Ultra Comfortable Bandages set new standards for wearing comfort. Under development are tapes, specialty dressings, and skin treatments that will reinforce and broaden the company's leading market positions and accelerate sales growth.

- In pharmaceuticals, MMM is a global leader in technologies for delivering medications that are inhaled or absorbed through the skin, and the company is expanding its horizons in new molecule discovery.

Total assets: $14,153 million
Current ratio: 1.44
Common shares outstanding: 401 million
Return on 1998 shareholder's equity: 25.6%

	1998	1997	1996	1995	1994	1993	1992	1991
Revenues (millions)	15,021	15,070	14,236	13,460	15,079	14,020	13,883	13,340
Net income (millions)	1,526	1,626	1,516	1,359	1,345	1,263	1,229	1,154
Earnings per share	3.74	3.88	3.63	3.23	3.18	2.91	2.82	2.63
Dividends per share	2.20	2.12	1.92	1.88	1.76	1.66	1.60	1.56
Price: high	97.9	105.5	85.9	69.9	57.1	58.5	53.5	48.8
low	65.6	80.0	61.3	50.8	46.4	48.6	42.8	39.1

INCOME

National City Corporation

P. O. Box 5756, Dept. 2101, Cleveland, OH 44101-0756 ❑ Investor contact: Julie I. Sabroff (800) 622-4204 ❑ Dividend reinvestment plan available (800) 622-6757 ❑ Web site: www.national-city.com ❑ Listed: NYSE ❑ Ticker symbol: NCC ❑ S&P rating: A- ❑ Value Line financial strength rating: A

National City Corporation is a major diversified financial services company based in Cleveland, Ohio. NCC operates banks and other financial service subsidiaries, principally in Ohio, Kentucky, Michigan, Indiana, and Pennsylvania.

Since David A. Daberko was named chairman and chief executive officer of National City Corporation in mid-1995, the company, once known only to Ohioans, has more than doubled in size through acquisitions. The closing of 1998 deals makes NCC the nation's thirteenth largest bank, with assets of $88.2 billion, in contrast to $35 billion in mid-1995.

National City subsidiaries provide financial services that meet a wide range of customer needs, including commercial and retail banking, trust and investment services, item processing, mortgage banking, and credit card processing.

Retail Banking
The retail banking business includes the deposit-gathering branch franchise, along with lending to individuals and small businesses. Lending activities include residential mortgages, indirect and direct consumer installment loans, leasing, credit cards, and student lending.

Fee-Based Businesses
The fee-based businesses include institutional trust, mortgage banking, and item processing.

● Institutional trust includes employee benefit administration, mutual fund management, charitable and endowment services, and custodial services.

● Mortgage banking includes the origination of mortgages through retail offices and broker networks and mortgage servicing.

● Item processing is conducted by National City's majority-owned subsidiary, National Processing, Inc. (NYSE:NAP) and includes merchant credit card processing, airline ticket processing, check guarantee services, and receivables and payables processing services.

A Review of 1998
National City Corporation reported net income of $1,070.7 million, or $3.22 per diluted share, in 1998, compared with $1,122.2 million, or $3.42 per diluted

share, in 1997, and $993.5 million, or $2.95 per diluted share, in 1996.

Included in reported net income were after-tax merger and restructuring expenses of $261.9 million, or $.78 per diluted share, in 1998, $34.9 million, or $.11 per diluted share, in 1997, and $49.1 million, or $.15 per diluted share, in 1996.

Excluding merger and restructuring expenses, net income in 1998 of $1,332.6 million, or $4.00 per diluted share, increased 15.2 percent over 1997. Results for 1998 and 1997 reflect strong loan and noninterest income growth and lower credit costs.

Excluding merger and restructuring expenses, return on average common equity was 19.18 percent in 1998, up from 18.77 percent in 1997 and 17.53 percent in 1996. On this same basis, return on average assets was 1.66 percent in 1998, compared with 1.61 percent in 1997 and 1.47 percent in 1996.

Merger and restructuring expenses in 1998 related to the merger with First of America Bank Corporation and the acquisition of Fort Wayne National Corporation.

All things considered, 1998 was an excellent year for National City, but years ahead have the potential to be even better. With the merger integration effort behind the bank, and year 2000 systems readiness activities taken care of, National City will benefit from significantly lower overhead expenses, while at the same time realizing merger-related revenue enhancements from offering the bank's products and services to the new markets.

Customer Needs and Preferences

To gain insight into customer preferences, National City has been making substantial investments in data warehouse technology to more effectively capture and manage customer information. This capability has already resulted in more effective cross-selling and has given the bank tools to better understand and predict customer needs and preferences.

The bank is well aware that customer demand for financial services transcends traditional time-and-place limitations. To that end, the company initiated a multi-year plan to reconfigure its branch delivery system, reducing traditional, full-service branches while expanding nontraditional alternatives. This includes in-store locations, limited-service facilities, and off-site ATMs, which, along with better call-center capability, makes it easier and more convenient for customers to do business with National City.

Shortcomings to Bear in Mind

- National City has a lackluster record of growth. In the 1988–1998 period, earnings per share expanded from $1.92 to $4.00, a compound annual growth rate of 7.6 percent. In the same ten-year span, however, dividends per share outperformed EPS growth, climbing from $.75 to $1.94, a growth rate of 10.0 percent.

- Looking ahead, banks are finding it increasingly difficult to expand revenues. Those with the broadest product mix are more likely to have an easier time registering top-line growth. In addition, savings from cost-cutting efforts, which have propelled earnings for many large banks in recent years, are becoming more difficult to come by, placing greater emphasis on top-line growth. Loan growth also remains a regional phenomenon, with strength in areas of the Southeast and Midwest, where economies continue to grow at a rate above the national average.

Reasons to Buy

- In corporate banking, National City's second-largest business, the bank has worked hard to retain its position as the number-one middle-market lender in its region. The bank's markets have been economically vibrant, as evidenced by low rates of unemployment and significant growth in small and medium-size businesses over the past several years. The bank's decentralized system of credit approval permits quick responsiveness to customer needs. At the same time, the company's product capability is second to none. For example, NCC introduced an innovative lending product, Corporate Select, that utilizes built-in interest-rate protection options inside a conventional loan. This helps companies manage risk in a seamless, straightforward manner. Corporate Select offers a competitive advantage in winning and strengthening customer relationships. There is no comparable product currently available in the market. Through initiatives such as these and a strong team of relationship managers, National City has been able to maintain or increase market share in virtually all of its markets. What's more, the company has been particularly successful in western Pennsylvania, which it entered through the merger with Integra Financial Corporation in 1996.

- A new challenge for National City developed in 1998, following the merger with First of America Bank Corporation, which was announced late in 1997. First of America, which has $21 billion in assets and is based in Kalamazoo, Michigan, dramatically bolsters the National City franchise through the addition of over 3 million customers in markets across Michigan, central Indiana, and key Illinois cities outside Chicago. Although the one-time charges temporarily disrupted National City's earnings per-share growth record in 1998, management expects a resumption of earnings growth in 1999 and beyond, through the rollout of National City products and services to First of America's markets and customer base.

- In early 1998, the bank announced an agreement to acquire Fort Wayne National Corporation, a $3-billion in assets banking company that has the number-one and number-two market share, respectively, in the attractive northern Indiana markets of Fort Wayne and South Bend. This franchise will significantly enhance the company's Indiana banking presence.

- To better serve the growing base of affluent individuals and households, NCC created the Private Client Group, which combines the former personal trust and private banking divisions into a single, customer-driven entity.

The remainder of the former Trust Group, principally asset management, employee benefits, and corporate trust services, has been reorganized into Institutional Trust, focusing on corporate clients and providing investment management services to the Private Client Group.

Total assets: $88,246 million
Return on assets in 1998: 1.66%
Common shares outstanding: 326 million
Return on 1998 shareholders' equity: 19.2%

	1998	1997	1996	1995	1994	1993	1992	1991
Loans (millions)	58,011	39,573	35,830	25,732	22,566	20,843	18,354	15,216
Net income (millions)	1,333	807	733	465	429	404	347	231
Earnings per share	4.00	3.66	3.27	2.64	2.60	2.59	1.76	1.38
Dividends per share	1.94	1.67	1.47	1.30	1.18	1.06	.94	.94
Price: high	77.5	67.6	47.3	33.8	29.0	28.1	24.8	21.1
low	56.9	42.5	30.6	25.3	23.8	23.1	17.9	13.9

New Plan Excel Realty Trust, Inc.

1120 Avenue of the Americas, New York, NY 10036 ❐ Investor contact: Dean Bernstein (212) 869-3000 ext. 314 ❐ Dividend reinvestment plan available (212) 869-3000 ❐ Web site: www.newplanexcel.com ❐ Listed: NYSE ❐ Ticker symbol: NXL ❐ S&P rating: not rated ❐ Value Line financial strength rating: A

New Plan Excel Realty Trust is the product of a merger between New Plan Realty Trust and Excel Realty Trust. The combined entity is one of the nation's largest owners of retail strip shopping centers. The merger took place in the fall of 1998.

The creation of New Plan Excel provided its shareholders with the security of $2.9 billion in total assets, more than $419 million in annual total revenue, and an investment-grade credit rating of A/A2 by Standard & Poor's and Moody's, respectively, a credit rating not exceeded by any REIT in the nation.

The strength of the balance sheet has created significant financial resources for New Plan Excel. The new company has 357 properties in thirty-one states, comprising more than 4,500 tenants in a retail portfolio of about 38 million square feet of gross leasable area and 55 garden apartment communities. The asset size, coupled with tenant and geographic diversity, provides a stability and momentum that few real estate organizations in the world can match.

Management believes the combined company boasts a number of competitive advantages that neither of the predecessors could claim. The first is a national portfolio, which permits NXL to compete effectively for national and regional tenants by offering a wide selection of sites. In addition, the company has significant concentrations of properties in certain markets, enabling it to negotiate favorable lease terms with existing and prospective tenants. Also, potential synergies resulting from complementary property management offices and expected operating efficiencies should enhance New Plan Excel's overall competitiveness.

Community shopping centers range from 100,000 square feet to 600,000. They are typically anchored by a supermarket and/or a drug store. Other merchants might include a dry cleaner, a stationer, apparel shops, restaurants, and so on. Community centers tend to be recession-resistant, because most goods and services sold by tenants are considered consumer necessities. Also, these merchants are not likely to compete with those that deal on the Internet.

Garden apartments are two-story apartments with landscaped common areas and amenities such as tennis courts and swimming pools. In the past, New Plan's acquisition strategy has focused on buying middle-income properties away from metropolitan areas for less than replacement cost. Management believes that tenants in these buildings move less frequently, and that below-market rents provide room for future rent hikes.

Still Room to Grow

Most of the commercial real estate in the United State is owned by private groups or individuals: 96 percent of the office buildings, 95 percent of industrial warehouses, 93 percent of rental apartment buildings, and 78 percent of retail malls. There is somewhere between $2 trillion and $3 trillion worth of commercial real estate, and very little of it is publicly owned. Suddenly, and at an accelerating rate, this last great trove of assets and cash flow is becoming available to investors.

Call it REIT fever. Meanwhile, many of the great realty magnates are approaching retirement and want to diversify their assets. The vehicle for unlocking these assets has been around for thirty-five years, real estate investment trusts or REITs. An REIT is a company that owns and manages many forms of real estate, such as office buildings, apartment buildings, nursing homes, hotels, restaurants, and warehouses.

Shares of REITs trade like the stock of other public companies, but they have a hybrid nature, part bond, part common stock, that many investors don't fully understand. REITs can avoid paying corporate income tax if they pass on nearly all of their net income to shareholders in the form of dividends. These dividends create a steady stream of income, typically 5 percent or more, that is similar to yield investments such as bonds. But, unlike bonds, shares of REITs can increase in value if the underlying property appreciates and if the REIT can raise rents.

As recently as 1992, all equity REITs in the United States had a combined market value of just $10 billion, less than the market value of one stock, such as McDonald's Corp. In the past five years, however, that figure has grown to $200 billion, but it still pales in comparison with the size of the commercial realty industry.

A Glimpse of New Plan Exel Realty Trust

Celebrating its seventy-third year in real estate, New Plan went public in 1962 and became a Real Estate Investment Trust (REIT) in 1972. It owns and operates retail and residential properties largely in the eastern half of the United States. As one of the oldest and largest real estate investment trusts, New Plan became the nation's first billion-dollar REIT in 1992, based on market capitalization.

Shortcomings to Bear in Mind

- Since 1991, more than 150 REITs have gone public, and the industry's market capitalization has soared from $13 billion to $200 billion. In 1998, however, fears of overbuilding, recession, and a credit crunch drove REIT shares down. That sidelined REITs as real estate buyers, and for the first time since the mid-1990s, pension funds and other institutional investors overtook REITs as the top buyers of commercial real estate, according to Institutional Real Estate, Inc. When are REITs coming back? That is the $64 billion question.

Reasons to Buy

- Utilizing the strategy known as "spread investing," New Plan adheres to the practice of using balance sheet strength to raise low-cost capital for investment in higher-yielding real estate. Typically, the initial return from a newly acquired property increases further as the property is improved, the tenant roster is upgraded, rents are increased, and vacancies filled.

- According to analysts, real estate investment trusts are, by their very nature, less risky than other sectors and the stock market as a whole. In good times and bad, REIT performance across all real estate sectors traditionally is less volatile than the Standard & Poor's 500, moving at about half the rate of the popular index. For stockholders, the predictable performance of REITs offers a safer haven in times of turmoil. Because income is generated from rent on leased space, REITs have a fairly steady revenue stream, says one analyst.

- New Plan's management prefers to buy property at a significant discount to its replacement cost, in areas of proven stability, rather than pay what it considers to be excessive prices for more glamorous locations.

- The REIT industry has proven itself to be a particularly successful form of ownership. The reasons for that starts out with the 1960 Act of Congress that enabled the REIT industry to get started. What it did was to provide a structure that is free of income tax, similar to the mutual fund industry. It is a pass-through type of structure, which means that by law, REITs are to distribute 95 percent of their taxable earnings to their shareholders, and the main reason for their existence is that Congress felt that REITs would enable the small investor to participate in the benefits of real estate ownership.
- One of the drawbacks of real estate has always been the lack of liquidity. With a REIT, you have complete and instant liquidity. Another point is that syndicators require large individual investments from participants. With REITs, you can buy one share or a million shares, so you have an ability to buy into the largest pieces of property with the smallest amount of money. You also have diversification, in this instance nearly 360 different properties.
- New Plan Excel's portfolio presently enjoys a low vacancy rate of only 7.7 percent.
- The majority of the company's leases contain provisions to mitigate the adverse impact of inflation. Such provisions include clauses enabling the company to receive percentage rents that generally increase as prices rise, and/or escalation clauses that are typically related to increases in the consumer price index or similar inflation indexes.

  In addition, the company believes that many of its existing lease rates are below current market levels for comparable space and that upon renewal or rerental such rates may be increased to current market rates. This belief is based upon an analysis of relevant market conditions, including a comparison of comparable rental rates and upon the fact that many of such leases have been in place for a number of years and may not contain escalation clauses sufficient to match the increase in market rental rates over such time.

  Most of the company's leases require the tenant to pay its share of operating expenses, including common area maintenance, real estate taxes, and insurance, thereby reducing the company's exposure to increases in costs and operating expenses resulting from inflation.
- New Plan has an impressive record of dividend increases. At the end of 1998, the company had raised its dividend for seventy-nine consecutive quarters. This would appear to be a record nearly impossible to equal or exceed.

Total assets: $2,894 million
Common shares outstanding: 88 million
Return on 1998 shareholders' equity: 9.1%

	1998	1997	1996	1995	1994	1993	1992	1991
Rental income (millions)	419	202	163	126	96	65	48	41
Net income (millions)	154	77	70	63	51	42	39	35
Earnings per share	1.49	1.31	1.25	1.19	1.04	.87	86	.92
Dividends per share	1.62	1.44	1.40	1.36	1.32	1.28	1.21	1.13
Price: high	26.1	26.0	25.6	23.0	24.4	26.4	26.1	24.5
low	17.9	21.4	19.9	19.6	18.8	21.5	19.6	16.1

Newell Rubbermaid Inc.

29 E. Stephenson Street, Freeport, IL 61032 ❑ **Investor contact: Ross A. Porter, Jr. (815) 381-8150** ❑
Dividend reinvestment plan available (800) 317-4445 ❑ **Web site: www.newellco.com** ❑ **Listed: NYSE** ❑
Ticker symbol: NWL ❑ **S&P rating: A+** ❑ **Value Line financial strength rating: B++**

Newell Rubbermaid (formerly Newell Company) acquired Rubbermaid Inc in 1999. It is the company's largest acquisition to date. The resultant company should be a formidable competitor in the housewares industry. This merger created an entity that should benefit from both companies' prior strengths: Newell's operational efficiency and dedicated customer service, coupled with Rubbermaid's innovative product development and brand name.

Rubbermaid's Product Lines

Home Products includes housewares, hardware, storage and organization, and leisure and recreational products sold primarily to retailers under the Rubbermaid and Curver brands in the United States and Europe. This is Rubbermaid's largest operation, with 1998 sales of some $1.3 billion.

Infant Products includes car seats, strollers, portable playpens, and other infant products sold primarily to retailers in the United States under the Century and Graco brands. Sales were about $400 million in 1998.

Juvenile Products includes children's toys, playground equipment, recreational products, and other related items sold primarily to domestic retailers under the Little Tikes label. Sales in 1998 were about $350 million.

Commercial Products includes commercial, industrial, and sanitary maintenance, home health care, and food service products sold mostly to institutional accounts in the United States under the Rubbermaid brand. Sales were about $400 million in 1998.

Newell's Product Lines

Newell manufactures and markets a variety of consumer products, primarily through volume retailers, such as Wal-Mart, Sears, Kmart, and Costco. The company operates in three main categories: Hardware and Home Furnishings, Office Products, and Housewares Products.

Virtually all of Newell's products are branded, highly visible market leaders, ranking number one or number two. Newell's product are manufactured and sold by twenty-six operating divisions. Each division has high-volume manufacturing capabilities, an unwavering customer service focus, and innovative merchandising. Among Newell's brand names are Sanford, Rolodex, Ace, Goody, Anchor Hocking, Pyrex, Wearever, Panex, Eberhard Faber, and Wilhold.

Newell's largest customer, Wal-Mart, recently opened a large store in Mexico City. Newell's sales continue to grow, both at home and abroad, as major mass retailers consolidate and expand in a worldwide marketplace. Other leading customers include Kmart, Home Depot, Target, Toys R Us, Office Depot, Lowe's, JC Penney, United Stationers, and Staples.

Newell strives to penetrate high-volume mass merchandisers with moderately priced, branded consumer staples and is constantly expanding its multi-product offering through acquisitions and modifying existing lines to achieve maximum profit. The company emphasizes high-quality, low-tech, recession-resistant, and highly recognized brand-name consumer products that generally hold leading shares in their respective markets. Newell operates under the axiom that high-margined products are better than lower-margined items; therefore, it is constantly upgrading existing lines, adding products and weeding out the less-profitable.

Shortcomings to Bear in Mind

- The acquisition of Rubbermaid is expected to be dilutive in 1999. And, since it is by far the company's largest venture, it may be more difficult to complete Newellization.

Reasons to Buy

- For more than thirty years, acquisitions have been the company's primary vehicle for growth—1998 was no exception. Newell completed five major acquisitions in 1998, accounting for about $700 million in annualized sales, further expanding Newell's international leadership in window treatments, aluminum cookware, and writing instruments.

  Newell bolstered its European drapery hardware and window treatments offering with two significant acquisitions in 1998. In March, the company completed the acquisition of Swish Track & Pole and in August the acquisition of Gardinia. Combined with Kirsch, acquired in 1997, these additions give Newell leading drapery hardware market positions in most major European countries, with annualized sales of about $400 million.

- The company also expanded its offering of cookware and bakeware into gourmet and Latin American markets. In May 1998, Newell completed the acquisition of Calphalon, a manufacturer of gourmet cookware marketed to specialty and department stores.

  The company further expanded its cookware offering in June of 1998 with the acquisition of Panex, based in San Paulo, Brazil. Panex is the leading South American cookware maker, with brands such as Panex, Penedo, Rochedo, and Clock. Newell now boasts a worldwide cookware and bakeware business with sales approaching $500 million.

- The company also added to its writing instrument offering in 1998 with Rotring, acquired in September of 1998. Based in Hamburg, Rotring is a leading manufacturer and supplier of writing and drawing instruments and art supplies sold under the Rotring, Koh-I-Noor, and Grumbacher brands. With strong distribution in over one hundred countries, Rotring gives Newell an impressive platform to introduce a full line of writing instruments to Europe. Currently, Newell's global writing instrument business exceeds $900 million in annualized sales.

- In March of 1999, the company completed the acquisition of Rubbermaid. Newell's offering of hardware and home furnishings, office products, and housewares complements Rubbermaid's $2.45 billion offering of home, infant, juvenile, and commercial products. Newell's management believes that "our disciplined approach and focus on consumer service, combined with Rubbermaid's innovative new product capability, makes the acquisition an excellent strategic fit."

- During 1998, the company strengthened its financial position as a result of three strategic transactions. In March, Newell sold its stake in Black & Decker, resulting in net proceeds of almost $400 million. In July and August, respectively, the company divested its Stuart Hall and Newell Plastics divisions, resulting in net proceeds of about $200 million. The proceeds from these divestitures were used to pay down debt, leaving the company with a strong, flexible, and conservative balance sheet, positioning Newell for future growth.

- Consolidation continues in the markets where Newell competes, and mass merchants are beginning to expand globally. These trends support the company's multi-product-line strategy and contribute to growth with its major customers. Retail consolidation also reinforces Newell's strengths, which include extensive manufacturing capabilities, leading-edge merchandising, and the ability to provide superior customer service to the company's ever-expanding customer base. These major customers want fewer, larger, and stronger suppliers who are nimble enough to adapt to an ever-changing and growing global environment.

■ Newell typically acquires companies with a history of underperformance—this indicates unrealized profit potential. As soon as a company or product line is acquired, Newell begins a concentrated effort to quickly integrate the new operation and make it a profitable member of the Newell family. This process of bringing newly acquired product lines up to Newell's high profitability standards even has a name: Newellization.

The first step in that process, after improving customer service, is the establishment of a focused business strategy. In some cases, the business objectives that once make these acquired companies great have been obscured or lost. Acquisitions that were once part of other companies may have had goals that were in conflict with those of the parent company, hurting sales and profitability at the product line. By installing a focused business strategy, Newell makes these new acquisitions concentrate on core growth opportunities, setting them firmly on the path to profitability.

The Newellization process involves administrative changes that increase operating margins, including eliminating corporate overhead by centralizing office functions, tightening financial controls, and trimming excess costs.

In the factory, Newellization means improving manufacturing efficiency, pruning nonproductive product lines, reducing inventories, and increasing trade-receivable turnover.

At the customer level, profitability is increased by providing better customer service, building partnerships, and improving sales mix profitability through the application of program merchandising techniques.

In most cases, experienced Newell managers are placed in key positions at the new company. These executives bring Newell controls and culture and instill a team spirit to improve product quality, customer service, and profitability. The integration effort, which typically takes about two or three years, is always underway at some recently acquired product lines of Newell. The changes the company makes are specific to the needs of the newly acquired business, whether foreign or domestic.

■ Newell has grown dramatically over the last decade. In the 1988–1998 period, earnings per share climbed from $.51 to $1.94, a compound annual growth rate of 14.3 percent. In the same ten-year span, dividends per share climbed from $.14 to $.72, a compound annual growth rate of 17.8 percent. Nor were there any years in which earnings declined in the 1981–1998 period.

■ Only seven of the world's top retailers are currently major customers of Newell. Management is convinced that this "presents a huge opportunity for growth." Its current customers include: Wal-Mart, Sears Roebuck, Kmart, J. C. Penney, Dayton Hudson, Home Depot, and Costco.

Total assets: $4,328 million
Current ratio: 1.94
Common shares outstanding: 281 million
Return on 1998 shareholders' equity: 23.0%

	1998	1997	1996	1995	1994	1993	1992	1991
Revenues (millions)	3,720	3,234	2,873	2,498	2,075	1,645	1,452	1,259
Net income (millions)	320	290	256	222	196	165	163	136
Earnings per share	1.94	1.82	1.62	1.41	1.24	1.05	1.05	.89
Dividends per share	.72	.64	.56	.46	.39	.35	.30	.30
Price: high	55.2	43.8	33.8	27.3	23.9	21.5	26.5	22.9
low	35.7	30.1	25.0	20.3	18.8	15.4	16.5	11.5

INCOME

Nicor Inc.

P. O. Box 3014, Naperville, IL 60566-7014 ❐ **Investor contact: Mark Knox (630) 305-9500, ext. 2529** ❐
Dividend reinvestment plan available (630) 305-9500 ❐ **Web site: www.nicorinc.com** ❐ **Listed: NYSE** ❐
Ticker symbol: GAS ❐ **S&P rating: A-** ❐ **Value Line financial strength rating: A+**

Nicor is a holding company. Its principal business is Nicor Gas (previously Northern Illinois Gas), the nation's fifth-largest gas distribution company. Nicor Gas delivers natural gas to more than 1.9 million customers, including transportation service, gas storage, and gas supply backup to about 40,000 commercial and industrial customers who purchase their own gas supplies.

The Nicor Gas subsidiary operates in a 17,000-square-mile territory, covering 544 communities in northern Illinois, excluding Chicago.

The company operates seven underground gas storage facilities. On an annual basis, GAS, the company's ticker symbol, cycles about 130 billion cubic feet (Bcf) in and out of storage. Having ample storage is particularly important during cold winter months when there is a huge demand on the pipelines. Nicor has one of the most extensive storage facilities in the industry.

Nicor Gas's service territory has a stable economic base that provides strong and balanced demand among residential, commercial, and industrial natural gas users. Residential customers account for about 40 percent of deliveries, while industrial and commercial customers account for about 35 percent and 25 percent of deliveries, respectively.

Nicor also owns Tropical Shipping, which transports containerized freight between the Port of Palm Beach, Florida, and twenty-six ports in the Caribbean and Central America. Tropical Shipping is recognized as a dependable, on-time carrier in its operating region.

With a fleet of fourteen vessels serving twenty-six Caribbean ports, Tropical Shipping is one of the largest carriers of containerized cargo in the region. The company has a reputation for providing quality, on-time service and has established dominant market shares in many of the ports it serves. Markets include the Bahamas, the Cayman Islands, the Dominican Republic, the Virgin Islands, and the Eastern Caribbean.

To improve profitability, Tropical plans to increase vessel utilization and reduce costs. Future growth is anticipated, mostly from higher-margin services to existing and new markets. Tropical Shipping accounts for 11 percent of Nicor's operating income.

Shortcomings to Bear in Mind

■ By their very nature, public utilities are for conservative investors who are seeking above-average yield. However, growth is modest. In the 1988–1998 period, for instance, Nicor, like most utilities, did not enjoy explosive growth. In that stretch, earnings per share advanced from $1.74 to $2.42, a compound annual growth rate of 3.4 percent. On the other hand, this was better than many others in the industry. Unfortunately, Nicor chose to cut its dividend in 1986 when some of its nonutility segments fell on hard times. In the ten-year period since the cut, dividends per share advanced from $.94 to $1.48, a compound growth rate of 4.6 percent, which is satisfactory.

■ All public utilities are vulnerable to shifts in interest rates. In fact, interest-rate changes are the most potent factor affecting the action of utility stocks. There are two reasons: utilities borrow a lot of money, and higher interest rates can hurt. Second, many investors buy utilities for income. If they are convinced that they can do better elsewhere, they may be tempted to sell their utility shares, thus depressing them to lower levels.

■ The weather has an impact on electric as well as natural gas utilities. Electric companies like hot summers so they can sell more air conditioning. They like cold winters so they can sell more space heating. For their part, natural gas utilities don't worry much about the summer, since they typically lose money during those months. But in the winter, they want plenty of cold weather. If they don't get it, their profits are hit hard.

Reasons to Buy

■ 1998 was a challenge because of extremely warm weather and the impact it had on the company's natural gas distribution business. In Northern Illinois, weather was 21 percent warmer than normal, making 1998 the warmest year of the century. Despite this, diluted earnings per common share declined only 7 percent. Had the weather been normal, Nicor would have easily exceeded its 1997 earnings-per-share level.

■ Nicor Gas typically accounts for about 90 percent of Nicor Inc.'s consolidated operating income. The company is widely regarded as one of the best companies in the natural gas distribution industry, and it consistently ranks at or near the top of its industry in terms of operating efficiency and financial returns.

■ Changes in the energy industry made it possible for Nicor to enter the market for energy services, and as those changes continue, other opportunities have emerged. One of those opportunities is in the market for electric power generation. The company believes power generation is a logical extension of Nicor's strategic focus as it establishes Nicor as a total energy provider, increases deliveries in its regulated gas distribution business, and builds on the knowledge it has developed from cogeneration projects over the years.

Nicor looks at the power generation market in terms of three primary segments—small commercial generation, midsize commercial generation, and large industrial or wholesale generation. In 1998, the company took steps that put Nicor in position to be a participant in all three market segments.

In one of 1998's most significant developments, Nicor formed an alliance with Dynegy that gives the company the ability to develop large electric power generation projects in the Midwest. In January of 1999, Nicor and Dynegy announced plans for the first such project: a 250-megawatt, natural gas-powered electric generation plant in northern Illinois. Electric power from the plant will be sold to investor-owned utilities, electric cooperatives, and municipalities during high-demand periods.

- Public utilities generally rely on a greater amount of debt in their balance sheets than industrial companies. For its part, Nicor is exceptionally strong, with 57.5 percent of capitalization in the form of shareholders' equity. At the other extreme, some utilities have only 35 percent in equity.

- One of the reasons Nicor Gas has been able to increase gas deliveries in recent years is the upward trend in diversified uses of natural gas. The company continues to make steady inroads in such markets as electric power generation, cogeneration, and large-tonnage gas air conditioning.

- At Nicor Gas, earnings growth will come from a combination of customer additions, increases in gas deliveries to existing customers, and efforts to minimize costs.

  Beyond the company's traditional gas distribution business, Nicor has developed several new sources of revenue. Examples include utilization of its transmission network and storage facilities to provide services to pipelines, gas distribution companies, and gas marketers. The company has also established several unregulated businesses that provide value-added services to Nicor's customers.

- Even with its 1996 rate increase, Northern Illinois Gas prices remain among the lowest in the nation. Low gas prices are important because continued deregulation of the utility industry will likely result in more competitive pricing between natural gas and electricity. For Nicor Gas's residential and small commercial customers, natural gas costs are currently about one-third the cost of using electricity, and the company expects to maintain a competitive advantage compared with electricity in the years ahead.

- Nicor has a flexible supply position. Nicor Gas has interconnects with five interstate pipelines, providing access to most major gas-producing areas in North America. This allows for a diverse supply portfolio, which helps assure reliability and competitive pricing.

- Largely because of its location on the nation's pipeline grid, Nicor Gas has been able to use its transmission and storage assets in nontraditional ways through operation of the Chicago Hub and by providing transportation and storage services for others.

- In 1998, Tropical Shipping again achieved record volumes shipped, revenues, and income. Operating income was $27.6 million, up from $25.3 million in 1997, due to an increase in volumes shipped and higher average rates.

  The company continued its efforts to increase efficiency and reduce costs. Tropical Shipping operates a fleet of thirteen owned and five charter vessels. In 1998, the company modified its vessel schedule in order to reduce the number of weekly port calls, streamline the handling of containers, and free up vessel capacity.

Total assets: $2,365 million
Current ratio: 0.74
Common shares outstanding: 48 million
Return on 1998 shareholders' equity: 15.3%

	1998	1997	1996	1995	1994	1993	1992	1991
Revenues (millions)	1,465	1,993	1,851	1,480	1,609	1,674	1,547	1,457
Net income (millions)	116	126	121	100	110	109	95	100
Earnings per share	2.42	2.55	2.42	1.96	2.07	1.97	1.67	1.70
Dividends per share	1.48	1.40	1.31	1.28	1.26	1.22	1.18	1.12
Price: high	44.4	42.9	37.1	28.5	29.3	31.6	25.8	23.8
low	37.1	30.0	25.4	21.8	21.9	24.1	19.0	19.5

CONSERVATIVE GROWTH

Nordson Corporation

28601 Clemens Road, Westlake, OH 44145 ◻ Investor contact: Barbara T. Price (440) 414-5344 ◻ Dividend reinvestment plan available (800) 622-6757 ◻ Web site: www.nordson.com ◻ Fiscal year's end about October 31 ◻ Listed: Nasdaq ◻ Ticker symbol: NDSN ◻ S&P rating: A- ◻ Value Line financial strength rating: A

Nordson Corporation designs, manufactures, and markets systems that apply adhesives, sealants, and coatings to a broad range of consumer and industrial products during manufacturing operations. Nordson's high value-added product line includes customized electronic-control technology for the precise application of materials to meet customers' productivity, quality, and environmental management targets. Nordson products are used around the world in the appliance, automotive, construction, container, converting, electronics, food and beverage, furniture, graphic arts, metal finishing, nonwovens, packaging, and other diverse industries.

Nordson markets its products through four international sales divisions: North America, Europe, Japan, and Pacific South. These organizations are supported by a network of direct operations in thirty-two countries. Consistent with this strategy, nearly 60 percent of the company's revenues are generated outside the United States.

Nordson has manufacturing facilities in Ohio, Georgia, Alabama, California, Connecticut, Germany, the Netherlands, Sweden, and the United Kingdom.

Company Background
The U.S. Automatic Company, the parent of Nordson, was founded in Amherst, Ohio, in 1909. Initially, the company specialized in high-volume, low-cost screw machine parts for the burgeoning automotive industry.

In the years following World War II, Walter Nord, along with sons Eric and Evan, searched for a proprietary product to serve as a basis for future growth. This resulted in the acquisition of patents covering the "hot airless" method of spraying paint and other coating materials. The company later expanded its product line to include air-spray equipment and incorporated the highly efficient electrostatic process in both airless and air-spray painting systems.

Beginning in the late 1960s, Nordson pioneered the technology and equipment for applying powder coatings with the development of the compact and efficient cartridge-type recovery/recycle systems. Nordson has steadily refined its cartridge-booth technology and is an innovator in all aspects of the powder coating process for both organic and porcelain enamel applications. Today Nordson is the acknowledged industry leader in powder coatings systems.

Each year, the worldwide appliance industry transforms millions of square feet of prefinished sheet steel into consumer durables, including refrigerators, ranges, washers, and dryers. Before appliances are assembled, manufacturers use Nordson flatline powder coating systems to apply flexible porcelain enamel "powder paint" that quickly turns steel into gleaming panels of white, almond, and black metal that can be bent and wrapped to achieve new model designs. The benefit to manufacturers is increased line speed, higher quality, and lower operating costs. Consumers benefit, too: these uniformly coated appliances are more attractive and less prone to corrosion.

Shortcomings to Bear in Mind

- Although 1998 revenues reached $661 million, marking the thirteenth consecutive year of record sales growth, the company's earnings were static. Volume gains exceeded 7 percent, but the impact of the strong dollar on currency translations reduced reported sales growth by 3 percent. Earnings per share on a diluted basis before nonrecurring charges of $2.85, essentially the same as 1997. After the effect of nonrecurring, pretax charges totaling $33 million, earnings per share on a diluted basis were $1.25.

  On the other hand, sales volume in North America grew 12 percent in 1998, primarily enhanced by strong sales in the company's electronics and powder-coating businesses. Local sales volume advanced 14 percent in Europe, with strong sales across all the company's European businesses. However, economic challenges in Japanese and Asian markets reduced Nordson's sales volume in Japan by 12 percent and in the company's Pacific South Division by 10 percent. On a more positive note, Mexico, which accounted for more than 15 percent of revenue in the company's Pacific South Division, has emerged as one of Nordson's strongest industrial markets.

Reasons to Buy

- During 1998, Nordson made a number of improvements to raise the quality of its products, simplify business processes that were not adding value, and eliminate waste. For example, management was not satisfied with the quality and efficiency the company was getting from its printed-circuit-board assembly plant. As a consequence, it was shut down, and the company began outsourcing all of its circuit board requirements.

  Nordson also implemented a number of restructuring actions that reduced costs and shifted its organizational focus toward global customers and markets. In the European Division, for instance, Nordson restructured its operations in anticipation of changes that have followed the adoption of the euro as a common currency and the continent's continuing evolution into a single business community.

- "Finishers of consumer and industrial products come to Nordson for the most efficient methods to apply liquid paints and powder coatings," says Sam Dawson, vice president of Nordson. "Spraying coating materials is the easy part . . . our ability to control their precise application is where we deliver real value to our customers."

  Nordson markets complete material application systems that help manufacturers improve product quality while lowering material usage.

"Today, finishers want to reduce the environmental impact of their operations," says Dawson. "That's why Nordson focuses on providing systems that apply solvent-free powder coatings and low-solvent liquid paints. Finishers who convert to these finishes can meet environmental goals and reduce waste-disposal costs without sacrificing quality.

"Proactive involvement in the industries we serve, through memberships in professional associations and relationships with coatings suppliers, is key to understanding our customers' needs," Dawson adds. "This involvement, combined with our experience base, gives Nordson two competitive advantages—the best equipment available and the fastest new-product cycle time."

- Nordson technology simultaneously delivers precise applications of both hot and melt adhesive and cold glue to tightly seal cases of agricultural products, beverages, and consumer packaged goods. The hot-melt adhesive delivers an instant bond to seal the cases. At the same time, the slower-setting cold glue permeates the paper fiber, to ensure that packages remain intact regardless of the environmental conditions. This dual-gluing process ensures that shipments won't be rejected due to carton failure during transit, a substantial customer benefit.

- Nordson's strategy is to participate in the higher-growth segments of the global economy by expanding its expertise to electronic assembly and printed circuit board coating. In the future, as electronic parts become smaller, labor rates continue to increase in emerging countries and electronics assembly become more complex, we will continue to see more highly automated electronic assembly processes. Management is convinced that Nordson will be a major participant in the market for electronics assembly equipment with internally developed products and acquired businesses.

- Just five years ago, Nordson's electronics systems business accounted for less than 2 percent of annual revenues. Today, the number has expanded to more than 10 percent, owing chiefly to new technologies for dispensing fluid materials during the manufacture of printed circuit boards, semiconductors, and electronic components. To meet demand, the company increased manufacturing capacity by 45,000 square feet in 1998 at its Carlsbad, California, location. This expansion will be supported by new application engineering and demonstration centers located in Amherst, Ohio; Maastricht, the Netherlands; Taiwan; and Singapore.

Total assets: $538.9 million
Current ratio: 1.59
Common shares outstanding: 17 million
Return on 1998 shareholders' equity: 22%

	1998	1997	1996	1995	1994	1993	1992	1991
Revenues (millions)	661	637	609	581	507	462	426	388
Net income (millions)	47	50	53	53	47	41	40	34
Earnings per share	2.86	2.85	2.92	2.84	2.45	2.13	2.03	1.77
Dividends per share	.88	.80	.72	.64	.56	.48	.44	.40
Price: high	52.4	65.0	65.0	61.0	63.0	54.8	57.0	46.0
low	42.3	47.1	45.5	53.8	52.0	38.3	43.0	22.1

Norfolk Southern Corporation

Three Commercial Plaza, Norfolk, VA 23510-2191 ◻ Investor contact: Christopher R. Neikirk (757) 629-2861
◻ Dividend reinvestment plan available (800) 432-0140 ◻ Web site: www.nscorp.com ◻ Listed NYSE ◻
Ticker symbol: NSC ◻ S&P rating: A ◻ Value Line financial strength rating: A+

Norfolk Southern Corporation is a Virginia-based holding company that owns all the common stock of and controls a major freight railroad, Norfolk Southern Railway Company, and a natural resources company, Pocahontas Land Corporation. The railroad system's lines (before adding in Conrail) extend over more than 14,400 miles of road in twenty states, primarily in the Southeast and Midwest, and the Province of Ontario, Canada.

After June 1, 1999, the railroad began operating a portion of Conrail's lines. Thus, the system now extends over about 21,600 miles of road in twenty states, the Province of Ontario, Canada, and the District of Columbia.

Pocahontas Land manages about 1.2 million acres of coal, natural gas, and timber resources in Alabama, Illinois, Kentucky, Tennessee, Virginia, and West Virginia.

Highlights of 1998
- Railway operating revenues were $4.22 billion, nearly even with 1997. General merchandise revenues increased $55 million or 2 percent. However, coal revenues decreased $49 million, or 4 percent, because of declines in export and domestic metallurgical coal traffic. Intermodal revenues declined $8 million, or 1 percent.
- The increase in general merchandise revenues was driven by a $74 million, or 15 percent increase, in automotive revenues. Metals and construction revenues increased $5 million or 1 percent. Chemicals revenues decreased $11 million or 2 percent; agriculture, consumer products, and government revenues decreased $8 million or 2 percent; and paper, clay, and

forest products revenues decreased $5 million, or 1 percent.
- Norfolk Southern took top honors in the E. H. Harriman Memorial Safety Awards for the ninth consecutive year for having the safest employees in 1997 among the major railroads. The carrier had 0.92 reportable injuries for every 200,000 employee-hours worked.
- Norfolk Southern was designated "America's Most Admired Railroad" by *Fortune* magazine in 1999, making it the fifth time in the past six years that the carrier was singled out for this award.
- The new Ford mixing center network contributed to a 15 percent revenue increase for the company's automotive traffic.
- Norfolk Southern and Kansas City Southern opened a joint intermodal facility at Port Arthur, Texas.
- Norfolk Southern and Guilford Rail System launched a competitive new intermodal service for New England.
- The company received a citation from the Smithsonian Institution and *Computerworld* magazine for innovative application of technology associated with the company's Strategic Intermodal Management System.
- In March of 1998, Norfolk Southern completed the sale of its North American Van Lines unit to Clayton Dubilier and Rice, Inc. for $200 million. The sale resulted in a $105 million after-tax gain.

Shortcomings to Bear in Mind
■ The consolidation of two companies is always complicated. But creating a new

Norfolk Southern in this transaction was even more challenging. Integrating a part of the Conrail network and a substantial portion of its workforce has been the carrier's greatest challenge. For one thing, proper preparation required substantial investments in assets, in people and training, in tools and physical plant, and in systems to assure both compatibility and the company's capability to successfully implement a sophisticated operating plan.

Unfortunately, those investments have a short-term and significant impact on Norfolk Southern's profits. Including the sale of North American Van Lines, net income in 1998 was $734 million, up only slightly from the prior year. Results from continuing operations reflect the added costs of preparing for Conrail. On the plus side, according to management, "We believe the sacrifices we are making will enable us to realize unparalleled, long-term opportunities."

- Chemicals traffic volume decreased 1 percent, and revenues decreased 2 percent in 1998, the first decline since 1989. The weak economies of Asia and softness in certain domestic markets hurt shipments of products for vinyl, polyester, and pulp markets. In addition, nationwide rail service problems caused some customers to divert traffic to trucks and barges. However, several Norfolk Southern-served facilities with new and expanded plant capacity increased shipments of plastics and petroleum products, somewhat offsetting these negatives.

Reasons to Buy

- The acquisition of some 58 percent of the Conrail system will provide greater access for Norfolk Southern to the Northeastern markets of New York City, Baltimore, and Philadelphia. It also will provide the carrier with better connections to western rail systems. What's more, with longer, single-systems routes, Norfolk Southern hopes to divert intermodal and auto shipments away from motor carriers by offering shorter transit times between the Northeast and Southeast. The company projects a $423 million in net new traffic by the year 2000 from the Conrail routes.

- Utility coal traffic increased 9 percent in 1998, due to rising electricity production in the company's service area, the return of some traffic to rail, and increased business from several customers. The near-term outlook for utility coal remains positive. Domestic demand for electricity continues to increase at a rate greater than generation capacity is being added, and coal-fired generation continues to be the cheapest marginal source of electricity. Coal revenue represented 30 percent of total railway operating revenues in 1998, and 89 percent of coal shipments originated on Norfolk Southern's lines.

- In 1998, Norfolk Southern added line capacity, locomotives, equipment, and terminals. In order to provide better service, moreover, the company also redesigned its intermodal network and invested in the most modern technology in transportation.

- Automotive carloads increased 35 percent, and revenues increased 15 percent in 1998, exceeding the record levels achieved the prior year. Finished vehicles led the growth, as carloads increased 54 percent and revenues increased 19 percent, primarily due to new business through the Ford mixing centers. Full production volume at the Mercedes-Benz plant in Vance, Alabama, and the Toyota minivan line at Georgetown, Kentucky, also contributed to the increases. Finally, vehicle parts traffic volume and revenues remained steady despite the effects of the midyear strike at General Motors.

- Over time, the absence of competitive single-line rail service across the East has forced large volumes of freight onto highways. Norfolk Southern's management believes that one great benefit of the Conrail transaction will be the shift of freight from the highway back to rail. It will be substantial and probably will translate into fewer highway accidents. Further, it will translate into fuel savings, estimated conservatively at 80 million gallons each year. It will also translate into fewer emissions, reduced highway congestion, and savings on highway maintenance.
- The flow of goods between the Northeast and South and between East and West will improve dramatically as a result of the Conrail transaction. Some 56 million consumers living in the expanded Norfolk Southern territory can expect to benefit.
- During a 16-month period, mostly in 1997, Norfolk Southern designed and implemented a comprehensive distribution network to deliver 3 million Ford Motor Co. vehicles annually. The network began operating in early 1998. This represents a completely different logistics methodology that encompasses every step of transporting vehicles from Ford's twenty North American assembly plants to its national dealer network. The project is expected to increase significantly the carrier's motor vehicle

business with Ford, under a twelve-year, $3-billion contract to coordinate the transportation network. It is the largest single transportation project ever undertaken by Norfolk Southern.

Using a hub-and-spoke model, the company serves four "mixing centers" expected to help Ford reduce plant-to-dealer delivery times by more than 30 percent.

- Intermodal traffic has been very successful for railroads in general. This involves moving truck trailers and containers that normally would be hauled over the highway. In the past, intermodal business did not apply to shorter hauls, those of 500 miles or less. More recently, railroads have even been competing successfully in this sector as well. One reason for growth in intermodal business is the problem that truckers have had in hiring drivers. Turnover among drivers has been high because drivers are averse to being away from home several weeks at a stretch. As a result, trucking firms, such as J. B. Hunt and Schneider, have signed contracts to cooperate in the carrier's intermodal business. In 1997, the carrier's intermodal revenues increased $60 million, or 12 percent, over the prior year. Volume growth was 11 percent, making 1997 the third year of double-digit growth in four years.

Total assets: $18,100 million
Current ratio: 0.82
Common shares outstanding: 370 million
Return on 1998 shareholders' equity: 12.9%

	1998	1997	1996	1995	1994	1993	1992	1991
Revenues (millions)	4,221	4,223	4,770	4,668	4,581	4,460	4,607	4,451
Net income (millions)	630	771	779	715	668	595	558	528
Earnings per share	1.93	1.90	2.03	1.82	1.63	1.42	1.31	1.19
Dividends per share	.80	.80	.75	.69	.64	.62	.60	.53
Price: high	41.8	38.1	32.2	27.2	24.9	24.1	22.5	21.9
low	27.4	28.2	25.5	20.2	19.5	19.8	17.8	13.3

Pfizer Inc.

235 East 42nd Street, New York, NY 10017-5755 ❐ **Investor contact: Ronald C. Aldridge (212) 573-3685** ❐
Direct dividend reinvestment plan available (800) 733-9393 ❐ **Web site: www.pfizer.com** ❐ **Listed: NYSE** ❐
Ticker symbol: PFE ❐ **S&P rating: A** ❐ **Value Line financial strength rating: A++**

Pfizer traces its history back to 1849 when it was founded by Charles Pfizer and Charles Erhart. In those early days, Pfizer was a chemical firm. Today, it is a leading global pharmaceutical manufacturer, creating and marketing a wide range of prescription drugs. PFE also has an important stake in hospital products, animal health items, and consumer products. Pfizer's growth over the past half century was paced by strategic acquisitions, new drug discoveries, and vigorous foreign expansion.

Highlights of 1998
For the forty-ninth consecutive year, Pfizer's sales increased, and for the first time, revenue topped $13.5 billion, up 23 percent over 1997. On a reported basis, which includes the impact of the Medical Technology Group (MTG) divestiture, net income for the full year was $3.35 billion, and diluted earning per share were $2.55.

Pfizer's achievements in 1998 attracted a great deal of recognition. For the second year in a row, *Fortune* named Pfizer one of the most-admired companies in the world and the world's most-admired pharmaceutical company. *Chief Executive* rated Pfizer's board of directors as one of the five best in America, and in January of 1999, *Forbes* named Pfizer "Company of the Year."

Shortcomings to Bear in Mind
- Like most stocks with bright prospects, Pfizer often sells at an elevated price/earnings ratio.
- In May of 1999, the FDA asked Pfizer to revise its label on Trovan, an antibiotic, to include a warning about rare cases of serious liver damage. Some 140 cases of liver problems have been reported among patients who have taken Trovan since February 1998. Most of those cases were resolved after the patients stopped taking the drug. One analyst said that these warnings may significantly slow growth of new Trovan prescriptions in the United States, and they also could delay or prevent approval in countries where Trovan is not yet marketed.
- Although Pfizer is eminently successful, not everything the company touches turns to gold, at least initially. In a surprise setback for one of its new products, the FDA recently rejected its antipsychotic drug Zeldox, setting back the product launch, which was originally scheduled for the last quarter of 1998. That marked the second time in two years that Pfizer hit a wall at the FDA with a high-profile drug in development. In May 1996, the FDA turned down its arthritis treatment, Tenidap, forcing the company to end efforts to commercialize it.
- Nearly everyone knows about the success Pfizer has had with Viagra. A successful product begets imitators. Pfizer's CEO, William C. Steere, Jr., responds to this concern, "Everybody is going to be in this now that it's been demonstrated it's such a good market. I imagine it's going to be years before anybody is going to come out with a better Viagra. Viagra is about 70 percent effective. It's safe. Side effects are all very minimal. A better Viagra in my view wouldn't be one that's safer, it

would be one that's 98 percent effective instead of 70 percent effective. This is a very safe product."

- The odds of discovering a new drug are staggering. Out of every 7 million compounds screened, only 1,000 hold promise. Of that 1,000, only 12 compounds actually become candidates for development. And of those 12, only 1 makes it to market.

Reasons to Buy

- Building on the strength of Pfizer's in-line products, the company is forging ahead with an ambitious R&D program, with more than 170 research projects in discovery and development, more than at any time in its history.
- In 1998, Pfizer acquired the rights to help develop and market a new arthritis drug being developed by Monsanto, setting up a race among Merck, Johnson & Johnson, and Pfizer to market the first new class of prescription painkillers in more than two decades. These new drugs are called COX-2 blockers and are expected to relieve pain without causing stomach distress and other problems associated with existing anti-inflammatory drugs. In addition to treating arthritis, the new drugs have potential to prevent certain cancers and even Alzheimer's disease.
- The FDA approved Pfizer's Viagra in March of 1998. This pill (chemically sildenafil citrate) is the first nonsurgical treatment for impotence that doesn't have to be either injected or inserted directly into the penis. Unlike other remedies, it does not cause an erection unless the man is sexually stimulated. Viagra sells for $7 per pill wholesale and about $9 retail. Impotence specialists hope the pill will encourage more patients to seek medical help. Only 5 percent of the estimated 10 million to 20 million impo-

tent Americans get treatment, but the pill could increase that number to 20 percent very quickly, said Dr. Harin Padma-Nathan of the University of Southern California.

Viagra was first identified by scientists at Pfizer's laboratory in Sandwich, England. They first saw it as a new agent to treat angina, the painful heart condition caused by constricting or clogging heart arteries. But after seven clinical trials on numerous test subjects, the researchers were forced to concede that the drug was not going to make it. "We could have easily let it die," one of the scientists said.

The program was about to be shelved permanently in 1993 when Pfizer researchers noticed something quite unexpected: Several men who had received higher-than-usual doses in a small study told doctors they had achieved improved and more frequent erections than before. At the time, it seemed like an objectionable side effect, rather than a remedy. However, the Pfizer scientists, trying to salvage a drug they had worked on for years, believed the erection effect might represent a significant advance. Early trial results in treating impotence were so dramatically successful that the company quickly moved into larger-scale testing. There were a number of impotence treatments before Viagra, but all carried one or more drawbacks that the drug does not have: a need for surgery, interruption of lovemaking, or pain.

Doctors caution that Viagra will not make normal men sexual virtuosos. There is no reason to believe that it will revive flagging sex drive or allow men to partake in sexual endurance feats. "This drug does not alter libido or desire," Dr. Padma-Nathan said. "It does not create prolonged erections. And if you have normal erections, it will not make you feel more rigid." Viagra, he said, "is not a sexual revolution."

- Selling drugs is more complicated than selling, say, soap. You need to interest consumers, but first you must win over doctors. Though it ranks only fourth in worldwide drug sales, Pfizer deploys the largest sales force in the industry: 5,400 marketers pushing free samples. Their ranks are filled with gung-ho former military men and women urged to ever greater effort with the carrot-and-stick of hefty bonuses and multiple quotas.

- Pfizer's Consumer Health Care Group (CHC) is a worldwide marketer of leading over-the-counter (OTC) health care products. Among the category-leading U.S. OTC brands are Visine in eye care, Cortizone anti-itch medicines, BenGay topical analgesics, Desitin diaper rash treatments, Unisom sleep aids, and Rid for killing lice.

  In recent years, Pfizer has launched three prescription drugs for over-the-counter use: OcuHist, an antihistamine eyedrop; Zyrtec, an antihistamine for allergies, called Reactine in Canada; and Diflucan, a one-pill treatment (sold in the United Kingdom) for vaginal yeast infections.

- Pfizer's Animal Health Group (AHG) in not only one of the largest in the world, but is also noteworthy for the breadth of its product lines and its geographic coverage. Innovative marketing has become an AHG hallmark in its efforts to succeed in a highly competitive market. An independent survey of U.S. veterinarians, for example, named the Pfizer sales force the best in the industry.

- Pfizer pins its hopes for the future on five major products already on the market, plus a half dozen in the pipeline. Those now on the drug store shelves:

- Norvasc is a treatment for hypertension and angina. Project sales for 1999: $3 billion. Its patent expires in 2007.

- Zithromax, a treatment for chlamydia and other bacterial infections. Projected 1999 sales: $1.2 billion. Its patent expires in 2005.

- Zoloft is a treatment for depression and obsessive-compulsive disorder. Project sales for 1999: $2.1 billion.

  Its patent expires in 2005. Sales are closing the gap on Lilly's Prozac.

- Trovan is a treatment for fourteen kinds of bacterial infections. Projected sales for 1999: $440 million. Its patent expires in 2011.

- Viagra for erectile dysfunction. Projected sales for 1999: $1.4 billion. Its patent expires in 2011. Approval for female sexual dysfunction would be a big plus for sales.

In the works are the following:

- Zeldox, a treatment for schizophrenia, a disease that affects some 2.7 million. Approval is possible in 2001.

- Relpax is a treatment for migraine headaches. There are 11.9 million people afflicted with this painful affliction. Approval is looked for in mid-1999.

- Insulin that can be inhaled, rather than injected. Some 8.7 million people have this disease. Approval is estimated to occur in 2001.

- Tikosyn treats heart rhythm disorder. About 8.8 million suffer from this malady. Approval is likely in 1999.

- Alond is a treatment for diabetes-related disorders; about 8.7 million suffer from these disorders. Alond could hit the market in 2001.

- Droloxifene is a treatment for osteoporosis. There are some 23 million with this disease. It could be ready for the pharmacy shelf in 2001.

Total assets: $18,302 million
Current ratio: 1.36
Common shares outstanding: 1,298 million
Return on 1998 shareholders' equity: 40.0%

	1998	1997	1996	1995	1994	1993	1992	1991
Revenues (millions)	13,544	12,504	11,306	10,021	8,281	7,478	7,230	6,950
Net income (millions)	2,627	2,213	1,929	1,554	1,298	1,180	1,094	917
Earnings per share	.67	.57	.50	.41	.35	.31	.27	.23
Dividends per share	.25	.23	.20	.17	.16	.14	.12	.11
Price: high	43.0	26.7	15.2	11.1	6.6	6.3	7.3	7.2
low	23.7	13.4	10.0	6.2	4.4	4.4	5.4	3.1

GROWTH AND INCOME

Philip Morris Companies Inc.

120 Park Avenue, New York, NY 10017 ◻ Investor contact: Nicholas M. Rolli (917) 663-3460 ◻ Dividend reinvestment plan available (800) 442-0077 ◻ Listed: NYSE ◻ Web site: none ◻ Ticker symbol: MO ◻ S&P rating: A ◻ Value Line financial strength rating: A+

Philip Morris is the largest cigarette manufacturer in the United States. It is also the fastest-growing tobacco company in the world and has doubled its worldwide market share in the last decade to 13.9 percent. At the same time, it is also the largest domestic food processor (Kraft) and is the second-largest brewer (Miller Brewing Co).

Realistically, however, Philip Morris is primarily a tobacco company, with such major brands as Marlboro (the top-selling brand in the United States), Merit, Virginia Slims (the best-selling women's cigarette), Benson & Hedges, and Parliament. Philip Morris has a 49.4 percent share of the domestic tobacco market. Outside the United States, the company also has well-known brands, such as L & M and Lark.

The company's other large operation is food, as a result of prior acquisitions of General Foods (1984) and Kraft (1988). Some well-known names include Jell-O, Shake 'n Bake, Lender's Bagels, Philadelphia Cream Cheese, Post cereals, Velveeta, Kool-Aid, Miracle Whip, Oscar Mayer, Cracker Barrel cheese, Tang, and Maxwell House coffee.

Ranking third is the company's beer business, featuring such brands as Miller Lite, Miller Genuine Draft, Miller, Icehouse, Red Dog, Lowenbrau, Meister Brau, and Milwaukee's Best. During 1997, Miller sold its equity interest in Molson Breweries in Canada and 49 percent of its ownership of Molson USA, which holds the rights to import, market, and distribute the Molson and Foster's brands in the United States. Currently, Miller holds a 21 percent share of the domestic beer market. Finally, Philip Morris also has a stake in financial services (Philip Morris Capital Corp.), with assets of $6.5 billion.

Shortcomings to Bear in Mind

- In 1998, Philip Morris suffered from the negative impact of two major external factors: weaker foreign currencies, which lowered the company's pretax income by $365 million; and economic downturns in much of Asia and Eastern Europe (especially Russia) and in certain parts of Latin America.

- At Miller Brewing Company, an intensely competitive environment brought about disappointing volume and share declines in 1998. However, Miller is taking steps to improve its marketing and capitalize on its proven expertise in brewing operations. According to the company's CEO, Geoffrey C. Bible, "These actions should help lead to improved results."

■ As most investors are aware, Philip Morris is being besieged by the many pressures facing the U.S. tobacco industry: public smoking restrictions, possible excise tax hikes, the threat of FDA regulation, congressional hearings, negative media coverage, and litigation. Still, we should remember that the company's tobacco segment has faced similar threats before and has overcome them. Finally, it's important to note that over the past forty years, the tobacco industry has rarely lost or paid to settle a smoking-health product liability case.

More recently, however, that seems to be changing. In early 1999, a jury in San Francisco awarded $1.5 million in damages to compensate a former smoker with lung cancer, the largest such award against the tobacco industry and the first against Philip Morris. The verdict, following a month-long Superior Court trial, served abrupt notice to the tobacco industry that it remains vulnerable to suits brought by individual smokers, despite a $206-billion settlement with states in 1998 that ended their efforts to recoup health outlays linked to smoking-related illnesses.

■ Unprecedented in its scope and complexity, the historic settlement between the major domestic tobacco companies and forty-six state attorneys general and representatives of other U.S. Jurisdictions, added to previous settlements with four states, essentially puts an end to many of the claims made or threatened against the company's domestic operations by the states.

According to Mr. Bible, "Obviously, the 1998 settlement is a costly, bitter pill to swallow. And obviously, we still have some considerable hurdles to overcome as we seek to create a more stable and predictable business environment and find common ground with our critics."

Reasons to Buy

■ In 1998, seventy-three of the company's brands each generated revenues of more than $100 million. Of these star performers, twelve mega-brands each generated more than $1 billion in revenues, led by Marlboro, which Philip Morris believes "is one of the most successful brands in the world."

■ According to Mr. Bible, "Our brands do not just grow by momentum: We build them and protect them with world-class marketing and expertise." For example, in 1998, the company bolstered Marlboro's leadership position with the national introduction of Marlboro Ultra Lights, a new product so successful in the United States that the company has already launched it in Germany and Switzerland.

In the food sphere, Oscar Mayer Lunchables lunch combinations, which generated half a billion dollars in domestic operating revenues in 1998, have become a cornucopia of new products both in North America and more recently in selected European markets.

■ In the company's international tobacco business, income grew a solid 10 percent in 1998, fueled by higher pricing and volume gains in established markets. The strength of the company's brands again sustained it, as volume for Marlboro increased 3.8 percent.

■ Philip Morris's outstanding brands, marketing, and infrastructure have made the company the market leader in tobacco in the United States and in thirty other major markets around the world. They have also won the company first place positions in eighteen of its twenty most profitable food categories in North America and in more than 40 of its major coffee, confectionery, cheese and powdered soft drink businesses.

- Despite the never-ending strife against antismoking forces, Philip Morris has been a most successful company. Unlike many other huge companies, Philip Morris is growing at a consistent and impressive pace. In the 1988–1998 period, earnings per share climbed from $.74 to $2.20, a compound annual growth rate of 11.5 percent. Similarly, dividends per share expanded from $.34 to $1.68, a growth rate of 17.3 percent.

- It goes without saying that the fear of antitobacco legislation haunts Philip Morris and has kept the stock at a low multiple. Even so, many big investors hold huge stakes in Philip Morris. For instance, MO is the largest position in a few billion-dollar mutual funds. In the words of one portfolio manager, "To buy a stock when other people worry is part of our investment discipline." Still another professional is unfazed by the furor over tobacco. He says he has seen it all before. "In 1985 and 1986," he points out, "there were great litigation concerns and just as many negative stories. While 1985 was not a banner year for the stock, in 1986 it was up about 100 percent."

- Analysts believe that Philip Morris is poised for earnings per share growth over the next several years, as earnings are projected to increase in all major business units. Key to the company's ability to achieve large EPS gains are the following factors:

- Strong earnings gains from the company's international cigarette business, with units estimated to grow at an 8 percent per year rate over the next few years.

- Further margin expansion in the company's domestic tobacco business.

- Large-scale share repurchases made possible by a high rate of excess cash generation.

- Philip Morris' extensive worldwide network of manufacturing plants and distribution channels insures that it can quickly meet shifting consumer demand in each of the more than 180 markets where it does business.

- Kraft is one of the largest coffee companies in the United States. Major brands include: Maxwell House, Yuban, Sanka, Maxim, and General Foods International Coffees.

- Kraft Foods International is among the largest food businesses in Europe, and the largest U.S.–based food company in the Asia-Pacific region.

- In 1998, Kraft's North American food business turned in another good year, as new products and effective marketing drove strong volume and income growth. Underlying income rose a solid 7.2 percent to $3.1 billion, fueled by strong 3.4 percent volume growth and continued productivity savings, despite record high dairy costs.

Kraft's beverage business served up double-digit volume growth, led by ready-to-drink Capri Sun, Kool-Air Bursts, and Kool-Aid Splash beverages. In the powdered soft drink category, new products such as Country Time lemonade iced teas more than offset declines for Kool-Aid powdered soft drinks.

Post cereals scored solid volume gains and market share climbed to 17.2 percent, driven by the success of Honey Nut Shredded Wheat, introduced in the second half of 1997, and Oreo O's cereals, launched in 1998. Volume also grew for established ready-to-eat cereals such as Honey Bunches of Oats, Great Grains, and Honeycomb.

Volume grew in the company's cheese business, with good gains for most product lines, including Kraft Singles, Velveeta Loaves, Kraft Natural Cheese, and Knudsen and Breakstone's sour cream and cottage cheese. New products such as Kraft Natural Cheese Cubes and Cheddar Melts Cheese also contributed to volume growth.

■ At Philip Morris Capital Corporation, underlying income from operations was up an impressive 14.4 percent to $183 million in 1998. These results exclude a 1997 $103-million pretax gain on the sale of Mission Viejo Company, the former real estate subsidiary. Finally, Philip Morris significantly increased investments in both of its domestic and international portfolios, as total assets grew 10 percent, to $6.5 billion.

Total assets: $59,920 million
Current ratio: 1.24
Common shares outstanding: 2,431 million
Return on 1998 shareholders' equity: 33.2%

	1998	1997	1996	1995	1994	1993	1992	1991
Revenues (millions)	74,391	72,055	69,204	66,071	65,125	60,901	59,131	56,459
Net income (millions)	5,372	6,310	6,303	5,478	4,725	3,568	4,939	4,202
Earnings per share	2.20	2.58	2.56	2.17	1.82	1.35	1.82	1.51
Dividends per share	1.68	1.60	1.47	1.22	1.01	.87	.78	.64
Price: high	59.5	48.1	39.7	31.5	21.5	25.9	28.9	27.3
low	34.8	36.0	28.5	18.6	15.8	15.0	23.4	16.1

GROWTH AND INCOME

Pitney Bowes Inc.

1 Elmcroft Road, Stamford, CT 06926-0700 ◻ Investor contact: Charles F. McBride (203) 351-6349 ◻ Dividend reinvestment plan available (800) 648-8170 ◻ Web site: www.pitneybowes.com ◻ Listed: NYSE ◻ Ticker symbol: PBI ◻ S&P rating: A+ ◻ Value Line financial strength rating: A

A pioneer and world leader in mailing systems, Pitney Bowes is a multinational manufacturing and marketing company that provides mailing, shipping, dictating, copying, and facsimile systems; item identification and tracking systems and supplies; mailroom, reprographics, and related management services; and product financing.

The key to Pitney Bowes will probably continue to be consistency rather than spectacular growth, in view of the maturity of its highly profitable postage meter rental business and the moderate growth of some of its other annuity revenues, such as

service. On the other hand, analysts believe that the stock has limited downside risk; it should appeal largely to long-term investors.

Pitney Bowes is best known as the worldwide leader in mailing systems. It markets a full line of mailing systems, shipping and weighing systems, addressing systems, production mail systems, folding and inserting systems, as well as mailing software.

Pitney Bowes Software Systems, a division of Mailing System located in Illinois, offers a full range of advanced software and services for business communications, and marketing and mailing applications to Fortune 1000 companies.

Shipping and Weighing Systems (SWS) provides parcel and freight information and automation systems for the shipping and transportation management functions of the logistics market. SWS's products are marketed through Mailing Systems's worldwide distribution channels, with particular emphasis on North America. Service is provided by specially trained service representatives and a National Remote Diagnostic Center.

Pitney Bowes Transportation Software, a division of Pitney Bowes located in Minnesota, markets and develops logistics management solutions and provides consulting services.

Other Businesses of Pitney Bowes

The company's other businesses are also important. A brief description of each follows.

Pitney Bowes Management Services (PBMS) is a leading provider of facilities management services for the business support functions of creating, processing, storage, retrieval, distribution, and tracking of information, messages, documents, and packages. Using the latest available technology, PBMS manages mail centers, copy and reprographic centers, facsimile services, electronic printing, and imaging services and records management services for customers across the United States, as well as in Canada and the United Kingdom.

Pitney Bowes Facsimile Systems is a leading supplier of high-quality facsimile equipment to the business market. It is the only facsimile system supplier in the United States that markets solely through its own direct sales force nationwide.

Pitney Bowes Copier Systems concentrates on serving larger corporations with multi-unit installations of its full line of equipment.

Pitney Bowes Financial Services provides lease financing programs for customers who use products marketed by Pitney Bowes companies.

Shortcomings to Bear in Mind

- Several small newcomers are racing to develop a computer-generated stamp that would replace the old, expensive system of stamping inky, eagle-adorned postmarks onto envelopes. The new "stamps" would include a bold, black bar code below the traditional postmark. Instead of going to the post office to purchase postage in bulk, users would save time by simply ordering and downloading stamps off the Internet and printing them onto envelopes.

Reasons to Buy

- Some observers are concerned that the volume of mail may be declining, as people rely more on the telephone and their connection with the Internet.

  Pitney's CEO, Michael Critelli, responds to this concern, "Outside experts confirm our internal findings that mail volumes worldwide will continue to increase for the next ten years. Lots of paper-based communication is going away, but it is more than being offset by growth engines."

  According to Mr. Critelli, there is explosive growth in the direct mail marketing. To be sure, individual mailings are falling a couple of percent each year. On the other hand, direct mail is climbing at a far faster pace, between 6 and 8 percent a year. As a result, says the Pitney CEO, the overall volume of mail is going up each year. What's more, the same trend is visible in other developed markets. In the developing world, moreover, the growth of mail is even more explosive. China, for example, is registering increases of 25 percent a year.

- Pitney Bowes has a consistent record of earnings growth. In the 1988–1998 period, earnings per share mounted from $.75 to $2.03, an annual compound growth rate of 10.5 percent. In the same ten-year span, dividends per share climbed from $.23 to $.90, a growth rate of 14.6 percent.
- As the largest business unit of Pitney Bowes, Mailing Systems is the world leader in helping customers manage their messages through mailing solutions. These systems are marketed to businesses of all sizes, from the smallest office to *Fortune* 500 companies. With over 2 million customers worldwide, Pitney Bowes Mailing Systems is focused on keeping business messages moving and its customers ahead of the curve.

  With products such as the DocuMatch Integrated Mail System, Paragon II Mail Processor, and the AddressRight System, large mailers are provided the tools they need to drive their businesses and enhance competitiveness. The Galaxy Mailing System and Series 3 Folder and Inserter address similar needs in midsize organizations. With DirectNet, a hybrid mailing service, the company is able to assist customers of all sizes with value-added capabilities to improve the efficiency and impact of their messaging applications.
- The company's fastest-growing division, Pitney Bowes Business Services, provides customers with on-site and off-site business support services, including mail, reprographics, facsimile, records, electronic document management, and mortgage financing services. The Management Services subsidiary is the outsourcing leader in the legal market and a leading provider to *Fortune* 500 companies.
- Still another development revolves around infrastructure. Along with the much-desired provisions of telephones, gas, water, or electricity come less-welcome bills for these services. This makes Michael Critelli respond enthusiastically, "The number of telephones in emerging markets is going to double over the next five years. We love the monthly billings."
- Deregulation is another growth engine for Pitney Bowes. When governments sell off their ownership of businesses, private businesses step in and mail soars. Critelli points to Thailand, where government deregulation of the insurance market three years ago produced "astronomical" increases in the number of newly issued insurance policies, all involving regular billing.
- Operating profits at Pitney Bowes's largest business, mail systems, should benefit from a host of new products, along with greater operating efficiencies. New software-driven equipment and systems utilize advanced digital technology, which, in turn, is derived from both its own research program and joint ventures with various partners, including IBM.
- R&D continues to drive the company's momentum, with 124 new patents in 1998. Pitney Bowes has a thirteen-year unbroken track record as one of the top 200 corporations receiving domestic patents, with more than 3,000 patents in its portfolio.
- A recent Pitney Bowes/Gallup survey revealed that mail center expenditures account for more than 9 percent of *Fortune* 500 companies' total operating costs. PBI's new addressing and postal coding products provide cost-effective solutions by allowing mailers to increase productivity, improve efficiency, and take advantage of United States Postal Service work-sharing discounts.
- In the United States, 90 percent of businesses have fifty or fewer

employees. Significantly, the vast majority do not have mailing systems. Pitney Bowes views this as an opportunity to bring cost-effective mailing solutions to the fastest-growing market in the country. As a consequence, in 1994, PBI introduced a series of new mailing products specifically designed for small businesses.

■ Of the more than 2,500 stocks traded on the New York Stock Exchange, Pitney Bowes is one of only eighteen common stocks that have consecutive double-digit dividend increases from 1983 through 1998.

■ Pitney Bowes has a number of businesses that lag the economic cycle, but they should also resist a downturn. About two-thirds of total revenues come from annuity sources such as postage meter rentals, rentals of other mailing and business equipment, facilities management, rental, finance, service, and supply revenues.

■ Pitney Bowes Management Services is expanding its existing business by incorporating technology-based services, such as on-demand document printing from electronic data provided by customers and services to enhance the processing and distribution of computer-generated mail, messages, and documents.

Total assets: $7,661 million
Current ratio: 0.97
Common shares outstanding: 273 million
Return on 1998 shareholders' equity: 35.0%

	1998	1997	1996	1995	1994	1993	1992	1991
Revenues (millions)	4,221	4,100	3,859	3,555	3,271	3,543	3,434	3,333
Net income (millions)	568	526	469	408	348	369	312	288
Earnings per share	2.03	1.80	1.56	1.34	1.11	1.16	.98	.90
Dividends per share	.90	.80	.69	.60	.52	.45	.39	.35
Price: high	66.4	45.8	30.7	24.1	23.2	20.5	16.4	13.4
low	42.2	26.8	20.9	15.0	14.6	18.1	14.0	9.5

CONSERVATIVE GROWTH

PPG Industries, Inc.

One PPG Place, Pittsburgh, PA 15272 ▫ Investor contact: Douglas B. Atkinson (412) 434-2120 ▫ Dividend reinvestment plan available (800) 648-8160 ▫ Web site: www.ppg.com ▫ Listed: NYSE ▫ Ticker symbol: PPG ▫ S&P rating: A- ▫ Value Line financial strength rating: A++

PPG Industries, a diversified global manufacturer, is a leading supplier of products for manufacturing, building, automotive, processing, and numerous other world industries. Established in 1883, the Pittsburgh-based company makes decorative and protective coatings, flat glass and fabricated glass products, continuous-strand fiber glass, and industrial and specialty chemicals.

PPG is a leading worldwide producer of chlorine and caustic soda, vinyl chloride monomer, and chlorinated solvents. Specialty chemicals include silica compounds, surfactants, photochromic lenses, and fine chemicals, such as optical resins, pool and water-treatment chemicals, phosgene derivatives, and flame retardants.

PPG operates seventy-seven major manufacturing facilities in Australia,

Brazil, Canada, China, France, Germany, Ireland, Italy, Mexico, the Netherlands, Portugal, Spain, Taiwan, Turkey, the United Kingdom, and the United States.

To benefit its customers through leadership in technology, the company conducts research and development at ten facilities throughout the world.

Competitive Position
- Among the world's leading suppliers of automotive and industrial coatings
- Major supplier of architectural and packaging coatings
- World's second-largest producer of continuous-strand fiber glass
- Among the leading producers of float glass
- Major global supplier of automotive transparencies
- World's leading supplier of aircraft transparencies
- World's third-largest producer of chlorine and caustic soda
- World's leading producer of optical monomers
- World's leading maker of changeable-tint lenses, through Transitions Optical, Inc
- World's leading producer of amorphous precipitated silicas

Shortcomings to Bear in Mind
- Although PPG is less susceptible to the business cycle than it has been in the past, it is still vulnerable to vagaries of the automotive and housing markets.
- PPG is not a classic growth stock with steadily increasing earnings. For instance, earnings fell from the prior year twice in the last ten years (in 1989 and 1991).
- In the past decade, investors have seen examples of remarkable improvements in turnaround situations (such as AlliedSignal, IBM, AT&T, Sears Roebuck, Union Carbide, and Goodyear)

when companies cut costs, sold poorly performing businesses, eliminated levels of bureaucracy, and sent thousands of employees packing. These actions often produced dramatic reversals in earnings per share. By contrast, PPG has been well run for a long time, so there is no apparent need nor opportunity for a drastic restructuring, with the resultant escalation of earnings. To be sure, cost reductions are expected to continue in most PPG units. However, analysts expect these cost savings to be similar to the overall industry. Thus, cost reductions will help PPG stay competitive, rather than significantly improve profitability.

Reasons to Buy
- PPG has paid uninterrupted dividends since 1899. Equally impressive, the company has increased its dividend for twenty-nine consecutive years. In the 1988–1998 period, dividends per share climbed from $.64 to $1.42, a compound annual growth rate of 8.3 percent. In the same ten-year span, earnings per share advanced from $2.13 to $4.13, a growth rate of 6.8 percent.
- According to analysts, acceleration of PPG sales and growth is likely to be driven by acquisitions in coatings and specialty chemicals, PPG's top-priority businesses. Fortunately, there are plenty of consolidation opportunities in this fragmented market. Analysts look for the company to make aggressive moves in acquiring European-based paint businesses, as well as improving profitability through leveraging the company's existing customer base with PPG products. In the past, the company has demonstrated the ability to accomplish that goal. What's more, PPG has a strong balance sheet, which should enhance its ability to make a large acquisition, such as $2 billion or more.

- In the past two years, the company completed twelve acquisitions. Management expects they will generate close to $1 billion in profitable sales by 2000.
- As a result of PPG's strong concentration on research and development, about 35 percent of fiberglass sales stem from products introduced in the past five years. Much of the company's R&D effort focuses on engineering plastics, the fastest-growing segment of the reinforcement arena, with an annual growth rate of 8 or 9 percent.
- The company's employees own 17 percent of its common shares. What's more, in 1998, PPG launched an innovative program granting more than 30,000 employees worldwide an option to purchase one hundred shares of company stock. Workers with a stake in the company are normally more motivated.
- In 1998, for the third time in the three years of its competition, *Industry Week* magazine ranked PPG as one of the world's one hundred best-managed companies. Among other awards, *R&D* magazine selected the company's *Sungate* antenna windshield and automotive powder clear coats as two of the year's top one hundred technical achievements. *Automotive Industries* magazine presented the company with Quest for Excellence awards for being the best supplier of glass and coatings. Finally, the International Customer Service Association again bestowed the Award of Excellence on PPG's chloralkali and derivatives business.
- Through the Value Focus process, PPG has been able to drive down production costs. This activity aims for breakthrough improvements in such areas as production yields, cycle times, and in-process inventory. Highlighting activities in automotive replacement glass, PPG opened a second, advanced-technology call center to accommodate the growth in LYNX Services from PPG.

With this addition, LYNX Services will handle more than 20 percent of the insurance industry's auto glass claims yearly, making the company a national leader in managing automotive claims for insurance companies.

- With the acquisition of the largest automotive and industrial coatings business in Australia and New Zealand, PPG expanded its global presence in auto refinishes. Also contributing was their extension of operations in South America, including an expanded sales program and opening of customer training centers in Argentina and Brazil.
- Acquisition of a portion of the Courtaulds packaging coatings business from Akzo Nobel in late 1998 and substantially all of the remainder in 1999 established a global presence for PPG in this promising product line. Also during 1998, the company achieved the first commercial application of two-way barrier coatings for plastic beverage bottles. The coatings retain the carbonation within the bottle and keep oxygen out for a much longer time.
- In November of 1998, the company acquired from Akzo Nobel the Courtaulds Porter Paints business, which includes a manufacturing plant in Louisville, Kentucky, and a chain of more than 125 U.S. retail stores located primarily in the Midwest and Southeast. Porter Paints supplies a broad line of interior and exterior paints, mainly for contractors. This acquisition builds a presence for PPG in retail store channels, allows the company to serve contractors more efficiently, and provides other cost benefits. The Porter paints brand has been on the market for more than seventy years.
- At the company's joint-venture plant in Taiwan, PPG began construction of a third large melting furnace. When completed in 2001, the unit will increase

capacity by 50 percent. Virtually all of the new production will be used for printed circuit boards, which are growing in demand for computers, cell phones, automotive components, and other electronic items.

- PPG's emphasis on chemicals centers on shifting toward specialty products. This includes strengthening its leadership in changeable-tint optical lenses, expanding the company's presence in pharmaceutical intermediates, and developing new, high-value-added products.

- Within fine chemicals, a key strategy involves strengthening relationships with major customers for the company's pharmaceutical intermediates. Reinforcing this strategy was the acquisition of Sipsy Chimie Fine, which supplies intermediates and related products. Based in France, the firm has expanded PPG's array of technologies and its presence in France.

- At the La Porte, Texas complex, construction began on a full-scale certified facility for producing pharmaceutical intermediates. This operation, which is scheduled for start-up in early 2000, represents the second expansion in the past two years.

- Silica products that made strides in 1998 included highly dispersible silica for several major makers of "green" or environmental-friendly tires, particularly in Europe, where this segment is growing rapidly. Silica lowers rolling resistance, which increases gas mileage and improves tread wear.

Total assets: $7,387 million
Current ratio: 1.39
Common shares outstanding: 176 million
Return on 1998 shareholders' equity: 29.4%

	1998	1997	1996	1995	1994	1993	1992	1991
Revenues (millions)	7,510	7,379	7,218	7,058	6,331	5,754	5,814	5,673
Net income (millions)	738	729	744	748	566	377	342	201
Earnings per share	4.13	4.06	3.96	3.70	2.67	1.78	1.61	.95
Dividends per share	1.42	1.33	1.26	1.18	1.12	1.04	.94	.86
Price: high	76.6	67.5	62.3	47.9	42.1	38.1	34.2	29.7
low	49.1	48.6	42.9	34.9	33.8	29.7	25.0	20.8

CONSERVATIVE GROWTH

Praxair, Inc.

39 Old Ridgebury Road, Danbury, CT 06810-5113 ❑ Investor contact: Joseph S. Cappello (203) 837-2073 ❑ Dividend reinvestment plan available (800) 432-0140 ❑ Web site: www.praxair.com ❑ Listed: NYSE ❑ Ticker symbol: PX ❑ S&P rating: Not rated ❑ Value Line financial strength rating: B++

Praxair, Inc. serves a diverse group of industries through the production, sale and distribution of industrial gases and high-performance surface coatings, along with related services, materials, and systems.

Praxair, which was spun off to Union Carbide shareholders in June 1992, is the largest producer of industrial gases in North and South America; it is the third-largest company of its kind in the world. Praxair's major customers include aerospace, chemicals, electronics, food processing, health care, glass, metal fabrication, petroleum, primary metals, as well as pulp and paper companies. As a pioneer in the industrial gases industry, Praxair has been a leader in developing a wide range of proprietary and patented applications and supply-system technology. The company's primary industrial gases products are atmospheric gases (oxygen, nitrogen, argon, and rare gases) and process gases (helium, hydrogen, electronics gases, and acetylene). Praxair also designs, engineers, and supervises construction of cryogenic and noncryogenic supply systems.

Praxair Surface Technologies provides metallic and ceramic coatings and powders used on metal surfaces to resist wear, high temperatures, and corrosion. Aircraft engines are its primary market, but it serves others, including the printing, textile, chemical, and primary metals markets, and provides aircraft engine and airframe component overhaul services.

The company was founded in the United States in 1907 as Linde Air Products Company.

Shortcomings to Bear in Mind
- Praxair's earnings growth stagnated in 1998. This reflects two factors. First, cheap, imported steel hurt the domestic steel industry, an important Praxair customer. This forced the company to cut back on manufacturing capacity. Second, Brazil has been in economic doldrums, with interest rates soaring to the 30 percent level, plus currency devaluations. To combat this difficult environment, Praxair has been improving its operations.

  Despite significant turmoil in the global economic environment during 1998, Praxair was able to deliver steady improvement in its operating results:
  - Operating profit increased 4 percent, to $885 million, excluding special charges.
  - Operating profit as a percent of sales topped 18 percent.
  - Operating cash flow rose 24 percent, to a record $936 million.

Reasons to Buy
- Praxair has been investing its resources to help its customers improve their operations, with special emphasis on those industry segments that represent the highest long-term growth potential for Praxair. Resource allocations are being made in favor of segments such as food and beverage and certain health care markets, which are less prone to economic swings. What's more, the company has been investing in Praxair Surface Technologies, which continues to exhibit solid growth and earnings potential. It earned top supplier recognition from American Airlines and Delta Air Lines.

  At the same time, the company is being more selective about geographic markets. Praxair has found that it generates the highest return where the company has a leading market share; a balanced distribution mix (on-site, merchant, packaged gases); and high operating rates. The company's investment program supports growth in already profitable markets in North America, southern Europe, and South America. Meanwhile, the company has been consolidating its position in established Asian markets, such as Korea and Thailand, while strengthening its presence in China and India.
- Praxair's South American subsidiary, S. A. White Martins, has a consistent record of profitability and strong operating performance in Brazil, in spite of economic and political uncertainties over the years. To be sure, the Brazilian environment was difficult in 1998. Despite these challenges, the company's White Martins operation actually improved its operating margin through an aggressive focus on productivity.
- At Praxair, continuous productivity improvement remains a top priority.

Global, regional, and local productivity made a substantial contribution to profits in 1998. For instance, the company was able to streamline procurement procedures and radically reduce the number of suppliers. In addition, PX has been optimizing cash flow through re-engineering programs in South America, northern Europe, Poland, and in the company's North American packaged gases operations.

A team focused on working capital achieved a $97-million reduction in 1998. In addition, some 400 local and regional initiatives contributed $80 million in savings during 1998.

- Since the spin-off in 1992, Praxair has:
  - Almost doubled sales
  - Raised market capitalization from $2 billion to more than $7 billion
  - Expanded its geographic reach from fifteen countries to forty
  - Increased its dividend every year
  - Invested a record $3 billion in new plants, acquisitions, and geographic expansion
  - Strengthened its balance sheet and credit rating
- The addition of carbon dioxide to Praxair's portfolio opens up new avenues for growth in relatively noncyclical markets: food preservation, beverage carbonation, and water treatment. Looking ahead, increased demand for beverage carbonation and water treatment, particularly in emerging South American and Asian markets, promises to generate continued growth. Supplying global beverage-carbonation customers also leads to opportunities in new markets for other Praxair products and technology. Use of carbon dioxide in new food-preservation markets, such as bakery goods and dairy products, also is on the verge of rapid growth.
- In recent years, Praxair has developed noncryogenic air-separation technology, which allows lower-cost delivery to customers who have smaller volume needs. By sacrificing a small amount of purity, these customers can purchase a gas that meets customer needs at a discount to the cost of traditional supplies of product in cryogenic liquid form. This product is less expensive for Praxair to produce and thus higher-margined relative to "cryo" liquid. Not least, demand is growing dramatically.
- The company has refocused strategies for the electronics market, which allows Praxair to capitalize on growth opportunities. Its packaged-gases strategies and geographic expansion enhance the company's ability to provide high-quality, total gas-management services to the worldwide electronics market.
- New developments in combustion and oxidation processes—with emphasis on steel, chemicals, glass, and pulp and paper markets—promise to increase the use of oxygen, much of which can be supplied through Praxair's state-of-the-art noncryogenic supply systems.
- Producers of wine bottles, light bulbs, and construction glass use Praxair's oxygen. Praxair's argon, krypton, neon, and xenon also are used in the production of light bulbs.
- Metal fabricators use Praxair's blended shielding gases to increase productivity and decrease fume levels. Based on argon, helium, or hydrogen, these blends are used to produce a wide range of products, from ships and chemical plants to milk containers and motorcycles.
- By the end of the decade, Praxair estimates that noncryogenic oxygen and nitrogen supply systems will achieve 40 percent penetration of liquid markets worldwide. In many markets, this will help optimize local business performance and moderate the need for new liquid capacity.

- As the world's largest supplier of carbon dioxide, Praxair is the leading global supplier to the food and beverage industries. The company gained a significant customer in Asia when Coca-Cola Shanghai approved Beijing Praxair Huashi Carbon Dioxide Co., Ltd. as the authorized supplier of food-grade carbon dioxide for its bottling plants in China.

  This joint venture started up the largest carbon dioxide plant in China during 1998. The company also added carbon dioxide capacity through Praxair India's acquisition of majority ownership in a carbon dioxide joint venture. What's more, business activity picked up in Thailand toward the end of 1998, where Praxair carbon dioxide helps freeze shrimp for export.

- Although steel production slowed in the face of increased imports during 1998,

Praxair's steady stream of new patented technologies continues to gain business for the company in this market segment. For instance, Praxair received two U.S. patents for its CoJet coherent jet technology and has licensed it to steel companies in the United States, Mexico, and Argentina.

The technology, which can save a typical steel mill about $1.2 million a year, is a new oxygen-injection system that delivers a laserlike jet of oxygen into the molten steel bath. This system provides energy savings, safety, productivity, and environmental benefits. Finally, CoJet has potential applications in about 300 electric arc furnaces around the world and is being licensed for use in other types of steel and nonferrous melting and refining furnaces.

Total assets: $8,096 million
Current ratio: 1.25
Common shares outstanding: 158 million
Return on 1998 shareholders' equity: 19%

	1998	1997	1996	1995	1994	1993	1992	1991
Revenues (millions)	4,833	4,735	4,449	3,146	2,711	2,438	2,604	2,469
Net income (millions)	425	416	335	262	203	118	(60)	107
Earnings per share	2.60	2.53	2.11	1.82	1.45	1.06	.64	84
Dividends per share	.50	.44	.38	.32	.28	.25	.125	
Price: high	53.9	58.0	50.1	34.1	24.5	18.6	17.5	
low	30.7	39.3	31.5	19.8	16.3	14.1	13.6	

CONSERVATIVE GROWTH

The Procter & Gamble Company

2 Procter & Gamble Plaza, TN-2, Cincinnati, OH 45202 □ Investor contact: James W. Martis (513) 983-9974 □ Direct dividend reinvestment plan available (800) 742-6253 □ Web site: www.pg.com/investor □ Listed: NYSE □ Fiscal year's end June 30 □ Ticker symbol: PG □ S&P rating: A □ Value Line financial strength rating: A++

Procter & Gamble is a uniquely diversified consumer products company with a strong global presence. Established in 1837, P&G today markets its broad line of products to nearly 5 billion consumers in 140 countries. Based in Cincinnati, the company has operations in more than 70 countries and employs 110,000.

Procter & Gamble is a recognized leader in the development, manufacturing, and marketing of superior quality laundry, cleaning, paper, personal care, food, beverage and health care products, including prescription pharmaceuticals. Among the company's more than 300 brands are Tide, Always, Whisper, Didronel, Pro-V, Oil of

Olay, Pringles, Ariel, Crest, Pampers, Pantene, Crisco, Vicks, Bold, Dawn, Head & Shoulders, Cascade, Zest, Bounty, Comet, Scope, Old Spice, Folgers, Charmin, Tampax, Downy, Crisco, Cheer, and Prell.

Procter & Gamble is a huge company, with 1998 sales of $37.2 billion. In the same fiscal year (which ended June 30, 1998), earnings per share advanced from $2.28 to $2.56. Dividends also climbed, as they have for many years, from $.90 to $1.01. Such outstanding results tend to dispel the notion that large companies are only for widows and orphans. In my estimation, Procter & Gamble is a "core holding," a term used by my profession to indicate a stock you must own.

Shortcomings to Bear in Mind

■ Procter & Gamble is behind on Chairman John Pepper's plan to double sales to $70 billion by 2005. In the year ended June 30, 1998, revenues rose only 4 percent. While P&G's sales are nothing to sniff at, the consumer-products powerhouse has been beset by myriad woes. For instance, there's the flu in Asia, where the company obtains 12 percent of revenues, turmoil in Russia and Latin America, not to mention the strong dollar.

For his part, John Pepper thinks P&G can boost emerging-markets sales by $8 billion over the next decade. At the same time, he looks for sales from core businesses to rise $15 billion and sales of new products such as fat substitute Olestra to climb $12 billion.

■ Procter & Gamble is a dynamo in virtually every consumer market it serves. But this is not the case for its 21-year-old pharmaceutical business. Drugs account for a mere $600 million in sales, a drop in the bucket for a company with total revenues of $37 billion. Compared with drug titans Merck and Pfizer, P&G is a small fry, ranking only thirtieth

worldwide in drug and other health care sales. Now, just over two years after launching a public campaign to dramatically bolster the company's drug business, CEO John E. Pepper is finding out that building up that market is a whole lot tougher than launching a new brand of toothpaste. Mr. Pepper has already pushed back a deadline for doubling drug sales by five years, to 2005.

■ The company's many attributes are no secret on Wall Street, which means the price of Procter & Gamble may be too high by historic standards.

Reasons to Buy

■ Anyone who thinks Japan doesn't offer opportunities for U.S. consumer products should look at how quickly Procter & Gamble cleaned up in the country's dish-soap market. Until 1995, P&G didn't sell dish soap in Japan at all. Now, it has Japan's best-selling brand, Joy, which commands a fifth of the nation's $400 million dish-soap market. That's impressive progress, given that the market had appeared to be classically mature—both shrinking and dominated by giant Japanese companies. How the Cincinnati company executed its coup provides lessons that transcend the kitchen sink. One big lesson: Mature Japanese markets can be surprisingly complacent. P&G offered new technology, something the two incumbents hadn't bothered to do for years. It developed packaging that let stores make more money. And it spent heavily on oddball commercials that created a buzz among consumers.

Before tackling the Japanese market, Procter & Gamble sent out researchers to study Japanese dishwashing rituals. They discovered one odd habit: Japanese homemakers, one after another, squirted out more detergent than needed. It was "a clear sign of frustration," with existing Japanese products, commented Robert A. McDonald, head of the company's Japanese operations. He saw the research as a sign that an "unarticulated consumer need" was more powerful soap. "We knew we had something to go after," he said.

- Procter & Gamble is prodding reluctant retailers that sell its soaps and diapers toward the World Wide Web with a new advertising campaign. P&G unleashed a new on-line program called "Store Link" in late 1998. It's a special Web site for retailers who want to sign up to get on-line. The idea is to coax wary retailers onto the Internet so the company's ads there won't exist in a vacuum. The goal: make it easier for consumers who see a Web ad to act on it.

- P&G concluded fiscal 1998 by increasing common share dividends by 13 percent, to $1.14, marking the forty-third consecutive year of increased dividends. Procter has been paying dividends without interruption since 1890. The compound growth rate over the past five years has been 13 percent.

- Procter & Gamble is consistently recognized as one of the best-managed companies in the world:
  - "World's most admired soaps & cosmetics company," *Fortune* magazine, 1997, 1998
  - "America's most admired U.S. companies" list, *Fortune* magazine, 1985–1996
  - "One of the top 25 managers in the world"—CEO John Pepper, *Business Week*, 1998

- In 1998, about 50 percent of the company's net sales came from outside North America. P&G has built a strong global presence by continuously improving some of the world's most-recognized brands, including Pampers, Pringles, Oil of Olay, and Pantene. Procter has the number one global market share in seven consumer product categories, including laundry, diapers, hair care, and feminine protection. What's more, P&G has the number one or number two brand in over thirty product categories in North America.

- Innovation enables Procter & Gamble to deliver the best possible products to the world's consumers. The company files for nearly 2,000 patent applications every year, ranking P&G among the most innovative companies in the world. More than 7,000 scientists, from nearly 600 colleges and universities work at P&G's eighteen research centers around the world.

   In 1998, the company invested over 4 percent of net sales into research and development efforts. As a result, Procter has more new ideas in its product pipeline than at anytime in the company's history.

- Operating margins have increased consistently over the past five years, as a result of the elimination of non-value-added costs by standardizing products, packages, and manufacturing processes throughout the world. For example, since October 1995, P&G has decreased the number of North American package varieties (e.g., sizes, versions) by 20 percent.

- Historically, Procter & Gamble has delivered consistent earnings per share growth (15 percent since 1994) and expanded its operating margins (over 100 basis points annual improvement during the last five years). Furthermore, return on equity has improved from 27 percent in fiscal 1994 to 31 percent in 1998.

- The company has split its stock eight times since 1950. The most recent was a 2-for-1 split in 1997.

- Today, about half of P&G's sales come from North America, yet 95 percent of the world's population lives *outside* that region.

According to CEO John Pepper, "If we can achieve these levels of success around the world in just our existing businesses, we'll more than double our current sales and profits."

"This tremendous potential for growth exists in category after category," states Procter & Gamble's annual report. Capitalizing on this potential will not be easy, but the company will pursue it by staying focused on the company's key value and globalization strategies, while placing particular emphasis on three fundamental areas:

• Better products at more competitive prices
• Deeper, broader cost control
• Faster, more effective globalization

■ Procter & Gamble is entering new categories and introducing new brands throughout the world. From new categories like fine fragrances to new brands such as Olay Body Wash and Olay Bath Bar, new P&G businesses are building a foundation for future growth.

■ In an effort to loosen its stiff corporate culture and free more cash for product development, P&G said in June 1999 that it would cut 15,000 jobs worldwide—about 13 percent of its work force—close ten plants, and take nearly $2 billion in charges linked to the reorganization. The company said the reorganization would spur future growth and save about $900 million a year by 2004.

What's more, management said that it is determined to overhaul how products are developed, tested, and introduced. That includes lengthy research and development and market testing of products in the United States before those products are turned over for redevelopment by overseas marketing groups. Now, all products will be developed by seven global brand groups and tested simultaneously around the world to shorten time to market.

Total assets: $30,966 million
Current ratio: 1.14
Common shares outstanding: 1,327 million
Return on 1998 shareholders' equity: 30.9%

	1998	1997	1996	1995	1994	1993	1992	1991
Revenues (millions)	37,154	35,764	35,284	33,434	30,296	30,433	29,362	27,026
Net income (millions)	3,780	3,415	3,046	2,645	2,211	2,015	1,872	1,773
Earnings per share	2.56	2.28	2.15	1.86	1.55	1.41	1.31	1.23
Dividends per share	1.01	.90	.80	.70	.62	.55	.52	.49
Price: high	94.8	83.4	55.5	44.8	32.3	29.4	27.9	23.8
low	65.1	51.8	39.7	30.3	25.6	22.6	22.6	19.0

Sara Lee Corporation

Three First National Plaza, Chicago, IL 60602-4260 ❑ Investor contact: Janet E. Bergman(312) 558-8651 ❑ Dividend reinvestment plan is available (800) 554-3406 ❑ Web site: www.saralee.com ❑ Fiscal year's end Saturday nearest June 30 ❑ Listed: NYSE ❑ Ticker symbol: SLE ❑ S&P rating: A- ❑ Value Line financial strength rating: A+

Sara Lee Corporation is a global manufacturer and marketer of high-quality, brand-name products for consumers throughout the world. Sara Lee has operations in more than 40 countries; it markets branded products in more than 140 nations.

Sara Lee is committed to the principle of decentralized management. The company is organized into a large number of discrete profit centers, each led by an operating executive with a high degree of authority and accountability for the performance of the business.

In fiscal 1998, Sara Lee Corporation announced that it was embarking on a program of de-verticalization, a plan to reshape the company by concentrating resources on the activities from which it derives the greatest value.

In essence, the company's new model for doing business is creating an organization that is less vertically integrated, owns fewer fixed assets, and uses knowledge-based skills to develop and market its products. Its intent is to divest low-return segments of its business, thereby allowing management to focus its attention on the product development and brand building that are the essential elements for its future.

A case in point: In January 1998, Sara Lee announced the divestiture of nine yarn and textile operations. In addition to generating cash flow benefits of about $600 million over three years, this de-verticalization effort has enhanced Sara Lee's competitiveness by allowing more emphasis on product development and marketing.

Sara Lee's Operations

Sara Lee, best known for its familiar baked goods, also boasts many other branded food and nonfood products, ranging from Ball Park franks to the Wonderbra.

The Packaged Meats division makes pork, poultry, and beef products sold to supermarkets, warehouse clubs, and other customers in the United States, Europe, and Mexico. Brands include Ball Park, Best's, Kahn's, and Hillshire Farm. The bakery division produces fresh and frozen Sara Lee brand baked goods and specialty items throughout the United States, the United Kingdom, France, Mexico, Australia, and many Pacific Rim countries.

Foodservice business is conducted principally under the PYA/Monarch name. Coffee and tea products (Douwe Egberts coffee, Pickwick tea) are sold mainly in Europe.

Branded apparel products include such personal products as hosiery (Hanes, L'eggs, Sheer Energy, Underalls, Dim, Pretty Polly); activewear (Beefy-T, Champion, Hanes Her Way); and underwear and intimate apparel (Bali, Dim, Just My Size, Hanes, Playtex). Household and body care includes such brands as Kiwi shoe care and Sanex skin care products.

The company owns the Coach brand of premier leather products. Sara Lee also has a stake in insecticides (Bloom, Catch, and Ridsect), air fresheners (Ambi-Pur), and oral care (Prodent and Zendium).

Shortcomings to Bear in Mind

- Coach, the company that makes upscale leather goods such as wallets and handbags, posted lower sales in 1998, principally because of market conditions in Asia. To improve sales and profitability, Coach is bringing stronger focus to its core branded leather goods, lowering its cost base, and continuing to respond to rapidly changing fashion trends. This last strategy includes significant product introductions, such as the first Coach luggage collection, which was launched in the 1998 holiday season.
- The company's balance sheet is somewhat leveraged, with common stock representing only 40 percent of total capitalization.

Reasons to Buy

- Sara Lee's return on invested capital reached 17.5 percent in fiscal 1998, the highest level ever. Similarly, cash flow from operations set an impressive record level of $1.9 billion that year. This exceptional cash flow was 25 percent higher than it was in 1997, reflecting benefits from the company de-verticalization efforts.
- In 1998, Sara Lee's sales increased to more than $20 billion for the first time. Adjusted for currency changes, sales expanded 6 percent, which is consistent with the company's sales growth over the past ten years. In addition, the company's net income increased at a faster pace than revenues. In the past ten years, moreover, the pace of income growth has been twice that of revenue growth. This performance reflects Sara Lee's ability to produce and sustain margin improvements throughout the company's many businesses. Finally, unit volume in 1998 increased by 3 percent, the strongest corporate unit volume increase in four years.
- With sales of $4.3 billion in fiscal 1998, Sara Lee Packaged Meats continued to hold a leading position in the $25-billion domestic packaged meats industry. Sara Lee also has considerable strength internationally in Europe and Mexico. Sales and profits benefited from lower commodity prices throughout the year. What's more, they expanded to record levels as Sara Lee Packaged Meats continued to focus on high-margin, value-added products. Finally, Sara Lee's brands hold number-one-market-share positions in a number of important categories of hot dogs, smoked sausage, and breakfast sausage, as well as in corn dogs, cocktail links, and breakfast sandwiches.
- Through a licensing agreement with Baker Furniture Company, Coach has launched a premium leather furniture line that includes sofas, chairs, ottomans, and accessory pieces in a variety of Coach colors and treatments. The furniture is classic with a modern edge. The line is available at Coach stores, select department stores, specialty stores, and Baker Knapp & Tubbs Showrooms throughout the country.
- In 1998, Coach opened five full-price and eight factory stores in the United States, bringing the total number of company-owned retail stores to 162. Internationally, Coach markets its products in more than 150 locations, in both freestanding stores and prestigious department stores. In 1998, coach renovated fifteen of its stores in Asia, strengthening in-store visual merchandising.
- Building on its position as the number one frozen baked goods brand in the United States, Australia, and the United Kingdom, Sara Lee Bakery posted sales of $1.1 billion in 1998. And it acquired businesses to expand its geographic presence and enhance its product lines, particularly in Europe.

Worldwide, the Bakery markets its product through multiple channels of distribution, including retail, bakery-deli, and foodservice. The segment's core products include frozen and fresh baked product offerings, such as cheesecake, pound cake, pie, and bagels.

- The venerable Kiwi brand continues to grow, with product line extensions and new global markets. Now in 122 countries, Kiwi is Sara Lee's most global brand, recognized for quality the world over.

- In the twenty years since Sara Lee acquired the 244-year-old Douwe Egberts coffee company, its leading coffee positions in the Netherlands and Belgium have been expanded and significant market shares in nine other countries have been secured. In those two decades, Sara Lee has built upon the Douwe Egberts heritage of brand leadership and quality with contemporary consumer market techniques. Today, European coffee lovers find Douwe Egberts coffee not only at their local markets, but also in Sara Lee-owned shops and on the Internet.

- The Just My Size apparel collection for plus-size consumers represents Sara Lee's response to a fast-growing but overlooked segment of the women's apparel market. Begun in 1984 as a line of plus-size hosiery, Just My Size has been expanded over the years to include intimate apparel, casualwear, and socks. Recent additions include a contemporary denim collection of jeans and other items.

- The company's namesake brand, Sara Lee, has been extended from frozen retail desserts to fresh-baked products and represents a growing lineup of meats and innovative home-meal-replacement products.

- Well-known Sara Lee intimate apparel brands, Playtex, Bali, and Wonderbra, have reinvented themselves under the company's guidance. Playtex and Bali are gaining new generations of consumers with exciting products that redefine fit and fashion. Wonderbra is growing up, blossoming into a lifestyle brand that goes far beyond push-up bras.

- In days gone by, savvy marketers needed only to place their products on store shelves; the rest was up to the consumer. Today, the delivery part of the equation is profoundly more complex. The task of getting product into consumers' hands requires innovation and accessibility.

The company's meats business, for example, has opened more than 250 Sara Lee Sandwich Shoppes in supermarkets, airports, and universities. Sara Lee Bakery has introduced retail kiosks in convenience stores, airports, and other venues to provide increased access to its baked goods. In the company's coffee businesses, it has expanded beyond grocery store sales to out-of-home systems and its own coffee shops in Europe and the United States, capitalizing on trends toward on-the-go consumption.

Sara Lee Direct Selling division has found it niche in developing economies through a door-to-door sales force of 500,000 people in more than twenty countries.

Total assets: $10,989 million
Current ratio: 0.94
Common shares outstanding: 913 million
Return on 1998 shareholders' equity: 59.1%

	1998	1997	1996	1995	1994	1993	1992	1991
Revenues (millions)	20,011	19,734	18,624	17,719	15,536	14,580	13,243	12,381
Net income (millions)	1,102	1,009	916	804	729	704	620	535
Earnings per share	1.11	1.02	.92	.81	.74	.70	.62	.54
Dividends per share	.45	.41	.37	.34	.31	.28	.31	.23
Price: high	31.8	28.9	20.3	16.9	13.0	15.6	16.3	14.5
low	22.2	18.3	14.9	12.1	9.7	10.5	11.7	7.4

CONSERVATIVE GROWTH

The Sherwin-Williams Company

101 Prospect Avenue, N. W., Cleveland, OH 44115-1075 ☐ Investor contact: Conway G. Ivy (216) 566-2102 ☐ Dividend reinvestment plan available (800) 432-0140 ☐ Web site: www.sherwin.com ☐ Listed: NYSE ☐ Ticker symbol: SHW ☐ S&P rating: A+ ☐ Value Line financial strength rating: A

Sherwin-Williams' shares are particularly suitable for investors seeking consistency of earnings growth and an exceptionally strong balance sheet, coupled with astute management. The company has displayed its ability to prosper through two full business cycles since Jack Breen and his management team took control.

Sherwin-Williams, which was founded some 130 years ago, is the largest architectural coatings company in the United States and the third-largest coatings company in the world. The company is a vertically integrated, multibrand, multichannel distributor.

Company Background

Sherwin-Williams has 2,254 company-operated paint and wall covering stores that sell Sherwin-Williams-labeled architectural coatings, industrial finishes, and associated supplies. These stores are situated in forty-nine states, Puerto Rico, and Canada.

The company manufactures and sells Dutch Boy, Martin-Senour, Kem-Tone, Dupli-Color, Cuprinol, and Krylon brands, plus private-label brands for mass merchandisers and home-improvement centers. Sherwin-Williams also produces coatings for original equipment manufacturers (OEMs) and special-purpose coatings for the automotive market, industrial maintenance, and traffic paint markets.

The Paint Stores Segment exclusively distributes Sherwin-Williams branded architectural coatings, industrial maintenance products, industrial finishes, and related items produced by the Coatings Segment of the company and others.

Paint, wall coverings, floor coverings, window treatments, spray equipment, and other associated products are marketed by store personnel and direct sale representatives to the do-it-yourself customer, professional painter, contractor, industrial and commercial maintenance customer, property manager, architect, and manufacturer of products requiring a factory finish.

The five divisions within the Coatings Segment (Coatings, Consumer Brands, Automotive, Transportation Services, and Specialty) participate in the manufacture and distribution or sale of coatings and related products.

The Coatings Division manufactures paint and paint-related products for the do-it-yourselfer, professional painter, contractor, industrial and commercial maintenance account, and manufacturer of factory finished products.

The Consumer Brands Division (now part of the Consumer Group) is responsible for the sales and marketing of branded and private-label products by a direct sales staff to unaffiliated home centers, mass merchandisers, independent dealers, and distributors.

The Automotive Division develops and manufactures motor vehicle finish and refinish products that are marketed under the Sherwin-Williams and other branded labels in the United States and Canada, through a network of 135 company-operated branches, jobbers, and distributors.

The Transportation Services Division (now part of the Consumer Group) provides warehousing, truckload freight, pool assembly, freight brokerage, and consolidation services primarily for the company and for certain external manufacturers, distributors, and retailers throughout the United States. This division provides the company with total logistics service support that allows increased delivery schedules, lower field inventory levels, and fewer out-of-stocks.

The Specialty Division competes in three areas: custom and industrial aerosols, paint applicators, and retail and wholesale consumer aerosols. This Division participates in the retail and wholesale paint, automotive, home-care products, institutional, insecticide, and industrial markets. A wide variety of aerosol products are filled, packaged, and distributed to regional and national customers.

The Other Segment is responsible for the acquisition, development, leasing, and management of properties for use by the company and others. Obtaining real estate in the proper location at the appropriate cost is a critical component for achieving the desired operating success, particularly for paint stores and distribution centers.

Shortcomings to Bear in Mind

- The Coatings Segment realized annual net sales of over $2.1 billion in 1998. This was a decrease of about $129 million, or 5.7 percent. The sales shortfall was primarily the result of a soft retail paint market, the 1997 loss of business due to price concessions the company was unwilling to make to keep the business.

  Also contributing to the downturn were weak out-the-door, do-it-yourself retail sales at some of the company's major domestic customers and the continued deterioration of market conditions in South America.

  Faced with these challenges, Sherwin-Williams made significant changes to the management structure and operations within the Coatings Segment to put the company in a stronger position to effectively compete, expand market share, and increase shareholder value in the future.

  At the beginning of 1998, Sherwin-Williams consolidated the Consumer Brands Division into the Coatings Division. This consolidation brought improvement in areas of research and development, production efficiency, product service levels, and the production process for new products.

  In the middle of 1998, the company further consolidated the Diversified Brands and Transportation Services Divisions into the Coatings Division, creating the Consumer Group. These consolidations have resulted in a single source of contact for the company's customers. By the end of 1998, the new Consumer Group started to realize selling, marketing, and administrative efficiencies.

- The lead liability concern periodically surfaces for former pigment manufacturers like Sherwin-Williams. The most noteworthy cases involving Sherwin-Williams have been dismissed. On the other hand, visibility of cases and actions can periodically affect the stock price.

Reasons to Buy

- Despite challenges faced in 1998, Sherwin-Williams posted its twenty-first consecutive year of earnings improvement. The company's consolidated net sales increased 1.1 percent, and net income increased 4.7 percent.
- The Paint Stores Segment continued to set the pace for the company in 1998 by achieving its seventh consecutive year of sales and operating profit improvement. Net sales increased 6.9 percent, to a total of nearly $2.8 billion. Comparable-store net sales increased 4.9 percent. The segment's operating profit for the year increased 10.4 percent, compared with 1997.

The improved results were due to a number of new products, productivity gains, new stores, improved product quality in product finishes, and better customer service. Gallon gains were achieved in the architectural, industrial maintenance, and product finishes categories. Meanwhile, SHW continued its store opening program by adding 59 net new stores, to bring the total number of stores at year-end to 2,254.

- The architectural coatings business is a fairly stable one, with a cyclicality much less pronounced than that of other building products. The reason for this consistency is that about 90 percent of demand for paint comes from the remodeling market, not from the new construction market. Moreover, the low cost of paint relative to other remodeling costs makes purchase of it less subject to delay in economic downturns.
- The company should benefit from operating leverage in manufacturing, as sales and distribution grow. What's more, its distribution will benefit from new or acquired products, product lines, and brand names.

To illustrate: the acquisition of DeSoto's manufacturing assets in 1990 brought state-of-the-art manufacturing and the capacity to more aggressively pursue the retail channel.

Krylon, purchased in 1990, expanded the company's participation in aerosol paints; Cuprinol, a well-recognized Northeastern and Northwestern regional stain brand acquired in 1991, was expanded geographically through Sherwin-Williams distribution.

- Although somewhat sensitive to interest rates, the company's overall business is not significantly affected by new home construction.
- To enhance its stores technologically in 1998, the Paint Store Segment completed the installation of a satellite network among its stores. This network brings all associated products into a perpetual inventory system along with the perpetual inventories for manufactured products, thus allowing this Segment to achieve purchasing efficiencies and better inventory data among the stores.

Total assets: 4,065 million
Current ratio: 1.36
Common shares outstanding: 172 million
Return on 1998 shareholders' equity: 17.1%

	1998	1997	1996	1995	1994	1993	1992	1991
Revenues (millions)	4,934	4,881	4,133	3,300	3,100	2,949	2,748	2,541
Net income (millions)	273	261	229	201	187	165	145	128
Earnings per share	1.57	1.50	1.33	1.17	1.08	.93	.82	.73
Dividends per share	.45	.40	.35	.32	.28	.25	.22	.21
Price: high	37.9	33.4	28.9	20.8	17.9	18.8	16.4	13.9
low	19.4	24.1	19.5	16.0	14.8	14.9	12.7	8.8

SIGCORP, Inc.

20 N.W. Fourth Street, P. O. Box 3606 ◻ Evansville, IN 47735-3606 ◻ Investor contact: Timothy L. Burke
(800) 227-8625 ◻ Dividend reinvestment plan available (800) 227-8625 ◻ Web site: www.sigcorpinc.com
◻ Listed: NYSE ◻ Ticker symbol: SIG ◻ S&P rating: A ◻ Value Line financial strength rating: A

SIGCORP, Inc. provides electric and gas service to Southwest Indiana and energy-related and telecommunications products and services to customers throughout the greater Midwest and elsewhere.

Nonregulated subsidiaries either extend SIGCORP's ability to reach new markets with energy and telecommunications products and services or provide opportunities for creating shareholder value by investing in other areas. These subsidiaries are projected to provide more than 25 percent of SIGCORP's earnings by the year 2002.

Utility Services

Southern Indiana Gas and Electric Company (SIGECO) is the largest and oldest part of the company. Its operations are focused in two areas to prepare for the deregulated market.

The first area is power supply. SIGECO's power-production plants have a generating capacity of 1,256 megawatts and have among the lowest operating costs in the industry. A planned cogeneration plant is projected to bring an additional 42 megawatts of capacity to the system by 2001. Power is marketed to municipalities, other utilities, and power resellers when it is not needed for retail customers.

The second area is energy delivery. This business unit serves more than 124,000 residential, commercial, and industrial electricity customers and 108,000 natural gas customers in a ten-county area in Southwest Indiana. SIGECO also generates revenues by transporting gas and electricity across its system for other marketers.

Energy Products

SIGCORP Fuels provides SIGECO's generating plants with a dependable, low-cost source of coal. It also markets coal to other utilities.

Southern Indiana Minerals processes power plant combustion by-products and markets these industrial minerals to the paint, coatings, and construction industries.

Energy Services

SIGCORP Energy Services markets wholesale natural gas to industrial and other large-volume customers throughout a seven-state region and offers customers a wide range of other energy management services.

Energy Systems Group, an affiliate owned jointly by SIGCORP, Indiana Energy, and Citizens Gas and Coke Utility, provides energy conservation savings to institutions, government units, and commercial entities through riskfree building improvements and equipment upgrades.

Air Quality Services, a joint venture firm owned by SIGCORP and Environmental Management Consultants Inc., was created in 1998 to offer air quality monitoring and testing services for industry and utilities in the region.

Telecommunications

SIGECOM, a partnership between SIGCORP and the Massachusetts technology company, UtiliCom Networks, is investing $60 million to build a fiberoptic-based network that offers leading-edge telecommunication services to greater Evansville. The project's first phase, when complete, will have the potential to provide service to more than 80,000 homes and businesses. SIGCORP Communications Services builds high-speed fiberoptic communications networks for municipal utilities, enabling them to manage power loads more efficiently and offer communication services such as cable television.

Financial

Southern Indiana Properties participates in structured finance and investment transactions, including leveraged leases of real estate and equipment, which have provided above-average returns to the company.

SIGCORP Capital provides financing and cash management services for SIGCORP's nonregulated subsidiaries.

The Merger with Indiana Energy

In mid-June 1999, Indiana Energy (a natural gas utility headquartered in Indianapolis) joined the energy industry's consolidation movement, agreeing to merge with SIGCORP in a transaction valued at $655 million. Terms of their accord call for the two neighboring Indiana utilities to form a new holding company, Vectren Corporation. The new company's business is about equally split between natural gas and electric distribution.

The agreement was between two fiscally solid partners positioned in relatively prosperous service territories. With industry deregulation looming, the nation's energy providers have been merging at an accelerating rate, seeking efficiencies to bolster their competitive position. The combined company will be headquartered in Evanston, Indiana.

Shortcomings to Bear in Mind

- Electric and natural gas utilities are both subject to a sharp earnings impact from the weather. If the summer is hot, electric utilities benefit, since they sell more power for air conditioning. In the winter, both types of utilities enjoy robust profits when the weather is cold. This is particularly true for natural gas distributors, since the bulk of their sales are for space heating. A mild winter can hurt earnings severely. Unfortunately, the weather is extremely difficult to forecast.

Reasons to Buy

- Since public utilities are virtual monopolies, it is necessary that they be regulated. Without regulation, a company without competitors might be tempted to charge whatever the traffic would bear.

  Unfortunately, regulators are often more interested in rate payers than they are in utilities. Each state has its own regulation; federal regulation is rarely a factor. Some states select commissions by the electoral process. This is particularly true in several southern states, among others.

  More often, commissioners are chosen by the governor and normally have to be ratified by the legislature. Brokerage houses often rate these regulators as to how well they treat the utilities within their borders. For its part, Indiana is generally accorded high marks. Of course, the utility itself can make a difference as well. In a sense, it's a matter of salesmanship. SIGECO has a history of cooperation and a straightforward approach that has allowed the company to settle major regulatory issues without the expense of protracted legal hearings.

- The health of the service territory should not be ignored when you are evaluating an electric utility. If power sales are to grow, it's necessary to have a thriving economy. Many public utilities play a key role in achieving this end, as they help to bring new businesses to the region.

  The utility's headquarter city, Evansville, is the largest city in the territory. It continues its rapid development as a service center. Educational, medical, retail, cultural, and other activities are expanding to meet the growing demand.

- SIGECO's ratio of dividend payout to earnings is about 57 percent, compared to the industry average of over 80 percent. SIG's management is convinced that a conservative dividend payout results in greater value for long-term investors. A low payout ratio enables the company to continue to raise dividends even when earnings are flat. It also gives management more capital to plow back into the business without resorting to outside financing.

- The low cost energy that the company provides, coupled with its aggressive economic development efforts, have played a large role in the area's significant growth. Major manufacturers such as Toyota, ConAgra, Bristol-Myers Squibb, Waupaca Foundry, and AK Steel are pouring billions of dollars of new investment and creating thousands of new jobs in southwestern Indiana.

- SIGECO remains a low-cost producer of electricity, with rates among the most competitive in the country. The company's fuel costs are low. Its plants meet all major Clean Air Act of 1990 requirements for the year 2000. According to most industry analysts, SIGECO has little or no "stranded," or unrecoverable, investment in its generating plants. What's more, the company does not face an immediate need to spend money to build additional generating capacity.

- SIGCORP's history as a utility has been one of lean operations and low production costs. In 1997, the company's electric production costs were eighth-lowest among all domestic investor-owned utilities. That translated to some of the lowest consumer electric rates in the industry. In 1998, the company's average retail electric rate was about 4.7 cents per kilowatt hour, or about 32 percent below the national average of 6.9 cents. This history provides a solid foundation in the company's efforts to continue to enhance productivity and prepare for competition.

- As a group, SIGCORP's nonregulated subsidiaries accounted for all of the company's 1998 increase in net income. These businesses contributed 15.9 percent of overall net income in 1998, compared with 4.1 percent the prior year. This moves the company closer to its previously announced goal of deriving 20 percent of consolidated earnings from nonregulated businesses by 2000.

- SIGECOM, the company's telecommunications partnership with UtiliCom Networks, exemplifies the significant long-term growth potential and community benefits to be gained by entering nonutility businesses. Formed in mid-1998, SIGECOM immediately began construction on a two-way fiberoptic-based network to provide high-speed data, voice, and video applications to greater Evanston.

  Business and residential customers will have the opportunity to buy expanded cable TV, local and long-distance phone service, and high-speed Internet applications all from the same local provider. The first phase of this $60-million project will make these "bundled" services available to more than 75,000 homes and 7,000 businesses by mid-2000. SIGECOM has received the necessary regulatory approvals to provide phone service and has established local cable television franchises. These new markets offer significant opportunity for SIGCORP. No other single communications company locally offers the option to bundle these telecommunication services.

Total assets: $1,030 million
Current ratio: 0.59
Common shares outstanding: 23.6 million
Return on 1998 shareholders' equity: 14.4%

	1998	1997	1996	1995	1994	1993	1992	1991
Revenues (millions)	557	433	373	339	330	328	306	323
Net income (millions)	50	47	43	49	41	40	37	38
Earnings per share	2.12	1.95	1.83	1.63	1.69	1.63	1.51	1.58
Dividends per share	1.21	1.18	1.15	1.13	1.10	1.07	1.04	1.00
Price: high	36.9	30.1	24.7	24.3	22.6	23.7	22.7	22.5
low	26.9	21.6	21.9	17.6	16.0	21.3	20.3	15.6

CONSERVATIVE GROWTH

Sysco Corporation

1390 Enclave Parkway, Houston, TX 77077-2099 ❑ Investor contact: Ms. Toni R. Spigelmyer (281)584-1458 ❑ Web site: www.sysco.com ❑ Dividend reinvestment plan available (800) 730-4001 ❑ Fiscal year's end June 30 ❑ Listed: NYSE ❑ Ticker symbol: SYY ❑ S&P rating: A+ ❑ Value Line financial strength rating: A+

As they go about their lives, many people encounter the familiar Sysco trucks, bearing giant blue lettering, delivering products to customers. Few are aware, however, of Sysco's far-reaching influence on meals served daily throughout North America. As the continent's largest marketer and distributor of foodservice products, Sysco operates seventy-two distribution facilities, serving more than 300,000 restaurants, hotels, schools, hospitals, retirement homes, and other locations where food is prepared to be eaten on the premises or taken away and enjoyed in the comfort of the diner's chosen environment. The company's distribution network extends throughout the continental United States, as well as portions of Alaska and Canada.

With annual sales of more than $15 billion, Sysco distributes a wide variety of fresh and frozen meats, seafood, poultry, fruits and vegetables, plus bakery products, canned and dry foods, paper and disposables, sanitation items, dairy foods, beverages, kitchen and tabletop equipment, as well as medical and surgical supplies.

Sysco 's innovations in food technology, packaging, and transportation

provide customers with quality products, delivered on time, in excellent condition and at reasonable prices.

Shortcomings to Bear in Mind

■ Over the years, the company's earnings have grown steadily, year after year. In the most recent ten-year span, earnings per share climbed from $.24 to $.95, a compound annual growth rate of 14.7 percent. Dividends also advanced smartly during the period, expanding from $.04 to $.33, a growth rate of 23.5 percent. This is indeed impressive, particularly when compared with the industry it operates in.

More recently, however, results have not been as dynamic. Total sales in fiscal 1998, for instance, reached $15.3 billion, a 6 percent increase. On a real basis, after adjusting for acquisitions and inflation/deflation, sales growth was 5.9 percent for 1998.

On a calendar 1997 basis (most recent data), the $158-billion foodservice distribution industry grew at a modest 2.1 percent, or at the lower end of its 2 percent to 3 percent historical annual growth rate. Sysco compares favorably at 4.3 percent for the same period and continues to grow at a faster pace than the industry because it offers an ever-expanding array of product choices, reliable delivery schedules, and services that assist customers in strengthening their profitability.

Reasons to Buy

- While Sysco does not manufacture or process any products, the company is dedicated to procuring products of the most consistent quality for America's diners. This ideal is reinforced by a team of more than 180 quality-assurance professionals unparalleled in the industry. Continually, they consult with 1,500-plus worldwide growers and manufacturers of Sysco Brand products, developing product specifications, monitoring production processes, and enforcing Sysco 's stringent standards.

- The SYGMA Network, Inc., Sysco 's chain restaurant distribution subsidiary, set a new sales record of $1.4 billion in fiscal 1998. This was 8.3 percent above the prior year and represented 9 percent of corporate sales.

  Sysco remains committed to serving growing segments of this market, as evidenced by a recent five-year agreement expanding service to some 1,700 additional Wendy's International, Inc. locations across the United States. This move should increase annual sales by about $600 million and expand the total Wendy's business to the $1 billion level, making Wendy's SYSCO's largest customer.

- Although acquisitions played a vital role in establishing geographic footholds in SYSCO's early years, the company's sustained growth in market share primarily reflects internally generated sales increases within each market served.

  While the acquisition pace has diminished, selective acquisitions that offer strategic advantages will continue to be vital in building share in certain markets. Recent examples include the acquisitions of the foodservice distribution division of Beaver Street Fisheries, Inc. and the Jordan's Foodservice Distribution Division of Jordan's Meat's, Inc. Based near Portland, Maine, Jordan's greatly expanded the company's New England coverage. Each of these companies generates about $130 million in annual revenues. Equally important, they provide access to a marketing associate-served base, a primary Sysco focus.

- Investment in facilities, fleet, and equipment were $259 million in 1998, higher than the $211 million the prior year. Facility and fleet purchases comprised 63 percent of the total.

- In fiscal 1998, the company repurchased 12.1 million shares of its own stock, bringing to 71 million the total number of shares repurchased since May 1992. A new 8-million-share buyback was authorized late in 1998. The company has been accelerating share repurchases to offset the 2 million shares issued annually in various benefit and compensation plans, as well as to increase earnings per share by reducing total shares outstanding. Increased operating earnings, along with fewer shares outstanding, resulted in a 23 percent return on average shareholders' equity and a 15 percent return on average total capital before an accounting change.

- As the largest distributor of foodservice products in North America, Sysco assists customers in creating a vast array of dining choices. Menus have greatly improved since a French chef named Boulanger offered a choice of soups, or "restoratives," to patrons who paused at his inn to refresh themselves as they traveled during the 1700s. The sign in French read "restaurant," and his establishment may have been the first to offer a menu.

Today's diverse menu choices could not have been imagined then: raspberries from Australia served fresh in Wisconsin in January, gourmet pesto sauce rich with garlic, fresh basil and pine nuts delivered to a Vancouver chef's doorstep, or artfully prepared hearts of lettuce served in an Arizona college cafeterias each day. Providing choices from soup to nuts, and everything in between, Sysco leads the way in helping chefs in restaurants, schools, business cafeteria, health care locations, lodging, and other facilities increase the variety and quality of food choices in North America.

- Whether dining in an upscale restaurant or picking up pasta as the entree for a meal at home, people spend less time on food preparation than ever before. They want variety and flavor in the foods they choose to eat, yet their time to prepare meals is constantly in competition with work and leisure activities. More than ever, people are turning to meals prepared away from home for greater convenience, quality and, most of all, choice.

It is a trend that started in World War II, as women began to work outside the home. Business cafeterias, coffee shops, school lunchrooms, and restaurants broadened the range of dining choices for people who were used to much simpler fare. Twenty-five years ago, not many consumers could identify kiwi fruit. During the past three decades, foodservice offerings have moved from fruit cocktail with a cherry on top to kiwi and other exotic fare; from steak and potatoes to fajitas with all the trimmings.

- Each day, the drivers of Sysco's nearly 5,800 delivery vehicles crisscross the cities and counties of North America to deliver more than two million cases of product. From the back alley door of a small deli in Los Angeles to the loading dock of a major hospital in St. Louis, Sysco distributes a range of 275,000 products systemwide that have been transported by rail, trucked, or flown from points near and far around the globe to Sysco warehouses. That foods are daily shipped so reliably and accurately is possible only because of advances in computer technology, transportation, refrigeration, and warehousing.

In the 1970s, the typical fleet unit was a 12- to 16-foot truck with modest refrigeration capabilities. Frozen and dry goods were the primary commodities of the foodservice industry. Today's 28- to 36-foot, single-axle trucks typically have three separate food storage compartments with the most reliable mechanical refrigeration systems available.

Total assets: $3,780 million
Current ratio: 1.65
Common shares outstanding: 335 million
Return on 1998 shareholders' equity: 23%

	1998	1997	1996	1995	1994	1993	1992	1991
Revenues (millions)	15,328	14,455	13,395	12,118	10,942	10,022	8,893	8,150
Net income (millions)	325	302	277	252	217	202	172	154
Earnings per share	.95	.86	.76	.69	.59	.54	.47	.42
Dividends per share	.33	.29	.25	.20	.16	.14	.10	.06
Price: high	28.7	23.6	18.1	16.3	14.6	15.5	13.9	11.8
Low	19.9	14.6	13.8	12.4	10.6	11.1	10.3	7.5

CONSERVATIVE GROWTH

Textron Inc.

40 Westminster Street, Providence, RI 02903 □ Investor contact: Mary F. Lovejoy (401) 457-2353 □ Dividend reinvestment plan available (800) 519-3111 □ Web site: www.textron.com □ Listed: NYSE □ Ticker symbol: TXT □ S&P rating: A □ Value Line financial strength rating: B++

Textron is a $10-billion, global, multi-industry company with market-leading businesses in Aircraft, Automotive, Industrial, and Finance. Textron has achieved an impressive record of consistent growth in earnings and superior returns to shareholders. Here are the company's four segments and a brief description of their products:

• Aircraft, with 1998 revenues of $3.189 billion, was responsible for 33 percent of the company's sales. Aircraft has a stake in commercial and military helicopters, tiltrotor aircraft, business jets, single-engine piston aircraft, and utility turboprops.

• Automotive was responsible for 25 percent of 1998 revenues, with sales of $2.405 billion. This segment concentrates on the manufacture of interior and exterior trim, fuel systems, and functional components.

• With sales of $3.722 billion, Industrial is Textron's largest segment, accounting for 38 percent of 1998 revenues. This part of the company makes fastening systems; fluid and power systems; golf, turf-care, and specialty products, as well as industrial components.

• By far the smallest part of Textron is Finance, with 1998 sales of $367 million, or 4 percent of the total. Finance has a stake in diversified commercial financing.

Highlights of 1998

• A 22 percent increase in earnings per share—the sixth consecutive year of double-digit increases and the ninth consecutive year of income growth

• A 12 percent increase in revenue—the third consecutive year of double-digit growth

• Return on equity of 19.6 percent

• A return of 13.7 percent on invested capital

• Free cash flow of $348 million, up from $234 million in 1997

• Textron shareholders realized a total return of 24 percent. Over the past nine years, total annual returns to Textron shareholders has averaged 26 percent, compared with 18 percent for the Standard & Poor's 500.

• These financial achievements are especially impressive when you consider that in 1998 the company acquired and integrated nine companies. At the same time, it announced two divestitures and put in place the leadership team to guide the company into the twenty-first century.

Shortcomings to Bear in Mind

■ Although I am impressed with the company's future prospects, I am not impressed with its record of growth in the 1988–1988 period. During those years, earnings per share advanced from $1.55 to $2.68, a compound annual growth rate of only 5.63 percent. In the same ten-year stretch, dividends made better progress, climbing from $.50 to $1.14, an 8.59 percent growth rate.

■ At least one analyst is not convinced the company made the right move when it sold Avco, its consumer finance business. "Although TXT's remaining businesses may possess greater revenue growth potential, they nonetheless generate lower profit margins, yet require higher capital expenditures to maintain ongoing operations."

Reasons to Buy

- In early 1999, the company completed the sale of Avco to The Associates First Capital Corporation for $3.9 billion, perhaps one of the most strategic moves in Textron's 75-year history. Driving this critical decision was the continued consolidation of the consumer finance industry, the high premiums placed on successful consumer finance franchises, and Textron's realization that significant capital investment would have been needed to generate the required returns on Avco.

  Textron redeployed the $2.9 billion in aftertax proceeds by allocating 40 percent to share buyback and 60 percent to acquisitions. Full deployment of this capital is expected by the end of 1999.

- In 1998, the company spent $1.1 billion on nine acquisitions. Textron expects to sustain this level of acquisition activity through 2001, complemented by aggressive internal growth focused on developing innovative products and technologies and penetrating new markets.

- In 1998, Textron's Aircraft segment delivered a 5 percent increase in revenue and an 8 percent improvement in operating profit, reflecting the continued strength of Cessna Aircraft. The introduction of four new aircraft highlights the power of Cessna's internal growth strategy. Bell Helicopter continues to invest in the development of breakthrough tiltrotor technology, which promises to be a growth driver early in the new century. Thanks to its impressive array of new products and technologies, the Aircraft segment now enjoys an unprecedented backlog of $5.9 billion, an indicator of the solid future that lies ahead.

- Bell Helicopter is the leading helicopter manufacturer in the world because of its unparalleled product reliability and responsive customer service. But to stay number one in this competitive industry, Bell must stay at the forefront of new technology. Bell is employing new tiltrotor technology in its commercial Bell Agusta BA 609 and military Bell Boeing V-22 tiltrotor aircraft. (The BA 609 program is a joint venture with Agusta, Italy's leading helicopter manufacturer. Agusta complements Bell's strengths with its European marketing, engineering, and manufacturing capabilities.) These aircraft will meet the needs of air travelers around the world by combining the speed and range of a fixed-wing aircraft with the flexibility of a helicopter.

- Automotive posted a strong year in 1998, with revenue increasing 13 percent and operating profit up 19 percent, led by Kautex's outstanding growth and improving margins in the company's trim business. Looking ahead, management's focus remains on developing technology-driven, integrated solutions, as the company continues to globalize this business.

- In 1998, the Industrial segment achieved an impressive 17 percent growth in revenues and a 19 percent increase in operating profit. This resulted from the introduction of innovative products, penetration of new markets, coupled with six strategic acquisitions in the United States and Europe. These acquisitions strengthen the company's geographic, product, and customer balance.

  The four groups within the Industrial segment contributed to 1998's performance:

  - Textron Fastening Systems, this segment's flagship group, is the global leader in its industry and is targeted to double in size over the next five years.

- The Fluid and Power Systems group reached an important milestone in 1998 with the acquisition of David Brown Group PLC, which propelled the group's annualized revenues to $1 billion and provides an important platform for the future.
- The Golf, Turf-Care, and Specialty Products group is maximizing internal synergies, while generating a steady stream of new products.
- In Industrial Components, new technologies are being developed that support rapidly expanding end user markets such as the data, voice, and telecommunications industries.

■ In the Finance segment, Textron Financial Corporation (TFC) is a well-established niche player in the commercial finance market. In 1998, TFC achieved its twentieth consecutive year of continuous earnings improvement. The company is committed to this business and plans to strategically invest in growth opportunities.

■ Bell and Cessna earned their success by building the most reliable, highest-quality aircraft in the world and by understanding and delivering what their customers want. Cessna's new Citation Excel is an excellent example. Product development began with a comprehensive survey of existing Citation owners. They were enthusiastic about the performance, versatility, low operating cost, and reliability of the Citation V. On the other hand, these owners wanted more cabin room, speed, and range. They also insisted upon the flexibility of operating in smaller airports with shorter runways.

The Excel responds to all of these needs. Adapting technology proven in other Cessna aircraft, the Excel provides an exceptional combination of operating versatility and performance. The use of existing technology sharply reduced development and tooling costs and resulted in a very competitively priced aircraft.

The market clearly approves. Firm order backlog for the Excel already exceeds 180 aircraft and extends to the last quarter of 2001. First deliveries were made in mid-1998.

■ Similarly, the Bell Boeing 609 tiltrotor started with Bell's research in the early 1990s among operators of fixed-wing aircraft and helicopters. The advantages of combining the maneuverability of helicopters with the performance of fixed-wing aircraft are impressive. Compared with conventional helicopters, tiltrotors can deliver twice the speed and range with greater passenger comfort and still improve cost-effectiveness. Tiltrotors are ideal for traveling to offshore oil rigs, particularly as these rigs move farther offshore. They're also well suited for search-and-rescue operations where their use could shorten missions by 40 percent and cut costs by up to 25 percent. The findings led directly to the 609, a highly flexible six-to-nine passenger aircraft designed primarily for executive transportation, offshore oil shuttle, emergency medical evacuation, government support roles, and disaster relief. Market response has been excellent. Bell has over 60 commitments and sees an opportunity to sell more than 1,000 aircraft over the next twenty years.

■ Another innovative product developed by TAC is a state-of-the-art automotive seat that automatically adjusts to the shape and size of each user. Developed by McCord Winn, the ASCTec seat was introduced on the 1998 Cadillac Seville and is now available on a number of other luxury cars. Finally, the technology has application in other areas, including airlines, home furniture, and hospital care.

Total assets: $13,721 million
Current ratio: 1.11
Common shares outstanding: 158 million
Return on 1998 Shareholders' Equity: 19.6%

	1998	1997	1996	1995	1994	1993	1992	1991
Revenues (millions)	9,683	8,683	7,179	6,468	6,678	6,271	5,617	5,210
Net income (millions)	443	558	482	416	366	299	252	238
Earnings per share	2.68	3.29	2.80	2.76	2.40	2.11	1.83	1.71
Dividends per share	1.14	1.00	.88	.78	.70	.62	.56	.52
Price: high	80.9	70.8	48.9	38.7	30.3	29.4	22.4	19.8
low	52.1	45.0	34.6	24.3	23.3	20.2	16.8	12.5

AGGRESSIVE GROWTH

United Technologies Corporation

One Financial Plaza, Hartford, CT 06101 ◻ Investor contact: Angelo J. Messina (860) 728-7000 ◻ Listed: NYSE ◻ Dividend reinvestment plan available (800) 519-3111 ◻ Web site: www.utc.com ◻ Ticker symbol: UTX ◻ S&P rating: B+ ◻ Value Line Financial Strength A+

United Technologies provides high-technology products to the aerospace, building systems, and automotive industries throughout the world. Its companies are industry leaders and include Pratt & Whitney, Carrier, Otis, Sikorsky, and Hamilton Standard. The latter two companies make up the Flight Systems segment.

Pratt & Whitney
Products and Services

Pratt & Whitney produces large and small commercial and military jet engines, spare parts, and product support; rocket engines and space propulsion systems; and industrial gas turbines; and provides specialized engine maintenance and overhaul and repair services for airlines, air forces, and corporate fleets.

Pratt & Whitney engines fly on more than half the world's commercial fleets. In 1998, Pratt's commercial engines alone logged more than 30 million flight hours. Pratt & Whitney's large commercial engines provide thrust for narrow- and wide-bodied aircraft. The company's new engine series, the PW6000, will serve growing demand for flights in the 100-to-120-passenger range.

Primary Customers

Pratt & Whitney's customers include commercial airlines and aircraft leasing companies; commercial and corporate aircraft manufacturers; the U.S. government, including NASA and the military services; and regional and commuter airlines.

Carrier
Products and Services

Carrier's products and services include heating, ventilating, and air conditioning (HVAC) equipment for commercial, industrial, and residential buildings; HVAC replacement parts and services; building controls; and commercial, industrial, and transport refrigeration equipment.

Carrier emphasizes energy-efficient, quiet operation and environmental stewardship in its new residential and commercial products. The new WeatherMaker residential air conditioner using Puron, a non-ozone-depleting refrigerant, provides the domestic market with low operating costs and sound levels, about the same as a refrigerator's. The Puron unit gives Carrier a healthy lead over competitors, as chlorinefree refrigerants become the standard.

Primary Customers

Carrier's primary customers are mechanical and building contractors; homeowners, building owners, developers, and retailers; architects and building consultants; transportation and refrigeration companies; and shipping operations.

Otis
Products and Services

Otis Elevator Company's products and services include elevators, escalators, moving walks, and shuttle systems, and related installation, maintenance and repair services; modernization products and service for elevators and escalators.

Otis took advantage of healthy market conditions in Europe and the Americas in 1998, more than offsetting Asia's economic problems. Yet despite a 42 percent drop in new equipment sales in Asia (50 percent in China alone), Otis had an excellent year, including several large contracts. For instance, the company captured its largest North American contract ever, a $68-million agreement for forty-three elevators, forty-eight escalators, thirty-four moving walkways, and a people mover for the new Northwest Airlines terminal at Detroit Metro Airport. The contract includes a ten-year maintenance agreement.

Primary Customers

Primary customers for Otis include mechanical and building contractors; building owners and developers; homeowners; and architects and building consultants.

Flight Systems
Products and Services

Products and services for the Flight Systems Group include military and commercial helicopters and maintenance services; engine and flight controls; propellers; environmental controls for aircraft, spacecraft, and submarines; space life support systems; fuel cells; and micro-electronics. Flight systems include Hamilton Standard, Sikorsky, and Sundstrand.

Hamilton Standard products are on the great majority of the world's fixed-wing and rotary aircraft, including more than 98 percent of large commercial airlines. In 1998, Hamilton Standard won additional competitions, including the air start and turbine-case cooling systems for Rolls Royce's Trent 500 engine, an upgraded, digital engine control for GE's F101 and F118 engines, and key controls components for Pratt & Whitney's new PW6000 and PW8000 engines.

The Sikorsky name is rooted in the history of flight; they founded the helicopter industry, built the world's first four-engine airplane, designed flying boats, and led in inaugurating airmail service and launching commercial air travel. Sikorsky's helicopters flew the first hoist rescues at sea, the first medical evacuation flights, and the first combat rescue missions. Building on that legacy, Sikorsky helicopters are flying in more than forty countries. In 1998, the company signed contracts or made deliveries to Brunei, Taiwan, Malaysia, Chile, Turkey, Israel, Korea, and Greece.

Primary Customers

Primary customers for Sikorsky include the U.S. government, including NASA, FAA, and the military services; non–U.S. governments; aerospace and defense prime contractors; commercial airlines; aircraft and jet engine manufacturers; hospitals; and oil and gas explorations companies.

Shortcomings to Bear in Mind
- I tried to find a shortcoming, but failed to discover anything of consequence. Maybe next year.

Reasons to Buy

- In 1999, the company made two major moves. In the spring, it sold its automotive parts division to Lear Corporation for $2.3 billion. UT Automotive, which had annual sales of $3 billion and 44,000 employees, is a major supplier of instrument panels, electrical wiring systems, and motors. The unit had become a laggard for United Technologies, as auto makers have become more demanding and competition more fierce. The sale of UT Automotive was viewed as being critical to the company's aggressive acquisition strategy.

  In February of 1999, United Technologies purchased Sundstrand Corporation for $4.3 billion. (Sundstrand was featured in the 1999 edition of this book when the stock was selling in the $40 range; it was over $70 in the spring of 1999.)

  Sundstrand was wrapped into United Technologies's Hamilton Standard Division and was renamed Hamilton Sundstrand. While United Technologies's roots in aerospace date back to the 1930s, the Sundstrand purchase is the company's first major acquisition in the business in many years. Analysts believe that defense budgets are growing, and Asian economies are stabilizing. Thus, they see robust growth for the industry.

  Sundstrand designs and manufactures power systems for commercial and defense aircraft. As one analyst puts it, "Automotive hasn't been a strong business for United, whereas Sundstrand is a growth business with a strong franchise in aerospace."

- Sunstrand's flagship product remains aircraft Electric Systems, including constant-speed drives, generators, controls, integrated-drive generators, and complete integrated electric systems. Systems are sized for each aircraft type, from regional jets such as the Canadair RJ-700 to widebodies such as the Boeing 767-400ER and Airbus A340-500/600. As aircraft evolve into derivative configurations, Sundstrand works with the manufacturer to tailor electrical systems and components. Many existing Boeing DC-10s are being reconfigured with new MD-11 cockpits and new Sundstrand electric system controls to emerge as Boeing MD-10 freighters.

  The company's design, development, testing, and manufacturing expertise enables airframe makers to depend on Sundstrand for the *best* system for their aircraft.

- All over the world, people want to be comfortable when it gets too hot or cold. So, Carrier employees from Indianapolis to Shanghai spend their waking hours building machines that satisfy that simple human need. Carrier is already the world's largest air conditioning manufacturer, but it is growing like a small company. Acquisitions totaling $623 million in the past three years have augmented Carrier's unsurpassed global presence, while bolstering operating profit margins by a hefty 29 percent.

- United Technologies is seeking to convince suppliers to make a greater effort to enhance quality and reduce prices. For those who fail, the penalty is not pleasant. The company is pruning the ranks of its suppliers. Its goal is to whittle them down from 60,000 to 10,000 by 2002. The annual cost savings to United Technologies could be as high as $750 million.

Total assets: $18,375 million
Current ratio: 1.21
Return on 1998 equity: 28.6%
Common shares outstanding: 450 million

	1998	1997	1996	1995	1994	1993	1992	1991
Revenues (millions)	25,715	24,713	23,512	22,802	21,197	21,081	21,641	20,840
Net income (millions)	1,255	1,072	906	750	616	487	486	319
Earnings per share	2.53	2.11	1.73	1.43	1.16	.83	.90	.59
Dividends per share	.70	.62	.55	.52	.48	.45	.45	.45
Price: high	56.2	44.5	35.2	24.5	18.0	16.6	14.5	13.7
low	33.5	32.6	22.7	15.6	13.8	11.0	10.4	10.6

CONSERVATIVE GROWTH

U.S. Foodservice

9755 Patuxent Woods Drive, Columbia, MD 21046 ▫ Investor contact: Robert W. Gillison, IV (410) 312-7512 ▫ Dividend reinvestment plan not available ▫ Web site: www.usfoodservice.com ▫ Listed: NYSE ▫ Fiscal year's end Saturday closest to June 30 ▫ Ticker symbol: UFS ▫ S&P rating: Not rated ▫ Value Line financial strength rating: B+

On December 23, 1997, JP Foodservice acquired Rykoff-Sexton to create U.S. Foodservice, the nation's second-largest broadline distributor of food and related products to restaurants and other foodservice establishments. The company distributes its products from thirty-seven full-service distribution centers across the continental United States, reaching over 85 percent of the U.S. population. In addition to its full-service distribution centers, U.S. Foodservice also operates a subsidiary that designs and equips restaurants and hotels throughout the country.

In the last three years, U.S. Foodservice has been the fastest-growing broadline distributor in the industry. When JP Foodservice (the predecessor to U.S. Foodservice) went public in 1994, the company's reported sales for fiscal 1994 were $1.029 billion. With reported sales for fiscal year 1998 of $5.507 billion, the company has increased reported sales at a compound annual rate of 52 percent.

U.S. Foodservice offers one of the industry's most comprehensive product lines, including more than 40,000 national, private, and exclusive brands of canned and dry foods, fresh meats, poultry, seafood, frozen foods, fresh produce, dairy and other refrigerated foods, paper products, cleaning supplies, restaurant equipment and other supplies. U.S. Foodservice sources products from all over the world to provide its customers the best products at competitive prices.

With more than 130,000 customers, including restaurants, hotels, health care facilities, cafeterias, schools, daycare centers, and sports arenas, U.S. Foodservice sets itself apart from the competition by providing superior service, high-quality products, and innovative value-added programs.

U.S. Foodservice is a key supplier to such firms as Subway, Pizzeria Uno, Ruby Tuesday, Old Country Buffet, Perkins Family Restaurants, Eurest Dining Services, Hard Rock Cafe, and Cheesecake Factory. It also does business with several Las Vegas casinos, as well as such establishments as Fenway Park, Kindercare daycare centers, and the U.S. Senate.

Shortcomings to Bear in Mind

■ One of the biggest post-merger challenges facing the new company is combining its private-label programs with

Rykoff and deciding which to take nationally. Private labels accounted for 20 percent of JP Foodservice prior to the acquisition, up from 16 percent in 1997. At Rykoff, they accounted for about 33 percent of sales.

- The costs incurred related to the acquisition of Rykoff-Sexton and the associated integration plan had a significant effect on U.S. Foodservice's financial results. These charges, which totaled $138 million on a pretax basis, included changes in control payments, severance payments, transaction costs, and writedowns of fixed assets, inventory, and accounts receivable resulting from the integration of the two businesses.

  However, it is important to note that only $62 million of these charges required the use of cash. Through the sale of redundant assets and the realization of the tax benefits from these charges, the company expects to raise over $85 million, more than offsetting the cash cost of the acquisition. Earnings per share, net of the effect of these charges, would have been $1.37 for the year.

- The company's gross profit margin decreased to 18.3 percent in the first quarter of fiscal 1999, from 19.1 percent in the comparable quarter of the prior year. The decrease was primarily attributable to a continuing shift in product mix from certain high-margin items to higher-turnover, lower-margin items. However, the effects of this shift were offset in part by the growth of the company's private and signature brand product sales in the 1999 quarter. Sale of these products, which generally have higher gross margins than national brand products of comparable quality, increased 3 percent in the 1999 period.

Reasons to Buy

- The acquisition of Rykoff-Sexton elevated the company to number two, from number five among the nation's restaurant, hotel, and institutional foodservice suppliers. It also nearly tripled the company's annual sales to $5.2 billion and boosted its client count to 130,000 from 35,000.

  What's more, U.S. Foodservice went from a regional focus, mostly serving the Northeast, to a service territory containing 85 percent of the nation's population. The company is now one of just three firms able to do business with national accounts. The other two are Sysco Corporation (also reviewed in this book) and Alliant Foodservice.

- In addition to the acquisition and integration of Rykoff-Sexton in 1998, the company also completed the fold-in of the Mazo-Lerch business that it acquired at the end of 1997. The company also closed three additional acquisitions.

  The fold-in of the Mazo-Lerch business into the company's Severn, Maryland distribution center greatly enhances the efficiency with which the company can service the important Baltimore/Washington market.

  In late 1997, U.S. Foodservice completed the acquisition of Outwest Meat Company, located in Las Vegas, Nevada. Outwest is the largest meat specialist in that market. Similarly, the company acquired Westlund Provisions in March of 1998. Westlund is a custom-cut meat specialist in Minneapolis, Minnesota. These two acquisitions complemented the company's existing operations in those two markets, enabling U.S. Foodservice to enhance its custom-cut meat offerings to its customers, while also giving the company the opportunity to cross-sell its broad product line of products to Outwest and Westlund customers.

  In January of 1998, U.S. Foodservice acquired Sorrento Foodservice, Inc., a broadline foodservice distributor located in Buffalo, New York. The acquisition of Sorrento expanded the company's geographic reach into northeastern Ohio, northwestern Pennsylvania, and northwestern New York.

- The acquisition of Rykoff-Sexton gives the company a much larger size, which enables U.S. Foodservice to renegotiate some of its contracts with suppliers.
- Before the big acquisition, JP Foodservice (its prior name) distributed some 30,000 products. That number has since expanded to more than 40,000.
- In mid-1998, U.S. Foodservice announced that it had signed a contract to become the prime supplier of all categories of food for Ruby Tuesday of Mobile, Alabama. The five-year agreement will run through March of 2002 (it is renewable at that time) and has an estimated value of $900 million over the five-year period. This more than triples the amount of business that U.S. Foodservice will do with Ruby Tuesday.

According to Jim Miller, the company's CEO, "Since our acquisition of Rykoff-Sexton in December 1997, we have been able to leverage our national presence to renew and expand relationships with several existing chain account customers."

U.S. Foodservice will service all units of Ruby Tuesday, which are situated throughout the United States. The company owns and operates 388 restaurants, including 320 Ruby Tuesdays, 47 An American Cafes, and 21 Tia's "Tex-Mex" restaurants, located in thirty-three states. Franchise operations include thirty-two domestic units and five international units.

- In 1998, four new facilities were opened by U.S. Foodservice in South Carolina; Las Vegas and Reno, Nevada; and Atlanta, Georgia. The Carolina facility is located on 100 acres in Fort Mill and contains more than 540,000 feet under roof. This structure is one of the company's largest and most modern distribution centers.

The Atlanta Division opened a new distribution center in Austell, Georgia, with more than 150,000 square feet of warehouse and office space.

Total assets: $1,732 million
Current ratio: 1.71
Common shares outstanding: 47 million
Return on 1998 shareholders' equity: 10.7%

	1998	1997	1996	1995	1994	1993	1992	1991
Revenues (millions)	5,507	1,692	1,243	1,108	*			
Net income (millions)	63	28	14	7				
Earnings per share	1.37	1.26	.88	.59				
Dividends per share	nil	nil	nil					
Price: high	49.3	37.2	28.8	19.8	11.5			
low	31.3	25.8	18.0	9.3	9.3			

* This table is incomplete, since the company's acquisition of Rykoff-Sexton makes comparable figures irrelevant.

The Valspar Corporation

1101 Third Street South, Minneapolis, MN 55415 ◻ Investor contact: Paul C. Reyelts (612) 332-7371 ◻ Web site: www.valspar.com ◻ Direct dividend reinvestment plan available (800) 205-8318 ◻ Fiscal year's end on the Friday before October 31 ◻ Listed: NYSE ◻ Ticker symbol: VAL ◻ S&P rating: A+ ◻ Value Line financial strength rating: B+

Valspar is one of the five largest domestic manufacturers of paints and related coatings. Founded in 1806 as the first maker of spar varnish in America, the company has expanded rapidly in the past decade, mainly through acquisitions, and has recently positioned itself for a strong push into the international realm.

Valspar's four business groups provide a balance to the economic cycle. The two largest business groups—packaging coatings and inks for the food and beverage industry and consumer coatings for the do-it-yourself market—stabilize Valspar's financial performance in weak economies. This balance and diversity of markets has enabled Valspar to achieve increased earnings every year since 1974.

Highlights of 1998
- The company completed its twenty-fourth year of consecutive earnings growth.
- Earnings per share climbed 9.4 percent to $1.63.
- Sales expanded 13.6 percent to $1.2 billion.
- The completion of several acquisitions: Anzol, Plasti-Kote, Hilemn Laboratories, and Phase 1 of Coates South Africa will increase annual sales by more than $100 million.
- The acquisition of Dexter's Packing and European Industrial businesses was announced.
- The company's MIDAS Program and Waste Minimization efforts showed continued progress, returning 43 cents per share to earnings. MIDAS is the company's

employee-led effort to optimize Valspar's global supply chain practices. It continues to stimulate cost-reduction opportunities to support and improve future earnings.
- The Consumer Group had another strong year, with sales increasing 15 percent as the company continued to improve its position with large home centers and mass merchandisers. In addition, sales of Valspar's Laura Ashley designer paint and McCloskey Special Effects coatings exceeded expectations.
- The Packaging Group, with nearly 30 percent of its sales outside North America, grew by 7 percent, despite difficult market conditions.
- Sales for the Industrial Group increased 19 percent, with about 16 percent of the sales increase coming from internal growth. This growth continues to be led by the company's Coil and Architectural Spray Coatings businesses.
- Special Product Group sales were also strong, up 16 percent over the prior year. Valspar Automotive Refinish again led this group, with 29 percent growth. EPS resin, Marine, and Federal Flooring sales were each up about 20 percent.

Valspar's operations break down into four categories:

Consumer Coatings Group
The Valspar Consumer Group develops, manufactures, and markets paints, stains, varnishes, and specialty decorative products for the do-it-yourself and contractor markets. Its primary markets include home centers, mass merchants, hardware wholesalers, and independent

dealers. Products are sold under the Colony, Valspar, Enterprise, Magicolor, McCloskey, BPS, and Masury trade names, as well as under private label. Through a successful partnership with each of its customers, the Valspar Consumers Group is able to offer a customized range of products best suited to their marketing strategy, pricing structure, and competitive environment.

Packaging Coatings Group

The Valspar Packaging Group is the largest coatings and ink supplier to the metal can industry worldwide. A leader in the North American can coatings industry for many years, Valspar now spans the globe to serve customers in Europe, Asia, Africa, and Australia. Joint ventures in Mexico, China, South America, South Africa, and licensees in other markets demonstrate Valspar's global leadership.

Industrial Coatings Group

The Valspar Industrial Coating Group develops environmentally compliant, protective and decorative coatings using a broad range of resins, application technologies, and cure methods. The Industrial Group's full-line capability, which serves more than twenty industrial markets, focuses on three primary areas: coil-applied and extrusion coatings, wood coatings, and general industrial coatings (including powder, UV cure, high solids, waterborne, and electrodeposition).

Special Products Group

The Valspar Special Products Group is a low-cost producer of customized paints, coatings, resins, and colorants. Customers include worldwide manufacturers of coatings, automotive refinish shops, and marine floor coatings users.

Shortcomings to Bear in Mind

- Titanium oxide, a key ingredient in Valspar products, has been rising in price, putting pressure on margins.

Reasons to Buy

- Valspar has been at the forefront of packaging technology for over half a century, from the first commercial beer can to today's cans, which require high-performance coatings and inks. Substantial annual investments in research and development enable the Packaging Group to introduce high-quality products year after year. Environmental awareness guides current innovation in radiation cure, high solids, and water-based and solventless paints.

- Valspar is the only coatings company in the beverage market that supplies coatings for the entire can: water-based interior sprays, basecoats, exteriors, and UV and thermal-cure inks. The Packaging Group also manufactures the broadest product line for the food can market and a comprehensive line of inks for the metal packaging industry.

- Because the Industrial Group's average product cycle is only two years, innovation and speed are critical to serving the company's customers. The Industrial Group has the ability to custom design and manufacture a broad range of environmentally compliant resin technologies. This expertise is built on a foundation of in-depth knowledge of application methods and cure technologies.

- Valspar Refinish is the market leader in "universal" intermix technology. Now automotive paint jobbers and body shops no longer have to invest in multiple mixing systems. Valspar helps its customers by helping their consumers; the nationwide "Commitment to Excellence" program provides lifetime warranties on auto refinish products at Valspar-certified body shops.

The Valspar Refinish Group also includes House of Kolor, one of the premier automotive custom paint lines in the world. These finishes have been used by world-renowned painters on custom hot rods, trucks, and motorcycles since the early 1960s. In addition, early in 1997, Sureguard became part of the Refinish team. Sureguard has been a manufacturer of quality finishes for over sixty years and currently supplies the OEM trailer market. The Plasti-Kote and Tempo spray can lines are a growing part of the automotive retail business.

- In the company's Marine segment, Valspar high-performance coatings are used when harsh environmental conditions require specialized marine coatings technology. Customers have been impressed with Valspar's "Zero VOC" zinc-rich primers, which provide excellent corrosion protection and high-speed welding capability, as well as with the company's superior tank coatings and surface-tolerant products. Marine's ability to service the needs of the North American marine industry is strengthened by a joint venture with Jotun Marine Coatings, a division of Jotun A/S Norway.

- The EPS Resin Group provides emulsions and resins for Valspar and other paint industry customers. EPS resin technology enables Valspar to vertically integrate raw material procurement and cost-effectiveness within the corporation. Many paint and coatings manufacturers turn to EPS for its leadership role in providing coating applications based on polymer chemistry.

- Valspar is one of the lowest-cost paint manufacturers and should continue to benefit from its strong relationship with Home Depot and Lowe's. In fact, its relationship with Lowe's is likely to improve, since the home center chain has recently acquired Eagle Hardware, another fast-growing chain.

- Valspar acquired Dexter's Packaging Coatings business at the end of calendar 1998. The Dexter operations has annual sales of just over $200 million. This purchase makes Valspar the largest supplier to the $1.7-billion food-and-beverage can coatings market. The deal provides Valspar with significantly larger global capacity and more cost savings from mass raw material purchases, along with the elimination of overlapping operations.

Total assets: $802 million
Current ratio: 1.54
Common shares outstanding: 44 million
Return on 1998 shareholders' equity: 22.7%

	1998	1997	1996	1995	1994	1993	1992	1991
Revenues (millions)	1,155	1,017	860	790	724	694	684	633
Net income (millions)	72	66	56	48	44	40	34	28
Earnings per share	1.63	1.49	1.26	1.08	1.00	.93	.79	.63
Dividends per share	.42	.36	.33	.30	.26	.22	.18	.15
Price: high	42.1	33.1	29.3	22.3	22.9	20.8	18.3	14.9
low	25.8	26.8	20.9	16.7	15.3	15.2	14.2	8.9

VF Corporation

P. O. Box 21488, Greensboro, NC 27420-1488 ▫ Investor contact: Cynthia F. Knoebel, CFA (336) 547-6189 ▫ Dividend reinvestment plan available (201) 324-1225 ▫ Web site: www.vfc.com ▫ Ticker symbol: VFC ▫ S&P rating: A ▫ Value Line financial strength rating: B++

VF Corporation is something of a stealth giant, a company that touches your life in dozens of different ways without your ever being aware of it. Among its broad line of apparel products, VF makes Lee, Wrangler, Britannia, and Rustler jeans. It sells about $2 billion of jeans a year, more than any other company.

VF also makes Timber Creek khakis, Vanity Fair and Vassarette underwear, Healthtex clothes for children, Jantzen bathing suits, JanSport backpacks, and Red Kap workwear (including mechanics's uniforms and bulky firefighter garb). The company's apparel is sold by department stores and mass-market retailers such as Wal-Mart and Target.

VF traces it origins to 1899, when it was incorporated under Pennsylvania law as the Reading Glove & Mitten Manufacturing Company of Reading, Pennsylvania. In 1919, that name was changed to Vanity Fair Mills, Inc. But in 1969 it was changed to VF Corporation. At this juncture, a new subsidiary under the Vanity Fair name was established to continue the corporation's intimate apparel business.

Highlights of 1998

In 1998, earnings per share hit a record $3.17, up 15 percent from the prior year. Net income increased 11 percent during the year, while sales grew five percent. In 1998, the company increased its dividend for the twenty-six consecutive year.

In 1998, consumerization helped VF continue to do what it does best: respond effectively to its customers. In the company's growth categories, jeanswear, domestic intimate apparel, workwear, and daypacks, sales climbed 12 percent. New products such as Lee Dungarees, Lee Pipes, Wrangler Khakis, and Brittania stimulated jeanswear sales. There was also solid growth from the Wrangler and Timber Creek lines in mass-merchandise stores.

International sales were up modestly in 1998, reflecting expansion in Latin America and Japan. On the other hand, soft sales in Europe were the result of weak consumer spending and jeans demand in Germany, the company's largest market, and increased competition from private label goods. On a more positive note, domestic intimate apparel sales recorded the biggest increase in 1998, due primarily to the acquisition of Bestform Group, Inc., whose brands include Bestform, Exquisite Form, Lily of France, and Enhance.

Recently, Vanity Fair signed a license agreement with NIKE, Inc. for a new line of high-performance sport bras, which were introduced in the summer of 1999. In 1999, the company announced that Bestform would be joining forces with Tommy Hilfiger Licensing, Inc. to produce and market a complete line of intimate apparel under the Tommy Hilfiger brand, which will hit the market in 2000.

In workwear, Red Kap's sales improved over 1997 levels. Acquisitions are a key component of VF's plans in workwear. In late 1998, the company completed the purchase of Penn State Textile Manufacturing, Inc., a market leader in service apparel whose products range from lab coats to aprons and other apparel and products for the restaurant industry. In 1999, VF Corp. acquired Fibrotek Industries, Inc., a maker of "cleanroom" products often used by personnel in the semiconductor, pharmaceutical, and automotive industries.

Shortcomings to Bear in Mind

■ Some analysts are concerned with new competition, particularly in the jeans market, on both the branded and private-label sides of the business. In response, Mackey McDonald, president and CEO, says: "After nearly a hundred years in the jeans business, competition is a way of life for us. If anything, we see a positive side to this: the jeans market is healthy and growing and attracting new players. But no one out there has the portfolio of brands that we do. Wrangler, Lee, Rustler, Riders, Brittania—they're some of the best-known brands in the world. And we see a tremendous opportunity to take this brand portfolio into new consumer segments, with fresh products and marketing. For example, Lee is following the successful introduction of Lee Riveted line with Dungarees, the biggest product launch in its history. Likewise, Wrangler is expanding its casual pant business through Timber Creek by Wrangler and Wrangler Khakis. And Riders continues to grow its market share among women who shop in discount stores."

■ VF operates in the apparel industry, which is well known for its volatility and uncertainty.

■ VF has a rather pedestrian record of growth. In the 1988–1998 period, earnings per share expanded from $1.33 to $3.10, a compound annual growth rate of 8.8 percent. Dividends advanced from $.43 to $.81, for a growth rate of only 6.5 percent. This, to be sure, is not impressive. However, the payout ratio is very conservative, as only 26 percent of earnings were paid out in 1998.

Reasons to Buy

■ In 1998, VF embarked on a multiyear strategy to invest $1.25 billion in brand marketing. What's more, the company is spending $150 million on new, state-of-the-art technology systems and is creating a simpler and more streamlined operating structure. The prior year, the company moved from seventeen decentralized divisions to five product-based coalitions: VF Jeanswear, VF Intimates, VF Knitwear, VF Playwear, and VF International. As part of its transformation, VF is investing heavily in training and education, emphasizing computer skills.

■ Close communications with the consumer—through in-home surveys, focus groups, and segmentation studies, as well as from sources like Lee's Web site (where about 1,000 kids a day provide product input) and Lee's Trend Leaders Panel, which is made up of thirty-five young men and women who are peer-group fashion leaders who share their views with the product development staff—leads to constant innovation.

For example, Lee Pipes (aimed at 10-to-14-year-old boys) launched its own sub-brand called Pipes BMX because consumers told them they were riding bikes more and were concerned about pant legs getting caught in their spike chains. As a result, the BMX line incorporates a cinch at the bottom of the leg.

To translate these ideas into products as quickly and accurately as possible, VF created cross-functional development teams, where the designers, engineers, and pattern-makers all work together simultaneously to turn concepts into products that meet the consumer's needs and make money for the brand.

Finally, the company's domestic plants have fast cycle times and a high level of flexibility, which means they can change product lines and produce volume in a short span of time. However, offshore has longer lead times. This is being corrected, according to a company official. "But we've still shortened it through strategically placed plants and groups of plants so that we can fill containers quickly and economically. In Costa Rica, for example, we have six plants that can load 10 to 12 containers a week. They also work multiple shifts."

- Timber Creek is central to the company's goal of being a leader in casual pants in discount stores. Designed to meet the needs of hard-working men who seek sturdy, stylish, comfortable clothes, Timber Creek extends the Wrangler franchise. This rapidly expanding line is among those the company has specifically targeted for growth.

- On the manufacturing side, VF Corp. has moved 57 percent of the sewing of products sold in the United States to Mexico, the Caribbean, and other cost-efficient locations, up from 45 percent at the end of 1997. The company plans to gradually increase this percentage over the coming years, to help offset rising labor costs and to combat continued pricing pressures.

- VF Corporation has been working to tie its supply chain management software with a enterprise-wide resource planning system (ERP) to optimize production, react promptly to retail sales during key selling seasons, and fine tune distribution to the stores. This was accomplished in mid-1999.

The supply chain management system enables VF to know what materials have been received and to optimize production at its ninety-three manufacturing facilities. This system, from i2 Technologies, Irving, Texas, exchanges data with a companywide resource planning system that encompasses merchandises, management and financials. The ERP system is from SAP in Walldorf, Germany.

For example, if a particular color of shirt is selling well at one retailer, the connected ERP and supply chain systems will enable VF to identify the need quickly and check materials and capacity to ramp up production on that particular garment. According to a company spokesman, "Prior to installing centralized manufacturing systems, each of our divisions did things independently, and the planning ranged from a sheet of paper to sophisticated PC-based spreadsheets. The diverse systems made it difficult to coordinate production on an enterprise-wide basis," he said.

Using the supply chain management and factory planning data in the ERP system helps the company meet the needs of individual retailers, assuring that the appropriate colors, sizes, and styles are produced and distributed to the retailers.

- VF Corp. views its balance sheet as a competitive weapon. To give the company the flexibility to make acquisitions, repurchase shares, and deliver an average annual dividend payout of 30 percent, VF targets a debt-to-capital level below 40 percent. For the past three years, this ratio has averaged 24 percent. Finally, careful inventory management is another VF hallmark and a key contributor to the company's strong cash flow from operations.

Total assets: $3,837 million
Current ratio: 1.79
Common shares outstanding: 119 million
Return on 1998 shareholders' equity: 19.7%

	1998	1997	1996	1995	1994	1993	1992	1991
Revenues (millions)	5,479	5,222	5,137	5,062	4,972	4,320	3,824	2,952
Net income (millions)	388	351	300	244	274	246	237	161
Earnings per share	3.10	2.76	2.32	1.88	2.10	1.90	1.90	1.38
Dividends per share	.81	.77	.73	.69	.65	.61	.56	.51
Price: high	54.7	48.3	34.9	28.6	26.9	28.2	28.8	20.8
low	33.4	32.3	23.8	23.4	22.1	19.8	19.3	8.8

GROWTH AND INCOME

Vulcan Materials Company

1200 Urban Center Drive, Birmingham, AL 35242 ▫ Investor contact: E. Starke Sydnor (205) 298-3202 ▫ Dividend reinvestment plan available (800) 519-3111 ▫ Web site: www.vulcanmaterials.com ▫ Listed: NYSE ▫ Ticker symbol: VMC ▫ S&P rating: A ▫ Value Line financial strength rating: A

Vulcan Materials is the largest domestic producer of construction aggregates (a product category that includes crushed stone, sand, and gravel). The company does not materially depend upon sales to any one customer or group of customers. Typically, its products are sold to private industry. However, most of VMC's construction materials are ultimately used in public projects.

From 330 aggregates plants and other production and distribution facilities, Vulcan provides a diversified line of aggregates, other construction materials, and related services to all parts of the construction industry in twenty states. Vulcan's principal product, crushed stone, is used in virtually all forms of construction.

Vulcan's Chemicals segment is a significant producer of basic industrial and specialty chemicals. Through its Chloralkali Business Unit, it produces chlorine, caustic soda, hydrochloric acid, potassium chemicals, and chlorinated organic chemicals. The food and pharmaceutical markets provide stable demand for several of chloralkali's chemical products.

Through its Performance Systems Business Unit, it provides process aids for the pulp and paper and textile industries and chemicals and services to the municipal, industrial, and environmental water-management markets. It also has a stake in the custom manufacture of a variety of specialty chemicals.

A Look at the Industry

Aggregates account for about 95 percent of the weight of each ton of asphalt that is used to pave highways and parking lots. Aggregates account for 85 percent of the weight of ready-mix concrete used for such projects as dams, highways, and foundations.

Vulcan quarries and processes the stone to various sizes so that it conforms to specific engineering standards. Independent truckers or customer trucks haul the stone to the construction site, rarely more than twenty or thirty miles away.

There are two major exceptions to this rule. The first exception is the Reed quarry, which ships a large portion of its production great distances, mainly by barge on the Mississippi River system. A much smaller portion is shipped by rail.

The company's so-called Crescent Market Project is the second exception to the local-market rule of thumb. Because aggregates deposits along the Gulf Coast are limited, most aggregates are supplied from inland sources 70 or more miles away. Consequently, transportation costs increase the product's delivery prices substantially.

Vulcan participates in a venture that produces crushed limestone at a quarry near Cancun, Mexico, ships the product to the U.S. Gulf Coast, and markets the stone in a number of cities, including Houston, Galveston, New Orleans, Mobile, and Tampa.

The economics of the project work because ocean shipping costs much less than truck or rail transportation, even though the distance is much greater.

The largest end-use for aggregates is highway construction and maintenance. Crushed stone is used as a highway base material and as the major portion of the asphaltic concrete and ready-mixed concrete used as a surface material.

Crushed stone is the company's largest product; it accounts for three-fourths of Construction Materials sales. Vulcan also produces sand and gravel, asphaltic and ready-mix concrete, and numerous other, less-significant products.

Shortcomings to Bear in Mind

- The company's Chloralkali unit is part of its commodity chemicals business. A commodity differs from a proprietary product in that it is not differentiated from the products of its competitors. In order to survive in a commodity business, you should be a low-cost producer or offer a unique service, such as quick delivery.
- Demand for aggregates is both cyclical and mature.

- Caustic soda prices tend to be volatile. For instance, prices peaked in April 1991 at nearly $300 per ton; then they plummeted to $61 in March of 1994. In the spring of 1997, the price was about $130 per ton, well below earlier levels. The reason for the decline was too much of the chemical in the marketplace. Vulcan sells nearly all of the caustic soda it produces. As a consequence, any price change can impact earnings significantly.

Reasons to Buy

- In 1998, the company's Construction Materials segment generated its fifth consecutive year of record financial performance. Strong infrastructure spending and demand for construction aggregates will likely continue and may increase as federal spending for highways intensifies. The passage in 1998 of federal legislation for highway construction, known as TEA-21, authorizes the federal expenditure of $157 billion for highway construction over the next six years. According to management, the new legislation will increase spending in the states served by Vulcan by 53 percent in the next six years, compared with the prior six years. By contrast, the increase will be only 35 percent in states where Vulcan does not operate, such as New England, the Northeast, and the upper plains states.
- In January of 1999, Vulcan Materials completed the acquisition of CalMat Company, California's leading producer of aggregates and asphalt mix and a major producer of ready-mixed concrete. California is the largest beneficiary of TEA-21, with an average annual allocation of $2.4 billion, a 46 percent increase over the prior legislation.

  CalMat finished 1998 with significantly stronger earnings from operations. CalMat's robust earnings during the second half of 1998 indicate greatly improved construction markets in California. CalMat's sales increased 16 percent for the year and 26 percent in the fourth quarter.

- In addition to the CalMat acquisition, Vulcan stepped up the pace of property additions. During 1998, the company acquired six stone quarries in Georgia, Illinois, and Tennessee, and began production of greenfield (new) aggregates operations in Alabama, Georgia, and Indiana.

The company began accelerating the rate of property additions in the latter part of 1997 when it acquired two quarries in Texas, one in Arkansas, and one in Georgia. At the same time, Vulcan began sales at a greenfield lime plant in Illinois. In the early part of 1999, the company purchased five quarries in Arkansas, three in Georgia, and two in North Carolina.

- In mid-1998, the company announced the formation of a joint venture with Mitsui & Company, Ltd. to construct a new chloralkali plant and expand ethylene dichloride (EDC) capacity at Vulcan's current manufacturing site in Geismar, Louisiana. In addition to leveraging Vulcan's existing infrastructure, the project is structured to provide attractive and relatively stable returns over the chloralkali business cycles and the life span of the joint venture.

The project focuses each partner on its strength. Vulcan, a 51-percent owner of the joint venture, will operate the plant and market its caustic soda production through existing sales and distribution networks. Mitsui, a Vulcan customer for over twenty years and the largest EDC trader in the world, will buy all of the EDC output from the Geismar facility. EDC is a precursor to vinyl chloride monomer and polyvinyl chloride (PVC) products.

- Earnings per share have moved ahead steadily in recent years, with only one significant drop (in 1991, EPS slumped to $.46 from $1.03). In the 1988–1998 period, earnings per share expanded from $1.10 to $2.44, a compound annual growth rate of 8.3 percent. In the same ten-year stretch, dividends per share climbed from $.33 to $.69, a growth rate of 7.7 percent.

- The aggregates industry has undergone significant ownership and concentration changes in recent years. In 1985, the top 10 producers in the United States accounted for about 13 percent of total domestic sales.

Ten years later, the top ten producers shipped about 22 percent of the U.S. market. Vulcan, the industry leader with an estimated 6.3 percent of the U.S. aggregates market and an estimated 10.4 percent of the crushed stone market, currently serves geographic markets with about 25 percent of the U.S. population. Notwithstanding the recent consolidation, the aggregates industry remains highly fragmented and contains significant growth opportunities.

- Historically, Construction Materials enjoys good results when housing starts are strong. Conversely, Chemicals enjoys its best results when caustic soda prices are high. The inverse relationship between changes in housing starts and caustic prices has been almost perfect for the last twenty-five years.

The relationship occurs because the demand for chlorine is heavily dependent upon economic activity, especially construction. Demand for caustic is much less cyclical because of the diverse nature of its end-use markets. Hence, when economic activity is strong, chlorine demand increases sharply, putting caustic in an oversupply situation.

However, when the economy is slack, chlorine production is curtailed, thus reducing caustic production and creating a shortage of caustic.

- Vulcan manufactures sodium chlorite at a world-class facility in the company's Wichita, Kansas chemical complex. Vulcan is the largest North American producer of sodium chlorite and the world's second-largest. Sodium chlorite is used in a variety of applications, including drinking and industrial water treatment, air scrubbing, and paper, textile, and electronics manufacturing.

Total assets: $1,659 million
Current ratio: 2.73
Common shares outstanding: 101 million
Return on 1998 shareholders' equity: 21.5%

	1998	1997	1996	1995	1994	1993	1992	1991
Revenues (millions)	1,776	1,679	1,569	1,461	1,253	1,134	1,078	1,008
Net income (millions)	248	209	189	166	98	88	91	53
Earnings per share	2.44	2.03	1.79	1.54	.89	.80	.80	.46
Dividends per share	.69	.63	.56	.49	.44	.42	.40	.40
Price: high	44.7	34.6	22.2	20.1	18.8	18.7	16.5	13.3
low	31.3	18.4	17.7	16.0	14.7	13.4	12.0	10.1

GROWTH AND INCOME

Wachovia Corporation

100 North Main Street, Winston-Salem, NC 27150 ☐ Investor contact: James C. Mabry (336) 732-5788 ☐ Dividend reinvestment plan available (800) 633-4236 ☐ Web site: www.wachovia.com ☐ Listed: NYSE ☐ Ticker symbol: WB ☐ S&P rating: A- ☐ Value Line financial strength rating: A+

Wachovia Corporation is an interstate bank holding company. It has dual headquarters in Atlanta, Georgia and Winston-Salem, North Carolina. The company's properties are situated in the Southeast and include operations headquartered in Atlanta; Winston-Salem; Columbia, South Carolina; and Wilmington, Delaware.

At the end of 1998, Wachovia had assets of $64.1 billion, making it the sixteenth-largest banking company in the United States.

Wachovia's Heritage

Wachovia traces its roots deep into the European continent. Wachovia originates from the German word "Wachau," which is the name given by Moravians, a European Protestant sect, to land they settled in the Piedmont region of North Carolina. The Moravians chose the name because their new land reminded them of the Wachau Valley along the Danube River, the ancestral home of their benefactor in Germany. As the settlers made the new area their home, "Wachau" was Anglicized into Wachovia (pronounced wah-KO-vee-yah).

The Moravians were the entrepreneurs of their day, organizing the First National Bank of Salem in 1866 to supply the growing need for financial services in the town of Salem. When nearby Winston experienced industrial growth, they moved the bank and renamed it Wachovia National Bank in 1879.

Wachovia's Operations

Major corporate and institutional relationships are managed by Wachovia Corporate Services, Inc. through banking offices in Georgia, North Carolina, and South Carolina and through representative offices in Chicago, London, New

York City, and Tokyo. The corporation maintains foreign branches at Grand Cayman, through its banking subsidiaries, and an Edge Act subsidiary in New York City.

Wachovia Trust Services, Inc. provides fiduciary, investment management, and related financial services for corporate, institutional, and individual clients.

Discount brokerage and investment advisory services are provided by Wachovia Investments, Inc. to customers primarily in Georgia, North Carolina, and South Carolina.

Wachovia Operational Services Corporation provides information processing and systems development for Wachovia's subsidiaries. Finally, WB is involved in other financial services activities, in other financial services, including residential mortgage origination, state and local government securities underwriting, sales and trading, foreign exchange, corporate finance, and other money market services.

Highlights of 1998

For the full year, operating earnings were $4.45 per diluted share, compared with $3.96 in 1997. Operating net income totaled $929.8 million, up from $799.9 million the prior year. Operating earnings exclude merger-related expenses of $85.3 million, pretax, for 1998 and special charges in the 1997 fourth quarter totaling $303 million, pretax, primarily for merger integration expenses. Including the special charges, Wachovia's net income for 1998 was $874.2 million, or $4.18 per diluted share, compared with $592.8 million, or $2.94 per diluted share for 1997.

On an operating basis, Wachovia's return on shareholders's equity was 18 percent, and return on assets was 1.45 percent, compared with five-year averages of 17.2 percent and 1.38 percent, respectively.

Average common equity to assets was 8.08 percent for 1998.

Net loan losses were .67 percent of average loans. Losses were .11 percent, excluding the credit card portfolio. At December 31, nonperforming assets were .40 percent of loans. Foreclosed property and the corporation's reserve coverage of nonperforming loans was 349 percent. Wachovia's overhead, or efficiency ratio, on a core operating basis was 52.7 percent.

The total return on Wachovia's common stock, including price appreciation and reinvested dividends, was 10.2 percent for 1998. This compares with 8.3 percent for the Keefe, Bruyette & Woods Index of 50 money-center and regional banks and 28.6 percent for the Standard & Poor's 500 Index. The five-year compound annual total return for Wachovia was 25 percent. For the KBW Index and the S&P 500 Index, it was 27.8 percent and 24.1 percent, respectively.

Strong revenue growth drove Wachovia's 1998 financial performance. Total revenue advanced $468.8 million for the year, with fee-based income contributing 47 percent of the growth. This diverse and robust revenue stream reflects Wachovia's ability to achieve growth in key lines of business.

At the end of 1998, Wachovia had relationships with 3.5 million households and 200,000 small businesses in the Carolinas, Florida, Georgia, and Virginia. In addition, Wachovia had 28,000 large and middle-market corporate relationships in its home markets, nationally and abroad. Wachovia's merger with Interstate/Johnson Lane, a leading regional securities firm in Charlotte, North Carolina, will add more customers and strengthen product and services capabilities for consumers and corporate capital markets customers. The merger was consummated in the spring of 1999.

Shortcomings to Bear in Mind

- As its in-state competitors have expanded aggressively through mergers, Wachovia has lost some ground. At one time, Wachovia was the largest bank in North Carolina, as measured by deposit share, but now ranks second.

Reasons to Buy

- All consumer programs are dependent on the most efficient and effective retail distribution systems to accommodate customers. This is being achieved in each market with the bank's Market Network model, which enables Wachovia to determine the best configuration of branches, ATMs, and nontraditional sales points such as the workplace and targeted supermarkets, complemented by telephone and Internet banking. Here are some highlights:
  - Wachovia's 752 banking offices and 1,372 ATMs are strategically located throughout five states.
  - Located primarily in Virginia and Georgia, 43 in-store banking centers serve customers at one-fourth the cost of a traditional branch.
  - Wachovia provides 182 bank-at-work ATMs that help build wallet share with employees, while enhancing overall corporate relationships, with a cost that is one-tenth of an in-branch transaction.
  - Wachovia On-Call, the telephone-based sale-and-service center, and Wachovia Phone Access, the fully automated telephone banking capability available 24-hours-a-day, seven-days-a-week, handled 48.2 million calls in 1998, 88 percent via automation.
  - Investors now can place securities trades 24-hours-a-day, seven-days-a-week through Wachovia's expanded automated telephone service.
  - www.wachovia.com offers Internet trading, on-line banking, on-line credit card applications, mortgage rates updated daily, and a host of other interactive financial services. It has been voted one of the best Internet banking sites by *Smart Money*, the *Moneypage*, and *Bank Rate Monitor*.

- For years, Wachovia has enjoyed a reputation as a "banker's bank." It consistently generates a high return on equity. Its discipline in keeping overhead costs low puts it among the elite of efficient banking institutions. What's more, Wachovia's conservative stance when granting credit helped it sidestep the loan losses that bedeviled rivals in the past.

- The bank's stripes have been changing under the leadership of a new CEO, Leslie "Bud" Baker, Jr. Since the 55-year-old president, who has been with Wachovia since 1969, took the reins in 1994, he has launched a quiet revolution, which some analysts contend is beginning to bear fruit.

  According to one analyst, "When Bud Baker came in, he was really faced with a pretty monumental task. He had to spend hundreds of millions of dollars to bring technology up to par."

  Mr. Baker carefully examined every part of the bank's operations and has been taking steps to discover the best way to proceed. For one thing, Wachovia is closing as many as 10 percent of its branches and reorganizing its trust operation. Mr. Baker says he believes that Wachovia will be able to exceed its historical target of 10 percent to 12 percent a year growth in earnings per share. The bank also plans to boost fee income to 50 percent of total revenue, up from only 32 percent, by introducing fee-based products and raising current charges.

- Some investors might complain that Wachovia has a low yield. However, it is well above average. But, more important,

WB has a fine record of growth, which means dividends are likely to move smartly ahead over the years. In the 1988–1998 period, earnings per share expanded from $1.81 to $4.45, with no dips during those years. The compound annual growth rate for earnings per share is a solid 9.41 percent. Dividends, moreover, climbed at an even better clip in this ten-year stretch, rising from $.58 to $1.86, a compound growth rate of 12.4 percent.

If you compare Wachovia's financial ratings with the twenty-five largest U.S. banks, the numbers are impressive.

FINANCIAL RELATIONSHIP	WACHOVIA'S RANKING
Total assets	16
Net income	15
Return on assets	7
Return on common equity	11
Common Equity Assets	8

Noperforming assets/loans + foreclosed property	4
Loan loss reserve/ nonperforming loans	13
Overhead ratio	4
Market capitalization	15
Market cap/asset	7
Prce/earnings ratio year-end 1998, based on 1999 estimates	7
Price/bookvalue 12/31/98	9

Wachovia is one of the leaders in addressing the growing issue of check fraud. WB's check fraud task force, with representatives from operations, product management, legal, and security, is helping bring industry associations together to focus on common loss prevention initiatives, conducting seminars to educate companies on risks and prevention measures, and seeking ways to leverage image processing and other technology capabilities to combat the problem.

Total assets: $64,123 million
Return on average assets: 1.45%
Common shares outstanding: 203 million
Return on 1998 shareholders' equity: 16.92%

	1998	1997	1996	1995	1994	1993	1992	1991
Loans (millions)	45,719	44,194	31,283	29,261	25,891	22,416	19,642	20,257
Net income (millions)	930	800	645	602	539	492	433	230
Earnings per share	4.45	3.96	3.81	3.50	3.13	2.83	2.51	1.34
Dividends per share	1.86	1.68	1.52	1.38	1.23	1.11	1.00	.92
Price: high	96.8	83.9	60.3	48.3	35.4	40.5	34.8	30.0
low	72.8	53.5	39.6	32.0	30.1	31.9	28.3	20.3

AGGRESSIVE GROWTH

Walgreen Company

200 Wilmot Road, Mail Stop #2261, Deerfield, IL 60015 ❐ Investor contact: John M. Palizza (847) 914-2972 ❐ Direct dividend reinvestment program available (888) 290-7264 ❐ Fiscal year's end August 31 ❐ Web site: www.walgreens.com ❐ Ticker symbol: WAG ❐ S&P rating: A+ ❐ Value Line financial strength rating: A+

Walgreens, one of the fastest-growing retailers in the United States, leads the chain drugstore industry in sales and profits. Sales for 1998 reached $15.3 billion, produced by 2,549 stores in thirty-five states and Puerto Rico.

Founded in 1901, Walgreens today has 90,000 employees and 45,000 shareholders of record. The company's drugstores serve 2.5 million customers daily and average $5.8 million in annual sales per unit. That's $567 per square foot, among the highest in the industry. Walgreens has paid dividends in every quarter since 1933 and has raised the dividend in each of the past twenty-two years.

Competition from the supermarkets has convinced Walgreens that the best strategy is to build standalone stores. Since the rise of managed care, many pharmacy customers now make only minimal co-payments for prescriptions. That leaves convenience as the major factor in choosing a pharmacy. The freestanding format makes room for drive-thru windows, which provide a speedy way for drugstore customers to pick up or drop off prescriptions.

On the other hand, the company's standalone strategy is more expensive. Walgreen insists on building its units on corner lots near an intersection with a traffic light. Such leases normally cost more than a site in a strip mall.

Highlights of 1998

• Walgreens opened a record 304 stores in 1998, 94 of which were relocations to more convenient sites. Well over half the chain is now freestanding. The average age of a Walgreen store today is seven years. By the company's one hundredth anniversary in 2001, that number will fall to less than six years.

• The company has entered forty-three new markets since 1992 and added several more in 1999.

• Walgreens filled 226 million prescriptions in 1998, about 9 percent of the U.S. retail market. Pharmacy, moreover, is now half the company's business.

• Drive-thru prescription service is now offered in nearly 1,200 Walgreen pharmacies, and one-hour photo processing is available in over 90 percent of the company's outlets.

• Walgreens Health Initiatives, the company's managed care division, increased sales 29 percent, to nearly $600 million in fiscal 1998. Its two mail service facilities dispensed nearly 6 million prescriptions—more than 19,000 per day.

• Walgreen Company ranked 108 on the *Fortune* 500 list in 1998. Among *Fortune* 500 retailers, the company's sales volume ranked fourteenth and its profits twelfth.

• For the fifth consecutive year, Walgreens was included on *Fortune* magazine's "Most Admired Corporations in America" list.

The company climbed from second to first place among food and drug retailers. What's more, it was number one in six of the eight categories measured: management quality, innovativeness, investment value, financial soundness, talent, and use of corporate assets.

Shortcomings to Bear in Mind

■ Often, Walgreen chooses a freestanding location on the site of an existing strip center, for instance, a piece of the mall parking lot. For the property's owners, this usually means an opportunity to charge more for the standalone space while renting out the old strip center space. Increasingly, however, supermarkets and other big retailers are starting to put exclusionary provisions in their leases, prohibiting a drugstore from occupying freestanding space on shopping center properties they anchor. Walgreen management says it has encountered such provisions but insists that they aren't yet "a real problem."

■ According to management, "Prescription margins continue to be pressured by managed care. The news, though, is better than a year ago. While our pharmacy margins haven't increased, they have leveled out. This is chiefly due to aggressive negotiation, including dropping six plans in the past six months because they didn't meet minimum profitability standards."

■ Another concern for Walgreen: the food chains are ringing up impressive sales in high-margin health care and beauty products, such as shampoo and toothpaste, long a vital profit center for drugstore retailers.

- The stock has performed so well in recent years that its P/E multiple is extremely high.

Reasons to Buy

- The company's new pharmacy system, Intercom Plus, is now up and running in all Walgreen stores across the country. This system, costing over $150 million, raises Walgreen's service and productivity to a new level. While providing increased patient access to Walgreen's pharmacists, it also substantially raises the number of prescriptions each store can efficiently dispense.
- Walgreen's management is heartened by the increase in prescription usage in the United States due to the dramatic aging of the population. Between 1995 and 2005, people age 55 or older in the United States will grow at a compound rate of 3.8 percent—double the rate of the rest of the population. The good news for Walgreen's is that these graying Americans need twice as many prescriptions per year as the rest of the population.
- Walgreen's net number of new stores in 1998, minus relocations and permanent closings, was a record 191. Between 1993 and 2000, the company opened a net of 1,250 stores. In addition, the company relocated 540 units during those seven years. In 1999, capital expenditures topped $750 million, most of which was targeted for store growth.

  The company's 3,000th store will open during the year 2000, and Walgreens has set a goal of 6,000 by the year 2010. Contrary to the consolidation so prevalent in the drugstore industry, Walgreens growth is internally generated; the company has not made a major acquisition since the mid-1980s.
- Every corner of Walgreen's strategy is focused on convenience: how fast people get into the store or be served in the drive-thru pharmacy, how fast they get out, how easily they find what they came to buy, how well Walgreen's clerks remind them of what they are forgetting to buy.
- Food departments are another example. Recently, a major grocery chain cited drugstores as a reason behind disappointing sales gains: "Fill-in shopping needs," said the grocery CEO, "are increasingly being satisfied in convenience and drugstores." Walgreens, with highly convenient, on-the-way-home locations, is on the receiving end of this trend.
- "The best thing about a new market is we start with an entirely clean slate," says one store manager. "Every store is sparkling, every manager is hand-picked. We can build the image we want . . . and what we want is terrific customer service."

  That's certainly worked in Las Vegas, the fifteenth market Walgreens has entered since 1992, and most new stores are successful. "Business took off from the get-go," says district manager Greg Wasson. "We opened our first store in August 1996 and of the dozen operating now, several have already posted profitable months. The package Walgreens offers—free-standing stores with drive-thru pharmacies—is totally unique to this market."
- Supplying Walgreen's broad merchandise mix requires technology that supports frequent replenishment of quantities as small as a few bottles of shampoo or a few packages of over-the-counter allergy medication. In addition to highly automated split-case picking machines, Walgreens has installed a proprietary pick-to-light system in its Orlando center. This was in place in all eight major DCs by 1999.

Total assets: $4,902 million
Current ratio: 1.66
Common shares outstanding: 499 million
Return on 1998 shareholders' equity: 19.6%

	1998	1997	1996	1995	1994	1993	1992	1991
Revenues (millions)	15,307	13,363	11,778	10,395	9,235	8,295	7,475	6,733
Net income (millions)	514	436	372	321	282	245	221	195
Earnings per share	.51	.44	.38	.33	.29	.25	.22	.20
Dividends per share	.13	.12	.11	.10	.09	.08	.07	.06
Price: high	30.2	16.8	10.9	7.8	5.7	5.6	5.6	4.8
low	14.8	9.6	7.3	5.4	4.2	4.4	3.8	3.1

AGGRESSIVE GROWTH

Wal-Mart Stores, Inc.

702 SW Eighth Street, Bentonville, AR 72716-8611 ◻ Investor contact: Steve Hunter (501) 273-8446 ◻ Direct dividend reinvestment plan available (800) 438-6278 ◻ Web site: www.wal-mart.com ◻ Listed: NYSE ◻ Fiscal year's end January 31 of the following calendar year ◻ Ticker symbol: WMT ◻ S&P rating: A+ ◻ Value Line financial strength rating: A+

Wal-Mart is the world's number one retailer, larger than Sears, Kmart, and J. C. Penney combined. At the end of fiscal 1999 (January 31, 1999), the company operated 1,869 domestic Wal-Mart stores, 564 domestic Supercenters, 451 Sam's Clubs, and 715 international units. Most of the company's outlets are in the United States, but it is moving abroad aggressively and has a presence in Canada, Latin America, Asia, and Europe.

In fiscal 1999, Wal-Mart completed its best year ever, with sales of over $137 billion, up 17 percent, which is nearly $20 billion more than the prior year. What's more, earnings per share shot up 27 percent. Return on assets improved to 9.6 percent, and the company paid dividends of almost $700 million.

Shortcomings to Bear in Mind

■ At 192,000 square feet, Wal-Mart Supercenters are about the size of four football fields. Wal-Mart quickly found that some customers have trouble navigating them. According to one shopper, "The stores are too big. It takes too long to get around." On the other hand, the

store's "really good prices" keep them coming back, but she warns, "We've just about decided we'll go somewhere else and pay more not to have to go through all the hassle."

Reasons to Buy

■ In June of 1999, Wal-Mart made a major international move with the $10.7-billion purchase of Britain's third-largest supermarket chain, Asda Group PLC. This acquisition doubles the company's international sales to $25 billion—some 17 percent of annual revenues. What's more, the Asda purchase gives Wal-Mart a second leg on which to build a continent-wide business, adding to the two German chains it acquired in the last two years. The company wants one-third of its growth over the next five years to come from international operations.

■ Two or three years ago, Sam's Club experienced some challenges, but it has bounced back of late. Sam's Club is a concept that was started back in 1983. The company entered the business because it was the retail innovation with the lowest-cost method of distributing merchandise. Unfortunately, according to Don Soderquist, senior vice chairman, "Over the years, the industry and Sam's as well, has lost some of its merchandising focus. The Sam's team used the last two years or so to reinvigorate the clubs and put some fun back into the operation, and with their new president, Tom Grimm, continue to improve the merchandise offering. I believe this is obvious by the acceleration in the sales increases as well as the number of new members and the renewal rates of existing members."

■ Wal-Mart's international operation has just completed its fifth year. In fiscal 1999, the division generated $12.2 billion in revenue and $551 million in operating profit. In addition to the seventy-four units in Germany (where the company has completed two acquisitions), the company also acquired four units in Korea and added another thirty-six units to the countries where Wal-Mart had existing operations. According to Bob Walton, chairman of the company, "We still have tremendous room for growth domestically, but we also want to offer the Wal-Mart shopping experience to customers around the world. Over the next five years, the International division should represent up to one-third of total sales and earnings growth of the company. In addition to being the largest retailer in Canada and Mexico, we now have stores in Asia, Europe, and South America and will continue to grow those markets as well as look for other areas where we can build on the Wal-Mart name."

■ Some ten years ago, Wal-Mart began experimenting with a retail concept called a "Hypermarket," which the company translated into its Supercenter. This concept took the idea of retailing both general merchandise and food in the same building and created the convenience of "one-stop shopping." According to the CEO of Wal-Mart, David Glass, "It has become our key domestic growth vehicle and will remain so for at least the next ten years. This year alone (fiscal 2000), we are going to open approximately 150 Supercenters in the United States as well as using it as a vehicle in our international growth. Supercenters effectively serve a large trade area, but we think there may be some business that we are not getting purely because they may be close to the customer or convenient for small shopping trips. That's where we think there may be an opportunity for the small grocery/drug store format where we are testing the Neighborhood Market."

Already, Wal-Mart's push into groceries is pressuring giants like Kroger Company and Safeway Inc. to cut costs and boost service. The pressures aren't coming merely from the Supercenters; add food and other grocery items sold through the Wal-Mart discount and Sam's Clubs units. One retail analyst estimates that groceries now account for more than $30 billion of Wal-Mart's total sales. According to still another analyst, "Wal-Mart is totally flanking the grocery industry. It is terribly threatening." He predicts that in ten years, Wal-Mart and Safeway will be the two largest food retailers in the United States, leaving such rivals as Kroger and Albertson's in the dust.

■ Wal-Mart makes a concerted effort to find out precisely what its customers want. To do this, the company relies on information technology. It does this by collecting and analyzing internally developed information, which it calls "data-mining." It has been doing this since 1990.

The result, by now, is an enormous database of purchasing information that enables management to place the right item in the right store at the right time. The company's computer system receives 8.4 million updates every minute on the items that customers take home—and the relationship between the items in each basket.

Many retailers talk a good game when it comes to mining data at cash registers as a way to build sales. Wal-Mart, since it has been doing this for the past ten years, is sitting on an information trove so vast and detailed that it far exceeds what many manufacturers know about their own products. What's more, Wal-Mart's data base is second in size only to that of the U.S. government, says one analyst. Wal-Mart also collects "market-basket data" from customer receipts at all of its stores, so it knows what products are likely to be purchased together. The company receives about 100,000 queries a week from suppliers and its own buyers looking for purchase patterns or checking a product.

Wal-Mart plans to use the data in its new Neighborhood Markets. Equipped with a drive-through pharmacy and selling both dry goods and perishables, the stores are a little smaller than typical suburban supermarkets. They are much smaller than Wal-Mart's Supercenters, the massive grocery-discount store combinations that Wal-Mart began opening in 1987.

This kind of information has significant value in and of itself. According to management, "Consider Wal-Mart's ability to keep the shelves stocked with exactly what customers want most, but still be able to keep inventories under tight control. Consider the common banana, so common, in fact, that the grocery carts of America contain bananas more often than any other single item. So why not make it easy for a shopper to remember bananas? In Wal-Mart grocery departments, bananas can be found not just in the produce section, but in the cereal and dairy aisles too."

- Most Wal-Mart customers hear a "welcome" when they enter a store. In some instances, to be sure, this may sound like Bienvenido or Willkommen or perhaps the welcome version in Chinese, French, or Korean. That's because Wal-Mart is doing business not only in the United States but also in Argentina, Brazil, Canada, China, Germany, and a host of other countries. According to Bob Martin, President and CEO of Wal-Mart International, "Wal-Mart is still very early in the curve, but we already are a proven global brand. The United States has only 4.5 percent of the world's population, so the way we see it, that leaves most of the world as potential Wal-Mart customers."

The International division's sales rose to more than $12 billion in fiscal 1999, an increase of 63 percent over the previous year's sales of $7.5 billion. And International's operating profit for the year was $551 million, for an increase of 110 percent from the year before.

In fiscal 1999, along with growing the company's business in such familiar venues as Mexico, Canada, and Puerto Rico, Wal-Mart also took its first steps into South Korea, acquiring a majority interest in four units previously run by the Korea Makro company; acquired the 74-unit Interspar hypermarket chain in Germany, approximately quadrupling the size of the company's operations there; and announced plans to triple the size of Wal-Mart's operations in China. According to Bob Martin, "In the markets we currently serve, there are significant expansion opportunities, and in the new regions we are exploring, there are millions of under-served customers."

- Wal-Mart is testing in-store coffee bars, hoping shoppers will take a quick break for a $2.25 cup of coffee. The company opened three cafes, called Cafe Tostino, in Supercenters in Indiana in the spring of 1999. They plan to open another ten to fourteen by year-end 1999. Though Wal-Mart executives say the company is just experimenting with the concept, Tostino operators envision opening their cafes in 1,000 Wal-Mart stores in a few years. Wal-Mart hopes the cafes will encourage shoppers to stay awhile and also draw in some customers who come for the coffee alone.

Tostino tries to stay slightly under Starbucks's prices, with muffins and cookies for $.99, apple and cherry turnovers for $1.49, and "jazzberry" strawberry-blueberry smoothies and mocha frappes for $3.95. Initially, the cafes are planned for Wal-Marts that are located far from a Starbucks or other upscale coffee houses.

Cafe Tostino builds on Wal-Mart's broader restaurant ambitions. In 1998, the company ended its agreement with McDonald's to put McDonald's in new stores, so Wal-Mart could expand its own "Radio Grill" restaurants, a 1950s-style diner where customers can eat at Wal-Mart prices. A hamburger sells for $1.58, while a hot dog and 32-ounce soda go for $1.47. The company says it has 1,477 Radio Grills and about 680 McDonald's in the United States.

Total assets: $49,996 million
Current ratio: 1.22
Common shares outstanding: 4,446 million
Return on 1998 shareholders' equity: 22.4%

	1998	1997	1996	1995	1994	1993	1992	1991
Revenues (millions)	137,634	117,958	104,859	93,627	82,494	67,345	55,484	43,887
Net income (millions)	4,430	3,526	3,056	2,740	2,681	2,333	1,995	1,608
Earnings per share	0.99	0.78	0.67	0.60	0.59	0.51	0.44	0.35
Dividends per share	0.16	0.14	0.11	0.10	0.09	0.07	0.05	0.04
Price: high	41.4	21.0	14.2	13.8	14.6	17.0	16.4	15.0
low	18.8	11.0	9.6	10.2	10.6	11.5	12.6	7.0

INCOME

Washington Gas Light Company

1100 H Street, N.W., Washington, DC 20080 ◻ Investor contact: Marie Frazzini (703)750-5636 ◻ Dividend reinvestment program available (888)269-8845 ◻ Fiscal year's end September 30 ◻ Listed NYSE ◻ Web site: www.washgas.com ◻ Ticker symbol: WGL ◻ S&P rating: A ◻ Value Line financial strength rating: A

Washington Gas Light Company often omits the word "Light" from its official name, probably because people sometimes mistakenly think WGL is an electric utility. In any event, Washington Gas is the energy company of choice in the Washington, D. C. metropolitan area and surrounding region. The company serves customers through about 820,000 gas meters in a franchise service area that covers 6,648 square miles in Maryland, Virginia, West Virginia, and the District of Columbia. The gas system contains over 22,000 miles of gas lines.

Meter growth on the Washington Gas system averaged 3.1 percent annually during the past five years, significantly higher than the rate for the gas industry. Residential and firm commercial customers provide a stable financial base, accounting for 72.34 percent of the company's therm deliveries in fiscal 1998 (ended September 30, 1998). The D.C. area, since it is the nation's capital, has a stable economy, often shielded from the ups and downs of more industrial cities.

Washington Gas has service agreements with eight interstate pipelines and connects directly to four. The company purchases gas from nearly seventy suppliers. This portfolio approach enables the company to benefit from competition among gas suppliers.

Washington Gas dates back to 1848. It has paid dividends for 147 consecutive years, a record matched by few companies on the New York Stock Exchange.

Washington Gas Light's service territory encompasses 6,648 square miles in and around the nation's capital. The franchise has a population of 4.4 million. It has been growing at an average annual rate of 1.3 percent over the past five years, driven by the expansion of such industries as the region's telecommunications, biotechnology, and information services. Most of the growth has taken place in the suburban areas around Washington, D.C., generating high levels of new home construction. What's more, WGL has been able to capture a majority share of all new single-family homes built within its service territory.

Highlights of 1998
• During 1998, the company added nearly 21,000 new customer meters and continued to grow at a rate significantly higher than the national average for the gas industry.

• Washington Gas Light began installing a major business system that integrates financial, human resources, and procurement information and resources; it upgraded and standardized all desktop computers, improved its computer network infrastructure, and implemented new standards for security and efficiency.

• Washington Gas Energy Services, the largest natural gas marketer in its region, increased its natural gas therm sales in 1998 by 65 percent as it continued to gain profitable market share.

• The company was awarded a major contract to install individual gas heating systems in forty-six buildings at the Patuxent River Naval Air Station in Southern Maryland. The company's Washington Gas Energy Systems affiliate will coordinate construction of this multi-million-dollar project.

• The company completed a major gate station upgrade and installed a new pipeline in the rapidly growing Germantown area of upper Montgomery County, Maryland. It installed four sets of "pig" (metal loss inspection devices) launcher and receiver assemblies for the 18 miles of 2,450 psig transmission piping system at the Hampshire Gas Storage Facility, which will enable internal inspection and cleaning of the entire pipeline.

Shortcomings to Bear in Mind

■ Over the past ten years, earnings per share advanced from $1.26 to $1.54, for a compound annual growth rate of 2.0 percent. In the same 1988–1998 period, dividends per share made only modest progress, rising from $.94 to $1.20, for a compound growth rate of 2.5 percent. These figures may not be a disconcerting as they seem. The weather comes into the picture. In fiscal 1998, the weather was mild during the winter, thus reducing revenues from space heating. As a consequence, earnings per share fell from $1.85 to $1.54.

Reasons to Buy

■ The company's franchise area possesses a significant number of conversion opportunities for Washington Gas Light to pursue. Conversion takes place when owners of older homes that use some other energy source (typically electricity or fuel oil) for their space heating are persuaded to convert to natural gas. The company now has about two-thirds of the business in existing structures in its service territory.

The conversion potential is a legacy of events that took place during the 1970s. This was when natural gas was perceived to be in short supply. To "cure" the problem, WGL's regulators imposed a moratorium on new gas hook-ups. This ruling prohibited Washington Gas from investing in facilities to serve new customers. With natural gas denied to them, homeowners turned to electricity. Electric heat pumps became a popular alternative for heating new homes built during the mid- to late-1970s. As a consequence, a thick ring composed of thousands of electrically heated homes sprung up around the company's service territory. Washington Gas calls this an "electric doughnut."

When the moratorium was lifted in 1980, WGL had to make large capital investments to extend its gas line beyond the doughnut so that it could provide service to new customers in the growing parts of its franchise area. Meanwhile, the electric heat pumps are now nearing the end of their useful lives. Consequently, with the favorable economics and greater effectiveness of natural gas heating, coupled with the presence of natural gas mains crossing through the area, the aging electric doughnut provides Washington Gas with a significant opportunity to tap into these lines to recapture this business from the electric company.

- Washington Gas enjoys the stability of a customer base that is made up of 92 percent of residential customers, with 95 percent of these using natural gas for space heating. Of the remaining 8 percent, most are small commercial accounts that also use natural gas for space heating. Lacking are the industrial customers that can make the territory sensitive to the ups and downs of the economy.

On the other hand, since WGL sells most of its gas for space heating, it is particularly sensitive to changes in the weather. To offset this weather sensitivity, the company features declining rate blocks. Translated, this means that successively higher levels of usage each month are charged lower incremental rates. In addition, there are other temperature-shielding rate mechanisms. Even so, the weather still makes earnings quite volatile.

To be sure, the vagaries of the weather also help or hurt other natural gas companies. Some of them have found a way to mitigate this volatility by making a deal with the regulators to set up a weather normalization scheme. Under this arrangement, the utility adds an extra charge during a warm winter and gives back a little when the heating season is abnormally cold. However, Washington Gas Light has rejected this idea, fearing that the various state commissions would lower their allowed rate of return as an offset.

- Washington Gas Light is expanding its customer base by working closely with area builders and developers. Today, more than 95 percent of the new homes sold by top builders in the Washington area use natural gas. The company has focused its marketing and development efforts on increasing the number of gas appliances installed in these new homes. Results have been impressive. Over the past five years, the number of new homes in its service territory featuring gas fireplaces or lot sets has more than doubled. What's more, the number of new homes with gas ranges has risen by 25 percent.

Total assets: $1,682 million
Current ratio: 0.70
Common shares outstanding: 44 million
Return on 1998 shareholders' equity: 11.2%

	1998	1997	1996	1995	1994	1993	1992	1991
Revenues (millions)	1,040	1,056	970	829	915	894	746	698
Net income (millions)	69	82	82	63	60	55	52	46
Earnings per share	1.54	1.85	1.85	1.45	1.42	1.31	1.27	1.14
Dividends per share	1.20	1.17	1.14	1.12	1.11	1.09	1.07	1.05
Price: high	30.8	31.4	25.0	22.4	21.3	22.9	19.6	17.3
low	23.1	20.9	19.1	16.1	16.0	18.1	15.6	13.7

INCOME

Washington Real Estate Investment Trust

6110 Executive Boulevard, Rockville, MD 20852-3927 ◻ Investor contact: Larry E. Finger (800)565-9748 ◻ Listed: NYSE ◻ Dividend reinvestment plan available ◻ Web site: www.washreit.com ◻ Ticker symbol: WRE ◻ S&P rating: Not rated ◻ Value Line Financial Strength B++

Washington Real Estate Investment Trust (WRIT), founded in 1960, invests in a diversified range of income-producing properties. Management's purpose is to acquire and manage real estate investments in markets it knows well and to protect the company's assets from the risk of owning a single property-type, such as apartments, industrial parks, or shopping centers. WRIT achieves its objectives by owning properties in four different categories.

The trust's properties are primarily situated in an area within a two-hour radius of Washington, D.C., that stretches from Philadelphia in the north to Richmond, Virginia, in the south. Its diversified portfolio consists of twenty office buildings, twelve shopping centers, eight apartment complexes, and sixteen industrial distribution centers. At the end of 1998, operating income from these properties was as follows: Office buildings, 48 percent; industrial properties, 15 percent; apartment buildings, 18 percent; and retail centers, 19 percent.

The REIT's goal is to continue to safely increase earnings and shareholder value. This approach has resulted in WRIT achieving thirty-three consecutive years of increased earnings per share, twenty-eight consecutive years of increased dividends per share, and twenty-six years of consecutive years of increased funds from operations.

Highlights of 1998

In 1998, Washington Real Estate Investment Trust achieved record earnings for the thirty-third consecutive year. Funds from operations (FFO), the measurement that most investment and banking specialists use to measure REIT performance, were up 21 percent over the prior year or 13.3 percent on a per-share basis.

Equally important, WRIT's share price performance in 1998, combined with its dividend, provided shareholders a total return of 18.7 percent for the year. By contrast, the REIT industry as a whole had a *minus* 17 percent total return for the year. WRIT had the second-highest total return of the 173 REITs tracked by the National Association of Real Estate Investment trusts.

WRIT's CEO, Edmund B. Cronin, Jr., believes the REIT industry in general is suffering the after effects of the mid-1990s misguided perception that REITs are growth rather than total-return investments. According to Mr. Cronin, "Over the last several years, momentum-focused analysts and investors have not been favorably inclined toward investing in WRIT because of our conservative strategy. In spite of those urging us to use our strong balance sheet aggressively to acquire assets and engage in speculative development, we have stayed with our proven business plan."

"This plan includes geographic focus, careful and judicious property acquisitions, property and tenant diversification, and concentration on improving our internal growth. We believe that investors' appreciation of this proven strategy is what caused WRIT's total return to dramatically outperform the industry in 1998. As in the past, our primary focus will be the management and improvement of what we own. At the same time, we are always looking for opportunities that meet our criteria for investment."

During 1998, WRIT acquired five properties, for a total purchase price of $81.6 million. These acquisitions should have a very positive impact on 1999 FFO. Continuing the company's diversification, it acquired two industrial properties, one office building, one retail property, and a two-building medical office complex. Concurrently, WRIT sold three properties for a total of $11.4 million, realizing a $6.8 million gain. Since these sales were incorporated into tax-deferred property exchanges, no current tax liabilities were incurred.

Shortcomings to Bear in Mind

■ There is an increased amount of new office building construction taking place in northern Virginia, more so than elsewhere in the region. Though a majority of the new buildings are preleased, several speculative buildings are under construction. Management comments on this development, "We will monitor that market carefully for signs of a downturn. Generally, the other markets and property types in which we invest are in equilibrium."

"Despite the construction described above, we anticipate 1999 real estate market conditions to be similar to 1998. Competition for new acquisitions should be keen, occupancy high, and rents should continue to escalate. However, later in the year, the Northern Virginia office market may see some flattening in rents when space becomes available as a result of tenants moving into the new buildings being built for their use. While we remain alert to market changes, 1999 should be another good year."

■ Some investors might fret that Washington Real Estate Investment trust lacks geographic diversification, since its properties are confined to the region around Washington. While this fear might seem valid, it is my belief that Washington's economy is less sensitive to economic fluctuations than most other large cities because of its close link to the federal government. What's more, the company's diversified holdings tend to offset its lack of diversification, since it does not rely on one type of property that might be out of favor for a period. If office buildings are not doing well, for instance, apartments or shopping centers may be thriving.

Reasons to Buy

■ Prior to acquiring a property, WRIT performs extensive inspections, tests, and financial analyses to gain confidence about the property's future operating performance, as well as any required near-term improvements and long-term capital expenditures. Upon completion of this evaluation, the company develops well-informed operating projections for the property. Accordingly, when the company announces an acquisition and its anticipated return on investment, it is confident that the property will meet or exceed its projections.

A review of WRIT's recent acquisitions confirms the value of its pre-acquisition analyses. In 1998, the fifteen properties the company acquired from 1995–1997 exceeded the 1998 returns originally projected for them by an average of 12 percent. Projections, of course, involve a number of uncertainties, and there is no assurance that future acquisitions will exceed projected returns. On the other hand, according to management, "As a result of our detailed analyses, hands-on management style, and in-depth knowledge of our markets, we have a high level of confidence in our projections."

■ One of 1998's key acquisitions was that of the Northern Industrial Park (NVIP), a 790,000-square-foot industrial distribution property in Lorton, Virginia. It was acquired for $30.35 million in cash and Operating Partnership Units. The property is strategically located in close proximity to I-95, the Capital Beltway, the newly completed Fairfax County Parkway, and U.S. Route 1.

NVIP provides WRIT with extraordinary value-added opportunities. Despite its prime location, the property's vacancy rate stood at 17 percent, due to deferred maintenance, inattention to tenant needs, and a lack of marketing. During 1998, WRIT invested $4 million into improvements, including facade renovations, new exterior lighting, signage, repaving, and roof replacement and repairs. When the property was acquired, rents averaged 15 percent to 25 percent below market for similarly situated, well-maintained properties,

depending on the level of tenant improvements in a particular space. In addition, the property includes a site with the potential for a 60,000-square-foot expansion. WRIT anticipates the park's return on investment to grow to over 10 percent within one year, due to the lease up of the 136,000 square feet of vacant space and the renewal of below-market leases. Leasing activity up until the spring of 1999 has resulted in reducing the unleased space by nearly 25 percent since acquisition. The $5.38 average rent on these transactions is 27 percent above the average rent in the property on the date of acquisition.

■ In late 1997, the company acquired the 7900 Westpark Drive office building in Tysons Corners, Virginia. At the time, management noted the opportunity to build about 49,000 square feet of additional space above the parking deck. As of early 1999, construction is underway, the space is 100 percent preleased, and the company expects occupancy in the third quarter of 1999.

Also during 1998, the company began the exterior renovation of the Bradlee Shopping Center, which is now complete. This renovation is enhancing the appearance and increasing the revenue from the Bradlee Shopping Center.

■ In 1999, Washington Real Estate reported that "Our properties are performing extremely well. We have never seen such a broad-based and consistent ability to maintain high occupancies and rental rate growth. The office building sector is particularly strong. At year-end, the overall portfolio was 95 percent leased. The office sector, at 98.6 percent leased, is our best performer in terms of occupancy and rental rate growth."

Total assets: $559 million
Current ratio: not relevant
Return on 1998 equity: 13.5%
Common shares outstanding: 36 million

	1998	1997	1996	1995	1994	1993	1992	1991
Revenues (millions)	104	79	66	53	46	39	34	33
Net income (millions)	34	30	28	26	23	22	20	18
FFO per share	1.39	1.23	1.13	1.05	.96	.93	.89	.88
Earnings per share	.96	.90	.88	.88	.82	.80	.76	.75
Dividends per share	1.11	1.07	1.03	.99	.92	.89	.84	.79
Price: high	18.8	19.6	17.5	16.6	21.1	24.8	21.3	18.5
low	15.1	15.5	15.3	13.9	14.9	18.6	14.9	10.9

INCOME

Weingarten Realty Investors

2600 Citadel Plaza Drive, P. O. Box 924133 Houston, TX 77292-4133 ◻ Investor contact: Steve Richter (713) 866-6054 ◻ Dividend reinvestment program available (888) 887-2966 ◻ Web site: www.weingarten.com ◻ Listed: NYSE ◻ Ticker symbol: WRI ◻ S&P rating: not rated ◻ Value Line financial strength rating: B++

Weingarten Realty Investors is an equity-based real estate investment trust (REIT). The company focuses primarily on the development, acquisition, and long-term ownership of anchored neighborhood, community shopping centers, and, to a lesser degree, industrial properties.

At the end of 1998, its portfolio included 217 income-producing properties, totaling 26.1 million square feet in thirteen states. Except for Maine and Tennessee, the company's properties are west of the Mississippi. The other states are: Nevada, Colorado, Arizona, New Mexico, Kansas, Oklahoma, Texas, Arkansas, Louisiana, Missouri, and Illinois.

By far the largest concentration of WRI's properties are in Texas, particularly Houston and Harris counties. Of the company's 217 properties, a total of 162 are in Texas.

Founded in 1948, Weingarten restructured itself into a real estate investment trust and listed on the New York Stock Exchange in 1985. Its performance as a public company has been among the best in the industry. This is a product of fifty years of real estate experience (in both growth and recessionary cycles), combined with a seasoned management team focused on specific segments of real estate. In addition to developing and acquiring properties, Weingarten adds value to them through consistent, high-quality operations that incorporate renovation, retailer recycling, and ongoing asset management.

Some History

Weingarten Realty Investors was founded in 1948 with two part-time employees, $60,000 in cash, and a portfolio of supermarket buildings totaling 51,000 square feet. The company was created to develop freestanding stores for J. Weingarten, Inc., a fast-growing grocery chain that was owned by the Weingarten family.

In addition to developing the stores, the company was charged with the responsibility to acquire raw land for future development and expansion. As a result, management was in an ideal position to take advantage of the trend to develop "clusters of stores" as the evolution of the "shopping center" began to take shape in the early 1950s.

As Weingarten began its new course, it focused on the neighborhood and community shopping center that ranged in size from 100,000 to 400,000 square feet and was "anchored" primarily by supermarkets.

This practice is still continued today, with the company also focusing on certain industrial properties, as well.

In 1980, the J. Weingarten supermarket chain was sold, and the realty company began to diversify and expand its relationships with other grocers and general retailers throughout the United States. Today, it boasts a diversified tenant roster of over 2,900 different tenants, many with multiple locations. During the fifty years of Weingarten's existence, the company has emerged as one of the largest REITs listed on the NYSE. Its portfolio has expanded from four properties to 217 at year-end 1998. The company's square footage has increased from 51,000 to more than 26 million, and the company has expanded its holdings from one city and one state to more than fifty-five cities in thirteen states. Likewise, Weingarten's revenue, funds from operations and dividends have increased significantly over the thirteen years of being a REIT. From the $60,000 that it began with, its total market capitalization today is over $1.9 billion.

Funds from Operations

Investors in common stock use "net income" as a key measure of profitability. However, in measuring a REIT, most investors prefer the term, "funds from operations" or FFO. This is because earnings and expenses of a real estate investment trust must be looked at differently.

The Securities and Exchange Commission has a blanket requirement that all publicly traded companies file audited financial statements. On a financial statement, the term "net income" has a meaning clearly defined under generally accepted accounting principles. Since a REIT falls under the classification of a publicly traded company, net income therefore appears on a REIT's audited financial statement.

For a REIT, on the other hand, this figure is less meaningful as a measure of operating success than it is for other types of corporations. The reason is that, in accounting, real estate "depreciation" is always treated as an expense. In the real world, most well-maintained quality properties have retained their value over the years. This is because of rising land values. In other words, it is because of steadily rising rental income, property upgrades, or higher costs for new construction for competing properties. Whatever the reason, a REIT's net income, since it suffers from a large depreciation expense, is a less-than-meaningful measure of how a REIT's operations have actually fared. It is because of this reasoning that FFO is often a better way to judge a real estate investment trust than traditional net income. You will note that I have used this alternative term in the table at the end of the article and so for the other REITs in the book.

Shortcomings to Bear in Mind

- Weingarten Realty Investors is primarily an income stock that often yields 6 percent or more. In terms of growth, however, it is not exciting. In the 1988–1998 period, funds from operations advanced from $2.24 to $3.60, a compound annual growth rate of only 4.9 percent. Similarly, dividends during this ten-year span advanced from $1.68 to $2.68, a growth rate of 4.8 percent.
- There is no way to avoid risk completely. Real estate ownership and management, like any other business, is subject to all sorts of risks. Mall REITs, for instance, are subject to the changing tastes and lifestyles of consumers.
- Although the company operates in thirteen states, it is predominantly situated in Texas and thus lacks effective geographic diversification.

Reasons to Buy

- Funds from operations increased to $96.6 million, from $89.2 million in

1997. On a diluted per-share basis, FFO increased to $3.60 from $3.33. Restating both 1998 and 1997 to reflect the effect of a new accounting regulation, FFO in 1998 would have increased 30 cents per share over the prior year, or 9.1 percent.

- Revenues increased by 13.7 percent in 1998.
- One of the many accomplishments of 1998 was the continued improvement of the company's existing portfolio. Occupancy of its 19.6 million square feet of retail properties was 93.3 percent at the end of 1998, up significantly from 91.5 percent at the end of the prior year. The occupancy of Weingarten's 6.4 million square feet of industrial portfolio was relatively unchanged, at 92.5 percent. Occupancy of the total portfolio at the end of 1998 was 93.1 percent, as compared with 91.8 percent at the end of the prior year.
- In 1998, the company completed 830 new leases and renewals, comprising 3.4 million square feet, with rental rates on a same-space basis increasing an average of 5.8 percent. After deducting the amortized portion of capital costs for tenant improvements, the increase was 3.2 percent.
- The company's primary focus is on neighborhood and community shopping centers. Almost all of the centers are anchored by supermarkets, drugstores, discount stores, and other "necessity" type retailers that have wide consumer appeal through all economic cycles.

- As a long-term owner of its properties, WRI maintains a program for renovating, re-merchandising, or recycling its existing centers in order to keep each competitive within its trade area. For instance, Wyoming Mall located in Albuquerque, New Mexico was acquired by the company in 1995 and renovated in 1998. The half-million-dollar redevelopment included additional landscaping, increased lighting, and a 36,600-square-foot Stein Mart.
- WRI acquired a 35 percent interest in the 178,000 square-foot Markham West Shopping Center in Little Rock, Arkansas, in 1998, bringing the total number of properties owned in that city to five. Currently 100 percent leased, Markham is anchored by Mega Market supermarket and Michael's Crafts. In total, the company's 1998 acquisitions numbered twenty-five and added about 3.6 million square feet to the portfolio.
- In addition to the company's strong acquisition performance, it continued to increase its new development activity. In 1998, Weingarten Realty completed construction of 26,000 square feet adjacent to an occupant-owned supermarket at a newly developed shopping center in Phoenix and also completed construction of a 162,000-square-foot bulk warehouse facility in its Railwood Industrial Park. The company currently has several other facilities under development, including four retail centers, an industrial office/service center, and a 260-unit luxury apartment project.

Total assets: $1,107 million
Current ratio: NM
Common shares outstanding: 27 million
Return on 1998 shareholders' equity: 10.2%

	1998	1997	1996	1995	1994	1993	1992	1991
Rental income(millions)	195	169	145	125	112	94	83	74
Net income (millions)	61.8	55.0	53.9	44.8	43.8	36.2	21.2	18.0
FO per share	3.60	3.32	3.09	2.82	2.71	2.40	2.36	2.22
Dividends per share	2.68	2.56	2.48	2.40	2.28	2.16	2.04	1.92
Price: high	46.9	45.6	40.8	38.5	40.5	45.3	38.0	32.9
low	35.9	38.8	34.3	33.4	32.8	36.5	29.5	24.1

Weyerhaeuser Company

P. O. Box 2999, Tacoma, WA 98477-2999 □ **Investor contact: Richard J. Taggart (253) 924-2058** □
Dividend reinvestment plan available (800) 561-4405 □ **Web site: www.weyerhaeuser.com** □ **Listed: NYSE**
□ **Ticker symbol: WY** □ **S&P rating: B+** □ **Value Line financial strength rating: B++**

Dating back to 1900, Weyerhaeuser is primarily engaged in the growing and harvesting of timber and the manufacture, distribution, and sale of forest products. It is also in real estate development and construction.

The company's wood products businesses produce and sell softwood lumber, plywood, and veneer, composite panels, oriented strand board, hardboard, hardwood lumber and plywood, doors, treated products, logs, chips, and timber.

These products are sold primarily through the company's own sales organizations. Building materials are sold to wholesalers, retailers, and industrial users.

Weyerhaeuser's pulp, paper, and packaging businesses include:

• Pulp—manufactures chemical wood pulp for world markets.

• Newsprint—manufactures newsprint at the company's North Pacific Paper Corporation mill and markets it to West Coast and Japanese newspaper publishers.

• Paper—manufactures and markets a range of both coated and uncoated fine papers through paper merchants and printers.

• Containerboard Packaging—manufactures linerboard and corrugating medium, which is primarily used in the production of corrugated shipping containers, and manufactures and markets corrugated shipping containers for industrial and agricultural packaging.

• Paperboard—manufactures bleached paperboard that is used for production of liquid containers and is marketed to West Coast and Pacific Rim customers.

• Recycling—operates an extensive wastepaper collection system and markets it to company mills and worldwide customers.

• Chemicals—produces chlorine, caustic, and tall oil, which is used principally by the company's pulp, paper and packaging operations.

Shortcomings to Bear in Mind

■ The major markets, both domestic and foreign, in which the company sells its products are highly competitive, with numerous strong sellers competing in each realm.

Many of Weyerhaeuser's products compete with substitutes for wood and wood fiber products. The real estate and financial services subsidiaries, moreover, also compete in highly competitive markets, competing with numerous regional and national firms in real estate development and construction and in financial services.

■ In 1998, the company's domestic oriented strand board and plywood markets benefited from another year of robust housing starts. This was offset, however, by the effects of the Japanese economy on lumber. Weak demand from Japan pushed import and domestic lumber into the U.S. market, resulting in low prices, despite high demand.

■ In 1998, Weyerhaeuser felt the effect of the Asian economic situation. Prices for both export and domestic logs dropped in response to lower Asian demand and higher inventories in the United States. However, this drop was offset somewhat by higher stumpage values in the southern United States.

Reasons to Buy

■ Weyerhaeuser is uniquely positioned in its industry. It manages more privately owned timber than any other company.

Likewise, Weyerhaeuser leads the industry in private forestry, having launched, nearly a generation ago, a program to maximize timber yield on every acre of planted forest land.

- To build on the timber assets and increase shareholder value, Weyerhaeuser is following a strategy that contains several elements:
  - Sell or dispose of nonstrategic assets
  - Work assiduously to upgrade the company's portfolio of land, mills, and other facilities
  - Ally strategically with domestic and international partners
  - Emphasize value-added products
  - Continually improve product quality and the cost efficiency of production
- In 1998, the company bought a pulp and paper mill and related assets from Bowater Inc., located in Dryden, Ontario. The Dryden mill has the capacity to produce 380,000 short tons of fine paper per year. According to management, "Our purchase of the Dryden facilities significantly enhances our Fine Paper business and augments our Canadian lumber position."
- The company is improving its returns on its Pulp, Paper, and Packaging sector by reducing its exposure to commodity grades, improving process reliability, and maintaining tight controls on capital spending.
- For nearly one hundred years, Weyerhaeuser has managed its timberland assets for growth. What started out as 900,000 acres in 1900 now encompasses more than 5.3 million acres throughout the United States. It also has timber licenses on 27 million acres in Canada. According to management, "We've also grown internationally with joint ventures in New Zealand and Uruguay. During 1998, this focus on growth once again produced strong results from our Timberland sector."
- The company believes that it has good prospects in the Southern Hemisphere, especially New Zealand and South America. Weyerhaeuser owns a 51 percent interest in 193,000 acres of managed forest land and related assets in New Zealand. As the majority owner, the company is responsible for the management and marketing activities of the joint venture.

In 1998, the company also made additional investments through its partnership with institutional investors known as the World Timberfund. This partnership currently holds a 97 percent interest in a venture that has acquired 234,000 acres of private agricultural land in Uruguay that is being converted into plantation forests.

- Weyerhaeuser has been narrowing its business focus since 1990. The company divested its milk carton, personal care products, insurance, nursery products, and gypsum wallboard businesses. What's more, WY reduced its investments by selling selected real estate assets.
- Extensive restructuring, carried out by former CEO John W. Creighton, Jr., since he took the reins in 1991, has transformed Weyerhaeuser, a one-time laggard, into one of the industry's most profitable players. In years past, investors scorned Weyerhaeuser as unwieldy and paternalistic. It was loaded down with outdated mills. What's more, it was hobbled by a host of noncore subsidiaries making everything from milk cartons to disposable diapers. Besides jettisoning these business, Creighton led his managers through an 18-month re-engineering in which each mill and tree farm had to redesign the way it worked. Creighton's goal: to add $700 million to operating earnings by 1995—a goal he achieved a year earlier than planned.
- Weyerhaeuser owns or manages an enormous expanse of highly productive forest land in North America. Thirty years ago, the company had the foresight to pioneer the High Yield Forestry programs. As a result, the company will see a dramatic increase in its timber harvest over the next twenty years. By the year 2020,

the timber harvest from the land WY owns and manages in the United States will increase by about 70 percent from 1995 levels and significantly enhance cash flow from this source. Meanwhile, Weyerhaeuser's manufacturing facilities are operating more efficiently and producing higher quality products than ever before.

■ The company is also differentiating other parts of its product line. For instance, Weyerhaeuser's Containerboard Packaging business began exploring new packaging solutions for customers. What's more, its Pulp operation is working on new absorbency fibers. Both efforts will help the company develop higher-value products capable of producing new growth opportunities and higher margins. New absorbency fibers, for instance, improve product function and provide manufacturers with greater flexibility and speed in commercializing their product upgrades. Management is convinced this will allow providers to develop a greater range of products and increase demand for its own products.

■ Analysts have considerable confidence in Weyerhaeuser's new CEO, Steven R. Rogel, who took the reins of the company in December of 1997. He succeeded John W. Creighton, Jr., who retired. Mr. Rogel is a thirty-two-year veteran of the forest-products business. He previously held the post of CEO with Willamette.

■ In 1998, the Real Estate sector reported earnings of $124 million. This compares with $66 million in 1997, before a gain associated with the sale of Weyerhaeuser Mortgage Company.

WY's real estate business focuses on home-building and land-development. In 1998, improved earnings resulted from increased operating efficiencies and improved margins and inventory turnover. During the year, the backlog of homes sold, both in absolute terms and as a percentage of in-process inventory, was increased to record levels. With home-building and land-development activities in Southern California, Las Vegas, Houston, Maryland, Virginia, and the Puget Sound area in Washington state, Weyerhaeuser Real Estate Company continues to be among the largest home builders in its selected markets.

■ Weyerhaeuser, in a June 1999 move that further consolidates the forest-products industry, agreed to acquire Canadian-timber concern, MacMillan Bloedel Ltd., in a stock swap valued at $2.36 billion. The new Weyerhaeuser is now one of the largest forest-products companies in North America. Its timber holdings on the continent increased to 39.2 million acres, from 32.3 million, with annual sales jumping to $13.3 billion, from $10.8 billion. Analysts praised the deal, saying the operations of the two companies would complement each other.

Total assets: $12,834 million
Current ratio: 1.45
Common shares outstanding: 199 million
Return on 1998 shareholders' equity: 6.4%

	1998	1997	1996	1995	1994	1993	1992	1991
Revenues (millions)	10,766	11,210	11,114	11,788	10,398	9,545	9,219	8,702
Net income (millions)	339	351	463	983	589	463	372	182
Earnings per share	1.70	1.76	2.34	4.83	2.86	2.26	1.83	.90
Dividends per share	1.60	1.60	1.60	1.50	1.20	1.20	1.20	1.20
Price: high	62.0	63.9	49.9	50.4	51.3	46.5	39.3	30.6
low	36.8	42.6	39.5	36.9	35.8	36.3	26.6	20.1

INDEX

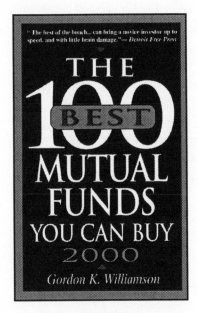

Money Without Madness

by Karen Brigham, CPA, MBA

Trade paperback, 1-58062-050-7,
$9.95, 220 pages

Money Without Madness
combines practical
money solutions with
basic human nature. If you are
ready for the rewards and confidence that come from gaining
control of your money, you will
benefit from this book. Written
with warmth and humor, *Money
Without Madness* is the first book to
offer an alternative to budgeting.

Find more on this topic by visiting BusinessTown.com

Developed by Adams Media, **BusinessTown.com** is a free informational site for entrepreneurs, small business owners, and operators. It provides a comprehensive guide for planning, starting, growing, and managing a small business.

Visitors may access hundreds of articles addressing dozens of business topics, participate in forums, as well as connect to additional resources around the Web. **BusinessTown.com** is easily navigated and provides assistance to small businesses and start-ups. The material covers beginning basic issues as well as the more advanced topics.

✓ **Accounting**
Basic, Credit & Collections, Projections, Purchasing/Cost Control

✓ **Advertising**
Magazine, Newspaper, Radio, Television, Yellow Pages

✓ **Business Opportunities**
Ideas for New Businesses, Business for Sale, Franchises

✓ **Business Plans**
Creating Plans & Business Strategies

✓ **Finance**
Getting Money, Money Problem Solutions

✓ **Letters & Forms**
Looking Professional, Sample Letters & Forms

✓ **Getting Started**
Incorporating, Choosing a Legal Structure

✓ **Hiring & Firing**
Finding the Right People, Legal Issues

✓ **Home Business**
Home Business Ideas, Getting Started

✓ **Internet**
Getting Online, Put Your Catalog on the Web

✓ **Legal Issues**
Contracts, Copyrights, Patents, Trademarks

✓ **Managing a Small Business**
Growth, Boosting Profits, Mistakes to Avoid, Competing with the Giants

✓ **Managing People**
Communications, Compensation, Motivation, Reviews, Problem Employees

✓ **Marketing**
Direct Mail, Marketing Plans, Strategies, Publicity, Trade Shows

✓ **Office Setup**
Leasing, Equipment, Supplies

✓ **Presentations**
Know Your Audience, Good Impression

✓ **Sales**
Face to Face, Independent Reps, Telemarketing

✓ **Selling a Business**
Finding Buyers, Setting a Price, Legal Issues

✓ **Taxes**
Employee, Income, Sales, Property, Use

✓ **Time Management**
Can You Really Manage Time?

✓ **Travel & Maps**
Making Business Travel Fun

✓ **Valuing a Business**
Simple Valuation Guidelines

http://www.businesstown.com

About the Author

John Slatter is an independent investment advisor who operates his own business near Burlington, Vermont. He has a varied investment background and has served as a stockbroker, securities analyst, and portfolio strategist. Mr. Slatter's clients include investors who have stock portfolios worth $100,000 or more.

John Slatter has written hundreds of articles for such publications as *Barron's*, *Physician's Management*, *Ophthalmology Times*, and *Better Investing*, as well as for brokerage firms he has worked for, including Hugh Johnson & Company and Everen Securities. His books include: *Safe Investing*, *Straight Talk About Stock Investing* and three prior editions of *The 100 Best Stocks You Can Buy*.

John Slatter has been quoted in such periodicals as the *Cleveland Plain Dealer*, the *New York Times*, the *Gannett News Service*, the *Burlington Free Press*, the *Wall Street Journal*, the *Cincinnati Enquirer*, the *Toledo Blade*, the *Christian Science Monitor*, *Money* magazine, the *Dayton Daily News*, and the *Buffalo News*. He has also been quoted in a number of books, including *The Dividend Investor* and *Stocks for the Long Run*.

In August of 1988, John Slatter was featured in the *Wall Street Journal* concerning his innovative investment strategy that calls for investing in the ten highest-yielding stocks in the Dow Jones Industrial Average. This approach to stock selection is sometimes referred as "the dogs of the Dow," a pejorative reference that he does not believe is justified, since the stocks with high yields typically include such blue chips as Merck, IBM, 3M, General Electric, AT&T, Caterpillar, DuPont, Exxon, J. P. Morgan, and Philip Morris.

John Slatter may be reached by calling (802)872-0637, Fax (802)878-1171 or by writing him at 70 Beech Street, Essex Junction, Vermont 05452. His Web site is: http://homepages.together.net/~bluechip